A Psychoanalytic Mind:
Selected Papers of Harold P. Blum, M.D.

A Psychoanalytic Mind: Selected Papers of Harold P. Blum, M.D.

Selected by Elsa Blum, Ph.D., and Lawrence Blum, M.D.

With an Introduction by Lawrence Blum, M.D.

IPBOOKS.net
International Psychoanalytic Books

International Psychoanalytic Books (IPBooks)
New York • http://www.IPBooks.net

A Psychoanalytic Mind: Selected Papers of Harold P. Blum, M.D.

Published by IPBooks, Queens, NY
Online at: www.IPBooks.net

ISBN: 978-1-956864-72-4

Contents

DEVELOPMENT

DREAMS

HISTORY

RECONSTRUCTION

THEORY AND TECHNIQUE

Introduction

by Lawrence D. Blum, M.D.

When Harold Blum died, in March, 2024, a few months short of his 95th birthday, he left a professional legacy of remarkable breadth and depth. He authored almost two hundred published papers, and he wrote or edited ten books. He gave invited lectures and taught students and colleagues across four continents. He was the second Editor-in-Chief of the Journal of the American Psychoanalytic Association and then Executive Director of the Sigmund Freud Archives. He thus had a major, and continuing, influence on psychoanalysis. That I am in the "family business," a psychiatrist and psychoanalyst, says something about my esteem for my father and has provided me a first-hand perspective on his contributions to psychoanalysis. Before turning to those contributions, I'll say a few words about his life.

Harold was born in 1929 in Brooklyn, N.Y, the middle child of Eastern European Jewish emigrees who valued education, though having little of it themselves. Many who knew him would be surprised to learn that he was tenth man on his high school basketball team, but education was always the priority, and he began college at Cornell in 1945, at age 16. He majored in chemistry, a subject in which he seems to have rapidly lost interest. More importantly, at Cornell he met Elsa Fienberg, in whom he never lost interest. Their marriage, in 1952, led to three children, five grandchildren, and (as of this writing) one great grandchild. Harold attended Boston University Medical School and decided to go into psychiatry. That the medical school dean admonished him for wasting a good medical mind by choosing psychiatry did nothing to dissuade him, and the dean's tragic suicide a couple of weeks later perhaps reinforced his decision.

After an internship at NYU, Harold served two years in the Navy, stationed in Washington, D.C. After his military service, he began his psychiatry residency at Yale, but left after a year for Downstate Medical Center, in Brooklyn, because at the Psychoanalytic Association of New York he could begin psychoanalytic training right away. It was while in the Navy, however, that he wrote his first psychoanalytic paper, a study of Van Gogh's Chairs, in 1955, the year of my birth. How he managed to write a still-cited psychoanalytic paper before starting psychiatric, let alone psychoanalytic training, has never been clear. When I asked him about the timing of the paper, he said, "I was probably competing with your mother!" His reply displayed his characteristic warmth, candor, and humor, but it was also psychoanalytically significant: despite having an analysis with an analyst who was mainly oedipally focused, in an era that was similarly focused, the comment bespeaks a casual awareness that a man may identify with a woman, and also envy or compete with a woman's (re)productive capacity.

His quip about his first paper is also consistent with his later work on pre-oedipal development and female psychology. At some point after his analysis, Harold recognized the inattention in it to pre-oedipal (and post-oedipal) development and managed some self-analytic understanding in these areas. During his childhood, his mother would at times take to bed for extended periods with minor ailments. I have a sense that in some way she was difficult to understand and that this difficulty, a kind of un-knowability, contributed to Harold's sensitivity to early development. I wonder if curiosity about his mother and her origins may also may have contributed to his interest in psychoanalytic history, as so many of the psychoanalytic pioneers were, like his parents, eastern European Jews who emerged from poverty and struggles with antisemitism.

Harold's interests in early development and in history both merit further comment.

Many of Harold's papers seem to me to have been written as "correctives," efforts to address what he saw as trends toward excess in the evolution of psychoanalysis. While never one to overlook oedipal dynamics, Harold was acutely aware of the problems in psychoanalysis of attending exclusively to them, and in fact the case vignettes in his articles routinely draw attention to a wide variety of pre-oedipal conflicts and traumas as well as maternal transferences. To draw attention to the importance of pre-oedipal influences, he wrote "The Prototype of Pre-Oedipal Reconstruction," using Freud as an example, and reasoning that if Freud himself was interested in reconstructing his own pre-oedipal influences, even the most orthodox psychoanalysts might consider their importance. His paper on "The Borderline Childhood of the Wolfman" likewise attends to under-emphasized early developmental influences. And his paper co-authored with Elsa, a clinical psychologist, pointed out how much superego development related to mother as well as father, and occurred before the traditionally highlighted resolution of the Oedipus complex. Harold's interest in development also contributed to his friendships across generations with Margaret Mahler and Anna Freud. I recall his pride at winning the inaugural Mahler Literature Prize in 1976.

Harold's knowledge of early psychoanalytic history was possibly unparalleled. If there was a book on Freud or an early psychoanalyst he hadn't read, it's because he hadn't found it yet. While there are many biographers and historians of Freud, other early psychoanalysts, and their era, I have a feeling that some understanding of those pioneers that was lost when my father died may never be recovered. A variety of his papers draw on his knowledge of psychoanalytic history, and his interest in reconstruction underlines his recognition of how history is alive in the present, and thus the importance of understanding history to make sense of the present.

Harold's immersion in psychoanalytic history, along with his level-headedness, made him a logical choice to become Executive Director of the Sigmund Freud Archives at time of controversy and struggle there. As Executive Director, he worked to open to scholars and the public materials that had been embargoed for unduly long periods of time. In relation to his interest in analytic history, I always appreciated the fact that along with his enjoyment of the genius of Freud, and of the contributions of other early psychoanalysts, Harold was also keenly aware of their flaws and misdeeds; a full understanding of reality, rather than idealization, was the aim.

Harold's work is itself a significant contribution to psychoanalytic history. Precocious as he was with writing psychoanalytic papers, he was appointed editor of the Journal of the American Psychoanalytic Association in 1972, at the psychoanalytically tender age of 41. He promptly began soliciting papers from a wider variety of contributors than had been typical. In 1976, perhaps with a nudge from my mother, who had always considered much of then-current psychoanalytic ideas about the psychology of women to be rubbish (a more polite word than she may have used), he published a special issue of JAPA devoted to updating analytic theory on this subject. There is a large landing on the staircase of the Freud Museum in London where Anna Freud spent a lot of time reading and writing, and on a visit to the museum I was very pleased to see a copy of that special issue in her small library there.

It may not be well known that that issue of JAPA was not only regarded by many as welcome, perhaps even overdue, but was regarded by some as a heretical attack on Freud, leading Harold to receive a good bit of abusive criticism. Challenging psychoanalytic orthodoxy was not new to him. At the time at which he trained, the Psychoanalytic Association of New York required its trainees to see their psychoanalytic patients at PANY's offices in Brooklyn, which at times necessitated needless commutes through traffic for both the trainees and their patients, giving him ample time and encouragement to doubt the wisdom of the analytic authorities. A matter of psychoanalytic orthodoxy that particularly irked him was the antiquated, anti-psychoanalytic practice of the reporting analyst (i.e., the trainee's analyst reporting to the institute on the trainee's progress, or lack thereof, in analysis). The only political matter at his institute that I recall him caring about deeply, and involving himself with, was the move to end that practice. Another early example of disdain for psychoanalytic (and other) authoritarianism that I remember occurred when on one of his first experiences as a visiting analyst, the case that was presented to him involved the trainee treating the patient in an authoritarian fashion, and Harold felt obliged to point out that this mirrored the way the senior supervisor treated the candidate in the visiting analyst conference.

It thus was interesting to learn that at some point Harold came to be regarded as part of the psychoanalytic orthodoxy. I had grown up hearing jokes about overly abstemious analysts, and I didn't realize the extent to which, unfortunately, they still existed. As far as I recall, for Harold the interpersonal aspects of the treatment were always present. Decades ago, he had for a while worked with a very religious patient, and at one point, after the patient had animatedly discussed heaven and hell, and who might end up there, Harold asked him, "Where does that leave you and me," which evidently provided them both a good laugh as well as a route to further understanding. At the same time, while emotionally engaged as an analyst, he certainly wanted the sessions to reflect the patient's contributions as much as possible, and he was concerned about problems of analytic solipsism. His paper on "The Position and Value of Extra-Transference Interpretation" was in part a caution against the spreading influence of Merton Gill's position that the transference was always the pre-eminent matter, in which Harold saw the danger of analytic self-indulgence.

Harold's emphasis on insight, reconstruction, and the contributions of all phases of development is not popular in all schools of psychoanalysis these days, but they are central psychoanalytic ideals that I think are likely to endure the various inevitable analytic pendulum swings. Perhaps his greatest psychoanalytic gift to me, as well as his students, colleagues, and readers is the unstated, but ever-present need to try to understand people comprehensively. The past and the present, and likewise, the intrapsychic and the interpersonal, are always both important, interacting with each other. Understanding development is essential, and all developmental phases matter. Drive and defense conflicts and object relations are heuristically distinguishable but in practice complementary and intertwined. I never heard Harold say any of the preceding three sentences – I don't think it occurred to him that such fundamental principles could need to be explicitly stated.

The selection of papers for this volume from among the nearly two hundred Harold has written is necessarily somewhat arbitrary. The division of them into this book's sections is somewhat arbitrary as well, especially since many of the papers readily fall into multiple categories. As foreshadowed by his first paper on Van Gogh, Harold's interest in psychoanalytic understanding of art has spanned his entire career. His native interests and his work as Vice

President of the International Psychoanalytic Association led to his chairing five international symposia on Psychoanalysis and Art in Florence, Italy. A glance at his papers on art, however, quickly shows that they overlap with his interests in early development and reconstruction.

Harold's papers in the Development section of this book cover a characteristically wide range of subjects, including intergenerational transmission of trauma and neurosis, hate, paranoia, superego development, and psychoanalytic history. The papers on Dreams are similarly diverse. The papers on Reconstruction are necessarily all also related to understanding development. A unifying theme is the need to understand how the past is influencing the present (and how the present influences understanding of the past). Harold clearly felt that insight about the past is not only essential to enable the greatest freedom from the past in the present, but also facilitates achieving genuineness and wholeness as a person.

The Theory and Technique section also has papers of substantial variety, but as always there is attention to development and to understanding the enduring influence of the past. Some of the papers, including the 2010 paper on object relations, convey his concern that this can be overlooked with contemporary trends that focus too narrowly on the current patient-analyst relationship. The three papers in the Case Reports section illustrate Harold's thorough approach to understanding his patients, as well as his concern for how clinical practice relates to theory. His presentation of a patient with postpartum depression remains the most comprehensive such report in the literature. His analysis of a patient who began treatment with a remarkable lie shows his flexibility in helping a patient with quite an inauspicious initial encounter. The "Childhood Trauma" (2019) paper demonstrates not only Harold's customary clinical acumen, but also the complexity of his understanding of trauma as well as his interest in how trauma may be overcome and turned to creative purposes.

Many of Harold's papers follow from his remarkable knowledge of psychoanalytic history. Two specifically historical papers are included here. The "Confusion of Tongues" paper, obviously referring to Ferenczi, conveys a great deal of analytic history, including how both Freud and Ferenczi dealt (or didn't) with their serious illnesses, as well as discussion of how the

Freud-Ferenczi tensions relate to current psychanalytic controversies about trauma, development, and technique. The second paper in this section, about antisemitism in the background of Freud's cases, I believe could only have been written by Harold. This article was enabled by in-depth knowledge not only of Freud and his milieu, but also of Freud's patients and their backgrounds, that no one else may have ever possessed.

In closing, I'd like to mention one of Harold's lesser-known papers, one that I use often in teaching, "Psychoanalytic Understanding and Psychotherapy of Borderline Regression." It reports the case of an aging pharmacist with an underlying borderline personality organization who has a new outbreak of severe obsessive-compulsive symptoms. One reason I like to assign it is that most trainees have been schooled to think that obsessive-compulsive disorder is an entirely biological matter, and in this instance the onset of the patient's symptoms as well as their resolution are clearly determined in great measure by his specific emotional conflicts. The paper also, however, nicely illustrates Harold's comprehensive approach. He conducts what he calls a supportive psychotherapy, carefully considering the frequency of sessions, his role as an "auxiliary ego," and which conflicts are interpreted or best left uninterpreted. In the course of these decisions, he addresses his patient's developmental history, significant traumas, and personal vulnerabilities; how these interact with his current environment and stage of life; how his object-relational difficulties influence his current adaptational possibilities; and lastly also transferential aspects of the treatment - and does so to a much greater extent than one often sees in reports of full psychoanalyses. It takes a characteristically comprehensive approach to understanding both the patient and the therapy, without ever calling attention to doing so.

While this selection of papers cannot take a full account of Harold Blum's contributions, it illustrates the scope of his interests and the depth of his thinking, and it celebrates a remarkable lifetime of psychoanalytic accomplishment. I hope you enjoy it.

CHAPTER 1

Van Gogh's Chairs

(1956). *Am. Imago,* 13(3):307–318.

Vincent Van Gogh was highly ambivalent toward Paul Gauguin. Gauguin, five years older, and a more experienced artist, aggravated this ambivalence with a supercilious and condescending manner. Van Gogh called him "Master" and considered him the greater artist and intellect. However, Van Gogh argued with him intensely and would not accept Gauguin's art criticism; when they exchanged self-portraits, Van Gogh claimed his own as artistically equal. (1, 2) He was keenly aware that Gauguin was more successful at the local brothel (3, 4) and felt that his own impassioned painting drained his sex desire. (5) He had been twice rejected as a serious suitor and though he had lived with a fertile mistress, he had never sired any children. He knew that Gauguin had attained marriage and paternity. (6, 7) He was admiring, yet envious of Gauguin's superior virility and sexual success.

Psychoanalytic considerations of their relationship also indicate that Van Gogh was homoerotically attracted to Gauguin and transferred to him the desire to be reunited with the powerful father. (8, 9, 10) Having first met Gauquin in Paris, he had insistently urged Gauquin to join him in Aries, France, and invited him to live in his house. (11) He prepared the guest room like a boudoir for Gauguin's arrival in October, 1888. (12)

Two days before Christmas, 1888, Van Gogh spontaneously flung a glass in Gauquin's face in a cafe. The next evening, Christmas Eve, Van Gogh threatened Gauguin with a razor but then turned from physical combat. Instead, he cut off his own ear and gave it wrapped as a gift to a prostitute at the local brothel. (13, 14) This has been interpreted as a substitute castration following assault on the

9

father-figure. The symbolic penis was then presented to the mother figure. (15, 16) It is noteworthy that Van Gogh occasionally painted his own ear injected, and in a self-portrait (1886–1887) one ear is seen flushed and engorged.

The time as well as the circumstances of the assault was related to a father conflict. Van Gogh was depressed and often quarreled with his cleric father on Christmas. He had tried to emulate his father in studying for the ministry, and failing in that, went to work as an impoverished Christlike evangelist in Christmas 1879. On Christmas Eve, 1881, his father asked him to leave home following a violent altercation. (17) Strife tended to occur at Christmas because Van Gogh, who identified with Christ, then demanded equality with the Divine Father, the omnipotent father of his infancy.

The emotions involved in Van Gogh's Christmas assault on Gauquin have been reconstructed psychoanalytically primarily from Van Gogh's letters, but not from his painting of that period. Should not Van Gogh have manifestly expressed such agitated emotions in his art at that time? The striking symbolism of that period's paintings stimulated this investigation.

In two extraordinary paintings on his easel (December 1888–January 1889) during his acute conflict with Gauguin, Van Gogh depicted his feelings about their relationship. These are the famed chairs, "Van Gogh's Chair", also called "The Chair and The Pipe" (Figure 1) and "Gauguin's Armchair" (Figure 2).

He began the chairs at a time of overt contention with Gauguin shortly before the catastrophic climax of their relationship. Actually, he first painted his own chair the very day he ran out on the fields for six hours after pleading with Gauguin to "be a good chap". (18)

Art critics have exclaimed how these chairs portray and compare the two personalities. (19) One critic found in the chairs a fundamental contrast "as between male and female", (20) and another thought there was a symbolic connection between Van Gogh's chair and his pipe. (21) The chair paintings are indeed a pair of still lifes alive with the symbolic essence of their creator's turmoil. Van Gogh's chair is crude and simple; it supports his pipe and tobacco pouch. This same chair is also seen in the background of his painting of his bedroom at Aries. Gauguin's armchair is more elaborate, dignified, and graceful as would befit the "Master". Van Gogh had procured the furniture and undoubtedly bestowed this chair on Gauguin.

The pipe and tobacco pouch on Van Gogh's chair and the lighted candle with two books on Gauguin's chair, are genital symbols. They are located in the positions of the genitals of their two invisible sitters. Van Gogh has depicted his feelings of impotence, sterility, and inferiority with his small downcast phallus and old worn scrotum. Contrast Gauguin's candle, a larger, erect, responsive (glowing) penis. Van Gogh's pipe is not lit, and there is no residual smoking. There is no glow of active life nor suggestion of recent activity. Gauguin's phallus stands next to the two large testicular symbols, books—artistic creations, though the phallic candle is the cynosure. Van Gogh was envious of Gauguin's phallus and admired it immensely. In this connection, an armchair alone is patently more phallic than a simple chair, the very word emphasizing an appendage. (The father in our society often uses the only armchair at the table.)

Significantly, the pipe and tobacco pouch symbolism first appears in a still life done just after the death of the artist's father in 1885. Van Gogh portrayed his father's pipe and pouch on a table with a vase of flowers. (22) The flowers mourn the father's castration and death, but also implicit is the resurrection of the adored genitals through art with the associated idea of the immortality of seed and flower of genitalia and offspring, male and female. Here, inchoate, is the artist's later theme of the sower fertilizing the earth (father making mother earth flower).

The chairs had a long latent history in Van Gogh's unconscious.

At twenty-four, after a visit from his father, he wrote: "And when…. I saw father's chair… and though I knew we should see each other again pretty soon, I cried like a child". (23) In 1882, at twenty-nine, he expressed great interest in a reproduction of Filde's woodcut of Charles Dickens' empty chair, done just after Dickens' demise. (24, 25, 26) Van Gogh eulogized Dickens with superlatives analagous to those he then applied to his idol, father. "Dickens paints with words", "There is no writer comparable". (27) Dickens was a symbol of the creative father. Many a son is intrigued by his father's chair, and may overtly demand to sit in it. Van Gogh yearned for his father's seat, and saw an invitation in the chair's emptiness. The artist was morbidly fascinated by the empty chair which reminded him of the lost or dead father, and unconsciously symbolically retained the father's presence at the same time. The empty chair signified the fulfillment of the death wish toward the father-figure, but also served as a monument for his preservation. Van Gogh's execution of his own empty chair was symbolic of his hostile identification with father and his acceptance of the supreme penalty for this hostility. His chair alone was a comparison between himself and his unconscious image of his seated father. Undoubtedly, he had been very impressed as he stared at father's genitals or their bulging outlines. The comparison becomes manifest when he simultaneously paints father Gauguin's chair with his own.

In December, 1888, at thirty-five, Van Gogh combined the chair and pipe theme into one painting. He had been deeply concerned with the empty chair of the father-figure Dickens and the pipe and pouch of his real father after their respective demises. They were memorials unconsciously linked together in homoerotic attraction and in denial of castrating death wishes. It is no accident that these symbols are united in the artist's painting years later when the same murderously ambivalent feelings transferred to father Gauguin burst to the surface. Significantly, in Van Gogh's first comment after the coma following his self-mutilation, was a request for his pipe and pouch. (28) Possessing his pipe and pouch, he pacified himself and recovered stability through denial of his own castration and the simultaneous oral satisfaction of smoking. After he had fatally shot himself, he also asked for his pipe and smoked while awaiting death. (29)

Figure 1. Van Gogh's chair

Figure 2. Gaugin's chair

Figure 3. Van Gogh's chair with tobacco and onions

Van Gogh's chair paintings, reminiscent of father and his paternal sexuality, are painted with an ardor appropriate to the awesome feelings invested in them. The chair reflect the same scoptophilic intensity with which Van Gogh must have studied his seated father. The figures in the chairs are blocked out except for the genitals which become most prominent, though symbolically disguised. In painting the chairs, Van Gogh compared his weak sexuality with his virile omnipotent father-substitute, murdered and mourned the castrating father, revered the paternal penis, and sublimated his longed-for union with father and father's phallus. Although Van Gogh paints books elsewhere, the chair Dickens association may further explanation of the choice of book symbols in the armchair.

Van Gogh wrote that his chair was of white wood. (30) That he painted it pale yellow in daylight (sunlight) indicates his attempted identification with father and paternal energy, since several analysts have deduced that yellow and sunlight symbolized both father and libido. (31, 32)

However, there are indications that pale yellow has another meaning, even if derived from yellow. Though the unconscious is not rational, it appears that to Van Gogh, pale yellow really represents an anemia of yellow, and logically suggests inadequate father identification, impotence, and castration. Concerning his painting, "Night Cafe", September 1888, he wrote that he "tried to express the terrible passions of humanity be means of red and green.... in an atmosphere like the devil's furnace, of *pale sulphur*". In this setting, he asserted that "one could run mad or commit a crime". (33, 34) The devil's furnace of pale sulphur is Van Gogh's inner world of guilt, rage, and depression centered about castration conflict. He wrote of his painting "The Keaper" that it was "a fair pale yellow" and that he had tried for an overall effect of "sulphur". (35) "The Reaper", pale yellow like his chair, has been interpreted as symbolic of castration and death in punishment for arrogating paternal power in "The Sower". (35)

Van Gogh also wrote that Gauguin's armchair had a "red and green night effect", (37) a menacing association to dark forbidden impulses, and corresponding to his later description of a pictorial image of anxiety. In analyzing his anxiety and tranquility states in the Insane Asylum, 1889, he wrote of a representative anxious painting: "This combination of ochre red, of green with a grey shadow over it and black contours, produces the feeling of anguish.... Moreover, this idea is confirmed by the motif of the huge tree struck by lightning." The struck tree was "sawn off". (38) Evidently, "red and green night effect" (grey shadows and black contour—night) refers in particular to castration anxiety.

Actually, aside from Van Gogh's chair, the predominant colors of both paintings are red and green, emblazoning "the terrible passions of humanity" which the artist sensed in himself and Gauguin. The overall color scheme together with the rival chairs expresses the tortured artist's feelings of oedipal jealousy, castration fear and impotence, homoerotic attraction and denial, narcissistic insult, depression and rage. The patterned tile and repetitive ornamentation in Van Gogh's chair and Gauguin's armchair, respectively, are schizoid compulsive defenses against the dangerous, frightening conflicts. The defenses fail and Van Gogh "runs mad" and threatens criminal assault on Gauguin while painting the chairs. Shortly after the assault, in January, 1888, he mentioned working on the chairs in the same letter in which he wrote, "Fortunately, Gauguin and I… are not yet armed with machine guns and other destructive weapons". (39)

A fantasy relating to Gauguin's loss is expressed in the painting "Still Life with Onions", January 1889 (Figure 3). This was one of the first paintings done after Gauguin's immediate departure following the ear episode. Gauguin's presence at the table is inferred from the kettle and contiguous candle; the presence of Van Gogh, seated opposite, is inferred from his representative bottle, pipe, and pouch. The homoerotic symbolic display in an oral milieu is perhaps suggestive of latent fellatio wishes (as is his pipe-smoking, not pertinent for discussion here). The letter-opener lies adjacent to the candle, suggesting again the knife against the penis, the desire to castrate Gauguin. But the knife-point is blunted, for here the "hatchet is buried". In fantasy, Gauguin has returned, and the tears and bitterness in the onions between them are to be devoured. (The sprouting onions are also genital symbols on a deeper level). It is known that Van Gogh very much hoped Gauguin would return and disclaimed any rancor toward him. (40)

These paintings, especially the chairs, present Van Gogh's terrible and passionate conflicts. He has expressed his most powerful emotions in his painting, as we would expect. Through psychoanalytic insight, we penetrate his particular choice of content, color, and composition, though not his genius at transforming these elements into great Art.

REFERENCES

Meier-Graefe, J.: "Vincent Van Gogh" The Medici Society, 1926, Vol. II, p. *11, 12, 30.*

Van Gogh-Bonger, J.: "The Letters of Vincent Van Gogh to His Brother" Vols. I and II, London & Boston, 1927; continued as Vol. III: "Further Letters of Vincent Van Gogh to His Brother", London and Boston, 1929, letters *544 and 545.*

"Further Letters of Vincent Van Gogh to His Brother", London and Boston, 1929, 1560.

Schneider, D.E.: "The Psychoanalyst and The Artist", Farrar, Straus, NY, 1950, Chapter 9.

Letters to Emil Bernard (by Van Gogh). The Museum of Modern Art, NY, 1938, pp. 40, 70.

Meier-Graefe, Letters to Emil Bernard (by Van Gogh). The Museum of Modern Art, NY, 1938, p. *5, 10*; also description of Van Gogh's affairs with Sien in Vol. I

Nordenfalk, Carl: "The Life and Work of Van Gogh", Philosophical Library, NY, 1953.

Schneider, "The Life and Work of Van Gogh", Philosophical Library, NY, 1953.

Westerman-Holstijn, A. J.: "Psychological Development of V. Van Gogh", *Amer. Imago*, 1951, Vol. 8, p. *239* (A reprint of his brilliant 1924 paper).

Schnier, J.: "The Blazing Sun: A Psychoanalytic Approach to Van Gogh", *Amer. Imago*, 1950, Vol. 7, p. *143.*

1Van Gogh-Bonger, "The Blazing Sun: A Psychoanalytic Approach to Van Gogh", *Amer. Imago*, Vol. I, p. *li.*

Van Gogh-Bonger, "The Blazing Sun: A Psychoanalytic Approach to Van Gogh", *Amer. Imago*, Vol. I, L. *534.*

Meier-Graefe, "The Blazing Sun: A Psychoanalytic Approach to Van Gogh", *Amer. Imago*, Vol. I p. *29–32.*

Gauguin, P.: "Avant et Apres", Paris, 1924.

Westerman-Holstijn, "Avant et Apres."

Schneider, "Avant et Apres."

Perry, I. H.: "Vincent Van Gogh's Illness", Bulletin History of Medicine, 1947, V. 21, p. *146*.

Meier-Graefe, "Vincent Van Gogh's Illness", Bulletin History of Medicine, 1947, V. 21, p. *15*.

Schapiro, M.: "Vincent Van Gogh", Library of Great Painters, NY, 1950, p. *90*.

Nordenfalk, "Vincent Van Gogh", Library of Great Painters, NY, 1950, p. *156*.

Estienne, C.: "Van Gogh", Skira, 1953, p. *65*.

Van Gogh-Bonger, "Van Gogh", Skira, 1953, L. *398*.

Nordenfalk, "Van Gogh", Skira, 1953, p. *33*.

Nordenfalk, "Van Gogh", Skira, 1953, p. *156*.

Van Gogh-Bonger, "Van Gogh", Skira, 1953, L. *220*.

"Letters to An Artist" (Van Gogh to Van Rappard) Viking Press, NY, 1936, p. *92*.

"Letters to An Artist" (Van Gogh to Van Rappard) Viking Press, NY, 1936, p. *139*.

Gauguin, "Letters to An Artist" (Van Gogh to Van Rappard) Viking Press, NY, 1936.

Terrasse, C.: "Van Gogh", Librarie Floury, Paris, 1947, p. *73*.

Van Gogh-Bonger, "Van Gogh", Librarie Floury, Paris, 1947, L. *534*.

Westerman-Holstijn, "Van Gogh", Librarie Floury, Paris, 1947.

Schnier, J., "Van Gogh", Librarie Floury, Paris, 1947.

Van Gogh-Bonger, "Van Gogh", Librarie Floury, Paris, 1947 L. *533*.

Van Gogh-Bonger, "Van Gogh", Librarie Floury, Paris, 1947, L. *534*.

Van Gogh-Bonger, "Van Gogh", Librarie Floury, Paris, 1947, L. *604*

Schnier, "Van Gogh", Librarie Floury, Paris, 1947, p. *159*.

Van Gogh-Bonger, "Van Gogh", Librarie Floury, Paris, 1947, L. *563*.

Letters to Emil Bernard, "Van Gogh", Librarie Floury, Paris, Nov. 1889, p. *98–99*.

Van Gogh-Bonger, "Van Gogh", Librarie Floury, Paris, Nov. 1889, L. *571*.

Van Gogh-Bonger, "Van Gogh", Librarie Floury, Paris, Nov. 1889, L. *567, 571*.

CHAPTER 2

Psychoanalytic Studies and *Macbeth*—Shared Fantasy and Reciprocal Identification

(1986). *Psychoanal. Study Child*, (41):585–599.

Shakespeare's Macbeth is a larger than life tragedy that for its brevity and rapidity of action is probably unparalleled in its dramatic scope and study of character, motive, and conflict. *Macbeth* is scrutinized not only for application of psychoanalytic discoveries, but as an artistic depiction of the most primitive and most advanced aspects of the human psyche which inspires as well as illuminates psychoanalytic insights.

This paper explores *Macbeth* in terms of shared fantasies and the reciprocal identifications intrinsic to their formation and structure. Freud (1908) introduced shared fantasies in discussion of aesthetic communication by poets and artists and in terms of group psychology. The poet conveyed his daydreams and dreams to the audience, awakening similar fantasies in the audience and inviting identification with the character and content of his own fantasy creation. Furthermore, myth, legend, and folklore were shown to converge with the fantasies disguised in literature and art. The primal fantasies of all cultures (Freud, 1916–17, p. 371), the universal fantasies of incest and parricide, matricide, pregnancy, birth, death, castration, omnipotence, etc., were all shared between writer and reader.

Shared fantasies exert a selective influence on the growth and development of personality functions. They facilitate, impede, or inhibit some lines of development while fostering other developmental potentials. The impact of the parents' feelings and fantasies will so selectively influence development as to make that child the child of that particular caretaker (A. Freud, 1965, p. 86) and culture. Whether shared fantasies exert unusual developmental influence will likely depend upon the identification investment and exclusive attachment of the parent, usually the mother, and the developmental phase, sensitivity, and proclivities of the child. Shared fantasies tend to shape personal, familial, and social history (Blum, 1985). The personal myth (Kris, 1956) may be overdetermined and affirmed by shared intrafamilial fantasy such as a child being chosen for great deeds to fulfill parental ambition, or for a scapegoat function, or as a replacement child, etc.

Following Freud's investigation, I shall turn to the applied analysis of *Macbeth* for elucidation of shared phallic narcissistic fantasy, though with changing developmental vicissitudes and with idealization of masculine aggression. In the course of this condensed commentary on the play, it will be clear that our understanding of *Macbeth* parallels the growth of psychoanalytic knowledge and insight. Each generation of analysts will interpret the play, like the Irma dream, in the light of new understanding which should enlarge rather than diminish its analytic and aesthetic appreciation. Freud (1916) regarded Shakespeare as the greatest of poets and used characters of Shakespeare's plays in his study of character types. Clearly intrigued by *Macbeth*, he told Ferenczi, "I have begun to study *Macbeth* which has long tormented me without my being able to find a solution" (Jones, 1955, p. 372). Freud (1916) quoted the play at great length, summarized the plot, and then referred to the "triple layer of obscurity into which the bad preservation of the text, the unknown intention of the dramatist, and the hidden purport of the legend have become condensed" (p. 323). Nevertheless, he stated that while the dramatist can overwhelm us by his art, "he cannot prevent us from attempting subsequently to grasp its effect by studying its psychological mechanism" (p. 323). Freud did not deal with methodology, although he was aware of the limits to inference with created characters (Baudry, 1984). Lady Macbeth is given as an example of a person who is wrecked by success, "after striving for it with single-minded energy … Beforehand there is no hesitation, no sign of any internal conflict in her … She is ready to sacrifice even her womanliness to her murderous intention" (p. 318). Lady Macbeth is ultimately destroyed by the very "vaulting ambition which overleaps itself" (I, 7), in the crimes committed in order to become queen and make her husband king. Oedipal victory could not be tolerated since it resulted in unconscious guilt and self-punitive destruction.

Actually, Freud gave several explanations for the basic motives in the play in addition to unconscious oedipal guilt, and these complementary and competing explanations have been largely overlooked. In this connection he also pointed to the disappointment of childlessness "to break the woman down and drive the man to defiant rage" (p. 322) so that childlessness drives the couple to crime. Freud comments that only a childless person could kill children, a remark that is strangely contradictory to his awareness of parental infanticide and filicide. In another explanation, Macbeth's childlessness and Lady Macbeth's barrenness are poetic justice, talion punishment for their crimes against the sanctity of generation so that childlessness is not the cause but the consequence of the crime.

The father-son relationship is also invoked by Freud with the murder of Duncan clearly noted as parricide. In Banquo's case Macbeth kills the father while the son escapes, and Macduff's children are killed while the father escapes. Lady Macbeth would have killed Duncan herself had he not resembled her father, and suspicion for his murder falls on his sons: "who cannot want the thought how monstrous it was for Malcolm and for Donaldbain to kill their gracious father? Damn fact!; so the sons of Duncan are thought to have murdered their father, the King, and Banquo's son, Fleance, is under suspicion and fleeing from his father's death" (III, 6). In putting her husband in her father's place, Lady Macbeth is clearly implying a hidden incestuous relationship. It seems to me that there can be no doubt that the play expresses derivatives of oedipal conflict with talion punishment for oedipal crimes. The punishment is childlessness, castration, and death, as Freud indicated. Parricide is virtually a manifest theme.

Numerous other explanations of this extraordinary drama have been offered. Calef (1969) invoked the concept of one crime, parricide, defending against another crime, incest, and the need to conceal and destroy the fruits of incestuous transgression. More recently, authors have discussed the play in terms of preoedipal themes, disregarding the earlier oedipal formulations. Newer work builds on Freud's formulation that Macbeth and Lady Macbeth are split characters which are not completely understandable until brought together into a unity. Macbeth is weak-willed and acts like a feminine man, and is goaded to brutal, fearless masculinity by his wife, while she is unsexed and becomes a masculine woman. Freud (1916, p. 324) noted: "It is he who has the hallucination of the dagger before the crime; but it is she who afterwards falls ill of a mental disorder … Macbeth does murder sleep… and so 'Macbeth shall sleep no more'; but we never hear that *he* slept no more, while the Queen… rises from her bed and, talking in her sleep, betrays her guilt. It is he who stands helpless with bloody hands, lamenting that 'all great Neptune's ocean' will not wash them clean, while she comforts him: 'A little water clears us of this deed'; but later it is she who washes her hands… and cannot get rid of the bloodstains: 'All the perfumes of Arabia will not sweeten this little hand.'… she becomes all remorse and he all defiance… like two disunited parts of a single psychical individuality, and it may be that they are both copied from a single prototype." Extending Freud's formulations, I wish to emphasize the importance of both oedipal and preoedipal determinants. I shall comment on the relationship of the different developmental phases to each other.

The understanding of this extraordinary, enigmatic drama is enlarged through consideration of the shared, phallic-narcissistic fantasy of the Macbeths, a fantasy system which undergoes regressive and progressive transformation. The Macbeths are paired as husband-wife, and unconsciously as mother-son. Lady Macbeth is the bewitching oedipal mother, but she is also the incompletely separated preoedipal mother. Lady Macbeth is not fully differentiated from Macbeth or from the witches. She is the most real and differentiated witch, the least and greatest, most benign and malignant of the witches. The witches reproject Macbeth's forbidden fantasies and ruthless ambition. The apparent validation of the witches' prophecies is comparable to the validation of shared fantasies of reciprocal projection and identification across indistinct boundaries.

Lady Macbeth is initially more determined and unscrupulous than Macbeth, who is conflicted and hesitant to perpetrate parricide-regicide. Lady Macbeth uses Macbeth as her own deadly instrument, her dagger, her murdering minister. Macbeth is initially overwhelmed by Duncan's murder, while Lady Macbeth remains concerned only with the details of what is to be done to maintain appearances and fabricate a cover-up. Darkness and blood pervade the drama, and the murder is carried out as a primal scene, with the stabbing in the dead of night, uncertain as to who committed the crime and blood dripping down the stairs until Macbeth will stand in a sea of blood. All Scotland bleeds, and forms become blurred in a murky, sleepless, sinister atmosphere. As Lady Macbeth grows remorseful, she still believes that a little water will dissolve the guilt. Fearful of attempts at retaliation and seeing others now trying to usurp the very throne which he has just seized, Macbeth descends into violent assaults as he becomes a hardened criminal.

The many references to Macbeth's being planted and full of growth (I, 4) and to the "pendant bed and procreant cradle of her castle" (I, 6) contrast with Macbeth's sterility and his extinction of life and lineage. One murder begets another, and Macbeth destroys rather than creates, unable to stop, though he has "supped full of horrors" (V, 5). Banquo is murdered, and then Lady Macduff and her children are murdered as Macbeth attempts to annihilate Macduff's entire extended family. Lady Macbeth collapses into suicidal depression, and poetic intuition of rudiments of analytic therapy follow. Macbeth admonishes her physician, "cure her of that. Can'st thou not minister to a mind diseased, pluck from the memory a rooted sorrow, raise out the written troubles of the brain." And the doctor replies, "Therein the patient must minister to himself" (V, 3). Believing in his invulnerability, Macbeth proclaims, "I bear a charmed life" (V, 7). According to the witches' prophecies he cannot be vanquished by "any man of woman born" and is safe so long as Burnham Wood comes not to Dunsinance Castle. Macbeth goes off to his final battle with avenging forces. The armies advance using Burnham Wood as camouflage and Macbeth is beheaded by the avenging Macduff who "was from his mother's womb untimely ripped" (V, 8). The curtain falls as the rightful heir is restored to the throne.

Macbeth is a study of regicide, as Hamlet, with attempts to usurp the throne, the paternal position, power, and penis. Critics have also noted the relationship of Macbeth to the Elizabethan era. Freud commented on Elizabeth's childlessness which resulted in her making the son of Mary Stuart, whom she had executed, her successor to the throne. Freud noted that this was similar to the prophecy of the Weird Sisters that Macbeth would be King without successors, but that Banquo's children should succeed to the crown. Macbeth laments, "Upon my head… a fruitless crown… a barren sceptre in my grip" (III, 1). Macbeth is incensed and violently jealous, since he wishes to found a dynasty. When's Banquo's eight descendants appear to Macbeth in the witches' cavern, he exclaims, "What, will the line stretch out to the crack of doom" (III, 1). His jealousy of parents and envy of their progeny contribute to his destructive rage against parents and children, particularly those in the dynastic line.

The promptings of the Weird Sisters, the witches, are closely related to the instigation, provocation, and goading of his wife. Lady Macbeth is an awesome figure, one of the great characters of literature. Macbeth readily succumbs to Lady Macbeth's influence, and at the same time struggles to free himself from the dangers of her domination and femininity. If Lady Macbeth is wife and mother, the pair form a mother-son latent relationship, but one of a very special type. Barron (1960) first noted that they were not only a composite character, they failed to differentiate from each other and had failed to achieve separate identities. Actually, the separation-individuation issues are intertwined with the oedipal themes and give a particular cast to the oedipal drama. Muslin (1984) explicates the play in terms of self-psychology and sees Lady Macbeth as a selfobject. Following the murder of Duncan, Muslin presumes that Lady Macbeth undergoes fragmentation of the cohesive self. Macbeth then loses her as an idealized parental selfobject responsible for his own self-cohesiveness and narcissistic equilibrium.

To my mind, important transformations occur at the beginning of the play, prior to Duncan's murder, and continue in an unfolding sequence. Macbeth is involved with the witches at the inception of the drama as they reflect his own grandiose ambitions which are shared in letter and speech with Lady Macbeth. Lady Macbeth is transformed, almost at once, from devoted wife to the bewitching, beguiling, seductive, oedipal mother and then to the arch witch, the preoedipal mother. Lady Macbeth becomes a mirror of Hecate, Goddess of Witches. Hecate admonishes the witches, "all you have done hath been but for a wayward son, spiteful and wrathful, who as others do, loves for his own ends, not for you" (III, 5). The preoedipal witch-mother is both an idealized and persecutory narcissistic object. "Fair is foul and foul is fair" (I, 1), and the drama is replete with reversals, splits, bisexuality, and paired opposite identifications. Regressive transformations are punctuated by some progressive reorganization which makes it easier for the audience to identify with the villainous heroes (antiheroes) of the drama.

The rampant entitlement, seizure, and abuse of power begin as a *folie à deux*. Peering through the thick fog on the heath that envelopes the play, Macbeth's descent into barbaric cruelty and tormented tyranny parallels that of Lady Macbeth. Semen and milk turn into blood. Lady Macbeth, anticipating ambitious fulfillment with "her dearest partner of greatness" (I, 5), nevertheless fears his nature, "it is too full of the milk of human kindness" (I, 5). She is ready to pour spirits into his ear, "and chastise with the valor of my tongue all that impedes thee" (I, 5). Lady Macbeth then undergoes one of the most dramatic and terrifying transformations in literature, "Come, you spirits that tend on mortal thoughts, unsex me here, and fill me, from the crown to the toe, topped full of dirous cruelty! Make thick my blood. Stop up the access and passage to remorse, that no compunctuous visitings of nature shake my sole purpose … Come to my woman's breasts and take my milk for gall, you murdering ministers" (I, 5). Unsexed, she is a masculinized woman like the bearded witches of ambiguous gender. She represents the murderous preoedipal mother, with both phallic and castrating attributes. She will then go on to ridicule her husband's vacillation, impugning his masculinity, and asserting those gripping lines which Freud also cited, "I have given suck, and know how tender 'tis to love the babe that milks me; I would, while it was smiling in my face, have plucked my nipple from his boneless gums, and dashed the brains out, had I so sworn as you have done to this" (I, 7).

These lines, so applicable to child abuse and infanticide (Blum, 1980), may also serve as a developmental metaphor crucial to a deeper understanding of the drama. The child may always have felt threatened and pressured to meet his mother's expectations, or projected such demands onto her. He fears betrayal or being dethroned by his mother or a rival at her breast. Motherliness unpredictably disappears, to be replaced by a devouring oral envy and greed. As Lady Macbeth is milked, she is depleted of nurturance and kindness; both Macbeths become mercilessly cruel. Lady Macbeth discards her conscience with her baby, although her unconscious superego will later assert itself with savage force and overpowering punishment. It is unconsciously fitting that as the instigating mother figure, the power behind the throne, she assumes the guilt. There is splitting between good and evil, male and female, creativity and destruction, generativity and sterility. Everything that is cruel, merciless, and murderous is associated with masculinity; everything compassionate, tender, motherly, and merciful is feminine (Martin, 1984).

Macbeth is initially the proxy agent and passive partner to Lady Macbeth's ruthless, phallic narcissism. He tries to cling to the passive position of the child without responsibility, directed by others and external forces. "If chance will have me king, why chance may crown me, without my stir" (I, 3). As he disengages from his initially dominant and controlling wife-mother, he emerges as the ruthless, omnipotent tyrant, unable to experience real grief or guilt, but experiencing persecutory visions and afraid of external retaliation. He wishes for and fears merger and femininity and defends to the death (or separation merger) his masculine autonomy. His regressively transformed witch-mother represents the infantile dangers institutionalized in witchcraft. (It is significant that suicides in the Elizabethan era could be ambivalently regarded as martyrs or as demonic sinners. "Sinful" suicides could be buried at night by crossroads with a stake driven through the heart [Forbes, 1970]. Lady Macbeth's suicide would then confirm her as a witch, and her death would match as well as atone for Duncan's midnight stabbing murder.)

The unintegrated bisexuality is of critical importance and related to the incomplete separation-individuation and lack of oedipal resolution. Lady Macbeth is disappointed in womanhood, hostile to her own mother and her child. Men also inevitably fail her, as Macbeth is later failed by his wife and the witches. She idealizes only her own possessed, illusory, omnipotent penis, her husband-son. Macbeth recognizes her masculine drive, identifies with it, and tells her to "bring forth men-children only! For thy undaunted mettle should compose nothing but males" (I, 7). He will ambivalently live out her grandiose omnipotent fantasies, redeem her disappointments, and be the weapon that avenges her fantasied injuries. (Banquo has a similar shared fantasy enjoining his son to revenge [III, 3].) There is a hidden shared fantasy that this son is his mother's phallus and omnipotent object.

If we look at Lady Macbeth's tormenting dialogue, the dialogue (Spitz, 1965) between mother and infant, he is massively threatened by nonconformity with her aspirations and will be thoroughly rewarded, yet threatened anew, with compliance. At the very moment when his smile should elicit maternal affection and increasing attachment, the infant is faced with malignant loss of face, breast, and nurturance. The smile and eye contact do not elicit the reciprocal smile which should be an organizer for the mother as well as the infant. The infant's smile is negatively perceived and becomes an aversive cue, evoking insufferable demand and feelings of angry accusation in the mother. Instead of providing a holding environment (Winnicott, 1965), she will cast the child down, just as later, "The sweet milk of concord" (IV, 3) will be poured into hell. Actually, the play is replete with images of mothers turning into witches and milk into gall. Security and safety are offered only to be suddenly and unpredictably withdrawn; such an unreliable frame of reference tends to impede differentiation and the achievement of self and object constancy. The witches themselves, bearded, undifferentiated, demonic, and divided from more mature nurturant images of motherhood, are unmistakably both maternal and antimaternal. As with betrayal at the breast (Erikson, 1959); (Bachmann, 1978), Macbeth imbibes the witches brew, inspires their air and is inspired by their prediction, and swallows the narcissistic supplies which he demands. The cauldrons represent pregnancy, the breast, and feeding, but the milk is poison and the brew is intoxicating and toxic. The witches and Macbeth have the shared fantasy of phallic-narcissistic grandeur and ruthless entitlement, murder, and retaliation.

Macbeth disengages from Lady Macbeth only to turn to the witches and from the witches back to Lady Macbeth and then to a "bold, bloody resolute" and rageful independence. The witches continue Lady Macbeth's threatening dialogue and dichotomy between murdering and nurturing infants: "finger of birthstrangled babe, ditch delivered by a drab" and "sow's blood that have eaten her nine farrow" (IV, 1) illustrate that the theme of childlessness also refers to infanticide. The sow is the preoedipal witch who cannot feed, but feeds on and as a cannibal devours her offspring. The infanticidal Lady Macbeth vicariously lives on and through the oedipal Macbeth who is the son who killed the father and the father who kills the son.

Many representations are split into opposites. The wicked witches augur harm, but Edward the Confessor's prophecies heal. Lady Macduff is the split-off nurturant mother who tries to support and comfort her children. Duncan is the venerated father who is trusting and trustworthy. Macbeth, distrustful and destructive, is the parricidal son and filicidal father. Macduff is both the deserting father who has failed to protect and the avenging father, the superego precursor, who will make Macbeth pay for his horrible crimes. But Macduff has been untimely ripped from his mother's womb, and exception in the form of a Caesarean birth, untainted with incestuous passage through the birth canal and a child who could not have been expected to live in that era. Only a Caesar could then survive a Caesarean birth. He is the avenger of the children whose lives were early aborted, on the oral level representing rivals at the breast, who are omnipotently destroyed by a voraciously greedy and envious Macbeth. Macbeth's narcissistic rage requires that the envied rival should disappear without possible return or replication; the extended family of kinsmen must also be killed, akin to genocide, so that no avenger could arise. Macbeth is the babe that milked Lady Macbeth of human kindness, the toddler whose rage threatens to consume and destroy everyone and everything. Macbeth retains awareness of some potential for moral revulsion, but his oral-narcissistic rage predominates: "I have supped full with horrors: Direness, familiar to my slaughterous thoughts, cannot once start me" (V, 5). Like Macbeth, Duncan's horses turn wild and devour each other after Duncan's murder (II, 4). The sterility of the Macbeths is associated with the infantile depletion and consuming destruction.

It is also possible to understand that to be untimely ripped from the womb is a metaphor for premature separateness with increased separation anxiety, oral regression, and coercion of the preoedipal mother to whom omnipotence is delegated. Helplessness is magically avoided by incorporating or being incorporated by the omnipotent witch, i.e., through merger with the preoedipal mother who is and who controls life and death. The drama depicts, with consummate artistic perception, the great dilemmas of separation individuation (Mahler et al., 1975) in concert with oedipal conflict. Macbeth, as the conquering hero toddler, becomes painfully aware of separateness, helplessness, and vulnerability. The more he recognizes how dependent and vulnerable he is, the more he turns to the witches for omnipotent reassurance and protection (Muslin, 1984). Their prophecies assure his invulnerability. If he is their sword, they are his shield. But they simultaneously threaten omnipotent retaliation, superego precursors that both reward and punish (Mahler and McDevitt, 1980). He can only be vanquished by someone like Macduff who has mastered the vulnerability of sudden premature separation. His magical dyadic orbit is omnipotently secure, and his space cannot be invaded nor lost through merger so long as Burnham Wood comes not to Dunsinane. The daggers in men's smiles (Bachmann, 1978), the treachery present in every form of intimacy, and the primal scene of mutual destruction (bodies locked in deadly combat) overweigh the unbridled narcissism of a frightened, enraged child who lacks self-definition and confidence, and the assurance of oral-narcissistic supplies. Macbeth attempts to ward off the awareness of anxiety, separateness, and helplessness, entreating and coercing the witches, holding on to them, darting away from them, having no comprehension or control of their mysterious appearance and disappearance. He is remorseless and furious when his magic fails and his mother will not function as an extension of himself and does not automatically understand or fulfill his unspoken wishes. "Be these juggling fiends no more believed" (V, 8). Reality has mercilessly intruded and the mighty tyrant has fallen from grace. Extreme disillusionment follows after infantile awe and idealization. Reality and omnipotence coexist and clash.

How are the crises to be resolved? Development will be determined by the prophecies which Macbeth drinks from the witches' cauldron. Here is a beautiful poetic metaphor for the character of the ego being determined by identification modeled on oral incorporation. Macbeth and Lady Macbeth demonstrate reciprocal identifications between marriage partners, parents, and parent and child. Macbeth drinks in her ruthlessness and infanticidal rage, as she appears to be drained and deprived. He is identified either with an object distorted by the projection of his own oral aggression or possibly with a mother who has undergone a profound oral regression concomitant with maternity. Lady Macbeth is identified with an ambivalently hated and feared mother and is unable to be consistently holding and nurturant. She is perceived as threatening rather than protective, perhaps threatened by a demanding infant with low frustration tolerance and circular, contagious anger within the dyad. Macbeth and his Lady cannot soothe or console each other. Macbeth's identification with Lady Macbeth's murderous attitudes may also be understood as an identification with the aggressor and her aggression. As in the formation of the superego, the identifications are based upon the parents' real and fantasied qualities; the image of a tyrannical, sadistic, and punitive parent may be based upon a child's primitive defenses and impulses, on problems in the child or the maternal environment, or on special problems within that particular dyadic relationship. The dyadic dimension of the drama may be read with emphasis on the demanding mother, the insatiable child, the particular mix and match, or the regressive relationship and reciprocal identification. Where there are serious preoedipal fixations and separation individuation is incomplete, there tends to be a distortion of the oedipus complex and often a fusion of oedipal and preoedipal issues (Kernberg, 1980). Parental images, normally split in the family romance, undergo extremes of idealization and devaluation. Castration anxiety covers and simultaneously represents separation anxiety, and phallic aims and objects continue preoedipal strivings as represented in the breast-penis equation. Oedipal disappointment and jealousy are likely to be intolerable since they are infiltrated with unresolved narcissistic frustration and oral greed, envy, and rage. The intensified and validated oedipal and castration fantasies present in each partner of a sterile couple are associated in *Macbeth* with much earlier, unresolved, parental ambivalence and infanticidal attitudes. The "milk of human kindness" has been depleted and replaced by a consuming exploitation and annihilation of narcissistic objects and oedipal rivals. Macbeth is the sterile child whose demands, envy, and rage can destroy the whole family. Macbeth is one of the rare dramas that approaches the theme of genocide, suggesting major underlying motives. Sterility is a motive, representation, consequence, and retribution for his villainy.

Macbeth has gone to the three Weird Sisters, the past, present, and future, and Freud's three fateful visions of mother, "to know by the worst means the worst" (III, 4). He received feedback steeped in omnipotence and in the blood of consuming hostility. After Lady Macbeth's demise, Macbeth is again prematurely separated, "She should have died hereafter. There would have been time for such a word" (V, 5). With separation and separateness he is alone with his inner anxieties and demons. As he acknowledges loss while defending against its affective meaning, time and life are suspended as "tomorrow, tomorrow, and tomorrow creeps in its petty pace from day to day, to the last syllable of recorded time" (V, 5). Deadened and dehumanized, he does not mourn but proclaims in anger and apathy that life is "a tale told by an idiot, full of sound and fury, signifying nothing" (V, 5). But in the age of psychoanalysis, even nothing has significance (Lewin, 1948). Nothing may mean the absent penis or flatus, but may also represent the helplessness of separateness (Abrams and Shengold, 1974). The shared phallic narcissistic fantasies which dominate the unresolved oedipal conflicts have their roots here in preoedipal dyadic issues. The unavailable narcissistic object is devalued and discarded. Macbeth repudiates his feminine identification, struggles against any weakness which is seen as being like a "baby girl" (III, 4), and simultaneously denies separation, castration, and death anxiety. His narcissism demanded descendants and now demands immortality through not dying. As the drama concludes, the cruel and remorseless coercion of the deflated toddler gives way, and the curtain falls on the "watchful tyranny... of this dead butcher and his fiend-like queen" (V, 8). The drama, ranging from the most profound and advanced levels of philosophical thought to the dyadic beginnings of the dialogue, grips the audience in shared fantasy and trial identification. Development may become deviant in the very vulnerable dyadic phase and wrecked if the postoedipal reorganization does not eventuate in reparative correction and benevolent transformation. "The instruments of darkness tell us truths" (I, 3). Macbeth illuminates analytic understanding of extreme hostility and sterility versus the harmony and fertility that are nurtured by the "milk of human kindness" and the internalization of benevolent parental attitudes and authority.

REFERENCES

Abrams, S. & Shengold, L. (1974). The meaning of nothing. *Psychoanal. Q.*43: *115–119.*

Bachmann, S. (1978). "Daggers in men's smiles.." *Int. J. Psychoanal..* 5:*97–104*

Arron, D. (1960). The babe that milks *Amer. Imago 17133–161.*

Baudry, F.D. (1984). An essay on method in applied psychoanalysis. *Psychoanal. Q.* 53:551–581.

Blum, H.P. (1980). The maternal ego ideal and the regulation of maternal qualities, In *The Course of Life*, ed. S. Greenspan and G. H. Pollock., *391–114* Washington, D.C.: National Institute of Mental Health.

——— (1985). Shared fantasy and reciprocal identification In *Unconscious Fantasy,* ed. H.P. Blum, Y. Kramer, A. Richards. New York: Analytic Press (in press).

Calef, V. (1969). Lady Macbeth and infanticide *J. Am. Psychoanal. Assoc.* 17: *528–548.*

Erikson, E.H. (1959). *Identity and the Life Cycle*, New York: Int. Univ. Press.

Forbes, T. (1970). Life and death in Shakespeare's London. *Amer. Scientis t58511– 520.*

Freud, A. (1965). Normality and pathology in childhood .W. 6.

Freud, S. 1908 Creative writers and day-dreaming, S.E. 9 141–153.

——— (1916). Some character-types met with in psycho-analytic work. *S.E.* 14 309–333.

——— (1916–17). Introductory lectures on psycho-analysis. *S.E.* 15 & 16

Jones, E. (1955). *The Life and Work of Sigmund Freud vol. 2.* New York: Basic Books.

Kernberg, O.F. (1980). *Internal World and External Reality..* New York: Aronson.

Kris, E. (1956). The personal myth. J. Am. Psychoanal. Assoc. 4:*653–681.*

Lewin, B.D. (1948). The nature of reality, the meaning of nothing, with an addendum on concentration *Psychoanal. Q.* 17:*524–526.*

Mahler, M.S. McDevitt, J.B. (1980). The separation-individuation process and identity formation In *The Course of Life,* ed. S. Greenspan. G. H. Pollock, 1*395–406* Washington, D.C.: National Institute of Mental Health.

——— Pine, F., Bergman, A. (1975). *The Psychological Birth of the Human Infant. New* York: Basic Books.

Martin, J. (1984). Discussion of *Macbeth,* by H. Muslin. *American Psychoanalytic Association.*

Muslin, H. (1984). *Macbeth.* Read at the American Psychoanalytic Association.

Spitz, R.A. (1965). *The First Year of Life.* New York: Int. Univ. Press.

Winnicott, D.W. (1965). *The Maturational Processes and the Facilitating Environment.* New York: Int. Univ. Press.

CHAPTER 3

Van Gogh's Fantasies of Replacement: Being a Double and a Twin

(2009). *J. Amer. Psychoanal. Assn.*, (57)(6):1311–1326.

The replacement child, often given the name of the deceased, is prone to fantasies that he or she is the embodiment of the dead child. Vincent van Gogh was born one year to the day after a stillborn brother of the identical name, including the middle name, Willem. In the parish register van Gogh was given the same number twenty-nine as his predecessor brother. Van Gogh's fantasies of death and rebirth, of being a double and a twin, contributed to both his psychopathology and his creativity. The replacement theme in van Gogh's life and work is evident in his voluminous correspondence containing drawings and references to his art. His parents and his brother Theo are viewed as having shared a familial fantasy system. Van Gogh's self-portraits are regarded as relevant to his being a replacement child. No single fantasy or theme can account for the complexities of development, disorder, or creativity. Van Gogh's art was vastly overdetermined, including extraordinary endowment and the motivation of a replacement child to justify his survival, surpass his rival double/twin through great achievement, repair parental depression, and defy death through immortality.

This paper explores the fantasies and themes of rebirth and replacement, separation, and being a double or a twin in the life and art of Vincent van Gogh (1853–1890). His stillborn brother, of the identical name including the middle name, Willem, was uncannily born exactly one year earlier, on March 30, 1852. In the parish register he was given the same number twenty-nine as his predecessor brother. That his parents gave him the exact same name and parish number strongly suggests the psychological significance of a replacement child to them and thus later to the artist. Though absent, this first Vincent was an invisible presence. Fantasies of death, resurrection, and reincarnation influenced much of van Gogh's art and permeated his life as well. His unconscious fantasies of birth and death, of being buried alive, of being "the life and the resurrection," were importantly represented in his psychopathology and his art. As a replacement child, van Gogh did not simply represent the replacement of all parents by their progeny, or a child given the name of a deceased member of the family according to a religious or cultural tradition.

Relating the effect of van Gogh's fantasies as a replacement child to his art, I will discuss the artist's self-portraiture and his preoccupation with self-definition and identity. The artist's self-portrait embodies both the external self and the internal private sense of self and identity, influenced by conscious and unconscious self- and object representations, as well as by more enduring aspects of character. Intrapsychic representations undergo change depending on developmental, psychological, and physical determinants, (Woods-Marsden 1998).

The Replacement Child and Bereaved Parents

As I use the term here, *replacement child* refers to the child of parents bereaved by the loss of another child, who have conceived the child as an intended replacement. Although the parents anticipate that the replacement will console them and relieve the pain of their loss, the replacement child may in fact either impede or facilitate their mourning. Depending on the interval between the child's death and the coming of the replacement, there may not have been adequate time for a mourning process. Parental reactions may require that the replacement child and the deceased child be of the same gender, be a biological child, or be an adopted child. Thus, there may be intervening births between the deceased child and the replacement child. The parents may be more depressed and traumatized if the deceased child was an only child or if several children had died, as in war, the Holocaust, or a natural disaster. The threat of further loss, as in past times of high infant mortality, may exacerbate the parental response. Appropriate mourning favors recognition of the new child as different from and independent of the lost child, rather than being a confusing and confused reincarnation, the living dead.

The parents' response to their child's death and to the birth of the next child as a replacement will have a major psychological and perhaps neurobiological influence on the replacement child. Parental trauma may be transmitted to the next generation. Not all parents insist on magical replacement, nor do all replacement children manifest significant psychopathology. While a replacement child may resent, or even rage against, being assigned the impossible mission of repairing the parents' injury, he or she may nevertheless compensate for their loss and ameliorate their bereavement. The parents' fantasy of an existing child replacing a deceased child has psychological consequences different from the effects of the replacement fantasy on a child conceived as a replacement. The unconscious fantasy of an only child that he or she has killed and replaced rivals (Arlow 1972) is not comparable to the fantasies of the child born to bereaved parents to replace an actual deceased sibling. The replacement child is influenced by the parents' persisting unconscious reactions, including their fantasies and expectations regarding the often idealized deceased child, as well as by his or her own replacement fantasy (Blum 2001).

Van Gogh as a Replacement Child

While personality and character are of course multidetermined, van Gogh's history and oeuvre suggest the profound influence of his role as a replacement child. Possibly the deceased Vincent was idealized in the parents' fantasy, predisposing them to disappointment as well as pleasure in the artist son who was his replacement. Van Gogh often acted as if he had an important, urgent mission in life, justifying his existence and his special status as a replacement child. He was an exception, and had to be exceptional to equal or exceed his fantasized rival double/twin. The replacement theme was interwoven with other determinants in the personality of this very complicated individual with a unique biological, artistic, and intellectual endowment. His letters (Van Gogh-Bonger 1959) demonstrate his unusual verbal gifts, replete with visual imagery. Very likely of great developmental significance, the replacement child theme appears to have been incorporated into a personal myth.

Familial Shared Fantasy

Van Gogh's personal myth as a replacement child is consistent with a parental shared fantasy. If indeed his mother had been depressed after losing the first Vincent (Lubin 1972), the artist would then have lacked her affectionate attunement, presumably attempting to find a responsive surrogate (e.g., his brother Theo). Vincent may have resurrected his namesake in fantasy and art to comfort and console his mourning parents. In his painted images the sorrowful, suffering *mater dolorosa* can be contrasted with the opposite figure of the comforting mother rocking the cradle. *The Cradle*, painted about the time he cut off his ear, depicted van Gogh's double identification with the caregiving mother and with her child. His bereaved mother could have been ambivalently afraid to readily bond with the new infant Vincent, since possibly he too would be lost. Historically, infant mortality rates were then very high. The first Vincent may have persisted as a ghostly presence in the family, specifically identified with his namesake in both the artist's and his parents' unconscious fantasy. Within his religious family, van Gogh was "the resurrection and the life …. though he were dead, yet he shall live," a biblical passage (John 11: 25) that his father preached as a minister. Death, rebirth, and immortality coalesce in the familial replacement theme, a proposed collective fantasy. Theo named his son for his brother Vincent, perhaps sharing the rebirth fantasy of his parents, who gave the artist the same name as their stillborn son. Although van Gogh's sister Anna, two years younger, was the next sibling, the artist's symbiotic fantasies were focused on Theo, his four-years-younger brother. Theo had been given the same name as his father, and Anna the same name as her mother. If resurrection had both psychological and religious significance in this family of pastors, then the parents reproduced themselves and their lost son in their first three children. The artist's concerns with blue sky and brown soil, the starry sky, and miners and sowers in the earth would then relate to his namesake's grave and his resurrected soul in heaven.

Preoccupation with Death

There is much evidence of van Gogh's preoccupation with death in his writings, his work in the mines, and his frequent visits to graveyards. The assumption that the artist had almost certainly seen the gravestone of his predecessor, with the name vincent van gogh inscribed on it (it stood in the graveyard of his father's church adjacent to his residence), during his childhood and on subsequent visits, has been confirmed. In a remarkable condolence note, recently discovered, dated August 3, 1877, sent by van Gogh to H. Tersteeg, his manager at an art gallery in The Hague, whose three-month-old daughter had died, van Gogh wrote: "I recently stood early one morning in the cemetery in Zundert next to the little grave on which it is written: Suffer the little children to come unto Me, for such is the kingdom of God" (Jansen et al. 2003). This biblical quotation (Luke 18: 16) is inscribed on the tombstone in Dutch under the name of his deceased brother. The note is not emotionally expressive. The art historians who studied it inferred that van Gogh was not in any sense plagued by the guilt that can often occur in a replacement child. They did not, however, take into account the artist's repression, suppression, and disguise of his emotional reactions. The bland note may well have defended against the powerful passions associated with the unconscious fantasy of being a magical replacement child. The replacement child who lives because a sibling has died can have survivor guilt, can readily imagine experiencing the same fate, and can also fantasy the revenge of the replaced child. The artist's lack of conscious connection between himself and the stillborn Vincent was perhaps further potentiated by the artist's exposure to the gravestone selected by his parents, which displays the year 1852 without giving the customary dates of birth and death. Presumably his parents chose to omit the date, and there is no known family reference to or observance of the fateful common birthday.

Van Gogh's confronting the gravestone of his predecessor is analogous to the childhood experience of Heinrich Schliemann, famous for unearthing ancient Troy (Niederland 1981). Schliemann, who like van Gogh had replaced and been given the name of a deceased brother, later visited and studied numerous catacombs and tombstones. Resurrection fantasy was apparently a determinant of Schliemann's becoming an archaeologist, as it was of van Gogh's becoming a painter. Van Gogh similarly visited many cemeteries, remarking on the overgrown graves bearing the names of the deceased (letters of September 17 and September 22, 1883). He had pictures of women in mourning and of the tomb of Anne of Brittany on the walls of his rooms. Suggestive of the significance of the tombstone of his deceased brother, he referred to an inscription on an ancient tombstone in Provence. In 1887 van Gogh wrote to his sister Wilhelmina about grains of wheat and corn that ripen and return to earth to germinate and become new plants. In the same letter he stated, "I believe, Jesus himself would say to those who sit down in a state of melancholy… get up and go forth. Why do you seek the living among the dead?" His inner preoccupation with the living dead is apparent also in his references to apparitions. In June 1890, shortly before his death, van Gogh wrote to his sister, "I should like to do portraits which will appear as apparitions to people in a hundred years' time …." In his last letter to her, later the same month, he wrote, "there are modern heads which people will go on looking at for a long time to come, and which perhaps they will mourn over after a hundred years." The references to apparitions, loss, and prolonged mourning are pertinent to the fantasy of a replacement child.

At the age of thirty, on August 8, 1883, van Gogh wrote, "I must complete a certain amount of work in just a few years." His premonition of his early death may have had suicidal implications, especially since, as I now believe, he had a bipolar disposition. In his frenzied artwork he was apparently manic. In his personal life there were marked depressive and masochistic trends prior to his psychotic episodes. Given the levels of ambiguity and complexity, it is not possible to arrive at a definite diagnosis (Meissner 1992b) or to clarify the relationship between his psychopatholgy and his creativity. "Before the problem of the creative artist analysis must, alas, lay down its arms" (Freud 1928, p. 177).

The Self-Portraits

Being a replacement child colored many aspects of van Gogh's life as an artist. Replacement fantasies affected his need to create art, as well as the content of his creations. While van Gogh could not afford models, that alone hardly explains his prolific self-portraiture. As a child he frequently studied himself in the mirror and drew sketches, long before he became a painter at age twenty-seven or -eight, relatively late in life for an artist. During the impoverished period of his ministry, he quoted the biblical text "For now we see through a glass, darkly; but then face-to-face: now I know in part but then I shall know even as also I am known" (Corinthians 13: 12). The biblical text would appear to have had special significance for van Gogh, whose self-portraits were face-to-face encounters with self, twin, internalized mother, and fantasized spectator. Van Gogh's use of himself as a model reflects his unconscious fantasies of replacement, doubling, twinship, and rebirth. Looking in the mirror and painting self-portraits, he sought to confirm his identity, stabilize his ego, regulate affects, and magically restore his self-worth and narcissistic object ties (Elkisch 1957; Shengold 1974). His self-portraits may be considered a symbolic mirror, perhaps representing the mirroring mother of infancy. In producing his art he could suffer, yet blunt, the power of his harsh, self-debasing conscience. Van Gogh's art, particularly his self-portraits, served his self-expression, his self-exploration, and his efforts at self-healing—a virtual art therapy (Meissner 1993, 1994). Van Gogh once stated that he felt alive only before his easel.

Figure 4. Van Gogh with bandage

Figure 5. Van Gogh portrait with vest

Figure 6. Van Gogh clean shaven

Conflicts regarding identity and identification are especially apparent in these self-portraits. The self-portraits also represent an identification and dialogue with his past masters, especially Rembrandt and Hals. After seeing the Louvre exhibition of self-portraits in February 1888, he soon depicted himself in his professional identity as an artist (Dorn 2000). During his two years in Paris, van Gogh completed nearly two dozen self-portraits, and over his career a total of more than forty. While the self-portraiture varies in each painting, he remains readily identifiable. In this respect the works differ from covert self-portraits like his portrait of Paul Gachet. This work has been considered a projection of himself, identified with Gachet, whom van Gogh referred to as a brother (Sund 2000).

How curious that van Gogh never painted a portrait of his brother, or of his "brother" Gauguin, even while living with each of them (and though Gauguin painted van Gogh). Was he afraid of disappointing Theo, arousing his intense sibling ambivalence, and awakening childhood revenants, or did he wish to deprive Theo of fantasized immortality in art? Van Gogh appears to have been jealous of, and deeply conflicted by, Theo's marriage and fatherhood, undercurrents in the expressive tension of his last self-portraits. In my view, Theo was unconsciously represented in the self-portraits, as secret sharer in Vincent's art, and its fantasy co-creator.

Van Gogh was afraid of both success and failure. Emotionally wrecked by feeling like a failure, he also feared being wrecked by success as a great artist. Though lacking recognition and respect in his foreshortened lifetime, the self-portraits of van Gogh, created in just a few frenetic years, would radically change traditional portraiture. For example, his use of nonrealistic and highly contrasting colors, heavy sinuous brushstrokes, undulating lines, and swirling rhythm, the achievement of intense affective expression, all influenced later portraiture. The prominent brushstrokes and thick, textured paint surface tend to evoke kinesthetic and tactile responses in the spectator. The depiction of a traumatized and tormented self-anticipated the twentieth-century art of self-dissolution and existential anxiety.

In December 1882 van Gogh painted *Orphan Man in Sunday Clothes with Eye Bandage*, a possible precursor of his self-portrait with his ear bandaged.

Although he had painted a bandaged person with a missing eye, van Gogh mutilated his ear. The ear was sacrificed, but he deliberately did not damage the eye of the artist (Walther and Metzger 1993). His visual conflicts were displaced onto the ear. As a child he would shun his family by keeping his eyes half-shut, a practice intermittently continued into his adult life (Lubin 1972). He regarded working on his self-portraits as contributing to his recovery after his near demise. Artists have painted self-portraits with a variety of motivations and meanings. In van Gogh's final self-portrait, the wavy vibrating lines, the intense, agitated motion and emotion, the contrasting colors, are nonetheless ordered and organized. The art was sustained despite his precarious psychological disorder. The final self-portraits were ghosts from the past, reincarnations given new life in the present and preserved for a timeless future. The portraits tend to evoke a dialogue with the spectator. There is an ambiguity in the identity of van Gogh's self-portraits. Who is the subject and who is the object? Which Vincent is the painter, and which Vincent was painted? Who is within and behind the portrait?

The Theme of the Double

As a re-creation and reincarnation of his brother Vincent, van Gogh had a split identity, a double identity, and/or a pseudo-identity, a false self (Winnicott 1960; Cain and Cain 1964). His remorseless, relentless self-scrutiny did not resolve his survivor triumph and survivor guilt. He was burdened by the unconscious fantasy of his being responsible for the life and death of his deceased brother, his fantasized double and ghostly imaginary companion (Nagera 1967; Lubin 1972; Anisfeld and Richards 2000). Sabbadini (1988, p. 531) noted the significance of the theme of the double in literature; among artists, both Salvador Dali and van Gogh were replacements. Sabbadini quotes Dali: "I lived through my death before living my life. At the age of seven my brother died of meningitis, three years before I was born. This shook my mother to the very depths of her being…. She was never to get over it. My parents' despair was assuaged only by my own birth, but their misfortune still penetrated every cell of their bodies…. I deeply experienced the persistence of my brother's presence as both a trauma—a kind of alienation of affections—and a sense of being outdone" (Dali and Parinaud 1973, p. 14). Sabbadini (1988) remarks that "a child might elaborate to an abnormal degree some specific fantasies that are also common in normal children:… that a double exists somewhere, which is one's real self, and of which one is only a shadow or a dim mirror reflection. This double has strong narcissistic connotations, and as 'immortal self' it has the function of defending the ego from the fear of death and annihilation" (p. 537). Conscious awareness by Dali and his bereaved parents of his being a replacement child invites comparison with van Gogh. The latter's replacement fantasies were apparently not in conscious awareness. Confused in his identity, the double was for van Gogh both protection against death and a lurking harbinger of death.

Van Gogh's signing with his first name only, though in the tradition of Rembrandt, may also allude to the many Vincents in his family. His father too had had a brother Vincent, a favorite brother who had helped support him, just as Theo (a fantasized twin), supported his artist brother Vincent. Using only his first name may also have facilitated efforts at separation-individuation. The soft, curvilinear *V* that he used in his signature in the middle of 1888 in Arles, replacing for a time the sharply angled *V*, may also represent his identity flux.

Sacrificing his health, depressed and disorganized in his personal life, van Gogh was controlled and creative in his art. This split between his personal and artistic identity can be conceptualized as a split between a true and a false self (Winnicott 1960). In his authentic artistic self he was able to sublimate his unconscious fantasies of rebirth and re-creation. Perhaps his artistic self/identity and his personal self were on different developmental lines. Possibly his identity as an artist tended to be adaptively maintained in the more conflict-free sphere of the ego (Hartmann 1964).

Van Gogh painted frantically and frequently all day and far into the night, sometimes forgetting to eat. Compounding his actual financial impoverishment was a depressive, masochistic quality reminiscent of his self-deprivation as a missionary. Starvation and malnutrition resulted in physical deterioration and the rotting of his teeth. His physical and mental condition was further damaged by smoking, by substance abuse including alcohol (notably absinthe), and by both inhaling and swallowing paint pigments.

Van Gogh, in addition to having the unconscious fantasy of being a double of his deceased brother, consciously fantasized that he had a double nature. In October 1888, essentially coincident with Gauguin's arrival in Arles, van Gogh wrote to Theo: "I am again pretty newly reduced to the madness of Hugo van der Goes …. if it were not that I have almost a double nature, that of a monk and that of a painter …." His fantasy of the double took many forms. It was displaced from the first Vincent to his brother Theo, as well as to Gauguin, a fantasy that haunted their relationship from the start. Aspects of the "double" are apparent also in van Gogh's identification with various artists. He wrote to Theo about the resemblance of a Delacroix portrait to himself and Theo (letter 564, December 1888). In the portrait by Delacroix, "a gentleman with red beard and hair, uncommonly like you or me… made me think of that poem by de Musset, 'Whenever I touched the earth—a miserable fellow in black sat down close to us, and looked at us like a brother.'" This citation evokes the original double, the first Vincent's gravestone, touching the earth as it were (Collins 2001).

After Vincent received his sister's notice in memory of the deceased artist Mauve, he wrote in a letter to Theo (March 31, 1888) that he had signed a canvas "souvenir de mauve / vincent theo." However, this painting (in the Kroller-Muller Museum, Otterloo, Netherlands) does not show Theo's name, only Vincent's. Did he retreat from the fantasized fusion of the two brothers?

This bonding or fusion fantasy could have been another disguised reference to his deceased namesake.

Object Relations

Concomitant with van Gogh's fantasies of doubles were pervasive difficulties in his relationships with others. Van Gogh was not an easygoing or cheerful individual; he manifested an abundance of inner turmoil and torment. In July 1882 he wrote to Theo, "I am often terribly melancholy, irritable, hungering and thirsting, as it were, for sympathy; and when I do not get it I try to act indifferently, speak sharply, and often pour oil on the fire. I do not like to be in company and often find it painful and difficult to mingle with people, to speak with them." He wrote of painful estrangement from friends, family, and social contacts. Lubin (1972), emphasizing van Gogh's endless struggle with depression, alienation, loneliness, and fragile self-esteem, indicated that his subject's sense of deficit and inferiority, shame and humiliation, defended against contradictory unconscious infantile omnipotence and narcissistic grandiosity. Hidden by masochism and martyrdom, grandiose expectations may have been reinforced by familial expectations for the replacement of an idealized deceased child. Born to a family who highly valued both religion and art, van Gogh continued his earlier religious fervor in his feverish devotion to art.

These relationships were colored by blurred boundaries and extreme dependency, particularly on his brother Theo. Van Gogh had for years been upset by disturbance in his bonding and dependency on Theo (Mauron 1976), and at one point anticipated the loss of both Theo and Gauguin to rival affections and interests. This sense of impending loss exacerbated his unconscious separation and castration conflicts. Although distressed that Gauguin planned to leave him, of even greater significance was his brother Theo's concurrent engagement to be married, which he announced in December 1888. Denying the impending loss of Theo to his fiancée, Vincent did not want to see, hear, or know about it. Displacing his dependent needs and angry demands from Theo onto Gauguin, he menaced the latter on December 23, 1888, just before Christmas, and, turning the aggression on himself, cut off half his left ear. Theo married on April 17, 1889, and two days later van Gogh wrote that he preferred to spend two or three months in an asylum. Learning in July that Theo's wife was pregnant, Vincent decompensated into psychotic depression. Theo's engagement, marriage, fatherhood, and subsequent physical illness were determinants of Vincent's subsequent severe regressions and suicidal behavior. Relevant to his attacking behavior, he had earlier written to Theo (in January 1884), "If I should drop dead .... you would be standing on a skeleton, and this would be a damned insecure standpoint .... as we are brothers, let us avoid killing each other …. I am forced to shoot at your side— however, I shall try not to hit you. You are forced to shoot in my direction—do the same." The correspondence strongly suggests a hidden reference to the skeleton of the first Vincent. "Standing on a skeleton" may have prefigured his later joining with the first Vincent through suicide, as well as fratricidal fantasy displaced onto Theo. Vincent had earlier reconciled a quarrel with Theo in a reunion of the brothers in an Amsterdam graveyard.

Christmas, too, reactivated ambivalently charged self- and object representations of Christ and God. Vincent as the divine son and his minister father as God the Father had often quarreled on Christmas (Blum 1956). Indeed, the light on van Gogh's forehead in some of his self-portraits has a subtle halo effect. He appears to have been identified with the dead and resurrected Christ, evident when he was an evangelist, and later in many of his letters and paintings (e.g., *The Pieta* and *The Raising of Lazarus*). The double identity as the dead and living Vincent is inferred as represented in the painting of loss and death in *The Pieta* and *The Reaper* and of rebirth and renewal in *The Sower* (after Millet) and *The Raising of Lazarus*. Van Gogh's paintings of the chair of Gauguin and his own chair were on his easel at the time of the cut ear episode. Object loss and death, as well as the implied presence of his brother and Gauguin in absentia, were symbolized by the empty chairs.

Supported by his younger sibling Theo, Vincent, in a role reversal, had become the child, with the younger brother the nurturing, stabilizing, surrogate parent. The last two self-portraits point not only to splitting but also to the reconstitution of the self in relation to Theo. Boxes and sarcophagi in his paintings may also refer to the graves of the two Vincents, as well as the conjoint "Vincent Theo." The twinship theme had appeared in his proposals that Theo join him, as a fellow artist, and that they even share the same mistress. Sharing the same mistress had unconscious oedipal, bisexual, and narcissistic determinants. The brothers' lives were interlaced like the pairs of shoes Vincent drew.

Theo, Vincent's alter ego and partner in his art, may also have represented the deceased brother Vincent, while protecting the artist from his ghostly rival. Yet displacement from conflicts with Theo onto the infant rival who was replaced must also be considered. The unconscious fantasized double can be the repository of conflicts with other important objects. Van Gogh's attachment to the artist Monticelli appears to be a disguised representation of his tie to Theo as a double, and as a resurrected brother. Vincent imagined he was a brother or son of Monticelli, or Monticelli himself. He thought of walking the same streets as Monticelli and dressing exactly like him. Writing to his sister Wilhelmina early in October 1888, van Gogh described the deceased Monticelli as cracked and impoverished, but with an extremely refined taste as a colorist. In a fantasy of being the dead Monticelli reborn, he then stated, "But isn't there another fatality which is charming? And what do we care whether there is a resurrection or not, as long as we see a living man arise immediately in the place of the dead man? Let us take up the same cause again, continuing the same work, living the same life, dying the same death."

Theo apparently shared a fraternal or familial fantasy with Vincent; he must have been psychologically dependent on Vincent to forge their almost symbiotic bond and to sustain Vincent's dependent attachment. The two brothers were the "parents" of van Gogh's art, though van Gogh was primarily Theo's dependent child. One may conjecture that van Gogh may also have fantasized that his paintings were their children or his own children in rivalry with Theo as biological father.

Van Gogh's disguised reference, in the letter of January 1884 ("standing on a skeleton"), to the first Vincent was followed by an assertion that their characters were not identical. That they were but also were not identical twins affirmed the artist's self-definition, and need to not only attach but to separate and individuate (Mahler, Pine, and Bergman 1975). Individuation was defended in action by being negative and oppositional, by provoking quarrels and preserving psychological and geographic distance from Theo. The fantasy of undoing the death of the first Vincent as his living embodiment protected against his hostile aggression.

Conclusion

Van Gogh had a confused double identity as **a** re-created, creative replacement, and as a ghost of himself and his deceased brother. The double represented triumph over loss and death, but was also a menacing harbinger of death. Theo joined Vincent in living out the parental shared fantasy of a twinship, a double, and eerily soon joined his brother in death. (Theo's death has now been attributed to tertiary syphilis. His body was moved by his widow to Auvers, France, where the brothers are buried beside each other.)

Van Gogh experienced an acute psychotic episode shortly after learning of the pregnancy of Theo's wife. He committed suicide in July 1890, six months after this new Vincent van Gogh's birth. The replacement child was replaced by "Vincent van Gogh," and this repetition contributed to his final psychological decompensation. With a despondent sense of failure as an artist, and anticipating Theo's loss, van Gogh succumbed to depressive hopelessness. He had taken refuge in paintings of fantasized merger with Mother Earth, his namesake in the earth, and his idealized narcissistic objects in the heavenly blue sky. "We take death to reach a star .... we cannot reach a star while we are alive" (letter to Theo, August 3, 1888). His suicide enacted the fantasy of merger, as well as murderous aggression against himself and his object world.

REFERENCES

Anisfeld, L., & Richards, A. (2000). The replacement child. *Psychoanalytic Study of the Child* 55:*301–318*.

Arlow, J. (1972). The only child. *Psychoanalytic Quarterly* 41:*507–536*.

Blum, H. (1956). Van Gogh's chairs. *American Imago* 13:*307–318*.

——— (2001). Psychoanalysis and art, Freud and Leonardo. *Journal of the American Psychoanalytic Association* 49:*1409–1425*.

——— (2003). De l'auto-portrait chez Vincent Van Gogh. *Revue Française de Psychanalyse* 67:*673–683*.

Cain, A., & Cain, B. (1964). On replacing a child. *Journal of the American Academy of Child Psychiatry* 3:443–456.

Collins, B. (2001). *Van Gogh and Gauguin.* Boulder, CO: Westview Press.

Dali, S., & Parinaud, A. (1973). *The Unspeakable Confessions of Salvador Dali,* transl. H.J. Salemson. London: Allen, 1976.

Dorn, R. (2000). The Arles period: Symbolic means, decorative ends. In *Van Gogh Face to Face.* Detroit: Institute of Art, pp. *134–171.*

Elkisch, P. (1957). The psychological significance of the mirror. *Journal of the American Psychoanalytic Association* 5:235–244.

Freud, S. (1928). Dostoevsky and parricide. *Standard Edition* 21:*177–194.*

Hartmann, H. (1964). Essays on Ego Psychology. New York: International Universities Press.

Jansen, L., Luijten, H., & Bakker, N. (2003). Self-portrait between the lines: A previously unknown letter from Vincent van Gogh to H.G. Tersteeg. *Van Gogh Museum Journal,* pp. *99–113.*

Lubin, A. J. (1972). *Stranger on the Earth: A Psychological Biography of Vincent van Gogh.* New York: Holt, Rinehart, & Winston.

Mahler, M.S., Pine, F., & Bergman, A. (1975). *The Psychological Birth of the Human Infant: Symbiosis and Individuation.* New York: Basic Books.

Mauron, C. (1976). *Van Gogh: Etudes psychocritiques.* Paris: Corti.

Meissner S.J., W.W. (1992a). The childhood of an artist. *Annual of Psychoanalysis* 20:*147–169.*

——— (1992b). Vincent van Gogh's suicide: A psychic autopsy. *Contemporary Psychoanalysis* 28:*673–694.*

——— (1993). Vincent: The self-portraits. *Psychoanalytic Quarterl y*62:*74–105.*

——— (1994). The theme of the double and creativity in Vincent van Gogh. *Contemporary Psychoanalysis* 30:*323–347.*

Nagera, H. (1967). *Vincent van Gogh: A Psychological Study.* New York: International Universities Press.

Niederland, W. (1981). An analytic inquiry into the life and work of Heinrich Schliemann. In *Lives, Events and Other Players,* ed. J. Coltrera. New York: Aronson, pp. *175–201.*

Sabbadini, A. (1988). The replacement child. *Contemporary Psychoanalysis* 24:528–547.

Shengold, L. (1974). The metaphor of the mirror. *Journal of the American Psychoanalytic Association*2 2:97–115.

Sund, J. (2000). Famine to feast: Portrait making at St. Remy and Auvers. In *Van Gogh Face to Face*. Detroit: Institute of Art, pp. *182–227*.

van Gogh-Bonger, J., ed. (1959). *The Complete Letters of Vincent van Gogh. 3 vols.* Greenwich, CT: New York Graphic Society.

Walther, I., & Metzger, R. (1993). *Van Gogh: The Complete Paintings. 2 vols.* Taschen.

Winnicott, D.W. (1960). Ego distortion in terms of true and false self. In *The Maturational Processes and the Facilitating Environment*. New York: International Universities Press, 1965, pp. *140–152*.

Woods-Marsden, J. (1998). *Renaissance Self-Portraiture: The Construction of Identity*. New Haven: Yale University Press.

CHAPTER 4

The Creative Transformation of Trauma: Marcel Proust's *In Search of Lost Time*

(2012). *Psychoanal. Rev.*, (99)(5):677–696.

Hidden childhood trauma beneath poignant memories is a central aspect of In Search of Lost Time. Marcel Proust's magnum opus may be psychoanalytically understood as an extraordinary literary transformation of severe trauma and associated unconscious conflicts. Proust's nearly fatal childhood asthma and concomitant medical mistreatment contributed to an intense ambivalent bond and bondage with his mother, replicated in the ambivalent relationships depicted in his novel. The retrieved and re-created past is relived in the novel's fantasy playground of time and space. Proust's intuitive grasp of significant aspects of time, memory, trauma, and transference was consistent with psychoanalytic thought. In the vast novel, the narcissistic mortification and losses of the protagonist are mourned, worked through, and partially redeemed. I interpret the famed joyous tasting of the madeleine in tea as an artfully disguised, temporally displaced, and affective reversal of life-threatening trauma. This article probes the role of Proust's intractable asthma in his breathless journey to ego mastery and timeless creativity.

In Search of Lost Time is the correct English title of Marcel Proust's (1871-1922) novel, À la Recherche du Temps Perdu. This epic masterwork comprises seven interwoven volumes of some three thousand pages (Proust, 1993). It was originally translated from the French into English as *Remembrance of Things Past,* a title apparently chosen by the translator and English publisher of the work. The English title was taken from Shakespeare's Sonnet 30, so aptly applied to the poetic prose of Proust:

When to the sessions of sweet silent thought
I summon up remembrance of things past,
I sigh the lack of many a thing I sought,
And with old woes new wail my dear times' waste:
Then can I drown an eye, unus'd to flow,
For precious friends hid in death's dateless night,

… … … …
But if the while I think on thee, dear friend,
All losses are restored and sorrows end.

Swaddled in blankets, lying in bed in his isolation chamber—his cork-lined, soundproofed, shuttered, bedroom—Marcel Proust wrote *In Search of Lost Time.* The setting of Proust's novel spans the time from 1878 to 1922, enveloping a vast personal, literary, and artistic terrain. To comprehend at all his life of infirmity and creativity it will be necessary to follow many diverging and converging paths through his intricate narrative. Because of the complexity and scope of Proust's magnum opus, it is impossible to do justice to its many themes. This article explores Proust's mastery of trauma in the creation of his masterpiece. While aspects of his illnesses have been noted with respect to his life and work, the pervasive influence of trauma and its mastery are illuminated here with new psychoanalytic exploration and biographical information. His vast novel may be described as autobiographical fiction, culminating in the integration of the sequential series of novels (Alexander, 2007).

Marcel Proust and Sigmund Freud never met nor, so far as is known, read each other's work, nor corresponded. Proust intuited the importance of retrieved memory, the reconstruction of childhood, and transference. His artistic reconstruction is especially relevant now when psychoanalysis has tended toward major emphasis on the here and now, and on intersubjectivity in the analytic relationship. He recorded vivid dreams, daydreams, and networks of associations. He noted that dreams in a flash permitted him to observe remote periods of his past life with all their emotion, shock, and brilliance. For Proust dreams were a nocturnal muse, and a reservoir of childhood wishes, memories, and fears.

Proust describes his own writing process in the opening pages of the first volume in the series, *Swann's Way*:

> *… for a long time I would go to bed early …. I would make as if to put away the book which I imagined was still in my hands …. It seemed to me that I myself was the immediate subject of my book …. I would ask myself what time it could be… I could hear the whistling of trains which now nearer and now further off… showed me in perspective the deserted countryside through which a traveler is hurrying to the nearby station, and the path he is taking will be engraved in memory …. (Proust, 1981, pp. 1-2)*

Time, memory, and a journey into the childhood past are hallmarks of Proust's monumental work. Though Proust grew up in Paris, he vacationed with his family in a rather obscure, picturesque village in the countryside near Chartres. Childhood is dramatically evoked in the old country home of his father's family, called Combray in the novel. The real name of the village is Illiers, now known as Illiers-Combray, France officially honoring Proust in a formal conjunction of art and life.

Proust's Traumatic Illness

Marcel Proust was born to a wealthy, sophisticated Jewish mother, Jeanne Weil-Proust, and a Catholic father, an eminent physician. Pregnant during the Franco-Prussian War, his mother suffered from malnutrition; his father was almost killed by a stray bullet. Marcel was a very sickly infant who was initially regarded as not likely to live. He became very closely attached to his anxious mother, concerned about the survival of her new family. Proust later attributed his vulnerability to illness to his precarious infancy, and there may well have been initial difficulties concerning a secure holding environment (Winnicott, 1965). Proust spent a considerable part of his childhood in bed or reclining in a chair, ill and asthmatic, or recovering from asthma and interrelated complications. His only sibling, Robert, was born two years after Marcel, in the changed setting of postwar calm and prosperity. In contrast to Marcel, Robert was a healthy, outgoing child.

Proust's illnesses permeate the form and content of his entire novel. He had severe allergies from early childhood; his nose was cauterized some one hundred times in a relentless attempt to cure his hay fever. At age nine he suffered his first and nearly fatal attack of bronchial asthma, for which he was hospitalized virtually comatose. His airways may have been scarred, and thus even more susceptible to allergens and infections (Shama, 2000). Often gasping for breath, he was repeatedly in danger of asphyxiation; frightened, he would lie still, as though dead. While afraid of death, he may have imagined escape into death, as well as being reborn free of illness. Sleep was sometimes interrupted by bouts of asthma; a severe attack, from which he and his parents feared he might never recover, could last 36 hours. Each attack could reactivate and intensify the preceding trauma, with the possibility of protracted, exceedingly dangerous forms of asthma. Complications such as emphysema were superimposed on the underlying asthmatic bronchitis. His asthma was unpredictable and unavoidable despite desperate attempts at prophylaxis; it was debilitating, emasculating, and developmentally disruptive. Proust's experience of choking and suffocation would have been associated with altered states of consciousness and an altered sense of time, which are incorporated in the novel. Catching his breath, Proust may have written the longest sentence in the French or English language, more than nine hundred words. Proust became prone to anxiety and depression and lost self-confidence, self-esteem, and self-reliance. Fortified by shared apprehension concerning Proust's safety and survival, an intense interdependence evolved between Proust and his mother. They became adhesive in their closeness to each other, often too close for each other's comfort. Proust wrote letters to his mother even when they were both home, and in her letters to Marcel, she regularly requested details of his health, illness, and treatments. Marcel Proust's mother was loving, hypervigilant, overprotective, and at times irritated and exasperated. Chronic asthma and severe acute attacks of asthma depleted the caregiver as well as the ill child. The family, attuned to early warnings of respiratory distress, became engaged in heroic efforts to limit allergens and to avoid asthma by any means possible. His mother alternated between infantilizing and reproaching Marcel. The secondary gains of his asthmatic illness became imbricated in Proust's personal, familial, and social life. Asthma became an alibi for evading unwanted tasks and social engagements, masked by a façade of indifference. The narcissistic wounds of illness were compensated by narcissistic entitlement, which coalesced with devouring and incestuous demands for his mother's total affection and attention. Identifying with his mother and his maternal grandmother, he assimilated their literary and artistic interests and taste, inspiring the future Marcel Proust. The etiology and unpredictability of asthma were not understood, and his physician father conjectured that Marcel might be suffering from neurasthenia or even masked malingering.

The slaughterhouse in Proust's novel referred to his own concerns with illness and the apprehension, shared by his parents, of an untimely demise. Lost time was a deeply important issue for Proust, as apparent from the title of his novel. Time had many conscious and unconscious meanings for Proust (Kristeva, 1993). Young, sickly Marcel actually lost time for school, socialization, and play. He missed time in school, was prohibited from engaging in rough-and-tumble sports and was admonished by medical authorities to avoid pets, flowers, fumes, and so on. He could not participate with friends in their ordinary active pastimes.

As a child and in later life, Marcel's psychological and physical problems were seriously aggravated by the medical management of the time (Strauss, 1980). The presumably well-intentioned but misguided treatment was highly harmful and hurtful. The etiology and treatment of asthma, still complex issues, were then unknown. Allergy and autoimmune illness awaited modern concepts; early formulations of psychosomatic causes proved naïve and oversimplified (Gottlieb, 2003). The eminent physicians who were then consulted recommended a restricted diet of milk and protracted bed rest. They thought that purges would purge the asthma, and consequently Marcel was sometimes subject to several enemas a day. The treatment might have led to electrolyte imbalance as well as malnutrition. What was prescribed had unrecognized toxicity in the form of castrating, emasculating assaults, anal rape, and narcissistic mortifications. He wrote to his mother in 1902, " … whether my asthma might be caused by worms—if Father thinks my ideas possible, would he please make a choice between… sugar or glycine enemas?" (Proust, 1971, p. 129). In a following letter (p. 134), he wrote, "Unfortunately, the only thing that has kept its appointment is an attack as asthma—I don't know whether to blame lack of sleep or lack of enemas" (Proust, 1971, p. 134). Proust had made friends with the enemas, and they had become familial exchanges, erotized penetrations and humiliations. The asthmatic illness and its mistreatment were associated with loss of autonomous control of body functions and contents and with both real and fantasized sadomasochistic submission and domination. Little wonder that Proust developed contempt for the medical profession, the profession of his father and brother. Apropos of his enema treatments, one of his favorite curses was "I will drown you in a sea of shit." In this very witty epithet in French, *mer,* sea or ocean, *mere,* or mother, and *merde,* or feces, are all close in sound and spelling, and psychologically connected. Illness and medical abuse were likely additive determinants to Proust's earlier bisexual and later homosexual disposition. During his adolescence his father hoped, according to conventional notions, that Marcel's gay tendencies could be cured by visiting a brothel. Marcel complied, and compared the brothel to a slaughterhouse. His fear of dying because of forbidden sexual activity and his sadomasochistic reaction to the brothel were incorporated in his novel.

Proust and His Mother

Proust's closest childhood relationship was with his mother, and continued throughout her life; he felt that he remained "little Marcel" in their interdependent interaction. His mother, however, had failed to give magical protection from the constant threat of the recurrence of asthma. Moreover, the birth of his brother, Robert, when he was two years old, seems to have intensified his ambivalent clinging to his mother, with feelings of betrayal and loss, sibling rivalry, and jealousy. When his brother married in 1903, Proust was so enfeebled that he could barely manage to attend the wedding, and was unable, or unwilling, to participate in the associated festivities.

All of the female characters in the novel disappoint and hurt the narrator through disloyalty, desertion, desecration, and ultimately the irreversible abandonment of death. Proust's ambivalence toward his mother is apparent in his letters, and toward all girls and women apparent in his novel, for example, in the relationships with Gilberte and Albertine. The rival males were emasculated and killed in the war. (The bisexual implications of the names of these women have long been noted.) There were many quarrels with his mother, followed by affectionate reconciliation. In his posthumously published, unfinished early novel *Jean Santeuil,* the thinly disguised autobiographical protagonist smashed a Venetian glass his mother had given him in an argument with his parents. Though the protagonist was expecting a reprimand, his mother whispered in his ear that it will be as in the temple, symbolizing an indestructible union. The reference to the breaking of a glass as at the conclusion of a Jewish marriage ceremony seems strongly suggestive of incestuous maternal seduction. The wish for, retreat from, and defense against incestuous union is an unconscious thread throughout the search for lost time and lost love. Oedipal conflict is condensed with unresolved preoedipal issues of attachment, separation individuation, infantile narcissism, fixation, regression, and progression (Halberstadt-Freud, 1991). Marcel's bond and bondage with his mother is displaced and modified in a number of relationships in the novel. Baron Charlus is first presented as masculine, with shades of Marcel's father and brother. Later, Charlus is effeminate, a phallic woman, and a masochist. He lusts after an older tailor and a youthful violinist. The Baron invested in a male brothel where he paid to be chained and beaten. Proust's illness itself was probably experienced as a punitive and persecutory object, primarily invested with his own projected aggression.

To deal with the aggression and sadomasochism exacerbated by his cumulative recurrent traumata, Proust split the maternal representation into the polarized extremes of good and bad, omnipotent punishment or protection. In *Swann's Way,* the first novel of the larger work, on his walk the hero observes a forbidden lesbian relationship (Mlle. Vinteuil and her lover) in which Mlle. Vinteuil spits on her father's photograph. Here, our protagonist is identified with a desecrating, destructive attitude toward the parent, with fears of retaliation. Madame Proust was accused of loving Marcel only when he was ill. When he was ill, he was ill disposed toward his mother, and she incurred his unconscious rage and hate. He thought he would die if he did not get his mother's good-night kiss, but he was unaware of his unconscious fantasy of killing her when she was experienced as disappointing and punitive. In À la Recherche, his grandmother dies a very cruel death. Albertine, a bisexual mother figure, is forced to confess her betrayal and desertion of the protagonist to another lover. Albertine is finally killed off in a fall from a horse, and so died as a fallen woman. The spitting on the parent's photograph in the novel may be related to Proust as a collector of photographs of persons he ambivalently admired. The spitting can be conceptualized as his projection of his hatred, perhaps modeled on the spitting of sputum during repeated bouts of asthmatic bronchitis. The idealized love object is profaned in the ambivalent spitting, which also might be understood symbolically as ejaculating on or into the mother figure. Madame Proust forbade her asthmatic son from going on outings or picnics, which interfered with Marcel's efforts at separation and independence, as well as fortifying the bilateral incestuous bond. Partly because of her prohibitions, Proust considered his mother a despot, but his asthma at times gripped him in a fearful, despotic chokehold. His own tyrannical hostility was projected and transferred in the novel onto women and other degraded, homosexual partners. His ambivalence to his parents is indicated in the novel, displaced onto other characters.

The Famed Magical Madeleine

The loving side of Proust's feelings toward his parents is most prominently expressed in the famous episode of the protagonist in *Swann's Way* tasting the madeleine and remembering the ones he used to dip in his aunt's warm tea. This radiant experience was overdetermined with multiple meanings and ramifications within the vast novel. The protagonist was an adult when the madeleine stirred the resurrection of the past, glowing in the present. For Proust this was a "privileged moment," when past and present coalesce outside of chronological time, analogous to the psychoanalytic concept of transference.

> When the 33-year-old narrator was offered the madeleine, he at first declined it, and then for no particular reason, changed my mind… no sooner *had the warm liquid, and the crumbs within it, touched my palate than a shudder ran through me …. An exquisite pleasure had* invaded my senses,… with no suggestion of its origin …. Whence *could it have come to me, this mighty joy?… What did it signify? How could I seize upon and define it?… I can measure the resistance, I can hear the confused echo of great spaces traversed… the object of my quest, the truth, lies not in the cup but in myself… I put down my cup and examine my own mind… but How?" (pp. 48-51).*

Proust struggles with inner resistance in a literary inquiry that reveals the great truth that the childhood past is still alive within us. The form and plotline of the novel is discontinuous, with flights of thought suggestive of free association. The protagonist states that he will postpone discovery of why the madeleine made him so happy, approaching Freud's formulation in his letter to Fliess of May 28, 1899, that "happiness comes only with the fulfillment of a childhood wish" (Masson, 1985, p. 353). More intense evocative recollections emerge, all consciously connecting to surprise and joy rather than pain and panic. The magical potion of the cake and tea symbolized maternal nurturance, the breast and milk, and also represented a regressive, incestuous union with his mother.

The indelible "tea time" brought back a flood of involuntary, that is, spontaneously recovered memories. These memories dramatically flooded the protagonist's consciousness. The retrieved memories were woven into a reconstructive tapestry. As he noted, the luminous world of his childhood appeared to magically arise from the teacup. His radiant recollection was associated with intense pleasure and curiosity. He was transported back to the country home in Combray, and preoccupied with obtaining his mother's treasured good-night kiss at bedtime. Waiting for her kiss seemed like an eternity, and without her kiss he would have anxiety and insomnia. After the doorbell signaled the departure of Swann, the first interloper who had come to dinner, little Marcel was concerned about his father as a rival for his mother's attention. He anticipated his father's irate opposition to his mother's going upstairs to give him his good-night kiss. His father is then transmuted from the forbidding object, instead excluding himself and urging his wife to attend to the child protagonist in his upstairs bedroom. The dinner scene with the guests is strongly suggestive of a primal scene, from which the child was excluded. By incorporating the madeleine and tea, the protagonist finds that loss, separation and narcissistic injuries were magically undone.

The critical unconscious significance of the madeleine memory has been essentially overlooked in Proust studies and psychobiography. I infer that Proust artistically transformed nearly fatal shock trauma (and cumulative trauma) into the opposite representation of a joyous recollection. Frightening asthma with wheezing and gasping for air is defensively and adaptively replaced in the novel by highly pleasurable sensations and affects aroused by the warm tea with the petite madeleine. Trauma is seemingly reintegrated and creatively transformed in triumphant literature. The transformation of trauma is facilitated by the author's fluid self, object, and temporal boundaries in a new developmental organization. I also interpret the central madeleine memory as a poetically disguised repetition of shock trauma, in which time is frozen. In an imaginary escape from overwhelming traumatic anxiety, the madeleine scene is projected backward in time to age seven, before Proust's first massive asthma attack at age nine. The novel freely alters linear, chronological time to the subjective time of fantasy and art. The narrator is transposed to an earlier, partly legendary, charming childhood into which the reader is invited on the beguiling paths of *Swann's Way*. Children want their mother's comforting, curative kiss in response to illness and injury. Imploring mother's good-night kiss might be understood as the magic cure, the antidote to the kiss of death. The petite madeleine might also signify the wafer of the Catholic mass, offering absolution and salvation from the punishment and peril of recurrent trauma.

Proust recovered memories of his first erotic crushes and his childhood masturbation. His fear that he could not possess or control his mother, or her surrogates, was evident. The affectionate ambiance of his aunt's home may also be contrasted with conservative society, which denigrated and stigmatized the infirm, gays, and Jews. His narcissistic rage was generally stifled with later attempts to cover frowns and scowls with wit, sarcasm, and humor. Narcissistic injuries promoted feelings of narcissistic entitlement, with abrasive demands for affection and admiration. Brilliant classmates were in awe of his intellect, but could tease and disparage him. He could alienate adolescent friends such as his close classmate Jacques Bizet (son of the composer) with seductive overtures (Carter, 2006). The sickly outsider concealed and compensated for his feelings of inferiority through the guise of a supercilious social climber and snob. He would later become a very satirical critic of the vain, arrogant aristocracy to which he had aspired. The aristocratic salons of the time, divided in part by pro and anti-Dreyfus attitudes, are brought to life in the novel in their ostentatious display and pretentious elitism.

Traumatic Object Loss, and Recovery

Proust's preoccupation with the relentless march of time and transience was intensified after the death of his parents; his father died in 1903, and his mother died in 1905. After his mother's death, Proust wrote, "I'm so incapable of living without her, so vulnerable in every way" (Davenport-Hines, 2006, p. 81). Temporally destabilized from her loss, he spent six weeks in a sanatorium. About 1907-1908, Proust began writing À la Recherche du Temps Perdu. He needed sufficient mourning and self-confident independence to begin the great literary enterprise without external support. His writing served as a form of unconscious reunion with his mother (Aciman, 2004), while fostering his own developmental progression and delayed individuation. With his parents deceased, he could write one of the first major novels containing numerous bisexual characters, without concern for parental antipathy and embarrassment. Writing his novel might have recapitulated his innumerable letters to his mother, a symbolic continuation of their love/hate communication, transposed into the realm of his creative imagination.

In 1906, Proust moved from his mother's apartment to his own apartment at 102 Boulevard Haussmann, a building that now preserves his abode as a monument. Situated on a busy, dusty, noisy thoroughfare, the apartment was hardly a salutary venue for the hypersensitive, asthmatic author. Weeks of childhood bed rest and lonely reverie prefigured his life as a secluded, isolated novelist. Having the apartment compulsively cleaned repeated the dusting, washing, and fumigation of his childhood rooms. Sleeping much of the day, he worked at night, attempting to avoid recurrent asthma. Phobic of dust and germs, he usually shook hands wearing gloves, cleaned envelopes before they were opened, and had his towels specially laundered. His life in his protective cocoon resembled a quarantine that his epidemiologist father recommended to prevent the spread of contagious disease, such as typhoid and cholera. He may have identified with his demanding chronically ill aunt in their Illiers/Combray home. His aunt had subjugated the maid, as Proust did later with his own housekeeper, an aunt/mother figure. He was not above trying to impose his own agenda on family and friends. He ventured out in the late evening when few carriages would spew road dust, and occasionally toured the countryside in a sealed car. Trying to prevent asthma, and guarding his privacy in order to have uninterrupted writing, he was phobic and quasiparanoid about boundary intrusion by invisible pathogens and invasive visitors. Proust's idiosyncratic lifestyle as a recluse may well have facilitated his internal reconstruction and re-creation of a lived, and living past.

Proustian Memory

Proust had a deep affective investment in memory, its registration, retrieval, functioning, and reconstruction. Proust's self-analytic search of forgotten memory, in search of a lost self and object world, was subject to poetic license with artistic transformation and transposition of characters and their character traits. He intuitively understood that memory was subject to various forms of distortion, and that even accurate memory could have a screening function (Freud, 1899; Schacter, 2001). Proust claimed that involuntary, spontaneous memory was superior to intentional recall. He implicitly recognized happy memories could dilute and defend against painful memories, and could have beneficial developmental influence. It should be noted that the Proustian ideal of involuntary memory is quite different from the summing up of remembrance of things past of Shakespeare's sonnet and the original English title of his novel.

"To summon up memory" is to intentionally recapture rather than to spontaneously retrieve memory. However, Proustian memory had many facets, in many respects anticipating modern concepts. Proust is primarily concerned with autobiographical (episodic memory) rather than factual semantic memory. However, autobiographical memory, as Proust surmised, is always subject to wishful thinking, defensive distortion, and historical/cultural context. Memory could be fallible, merged with imagination, modified over time and the process of retrieval and recall. Autobiographical memory retains some accurate details, but is never an exact reproduction of the past (Blum, 1998; Damasio, 1999). Proust's focus on sensory perception, especially taste and smell, in memory retrieval is consistent with current neuroscience. Taste and smell neurons are closely connected to the hippocampus, where long-term memory is stored (Lehrer, 2007).

"Proustian" memories are generally in the preconscious autobiographical category modified by traumatic experience, unconscious fantasy, and literary license. Proustian memory does not directly represent a return of the repressed. The long-lost memories evoke unconscious derivatives as well as associations that become pathways into the past. For example, waking up in Paris as an adult in the present, the narrator of Swann's Way states, "I usually did not go to sleep again at once, but used to spend the greater part of the night recalling our life in the old days at Combray .... Recalling all the places and people that I had known, what I had actually seen of them, and what others had told me" (Proust, 1981, p. 9). In this context, the two different paths in Swann's Way represent different sets of child and adolescent memories, fantasies, and perspectives as well as different ethnic, sexual, and social orientations. Memory systems probably interact with each other and are subject to the influence of endowment, development, and culture. For Proust, memory is fluid, leading to variable reconstruction, in part because in his view there are many selves, with varying recollection. Proust was probably influenced by Montaigne, and by his distinguished cousin by marriage, Henri Bergson, for whom the psyche was in constant flux.

Proust's sensory memories have been described as screen sensations, which evoked an upsurge of screen memories (Anthony, 1961). What is also significant is that Proust closely connects the sensations with powerful affects. Proust's recall of the uneven pavement in St. Mark's square when he visited Venice with his mother was linked to the irregular flagstones on which his protagonist tripped while entering the Guermantes mansion. Unconsciously, he could be punished for forbidden trespass. These memories were associated with the sound of a butler striking a spoon against a plate, and with wiping his mouth with a napkin. He then had an immediate visual impression of rounded, bluish breasts. The oral imagery of the madeleine in the tea, the spoon against the plate, and the napkin on the mouth can be connected to the dearly desired kiss of his mother and little Marcel's reciprocal desire to kiss an exact spot on his mother's cheek. Past and present converge in the oral-breast imagery, the Proust home dinner, with Swann as the guest, and the party with butler, spoon, plate, and napkin. For Proust the past was then activated and condensed in the present privileged moment, and therefore considered outside the objective, linear order of time. Proust seems to have intuited the absence of time in the unconscious, as well as the past persisting as a powerful determinant of the present and future. Proust wants to be nurtured and loved by his family, his lovers, his housekeeper, secretary, and readers, all represented in his created characters. The oral imagery cloaked the oedipal fantasy of the good-night kiss, and the incestuous tea for two.

Trauma, Time, and Loss

Proust's highly emotional reactions, his painful longing for love, his separation anxiety, anger, jealousy, and feelings of betrayal by his ambivalent love objects are vividly represented in the novel (Wimmers, 2003). The narrator

Marcel feels betrayed by his lovers, Gilberte and Albertine, and identifies with Swann's betrayal by his promiscuous partner, Odette. The narrator suspects Albertine of having a lesbian lover, inquires about her every word and action, and tries to divine her every thought and feeling. He needs to insistently confirm his suspicion with her confession. She must assert that the narrator is devotedly loved above all others. The novel mirrors Proust's internal and external demands on his mother and the surrogate objects in his life and art. He accused his mother of withholding her love and money; she could not love or comfort him enough when he was ill or well. "As soon as I feel well you destroy everything until I feel bad again… it is sad that I cannot have your affection and my health at the same time (Proust, 1971, p. 105). After inheriting his parent's wealth, Proust tipped waiters extravagantly, buying their attention, respect, and insurance against rejection. Needy and jealous, he hired a private detective to find and report on the activities of his wayward secretary and companion, Albert Agostinelli (a model for Albertine).

Time flows in all directions in the novel, for example, toward the timeless in the unconscious and in art, and toward the end of time in mortality. Proust has artfully mastered the tendency for the halting and freezing of time by trauma. Time is a dimension of trauma, conflict, and compromise, subjectively influenced by pleasure and unpleasure, and objectively regulated by the reality principle (Kristeva, 1993; Levine, 2008). Many of the characters die or disappear in the novel. Concerned with mortality, Proust wrote feverishly against the clock, racing against time to finish his magnum opus. His internal clock was repeatedly reset by trauma. Thieves of time, his asthma and infirmities were correlated with ever more time needed to develop and organize the novel. Extending the novel while concluding the novel, he evaded a decisive termination. For the severely traumatized person, the past threatens to return in the repetition compulsion, for example, in anniversary reactions, nightmares, frightful memories, fantasies, and flashbacks. Diminished belief in a hopeful future may contribute to the search for and construction of an idealized past. Proust equated ending his life's work with ending his life and his object relations. The counterpoint to personal death was to have an indestructible identity in art, to become one of the timeless immortals (Pollock, 1980). In writing his novel, lost time could be regained, traumatic injury could be repaired, and object loss could be reversed. Time could be a symbolic self or object as in "Father Time" with his scythe, or mother time exemplified in the three fates, the Horae, hours. Time could be lost or found, killed or saved, fleeting or forever. Time could be killed instead of self or object. In the novel, time is both compressed and expanded, and, in my view, telescoped into the subjective past. Pertinent to Proust's asthmatic coma, persons who have had near-death experiences have frequently reported altered experiences of consciousness and time, such as time standing still. Less frequent, striking reports of near-death experiences feature spontaneous images of long-forgotten happy scenes from early childhood (Hartocollis, 1983). These reports appear to be consistent with my thesis of the screen scenes evoked by the protagonist imbibing the magical warm tea with the madeleine. Proust's captivating, charming memories and reconstruction, retrieving and re-creating scenes of childhood (Blum, 1994), modulate the underlying depressive tone of separation and traumatic loss.

In his self-imposed solitary confinement, Proust turned inward into memory and constructed a world in which time is subordinated to his artwork (Levine, 2008). In search of lost time, Proust referred to more than two hundred works of art, from the thirteenth to the twentieth centuries (Karpeles, 2008). Trauma and mourning can be assimilated only over time, and Proust attempted to conquer the tyranny of trauma and time in an aesthetic reconstruction. Proust has intuitively represented regressive revival of the past, and progressive development to the present. He is not a traveler into the timeless unconscious, but he is deeply influenced by unconscious fantasy as well as conscious considerations of his art and literary goals. Greenacre (1971) noted the double orientation in the creative artist to fantasy and reality, childhood and adulthood, as well as an unusual facility in being able to shift into different developmental phases. The creative writer and artist can reinstate the thinking, feeling, and fantasy of all developmental phases. Regulated regression may have permitted the narrator-writer to use his seclusion room as a symbolic gestating womb. Proust may have been living in a fantasized timeless merger that would simultaneously disguise the incestuous fantasy of being inside his mother. Separation would impose time limits. The world outside his apartment was regarded as cold and comfortless, a dissociated bad object. The dangers of separation, illness, and incest seemed to emanate from a bad object world. His mother could withdraw love, or insinuate incestuous love.

As time flows and his artful journey proceeds, sadomasochism and infantile narcissism emerge front and center, and then recede. His writing contrasts the idealization of the arts with the perverse and profane. In *Sodom and Gomorrah*, the fourth volume, sadomasochistic scenes reflect the reports of people to whom Proust confided perverse interests. He had dreamed of his parents as rodents, and he reportedly became sexually excited watching fighting rats (Tadié, 2000). His sadomasochism was sublimated in the writing of remarkably gripping chapters of the novel (Chasseguet-Smirgel, 1984). As an author, Proust maintained omnipotent control of character, impulse, affect, and object. Loss could be assuaged, endured, and restored. He created a world subject to his own laws and whims at the stroke of a pen. Realistic perspectives coexist with narcissistic omnipotence and entitlement. The narrator laments the vagaries and loss of love and loved ones, that one loves only what one cannot have, and that one loves the fantasy rather than the reality of the lover. Tormented love is inevitable. The rejected lover expresses grief and rage at abandonment, as well as guilt and self-hate for wanting revenge on the disappointing, unavailable partner. The protagonist may also reverse the position of passive victim into active perpetrator, rejecting the faithless partner.

Reconstruction and Reintegration

Proust's characters are not only killed, but as mentioned earlier are recycled, split, dissociated, and transposed among other characters. His characters also enjoy life and each other. The focus on his illness does not do justice to Proust's pointed sense of humor and capacity for play. He plays games with his characters, parties with his socialites, and satirizes the supercilious snobs. The architectural unity of the work is served by the recurrence of disparate themes and by the reappearance, but with alterations, of the same characters in several volumes. Narrator and protagonist may be well differentiated, or at times may alternate (Poland, 2003). For clarity, the narrator often suggests what the reader should infer. Early critics had disparaged Proust's novels as a somewhat disorganized, lacking form. However, Proust's absolute command of poetic prose, metaphor, and composition ultimately won critical acclaim. He painted with verbal imagery. Despite the repeated traumas during the long period of his writing the novel, his literary gifts remained intact. Since he had been a sickly, confined child, Proust's vicarious experience of life through literature was richly rewarding. Proust wrote in 1905, "On no days of our childhood did we live so fully perhaps… as those… that we spent with a favorite book" (1971, p. 3). He could commune with his favorite authors, and quote the classics like his mother and grandmother, while confirming the value of imagined experience. He alluded to the role of reading in the attempted mastery of trauma, stating, "There are certain cases… in which reading may become a sort of curative" (p. 3).

Until traumatic losses are regained, the protagonist is in danger of not being able to write his novel. Mourning these losses and composing his novel were accomplished over a long period of time. Proust once referred to himself as a perpetual patient. When his housekeeper was recuperating from childbirth, Proust wrote to her that she would soon be liberated from being a patient, but he was imprisoned in his illness. He was nevertheless inwardly aware of his growth and power as an artist/author.

In *Time Regained,* the seventh volume, the narrator, now named Marcel, and Marcel Proust coalesce into a culminating reintegration. Before, the narrator and protagonist sometimes represent a dissociation between active experience and reflective observation, analogous to what happens in the psychoanalytic process. Living outside chronological time in psychic reality and living within the time limits of external reality are now different, yet compatible perspectives.

The end of the novel is a beginning, with a feeling of generative rebirth, and the comforting illusion of immortality in his magnum opus. The protagonist dies in the novel after seeing Vermeer's painting "The View of Delft," a scene based upon one of Proust's last journeys, when he saw that painting in 1921.

(Proust importantly contributed to the rediscovery of Vermeer.) He fantasied triumph over death in identification with great artists and timeless art.

In November 1922, Proust died of bronchial pneumonia. Though haunted by sickness during his life, he expanded and orchestrated his novel to the end. What was the role of his illness in his motivation and dedication to be a free-spirited, innovative author? Proust reflected on this issue and wrote, "For those who, like me, believe the literature is the ultimate expression of life, if the illness has helped you to write the book in question, people will think you must have been only too happy to welcome the inspired collaborator" (Tadié, 2000, p. 555). Was the illness really a collaborator, a muse, a fostering object? Was asthma a coconspirator, along with other traumas and injuries? His resilience in the face of severe, protracted trauma was extraordinary. If Proust had been free of asthmatic illness, I surmise that he could have still created a masterwork. But it would not have been the breathless journey of *In Search of Lost Time*.

REFERENCES

Aciman, A. (2004). The Proust project. New York: Farrar, Strauss, & Giroux.

Alexander, P. (2007). *Marcel Proust's search for lost time: A reader's guide to "The remembrance of things past."* New York: Vintage.

Anthony, E. (1961). A study of screen sensations. *Psychoanal. Study of the Child*, 16:211–221.

Blum, H. (1994). *Reconstruction in psychoanalysis: Childhood revisited and recreated*. New York: International Universities Press.

Blum, H. (1998). The reconstruction of reminiscence. *J. Amer. Psychoanal. Assoc.*, 47:1125–1144.

Carter, W. (2006). *Proust in love*. New Haven, Conn.: Yale University Press.

Chasseguet-Smirgel, J. (1984). *Creativity and perversion*. New York: Norton.

Davenport-Hines, R. (2006). Proust at the Majestic. London: Bloomsbury.

Damasio, A. (1999). The feeling of what happens. New York: Harcourt.

Freud, S. (1899). Screen memories. In J. S. Strachey, ed. and trans., The standard edition of the complete psychological works of Sigmund Freud, 24 vols. London: Hogarth Press, 1953–1974. 3:*299–322*

Gottlieb, R. (2003). Psychosomatic medicine: The divergent legacies of Freud and Janet. *J. Amer. Psychoanal. Assoc.*, 51:*857–881*.

Greenacre, P. (1971). Emotional growth. New York: International Universities Press.

Halberstadt-Freud, H. (1991). Freud, Proust, perversion, and love. Amsterdam: Swets & Zeitlinger.

Hartocollis, P. (1983). Time and timelessness, or The varieties of temporal experience. New York: International Universities Press.

Karpeles, E. (2008). Painting in Proust. London: Thames & Hudson.

Kristeva, J. (1993). Proust and the sense of time. New York: Columbia University Press.

Lehrer, J. (2007). Proust was a neuroscientist. New York: Houghton Mifflin.

Levine, H. B. (2008). Time and timelessness: Inscription and representation. *J. Amer. Psychoanal. Assoc.*, 57:*333–355*.

Masson, J. (1985). The complete letters of Sigmund Freud to Wilhelm Fliess. Cambridge, Mass.: Belknap Press of Harvard University Press.

Poland, W. (2003). Reading fiction and the psychoanalytic experience: Proust on reading and on reading Proust. *J. Amer. Psychoanal. Assoc.*, 51: *1263–1282*.

Pollock, G. H. (1980). [Review of the book Dying: A psychoanalytic study with special reference to individual creativity and defensive organization]. *Psychoanal. Q.*, 49:*704–706*.

Proust, M. (1971). Letters to his mother. New York: Greenwood.

Proust, M. (1981). Swann's way. New York: Vintage.

Proust, M. (1993). In search of lost time. New York: Modern Library.

Schacter, D. (2001). The seven sins of memory. New York: Houghton Mifflin.

Shama, J. (2000). Marcel Proust (1971–1922): Reassessment of his asthma and other maladies. *Eur. Respiratory J.*, 15:*958–960*.

Strauss, B. (1980). Maladies of Marcel Proust: Doctors and diseases in his life and work. New York: Holmes & Meier.

Tadié, J-Y. (2000). Marcel Proust. New York: Viking.

Wimmers, I. (2003). Proust and emotion. Toronto: University of Toronto Press.

Winnicott, D. (1965). The maturational processes and the facilitating environment. New York: International Universities Press.

CHAPTER 5

Leonardo da Vinci and the Mona Lisa

(2024). Psychoanalytic Study of the Child 77:212–216.

Abstract: This paper is a tribute to the late Fred Pine, Ph.D. Relating to Dr. Pine's original exploration of pre-oedipal and pre-verbal development, it discusses and amplifies Freud's interpretation of Leonardo's dream. It further explores Leonardo's early development and regards the Mona Lisa as a representation of his biological mother. It is a springboard for considerations of early development and object relations.

Preface

This paper is a tribute to the late Fred Pine, for his outstanding contributions to clinical psychoanalysis, analytic psychotherapy, and psychoanalytic developmental knowledge. Fred Pine was a truly independent thinker both as a clinician and researcher. Maintaining his own autonomous vision, he was open to multiple perspectives, considering a variety of psychoanalytic and neurobiological frameworks. A co-author of Margaret Mahler's description of the phases of separation-individuation (Mahler, Pine, and Bergman, 1975) and their relation to personality characteristics and psychopathology, he was not fixated to the Oedipus complex and emphasized the fundamental bases of the pre-Oedipal and pre-verbal development. His research in this area was in the forefront.

The relevance of Dr. Pine's contributions to the evolution of my own thought will become apparent in the paper that follows. Leonardo da Vinci's pre-oedipal experience and consequent object relations is emphasized and is key to my interpretations. It also demonstrates Freud's early interest in pre-verbal memory and experience.

Background

Leonardo da Vinci was a universal genius, a heroic ego ideal with whom Freud identified. He referred to Leonardo as his latest analytic patient (Freud letter to Jung, 10/17/1909) and wanted to learn as much as possible about Leonardo's life and work. Freud's essay "Leonardo da Vinci and a Memory of his Childhood" is a pioneering classic of psychobiography and psychohistory. Freud was formulating what came to be known as "applied analysis", a non-clinical though mutually enriching contribution.

Leonardo's memory or screen memory, which so intrigued Freud was: In my cradle a vulture came down to me and opened my mouth with its tail and struck me many times with the tail against my lips". Freud (1910, p.86-89) inferred "What the phantasy conceals is merely a reminiscence of suckling or being sucked at his mother's breast." This daring pre-verbal interpretation was introduced concurrent with the formulation of the oedipal phase of development. Freud's essay was nevertheless subject to the limitations of psychoanalytic theory, still in statu nascendi as well as the limited knowledge of Leonard's birth, life, and education at that time. Freud (1910, p. 107) had already formulated "Kindly nature has give the artist the ability to express his most secret mental impulses which are hidden even from himself by means of the work he creates". Freud had used subtle clues to unravel aspects of Leonard's psychobiography and first proposed the relationship between the artist's childhood and his adult art.

New Information

Relatively new data have significantly advanced our knowledge of Leonardo's mother, birth, childhood, family, society and culture of that time. These later contributions to the vast literature on Leonardo extend, modify, and correct earlier knowledge, permitting new formulations regarding Leonardo's life and work. This paper postulates that Leonardo's painting of the Mona Lisa, an icon of Western art, is a memorial to his biological mother, Caterina Lippi.

Leonardo's Background

Leonardo was an illegitimate child, born to a sixteen-year-old indigent orphan, April 15, 1452. Kemp (1989) and associates identified her as Caterina Lippi. His biological father was Ser Piero da Vinci, age twenty-five. An esteemed notary from an affluent social class, his having had a dalliance with an impoverished waif was not reproached. Leonardo was disinherited by Ser Piero, unlike the legitimate sons of subsequent proper religious marriages. Classified as a bastard, Leonardo could not attend a Church school, and was excluded from the guild of notaries in Florence. His only childhood formal education was at an abacus school, with a focus on basic mathematics. Caterina, as an unwed mother, was unworthy of mention at Leonardo's public baptism at his father's Catholic Church. The ceremony included ten godparents and other dignitaries from Florence and Vinci.

Soon after Leonard's birth in 1453 his mother married an obscure kiln worker nicknamed "Accattabriga", which translates as "trouble maker". He fathered Leonardo's maternal half siblings. Promptly pregnant, Caterina's next child was a daughter, born in 1454, and in quick succession three more daughters and a son. Leonardo was therefore confronted with and undoubtedly traumatized by his mother's pregnancies, five sibling rivals and a rival stepfather. His stepfather's and father's relationships with Leonardo has not been clarified. His ambivalence toward childbirth is supported by his arrest for sodomy after the birth of his father's first legitimate son (Collins, 1997). Perhaps he needed a comforting relationship after the birth of his new sibling rival. Leonardo could have been breast fed only briefly consequent to the rapid arrival of his maternal half-siblings. In a drawing of a nursing mother -infant pair there are heads of humans that turn into snarling biting lions and dragons. Leonardo's traumatic experience (Eissler, 1961) and suppressed or repressed rage at his mother and her other children is expressed and sublimated in the drawing.

Leonardo's childhood is an important background for his painting of the Mona Lisa. Baptismal and tax records confirm that Leonardo stayed in Vinci as infant with Caterina and in later childhood in the home of his paternal grandfather.

How did Leonardo survive and thrive in the uncertain, often dangerous world of the Renaissance? Despite her ambivalence, likely partly experiencing Leonardo as an unwanted embarrassing burden, Caterina was able to provide oral nutritional gratification, plus emotional support, affect discrimination and regulation. Leonardo was doubtless mirrored by Caterina, a good enough mother (Erikson, 1959, Hardin, 1988, Winnicott, 1965, Trosman, 1986, Blum, 2013.) "The experience of being mirrored enables patients to feel heard, seen, attended to, to feel they matter, or even exist as reflected in the eyes of the other" (Pine, 2021, p.953.) Among others, Pine's understandings encompass the mother-infant primary object relationship.

Leonardo advised artists to review their paintings in a mirror (Kemp, 1989). As a student of optics, Leonardo was obsessed by reflected light and drew hundreds of mirrors. Left-handed, he worked from right to left on a page and wrote each letter backwards. The hatching in Leonardo's drawings was unusual since his lines stared from the lower right, proceeding higher to the right. (Isaacson, 2017). Mirror writing was not then a rare practice. but appears to have special meaning to Leonardo. Mirror writing and reading and reflected images may have been significant for Leonardo in his identity, object relations, and concerns with fantasy, reality, and mastery of trauma.

Identification of the Mona Lisa with Leonardo's Mother

The external model for the Mona Lisa was Lisa Gherardini, wife of Francesco del Giocondo, a wealthy silk merchant. Similar to Caterina, she had married at age sixteen in 1495. Her husband was the same age as Leonardo's father at the time of his marriage. Francisco and Lisa had about the same number of children in rapid succession, as had Caterina. Leonardo therefore could have readily associated Lisa del Giocondo with Caterina. Mona Lisa is an abridged name of Madam or Madonna Lisa. (Isaacson, 2017). Leonardo had initially accepted Francesco's commission to paint his wife Lisa's portrait; possibly her not being of nobility was considered to permit Leonardo greater artistic freedom. Leonardo, however, declined payment and never parted from the portrait, which he had begun in 1503. A perfectionist who abandoned projects that did not meet his standards, Leonardo persisted in creating an ever more idealized Mona Lisa.

Yet his ambivalence was conveyed in her enigmatic smile. Smiles were evident in paintings in Verocchio's studio where adolescent Leonardo had apprenticed as well as in painting by other artists. The elusive, enigmatic smile of the Mona Lisa, suggesting multiple meanings, and was uniquely Leonardo's creation. Freud inferred the Mona Lisa's smile as eliciting Leonardo's early infantile memory of his mother which Freud described as both seductive and sinister, fascinating and puzzling, convergent with current knowledge of the developmental significance of the mother's face, smile, and eye contact. The Mona Lisa has elicited the intense reactions of generations of viewers, as it seems to follow the viewer's movements in the gallery. While there are portraits by other artists in which the painted eyes seem to follow the movements of the spectator, the more pronounced sense of movement in the "Mona Lisa" is sometimes called the "Mona Lisa effect". The Mona Lisa smile flickers with movements of the eye. (Isaacson, 2017). Leonardo's studies of mirrors, optics, light and perspective may have contributed to this singular effect. When first painting the Mona Lisa, Leonard's eyes would also have met the eyes of his model, as they had in his infancy, met the gaze of his mother. The eye is endowed with personal, cultural, and symbolic meaning (Freud,

1910b). Seeing, being seen, voyeurism, exhibitionism are all intrinsic to the visual arts. Poetically "the window of the soul", they may be may be assigned the attributes of hand, mouth, self or object representation or any erogenous zone. The all-seeing eye of the omnipotent parent is associated with magical qualities which may be displaced onto art.

Leonardo's complicated attitude towards his mother, and very likely the latter's ambivalence to her out- of wedlock child is apparent in their later overt relationship. In 1493 Caterina, then frail and ill, reappeared in the life of her renowned son. She was accepted into his home as had never been any other visitor, for even a day. Leonardo's servants were male and there were no other females in his household. Caterina died a year later in Leonardo's home. Freud (1910, p.14) noted that Leonardo arranged an elaborate funeral for his mother with a list of all the expenses. He recorded no affective response, no grief, separation anxiety, or depression. He changed the word "dead" to "entombed". His emotions and thoughts about Caterina's life and death were disguised and entombed in his meticulous account of her funeral expenses, including the cost of the casket, priest, etc. In this context Leonardo had recorded the hour of his father's death without affect or comment. Leonardo's inhibited and/or repressed reactions to Caterina's death were sublimated in his art. Leonardo, a perfectionist who abandoned projects that did not met his standards, persisted in creating an ever more idealized Mona Lisa.

Conclusion

In the background of the Mona Lisa a river meanders, almost in contact with her body. There are visible though distant rock formations, consistent with Leonardo's discovery of geological strata. The timeless flow of the stream may imply the wish for immortality of parent and child, self and object, of his art, and of the artist through his art.

Leonardo wrote that every portrait is also a self portrait - as the Mona Lisa, he could be bi-parental, predominantly maternal, with the fantasy of being a phallic woman. Childless, Leonardo may have unconsciously also regarded the Mona Lisa as his child, representing his feminine self, identified with his idealized biological mother. He defended against grief and separation by keeping her portrait by his side, never delivering the commissioned work of art. His impoverished orphan unwed mother was transformed into the iconic art of the Mona Lisa.

Leonardo kept the Mona Lisa portrait with him in his travels through and retained the painting until his death in Amboise, France in 1519. In France he lived adjacent to the country castle of his patron King Frances I. Having bought the painting from Leonardo's servant and companion who had inherited it upon Leonardo's death, King Francis I installed it in his castle at Fontainebleau. It was ultimately installed in his Paris castle which became the Louvre museum, where it has ever after been the pride of the art collection of the Louvre.

REFERENCES

Blum, H. (2004). Psychoanalysis and Art,, Freud and Leonardo in *Psychoanalysis and Art*, eds. E. Blum, HI, Blum, Amati, J. Madison, CT: International Universities Press.

Collins, B. (1997), *Leonardo, Psychoanalysis and Art History.* Evanston IL: Northwestern University Press.

Eissler, K. (1961). *Leonardo da Vinci: Psychoanalytic Notes on the Enigma.* NY: International Universities Press.

Erikson, E. (1959). *Identity and the Life Cycle.* New York: International Universities Press.

Freud, S. (1909). Letter to Jung, 10/17/1909. E.L. Freud, ed. *Letters of Sigmund Freud, 1873–1939.* NY: Basic Books, 1965.

——— (1910a). Leonardo da Vinci and a Memory of his Childhood. *S.E.* 11:57–137.

——— (1910b). The psychoanalytic view of psychogenic disturbance of vision. *S.E.* 11: 209–218.

Hardin, H. (1988). On the vicissitudes of Freud's early mothering. *Psychoanalytic Quarterly*, 57:72–86.

Isaacson, W. (2017). *Leonardo da Vinci.* NY: Simon & Schuster.

Kemp, M. (1989). ed, *Leonardo on Painting.* New Haven, CT: Yale University Press.

Mahler, M., Pine, F. and Bergman, A. (1975). *The Psychological Birth of the Human Infant.* New York, NY: Basic books.

Pine, F. (2021) A personal odyssey through psychoanalytic process and presence. *Journal of the American Psychoanalytic Association.* 69:941–963.

Trosman, H. (1986). Toward a psychoanalytic iconography. *Psychoanalytic Quarterly* 55:130–167.

Winnicott, D. (1940). *Playing and Reality.* London: Routledge.

CHAPTER 6

Childhood Trauma, Unconscious Conflict and Developmental Transformation

(2019). *International Forum of Psychoanalysis*, 28(3):165–172.

Trauma is the subject of increasing attention in contemporary psycho-analysis. Its complexities will be explored in a clinical case, emphasizing traumatic experience and unconscious conflict across developmental phases. The patient, a young adult white man began analysis complaining of anxiety and depression. Born to adolescent parents, he had experienced infantile stress and childhood traumatic illness. Needy, greedy, and dependent, he was gratified by the frequency and intimacy of psychoanalysis. Genetic interpretation and reconstruction were particularly important in the analytic process. Analytic progress with attenuation of unconscious conflict and developmental transformation proved enduring after termination.

Psychic trauma has been a subject of increasing interest and investigation in the second century of psychoanalysis. Traumatic experience is not isolated, but is a component of the compromise formation of unconscious fantasy. In a continuous interaction of fantasy and reality, traumatic experiences are distorted and elaborated by defense, developmental transformation, and structural regression. Cumulative trauma may be consequent to acute trauma merged with chronic stress. Every delusion has a grain of truth (Freud, 1913, 1937). The complexities of the psychological and developmental sequelae of trauma will be explored in a clinical case.

Past traumatic experience influences the transference. Although transference is basically a return of the repressed, the past appearing in the present, it is activated and influenced by the real and new analytic relationship, and the patient's life situation. Transference cannot be fully understood without its genetic roots, so that transference analysis and genetic reconstruction provide reciprocal illumination. Genetic interpretation and reconstruction were important in the analytic process of the case to be presented (Blum, 1994; Fenichel, 1945a, 1945b; Greenacre, 1981). The intersubjective dimensions were aspects of the analytic work only dimly recognized until the reorganization of psychoanalysis after World War II. The war, the Holocaust, and analytic and social studies of child abuse (originally called seduction trauma) all fostered a new focus on trauma and aggression alongside a reconsideration of countertransference (Blum, 2010; Bohleber, 2010; Kernberg, 2004). The concept of "deferred action" refers to a relatively neutral event, experienced as traumatic at a later phase of development. This, however, remains a controversial concept in psychoanalysis and neurobiology.

The clinical case reported in this paper illustrates many of the preceding issues. T, an adult white married male in his late twenties began analysis complaining of generalized anxiety and depressed moods. His symptoms had appeared or reappeared in adolescence; he thought he had been an anxious, tense child. He recalled a depressive yet devoted mother, who was his main caregiver during a serious childhood illness. Well functioning in many areas, he largely presented with constricted negative affect. He began analysis with gratitude for this opportunity, but quickly revealed his needy, greedy, demanding, and dependent character. He rapidly formed a therapeutic alliance, hoping for symptom relief, but not an analytic alliance in search of self-understanding and insight into his conflicts. Initially, he lacked trust in the reliability of the analyst and the efficacy of psychoanalytic therapy. Gratified by the attention and intimacy of the analytic situation, he was glad to have five sessions per week and would have liked to have had appointments on weekends and holidays as well. Whining and pleading for more time, he seemed like an overgrown little boy. He displayed, however, the capacity for warmth and interest in the outside world and current events.

He soon attacked psychoanalysis as existing for the wealthy doctors' fees and avaricious professionals. They profited regardless of whether their clients benefited. He emphasized the vast profits of medical personnel. His wife, however, was relatively well paid for her regular work and tutoring, which he reported as a sarcastic tease. Did I see higher paying patients on holidays?

Continuing his caustic critique, he insinuated that I was not truly devoted to my patients, implying that I should be at their beck and call. Psychoanalytic treatment was never sufficient, timely, or totally dedicated. Underneath the dependent demands, he elicited images of a sickly, petulant, whining crybaby. My interest in his welfare should be limitless and he should have narcissistic supplies ever available, like demand feeding and ever-attentive soothing, comforting, care. His affective development in the areas of frustration tolerance and self-comforting was at an infantile level in contrast to his superior cognitive capacities.

T soon casually revealed that he had suffered from a serious childhood systemic disorder. The illness at age five involved multiple systems, although without debilitation or pain. He had been confined to rest at home with restriction of his usual activity. Being on the couch in analysis may well have activated memories of his illness, when he often reclined on a couch. His mother was his caregiver, nurse, and nearly exclusive companion. His two and a half to three years younger sister was present, but was virtually eliminated in his lack of associations about her. It was as though she hardly existed. For an ill- defined number of months, he did not attend school, see playmates, or engage in any extended physical activity.

T had always feared bodily injury and was now reminded of a recent auto accident that had occurred while he had been daydreaming at the wheel. During the relative isolation and enforced passivity of his illness, he had frequently daydreamed of physical and intellectual exploits. By puberty, these daydreams were associated with frequent masturbation. During his adolescence, his erotic masturbation fantasies were of heterosexual conquests. They sometimes involved a woman or lesbians who seemed to have resembled his mother. Although pleasurable, on the one hand (pun intended), he had "irrational" ideas that masturbation could make one blind, enfeebled, or crazy. In later adolescence, he was aware of sexually transmitted disease; he disavowed but could not dismiss his fears of illness and physical damage. Very exciting masturbation fantasies continued into adulthood. He suggested that two lesbians could be his wife and mother, only as an afterthought thinking of his sister. The manifest content of voyeuristic excitement may have served to deny his having been a frustrated, disappointed witness to parental love-making or his mother nurturing his sister, which he would have observed.

T dreamt of a cut in his mouth, an upward displacement of his fantasy of castration as a punishment for masturbation, associating to his wife's menstrual period. The cut lip and mouth were interpreted as representing bleeding female genitals, an infantile symbol of castration. Interpretation of punishment for his insatiable oral demands and narcissistic entitlement was deferred to a later phase of his analysis. He also associated to compensation for loss in his persistent wish for a cut-rate fee demonstrating special care and affection. The secondary gains of his childhood illness had fueled his wish to be treated as an exception, entitled to the constant care of an idealized transference mother. His anger at what he experienced as a withholding mother was unconscious, in fantasy dangerous to himself and his mother. The imagined good caregiving mother and aggrandized self were dissociated from the neglectful bad mother and hostile self. Punishment through illness, injury, castration, and desertion were all too real in his childhood traumatic experience.

Instead of being told, as he had been at home, to stop complaining, as his father also rebuked his mother, he was permitted to own his fears and tears. and to vent his anger in analysis. In the safety and support of the analytic situation, he learned that he would not be abandoned, neglected, or punished. Sensitive to his parents' limited education and socialization, his speech was properly grammatical with general avoidance of vulgarity or obscenity. Analysis of his transference rivalry with his analyst led to his understanding of such feelings toward his parents. Clearly aware that his educational attainments and goals far surpassed his those of his parents, his pride was tinged with guilt.

Feeling superior simultaneously defended against his damaged weak self-image and his anxiety that he could not compete with paternal and peer rivals and with his analyst.

Nightmares reflecting his vulnerability to narcissistic injury as well as bodily injury recurred at times during adolescence and adult life. He dreamt of being shot in the back, with associations to an acquaintance who had in reality deftly evaded being stabbed in the back in a criminal assault. His illness had appeared without warning or preparation as though perpetrated by a thug. My comment that I was behind him and might attack without warning was summarily dismissed. However, he wondered if I would get back at him for his verbal darts and demands for more analytic time and progress. He pondered whether my attention and interest wavered. Did I daydream during the session or did I have other patients or persons in mind? Intense daydreaming during the imposed rest of his childhood illness may have influenced being accident prone as well as introspective. In his maternal transference, he was the exclusive partner, derived from a condensation of predominantly pre-Oedipal developmental phases with fantasized Oedipal eradication of rivals for mother's love and care. Narcissistic demands and entitlement continued to be prominent. He dreamt of my having a new rug in my office and associated to my rolling out a red carpet reception for him.

Aware of negative countertransference, I asked whether he was concerned that I was bored or alienated, or should prove my attention to him above all else and others. I did not disclose my countertransference reactions, for example concern and sympathy mixed with irritation and disparagement with regard to his infantile demands. Overall, I did not feel that I was escaping from his critical, nagging, pleading, and protesting negative transference. I regard self-disclosure by the analyst as all too often inappropriate, a countertransference intrusion in the analytic process. There are of course appropriate disclosures, such as when an analyst is ill, injured, impaired, absent, etc.

While T initially responded to my not answering personal questions as a "put down," he was gradually able to contemplate that he could actually regress to being a needy, greedy, petulant child. Developmental interference was circumscribed, but a tendency toward regression was evident throughout much of the analysis, although in many ways he functioned as an adult in his extra- analytic life. He had not behaved as a baby in college, or in his superficial social life. The transference regression was a pathway for reconstructing his childhood trauma and its aftermath. There was an ongoing interplay of interpretation in the here-and-now, inside and outside the transference and reconstruction of childhood sources of his transference reactions.

We reconstructed that, during his childhood illness, there had been developmental interference and he had regressed to infantile attitudes, feelings, and behavior. At rest and socially isolated during his illness, T had had his mother's nearly exclusive attention, but could wear her out with needy demands. He now worried that he might wear out his analyst's care and concern while unconsciously also pleased to exhaust his analyst. The analyst would have little energy remaining for rival patients.

He may well have experienced diverting his mother's attention from his baby sister to himself as a secondary gain of his illness. His dependency intensified his fear of aggression toward his mother, in addition to his and his mother's fears of bodily harm if he did not remain at rest. The powerful secondary gain of infantile dependent gratification was complicated by his and her ambivalence. We reconstructed that she too was prone to regression and could be exasperated and exhausted. In his later adult life, his mother was described as mildly depressive, dour, moody, and whining, with tendencies to be disappointed and dissatisfied. T's identification with his mother, especially in the transference, was apparent in the analytic situation and clarified in genetic interpretation. His mother's feeling drained had been exacerbated by her need to attend to his younger sibling. He defended against awareness of his murderous hostility toward the mother–sister dyad. He had attempted to eliminate his sister in thought, feeling, and fantasy. Erotic excitement by the fantasized lesbian relationship of mother and sister defended against his jealous rage. The interpretation of the recapitulation of T's childhood illness in the transference made him aware of the sequelae of his childhood illness. We compared and contrasted his medically imposed rest to his many hours on the analytic couch. His daydreaming and reveries were then connected to his dreams and associations, and to his sometimes feeling as though psychoanalysis promoted an altered state of consciousness. His traumatic experience had also appeared in nightmares and in acting-out outside the analytic situation, for example in the first car accident reported. He had another car accident, a minor rear-end collision. He thought a frontal collision might have resulted in more serious bodily injury, such as head or genital trauma. No one was actually hurt, however, and there was only minor damage. With regard to the "rear-ender," he thought of anal penetration. It could be dangerous to pick up a male trying to "thumb a ride." Was he being taken for a ride in his psychoanalysis?

Through interpretation and reconstruction, T grasped that his childhood illness had left him feeling castrated and emasculated, prone to fantasies of homosexual seduction. He could now comprehend that he unconsciously viewed the reduced fee or an extra session as a homosexual seduction. He had been fearful of "seduction trauma." In his homosexual fantasy, he would perform fellatio on his analytic partner. Thumbing a ride was offering his penis in exchange for a free taxi ride. In the analytic process, he would be fed in the maternal transference and incorporate the father figure's masculinity and power in the paternal transference. Homosexual transference was a compromise between accepting castration or gaining phallic masculinity. He referred to bleeding hemorrhoids and again to his wife's menstrual period. He was fearful of his fantasy of being a genitally damaged castrated female. As a teenager, he had had to learn that a girl's being called "unwell" when she had her period was not a form of illness

In the session following the report of the second auto accident, he reported a nightmare replete with images of bloody aggression and death. Was he then accident-prone? He dreamt of a terrible auto accident with a woman's body partly hanging out of a demolished car, her head split open. Since he was distracted, daydreaming of pretty young women while driving, the accident could have been his own doing. He associated to being punished for masturbation by going crazy, his head split open like bleeding female genitalia. A damaged head also referred to his mother's depression and his own fear of physical and psychological disorder. The repetitive nightmares of auto damage and death (auto = self) were variations on the theme of his childhood traumatic illness.

The same traumas in the nightmares were acted out in the accidents in a muted form. Retrospectively, they were part of the analytic process of working through his erotic and aggressive impulses, feelings of transgression, and seeking repair and reparation. I further interpreted his fear that his childhood illness could have been fatal. Injury to his body could lead to early death. His anxiety about death had possibly increased as he had better understood the meaning of death with less denial during adolescence compared to childhood. Moreover, had his parents similarly been fearful about his future? His mother had never discussed with him her own fears for his future. Would his health be impaired? His illness would likely have exacerbated his mother's symptoms.

Given the particularly close binding relationship between mother and son before and during his illness, the affect would have been prominently transmitted in non-verbal communication such as facial expression, posture, tone, and pitch of voice. Parents and child wanted omnipotent reassurance of his permanent recovery, undoing the threat of irreversible damage.

Related to T's thoughts and fears of bodily damage, he reported that he had bought an air-conditioner that was apparently damaged. He was distressed, then infuriated at the deal and at himself for the trouble of repair or replacement. He had bought an upscale brand, but had not been offered a guarantee. His anxious angry transference was interpreted; there were no guarantees in psychoanalysis, no matter who the analyst or which school or brand of analysis.

As analysis proceeded, adolescent developmental interference and regressive tendencies came into focus; T was shy and ill at ease with his peers, afraid of both intimacy and rejection. In a series of conscious sadomasochistic fantasies, T's wife was raped by two adolescent males or two adolescent girls were raped by a young man. The adolescent male was initially the patient, aroused and guilty about his interest in young women and his fantasized extramarital affairs. I asked if any particular adolescent girls came to mind, and he then to his surprise explicitly thought of his mother with shame and guilt.

T consciously contemplated, as though it had been a revelation, that he was the son of teenage parents. His mother had been a mother at about age 16. He wondered if his conception was consequent to voluntary copulation. Had his mother been coerced, raped by his father? Was his conception an accident? He had not connected his adolescent masturbation fantasies of seduction or rape with his family history. Anxious and guilty from the breakthrough of his incestuous wishes, he identified with his father as the second male adolescent in the dream. If he was the only adolescent male, he was in fantasy impregnating his wife as his mother and fathering himself (like Oedipus). The clinical and developmental implications of his birth to adolescent parents were doubtless highly significant. With both guilt and pleasure for his expanding understanding, he thought he might read the Greek myth of Oedipus. And with a typical barb, expressing his competitiveness, he proposed that analysis was perhaps all a myth! He wanted to deflate my pride in his development.

Underlying separation anxiety was manifest in his yearning for his wife's reassuring presence during the weekend break from psychoanalysis. Sexual relations were then sought to substitute and compensate for separation from the analyst mother as well as freedom from paternal analytic rivalry. He wished and feared union with mother in a coalescence of pre-Oedipal and Oedipal conflict. As the analytic work proceeded, he gained respect for his wife's accomplishments with ego-integration of his own femininity. He had gained insight into his identification with aspects of his mother and possibly his sister.

T retrieved lost, fragmented memories in conjunction with the transference as an edited form of remembering. Analyzing my countertransference helped me to better understand his unconscious conflicts. Countertransference was facilitating as well as interfering with the analytic process. T remained curious about and attuned to my attitudes, initially more able to observe me than himself. His increasing capacity to observe his own disturbing thoughts, feelings, and fantasies improved, and engendered freedom to bring them into analytic scrutiny. He then revealed that during sexual intercourse with his wife, he had an intrusive fantasy of a woman with his mother's face. The incestuous fantasy during intercourse was suffused with anxiety and guilt, more intense than his guilt over his masturbation fantasies. But the fantasy mother changed into a teenage girl. He was reluctant to confront erotic fantasy that was doubly prohibited, incest with a current mother figure and sex with an adolescent girl who represented his teenage mother.

Fixated on his mother, he did not associate to his sister.

Fantasies that had previously been repressed and suppressed proved to be a significant segue into genetic interpretation and reconstruction. I had either not asked or had not absorbed the significance of his parents' age when he was first interviewed, but its importance later became all too apparent. His mother had been pregnant at 16 years of age. She had been bereaved and burdened by her own mother's death a few years before T's birth. She subsequently cared for her younger siblings, probably ambivalently. T's father was about a year older than his mother, her high-school boyfriend. Both parents were ill prepared for parenthood, emotionally immature, and themselves still in need of parenting. T was neither a wanted nor a welcome baby. We reconstructed that his parents were stressed and distressed, lacking reliable psychological, social, and economic support. His mother may well have had prepartum and postpartum depression. Nor were the grandparents looking forward to their grandchild.

They were ambivalent, limited in their availability and their capacity to help emotionally or financially. The family situation might be different in prior historical periods and other cultures. However, in their own sociocultural setting, T's parents most likely experienced an admixture of shame and humiliation, acceptance, and sympathy.

Adolescent pregnancy can be both a thrust toward mature development and a source of developmental interference and regression (B. Blum, 1980).

Fortunately, T's father did not disappear or disavow responsibility, and the young couple agreed to marry. T's parents were responsible but limited in their adapting to a wholly new unexpected overburdened life situation. Was the pregnancy a result of impulsive adolescent behavior with little anticipation of possible consequences? It is also possible that the pregnancy was unconsciously desired by T's mother in an attempt to replicate her relationship with her own mother. Inwardly mourning and crying for affection, she was presumably overwhelmed as an ambivalent mother-surrogate for her younger siblings. Was abortion considered and then dismissed?

T could not recall viewing his parents as romantic affectionate partners during his childhood. As a couple, they were united in their familial obligations, tolerant, if not empathically sensitive to each other. Could they engage in pleasurable care and playful activities with their infant? How well could his mother respond to her infant's temperament, needs, and initiatives, when she was very likely stressed and depressed. Had his mother's own childhood and adolescence been revived when she was a pregnant adolescent? Attachment and separation–individuation of T as an infant may well have been initially compromised before his Oedipal development. Since he was in his parents' bedroom probably for the first two years of life, he would have experienced psychosocial and sexual intimacy. Actual exposure to the primal scene would have contributed to his bisexual identification, castration anxiety, narcissistic injury, and punitive fears, later activated and exacerbated by his childhood illness. His illness interfered with the resolution of Oedipal/pre-Oedipal conflict and fueled his dependent demands and defenses, yet also his striving to master trauma. In its terminal phase, T regarded his treatment as beneficial, while he repeatedly defended against his Oedipal and sibling transference jealousy. His renewed narcissistic entitlement was addressed in the transference and silently analyzed in complicated countertransference. He was ever more curious about my wife and children, identifying with the person of the analyst as well as his analyzing function. His voyeuristic inquiry and observation presumably had retained elements of probable primal scene experience. With greater caring, empathy, and appreciation of her positive attributes, his relationship with his wife improved during treatment.

Approaching the termination of treatment, T reported a vivid dream that remained in his awake mind. He dreamt of a triangle with the "H" at the ends of the base and a hardly legible "L" at the apex. He asked what I made of the diagram, and I countered by asking what he thought about the triangle. It reminded him of my first name initial, then his/her, then his/her joined together. He assumed his/her joined was myself and my wife, himself and his wife, and his idealized parents joined in sexual intercourse, conceiving him. "L" meant "locked" to him, so in the analytic transference we were locked together, as were his adolescent parents when he was conceived. He associated to "wedlock," and thought of his adolescent parents having been compelled to marry and thus locked together in life. In another transference fantasy, he and I were an analytic couple locked together, defending against termination. He was refusing to be locked out of the analytic situation. His protests against termination after six years of analysis became an important part of the analytic process.

Although T's parents had not been martinets during his childhood and adolescence, he was nevertheless afraid of his own projected aggression. Would I retaliate if he changed his mind and refused to terminate? When he thought of me as an orthodox psychoanalyst, he imagined that I would urge him to leave with the proverbial "God helps those who help themselves." Despite deep gratitude, he resented that he had to confront separation–individuation, Oedipal conflict, and adaptive mastery of trauma as an adult on his own. Dependent yearnings were aroused, and remnants of his childlike clinging reappeared. Confronting termination and loss of his analyst, he had begun to mourn. He was not consciously cognizant that he had internalized his analyst and elements of the analytic process. Reflecting about my feelings regarding termination, he wondered how much he would be missed and how long he would be remembered. He suggested a good-bye embrace, while disappointed about a non-analytic personal relationship that could never be.

To my great surprise, I encountered T in a non-clinical setting many years later. He had gained status, had an appropriately mature appearance and confident manner, and greeted me with a friendly smile. It was quite extraordinary to be suddenly together again, seeing each other and talking together in a social situation. He informed me of his success in his profession and his pride in his marriage and children. Any deeper exploration was impossible under the social circumstances. Post-termination encounters tend to revive transference and countertransference. Memories of his analysis and recall of our first and last analytic sessions flashed through my mind. Concern at termination about resistance to change was replaced by shared gratification in his progressive developmental transformation.

Discussion

Writing this paper evoked that affectively charged surprise encounter and fostered a theoretical overview that had not previously been formulated in the same depth and within a more contemporary framework. T felt he was "owed" extra affection and attention, just as he had had secondary gains, compensation, related to his childhood traumatic illness. He was probably overprotected and overindulged, imagining himself as an exception. The usual demands of self-regulation of school, home life, and childhood did not apply to him. Narcissistic entitlement was further exemplified in imperious demands for extraspecial treatment. I have referred to the condensation of the Oedipal and pre-Oedipal phases in his transference regression. Pre-Oedipal antecedents of oral hunger, especially for nurturance, for near-merger, with dependent demands were at least adumbrated. However, his muted crying and clinging, whining, and appealing for more and more exclusive devotion were powerful, repetitive pre-Oedipal themes. He reacted to separation as though object constancy, seemingly well established, had been subject to developmental interference, vulnerable to infantile regression. T's intrapsychic parental representations did not regularly afford comfort and security in the face of frustration and disappointment (Tyson & Tyson, 1993).

As his anxieties were worked through in his analysis, his feelings of confidence and competence increased. His mastery of separation anxiety, anger, and negative affects evolved in the analytic process. T's separation–individuation (Mahler, Pine, & Bergman, 1975) was hindered by maternal ambivalence. Was his mother's ambivalence intensified when she again was pregnant during T's second to third years of age? He did not show signs of disorganized attachment, but may have struggled with and overcome insecure attachment. Bowlby (1982), noted that insecure attachment could interfere with later positive development. His intrapsychic self and object representations were well integrated by the termination of analysis. and it seemed that ego-integration and his ego-synthetic function had improved.

What was the effect of his infantile experience on his later experience? Pre-Oedipal stress and strain infiltrated his subsequent Oedipus complex (Fenichel, 1945a; Oliner, 2012). Freud (1931) revised his idea of the significance of the pre-Oedipal phase.

A developmental perspective enriches theories of pathogenesis and transference as a compromise formation. Psychoanalysis traditionally proceeds with interpretation and reconstruction of unconscious conflict and trauma.

While childhood trauma imposes regression and developmental disturbance, the gradual analytic mastery of trauma may spur developmental advance and transformation. In turn, developmental transformation of the pathogenic past facilitates further mastery of protracted stress, trauma, and their sequelae.

Nevertheless, residues of severe protracted trauma may be relatively refractory to current analytic and/or pharmacological treatment and may be indelible.

Impressed by the long-term benefit of T's treatment, I considered whether some patients are able to use the analysis for continuing new development long after termination. Was there an interwoven process in which the benefits of analysis facilitate positive life experience, which in turn promotes resilience in encountering the exigencies of life?

New perspectives may be considered based upon contemporary neurobiology. Neurobiological and psychological phenomena are highly interactive during pregnancy, and body and brain are inseparable from conception. A stressful pregnancy with prepartum as well as postpartum depression may have an adverse influence on the neurobiological systems of mother, fetus, and nursing infant. Stress hormones elevated during pregnancy might affect the immune system of mother and fetus as well as their postpartum bonding and attachment. An unnoticed mild impairment of his infant immune system could have left T predisposed to autoimmune and physical illness. The adolescent father's struggles to psychologically and financially support his wife and infant son were not able to alleviate the stress on the already vulnerable mother and infant, and the quality of T's mother's care during pregnancy, delivery, and his early infancy are unknown.

Postscript

Childhood trauma and loss can also be a spur to creativity, as they may have spurred my patient's resilient recovery. This seemingly paradoxical connection of a sickly infancy and childhood and later extraordinary creativity characterized the life and art of Marcel Proust (and others). Proust's childhood illnesses (Blum, 2012) powerfully influenced his later masterpiece *"In search of lost time."* Proust's mother had been semi-starved and malnourished during the Franco- Prussian war, when she was pregnant with Marcel (akin to some pregnant teens). She was further stressed by her husband's absence in his nearly fatal military service, exacerbated by her lonely isolation from her own family and friends. Proust believed that his vulnerability to physical illness was consequent to the deprived frightening situation of his mother's pregnancy and his infancy. With his childhood outbreak of nearly fatal asthma, lounging in a chair was imposed by his doctors, including his physician father. They advised purges, as well as restricted activity and diet. Illness and treatment were then merged, as the treatment was a secondary illness. With persisting childhood illness, analogous to my patient, Proust missed school, playmates, and age-appropriate independence. He was indeed in search of lost vitality and lost time.

His nearly exclusive relationship with his mother was characterized by reciprocal ambivalence and maternal depletion and overprotection. Protracted rest was compensated by soaring flights of imagination. He wrote emotional letters to his mother while in the same home. He was able to express in letters and novels what was prohibited or inhibited in person. He suffered from recurrent nightmares, fear of going to sleep, and fear of asthmatic asphyxiation. His mother read to him, and he demanded her presence particularly at bedtime and times of sleep separation. Proust's illness most likely promoted his intense identification with his mother. His quasi- autobiographical masterpiece is an innovative fanciful reconstruction of a lost childhood, an attempted aesthetic mastery of childhood traumas.

The reconstructions of Freud and Proust of their own childhoods have some striking similarities, for example their creativity and methodology, including special attention to dreams and reconstruction of childhood. The reconstruction of trauma in different phases of development facilitates developmental advance and conflict resolution in psychoanalysis and in life itself.

REFERENCES

Blum, B. (1980). *Psychological Aspects Of Pregnancy, Birthing, and Bonding*. New York: Human Science Press.

Blum, H. (1994). Reconstruction. In *Psychoanalysis: Childhood Revisited and Recreated*. New York: International Universities Press.

——— (2010). Adolescent trauma and the Oedipus complex. *Psychoanalytic Inquiry* 30:548–566.

——— (2012). The creative transformation of trauma: Marcel Proust's "In Search of Lost Time." *Psychoanalytic Review*, 99, *677–696*. doi: 10.1521/prev. 2012.99.5.677.

Bohleber, W. (2010). *Destructiveness, Intersubjectivity and trauma*. London: Karnac.

Bowlby, J. (1982). *Attachment*. New York: Basic Books.

Fenichel, O. (1945a). *The Psychoanalytic Theory of Neurosis*. New York: W.W. Norton. Reprinted New York: Routledge, 2016.

——— (1945b). The concept of trauma in contemporary psychoanalytic theory. *International Journal of Psychoanalysis*, 26:33–44.

Freud, S. (1913) *Totem and taboo. S.E.* 13: 1–161.

——— (1931). *Female sexuality. S.E.* 21:225–243.

——— (1937). *Construction in analysis*. SE 23: 257–269.

Greenacre, P. (1981). Reconstruction its nature and therapeutic value. *Journal of the American Psychoanalytic Association*, 29, *27–46*. doi: 10.1177/000306518102900102

Kernberg, (2004). *Contemporary Controversies*. New Haven: Yale University Press.

Mahler M., Pine, F., & Bergman, A. (1975). *The Psychological Birth of the Human Infant*. New York: Basic Books.

Oliner, M. (2012). *Psychic Reality in Context. Perspectives on Psychoanalysis, Personal History, and Trauma*. London: Karnac.

Tyson, P., & Tyson, R. (1993). Psychoanalytic theories of development. New Haven, CT: Yale University Press.

CHAPTER 7

Reconstruction in a Case of Postpartum Depression

(1978). *Psychoanalytic Study of the Child*, 33:335–362.

This paper will explore problems of depression via analytic reconstruction. The investigation also involves corollary questions concerning the value and validity of preoedipal reconstruction, and the reconciliation and integration of analytic data and the data of direct infant observation. The clinical basis for this paper derives from the psychoanalysis of a woman with postpartum depressions; hence the study has the unique advantages, tempered by an awareness of the uniqueness, of a particular psychoanalytic case.

In view of the rich analytic literature on depression, and the expanding psychoanalytic studies of the psychology of pregnancy and parenthood, it is noteworthy that there have been few psychoanalytic investigations of postpartum depression. Postpartum depression is a significant and not uncommon condition occurring at a crucial point in the life cycle, with repercussions and implications of pathogenic vulnerability for both mother and infant.

Mild postpartum "blues" may be overlooked or rationalized in terms of physical fatigue and lack of sleep. The relative universality of postpartum psychological problems in both parents is often disregarded, except for more dramatic and serious syndromes such as agitated or psychotic depression (Asch and Rubin, 1974). Psychiatric hospitalization may influence descriptive and diagnostic considerations (Pugh et al., 1963).

There is little agreement about the true incidence and duration of postpartum depression because of wide variation in definition, recognition, and reporting of the syndrome. For some observers, postpartum depression may nonetheless include prepartum depression during pregnancy. Others consider postpartum depression as precipitated by childbirth and a syndrome limited in onset from the third to the tenth days postpartum. Still other surveys consider postpartum depression as appearing in the first three to even six months after parturition (Hamilton, 1962); (Melges, 1968). This paper concerns idiopathic postpartum depression and not the depression which may be anticipated with illness in the mother or neonate, or the birth of a defective child (Solnit and Stark, 1961).

Numerous other questions and possible correlations have been noted. No specific relationship has been confirmed between postpartum depression and the age of the mother, the number of her pregnancies and children, the interval between pregnancies, or the duration or difficulty of labor and delivery.

Because of the massive shifts in hormonal activity during pregnancy, and again in the postpartum period, endocrine factors have been implicated. The dramatic changes in body state and image and actual physiological upheaval have also led many observers to postulate an organic etiology or predisposition. The hormonal and other physiological alterations are also thought to contribute to other mood disturbances associated with the menstrual cycle, e.g., premenstrual depression and tension, menstrual and menopausal depression. The physiology of depression is a very important dimension of the problem and, as a facilitating force, has to be distinguished from somatic concomitants and consequences of depression. Such factors, however, have unfortunately remained obscure, and no consistent endocrine or neurophysiological finding or aberration has been established to be specifically linked with or contributing to postpartum depression or other psychological disorders of the female reproductive cycle. It seems likely that endocrine and neurophysiological factors are involved, but may not have a regular or perhaps even predominant role in some cases. The importance of psychogenic factors is further suggested in similar initial psychological reactions observed in adoptive parents (Bental, 1965).

Women who have had one postpartum depression are more likely to have another than might be expected without such an antecedent history, but is such depression specifically postpartum, or does it occur in other situations of life-stress or normative crisis? Are these women depression-prone, and were there depressive episodes or equivalents in childhood? Where the depressive psychopathology has not been mastered, are there masked subclinical depressions which may predispose and persist after the postpartum depression subsides? At least some of these patients are chronically depressed, beginning in early life, even if the condition has not been recognized or consciously identified.

I shall attempt to explicate some of these problems, simultaneously demonstrating the value of reconstruction in analytic work. I refer here to reconstruction of adult disorders about which the patient may be confused, as well as to the classical reconstruction of infantile development and disorder. Analytic reconstruction does not emphasize actual historical events per se, but their meaning and impact, their consequences and sequelae (Greenacre, 1975); (Kanzer and Blum, 1967).

Reconstruction has been a significant tool, not only in psychoanalytic treatment, but in the development and validation of psychoanalytic theory. Reconstruction leads to a unique way of understanding individual development and permits the reintegration of dissociated fragments of both the life experience and the inner world. During clinical psychoanalysis, parallel with the mastery of intrapsychic infantile conflict, infantile amnesia is uncovered, memory distortions are corrected, and a unique individual history is reassembled and reconstructed (Kris, 1956); (Ekstein and Rangell, 1961). Reconstructions are tested and remodeled by analyst and patient with increasing refinement of the initial hypotheses, and expanding explanatory value. The continuing comparison and integration of clinical reconstruction with developmental studies and other psychoanalytic research are important to the identification and resolution of controversy concerning infantile development and pathogenesis.

Recognizing all the problems inherent in reconstruction of this early phase of life with all its ambiguities and uncertainty, I shall present current clinical material and analytic inferences organized around a reconstruction of the organization and disturbance of mental life between 20 and 28 months of life, essentially within the preoedipal phase that Mahler et al. (1975) have designated as the rapprochement subphase of separation-individuation, overlapping with the anal phase of development. Psychoanalytic knowledge of drive and ego development, of infantile object relations and the process of separation-individuation will be utilized in the testing and interpretation of analytic data and inferences. The preoedipal focus in this case is partially for heuristic descriptive purposes, and is not meant to indicate a diminished significance of oedipal and later development. Similarly, the studies of separation-individuation are most pertinent to a deeper understanding of postpartum depression, and have enriched analytic insights into many related complex clinical phenomena.

The reconstruction here is also pertinent to theories of the origin of depression, enriching understanding, rather than detracting from the importance of the superego, guilt, and self-reproach in adult depression. Personality development can be peculiar and uneven, regressed and retarded in some areas, advanced and precocious in other areas, sometimes with a mosaic appearance rather than the neat layering of development or conflict that was once popular in analytic constructs. However, in adult analytic work with an analyzable patient, genetic reconstruction is based upon clues, derivatives, and patterns emerging in predominantly verbal data filtered through advanced ego structures and a post-oedipal organization.

There is no reason to expect that any of the later normal developmental phases of life or pathological states will exactly replicate in any point-to-point correspondence any of the subphases of separation-individuation or psychosexual development. The early phases of development are not literally recapitulated; various consequences are inferred in terms of residue and influences, of forerunners which undergo further developmental vicissitudes. The childhood precursors and roots of adult depression are not identical with adult depression, and careful study of the personality in the psychoanalytic process and the emerging life history are prerequisites for reconstruction of infantile pathogenesis and depressive predisposition. It is important to follow affective states and style, the form as well as the content of the transference, and behavior patterns.

In this case, there was a transference neurosis, albeit with periods of severe regression. Preoedipal determinants and traits were regularly observable along with narcissistic vulnerability. There was no evidence of psychosis, major structural defects, or inability to participate in a coherent psychoanalytic process. What I observed from the inception of treatment was a very complicated picture of a depressive personality with many preoedipal character traits and with an oedipal transference neurosis. (Actually, many cases of depressive neurosis are also oral characters, just as obsessives typically demonstrate anal character.) The transference frequently manifested preoedipal imprints and influences and brief fluctuating periods of dyadic quality. Preoedipal problems and some regressive ego fragility were nevertheless not of the severity usually found in the borderline personality.

Susceptibility to severe regression was balanced by latent ego resilience and capacity to reverse regression. Antecedent preoedipal development will influence the formation and form of the infantile neurosis that underlies the later transference neurosis. Preoedipal influences on the oedipus complex and character structure are universal. In a patient without major ego modification there is no artificial isolation between character analysis and transference neurosis or between preoedipal and oedipal analysis.

Case Report

Mrs. A., a tall, well-groomed, serious, and articulate mother in her early 30s, had three children. A postpartum depression followed the birth of each child. Feelings of depression, dejection, denigration, and lassitude lasted several weeks after each delivery. She had awakened from the obstetrical anesthesia crying on each occasion, although she had anticipated happiness and regarded the pregnancies as precious life experiences. A nurse had had to take over the mothering of her first child during the first two months after the baby was born, arousing great envy and further self-reproach in the patient. What Mrs. A. described as the postpartum blues gradually cleared and each time she resumed her maternal functions with great energy and single-minded dedication. The acute depression became a subclinical depression with serious recurrent depressive disturbances. When she was not subject to depressive episodes, there were "depressive equivalents" particularly in the form of insomnia and an eating disturbance.

At the height of her postpartum depression Mrs. A. could neither eat nor sleep. The insomnia resulted in drug abuse via sleeping medication to which the patient felt she almost became addicted. Feeling guilty about what she considered to be her inadequate maternal care and ashamed of her behavior, she became secretly alcoholic. She smuggled spirits into the house to calm her almost constant anxieties and to drown her sorrows in liquor. She made abortive and half-hearted efforts at obtaining help, but it was only after her family took note of her increasing depression and Mrs. A. felt increasingly desperate that she finally was referred to a psychotherapist and ultimately for psychoanalysis.

Shortly after she had begun her first analysis (in a different city with a different analyst), she noted that her crying had enormously increased. There were "buckets of tears" during the sessions, and the sessions were punctuated by crying before and after the hour. She was admiring and respectful of her analyst, but at the same time intensely ambivalent, with chronic feelings of irritation and anger. She was committed to her treatment, although she was again constantly guilty that because the analyst lived at some distance from her home she had to leave her children in the charge of baby-sitters or the maid. By this time she had given up her reliance on alcohol, but her mood disturbance, indecision, and inability to maintain consistency and child discipline were productive, she thought, of more guilt. As she rushed off to her analyst, or away from home, she felt even more that she was deserting her maternal responsibilities.

In her brief first analysis her constant crying was associated with pleas and demands for the analyst's love and approval. Her acting out was regarded as a defense against feelings of rejection and rage, as well as a disguised gratification of her erotic attachment to the analyst based upon her unresolved guilt-ridden incestuous longing for her father. Her tears and depression were related to her guilt over her prostitution fantasies, which appeared in her dreams and associations.

Mrs. A. felt she made some therapeutic strides and thought she was beginning to understand herself particularly in the area in which her guilt and inhibition over unacceptable sexual impulses had led to constriction, and strong feelings of disappointment and defeat. On the other hand, her crying and depression had not been relieved. She claimed that in her first analytic treatment there had been little if any discussion of her postpartum depressions or her later depressive and addictive reactions. Depression was regarded as a manifestation of oedipal guilt and defeat, but was not specifically tied to conflicts over her children and motherhood. Her reactive overconcern and difficulty in maintaining maternal attitudes toward her children were not interpreted, and her family life remained isolated from her transference attitudes toward her analyst. She also realized that she may have preferred not to discuss feelings of failure as a mother as part of a general avoidance of painful topics—an attitude for which there was a familial model. Mrs. A. had invested a great deal of her energy and effort in motherhood and her children. Despite some feelings of accomplishment as a mother, she also experienced feelings of failure in what she considered to be the most important sphere of her life. What was missing in her understanding of her relationship with her children was paralleled by her bafflement about her own childhood. When she moved to another city and began analysis with me, she was clearly confused, impetuous, demanding, and depressed. She had the history and the characteristics of an oral depressive personality, but with a sufficiently intact ego structure to participate in analysis.

In the analysis with me, at first she appeared to be very compliant and eagerly accepting of interpretations. She stated that she had grown up to be a conformist and had been regarded by her parents and friends as a very obedient, dependable, and serious girl. It developed that she handled my interpretations analogously to her food symptoms. She would have eating binges often followed by self-induced vomiting which she concealed from her family. During these times she would eat scraps of food from the table, sweets, and dairy products to the point of abdominal discomfort. Her reactions to interpretations were in some ways analogous to swallowing followed by spitting, but with more assimilation of interpretation as the analysis progressed. There were always complaints about feeling that she was passive toward life, that the analyst and her family acted upon her, and that she could not be decisive, authoritative, and consistent in her relationships. Her children tended to dominate and control her because she was unable to be firm with respect to such issues as play, study, and bedtime.

Given the history of the postpartum depressions, a great deal of conflict over motherhood could have been anticipated. These conflicts were revived in the transference, had often been repeated in various forms with her children, and could be discerned and elaborated in the developmental picture that slowly emerged in the analytic process. Analytic data were supplemented by developmental data that the patient herself was stimulated to elicit about her childhood. Though such extra-analytic data are often obtained from patients in analysis (Novey, 1968), their use requires careful evaluation to avoid their abuse and distortion of the analytic process.

Mrs. A.'s intense and profound separation reactions, her bouts of bulimia and vomiting were associated with introjective and projective processes and a good deal of denial. While high-level defenses including repression were most important, the preoedipal drive-defense constellations were readily evident.

She demanded and struggled against any dependency on the analyst, often denying and isolating dependent and affectionate feelings, as she had previously struggled against dependency on her mother and dependency on food and drugs. The first bout of eating and vomiting occurred during the last trimester of her first pregnancy during a separation from her husband. There had been minimal nausea and vomiting during the first trimester and one thereafter except following eating binges. For the most part she had adhered to the nutritional regime prescribed by her obstetrician, and the eating disorder was, in the main, in abeyance. Her bulimia was also despite and because of food and weight restrictions during pregnancy.

Her symptoms, transference, and dreams also indicated the doing and undoing of her incestuous impregnation and masturbation. But the deeper level concerned her unresolved symbiotic wishes and, in instinctual terms, oral greed and cannibalistic devouring with fears of retaliation as well as wishes to be eaten. Dreams of feasts and famines alternated with dreams of children lost and found. There were feasts of dreams and absence of dreams. A dream in which a female dog ate her puppies led to the patient's associations and dawning realization of her impulses to devour—to incorporate her own children. Her enormous guilt arose from the intense conflict between her maternal ego ideal and her infanticidal impulses (Blum, 1976).

At the same time she began to understand her need to feed herself in order to feed the children. The eating binges were discovered to have occurred mostly before the family dinner. She needed to be fed and comforted first, or she would feel she would be too depleted to be a giving mother. She constantly wanted to see herself as nurturant, yet identified herself with the hungry children who needed food and love. She was also envious of the affectionate care the children received, and again had to vomit back the food she in fantasy took from them since she had literally eaten off their plate. Finally, she ate not only their food, but symbolically the children themselves in an ambivalent mixture of primitive love and destruction. Her sleep disturbances were particularly related to her fears of being devoured, in her struggle against both the cannibalistic and passive wishes of the oral triad (to eat, to be eaten, and to sleep). If she did not vomit after incorporation, she might be devoured from within.

In both her symbolic behavior and fantasy she indicated her ambivalent wish for merger and her fear and rage at separation. She came to understand her longing for the narcissistic bliss of fusion with an idealized good mother. In one dream she reached orgasm eating lox and bagel, representing the feeding mother. In another, she controlled a pulley which moved a loaf of bread in and out of her vagina, offering her a never-ending "alimentary orgasm" (Rado, 1927).

She began to perceive the impossible and insatiable demands she made for therapeutic help and magical relief on her analyst and the nature of her irrational demands on and fantasies about her husband. In her husband she had wanted a mother, a preoedipal mother, who was screened behind the heterosexual oedipal father. She had split the image of her mother into the eternally benevolent and feeding supportive figure, the bread that was life, and the depriving, castrating, and punitive mother whom she associated with her anger and depression. The split between the pure mother and prostitute, faithless mother had been superimposed upon the earlier splitting of the maternal representation which she had failed to integrate completely and cohesively in later development.

The patient had defensively idealized her mother and motherhood, although her maternal ideals had other important determinants. In her conscious thoughts and daydreams there had been no more important ideal than that of becoming a perfect mother of angelic children. Her mother had emphasized the joys of motherhood and had wanted Mrs. A. to think of her as an ideal mother and an ideal daughter to the patient's grandmother. Although the patient in many ways rejected femininity, for example, crying when she developed breasts in adolescence, she also wanted many children. There had been intense and prolonged doll play centered around maternity and child care. The play was generally idealized and she had no conscious thoughts of doll injury or death.

This case is also of interest from the point of view of the knowledge of the early mother-child relationship that can be obtained in the analysis of mothers. A great deal can be learned about a mother's empathy and responsiveness to her children, about her mode of play and recreation, discipline, organization, and direction of the children's growth and development based upon her own resources and the intrusion of her own problems into the mother-child relationship. This woman constantly sought to be an ideal mother, a kind of supermother who struggled against her hostile feelings toward her own mother and her children. No one else was allowed to shop for the food which was carefully selected. Every family menu was deliberately planned and had to be properly executed and served. The bathing, washing, and dressing of the children; the purchase of their clothes; the necessary chauffeuring; the arrangements and plans for lessons; or special appointments—all were made by Mrs. A. The children were the objects and objectives of the specific ministrations of the mother. She lamented her husband's preoccupation with his profession, yet made it clear that the home was her domain. She wanted him to be much more helpful and invested in the children's care, but remained unconsciously controlling and possessive. She liked her husband's somewhat seductive and easygoing play with the children, but at the same time she was envious of his relationship with them. She was pained at the children's frustrations, and took great pleasure in their achievements. This mother was highly ambitious for her children, and they developed their own unusual talents and sensitivities as well as neurotic disturbances.

Each child starting school aroused feelings of loneliness and separation in this mother. Repeating the anxiety and depression of childbirth, every separation from the children, and later from the analyst, could reactivate this syndrome in muted form. Her oral regression and fusion fantasies were partial and reversible, so that in the transference and at the end of the hour or week, upon awakening from anesthesia, sleep, and dreams, ego boundaries and object relatedness were rapidly reinstated.

The patient's depression was associated with feelings of intense disappointment and disillusionment as well as intermittent feelings of failure and helplessness. She could never be the perfect mother she wanted to be, and every unhappy encounter with the children's anxiety, frustration, or anger left her feeling anxious and guilty. Whatever she did for them was never enough, and she was filled with self-reproach. She was not sufficiently attentive as a daughter, feeling selfish and insensitive, despite her daily telephone contact and the frequent visits with her own mother.

Her complaints that her husband's discipline tended to become "overkill" in the form of extended lectures and verbal reprimands projected her own impulses. The overkill really referred to the fear of the breakdown of her compensatory undoing in her "supermomism." Her unconscious hostility to motherhood and the children led to reaction formations of maternal overconcern and overprotection. Her own wishes to destroy or desert the children or to replace them and be mothered by them also led to fear of aggressive encounters with them as well as to close involvement with their activities. The constant preoccupation with the compulsory undoing of wishes to be rid of the children was confirmed repeatedly. When I was away at a research conference, children were lost in research libraries in her fantasies.

She had separation dreams and fantasies: mothers search for children, grandmothers search for mothers, children fall off bicycles, die in plane crashes, and so forth. In nightmares, she was pursued because children had been burned on the stove or abused by predators, crushed by cars.

Motherhood was a fulfillment of her ego ideal but also an oedipal crime in which she was guilty of replacing her mother. Childbirth also represented castration for this woman who had serious unresolved bisexual conflicts and castration anxiety (Zilboorg, 1958). She was fearful of injury, experienced intensified anger in connection with the anticipation of sexual intimacy, and had numerous dreams in which one foot was in a man's shoe or ski. At the same time, the castration anxiety was related to a profound separation anxiety, indicating unresolved preoedipal separation conflicts. The loss of food or feces signified castration, but also separation and object loss. The birth of the baby was less significant as castration than as a traumatic rupture of symbiosis; her postpartum crying was an identification with the crying baby, an expression of her depression, loss, and wish for maternal care and comfort on an oral level. In contradistinction to her conscious yearnings to be a mother, following the birth of her children, she felt incomplete and alone and came to understand in the analysis her longing to be the baby united with mother, "one and inseparable, now and forever."

Awakening crying from obstetrical anesthesia was in itself emergence from a state of symbiotic sleep, a fantasy of birth and rebirth which was realized in the actual concurrent childbirth. The loss of the fantasied state of fusion and of the biological fusion of pregnancy was intolerable, and associated with severe ambivalence, aggression, and regression. She had unconscious fantasies of the destruction and desertion of the child (as an external object) associated with wishes to restore the previous narcissistic fusion. Identifying with her child, a narcissistic object, she turned her aggression on herself and felt intensely guilty, self-accusatory, and masochistic.

The ambivalent relationship to her own mother, the ambivalent splitting into idealized "good" and denigrated "bad" maternal representations, was associated with repeated transference configurations concerning birth, feeding, and separation. Initially, the first analyst was the frustrating, rejecting, devalued

mother, and I was the feeding, approving, idealized mother. Global identifications with her mother appeared in repetitive dreams when Mrs. A.'s mother gave birth to the patient's sibling who was born 2 years after the patient. This could be dated precisely because of the events surrounding the birth of this sibling, who had a minor congenital anomaly. Attention was focused upon the new baby, dethroning the patient who had been the prior object of the parents' and grandparents' rather exclusive concern. It appeared that the mother's pregnancy and delivery during the patient's preoedipal (anal and rapprochement) development were not related to problems of actual physical separation from her mother, but rather to the mother's problems and withdrawal of interest and perhaps increased maternal pressure upon the little girl toward mature behavior in anticipation of another infant. She magically did not allow the new baby to cry, while she was fretful and a finicky eater. Her guilt was also related to her unconscious fantasy that she was the cause of her sibling's birth "injury." The patient had always felt she had to be compliant and "properly behaved" in the analysis—a transference which she viewed ultimately as her relationship to her mother. She could be defiant or "disrespectful" toward her mother only when she was inebriated, and the capacity to be assertive and to exert considerable self-interest developed slowly during her analysis. Doubtless the mother's own anxiety and guilt were intensified and communicated when her son's anomaly required medical attention and repair.

Mrs. A.'s own feelings of injury and envy, her fears of aggression and attack, were disguised, and her depression and regression, excessive clinging, crying, and complaining were rationalized by her parents as a terrible 2-year-old stage which she would outgrow. Her later depression, postpartum and in response to other real or fantasied separations or object losses, seemed to have crystallized as an enduring configuration at the time of her sibling's birth. The anlage of the adult postpartum depression was related specifically to her mother's pregnancy and sibling's birth. The configuration and depressive proclivity were latent during her too sober and serious childhood, but were reactivated when she gave birth to her own children. Becoming a mother revived not only unresolved oedipal conflicts, but deeply regressive unresolved preoedipal problems. Another consequence of feeling that her mother and mother's love had been lost or devoured by the new baby was that her deprivation entitled her to compensatory consolation, e.g., via boundless feeding and coercive dependency. In the postpartum depression she reversed roles with the baby who was a narcissistic self-object, and became the devouring infant rather than the nurturant mother. Her baby represented her externalized and disavowed demanding infantilism, and both her devalued self and sibling, while she was identified with the "frustrator," a depriving and deserting mother figure. In many disguised dreams she was pregnant with the food she had gorged, having all the ice-cream cones, father's penis and baby, but also mother's breasts and love for herself. Her sibling was devoured and eliminated in fantasy, and was an object of identification for infantile gratification and replacement.

Despite the tremendous difficulties in (both genetic and longitudinal) prediction, many analysts will have anticipated that this patient had a feeding disturbance in the earliest period of life. Mrs. A. was allergic to her mother's milk and was rapidly weaned to a bottle in the first weeks of life. Milk could not be found that would agree with her, and abdominal colic persisted for the first 6 months. In addition, her rigid mother followed the rigid feeding schedule prescribed by the pediatrician, allowing the patient to scream between the timed feedings. The colicky infant was relatively inconsolable and cried protractedly. She was skinny, frail, fretful, and petulant, and had an overconcerned, anxious mother who hovered over her nutrition. Mrs. A.'s mother had herself been fixated on food, and had also been very distressed during both her pregnancies with *hypermesis gravidarum*. This familial information about Mrs. A.'s first year of life and her mother's *hypermesis gravidarum* was not based upon analytic reconstruction or derivative recollection. Strict and careful about the patient's eating habits, the mother had bribed, cajoled, and demanded that the patient's food be finished. Though the little girl usually conformed with her mother's wishes, her sibling turned the meals into altercations.

After the finicky eating of early childhood, the patient was never satisfied with her weight, always considering herself either too fat or too thin. The great tension at meals would increase as the patient attacked her food slowly and carefully, not permitting herself the pleasure of this basic gratification while unconsciously prolonging it. Early in analysis she was aware of tension in her jaws, and antecedent brauxism had probably led to dental disorder, later requiring "oral reconstruction." Her unconscious rage was related to self-reproach that simultaneously punished her mother. She constantly attempted to draw her mother's attention and interest away from the envied younger sibling, and later mine from her transference rivals. Her fear of boring me concealed her wish for my exclusive affection and love, and competition with my family and other patients. Analytic discussion was associated with feeding, and silence with deprivation.

The anxiety and rigidity that characterized the feeding relationship continued into other areas of the mother-child interaction. Toilet training for bowel and bladder was reputed to have occurred very early, possibly before 18 months. Illness and constipation were both "dangerous" and treated by enemas. Prunes adorned the breakfast table to insure regularity. All the routines of the house were carefully regulated. Early elements of transference in which the patient attempted compliance and conformity to insure my approval apparently repeated important elements of her relationship with her mother. Spanking was rare, but the withdrawal of approval and affection was an ever-present silent threat. Moreover, aggression and hostility were denied, and only loving feelings among members of the family were acknowledged during childhood despite flagrant evidence of the mother's irritation and hostility. While there was undoubtedly genuine parental affection, to some degree parental hostility was disguised as discipline for the benefit of the child. "Eating for mother," demanded of Mrs. A. in childhood, in the analysis came to represent for the patient the confused mother-child dialogue. Recalling maternal threats to have the police take her away if she did not eat, she began to understand that this early mode of communication with her mother was suffused with anxiety and hostility, submission and covert defiance. The mother as aggressor in the feeding situation reinforced the patient's ambivalence, which was symbolized in her ambivalent attitudes toward food as object and object love (A. Freud, 1946). The oral struggle was also a regressive recapitulation of fantasies of symbiosis and independence.

In childhood, her unresolved separation conflicts were associated with difficulty falling asleep. Bedtime rituals (also related to the primal scene) disappeared during a favorable adolescent disengagement from her parents and further personality consolidation. However, severe insomnia appeared when the patient first left home to go to college, marking the beginning of her adult depressive disorder. It should be noted that for the most part the depression was subclinical, the patient being regarded not as a sad, but a sober and serious child and adolescent.

The colicky, comfortless, and crying child of the early years of infancy did not reappear until she had her own infant, beginning with the immediate postpartum depression. The immediate postpartum crying was a harbinger of the depression of the first postpartum months and preceded the massive physiological changes of the first days after delivery. While I do not rule out constitutional and physiological factors,[1] the reconstruction here points to the importance of the psychological disturbance which began in the last trimester of her first pregnancy, as she anticipated motherhood. The first eating binge occurred when her husband was away and when she began to worry that she had not gained sufficient weight during the pregnancy. The thought occurred to her that she could injure the unborn baby, a disguised version of her infanticidal thoughts and her inability to be truly nurturant as delivery approached. Her fears of starving herself and her infant represented a reversal of her devouring and withholding attitudes. How could she be the mother of a separate, living, unique individual when she wanted and dreaded to be fused with her mother, clinging and separating, and regressively eating, rather than

---

1 Genetic and constitutional factors might include the infantile colic and allergy, the low frustration tolerance, abnormal glucose tolerance, and metabolic lability, tendency toward mood disturbance, and other factors. The patient's strengths and inner resources doubtless were constitutionally determined, e.g., her capacity to reverse regression and efforts at reintegration. The complex determinants results in circular and cross-interactions between endowment and environment.

feeding and caring for her own infant?[2] It is of interest that her adult problems in mothering were not global, that there were many varied and changing areas of "good enough" mothering, and that apart from the postpartum depression, her reactions to each of the children were different.

Discussion

In this patient, the yearnings for the good mother of symbiosis coexisted with more mature object relations, just as many areas of archaic ego functioning coexisted with advanced and intact ego functions. The reconstruction of the trauma surrounding her own mother's pregnancy and the birth of her sibling during the anal phase and the rapprochement subphase of separation-individuation is consistent with the intrapsychic assessment of the patient's deficient ego strength and other areas of positive ego development.

The specific reconstruction I wish to emphasize here concerned not a shock trauma of her sibling's birth, but rather the extended strain in the mother-child relationship in the months before and after her sibling's birth when she was 2 years old. The first 18 months of life were already indicative of preceding strain in the dyadic relationship: this patient's rigid, controlling mother was intolerant of the child's aggression and regression, while the child was allergic and "hypersensitive."

The oral phase extends into and influences later development, and every developmental advance is also associated with regression. The rapprochement

---

2 It is of interest that Freud (1892–1893) provides an illuminating preanalytic description of a similar patient, successfully treated by hypnosis. It was a case of a mother who was unable to feed her newborn baby. She had serious postpartum psychopathology following each of three pregnancies. The mother attempted to breast-feed, but she lost appetite and also developed insomnia. She vomited all her food and became agitated when the baby was brought to her bedside. Freud's first intervention was a suggestion that the patient would be able to feed the baby, and that the baby would thrive. The patient improved, but soon relapsed. Freud's next hypnotic intervention was in a sense a remarkably intuitive interpretation. "I told the patient that five minutes after my departure she would break out against her family with some acrimony: what had happened to her dinner? did they mean to let her starve? how could she feed the baby if she had nothing to eat herself? and so on" (p. 120). The patient had been very depressed and "furious at her inability to feed the baby" (p. 119). Freud's suggestion was an implied acceptance of her anger and interpretation of her aggression and wishes to be fed. His uncanny insight preceded his self-analysis.

phase is ushered in with oral regression, revived stranger anxiety, and increased separation anxiety (McDevitt, 1975), and the preceding problems accentuated the crisis potential. The fear of loss associated with anourethral and early castration conflicts is also confluent. The mother's pregnancy and birth of a sibling compound the child's conflicts, and the predisposition at that time to negative affect and a basic depressive mood (Mahler, 1966). Ambivalence is intensified and clinging to and coercion of the object may be associated with strenuous efforts to protect the relationship from the child's hostility and anal sadism.

This patient's feelings of loss of maternal closeness and support, separation panic, helplessness, and "negative ambivalence" predisposed her to her adult depressive neurosis. The interference with development at this time can be conceptualized in terms of oral regression to previous oral fixations, and to anal ambivalent struggles over the loss and preservation of the fecal (narcissistic) object. The evidence also points to a protracted rapprochement crisis, with pathogenic sequelae as a clinical inference rather than as literally recapitulated in adult life or psychoanalysis.

As stated previously, it is not to be expected that earlier psychosexual phases or the process of separation-individuation will be exactly recapitulated. Structuralization, differential progression and regression, defensive and adaptive alterations occur during development. Since the process of separation-individuation is closely connected to the formation of psychic structure, early forms of object relatedness and ego states neither persist unaltered nor reappear regressively in a specific phase organization, as occurs with libidinal drives. Instinctual regression usually follows more regularly defined patterns than ego regression. Highly variable regressive alternations occur among different ego functions. The determination of levels of regression and of ego development or deficit becomes a much more complex task than the more limited historical consideration of libidinal fixation and regression.

In this case, persistent transference and character configurations, the transference and genetic interpretation of dreams and symptoms were especially valuable guides to reconstruction. At 2 years of age, the patient was in an early verbal development phase, when words were becoming important in conjunction with gesture and affectomotor communication. It seems reasonable to assume reciprocal identifications between a vulnerable child and an anxious guilty mother with *hypermesis gravidarum*. The reenactment of the infantile trauma of her sibling's birth may be inferred in the patient's specific predisposition to postpartum depression. The preoedipal traumas were also determinants of her adult acting-out tendencies (Greenacre, 1950); (A. Freud, 1968); (Blum, 1976). Her preoedipal problems influenced and to some degree coexisted with later conflicts and advanced development. The importance of preoedipal determinants of depression (e.g., narcissism, orality, aggression, loss of object love, and self-esteem) outlined originally by Freud (1917) and Abraham (1924) are corroborated and extended.

The analytic data also are consistent with Mahler's formulations concerning unresolved rapprochement difficulties, leaving behind a depressive basic mood, persistent anger and overconcern which may become internalized. This is more likely to occur with protracted, intense rapprochement crises with persistent negative affects. The depressive proclivity may become structuralized and, if not later resolved, reactivated in later life. Differentiated from transient states of earlier infancy that resemble grief and sadness, the depressive affect of rapprochement and the feeling of loss and helplessness, narcissistic vulnerability, and ambivalent strivings toward symbiosis and separation with heightened separation anxiety suggests some preoedipal crystallization and specificity for the predisposition to neurotic depression. The outcome would be dependent upon antecedent and subsequent development, with epigenetic remodeling, and developmental transformations. In this respect, the patient's changing relationship with her father was quite significant, although not elaborated in the case report. The narcissistic injury when her sibling was born was a forerunner of her intense oedipal disappointment. She described her father as warm, devoted, and outgoing. Along with her grandmother, he was probably an alternative source of supportive nurturance, but was seductive in his play, and later withdrew from her and became more involved in activities with her sibling. Aggression toward the father was almost tolerable, but her mother was protected and idealized in Mrs. A.'s preanalytic conscious thoughts.

Tendencies toward splitting of the self and parental object representations may remain or regressively recur. In Mrs. A.'s case, excessive unneutralized aggression invested both the self and the object representations. Object constancy was not sufficiently stable to resist regression. Basic trust, confidence, and self-esteem were injured. Magical thinking, omnipotent and idealized fantasies were not sufficiently attenuated and replaced by secondary process, but a secure attachment to reality existed. The patient displayed severe separation anxiety with intense fears of and wishes for fusion, again analogous to the developmental problems of rapprochement. The 2-year-old readily regresses under stress, and is especially vulnerable during this period of psychic structuralization and rapid differentiation of ego functions.

The birth of the sibling in the second year of life heralded the loss of the throne to this princess, the partial loss of (undivided claim to) her parents, her family position, her feces, and fantasied penis. I would hypothesize that the normal danger situations of object loss and loss of love, and the depressive disposition of the rapprochement phase were reinforced by the preceding strain and the psychological stress of her sibling's birth on the patient and her parents. This appears to have led to the later crystallization of the infantile narcissistic depressive configuration.

She apparently felt lost, left, and bereft, and developed more of a negative affective state of depression rather than a defiant negativism with externalized aggression. An ambivalent dependency and exclusive possessiveness tended to persist instead of the more gradual relinquishment of claims upon the mother. Doubtless the picture was complicated by the patient's constitutional vulnerability, sensitivity, and oral fixations as well as by the lack of maternal empathy. Her yearning to re-create symbiotic omnipotence appeared to be associated with an awareness of separateness and a chronic resentment at the love objects she regarded as withholding themselves and narcissistic supplies from her.

Her hidden, repetitive, coercive, and resentful demands for contact and control were screened by characterological conformity and negative oedipal conflicts. Wishes to incorporate the penis, to have exclusive possession of mother or father, and to have babies by them may also defend against preoedipal wishes, e.g., for the breast instead of the penis, is not a revolutionary formulation. Both the oedipal and preoedipal problems require analysis, and it is an important technical issue to decide whether the transference is triadic or dyadic, how and in what form preoedipal material is to be interpreted. The patient was pessimistic with moments of despair, but never appeared to be on the verge of complete depressive collapse. There were always efforts to extract gratifications, supplies, and, on a higher ego level, interpretative understanding from the analyst.

The ambivalence and splitting of the object representation associated with the depressive mood also may have contributed to some of the superego problems observed in her adult depression. Frequent self-reproach and self-effacement were related to magical fears of retaliation, e.g., for her forbidden wishes toward her children, and earlier, her mother. The projection of her aggression contributed to the internalization of a harsh and punitive superego, while the fantastic and untamed idealization of the object led to ego ideals which demanded her impossible efforts and aspirations to be a perfect mother. The perfect and all-giving mother was the ideal omnipotent mother she wanted to have, incorporate, and become. The idealization also defended against the aggressive devaluation and envy of her mother and sibling (Kernberg, 1970). The sibling envy and rivalry contributed to her later inability to be a comforting, confident, and competent mother. She had not wanted her sibling to cry for the maternal attention that she demanded, and had wanted him taken away where he could not be heard or seen. She would be the only "crybaby." The unattenuated infantile ideals and fixation to archaic superego precursors left her with a primitive all-or-none value system which lacked perspective or proportion.

The evidence pointing to the crystallization of difficulty during this (rapprochement) developmental period is cohesive, internally consistent, and articulates with modern developmental theory and the psychoanalytic concept of depression as an affect and as a syndrome. (Consistency does of course not mean confirmation.) I do not see the material and formulations as competitive with the oedipus complex as the nucleus of neurosis or as a denigration of drive theory and the importance of the oral and anal phases of development. The process of separation-individuation does not compete with, but rather enriches and complements, psychosexual and other dimensions of developmental knowledge.

With more focus upon the drives, much more could be said about the patient's oral fixations and the constant anal struggle between retention and expulsion of the fecal narcissistic object. However, the coercive efforts to woo the object, the clinging and darting away, the awareness of helplessness and separateness, the wish to fuse and the fear of re-engulfment, the splitting of the self and object representations during rapprochement are different levels of discourse than "anal ambivalence," sadism, and negativism. Autonomous ego development, libidinal phases, and the processes of separation-individuation have overlapping, but also different orientations and timetables.

An integration of rapprochement considerations with ego and drive development is desirable, and my reconstruction is not limited to this developmental period or any one developmental line (A. Freud, 1965) in isolation. This is consistent with the contemporary reconstruction of psychic organization, of ego states and development, rather than simple drive-defense constellations or single traumatic situations. The oral fixations of the patient are apparent, as they are important to the understanding of adult depression. Her basic depressive mood, fears of loss of the object and the object's love, and narcissistic vulnerability at approximately 2 years of age were probably influenced by the preceding infantile colic and feeding disturbance during the first year of life. Does the "inconsolable" crying and helpless infant with oral-phase disruption develop a proclivity toward ego depletion and depression?

Mahler (1966) noted:

We could frequently observe that the "confident expectation" (Benedek, 1938) of those toddlers who were already, whether for extrinsic or intrinsic reasons, carrying over a deficit of emotional supplies from the previous subphases was more readily depleted during the second 18 months of life. They succumbed more easily than others to an increasingly angry mood, which was interpreted by Bowlby (1960) as "continual protest." In some instances, they seemed periodically to fall prey to a desperate feeling of helpless loss (from which, however, a child usually recovers intermittently, and with relative rapidity). The intrapsychic experience of loss is compounded by the affect-laden symbolic significance of toilet training, and by the advent of the castration anxiety of the phallic phase of psychosexual development [p. 162f].

Convergent with the increasing psychoanalytic understanding of depression (e.g., Freud, 1917); (Abraham, 1924); (Rado, 1927); (Lewin, 1950); (Bibring, 1953); (Mahler, 1966); (Jacobson, 1971), this material also indicates the convergence and synthesis of developmental knowledge and analytic reconstruction. Reconstruction utilizes and reciprocally influences the interpretation of analytic and developmental data.

A longitudinal survey which includes reconstruction of the patient's preoedipal problems permits an overview of the determinants and pathogenesis of adult (postpartum) depression. This patient's postpartum depressions were not discrete or isolated syndromes, but were acute manifestations of a persistent adult depressive disorder. Analysis revealed antecedent symptoms, e.g., during the last trimester of her first pregnancy, and in adolescence. The occurrence of an infantile depressive configuration and proclivity was reconstructed as a cautious approximation at the end of the second year of life, between about 20 and 28 months of age. The assignment of predisposition priority to this period rather than the first year difficulties is based upon analytic and theoretical considerations of structuralization and conflict.

During rapprochement ambivalence first appears, and intrapsychic conflicts may persist. Depression and other affects may also tend to persist in association with the child's newly developed capacity for fantasy, symbolic thought, and increasingly effective language communication. The child's sense of helplessness, separation, and narcissistic vulnerability can be correlated with the basic depressive mood (Mahler, 1966). Aggression directed toward the differentiated and well-defined object may be in conflict with superego precursors, favoring repression, reaction formation, and other defenses. The child's dependence upon the object and object's love, and both external and internal prohibitions, may foster internalization of aggression and/or splitting of aggressive and libidinal, "good and bad" object and self representations.

The presence of persistent ambivalence at this time in conjunction with loss of the now differentiated object helps explain the ego identification with the devalued worthless object and the anlage of the superego identification with the idealized omnipotently punitive object so commonly inferred in depressions (Jacobson, 1971, p. 226). This infantile period of increasing stability, consolidation of mental representations, and enduring structure and conflict significantly influences later development and the possibilities for mastery or pathogenic vulnerability (Mahler et al., 1975).

As previously stated, this patient's sensitivity to separation, object loss, and narcissistic injury was undoubtedly heightened by her earlier oral-phase problems. But the oral fixation per se does not explain her relatively intact ego, and the level of differentiated, albeit still narcissistic, object representation and relatedness she achieved. Her oral character and lifelong oral preoccupation, with hidden oral dependence and rage, imperative and devouring demands, is readily discerned. The understanding of her oral and aggressive conflicts in relation to her level of ego function and recapitulation of loss of a relatively well-defined object requires consideration of ego development and the process of separation-individuation.

The oral phase precedes, but contributes to, character formation. Many adult "oral characters" have different overall personality structures, and much depends on which defenses are later mobilized, and the parallel ego development. These issues involve fixation and regression, and also illustrate the importance of epigenesis, with preceding phase influence, later reorganization, and possible transformation on new developmental levels. In this case depressive tendencies and a basic depressive mood developed (at about 24 months), but many fascinating questions remain concerning earlier and later determinants of depression.

The meaning of loss, separation, and depression undergoes defensive and developmental changes, and is expressed and experienced differently at different phases of life. Given the complexities of development and structuralization, there are probably no simple infantile prototypes of adult depression, and later influences are very important. In analysis, the progressive influence of the working through of reconstructed material on new levels of development and ego synthesis can be observed. The reconstruction of preoedipal precursors of postpartum depression is significant not only for therapy, but for the testing and integration of new theoretical concepts of depression.

Summary

Postpartum depression is a common and very important disorder with implications for the mother-child relationship and maternal adaptation. Postpartum depression is not a discrete and circumscribed entity, but a symptom of an underlying preexistent disturbance. In the case described, the patient was a depressive character with masked depression before and between the acute postpartum depressions, and with related symptoms of appetite and sleep disturbance and addictive tendencies. While constitutional and somatic factors were doubtless involved, the case illustrates the importance of psychogenesis with depressive predisposition.

Reconstruction is a valuable therapeutic tool, but is also valuable in the testing and integration of new data and theory. Analytic reconstruction uncovered the presence of a preoedipal depressive configuration which developed during the period just before and after her sibling's birth when she was 2 years old. The reconstruction highlighted the role of this persistent infantile depressive configuration and predisposition, crystallizing during the anal phase and rapprochement subphase of separation-individuation. An intense negative ambivalence and depressive basic mood developed, associated with oral regression.

Developmental and analytic data also indicated significant oral fixation and oral-phase disorder. These formulations are consistent with classical psychoanalytic contributions to the theory of depression. The data articulate with and are illuminated by contemporary analytic theory, and point to the role of preoedipal influences on the oedipus complex, as well as superego and character formation. As anticipated by Freud and A. Freud, the utilization of both analytic and developmental data obtained from direct infant observation potentiates the investigation of early development and pathogenesis.

REFERENCES

Abraham, K. (1924). A Short Study of the Development of the Libido: Part I In: Selected Papers London: Hogarth Press, 1949 pp. 418–480.

Asch, S. Rubin, L. (1974). Postpartum Reactions Amer. J. Psychiat.13:1870–874.

Benedek, T.F. (1956). Toward the Biology of the Depressive Constellation J. Am. Psychoanal. Assoc. 4:389–427.

Bental, V. (1965). Psychic Mechanisms of the Adoptive Mother in Connection with Adoption Israel Annals of Psychiatry & Related Disciplines 324–34.

Bibring, E. (1953). The Mechanism of Depression In: Affective Disorders, ed. P. Greenacre. New York: Int. Univ. Press, pp. 13–48.

Blum, H. (1976). Masochism, the Ego Ideal, and the Psychology of Women J. Am. Psychoanal. Assoc. 24(Suppl.)157–192.

——— (1977). The Prototype of Preoedipal Reconstruction J. Am. Psychoanal. Assoc. 25:757–786.

Ekstein, R. & Rangell, L. (1961). Reconstruction and Theory Formation J. Am. Psychoanal. Assoc. 9:684–697.

Freud, A. (1946) The Psychoanalytic Study of Infantile Feeding Disturbances Psychoanal. Study Child2:119–132.

——— (1968). Acting Out Int. J. Psychoanal.49:165–170.

Freud, S. (1892-1893). A Case of Successful Treatment by Hypnotism S.E. 1:115–128.

——— (1917). Mourning and Melancholia S.E. 14 217–258.

Greenacre, P. (1950). General Problems of Acting Out Psychoanal. Q.19:455–467.

——— (1967). The Influence of Infantile Trauma on Genetic Patterns In: Psychic Trauma, ed. S.S. Furst. New York: Basic Books, pp. 108–153.

——— (1968). The Psychoanalytic Process, Transference, and Acting Out Int. J. Psychoanal. 49:211–218.

——— (1975). On Reconstruction J. Am. Psychoanal. Assoc. 23:693–712.

Hamilton, J. (1962). Postpartum Psychiatric Problems St. Louis: Mosby.

Jacobson, E. (1971). Depression. New York: Int. Univ. Press.

Kanzer, M.& Blum, H. (1967). Classical Psychoanalysis since 1939 In: Psychoanalytic Techniques, ed. B.B. Wolman. New York: Basic Books, pp. 93–146.

Kernberg, O.F. (1970). Factors in the Psychoanalytic Treatment of Narcissistic Personalities J. Am. Psychoanal. Assoc. 18:51–85.

Kris, E. (1956). The Recovery of Childhood Memories in Psychoanalysis J. Am. Psychoanal. Assoc. 11:54–88.

Lewin, B.D. (1950). The Psychoanalysis of Elation. New York: Norton.

Mahler, M.S. (1966). Notes on the Development of Basic Moods In: Psychoanalysis A General Psychology, ed. R.M. Loewenstein, L.M. Newman, M. Schur., & A.J. Solnit. New York: Int. Univ. Press, pp. 152–168.

——— PINE, F., Bergman, A. (1975). The Psychological Birth of the Human Infant. New York: Basic Books.

Melges, F. (1968). Postpartum Psychiatric Syndromes Psychosom. Med. 30:95–108.

Mcdevitt, J.B. (1975). Separation-Individuation and Object Constancy J. Am. Psychoanal. Assoc. 23:713–742.

Novey, S. (1968). The Second Look. Baltimore: Johns Hopkins Univ. Press.

Pugh, T.F., Jerath, B.K., Reed, R.B., Schmidt, W.M. (1963). Rates of Mental Disease Related to Childbearing New Eng. J. Med. 268:1224–1228.

Rado, S. (1927). The Problem of Melancholia. Int. J. Psychoanal .9:420–438, 1928.

Solnit, A.J. & Stark, M. (1961). Mourning and the Birth of a Defective Child Psychoanal. Study Child 16:523–537.

Zilboorg, G. (1957). The Clinical Issues of Postpartum Psychopathological Reactions Amer. J. Obst. Gyn.73:305–312.

CHAPTER 8

The Psychoanalytic Process and Analytic Inference: A Clinical Study of a Lie and a Loss

(1983). *Int. J. Psychoanal.*, (64):17–33. Presented at the 33rd International Psychoanalytical Congress, Madrid, July 1983.

Consideration for the dead, who, after all, no longer need it,
is more important to us than the truth, and certainly,
for most of us, than consideration for the living.
—Freud (1915a, p. 290).

The major route toward the solution of analytic problems and the resolution of unresolved controversies within the field has been clinical study; to return to analytic data, to suggest new formulations deriving from clinical evidence, to enlarge analytic knowledge from clinical experience, and to test the accuracy and validity of new hypotheses in the crucible of the analytic process. This paper represents clinical psychoanalysis as an intertwined therapy and scientific study, inseparable from analysis as a body of knowledge and a theory. I shall later give an example of an unique analytic process that had its inception with an extraordinary deception, and draw inferences from the analysis of a lie of object loss. The nature of analytic inference will be illustrated and reviewed in relation to the analytic process.

Clinical psychoanalysis remains the main research method and laboratory of psychoanalysis (though non-clinical observations have also informed and expanded psychoanalytic knowledge). Differences in the analytic process may produce different analytic data and evidence and the analytic process itself may colour the evidence obtained and subsequent inference.

Psychoanalytic observation, hypothesis, and theory are interdependent and reciprocal. There are implicit assumptions and points of view that underly any effort at analytic interpretation, so that it is neither possible nor desirable to propose hypothesis and inference entirely without any theoretical framework. 'The full meaning of clinical findings can only be developed in the framework of theory … All attempts at simplification, of which there are many, at a concentration on only one aspect at the expense of others, had to be paid for by a severe limitation on the explanatory reach and the predictive value of analysis' (Hartmann, 1958, pp. 134, 141). Psychoanalytic theory is a determinant of clinical experience. Problems and pitfalls ensue when there are gaps and inconsistencies between observations, hypotheses, and formulations; when description is confused with explanation; when different theoretical frameworks are combined without question of compatibility; and when there is a skewed selection of data and alternative inferences.

The classical psychoanalytic process is organized around free association and interpretation of all possible verbal and non-verbal data with a centre field of transference and countertransference. In this process, unconscious infantile conflicts and fixations will be traced to their genetic roots, with evidence of various forms of compromise formations and developmental transformations. Neurotic symptoms and behaviour will be revealed as a childish repetition of the past in the present, based upon persistent unconscious pathogenic conflicts. Connexions between past and present will be restored; the domain of the ego vastly expanded with progressive structural change. This is the essential core of the process and goals of psychoanalytic therapy.

The analytic process will depend upon the analyst's insight into transference and resistance and considerations of the totality of the analytic situation and process in making appropriate interventions. Work proceeds from the psychic surface which is ascertained from a consideration of all the available analytic data, the phase of analysis, and the patient's readiness for interpretation. Interpretation itself is an inference drawn from analytic evidence. Based upon understanding and conveying insight, it should be tactful and timely, flexible in application, and appropriately on target. The analyst should be aware of the effects, particularly on the transference, of interpretations and of all interventions and communications. The complex network of bilateral unconscious cues and communication in the analytic process means that evidence must be examined for artifacts and distortions of the process itself (Rangell, 1968); (Arlow, 1979).

The analytic attitude should be one of neutrality, with impartial objectivity toward the analytic data, with equidistance from id, ego, superego (A. Freud, 1937), and reality. A neutral analytic attitude will be associated with coexistent attitudes of candour and therapeutic commitment and 'sympathetic understanding' in the face of intense provocations of all sorts (Freud, 1913a, p. 140). Neutrality does not mean alienation or animosity, and actually fosters transference investment while avoiding transference contamination and gratification, transference-countertransference confusion, and constraints on the patient's free association and individuality. Neutrality is specifically related to the analyst's non-directive stance and the nonintrusion of the analyst's own problems and values into the treatment; 'we ought not to give up the neutrality towards the patient, which we have acquired through keeping the countertransference in check' (Freud, 1913b, p. 164).

Concerned with an impartial, objective analytic attitude in the selection of evidence, Freud (1912) stated, 'In making the selection, if he follows his expectations he is in danger of never finding anything but what he already knows; and if he follows his inclinations, he will certainly falsify what he may perceive' (p. 112). Freud (1912) further underscored the analyst's understanding of the transference-countertransference field when he stated, 'the doctor must put himself in the position to make use of everything he is told for the purposes of interpretation and of recognizing the concealed unconscious material without substituting a censorship of his own for the selection that the patient has foregone' (p. 115). Whereas this is relevant to all patients, it stands in bold relief when a patient deliberately seeks to deceive the analyst. Integrated analytic function and work depends upon analysing countertransference as an impediment. The analyst utilizes countertransference signals in conjunction with any other cues and clues as a guide toward comprehension of the analytic material. There is no guarantee of the validity of countertransference reactions or of the analyst's empathy, and these responses have to be subject to critical examination in relation to the patient (Beres & Arlow, 1974). Self-analysis should not be confused with analysis of the patient. The countertransference itself is a very broad topic related to the analyst's other reactions to the patient and the particular analytic situation (Kernberg, 1965). In the case to be described, countertransference analysis contributed to the illumination of the patient's unconscious denial and derision in his lie. The impact of the patient's deliberate deception of the analyst, and the potential for the analyst feeling 'fooled' and the victim of a fraud had significant countertransferential reverberations.

The circular transference-countertransference reactions and the interwoven fantasies and realities of the analytic situation are understood with macroscopic and microscopic, intrapsychic and external, transference and reality considerations (Rangell, 1979); (Sandler et al., 1973). Analytic work and 'the work of interpretation which transforms what is unconscious into what is conscious' (Freud, 1917b, p. 455) can then gradually and carefully extend from phenomenological patterns to metapsychological models.

As the analytic process gets underway with an analytic pact, an alliance develops between patient and analyst for co-operation and joint participation in the analytic work (Kanzer, 1981). This alliance arises from the correct attitude, position, empathy, and interpretive work of the analyst, from maintenance of the analytic framework, and from the patient's personality resources; it does not need special technical nurturance and is maintained and restored through appropriate interpretation. Such an alliance develops with difficulty, however, where there is a lack of mutual trust and where prevarication provokes countertransference. The acquisition of insight, the experience of new affectively meaningful understanding, has a powerful impact upon the patient's continuing interest and investment in the analytic process. Despite the negative transferences and inevitable resistance, there is a stimulation and excitement to beginning the discovery of the meaning of symptoms and understanding why, how, and under what circumstances the patient has fallen ill. It is an 'eye opener' for patients to discover their modes of self-deception, the ways in which they have defended against their anxieties, disguised their own motives, misunderstood their loved ones, and unwittingly contributed to their own difficulties. The pace of uncovering and discovery, its scope and depth, varies in each individual analysis, but it is one of the valuable effects of analysis which stimulates further curiosity and strengthens analytic inquiry.

The patient identifies with the analytic attitude, functions, and goals of analysis. Both analyst and patient must have the capacity for a 'therapeutic split' between observation and experience (Sterba, 1934) and for controlled regression in the service of the analysis. While providing a reliable stable 'holding environment' (Winnicott, 1965), analysis fosters a controlled regression. Analysis, however, is not a supportive psychotherapy and is in many respects a demanding, difficult, regressive and reorganizing experience.

Research issues concerning the analytic process and analytic evidence should be periodically re-evaluated with developments in psychoanalysis. While it has been sadly said that psychoanalysts remain better friends if they do not read and respond to each other's papers, it is apparent that there is an awakening of interest and a greater sharing of ideas when clinical material is presented and discussed at meetings. The evocation of real character and conflict, the challenge of organizing analytic data, the presentation of evidence that becomes coherent and convincing, and the shared search for understanding tend to diminish doctrinal differences and to break down barriers to analytic thought and inference. Moreover, we need a continuing commitment and investment in clinical analytic research by psychoanalysts in collecting and assessing analytic evidence and in reporting and publishing our analytic findings.

It is in this spirit that I turn now to the presentation of clinical material, material which complements my previous reconstruction of object loss (1980). This case presentation, of necessity compressed, is an overview of an analysis. It will enable us to contemplate further the nature of analytic evidence and inferences.

Clinical Presentation

The case that I shall present invited a serious question from the outset, namely, the question of analysability. Always a concern, analysability is dubious, at best, when a patient starts with fabrication. The patient was a young, married male in his thirties, a relatively successful engineer, who was noted to be extremely anxious in his initial consultation. He was more or less depressed, discontent, excessively concerned about being liked; he felt he couldn't get close to his family, and too often wondered and worried about death. His father died before the patient was 10 years old. The initial evaluation suggested that he could use and benefit from analysis and that analysis offered the possibility of a major exploration and reorganization of his personality with attenuation of his deep-seated conflicts and depressive tendencies. He seemed to accept the recommendation. Just before he was to begin analysis he telephoned the analyst stating, 'My mother died, and I will be in touch with you after the funeral'. I told him that I was very sorry and expressed condolence and said that I would wait to hear from him. He did not contact me for more than a year and a half. I later learned that during that time he had seen another therapist, and that therapist also advised psychoanalysis. The patient then telephoned asking for consultation to continue analytic treatment. He now really wanted to start analysis with me, and he had something to tell me at the outset.

He confessed that he had fled from analysis by invoking a completely false alibi: the story that his mother had died was not true; it was a fabrication, a 'big lie'. Could such a patient who begins analysis with dishonesty and with an 'outrageous lie' really be analysed? Was he a sociopath? Could he free associate and not be delinquent toward the fundamental rule? Would he lie throughout the analysis? Many patients initially withhold material such as an affair, an abortion, perverse tendencies, etc. but they do not start with a deliberate lie. In short, the question of selection and suitability was paramount. I was intrigued and perplexed with this remarkable behaviour. The patient seemed somewhat ashamed and expressed mild feelings of humiliation and guilt over having deceived the analyst. He could not explain the rather bizarre behaviour but asserted that he was not an habitual liar and he respected the truth.

What was interesting was not only his verbal communication but his non-verbal behaviour. The patient was so tremulous, so visibly agitated that the chair shook along with his head and torso. He looked as if he might 'jump out of his skin', and the room also seemed to vibrate. His mother had been ill with a possible malignancy at the time of the fabricated report of her death. Although he had wept when he learned of this news, the report of her death was entirely premature, and she was very much alive at the time the patient returned to me for possible analysis. It was progrostically positive that there was a feeling of relatedness and affective communication of his desire for help. The patient presented a kind of child-like pseudo-innocence, a plea to be accepted despite his delinquency, a fear of rejection coupled with a pathetic and almost desperate look that sought pity and protection.

I wondered about the lie in the service of denial and repression, the problems of acting out and other regressive potential, and the nature of the underlying superego pathology. His blatant lie, condoned and condemned meekly and after the fact, was a form of acting out through subversion of verbalization (Blum, 1976). Did he have to leave before he was left, and would he sustain analysis without interruption and repeated flight? What might be predicted about major resistances, transference constellations, and the ultimate explanation for such a fantastic fabrication? It seemed likely that the falsification and flight served an initial transference resistance and were probably part of an unconscious fantasy. I conjectured that the patient had committed a symbolic oedipal crime with an unconscious need for punishment and atonement. Simultaneously it was useful to ponder the limits of manifest content, first impressions, and initial explanation. 'It is not in the least our business to "understand" a case at once: this is only possible at a later stage, when we have received enough impressions of it. For the present we will suspend out judgement and give our impartial attention to everything that there is to observe' (Freud, 1909, pp. 22–23).

Other analytic considerations also influenced my assessment. The patient had, indeed, returned, had come back to 'the scene of the crime', having fled punishment with his 'alibi'. He came not only to confess but to understand behaviour that he considered alien and irrational. He knew he could have fled from analysis without any excuse, but had been compelled to invent the pathetic pseudology. The other factor was the nature of the fabrication itself, a truly outrageous lie. And it was a lie about the death of his mother; one of the most forbidden childhood wishes was nakedly expressed. It was so extreme and egregious that it had to have a prominent defensive function and could not simply be the primary expression of his undisguised matricidal wish. If the patient could be taken seriously when he said that he was not given to chronic lying in his adolescent or adult life, then when he told one it was a 'whopper'. Such a lie might 'testify' to denial in fantasy and in action and to the return from repression of some overwhelming traumatic experience. The lie was clearly related to the anticipated loss of his mother, and he had told me that his father had died when he was 9 to 10 years of age, in our initial interview.

The presence of many areas of well-integrated functioning held out hope for his ego strength and analysability. He showed appreciation and concern for his family and had honestly advanced his career and work. Having a trial of analysis in mind, I told the patient that I would accept him for treatment, and that if he and the treatment proved to be suitable for each other, we would hope to learn the reasons for his strange and unreasonable behaviour and to work out the conflicts and problems behind his anxiety and depression. He seemed relieved, promptly and regularly continued the analytic work. He initially associated to the analysis as a safety net and security blanket, at first seeking approval, affection, and absolution. While some patients with parent loss in childhood, fixated to the traumatic past, resist change, and new relationships, his initial attachment to analysis involved a transference fantasy of reunion with magical return of the lost parent. The analytic work was expectably difficult, but it was also analytically productive and rewarding with interpretation of his pathogenic conflicts, defences, and working through of childhood traumata leading toward a mutually acceptable 'termination' after approximately six years of analysis.

The leitmotiv of the lie and loss ran like a red thread through the analysis and was gradually understood from many different points of view and on different developmental levels, with major additional meanings gleaned in the final phase of treatment. Only certain salient features of the patient's analysis and of the life history which was reassembled from it will be presented here.

Appropriate and informal in manner and dress, he talked with pressure, smiled readily, had a quick wit and sense of humour. He liked to joke when he wasn't too anxious or depressed, and he needed to joke when he wanted to alleviate his depression. He was fun-loving and a potential 'killjoy', excitable and readily rejected and dejected. At the time we started treatment he was in his thirties, married, with a devoted worrisome wife of approximately the same age, and two small children. He was born into an immigrant Jewish family and grew up in another city. There were two siblings, a brother eight years older and a sister two years older than his brother. His parents had a general store and lived above the store. He recalled their spending very long hours in the store, leaving the young child in solitary play. His mother was remembered as chronically depressed, often tearful, sometimes crying. She tended to equate feeding and physical care with good mothering, and, retiring and withdrawn, she was often emotionally unavailable or insensitive. She was unable to inquire about the patient's feelings or to be very responsibe to his conversations and questions. He was very close to his father who was much more cheerful and, though very hardworking, given to jocular play and friendly, affectionate banter with the patient. The death of his father in the boy's tenth year was a terrible experience and followed a painful downhill course in which the father's vitality and vigour were lost in the advance of his malignant illness. Since there was a rather large age difference between the patient and the next older sibling, he had restricted contact with his siblings but was very pleased to have whatever attention was offered to him. Of great importance to his later development was his brother's interest in him in his late adolescence. The patient had not done well in school and was not prepared for work or a career until guided by his brother. The family had always been poor, and after the death of the father, their impoverished state was such that their life was a literal struggle for socioeconomic survival. His mother had trained for new work and again spent long hours away from home. His life was filled with loneliness, longing, sadness, and wish-fulfilling self-aggrandizing daydreams in which he achieved fame and fortune, admiration and esteem, and the conquest of attractive women.

A crucial question was whether the patient's initial fabrication was a symptom or part of a character defect. He did not lie in general, though he was given to bragging, particularly during the latency period. As a group phenomenon, his peer group told 'tall stories', and he was given to presenting himself as a far superior athlete than he was in reality. He wanted to be the biggest and the best with the mightiest bat and balls. His parents told little white lies to their relatives to avoid acknowledging their humiliating poverty. He disclaimed other dishonesty on the part of his parents or siblings. The patient had, on occasion, stolen little items from the 5/10c store until he was caught and reprimanded by his brother. As a little boy he had also once taken coins from his mother's purse and had lost money for which he was soundly spanked. The deprivations and punishments contributed to his feeling inadequate, disillusioned, and intimidated. Punishment and poverty unconsciously strengthened his selfdenigration, his homosexual submissive impulses toward his father as well as his unconscious rage and identifications with castrated, humiliated parents.

The patient recalled his mother's compassionate attempts to help the father after his father developed cancer. His mother became more depressed with an intensification of intermittent feelings of helplessness and hopelessness and yet with episodic efforts to provide tender care and offer comfort. These efforts often miscarried because of the mother's 'misery' and bouts of colitis with cramps and diarrhoea. This was often so severe that the patient remembered with disgust her excrement on the floor if she couldn't reach the bathroom in time. This was an area of familial silence and shame. He also emphasized the efforts at family closeness and warmth, the good times, particularly between himself, his father, and his brother, with shared laughter and games, occasionally playing tricks on each other.

He had, of course, 'tricked' me in the first session, and there was no question that there was an aggressive, derisive quality in making a fool of the fatherfigure. In its sado-masochistic provocation, the fabrication also represented a pathetic plea for sympathy; he thought he wanted to be pitied as a poor orphan and to avoid antagonizing a figure of authority. He invited punishment and humiliation and ran from pain and punishment. His anxiety and depression could be contagious, and his efforts at humour and joking could also be infectious. He had been the class comic and had attempted to disguise being a poor student by being the funny one and the wise guy. His curiosity and learning were clearly impaired by his neurotic problems, and his curiosity and motivation to learn rapidly were mobilized in the analysis. Although he lied to other people a few times during the analysis, mostly in the form of selfaggrandizing, bragging about his accomplishments, or by mentioning powerful people with whom he was associated, there were no further deliberate falsifications in the analysis. There were omissions and secretive reactions, e.g. delay in telling the analyst about masturbation, watching pornography, and temper responses to his family. The analyst was tested for sincerity and integrity, for his capacity to bear the patient's demands and depression, and for an analytic attitude rather than moral indignation or exoneration, for example concerning his initial lie.

The loss of his father with all its implications and ramifications rapidly emerged as a central psychological configuration early in the analysis. The patient had fantasies of playing dead with humorous revivals (like the fabrication of his mother's death). Far more worrisome were obsessive thoughts that he would return home to his wife and children whom he felt he loved so much, and find them massacred. This thought filled him with dread; he would want either to avoid going home or to rush home to make sure that everyone was all right.

There were repetitive dreams in which

his father fell off the roof, and the little boy standing behind him or at his side reached down, caught him, and magically pulled him back.

There was a child-like quality to his playfulness, although he could be described as adolescent in terms of many other features. He often thought about death, and his many 'sick' jokes lightly dismissed the dangers of severe illness, injury, and death. At the time he had consulted me he had been worried about the failing health of his mother and of his former therapist; they might die but he would live. He felt assured and yet not entirely free of worry about his analyst's health and longevity (typical of patients with childhood object loss). He had not been permanently lost but had come back to analysis. I interpreted that his leaving and returning were a form of enactment of his repetitive dream (of his father falling from a height and being pulled back to the roof by the patient).

One of the most significant meanings of the consultation drama of the lie, leaving analysis, and then returning, now emerged. The patient killed me off with the treatment and then resurrected me again! He too died and was rescued and resurrected while unconsciously killing the previous therapist in treatment. The theme of death, resurrection, and rebirth recurred throughout the analysis. The trauma of his father's death was re-enacted with an effort at mastery alongside the denial of the death. The denial concerned the meaning of death but included the denial of irreversible loss. The dramatization of the denial indicated the obligatory need to repeat in an episodic form of verbal and non-verbal enactment. The lie was a concentration of a fantasy and a magical alteration of reality. The patient confirmed Weinshel's (1979) formulation of fabrication as a means of not dealing with painful or potentially traumatic material. There were early indications that the fabrication had a screen function for pivotal traumatic events and important unconscious fantasies. The fantastic fabrication would serve as a vehicle for reconstruction and would be fitted into the nexus of his particular life history as described by Deutsch (1922). Much of the material was condensed and telescoped so that what is sketched in some sequence here was reorganized in the analytic process. Freud (1900) very early grappled with this problem in reconstruction and stated, 'If, during a child's prehistoric epoch, his nurse has been dismissed, and if soon afterwards his mother has died, the two events are superimposed on each other in a single series in his memory as revealed in analysis' (p. 255). Cycles of death, resurrection, and subsequent loss appear throughout the analytic material. In a slip of the tongue, when the patient remarked on where the analyst was born and bred, he said, 'born and dead'. He fantasied himself in a recurrent daydream as a girl floating on a leaf set adrift in the currents. This highly condensed image included his identifications with both parents, but particularly his identification with his mother and his being born as the girl she wanted. It also referred to identification with Moses and the Egyptian princess who bore him in a family romance. His father's and his own identification with the Jewish mythical hero and law-giver was a factor in his superego development. In this family romance, a narcissistic and oedipal creation, he was reborn as a great leader and saviour, along the lines of the myth of the birth of the hero.

Associations to falling off the roof were again symbolic, representative of both birth and death. He thought of movies of assassins, murders, and mayhem. He had actually seen death at firsthand which reminded him of his father and of his uncle. This brought to mind a terrible, vivid memory from his adolescence.

On the patient's sixteenth birthday, his uncle killed himself by jumping out of a window (cf. birth-death-falling). The patient had been due to visit his uncle and was obsessed with thoughts that he could have saved his uncle's life if he had indeed visited. Here again were birth and death, the fantasy of rescue, being rescued, and undoing the murderous deed. He developed suicidal ideation, insomnia, and had images of seeing his uncle's face in the coffin. After a single psychiatric consultation, the patient and his family were reassured that everything would be all right, that he was in effect just a nervous kid who would recover from the shock of the suicide. He thought of the crushed bodies of war victims and the dashed skull of a girl he had seen who had died as a result of a suicidal jump from a building. At the same time he thought of the assassination of President Kennedy and dreamt of:

operating on the bashed head of the President, reconstructing the brain (cf. analytic reconstruction).

He was gradually able to understand the revival of the loss of his father at the time of his uncle's death and his guilt over their deaths. He was the assassin who had unconsciously achieved an oedipal but pyrrhic victory over the father he ambivalently loved so very much. Bringing his father back from the dead was simultaneously an expression of his love and longing as well as his need to undo his fantasy destruction. He was like Freud's patient (1900, p. 260) who felt he was capable of wanting to push his own father off the top of a mountain and later developed obsessive self-reproaches after his father's painful illness and death.

At the time his father died, the patient had a cognitive grasp of death. Unlike Freud's 10-year-old (1900) who stated, 'I know father's dead, but what I can't understand is why he doesn't come home to supper' (p. 254);[1] my patient's father was consciously regarded as irreversibly lost. At the same time in the kind of split of the ego that Freud (1937) noted in connexion with denial, he continued to daydream and dream that his father would be back. He preferred his father to his mother and another unconscious meaning of the 'big lie' emerged. He had recognized, intellectually, that he probably harboured matricidal wishes, but they had no meaning to him at the beginning of the analysis. He later understood that the fabrication of her death served the double denial of his mother's illness and his father's death. He also would have preferred that his father had lived and his mother had died. If it were possible to make me believe that what was false was true, then the patient could also disregard the truth and believe in what was false (Fenichel, 1939). I reminded him of children's games of 'Let's Pretend'. The family shared suppression and denial concerning the father's cancer. He was not told the diagnosis, and the physician and family co-operated in the deception and the father's selfdeception. In his deliberate falsification with me, the patient repeated and reversed what the doctor and family had done to his father as a patient. There was a conspiracy of silence over the illness, as there had always been over money and sexual matters. The question of birth and death was connected with infantile sexual curiosity and theories. There was ample evidence of primal scene exposure and probably thinly disguised homosexual longing for his father and brother.

---

1 Freud (1900, p. 255), beginning developmental considerations of the child's concept of death, also described a 4-year-old girl's realistic idea of death as never coming back again.

Another traumatic experience condensed in the material of the first consultations was an adolescent experience of homosexual seduction by a father-figure which preceded the uncle's suicide. Longing for his father's love, reunion with him, and submitting to the father as a defence against his parricidal wishes, he was, at the same time, terribly guilty and ashamed of the experience. He would not only die because of the death wishes he harboured toward his father, but he would die of shame for having failed his father in not becoming a man. He felt impotent and castrated, used and abused like a 'fallen woman'. He had fallen from grace and should have 'dropped dead' instead of his father and uncle.

While maternal transference was intermittently present, the predominant transference object was that of the father, and the predominant developmental phase was that of the Oedipus complex. Pre-oedipal material appeared more frequently in oral regressive form and associated with maternal transference. He had caring thoughts about his mother; he remembered moments of warmth, her devoted efforts to feed and nurture, the tragic unhappiness of her life, and his wishes that she could have been far more nurturant and sensitive. The sights and sounds of the bathroom were associated with her colitis. His mother was prone to giving herself enemas; she would also give him enemas, despite his protests, if there were any signs of constipation or illness. Hidden behind the anger and discomfort, the excitement and mutual seduction was another aspect of his negative oedipal position as well as his castration at the hands of a phallic woman. The falling in his dreams was, therefore, also the loss of faeces representing the loss of potency, the penis, and both parents; falling also had the opposite symbolic meanings of birth and rebirth. He had lost his father through death and was afraid of losing his mother, and of his own castration and death. Paradoxically, he sometimes felt better when discussing an actual death which proved to be related to circumstances that reassured him that he was not responsible and was not a murderer. 'And death once dead, there's no more dying then' (Shakespeare, Sonnet 146). His great lie meant he was innocent, exonerated since his mother was really alive. His lie was also a repetition of the enema traumata, a submission to the therapeutic process followed by defying and deceiving me with the pseudo-production of 'bull-shit'. As a faecal object, the lie was 'living shit' and dead loss. His fleeing from homosexual submission protected against anal rape and robbery, and the revival of trauma, incontinence, crying, and expressive sadness were equated with a feared femininity.

As the analysis deepened, his disappointment, injury, and rage with his mother came more clearly to the surface. He remembered her sad, mournful face, her depression, her lamenting her hard life which had so much pain and grief. Again, she did not hesitate to inflict this upon her child who was, in many respects, an only child because of the great age difference between himself and his siblings. He was often reminded of his naughtiness, of his shortcomings. When he upset her, which was not difficult to do, or when she had an attack of colitis, he was told that she would die—he was giving her a cancer. In short, he was not only making her miserable, he was to be her executioner. This clarified some of his tormenting guilt and the sado-masochistic mother/son relationship. He was the youngest; he was more delicate, very special, and she loved him dearly. At the same time, he was her potential enemy. She felt bereaved; and he, in turn, felt bereaved and bewildered. What had he done to her, who was being cruel to whom? How could he cheer her up; how could he get rid of her contagious misery? His mother's inconsistent discipline, the loss of parental authority after his father's death, the many deprivations and nonbenign neglect, the feeling that he was an orphan who had to take matters into his own hands, had all contributed to a peculiarly harsh, brittle, and inconsistent superego. His deception was related to the psychology of the exception. An instability of regulation and control permitted the episodic enactments which intensified his guilt. His 'many superegos' permitted many truths (Ferenczi, 1927). The enactments were paradoxically the result of his unconscious entitlement and over-permissiveness, as well as his unconscious guilt and self-punishment. He unconsciously feared and wished for castration and death.

Though the oedipal organization and the superego were the most important analytic considerations in this case, the pre-oedipal determinants were also significant. His mother's depression compromised her caretaking and nurturance. Separation anxiety in childhood and the insomnia of adolescence were only partly mastered; and as an adult he had to guard his independence and autonomy. Analytic separations would result in either greater closeness and clinging to the analyst and to his wife, or provoking fights with his wife and then giving her the 'silent treatment'. He appeared to have earlier transferred his affection from the depressed mother to the more responsive father who was, in some respects, both a father and a mother. This was a further contribution to the understanding of the transferred ambivalence to the father as well as to the developmental insult suffered by the loss of the father. However, there was not a pervasive arrest at the level of development just prior to the father's death. The arrested mourning and reactivated conflicts did contribute to subsequent developmental disturbance and disharmony, but there was antecedent disturbance as well as later progressive gains along some developmental lines (cf. Altschul, 1968); (Furman, 1974); (Pollock, 1961).

The transference conflicts had concentrated in the father transference. This was related to the unconscious resurrection of the lost father, the activation of and struggle against mourning, and a defensive-adaptive shift from maternal transference and tendencies toward pre-oedipal regression. The father transference defended against maternal and pre-oedipal transference issues. Because of defence and developmental reorganization, the transference does not recapitulate the development of the neurosis and it cannot be the sole or whole guide to reconstruction. Following his exposition of the encompassing importance of the transference neurosis, Freud (1917b) contemplated the analytic process and cautioned: 'It will not be out of place to give a warning that we can draw no direct conclusion from the distribution of the libido during and resulting from the treatment as to how it was distributed during the illness. Suppose we succeeded in bringing a case to a favourable conclusion by setting up and then resolving a strong father-transference to the doctor. It would not be correct to conclude that the patient had suffered previously from a similar unconscious attachment of his libido to his father. His father-transference was merely the battlefield on which we gained control of his libido; the patient's libido was directed to it from other positions. A battlefield need not necessarily coincide with one of the enemy's key fortresses. The defence of a hostile capital need not take place just in front of its gates. Not until after the transference has once more been resolved can we reconstruct in our thoughts the distribution of libido which had prevailed during the illness' (pp. 455–6).

Both regressive alteration and progressive transformation complicate oedipal–pre-oedipal issues and relationships. The reconstruction of the infantile neurosis and its changes in life in the formation of the adult neurosis restores the complicated connexions between past and present, but proceeds on a higher level of synthesis and abstraction and at a greater distance from immediate analytic observation than transference analysis. But transference alone does not depict development or pathogenesis. Evidence for pathogenesis derives from the totality of the analytic process, and final reconstruction may be remodelled during termination or left to the analyst alone after the analysis is over.

As we shall see, the father transference in this case screened the underlying powerful developmental impact of his mother's depression. His mother's depression was a major pathogenic influence. The patient's tendency toward global identifications with her, his narcissistic fragility and compensatory narcissistic fantasies were based upon a pre-oedipal disturbance. Torn between dependent and autonomous strivings, he manifested oscillating clinging, coercive tantrums, and intense separation conflicts with modulated repetition in transference regression. His object relations and narcissism were particularly vulnerable to regression, with unstable self-esteem. A basic depressive mood and predisposition to depression were assumed to have developed prior to, and then in parallel with, the oedipal phase. The impression was that his primarily oedipal disorder had significant and detectable determinants arising from earlier psychosexual phases and the process of separation-individuation (Mahler, 1966), (1975). The depressive mood of his mother also contributed to his depressive tendencies and to an early proclivity toward denial, splitting of the ego to protect the narcissistic love object from rage, and to fantasies of fusion (later reunion) with the idealized object. In connexion with maternal depression, A. Freud (1965) noted, 'What happens is that such infants achieve their sense of unity and harmony with the depressed mother not by means of their developmental achievements but by producing the mother's mood in themselves' (p. 87). In some respects, he had remained an infant who had wanted immediate gratification and did not want to acknowledge the reality of what was unpleasurable. However, except in his dreams, there was never a manifest loss of object or self-constancy, so that some adequate structuralization, ego strengths, and resilient recovery from traumatization could be postulated for the infantile period. The multiple childhood traumata were nevertheless incompletely understood and mastered by the mature ego, and ego synthesis of traumatic states and consequences had not been accomplished.

His guilt was intensified after his father's death by the close, intimate, and unconsciously incestuous relationship with his mother. This was reproduced in fantasies about the analyst and analyst's wife, fears of retaliation for his incestuous wishes, and for his aggression against the mother on whom he was even more dependent as the only surviving parent. He wanted to possess and control her for both sexual and dependent gratifications and was afraid of his own anger toward her. The problems were also reflected in his marriage and his many problems with intimacy, closeness, and distance recapitulated in the transference. Afraid to be dependent, he was angry when dependent needs were not gratified inside and outside the analysis. He found that it was difficult for him to discuss death and explain it to his children. He compared his physical, emotional, and mental attributes with those of his mother and father. His resemblance to his father was emphasized as an assertion of his manhood as his father's unconscious resurrection and reincarnation. He would then be entitled to his mother which again aroused the spectre of death and the unconscious fear of his father's vengeance in the form of a similar malevolent fate.

In his closeness to his mother, his psychological atunement to her attitudes and moods, a new dimension of shared fantasy and affect appeared. His mother, forlorn and bereaved, had left many of her relatives behind in Europe. World War II had started at the time the patient entered the oedipal phase, and he recalled that his mother's grieving at this time continued into his later childhood and adolescence. She knew that her loved-ones were in mortal danger, and correctly suspected that these Jewish relatives had been murdered. The mother's intense bereavement actually preceded the onset of the father's malignancy. She was faced with multiple losses followed by the loss of her husband. The trauma of the father's death was, therefore, complicated by the mother's antecedent deep depression and mourning and her impotent rage about the massacre of her family.[2]

New meanings of the massacre fantasy of his own family surfaced towards the end of analysis. The patient was identified with his mother, i.e. his bereaved mother whose family had been massacred. At the same time, he was identified with the Nazis who were responsible for the massacre and who would eventually kill his mother (and him). After all, she also regarded him as the enemy who would destroy her with colitis and cancer. Behind the identification with the Nazis was the infantile identification with the aggressor and his infantile death-wishes for his mother. His mother's mourning hung like a pall over the family, an atmosphere which became ever more doleful with the illness and death of his father and the intensification of their psychological and economic impoverishment.

The central theme of death and resurrection, massacre and rescue appeared in a new light. His mother had occasionally lamented that she would have been better off dead, which the patient experienced as a reproach and rejection. He recovered a vague memory dating from the time when he was three or four years of age that there had been an incident with gas fumes at night. She might well have made a suicide attempt or even more than one attempt. His vague thoughts were entirely disconnected from the issue of the familial massacre. The timing of the suicidal attempt would have coincided with his mother's surmise that her loved ones in Europe were in grave danger or already killed. Her behaviour was not only suicidal but it could have resulted in the massacre of her own family here, jeopardizing the patient's life. He had survived his father but had earlier survivor guilt in identification with, and in relation to, his mother who survived her murdered relatives. In addition, he was identified with his mother as suicidal victim and homicidal executioner.

---

2 'The complement to this cultural and conventional attitude towards death is provided by our complete collapse when death has truck down someone whom we love—a parent or a partner in marriage, a brother or sister, a child or a close friend. Our hopes, our desires and our pleasures lie in the grave with him, we will not be consoled, we will not fill the lost one's place. We behave as if we were a kind of Asra, who die when those they love die' (Freud, 1915a, p. 290).

He might massacre his family, like his mother with her spouse and children, and as the Nazis did to his maternal relatives. The murderer represented his despised self and object images—his suicidal mother and vengeful father.

His siblings confirmed the mother's suicide attempt, and one of the siblings told him for the first time of the siblings' own suicidal ideation. His mother had never been able to complete mourning because of her own inner problems and because of the murder of her love objects. His mother had needed so much to be mothered and to be consoled for her multiple and cumulative losses. Her fragility and depression and his increased dependence upon the surviving parent made it particularly difficult for him to express aggression or criticism of her. His self-accusation represented her accusations which were internalized, as well as self-reproach for his hostility, his disappointing his mother and himself in his inability to comfort her, to redeem her deprivations, and to compensate for the familial suffering and sacrifices. He struggled against his identification with her and was unaware of their shared psychic reality and reciprocal fantasies. Fearful of failure, he had a special need to succeed. His hidden ambition was rooted in competitive wishes to outdo his father and siblings and, even more poignantly, to justify his survival. He and his mother were both survivors of each other's hostile fantasies, of his father, and of murdered relatives. His ambivalence to his mother was heightened by her depressive withdrawal, but also by her threat to destroy him with herself. The initial fabrication, therefore, screened multiple traumata from infancy to adolescence (Deutsch, 1922); (Weinshel, 1979) and simultaneously revealed a crucial dimension of his history. His mother was really ill at the time he first was moved to undertake analytic consultation. Her possible demise threatened to reactivate the trauma of her suicidal attempt, her (and his) rescue and survival. The patient shared the guilt of survival through his mother. Her suicidal behaviour intensified his primitive violent fantasies, fear of his aggression and his guilt over her suffering and self-destructiveness; but he also responded to unconscious expectations and hopes. There were mixed maternal messages passively to withdraw or die, to deny, to count blessings, and actively to compensate her for her missing objects, phallus, and self-regard. He would, with his siblings, achieve redemption and the rebirth of a new and far better life. It was fortunate that he did not feel these demands as an actual only child.

As a child he was identified with his mother as a remote victim and survivor of the holocaust (Bergmann & Jucovy, 1982). The incomplete mourning and life and death issues shared with his mother, the living with a *mater dolerosa* who was both 'alive and dead' in her feelings, attitudes, and withdrawal resulted in the far-reaching effects and transmission of trauma and the confirmation of primitive conflicts and fantasies. The paradoxical desire to kill or cure the parent permeated his early life and contributed to later adolescent attitudes of passive rebellion and social consciousness (Kestenberg, 1980). He wanted to deny and master the shock and strain trauma (Kris, 1956) that he and his parents experienced.

The holocaust themes, interwoven with his and his mother's fantasies, were partially denied in social reality, and this was probably interwoven with the deception and self-deception of the victims (as with his father's cancer). The cultural and psycho-historical facets of fabrication are significant in their impact upon particular individuals but are beyond the scope of this paper. The collusive silence, however, specifically applied to his mother's suicidal behaviour. There was no meaningful discussion of suicidal feelings or intent but an implicit cue not to question or report. Suspicion of concealment and fabrication of the attempt as an 'accident' was analytically inferred but not definitely confirmed. There was no effort to enlighten the confused, frightened child, to confront the threat of abandonment and overwhelming affective reactions. The family could not effectively cope with either the mother's anguished cry for help or feelings of betrayal, manipulation, and masochistic provocation. He felt his mother's rejection, the symbolic murder of self and love objects in her suicidal-homicidal behaviour, and this contributed to his own 'worthless' and self-punitive attitudes (Warren, 1966). The suicide of his uncle on the patient's birthday unconsciously represented the supreme rejection by the parent, particularly his mother, condensed with his oedipal guilt over displacing his father with his arrival. The adolescent experience screened the infantile traumata which were repeated in transference derivatives. Reconstruction of the early experience was necessary to deal with the denial and fragmented memories and to reassemble the experiences and reactions in a cohesive picture (Rosen, 1955); (Wallerstein, 1967). The sources of the edited transference repetitions and a causal, chronological, and developmental sequence for the legacy of his losses and the meanings of his symptomatic lie could then be understood.

The terminal phase of analysis reactivated all the feelings of abandonment and loss, with further mourning in the transference, with revived fantasies of death and resurrection as the oedipal victor. He remembered being locked out on the fire escape with his mother closing the window to the apartment; this broadened his understanding of their mutual feelings of desertion and rage and his identification with his fallen father. After the fall and the escape from analysis, he would be launched like an astronaut or athlete to new heights of phallic conquest and independent achievement. Working through on new developmental levels, he could find replacement and restitution in his current family and work. His imagery was replete with symbols of birth and death, sleep and walking, travel and homecoming. He anticipated termination with a peculiar bitter sweet admixture of grief and relief. Never lost, the dying of the analysis unmasked again the 'great lie' of humanity, the denial of death. His lie was a 'living lie', a lie that gave life to his parents and to his lost relatives. The impetus to fabricate may give rise to immortal works of art and fiction in creative individuals, and many writers have suffered parental loss in childhood (Kanzer, 1953).

Discussion

The analytic process bears a resemblance to a scientific experiment. The framework is relatively constant, reliable, stable, and interaction then occurs between the patient's varying communications and the analyst's variable interventions. Any session or sequence of sessions may be studied for its form and content, for the patient's language, affect, and gesture style, for particular subject preferences and personal linguistic forms of grammar and syntax. Dreams and daydreams, metaphor, imagery, objects, symbolism, the manner of opening and closing the session, etc. may be followed in each session and over the course of the analysis.

The myriad of derivatives of unconscious conflicts and fantasies are clarified and subject to analysis with working through and working to the underlying determinants. What appears to be rambled talk and jumbled images is actually dynamically and genetically determined. In the case described, as in all analytic cases, an enormous number of observations and various patterns can be followed through the treatment. While one session may be misleading in its implications, the course of the analysis is then corrective (Freud, 1937). Examining the criteria that transforms disconnected associations, thoughts, and affects into supportable hypotheses, Arlow (1979) noted the importance of the context of particular data. Form and sequence, repetitions, similarities and opposites, allusions, silences, and non-verbal communication lead to connexions and the gradual emergence of themes within the associations. In turn, this leads to an organization of the material into configurations.

Frequently, derivatives of a core conflict and central fantasy system become the 'leitmotiv' of treatment, like the Wolf Man's primal scene schema and the theme of death and its denial and undoing in this case.

Organization of analytic data into a meaningful integration is intrinsic to analytic methodology and later inference. Prototypical for analytic interpretation, Freud (1923) described the convergence of evidence. 'The analyst, too, may himself retain a doubt of the same kind in some particular instances. What makes him certain in the end is precisely the complication of the problem before him, which is like the the solution of a jig-saw puzzle … If one succeeds in arranging the confused heap of fragments … so that the picture acquires a meaning, so that there is no gap anywhere in the design and so that the whole fits into the frame—if all these conditions are fulfilled, then one knows that one has solved the puzzle and that there is no alternative solution' (p. 116).

This ideal solution applies to a central interpretive focus and often alternative interpretations and inferences have to be evaluated in terms of accuracy, priority, overdetermination, and level of explanation. New data may extend or amend earlier hypotheses. Insight itself is a circular, creative process which permits interpretation. It advances, and derives from the analytic process and analytic evidence (Blum, 1979).

The analyst listens and responds to the patient, reads and responds to the literature, and new analytic data resonate with his previous analytic education and experience. The evidence is subjected to analytic scrutiny and evaluation prior to explanatory hypothesis. The analysis of the transference is enlarged with other perspectives including consideration of the non-interpretive influence of the analyst (e.g. education, suggestion) (Stone, 1981), the phase and length of analysis, the phase and life situation of the patient, the effects of subtle unconscious adaptations by analyst and patient to each other's personality during a protracted analytic process. Every psychoanalytic situation has its own unique realities which need to be defined by analyst and patient (cf. the special situation of clinic and didactic analysis). The analyst scrutinizes the structure of the analytic situation, his own modes of participation and observation, the patient's utilization of the analyst and the process, to gather analytic data and determine valid evidence.

Concern with the nature of analytic evidence and inference, with our epistemology, should lead to more precise investigation and formulation and closer correlation between clinical inference and metapsychology (Kris, 1947). Waelder (1962) demonstrated six different levels of increasing abstraction ranging from the clinical discourse in the analytic process to the discourse of metapsychology. Analytic data are first observed, ordered, organized, abstracted, and generalized. At the level of clinical theory, inferences are drawn concerning defence, unconscious guilt, regression, etc. In conjunction with the theme of the 33rd IPA Congress, the analytic inferences I will present here will largely remain at the level of clinical theory with acknowledgement of inevitable subjective preference and implied assumptions. Many inferences can be drawn from this one case concerning the psychology of lying or deliberate falsification; the trauma of parent loss in childhood; the effects of maternal depression, the effects on the child of parental suicidal behaviour, etc. The material lends itself to the confirmation of many pertinent formulations. Freud (1917a) not only studied fundamental issues in 'Mourning and melancholia' but also made major contributions in other papers and letters to our understanding of object loss. A large and valuable literature on object loss has been added to Freud's pioneering formulations and will not be reviewed in detail here.

From the manifold inferences in this case, I shall select a few that I found of particular interest for further analytic reflection and investigation. The inferences move, as in analysis, from the more concrete clinical to the more abstract theoretical, and from the specific to the general, from the immediate present to the more remote past.

1. Because of the initial lie and flight from analysis, a negative assessment ofanalysability might be assumed. In this instance, the correct assessment would have to be based upon additional evidence. While we can predict definite nonanalysability in certain cases and have learned to predict analysability with greater understanding and reliability than in the past, a trial of analysis is still indicated in borderline situations.

2. The lie did not prove to be a manifestation of sociopathic character. In itsextremely childish character, it was analogous to Freud's (1913b) description of lies told by children. The case confirmed Freud's explanation that such lies were instigated by powerful unconscious motives which may give notice of disposition to future neurosis but should not be mistakenly regarded as prognostic for bad character.

3. The lie was simultaneously an unconscious confession. The truth was that hisfather was dead and his mother alive. The inner truths, akin to the truth in delusion, unknown to the patient, were his representation of his mother as already dead in her depressive withdrawal, and her perpetual mourning. The lie expressed the patient's matricidal wishes and protected him against her suicide-homicide threats. In fabricating his mother's death, he denied the meaning and finality of his father's death with his unresolved oedipal guilt. The lie itself could be understood as a resurrected lost object, a narcissistic triumph, and a disturbance of reality associated with trauma and denial.

4. The clinical inferences, beginning with the assessment of analysability, aredrawn within a framework of analytic knowledge and theory. The clinical study of a dramatic, deliberate, initial deception raised questions

about the patient's superego, and the structural hypothesis was used in the organization of the analytic data. In the course of analytic work, the patient's inconsistent and infantile superego was amenable to 'structural change'. The patient's conflicts over loyalty, justice, and responsibility were significantly related to contradictory parental identifications (e.g. loyalty versus betrayal) with reciprocity of clinical inferences, theoretical formulation, and validation of theory.

5. Parent loss in childhood may result in developmental arrest, deviation, ordisharmony but may also spur various forms of mastery and sublimation. The developmental disturbance in this case was highly selective as in the continued utilization of denial and undoing, while other areas showed progressive mastery as in the development of wit and humour. Much depends upon antecedent personality maturity and strengths, surviving object relationships, and the capacity to mourn. Mourning is not completed, and a child's partial mourning will be impeded by the unresolved mourning of the surviving parent.

6. The transference neurosis is ego edited and does not literally recapitulate the development of the infantile neurosis. Developmental sequence and consequence are inferred and then organized into coherent patterns with more or less priority and precision. Inferences concerning pathogenesis transcend the transference and encompass the modifications and complexities of development. In this case, the source of the intense father transference in adult analysis could not be fully understood without taking into account his mother's disturbance and their co-adaptation to his father's death.

7. The importance of reconstruction of *both* shock and strain trauma, i.e. of both nodal events and enduring patterns, as well as the interaction of external and psychic reality are emphasized. The traumatic experience of a parent's suicidal behaviour or the death of a parent in childhood is not simply revived in a transference pattern, and the lifting of denial and confusion, the restoration of cause and effect, depends upon both transference analysis in the here and now and reconstruction of the past. Case histories are not 'short stories' though an analytic

autobiography is constantly revised. Patients have real experience, real families, and an authentic, unique life with the most individual events, patterns, and meanings. Freud (1926) reaffirmed his earlier views, 'The correct reconstruction, you must know, of such forgotten experiences of childhood always has great therapeutic effect whether they permit objective confirmation or not' (p. 276).

8. In contemporary analysis, the patient's history is completed, corrected, andcreated, with reorganization of the personality. The past takes on elaborate new meaning in ways which could not and did not exist in childhood, so that experience and meaning are variously retrieved and reconstructed, reordered and created anew.

9. In this case the evidence pointed to the significance of the intrapsychic anddevelopmental impact of the traumata, the conflicts activated and validated, the fixation to trauma, and the compulsion to repeat trauma. These consequences of trauma can be differentiated with different clinical and theoretical implications. The transference revival of trauma was associated with derivatives of other traumata. The trauma of childhood parent loss and the mourning process are reactivated in analysis and repeated on different levels of development and throughout the life cycle. Developmental challenge may evoke regression, and/or renewed mourning with attempted mastery of trauma and conflict.

10. Inferences during and after the analytic process are at varying degrees ofabstraction and distance from the data of analytic observation. Observation, inference, and conclusion should not be confused with each other. The manifest meaning to the patient of the conscious fantasy of massacre was fear of reexperiencing death in the family. He was unaware of his own impulses, his confusion of past and present with a compulsion to repeat, the many other components of the fantasy as a compromise formation, etc. The massacre referred to the unconscious meaning of his father's death as parricide, to the formerly repressed and the largely reconstructed trauma of a family massacre threatened by his mother's destructive behaviour, and to the more remote reconstruction

of his mother's presumed reaction to the massacre of her relatives in the holocaust.

11. The more distant inferences are from the testing of the analytic process, and the earlier the inferences in terms of level of psychic development, the greater the need for articulation with other psychoanalytic knowledge, explanatory fit, and cautious extension. The representation of his childhood objects and the understanding of their contribution to his problems and to his strengths is at a different level of inference than transference conflict and its genetic interpretation.

12. The oedipal organization was hierarchically dominant, but analysis revealed important determinants of his neurosis from the early pre-oedipal period through adolescence. All evidence and developmental phases should be considered, e.g. so that the nuances of the relationship with the pre-oedipal mother are coordinated with his father's death in latency and his uncle's suicide in adolescence in drawing inferences concerning the origins of the patient's depression.

13. Though analytic insight is, in part, a created and creative attainment, the elucidation of latent motive and meaning from manifest content emerges from analytic evidence which can be shared with other analysts. Clinical psychoanalysis leads to recovery through discovery. The multiple meanings and functions of the patient's psychopathology, e.g. of a repetitive daydream of massacre, present prior to analysis, can also be understood relatively independently of the influence of the analytic situation and of the analyst's own personality.

14. The meanings of such a massacre fantasy at all developmental levels maybe inferred from analytic data with levels of inference at increasing distance from the clinical material. Analytic interpretation and reconstruction cannot be entirely free of suggestion or subjectivity. Nevertheless, interpretation is not arbitrary, preformed or mystical, but rather, conveys rational understanding of the irrational. Clinical inference is linked to analytic explanation which aims at objective comprehension of psychopathology and pathogenesis, personality development

and organization. Analytic explanation encompasses motivation and meaning, cause and consequence, fantasy and reality, and interdependent dimensions and levels of theory.

Summary

The nature of analytic evidence derived from the analytic process is illustrated and reviewed. The initial acting out of flight from analysis concomitant with an egregious lie later surprisingly proved to be analysable. The lie of loss was a leitmotiv in the analysis which revealed a neurotic structure strongly influenced by actual and threatened traumatic parent loss in childhood. Analytic explanation of psychopathology and pathogenesis is based on insightful inference at increasing distance from the direct analytic data. The meanings inferred and understanding achieved are progressively refined to minimize suggestion and subjectivity. Clinical inference may be tested in the analytic process, but inferences concerning the distant past, or on higher levels of abstraction or generalization require consistency and coherence and articulation with analytic knowledge and principles. The reconstruction of traumatic experience is re-emphasized as a significant dimension of analytic work, with reciprocal illumination of transference and resistance. In the case presented the evidence was drawn from the totality of the analytic process, in which shared inferences become a part of the process in which they are further evaluated and extended.

REFERENCES

Altschul, S. (1968). Denial and ego arrest *J. Am. Psychoanal. Assoc.* 16:301–318
Arlow, J. (1979). The genesis of interpretation *J. Am. Psychoanal. Assoc.* 27(Suppl.):193–206.
Beres, D. & Arlow, J. (1974) Fantasy and identification in empathy *Psychoanal. Q.* 43:26–50.

Bergmann, M. Jucovy, M., Eds. (1982). *Generations of the Holocaust*. New York: Basic Books.

Blum, H. (1976). Acting out, the psychoanalytic process and interpretation *Annual Psychoanal.* 4:163–184.

——— (1979). The curative and creative aspects of insight *J. Am. Psychoanal. Assoc.* 27(Suppl.):41–70.

——— (1980). The value of reconstruction in adult psychoanalysis *Int. J. Psychoanal.* 61:39–54.

Deutsch, H. (1922). On the pathological lie (trans.) *J. Amer. Acad. Psychoanal.* 10:369–386, 1982.

Fenichel, O. 1939 The economics of *pseudologia phantasitica* In *Collected Papers Second Series*. New York: Norton, 1954 pp. 129–140.

Ferenczi, S. (1927). The problem of the termination of the analysis In *Final Contributions to the Problems and Methods of Psychoanalysis*. New York: Brunner/Mazel, 1980 pp. 77–86

Freud, A. (1937). *The Ego and the Mechanisms of Defense*. New York: Int. Univ. Press, 1946.

——— (1965). Normality and Pathology in Childhood New York: Int. Univ. Press.

Freud, S. (1900). The interpretation of dreams *S.E.* 4/5.

——— (1909). Analysis of a phobia in a five-year-old boy *S.E.* 10.

——— (1912). Recommendations to physicians practicing psychoanalysis *S.E.* 12.

——— (1913a). On beginning the treatment *S.E.* 12.

——— (1913b). Two lies told by children *S.E.* 12.

——— (1915a). Thoughts for the times on war and death *S.E.* 14.

——— (1915b). Observations on transference-love *S.E.* 12.

——— (1917a). Mourning and melancholia *S.E.* 4.

——— (1917b). Introductory lectures on psychoanalysis *S.E.* 16.

——— (1923). Remarks on the theory and practice of dream-interpretation *S.E.* 19.

——— (1926). The question of lay analysis *S.E.* 20.

——— (1937). Constructions analysis *S.E.* 23.

——— (1940). Splitting of the ego in the process of defence *S.E.* 23.

Furman, E. (1974). *A Child's Parent Dies*. New Haven: Yale Univ. Press.

Hartmann, H. (1958) Comments on the scientific aspects of psychoanalysis *Psychoanal. Study Child* 13:127–146.

Kanzer, M. (1953). Writers and the early loss of parents *J. Hillside Hosp.* 2148–151.

——— (1981). Freud's "analytic pact": the standard therapeutic alliance *J. Am. Psychoanal. Assoc.* 29:69–188.

Kernberg, O. 1965 Notes on countertransference *J. Am. Psychoanal. Assoc.* 13:38–56.

Kestenberg, J. (1980). Psychoanalyses of children of survivors from the holocaust *J. Am. Psychoanal. Assoc.* 28:775–804.

Kris, E. (1947). The nature of psychoanalytic propositions and their validation In *Freedom and Experienceed*. Eds. S. Hook. M. Konvitz, eds. New York: Cornell Univ. Press.

——— (1956). The recovery of childhood memories in psychoanalysis *Psychoanal. Study Child.* 11:54–88.

Mahler, M. 1966 Notes on the development of basic moods: the depressive affect In The Selected Papers of Margaret S. Mahler Vol. II New York: Jason Aronson, 1979 pp. 59–75

Mahler, M. (1975). On the current status of the infantile neurosis *J. Am. Psychoanal. Assoc.* 23:327–333.

Pollock, G. 1961). Mourning and adaptation *Int. J. Psychoanal.* 42:341–361.

Rangell, L. (1968). The psychoanalytic process *Int. J. Psychoanal.*49:19–26.

——— (1979). Contemporary issues in the theory of therapy *J. Am. Psychoanal. Assoc.* 27 (Suppl):81–112.

Rosen, V. (1955). The reconstruction of a traumatic childhood event in a case of derealization *J. Am. Psychoanal. Assoc.* 3:211–221.

Sandler, J., Dare, C. Holder, A. (1973). *The Patient and the Analyst* London: George Allen Unwin.

Sterba, R. 1934 The fate of the ego in analytic therapy *Int. J. Psychoanal.*15:117–126.

Stone, L. (1981). Notes on the noninterpretive elements in the psychoanalytic situation and process *J. Am. Psychoanal. Assoc.* 29:89–118.

Waelder, R. (1962). Psychoanalysis, scientific method, and philosophy *J. Am. Psychoanal. Assoc.* 10:617–637.

Wallerstein, R. (1967). Reconstruction and mastery in the transference psychosis *J. Am. Psychoanal. Assoc.* 15:551–583.

Warren, M. (1966). Psychological effects of parental suicide in surviving children *Excerpta Medica Series* 117433.

Weinshel, E. (1979). Some observations on not telling the truth *J. Am. Psychoanal. Assoc.* 27:503–531.

Winnicott, D. (1965). *The Maturational Processes and the Facilitating Environment.* New York: Int. Univ. Press.

CHAPTER 9

Maternal Psychopathology and Nocturnal Enuresis

(1970). *Psychoanal. Q.*, 39:609–619.

Psychoanalytic contributions to the understanding of nocturnal enuresis have been repeatedly challenged; and organic factors such as allergies, urinary tract disorder, and central nervous system disturbance have been invoked to explain this perplexing problem. While I do not contest the fact of organic causes in some cases (5) and possible organic predisposition in many, I regard the child's inner emotional disturbance as fundamental in most cases. Anny Katan (2) and Melitta Sperling (7), summarizing many of the unconscious conflicts found in enuretic children, discussed the importance of developmental conflict in relation to trauma (e.g., physical illness, surgical operations, the birth of a sibling) and to passivity and passive expression of aggression. They also noted the relationship of enuresis to bisexuality and masturbatory conflict. The enuresis expressed both the state of castration and the bisexual wetting and being wet simultaneously. Katan mentioned one family in which seven out of eight children suffered from enuresis. The parents found it comparatively easy to accept the situation since they themselves had suffered from the same symptom. This emphasizes merely the acceptance, not the parental instigation of the enuresis.

The focus in this paper will be on the unconscious maternal conflict and its role in stimulating enuresis in the child.[1] Such maternal influences may be neither necessary nor sufficient for all cases of enuresis, but I believe that

---

1 In this paper enuresis primarily refers to its classical form of enuresis nocturna or bed-wetting.

they are sometimes of vast importance. The paper is based on data derived from the psychoanalysis of the mother of three enuretic children. The data, derived from associations, memories, dreams, transference, and the mother's direct observations, have an inner consistency and represent a confluence of what would otherwise seem to be diverging streams of unrelated facts and experiences. I shall show how the mother fostered, directed, and re-enforced the enuresis of her three daughters.

My patient's children were thirteen, ten, and four years old at the time she started analysis. The oldest was enuretic until she "outgrew" her symptom in prepuberty; the middle daughter was dry only during her third year of life; and the youngest achieved bladder control at seven during the third year of the mother's analysis. The conscious reasons for the mother's entering analysis were marital conflict, indecision about divorce, and depression attributed to her husband's withdrawal. She had no awareness of any relationship between her own problems and her children's enuresis. In fact the first mention of her children's enuresis emerged in association to repetitive water dreams. When the analyst confronted her with the recurrent images of dams bursting, rivers overflowing, falling into pools and puddles, rocking and floating in boats, among other fluid associations, the patient casually mentioned her house being inundated with her children's urine. She was initially resistant to seeing herself in these dreams, rationalizing that there was a constant urinary stimulus living in her home. She felt that the children stimulated her dreams. As the analysis progressed, however, the patient's fluid currents of thought and feeling made her aware of her own primary urinary preoccupations and her role as organizer of the enuretic household. The spontaneous emergence and convergence of the fantasies and memories wove a detailed picture of childish urinary preoccupation and its later influence on her own children.

The patient, thirty years old, was an attractive, well-groomed, intelligent, and highly verbal housewife. She rapidly developed an erotized transference. She announced that she had completely fallen in love with her analyst, that she was ready to leave her husband and drown her children if only the analyst would marry her and eliminate his family. This patient was not psychotic. Despite severe regressive tendencies she was gradually able to acquire insight into the nature of her transference and her life situation. She sustained a therapeutic alliance, and developed ambitions and idealistic analytic goals.

When she was a child her parents worked. She actually had two sets of parents since she was cared for by her grandparents at home. There was a particularly close and affectionate relationship with her grandfather who fed, cuddled, and adored this favorite granddaughter. Her grandfather accompanied her to the toilet as a little girl and took her to the public men's room when he had to urinate. This behavior was also fostered by the father, permitting the partial acting out of incestuous fantasies with excretion in both the grandfather's and the father's presence. When she became a parent, she tended to repeat with her own children derivatives of her earlier urinary overstimulation. This "benevolent intimacy" was never questioned until analysis. The mutual seduction of the generations led to an erotized transference and difficulty in distinguishing transference and real adult love. Fantasies had been verified by reality and the patient expected the same behavior from the analyst.

Other historical facts were of great importance: the patient was considered "the golden girl" who never caused difficulty and placated the parents during periods of family irritation. However, her sister, two years older, was enuretic and had a ferocious temper. An unmarried maternal aunt had a urinary tract disorder with chronic cystitis and urinary frequency, which often required catheterization of the bladder. So "sister," both to the patient and to her mother was associated with urinary incontinence.

The mother had early informed her that she was the survivor of an attempted abortion from which foetal tissue had been obtained. A boy twin had died. She had a central masturbation fantasy of being surrounded by admirers, standing on a table holding a torch, and then having simultaneous rectal-vaginal intercourse with two men. Doubly impregnated by father and grandfather, vaginally and rectally, she was in guilty search of her ambivalently loved twin. She considered herself a living abortion. She needed and expected special love as both unwanted and chosen. The parents had made no attempt to abort the older sister whom the patient unconsciously regarded as more loved by the mother. Her loving and appeasing attitudes covered her terror of abandonment and destruction at the mother's hands. The mother re-enforced the twin theme by describing how a male baby had been brought to her to nurse by mistake after the patient was born; and when both girls reached puberty, nearly simultaneously, the mother had them dress in twin clothes. She and her sister were treated by the mother as symbiotic complementary parts of the same individual. She was left-handed, the sister right-handed; she played, sister sang; she was beautiful, sister intellectual; she good-natured, sister ill tempered; she dry, the sister wet.

Water imagery embellished the mother's language. She was fond of talking in terms of "not having a pot to piss in" to describe the family's borderline indigence. The attempted abortion of the patient was related to the lack of money and the patient was to be "slopped into a bucket"; death itself was "going up the river" and economic security meant "the ship would come in". Her mother was always "up to her ears between the dishes and the douches". A huge borscht bowl was proof that they would always have a "pot to piss in". Later, as a mother, my patient spoke a water language to her own children and told them watery stories.

In one hour of the analysis she spoke in gushing imagery of a long line of dreams. In the last dream the content centered around a line of people waiting to use a telephone booth. The location, shape, and events surrounding the booth reminded her of a bathroom stall; and she associated the memory of wetting her underwear while waiting in line to use a ladies' room. On several occasions during childhood and adolescence the impulse to wet broke through during the day but never at night. On one of her earliest dates, too embarrassed to ask or look for a bathroom, she quietly urinated in a subway while standing next to her boy friend.

I have already alluded to the important masturbation fantasy of her standing on a table, holding a torch. This proved to be an identification with her sister, idealized as the beautiful Helen of Troy who had launched a thousand ships. The beautiful lady on the table was also the Statute of Liberty on a pedestal; and my patient urinated through her underpants at the top of the Statue of Liberty when she was six years old. This dramatized her identification with her enuretic sister. She had begun analysis nearly ready to drown herself in depression. Soon she was saying that she was ready to drown her daughters and, like Helen, run away with her lover (the analyst). She recalled that with the birth of each child she had frequent daydreams which were repeated in disguised variants in the transference. In these daydreams children were drowning and only the youngest was saved. During her fifth year her sister had nearly drowned in a pool and had been narrowly rescued, requiring artificial respiration. The patient had an intense ambivalence for her sister who also stood for her loved and hated dead twin. In identification with her mother this patient had several abortions during her marriage. Thus she attempted to master the trauma of being unwanted. The rupture of the membranes and gush of the waters at birth were the opposite of the drowning death.

She complained bitterly of her husband's continued preference for oral intercourse with ejaculation in her mouth. He was an ice-cold lover who "pissed in her face". He constantly humiliated and degraded her. A dream of bringing him a glass of water while he shaved in the bathroom led to a memory of her irritable uncle to whom, as a child, she had brought a glass of water directly from the toilet bowl. To her great delight and later shame, her uncle unknowingly drank the water. This savage revenge on a slighting uncle was associated with fantasies of talion retaliation. The dream also affirmed her fantasy of urinating not only in front of the parents but on the parent who eagerly incorporates the urine. Behind this were fantasies of the parents blissfully and angrily urinating on and into each other and of impregnation by drinking urine. She once dreamed of a physician urinating in torrents in front of the temple, inundating the community. The associations led to her pious grandfather, the patriarch of the entire family and in many respects more her father than her own father. Her urinating grandfather in her fantasies impregnated her grandmother, mother, and herself.

While the patient continued to deny her own enuretic interest, analysis of her adolescence lent further confirmation. Her menstruation was often hemorrhagic in onset. She recalled wearing a diaper to a camp masquerade in early puberty. In one of her dreams, she did not know whether to put a diaper or Modess on her daughter. Menstruation was a shameful form of enuresis, and the castrated genital was incapable of urethral control. She did not have a stopcock. At the time of menarche an important and frightening event occurred. In front of her visiting girl friends, she was so ashamed of her foreign speaking, aged, and poor grandmother that she did not permit her grandmother to cross the room to go to the bathroom. The old lady was forced to urinate into a bucket. That very night her grandmother died, and the next day the patient first menstruated. This first enuretic menstruation was "the punishment of God" for her despicable act. She felt sure that her grandmother had died of humiliation. This scene of humiliation, castration, degradation, and supreme punishment crystallized many aspects of her enuretic complex. She had made her grandmother incontinent, and this was a paradigm for her unconscious wish to make others incontinent, as she was later to do with her three daughters.

The patient was fearful of bleeding onto the couch during her period. This represented her wish to wet and soil, but also her dread of retaliation for making grandmother, sister, and children incontinent. During menstruation she dreamed of pulling away another woman's raincoat. The associations to raincoat led to tampons and condoms. She had unconsciously wished to expose both the premature ejaculation of her husband and also humiliate a girl friend who was having a menstrual period by stripping away sanitary protection and exhibiting her bleeding genital. She was fearful of uncontrolled urination, e.g., when sneezing or coughing. Early in analysis she had sought gynecological advice for possible stress incontinence. She would weep after orgasm. This she first connected only to her disappointment in marital love. Early interpretations of the equation of tears and semen with urine were met with denials: the analyst was "all wet". It was painful and guilt-provoking for her to gradually recognize that though she supported bowel-sphincter morality, she had corrupted her children's bladder control.

She dreamed of her daughter swimming and crying out that she had to urinate; the patient yelled to her daughter, "Go ahead, go ahead". In analysis she began to see that she must be sending such messages to the children. Though she instructed her children as toddlers to call her if they had to go to the bathroom at night, she would not apparently hear their call. This highly selective maternal withdrawal—she responded if the children were ill—

contradicted her verbal instruction and must have suggested condonement of the enuresis. At the same time, she unconsciously arranged for her husband to take the children to the bathroom and have them repeat her own experience as a young girl urinating in the presence of father or grandfather. Moreover, she encouraged her husband to bring the wet child into their bed. She cuddled the wet child who wet her and the parental bed. Thus, the children were rewarded for their enuresis with an undue degree of gratification and stimulation. She turned on the faucets when the children were to urinate, as if they needed extra stimulation. While she urged the children to achieve control, withheld fluids at night, and woke them up before going to sleep, she prided herself on never being rejecting and joined the children in a tolerant conspiracy of silence about their enuretic problem. Thus, she was able to foster and re-enforce enuresis in her daughters. She had the complicity of her husband who had been a childhood enuretic. His malice toward her and the children encouraged her to use the children as instruments of revenge, discharging her anger and sexual frustration. She used her children to urinate on her husband, as she felt he did on her.

Discussion

Analytic literature has been concerned with the analysis of enuretics, or individuals who were enuretic, rather than the psychoanalysis of the mother of enuretic children. My case was particularly illuminating because the mother was not an enuretic and had no awareness of her unconscious urinary fixation. Nor did she display any of the later derivatives of enuresis in the adult such as urinary tract disorder, spastic colitis, somnambulism, pyromania, frigidity, or delinquency. She was surprised during treatment to see the emergence of the urinary stream, even in the manifest content of her dreams. She was perplexed, amazed, and profoundly guilty to see the relationship between her unconscious impulses and their vicarious expression in her children's complementary enuresis (1), (3), (6). She might be described as a urethral character with a urethral identity. Her parents had contributed to this by referring to her as a "little pisher," "a long drink of water."

I have already described her close identification and rivalry with her enuretic sister who also stood for her aborted twin. She created her sister in her children, allowing them gratification of enuresis which she could vicariously enjoy. At the same time, she felt humiliation for them as she had for her sister. She identified with her mother who had an enuretic child and who used her own children for narcissistic purposes; and she identified with her mother's sister who had chronic cystitis. With her father and grandfather she participated in urinary exhibition. She had unconscious needs to create and to abort, to have her twin born and drowned, and to drown her own children. Her children filled the need of her missing penis and twin. She was disappointed in her daughters whom she regarded as castrated and defective like herself. She appeared to share both the mother's fantasies and guilt over the aborted twin. Her primal scene fantasies were elaborated in terms of urinating sadistically and being wet masochistically. The central masturbation fantasy of the Statue of Liberty revealed the phallic but enuretic woman. The enuresis represented both active and passive attitudes, male and female, phallic and castrated. But the primary emphasis was on castration, humiliation, and masochistic failure. However, while the mother's central unconscious fantasies were urethral, her influence on the children began during their bladder training and continued through their childhood.

How is it that she was able to remain free of enuresis, yet become the mother of enuretic children? A partial answer is that the tendency to act through a vicarious object or proxy (especially her sister) was established in childhood (8). She remained the "golden dry twin" while ambivalently re-creating the lost and enuretic twin. Later her unresolved urethral conflicts became the apparent focus of shared fantasies with her daughters. A vulnerable child may express for the mother what the mother does not display or dare to do, providing a complementary symptomatic action to the mother's fantasy. Mother and child then enjoy their special urogenital gratifications (6), (7) while the mother defensively disowns the forbidden evoked activity.

How did she communicate her urinary fantasies to the children? Through her urinary language, imagery, stories. Occasionally she even told her dreams to her children. Moreover, she was inconsistent in bladder training, condoned nighttime wetting, arranged for urinary exhibitionism with her husband, and had him bring the wet child to the parental bed, symbolically enacting a urinary primal scene. This mother unconsciously created a urinary climate which influenced her stimulation, discipline, and direction of the children.

The thesis of this paper does not rule out the possibility of a somatic basis for the predisposition to enuresis. Indeed, somatic compliance and psychological factors in mother and child are synergistic. In this case, the mother's use of her children to act out her unconscious enuretic fantasies seems to account for a major contribution to enuretic "psychophysiology" (4). The mother's unconscious conflicts interfered with mothering in a specific area and served to stimulate and re-enforce her children's enuresis. Her influence was far more subtle than overtly harsh, seductive, inconsistent, or apathetic bladder training.

Summary

Psychological determinants of nocturnal enuresis are many and diverse. This paper focuses on maternal influences.

Analysis of a mother of three enuretic daughters revealed unconscious conflicts over her own intense desires to wet. These conflicts were multidetermined and involved ambivalent childhood relationships with several figures, including her enuretic sister, her stillborn twin brother, and her father and grandfather. She played out her conflicts by having her daughters wet for her. Thus, she could enjoy wetting without awareness or apparent responsibility. With the help of her husband, she was able to organize a urinary household in which her daughters were stimulated and rewarded for their enuresis. The mother's fostering of her children's enuresis began during their prephallic toilet training and continued beyond the urethral phase into later childhood.

REFERENCES

Johnson, A.M. & Szurek, S.A. (1952). The Genesis of Antisocial Acting Out in Children and Adults. *Psychoanal. Q.* 21:323–343.

Katan, A. (1946). Experience with Enuretics. In: The *Psychoanal. Study Child,* Vol. 2 New York: International Universities Press.

Mahler, M.S. (1967). On Human Symbiosis and the Vicissitudes of Individuation. *J. Am. Psychoanal. Assoc.* 15:740–763.

Schur, M. (1955). Comments on the Metapsychology of Somatization. In: *The Psychoanal. Study Child,* Vol. 10 New York: International Universities Press.

Silberstein, R.M. & Blackman, S. (1965). Differential Diagnosis and Treatment of Enuresis. *Amer. J. Psychiat.*121:1204–1206.

Sperling, M. (1950). Children's Interpretation and Reaction to the Unconscious of their Mothers. *Int. J. Psychoanal.* 31:36–41.

——— (1965). Dynamic Considerations and Treatment of Enuresis, *J. Amer. Academy of Child Psychiatry* 1:19–31.

Wangh, Martin (1962). The 'Evocation of a Proxy': A Psychological Maneuver, Its Use as a Defense, Its Purposes and Genesis. In: The *Psychoanal. Study Child* Vol. 17. New York: International Universities Press.

CHAPTER 10

Clinical and Developmental Dimensions of Hate

(1997). *J. Amer. Psychoanal. Assn.*, (45):359–375.

Bridging concepts of aggression, affect, and attitude, hate emerges during the process of separation-individuation concurrent with ego development and persisting intrapsychic conflict and fantasy. Rage precedes hate developmentally, though later the two are amalgamated both developmentally and clinically. Hate is the negative pole of ambivalence and is a component of all self- and object representations and object relationships. When excessive and unmodulated, hate interferes with object relations and personality development. Paradoxically, hate may also subserve adaptation and personality organization. Transference hate is often a greater problem for the psychoanalyst or psychotherapist than is transference love. Transference hate threatens the analyst's narcissism and neutrality and tests the analyst's tolerance and patience. The patient's intense hate is often experienced as a direct assault on the analytic relationship and the analytic process.

Countertransference hate and the need to defend against it are of great clinical importance. Because it runs counter to analytic ideals and values, the analyst's hatred of the patient may be denied, minimized, rationalized, enacted, or vicariously gratified and may occasion great resistance to analytic self-scrutiny. Countertransference hate is often an unrecognized determinant in cases of analytic and therapeutic impasse. A classic contribution by D.W. Winnicott to the recognition and elucidation of countertransference hate is reevaluated.

Hate is an exceedingly important phenomenon, but it has not received the attention it deserves. There is a relative paucity of papers on the subject, especially compared to the extensive literature on love. Not addressed in the *Psychoanalytic Glossary* (Moore and Fine 1968) or *The Language of Psychoanalysis* (Laplanche and Pontalis 1967), the concept of hate has only recently been the subject of intense psychoanalytic investigation. The existence of hate between lovers, as well as between parent and child, tends to be denied. Hate is banished in the idealization of love or dissociated from the beloved and in a process of polarization attributed to the bad object (Akhtar, Kramer, and Parens 1995). Analysts, too, seem to have more difficulty confronting and conceptualizing hate than they do love, both inside and outside the psychoanalytic process. While "love makes the world go 'round," it is hate that might bring it to an end. Historically, aggression and hate were first subsumed under sexuality in the form of sadomasochism. Introduced as an independent drive only after World War I, aggression then was placed on an equal footing with the sexual drive, and hate was commonly encompassed within the former. The pioneer analysts had little to say about hate compared to the newly discovered importance of psychosexual development. Current interest in violence, child abuse, ethnic, religious and racial bigotry, and the Holocaust have stimulated analytic studies of hate.

Freud did not initially regard hate simply as an expression of aggression or as the reverse of love. Hate was originally considered neither a derivative of love nor its opposite, but was regarded as a different ego attitude. After describing the concept of a purified pleasure ego, Freud (1915) stated, "At the very beginning, it seems, the external world, objects, and what is hated are identical. If later on an object turns out to be a source of pleasure, it is loved but it is also incorporated into the ego; so that for the purified pleasure ego once again objects coincide with what is extraneous and hated" (p. 136). He added, "Thus, we become aware that the attitudes of love and hate cannot be made use of for the relations of the instincts to their objects, but are reserved for the relations of the total ego to objects" (p. 137). The preliminary stages of love were hardly to be distinguished from hate in the attitude of the ego toward the object. As Freud also observed, "The ego hates, abhors and pursues with intent to destroy all objects which are a source of unpleasurable feeling for it. Not until the genital organization is established does love become the opposite of hate.... The origins and relations of love make us understand how it is that love so frequently manifests itself as ambivalent—i.e., as accompanied by impulses of hate against the same object. The hate which is admixed with the love is in part derived from the preliminary stages of loving which have not been wholly surmounted; it is also in part based on reactions of repudiation by the ego instincts, which, in view of the frequent conflicts between the interests of the ego and those of love, can find grounds in real and contemporary motives" (pp. 138–139). After the introduction of structural theory, Freud associated hate with the death instinct, leaving the relationship between hate and aggression to be further clarified.

Subsequent to Freud, several concepts of hate emerged. Aggression aiming toward the injury or destruction of objects was considered a clinical manifestation of the death instinct. Aggression also began to be viewed as having both nondestructive aims, such as assertion, and hostile, destructive aims elicited by frustration as well as unpleasurable affects (Parens 1991). Hate was regarded as evolving from excessive aggression, with rage fostered by excessive unpleasure. Hate has also been regarded as a core affect "which contributes to the formation and organization of the aggressive drive" (Kernberg 1993). Here the affective dimension of hate is superordinate and emphasized.

It is clear that hate is known, felt, and experienced by every child and adult, but it is nonetheless a concept that is not easy to define. Hate has been conceptualized as an aggressive drive derivative, an affect, and an ego attitude. In my own formulation hate is linked to aggression and encompasses affect and attitude in an ego synthesis both comparable and antithetical to love. A person may be especially loving or hateful, affectionate or hostile, with hostility defined here as a mild form of hate.

Hate requires sufficient ego development for persistent affective states associated with differentiation of self- and object representations. Hate is the negative pole of ambivalence, and while in some individuals it predominates, it is internalized and colors self- and object representations in all. Hate may be overt or covert, object- or self-directed, or both self- and object-directed. The form of hatred described by Freud was extreme, and included an intent to destroy the object; it does not encompass a full spectrum of hate that would permit the consideration of less destructive aims. Lesser degrees of hate may not demand destruction of the object but may permit its preservation while making it suffer; this may range from massive humiliation to mild subjugation (Kernberg 1995).

The turning of hate away from completely destructive aims depends not only on the neutralization of aggression, but on a capacity for self- and object love. Aggression could be tamed and neutralized, and this would be much less likely to result in severe and persistent hate (Hartmann, Kris, and Loewenstein 1949; A. Freud 1972). A preponderance of object love over hate is necessary for the attenuation of ambivalence and the development of object constancy. Hate may be intensified through identification with hated or hating objects. Hate is readily elicited by narcissistic injury, frustration, powerlessness, and threats or injuries to one's self or one's love objects. Hate has also been proposed as arising from a sequence involving the frustration of infantile object love, hating the unloving object, and defending against the need for object love through hate (Balint 1952).

The word *hate* used to express intense dislike or aversion (e.g., hate of cold or of insects), may not have the identical meaning in different contexts. Also, hatred expressed toward nonhuman entities may have been displaced from self- and object representations.

The Development of Hate

Hate is developmentally inevitable; it is not pathological in its mild, more modulated forms. In fact, hate is to some degree normal and necessary, developing from responses to noxious stimuli and unpleasure and later functioning as a motivating force. Freud noted that it is important to be able to hate, and that one should have many hates rather than a single object of hatred. At one time he wrote that he was keeping a hate-list (letter to Max Eitingon, July 13, 1931). He early observed (Freud 1900) that he always had a need, not only for a close friend but for a hated enemy (p. 483). In the "non vixit" dream Freud, associating to unconscious ambivalence, remarked that "people of that kind only existed as long as one liked and could be got rid of ..." (p. 421); he added, "it has not infrequently happened that the ideal situation of childhood has been so completely reproduced that friend and enemy have come together in a single individual ... (p. 483). Freud's inferences are consistent with the notion that hate emerges during preoedipal development and the process of separation-individuation. The awareness of separateness and the loss of omnipotent control of the separate object, the awareness of relative helplessness, generate persistent hate (Mahler, Pine, and Bergmann 1975; Blum 1981).

The dangers of loss of the object, loss of the object's love, loss of self and identity, anal and phallic aggression, oedipal rivalry, and castration anxiety all contribute to infantile ambivalence. Hate and vengeful fantasies may coalesce in oedipal trauma, e.g., as a reaction to surgery or primal scene exposure (Arlow 1980). Once hate evolves, it participates in and influences all subsequent development and in turn is subject to further developmental influence. The neutralization and sublimation of hate would also be associated with the taming and control of rage. Hatred tends to elicit counterreactions and reciprocal hate. Because of its inciting qualities, intense hate may be contagious, qualities exploited by demagogues. Since all object love is ambivalent, hate is found in all relationships, as well as between generations, sexes, groups, etc.

Parent/Child Hate

Child/parent hate and aggression are normal experiences. The child's demands clash with those of the parents; the child inevitably encounters frustration, opposition, discipline, and the setting of limits at the hands of the parents. There is a developmental inevitability for children and parents to hate each other.

Children have not only patricidal wishes, so emphasized in discussions of the male oedipus complex, but also death wishes toward mothers and the siblings who share parental nurturance and protection. Oedipal and sibling rivalry stir hate as well as jealousy and envy. Mothers tend to be culturally and developmentally idealized, with hostility displaced onto other love objects or the self. Children are also objects and targets of their parents' hate, and such relationships may be suffused with hate and defenses against recognition and murderous expression of hate (Kramer 1995; Pine 1995). Historically, oedipal fathers have repeatedly sacrificed their sons in war. The hated child identifies with the hateful parent, yet another variation of "identification with the aggressor." Children also identify with parents who hate each other, as occurs in marital and divorce wars. Models of hateful authorities help explain how hate may become ego-syntonic and self-righteous. Intrafamilial death wishes may be acted out, and the most frequent objects of murder are family members. The first murder in the Bible is the fratricide of Abel by Cain.

Children's hatred toward the real or projected source of their unpleasure is often rather transparent. Infants with temperamental irritability and low frustration tolerance are often quite prone to temper tantrums. The infant or small child may lash out, hitting and kicking the parent or caregiving object. When crying or screaming or "choking with rage" does not suppress a child's verbalization, direct verbal expressions of hate are common. The child's capacity to modulate hate and rage is dependent on reciprocal love and identification with the caregiver's healthy parental functions. Violence has to be avoided and aggressive action contained. Older children need to learn limits to verbal expressions of hate; shouting, cursing, and hurling verbal insults and threats are immature and inappropriate. Primitive verbalization may be a prelude to, rather than a substitute for, uncontrolled action. Freud's famous dictum that the person who first hurled a word of abuse instead of flinging a spear was the founder of civilization is best understood in a developmental context.

Just as untamed hate is pathological, so is the inability to consciously hate or to relinquish hate. When hate cannot be appropriately expressed, it tends to go underground, often leading to somatization and self-hatred. Children who are thwarted by their caregivers and denied the expression of hate may turn hate and aggression back on themselves. This is readily seen when a child, reprimanded by a parent for expressing hate and aggression, engages in self scratching and -biting, verbal self-blame and self-denigration, etc.

The hateful child has often experienced excessive unpleasure, small comfort, little love, or excessive hate. The child may be helped to clarify and verbalize feelings that might otherwise be regarded as dangerous and relatively unspeakable. A child may hate to get up in the morning and hate going to sleep alone at night, hating the parental controls these demands represent. Distant or overprotective parents may defend against the unconscious hate they indirectly convey to their child. When hate is projected, either child or parent may misperceive the other as hateful. Children's experience of parents' hate should not, however, be considered merely a projection of the child's hate onto the parent. Parenting requires of parents the capacity to tolerate the child's aggression in the service of development and to maintain stability and regulation when confronting either their child's hate or their own.

Defensive and Adaptive Aspects

The capacity to hate may facilitate individuation, self-assertion, and mastery. When not excessive and when the caregiver is not depleted of love or provoked to counterhate, hate and aggression subserve the developmental process. To enhance individuation and object relations, the child needs the experience of safely hating the caregiver (Winnicott 1949; Bollas 1985). Hate may be an agent in the stabilization of individual identity, social adaptation, and anomalous forms of object relations (Pao 1965). Hate may facilitate ego organization and ward off disorganization (Gabbard 1993; Winer 1994). Paradoxically, excessive hate is a threat to preservation of the self or object, as well as to ego organization.

"A healthy hatred" could be consonant with the understanding that it is normal to hate one's enemies and tormentors or to hate those who tyrannize and torment others. Aristotle long ago asserted that "to enjoy the things we ought and to hate the things we ought has the greatest bearing on excellent character" (Bartlett 1982, p. 98). Hate may be mobilized in the service of higher ideals and values, as in the hatred of tyranny, poverty, brutality, and in self-defense and defense of family. "The Lord loves those who hate evil" (Psalm 97), and such hate wins love. People may hate offensive attitudes and actions, either their own or others'. As a response to danger situations, hate may be mobilized for purposes of defense. Hate may defend against forbidden love and dependency on the loved one. Conversely, reactive love may defend against the awareness and expression of hate. Adolescent mood swings, for example, are often both defenses against revived oedipal love-hate and a disguised expression of it. Love is ambivalent, as previously noted, but the intensity of hate and the love-hate balance are highly variable. People may hate their own negative affects, and hate may defend against such affects as anxiety, grief, guilt, and sadness. Hate and anxiety may feed on each other, as in fear of expressing hate and fear of retaliation. From the perspective of adaptation, hate may be preferable to panic, which threatens helplessness. Hate may help a person bear the unbearable, perhaps in association with efforts at mastery, hopes for escape, or plans for revenge.

Hate and Rage

There is no simple relationship between hate and rage, though the more intense form of hate is usually associated with rage. Advances in the neurosciences promise further delineation of an innate predisposition for rage reactions. Some children may be more innately disposed toward aggressive behavior, temper tantrums, and rage reactions. Male mammals appear more endowed with aggression than are females, at least in its externalized forms. A rage center is found in the human brain near the hypothalamic locus for sexual excitement. No such locus is known for the affect and attitude of hate. Rage may be regarded as a genetically "prewired," basic affect that precedes self object differentiation.

Primitive rage tends to be somatized and bodily centered. The kicking and screaming infant may be described as expressing rage before such an infant could be regarded as experiencing hate. Rage, thus, has a more direct neurophysiological foundation, in contrast to the more psychological basis of hate. Although subject to biological influence, hate appears to be a psychological response that emerges during the later preoedipal phases, with greater consolidation during oedipal development (McDevitt 1975).

As a motivational force, hate does not necessarily impel one toward immediate action or affectomotor discharge; these are more characteristic of rage. Hate does not necessarily or immediately incite rage and, unlike the latter, seems to require an object. Both may be either acute or chronic, but hate tends to be more persistent and less episodic. It may be inferred from these considerations that in the adult it would be possible to have hate without overt rage and vice versa. The activation of hate, however, is usually amalgamated with rage. These interrelationships have been depicted by writers and poets, as in William Congreve's *The Mourning Bride:* "Heaven has no rage like love to hatred turned ..." (act 3, scene 8). Disappointed or rejected love easily turns to hate, but turning hate back into love is far more complicated and difficult.

Superego Issues

Guilt and the pangs of conscience contribute to self-hate as well as to selfblame. Children may express self-hate for being "bad," and severe self-hate is often associated with depression and/or self-destructive behavior. In some individuals and groups, there is a delicate balance between the intensity of hate and capacities for defense, control, and regulation. In grave danger or sheer struggle for survival, object love and superego restraints may be regressively overwhelmed and overthrown, leading to the dominance of hate and expressions of rage. Hate may be morally condoned in righteous or self-righteous hatred. Hate can be taught, mobilized, directed, restrained, or released in group, social, and educational processes. It can be justified and fortified by indoctrination and identification, as in mobs and in the military. The military superego, the social sanction of war, may permit the unbridled expression of hate and rage, as well as sadistic pleasure in hateful destruction (Blum 1995; Pine 1995). Empathy with the enemy is suspended or severed. Hate projected onto others and displaced outside one's family or group fuels the search for scapegoats and enemies. This is reminiscent of children's games and their need for enemies and "bad guys" to be vanquished. Protection of self and love objects, familial group cohesion, and narcissistic aggrandizement have all too often utilized social stereotypes to externalize hate and denigration. A cause and consequence of violence, the social sanction and indoctrination of hate probably reached its malignant acme in the Holocaust. Hate became a way of life and a path to death. In the transformation of ideals and values, hate directed toward specific people or groups was not only justified but made expectable, respectable, and rewarded. This process is also depicted in the hate sessions and lessons of Orwell's *1984* and in the Rodgers and Hammerstein lyric "You've got to be taught to hate and fear, ...It's got to be drummed in your dear little ear...."

Clinical Issues

Many individuals are unaware of the intensity of their ambivalence and cannot admit their hatred. Hate may become manifestly or latently erotized, a development of special significance. Enduring hate may be experienced as pleasurable, and grudges may be nursed and vindictively gratified (Galdston 1987). In pedophilia, for example, although the term emphasizes the infantile love, the infantile hate in the sexual abuse of children is all too evident. Hate and destructive tendencies coalesce also within sadomasochistic relationships. Dehumanization and demonization appear to be a syndrome that permits the expression of hate and defends against experiencing guilt. The targeted person or group may be reduced to an object, a thing. In some perversions the attempted undoing of previous humiliation and hate is associated with reassuring sexual excitement and compensatory orgastic triumph over trauma (Stoller 1979).

Under certain circumstances, hate may become part of a stable tie to an inconstant object, replacing libidinal object constancy (Blum 1981). This is a pattern found in paranoid personalities, psychopaths, severe addictions, and related syndromes of malignant narcissism. As the object of hate in such cases is inherently a narcissistic object, it may be seen that self-hate, lack of self-esteem, and hatred of the narcissistic object are intertwined. Certain forms of love addictions and erotomanias defend against underlying paranoia, hateful self-defeat, and murderous impulses. The hidden hate in drug addiction and substance abuse is directed toward the self and the disappointing narcissistic object (Blum 1994). The drug may represent the ambivalently hated object on whom the addict depends.

The pioneering analytic formulation of paranoia—that conscious hate defends against repressed homosexual love—was promulgated in the Schreber case (Freud 1911). This formulation has limited validity, however, and circumvents the primary significance of pernicious paranoid hate. In paranoia, narcissistic rage and hate and omnipotent aggression are core issues (Blum 1994). Hate and rage may be projected, often with fear of retaliation and hypersensitivity to any hostile opposition. The paranoid dictator's fear of persecution is based on the projection of murderous persecutory wishes and fears of punishment and retaliation. The enemy, split off from any residual love object, becomes the bad object endowed with implacable malevolence (Klein 1946). In the presence of intense latent hate, any friend may become an enemy. The slightest insult or injury becomes all the more threatening because of the torrent of hate it may unleash. The need to undo, erase, reverse, or avenge an injury restores and expresses narcissistic grandeur and defends against overwhelming hate and uncontrolled narcissistic rage (Kohut 1972).

In contrast to the Schreber case, where hate was regarded as defending against love, love defending against hate was the formulation that Freud (1909) used in the case of the Rat Man. Undisguised in the extremes of homicidal and suicidal behaviors, persistent hatred may be found in all forms of severe personality disturbance and in various types of acting out, inhibition, and somatization. Hate is a determinant of human brutality, whether crude or refined, and of callous indifference to the needs and hurts of others.

There is often a close interrelationship between intense hate, ego dysfunction, and superego regression and dyscontrol. Blind rage and extreme hate may extinguish the rational ego. Pathological affective, cognitive, and control structures associated with intense hatred are commonly found in severely disturbed borderline and psychotic personalities. Such individuals are prone to self-hate and externalized hate, temper outbursts, rages, and violence. They may be consumed by their endless hate, indeed forming identities defined by that affect. Extreme hatred may have interfered with the development of psychic structure, or the failure of internalization and self-regulation has led to untamed hate and rage.

When hate is erotized or condensed with love, it is usually expressed in less extreme forms. Loving forms of hate may represent attempts to preserve object relations or to adapt to relationships characterized by abuse and neglect. Love-hate relationships may result in alternating attitudes or a "splitting of the relationship." Certain forms of seduction may be viewed as pseudo-loving forms of hate and abuse, often repeating childhood abuse. It is especially important to assess the risk of uncontrolled hate and rage in the analytic or therapeutic situation. The patient should become aware of his or her hate and the defenses arrayed against it. The patient may wallow in self-hate and may derive pleasure and other hidden satisfactions in hating and being hated (Bollas 1985; Kernberg 1995).

Transference and Countertransference

Transference hate, which is subject to change during different analytic phases, may be warded off or conscious, benign or malignant. Regressed patients whose transferences are dominated by hatred require a flexible yet consistent framework. Analytic tolerance, tact, and patience may be needed for the verbal expression of hate in the transference, which will then be subject to analytic clarification and interpretation. Exploring the reasons for a patient's resistance to such expression is generally a more productive first step than is its explicit encouragement. Understanding tends to defuse escalating hate and to restore reflection and reason. Clarification of paranoid transference, including fears of analytic retaliation, and the demonstration to the patient of repetitive patterns of hating, both within and without the analytic or therapeutic situation, help to forestall aggressive acting in or out. Clarification and appreciation of transference-countertransference hate may preempt stalemate or premature termination and deepens the analytic work. Hate may be both contagious and reciprocal in the analytic situation.

Raw hate is more likely to be disruptive than are expressions of infantile love. It is often much easier to tolerate a patient's demands for love and sexual gratification than to deal with a patient's implacable hatred and withering contempt. It is well known that idealization of the analyst may in fact mask hate and aggressive devaluation. When Freud developed cancer, the Wolf Man felt abandoned in retaliation for harboring death wishes against him. He regressed into a paranoid state and in hate and rage threatened to kill both Freud and Mack Brunswick.

Clinically, either the negative or the positive transference may defend against its opposite, but love is easier to tolerate in analysis as in life (Blum 1974, 1994; Kernberg 1995). After all, love is associated with caring and hate with destruction. Persistent transference and countertransference hate, inevitably registered and experienced by the patient, is a significant factor in analytic stalemates and failures. When the analyst's hate has been enacted, analytic integrity and the analytic process require candid clarification (Rangell 1984). Leaving a hateful transference-countertransference bind may be compared to leaving a marriage characterized by chronic hatred and smoldering rage. Such a marriage does not necessarily drown in a "sea of hatred" but can endure in highly ambivalent sadomasochistic bondage.

Until the post-World War II period there had been a dearth of attention to the ubiquity of the countertransference and its potential value, when analyzed, in furthering the analytic process. Similarly, scant attention was paid in the early literature to the analyst's hostility to the patient, though it was always understood that a treatment might founder if the analyst or therapist did not like the patient. Countertransference hostility is potentially significant in all analyses, though it more often becomes a crucial issue in cases in which hate predominates in the transference and/or in the extra analytic life of the patient. The intense acting out of hate (e.g., in child abuse or substance abuse) may diminish its appearance in the transference; when transference hate is initially expressed directly in the analytic situation, it signifies potential clinical progress.

Because the analytic relationship is so important in dealing with hateful patients, I shall comment on the "I hate you, you hate me" transference countertransference field. In a classic paper on countertransference hate, Winnicott (1949) courageously confronted and illuminated some of the relevant analytic issues. He attempted to distinguish between the analyst's typical countertransference reactions, based on unresolved neurotic conflicts and character disturbance, from what he called "objective countertransference reactions." He considered the latter to be not so much responses to the patient's transference as to the patient's actual personality and behavior. Winnicott shifted scrutiny of the countertransference from considerations of love to feelings of hate and from transference to reality. He believed there was objective foundation for the analyst's hatred of the patient, and that the patient's evocation of such hate could serve the analytic process.

Countertransference hate could be expected, recognized, and used to benefit both patient and analyst.

Winnicott was one of the pioneers of countertransference awareness, sensitivity, and honesty. Struggling with issues of enactment, he advocated that patients be informed about their analyst's particular countertransference. The analysis of some patients would be facilitated, he believed, by their knowing about the analyst's "objective hatred" and becoming aware of how and why they provoke countertransference hate. While many analysts would agree that analytic lapses and enactments should be candidly acknowledged, this openness should not extend to revelations of the analyst's fantasies about the patient (Greenson 1974). To this day, indications for countertransference disclosure remain ambiguous and controversial.

Winnicott appeared unaware that his thesis was problematic and his principal example even more questionable. Paradoxically, Winnicott, himself so fond of paradoxes, departed from his usually sensitive exposition of countertransference hate to depict it in this instance with little recognition of the implications and consequences of his own countertransference responses and behavior. He did not consider the analyst's countertransference as an acting out in collusion and identification with the hateful patient. Winnicott's extraordinary assertion that the analyst's hatred of certain patients is not only inevitable but desirable, and his radical proposition that the analyst's hate should be conveyed to the patient for the good of the analyst as well as the patient, were not further explored or questioned in his paper. Although Winnicott never again referred to his paradoxical notion of "objective countertransference," the paper has been repeatedly cited but rarely challenged. Justifying the analyst's hate, he clinically illustrated his thesis that in certain stages of certain analyses "the analyst's hate is actually sought by the patient, and what is then needed is hate that is objective" (p. 70). Countertransference, which is inherently subjective, is thus considered "objective" here, a rationalization, through reversal, of Winnicott's own loss of objectivity.

The vignette he offered is from his treatment of a nine-year-old boy evacuated from his own home during the war and taken into Winnicott's for three months. "The evolution of the boy's personality," Winnicott wrote, "engendered hate in me…. Did I hit him? The answer is 'No, I never hit.' But I should have had to have done so if I had not known all about my hate…. At crises, I would take him by bodily strength, without anger or blame, and put him outside the front door, whatever the weather or the time of day or night. There was a special bell he could ring, and he knew that if he rang it, he would be readmitted and no word said about the past…. The important thing is that each time, just as I put him outside the door, … I said that what had happened had made me hate him…. I think these words were important from the point of view of his progress, but they were mainly important in enabling me to tolerate the situation … without losing my temper and without every now and again murdering him" (p. 73).

Winnicott's case illustration includes denial of rage, a pact of silence, and acting out by the analyst. His incomplete exposition suggests collusive, abusive acting out. Winnicott was not only the therapist, but "in loco parentis" to this child. What were Winnicott's unconscious motives for home care and home treatment? Why did he take the child into his home? What were the reactions of Winnicott's wife to her husband's treatment plans, and to the child? Did the child evoke this response in Winnicott through "projective identification," or did Winnicott's rejecting, hostile countertransference attitude and behavior provoke the child's hate? Hate may be "justified," but not the analyst's acting out of countertransference hate. It is impossible to imagine that this child did not react to Winnicott's hate and rejection, cocreating a vicious cycle of reciprocal provocation and hate. Did he make brilliant inferences from the improvised treatment of a borderline child?

I was reminded of a patient who replaced physical beating of his child by leaving the child out in the freezing cold without a jacket. His child's chill and shivering were not acknowledged as satisfying the father's sadism and hate. After all, he hadn't hit the child, and there were no signs of physical abuse. Further, the child could apologize to his father and gain readmission to the house. Allowing the child back in was an act of paternal "kindness" that reactively disguised his continued abusive behavior. This patient, who was kind to one person and ruthlessly cold and cruel to another, had an overriding need to divide the world into allies and enemies. The patient aroused in me countertransference fantasies of hateful vengeance and child rescue, reactions that eventually contributed to further elucidation of the transference countertransference constellation, in which hate was prominent. The relationship was clarified in the analysis of hateful fantasies, but without discussing the countertransference with the patient.

Although Winnicott's paper catalyzed and greatly contributed to the hitherto rather forbidden exploration of countertransference hate, it also demonstrates the problem of countertransference and self-analysis. Hate mobilizes both reactive hate and reactive love, as well as potent defenses against their full recognition and impact. Etchegoyen (1991) critically inferred Winnicott's own countertransference, further noting that feeling hatred for a patient is human and understandable, but is a suspension of objectivity. Hate is especially likely to evoke and intensify intrapsychic and interpersonal conflict.

The analyst should be sensitive to the nuances of repressed and expressed hate and be aware of the reverberations of hate in the transference-countertransference field. The subtleties of hate may be particularly obscured in training analysis. Analysts should also be alert to their own vulnerability to be hated and to hate. Both analyst and patient may find hidden gratification through vicarious hate, while disavowing provocation. Defenses against recognition of hate in the countertransference may be particularly powerful, since hate runs counter to analytic ideals and values. Not only is it inappropriate to hate your patient; it is also neither rational nor right. The analyst's hate may subvert the goals of analysis and inflict hurt. The patient may defend against awareness of the analyst's hate, but at times not before first identifying it. Better to oversleep, to start late, and to dismiss the patient early than to confront the reciprocal hate in the analytic situation. On the other hand, the analyst may overcompensate, extending the session, reminiscent of the song "I hate to see you go,... I hope to hell you never come back...."

To deal with hate and the rage that often accompanies it, a setting of safety is necessary for both analysand and analyst. The analyst must be able to face both the patient's hate and his or her own without being defensive. The mere eschewal of retaliation or of abandoning the treatment, though necessary, is not equivalent to being able to empathize and "resonate" with the patient's hate. The calm, stable analyst retains or regains relative analytic objectivity. In the treatment of patients dominated by hate, it is necessary to maintain or reestablish a nonjudgmental analytic attitude. The analyst can then clarify the various motives and meanings of the patient's hate. The understanding of hate will inevitably involve the accompanying disturbing affects—anxiety, shame, guilt, etc. It should be noted that pervasive and malignant hate may not be analyzable. Here other forms of treatment should be considered, as well as whether certain patients, sociopaths for instance, are untreatable.

Lurking latent hate resurfaces at termination. One is reminded of the grateful patient who thanked the analyst profusely and then pulled out a gun to shoot him, saying, "But you know too much!" Nevertheless, the successful analysis of the conflicts in which hate is embedded will usually reveal in the patient at least a vestige of hope of loving and of being loved and valued.

REFERENCES

Akhtar, S, Kramer, S. Parens, H., eds. (1995). *The Birth of Hate*. Northvale, NJ: Aronson.

Arlow, J. (1980). The revenge motive in the primal scene. *J. Am. Psychoanal. Assoc.* 28:*519–541.*

Balint, M. (1952). On love and hate. *Int. J. Psychoanal.* 33:*355–362.*

Bartlett, J. (1968) *Familiar Quotations*. Boston: Little, Brown.

Blum, H. (1974). The borderline childhood of the Wolf Man. *J. Am. Psychoanal. Assoc.* 22:*721–742.*

Blum, H. (1981). Object inconstancy and paranoid conspiracy. *J. Am. Psychoanal. Assoc.* 29:*789–814.*

——— (1994). Paranoid betrayal and jealousy: The loss and restitution of object constancy. In *Paranoia: New Psychoanalytic Perspectives*, ed. J. Oldham S. Bone. Madison, CT: International Universities Press, pp. *97–114.*

Blum, H. (1995). Sanctified aggression, hate, and superego alteration. In *The Birth of Hatred*, ed. S. Akhtar, S. Kramer., H. Parens. Northvale, NJ: Aronson, pp. *15–37.*

Bollas, C. (1985). Loving hate. *Annual of Psychoanalysis* 12/13:*221–237.*

Etchegoyen, R.H. (1991). *The Fundamentals of Psychoanalytic Technique*. London: Karnac.

Freud, A. (1972). Comments on aggression. *Int. J. Psychoanal.* 53:*163–171.*

Freud, S. (1900). The interpretation of dreams. *Standard Edition* 4/5.

——— (1909). Notes upon a case of obsessional neurosis. *Standard Edition* 10:*155–318.*

——— (1911). Psycho-analytic notes on an autobiographical account of a case of paranoia. *Standard Edition* 12:9–79.

Freud, S1915). Instincts and their vicissitudes. *Standard Edition* 14:*117–140.*

Gabbard, G.O. (1993). On hate in love relationships: The narcissism of minor differences revisited. *Psychoanal. Q.* 62:*229–238.*

Galdston, R. (1987). The longest pleasure: A psychoanalytic study of hatred. *Int. J. Psychoanal.* 68:*371–378.*

Greenson, R. (1974). Loving, hating, and indifference toward the patient. *Int. Rev. Psychoanal.* 1:*259–266.*

Hartmann, H., Kris, E., & Loewenstein, R. (1949). Notes on the theory of aggression. *Psychoanal. Study Child* 3/4:*9–36.*

Kernberg, O. (1993). The psychopathology of hatred. In *Rage, Power, and Aggression,* ed. R. Glick & S. Roose. New Haven: Yale University Press, pp. *61–79.*

——— (1995). Hatred as a core affect of aggression. In *The Birth of Hatred,* ed. S. Akhtar, S. Kramer., H. Parens. Northvale, NJ: Aronson, pp. *53–82.*

Klein, M. (1946). Notes on some schizoid mechanisms. *Int. J. Psychoanal.*21: *125–153.*

Kohut, H. (1972). Thoughts on narcissism and narcissistic rage. *Psychoanal. Study Child* 27:*360–400.*

Kramer, S. (1995). Parents' hatred of their children. In *The Birth of Hatred,* ed. S. Akhtar, S. Kramer., H. Parens. Northvale, NJ: Aronson, pp. *1–14.*

Laplanche, L. Pontalis, J.-B. (1973). *The Language of Psycho-Analysis,* transl. D. Nicholson-Smith. New York: Norton.

Mahler, M., Pine, F. Bergmann, A. (1975). *The Psychological Birth of the Human Infant.* New York: Basic Books.

McDevitt, J. (1975). Separation-individuation and object constancy. *J. Am.Psychoanal. Assoc.* 23:*713–742.*

Moore, B. Fine, B. (1968). A Glossary of Psychoanalytic Terms and Concepts. New York: American Psychoanalytic Association.

Pao, P. (1965). The role of hatred in the ego. *Psychoanal. Q.* 34:*257–264.*

Parens, H. (1991). A view of the development of hostility in early life. *J. Am. Psychoanal. Assoc.* 39:*75–108.*

Pine, F. (1995). On the origin and evolution of a species of hate: A clinical literary excursion. In *The Birth of Hatred,* ed. S. Akhtar, S. Kramer., H. Parens. Northvale, NJ: Aronson, pp. *103–132.*

Rangell, L. (1984). The analyst at work. *Int. J. Psychoanal.* 65:*125–140.*

Stoller, R. (1979). Sexual Excitement. New York: Pantheon.

Winer, J.A. (1994). Panel report: Hate in the analytic setting. *J. Am. Psychoanal. Assoc.* 42:*219–231.*

Winnicott, D.W. (1949). Hate in the countertransference. *Int. J. Psychoanal.*30: *69–75.*

CHAPTER 11

Object Inconstancy and Paranoid Conspiracy

(1981). *J. Amer. Psychoanal. Assn.,* (29):789–813.

There remain many enigmas concerning the pathogenesis structure of paranoia and the different forms of paranoid psychopathology. This paper continues my investigation and reconsideration of the psychoanalytic theory of paranoia (Blum, 1980). My emphasis here will be on the mental representation of the persecutor and certain features of the paranoid persecutory system as viewed in a contemporary theoretical framework.

The paranoid personality tends to misperceive and distort reality in selected areas. Persistent fantasies of outer or inner danger coexist with unreasonable expectation and exaggeration of hostile threat and exquisite sensitivity to minor mishaps and injuries. Affection and commitment are unreliable, and disappointments in relationships are regarded as potentially menacing or malevolent.

Expectations or conviction of infidelity, betrayal, and conspiracy appear, with rage and hate directed at "disappointing" love objects or their disguised, symbolic representations. With paranoia, there is always a potential for conspiracy in which the patient will be victimized, and there is associated suspicion, distrust, and a readiness to accuse others of malice and to defend oneself. The conspiracy may be localized or general and may involve quite imaginary, composite, or fragmented figures. The therapist may be maintained outside the conspiratorial system as a protective object. However, the ambivalent paranoid patient is likely to become the fantasied hapless victim of the therapist, and with paranoid transference, the treatment itself may be regarded as a conspiracy. Narcissistic, negativistic, and aggressively disposed, the transference of the paranoid patient is then manifestly an embattled, omnipotent struggle with persecutory fantasy that is at least partially confused with current reality.

There are transitional paranoid states with varying degrees and reversibility of distrust, suspicion, and projected hostility as can be seen clinically and in forms of prejudice and social apprehension. Paranoid personality is compatible with advanced personality development in many other areas and the maintenance of intact language, logic, sublimations, etc. (Freud, 1911). Encapsulation of the paranoia protects the rest of the personality and the rest of the patient's interests and object relations from regressive invasion.

The disposition for the use of projection, particularly projection of aggression, criticism, and reproach is potentially present in everyone. Others may be blamed for any disappointment, injury, or transgression, and unacceptable impulses are externalized. Frustrations, misfortunes, psychological and physical injuries occur throughout life and, in childhood, are often blamed on the parents. In infancy, if aggression is not tamed or internalized, it is particularly directed toward and projected onto the mother and her surrogates. After ego, id and self-object differentiation and the later persistence of fantasy, affective reactions, and ego attitudes (McDevitt, 1980), some degree and focus of hate is ubiquitous, and a "safe" target for hatred is often needed for psychic equilibrium. With secondary defenses, irrational hatred may be rationalized and justified. Transient, regressive paranoid reactions, therefore, may occur in almost any patient, but this is a quite different situation than the fixity of paranoid ideation, projected hostility, and the malignant distrust of the paranoid personality.

The terror of persecution by perfidious witches or possession by the devil are historical analogues of individual paranoia. There may be, however, significant differences between the individual paranoid personality and group paranoia. While the particular individuals may be attracted to certain groups because of similar underlying paranoid psychopathology, the persecutory reactions of large groups dominated by a paranoid personality are not identical with individual paranoid dynamics. Furthermore, there is a certain variability in the personality structure of paranoid patients, and there are certainly differences from transient paranoid regression to paranoid states, to the fixed paranoid personalities referred to in this paper. Paranoid schizophrenia, though related to the paranoid personality, may be a different illness, classified as one of the schizophrenias.

Problems of fragmentation and fusion of intrapsychic representations, of unresolved and regressive symbiosis are more characteristic of paranoid psychosis. The paranoid personality usually displays greater differentiation and intact structure, but distortions of an incompletely negotiated separation individuation with precarious stability in some areas of ego function, intrapsychic self and object representations, and self-esteem regulation. Engulfment-enslavement conflicts here are not so much related to issues of fusion as to omnipotent demands concerning control, domination, intrusion, and possession of or by a narcissistic object endowed with overwhelming aggression. In the paranoid personality, fantasies of fusion or annihilation may be concurrent with maintenance of ego boundaries and organization. That boundaries and representations are unstable is related to aggressive defense of and continuing definition of boundaries. The patient may imagine that thoughts and feelings are deviously communicated to or from others and secrets stolen and betrayed. Paranoid fears of invasion and engulfment are paired with paradoxical fears of desertion and disloyal rejection so that neither intimacy nor separation are acceptable. There is no comfortable distance or position, and if the subject is not being watched and controlled, then the narcissistic object must be jealously guarded with monitoring of movement and direction. The use of projection may blur fragile ego boundaries, but may also be part of an enfeebled effort to master internal danger through externalization and external control.

Adult paranoid personalities have attained oedipal and further development. The quality and importance of the Oedipus complex and of postoedipal phases varies in different cases. Special forms of paranoia, as those following massive adult trauma, e.g., paranoia following a severe physical illness or in a holocaust survivor, may not be identical in etiology and underlying structure with other cases. In such survivors, later damage and regression may be more significant than infantile developmental deviation and deficit. In the more usual type of paranoid personality discussed here, the infantile features and determinants are likely to be predominant.

The final structure of the personality has features from all phases of development, all of which have contributed to the normal personality as well as the pathological paranoid deformations. However, infantile narcissism and preoedipal impairment of self and object constancy (Jacobson, 1964); (Mahler et al., 1975) may dominate the clinical picture. Oedipal regression in the transference and in external life is shaped and colored by preoedipal fixation and arrest. The Oedipus complex has set its own stamp on the personality, but has been reciprocally determined by unresolved antecedent developmental problems.

The paranoid's pathological object relations and the nature of the intrapsychic representations are related to difficulties in the process of separation individuation as well as in later development. The preoedipal predisposition and determinants are very important in paranoia and are responsible for severe narcissistic and sadomasochistic distortion and vulnerability to oedipal disappointments and castration threats that interfere with successful resolution of the Oedipus complex[1]. Oedipal conflicts, for example those connected with jealousy and envy, death wishes, and castration, will be expectable but should be understood as rife with narcissism, preoedipal aggression, and annihilation anxieties. Oedipal transference and particularly defenses against murderous and homosexual wishes may be in the foreground, but the latent core of the paranoid personality usually involves preoedipal problems which have led to the arrest and to the distortion of later development. The dangers of object loss and loss of the object's love, and later castration anxiety in all its forms, become for the paranoid personality overwhelming persecutory threats. The ego disturbance and the lack of

---

1 Freud (1932) cites a case of jealous paranoia reported by Mack-Brunswick, "which went back to a fixation in the preoedipus stage and had never reached the Oedipus situation at all" (p. 130). Freud's acceptance of the importance of preoedipal determinants is consonant with his evolving views of paranoia (cf. p. 120), although the problems then discussed would today extend to both sexes and to issues of developmental arrest and oedipal regression and distortion.

object and self-constancy leaves the patient prone to multiple conflicts and problems. Given that development involves interweaving and interpenetrating influences, the impaired object relations are also associated with disorders of narcissism, identity, and sexual identity.

These remarks may seem conventional, but they are worth stating at a time of analytic controversy concerning structural deficit and developmental deviation and arrest, preoedipal determinants, and a nuclear Oedipus complex. Theories of paranoia have variously emphasized primary deficits, core conflicts, and defensive impairments. An example of deficit would be in primary-process regulation and reality testing; core conflict involving homosexuality and masochism; defenses of projection with denial and regression, also leading to ego dysfunction. The narcissistic disturbance represents both developmental deviation and regression. Different cases may present varying admixtures of core conflicts and developmental failure. The problems are very complicated, and research has been restricted by the lack of current, reliable analytic data.

Most paranoid personalities are borderline or near-psychotic characters, and the majority of these cases are probably not analyzable, but may be treated by analytic psychotherapy.

Newer psychoanalytic developmental knowledge will be highlighted with clinical application toward enlarged understanding of preoedipal transference determinants and derivatives. Just as we know that id derivatives emerge only through the ego, so the preoedipal influences are filtered through oedipal and later developmental phases with accretions, overlay and overlap, reorganization, and transformations. This complicates transference analysis, but our appreciation of subtle dyadic transference issues where the analyst represents the preoedipal mother and a narcissistic object has greatly increased (Loewald, 1979). In addition, it is important to try to disentangle areas of developmental arrest from fixation and regression. The arrest and pathological distortion (Kernberg, 1975) of narcissism in paranoia, with "homosexual" self-love, can now be distinguished from the negative Oedipus complex though there are usually intense interrelated problems of phallic narcissism. Additionally, "homosexual panic" may represent fear of fusion with loss of boundaries.

Freud (1937) noted that persecutory delusions are rationalized with ego alteration, but that the delusions are also compensatory efforts at cure through restitution of the patient's relationship to the object world and to reality. Freud offered a number of explanations for the fixity and rigidity of paranoid ideation. Freud called attention to the element of historic truth and to the kernel of truth that also appeared to be confirmed by current experience (Freud, 1922), (1937). The paranoid may have actually had infantile experiences of threat to survival, of fragmented and disorganized ego states, and of primitive modes of experiencing and perceiving reality (Frosch, 1967); (Niederland, 1974). Anna Freud (1952), referring to the negativism in certain types of borderline patients, which would certainly apply to paranoid personalities, noted that the dread of passive surrender to the love object implied a threat of a primary identification with the loss of identity because of merger with the love object. The negativism was understood as a defense against the regressive disintegration or disorganization of the personality. A precarious self-definition was also maintained by opposition to objects and by defining the self by what one is not or by what one opposes (Wangh, 1964). The paranoid personality also demonstrates other problems with respect to the self-image and the experiencing self, e.g., problems in regulation of self-esteem and self-respect, exquisite sensitivity to narcissistic injuries and frustrations, with concomitant affective states of humiliation, shame, disgrace, and narcissistic rage (Kohut, 1972). Problems in object relations are parallel to these problems, and the lack of object constancy, so frequently encountered in the paranoid personality, is often partially represented and replaced by the constantly negative object relation with the persecutory object. In considering the inner representational world of the paranoid, it is important to keep in mind the degrees of differentiation of self and object, of new object and primary object, and of the libidinal and aggressive balance in the personality. Lack of consolidation of the highly aggressivized psychic representations is associated with the persistent tendency to split representations into idealized and devalued, good and bad, persecutory and protective object. This type of splitting, in conjunction with projection and denial, is indicative of defensive impairment of ego development and object relations.

To avoid becoming confused by dealing with these problems as intellectual abstractions, let us confront some of these issues as they become manifest in clinical material.[2]

The patient was a married woman in her late twenties who was treated in psychotherapy for one year, twice a week. Her past history included a period of hospitalization for psychological disturbance at nineteen, and psychotherapy as well as pharmacotherapy for her anxiety and tension. She warned her therapist of a terribly complex and difficult past treatment experience, but she was able to function in her external life and maintain her job as well as attempt to advance herself in graduate education.

As her psychotherapy progressed, the patient became increasingly preoccupied with thoughts about her therapist. What was he doing, where, and with whom? She spent her waking hours brooding and scheming, and hired a detective to follow the therapist. She learned where he lived and entered his home without his permission or knowledge. There were incessant telephone calls to the therapist, and telephone calls to his home and to his wife, on whom the caller immediately hung up. The therapist correctly assumed the latter were part of the patient's telephone activity. If she did not telephone and did not have him followed with her agent or herself chasing closely behind, she was afraid she might become incontinent. She derived a sense of power over the therapist and thought she avoided the humiliation of incontinence and a sense of helplessness. One month before, he had been away on vacation, and she was afraid he had died. That, she thought, was the beginning of murderous thinking on her part with the fear that she might lose control and kill him if he was not already dead. He could leave her, betray her, but she, at the same time, would not allow it. She not only called him at all hours, but there were days when she spent many hours in the waiting room, watching him and other patients come and go, and not incidentally, instilling anxiety in the other patients as well as the therapist. Sometimes she was confused between herself and the therapist. If they had shared thoughts

---

2 I am indebted to Dr. Rick Linchitz for permission to use the subsequent case material. Analytic data would greatly benefit research, but is scarce or unavailable for the reasons Freud (1911) described in the Schreber case.

and feelings, did they have an independent existence as different persons? She assured him he did not really have to worry; she would never kill him; if she were going to act destructively, she would kill herself first, equivalent to killing the poorly differentiated therapist as well.

At the same time that she was having these thoughts of suicide and homicide, she also thought that hiring a detective was a form of protection not only for herself, but for the therapist. She was protecting him through following and constantly watching over him. Her mother had died of a neoplastic illness when the patient was in her teens. The patient felt that because she did not exert precaution and watch her mother, she was then destined to find her mother dead. Now she would protect and watch over the therapist whom she also loved. She thought of him erotically when she was having sexual relations with her husband. Having found out that the therapist's wife was pregnant, she wanted to have something growing inside her, just as she wanted to be mother, to be with or become like her mother, in order to keep her mother alive. When confronted with the many intrusions into the therapist's setting and relationships, she realized that she was making the treatment impossible, but also indicated that she lacked the inner resources to restrain her need to possess and control the therapist.

It would be remiss in this case not to cite the patient's incomplete differentiation, yet with some preservation of ego boundaries. The patient demonstrates structural achievements, albeit with poor structural consolidation and concomitant with arrests and impaired ego functions. It is certainly possible to infer identification with the lost maternal object, the replacement of the mother with oedipal guilt, the intrusion into the house as into the forbidden primal scene, and the preoccupation with the therapist's infidelity with another woman who would unconsciously represent the homosexually loved partner. She had the therapist followed the way a jealous lover or spouse might hire a detective to check on the fidelity of the partner. It is well to keep in mind that this patient has an Oedipus complex, with oedipal conflicts and passions. However, I do not think that this is where the patient is fundamentally "understood," and that the central treatment issues and transference paradigms were primarily at an oedipal level. It is possible to infer some of the patient's adolescent and oedipal conflicts in the material, but it is also apparent that the patient had not surmounted many preoedipal problems, and that she had not successfully negotiated separation-individuation (Mahler et al., 1975).

Her oedipal organization was infiltrated by these distorting preoedipal influences. Oedipal jealousy continued and condensed her preoedipal possessiveness and envy, and oedipal disappointment and loss also represented her preoedipal separation conflicts and her injured, precarious self-esteem. Oedipal attachment and passion masked her symbiotic dependence, her longings for the omnipotent object and external nurturance. There was little affect modulation or capacity for delay and a propensity for rage when narcissistic and oral demands were thwarted.

Based on additional psychoanalytic knowledge of paranoia, of early development and structure formation, and more data from this patient and similar patients, the transference here to the therapist appears to be to the preoedipal mother who was also a narcissistic object. The patient's behavior and transference attitudes are strongly suggestive of a toddler who is clinging to the mother, shadowing the mother, occasionally ambivalently darting away, and whose basic mood is not one of established trust (Erikson, 1963), but a negative basic mood of distrust and lack of confidence (Mahler, 1971). Her infantile reactions are derivative of a need to keep the mother constantly within reach or within sight and hearing range—to dominate, control, and entirely possess the mother's interest and attention. Any move on the mother's part outside this narcissistic and omnipotent object orbit meets with increased negativism, opposition, and anger. To not have the organizing, omnipotent object within reach, at her beck and call, would be to confront the danger of not only separation anxiety, but of disintegration panic and the fear of overwhelming and disorganizing regression and aggression.

On the one hand the patient is all-powerful, consuming, controlling with numerous conspiratorial agents such as detectives at her command. The detective is an extension of her body ego, her perceptual and contact apparatus, her hand and eye. The detective is thus a narcissistic object and extension of herself. The patient is the omnipotent mother who will watch and protect the infant-therapist. The therapist must be protected from her own destructiveness and consuming desires. On the other hand, she is the helpless, separated infant who has not yet achieved object constancy and who must have the presence of the object to maintain ego integration. Her fear of losing sphincter control without the presence of the object is not only that she will become extremely apprehensive and enraged, but that she will regressively lose ego control and orientation without the presence of the organizing object. The patient demonstrates features that have been well described in the older literature in terms of the ambivalent conflict between retention and expulsion of the fecal object and Mahler's (1975) delineation of the rapprochement crisis and more general problems of development and structural consolidation in the second year of life. However, no specific locus of developmental failure is assumed or inferred here in the pathogenesis of paranoia.

In this case the mother blamed the patient for the mother's malignancy. The mother herself, therefore, was regressively lacking in empathy, used projection, and might have tended to see the patient as a real or potential persecutor. The daughter who was blamed in later life possibly also was regarded ambivalently as a threat to the mother's vitality during the patient's infancy. We may infer here that the patient was repeating in the transference a markedly disturbed infantile relationship. There were overt separation conflicts, severe regressive and panic potential, an inability to be comforted or to find self-comfort, and little experience of self-reliance in the mother's absence. The patient's behavior with the therapist is reminiscent of those children who do not permit the mother to leave the room, who demand constant attention and find reasons to be with the mother, to insist that the mother be there to feed, read, play, go to the bathroom, etc. This patient may be compared to the child who is exquisitely sensitive to mother's whereabouts at all times, who shadows the mother, and who displays the separation, sleep, and mood disturbances that may be precursors of serious developmental conflicts. Here are antecedents of later ideas of reference and delusions of being watched which are also explained and determined by primal scene exposure, superego pressures, etc. The darting away from the mother (that may alternate with coercive clinging) protects the patient not only against the revived threat of symbiotic engulfment, but may invite the mother to give chase (Mahler et al., 1975, pp. 82–89). Variable dyadic difficulties may ensue. Some infantile mothers may reciprocally cling to and shadow the child. Overly demanding infants may deplete the reserves of maternal nurturance. The mother may resent the infant's dependency (or autonomy), and the mother may demand that the infant function as a narcissistic extension of herself, while the infant may demand that mother and later objects function as an auxiliary ego and as a narcissistic omnipotent extension of himself. Various forms of aggressive, coercive, or negativistic behavior in the toddler may be followed by narcissistic withdrawal or other personality transformations that impede developmental potential, or by resumption of developmental progression and positive change.

With respect to the clinging, coercive children who will not leave mother or let her leave, who keep her within reach and sight, it is not possible to predict which of these children will later develop ideas of reference. There are many possible outcomes, and much depends on the capacity for developmental mastery and later beneficial influences and transformations.

These struggles for omnipotent control and possession have their analogues in conflicts in later development and adult life. Florid fantasies of oedipal infidelity may persist with oedipal disappointment, jealousy, and rage. In treatment as a transference-countertransference bind may develop in which the patient's jealous and tenacious watchful shadowing and clinging arouses anxiety and anger in the therapist. The patient then not only fears the therapist's rejection and desertion, but also may sense the therapist's actual anxiety and aggression toward the patient. With the interweaving of this type of transference and countertransference reactions, one may get escalating regression in both patient and therapist with paralysis or disruption of the therapeutic process. This type of escalating struggle may revive and recapitulate similar struggles between parent and child, sometimes with pathogenic developmental consequences. Areas of developmental failure or deficit and tendencies toward regression may be related to such pathogenic patterns and converging infantile trauma.[3]

The infantile omnipotence and narcissistic vulnerability to which I have referred is often partly due to narcissistic and ego arrest, and partly due to defense and the severe regression accompanying the precipitation or exacerbation of the patient's illness. The patient is often afraid of being engulfed and enslaved, of losing autonomy and identity. He may be afraid of his own tyrannical demands and may project his infantile attitudes and narcissistic wishes onto the therapist. The patient, as in the case just noted, may attempt in behavior (as well as fantasy) to engulf and enslave the therapist, trying to regain the lost narcissistic omnipotence and to become reunited with the narcissistic object who is regarded as essential for psychic survival. Such patients are abjectly dependent and want the omnipotent object, the early narcissistic preoedipal mother, to be a hovering guardian angel, ever nurturant, approving, and protective. Yet closeness or intimacy engenders the danger of invasion of ego boundaries and autonomy. The paranoid is guarded and distant, yet chronically resentful of narcissistic frustration.

The lack of internalization of the comforting, constant mother is associated with a lack of ego integration. Poor frustration tolerance and impulse control, fragile self-esteem, and unneutralized aggression leave the patient predisposed to severe sadomasochistic dispositions and rage reactions. When object constancy is not fully attained, there is also narcissistic arrest with untamed infantile omnipotence, and tendencies toward separation panic rather than signal anxiety (McDevitt, 1975).

In more regressed states, these patients refuse to recognize that the analyst or therapist is an independent object, just as it was difficult to accept their own mother as an independent object with her own needs and attitudes. (There may be greater or lesser degrees of boundary formation and differentiation or merger.) Simultaneously, the threat to the patient's sense of coping and the danger either of narcissistic fusion or of separateness and helplessness,

---

3 (1973) proposed an attachment to painful feelings prior to and overlapping with self-object differentiation, relevant to the pathogenesis of paranoia.

may mobilize various forms of intrapsychic defense and of regressive-adaptive behavior designed to ward off the catastrophe of loss of ego integration and dedifferentiation (or in the most regressed patients, structural fragmentation). In the therapeutic situation, separations or silence, questions or intrusiveness may be experienced by the patient as a major assault.

The murderous fantasies that so often appear at the juncture of object loss and narcissistic injury are indicative of the patient's inner lack of resources, and the feeling that the therapist does not or cannot or should not exist without the patient and affectively belongs to the patient; the patient cannot exist without the ego support and synthesis of the therapist who is a dyadic partner. The exquisite vulnerability of the patient may be compensated by fantasies of grandiosity, by ruthless exploitation of the object or substitute objects designed to demonstrate power and control over the object world and punishment of the disappointing object. To preserve the good object, the patient may split the object world and the self-representation into "good and bad" (Klein, 1932); (Mahler et al., 1975). The splitting of representations may be viewed either as an ego defect, as a defense, or both. What begins as a failure to achieve integration, possibly based on a constitutional deficit, may be utilized by the ego for defensive purposes (Kernberg, 1975). At the same time, the excessive utilization of such defenses as projection and denial severely interferes with both ego integration and reality testing.

While transference, idealizations, and hostile devaluations typically are linked to the family romance of the oedipal phase of development, in more narcissistically disturbed patients and those with more severe arrest and regression, the idealizations and devaluations are extreme, take on fantastic distortions, and are poorly differentiated from each other. Aggressor and victim, tyrant and slave, sadist and masochist, may be globally identified with each other or even fused as in the identification of the masochist with the sadist. This is usually unconscious, so that the conscious persecuted position is a defense against the opposite paired tendency (Kanzer, 1952).

From the point of view of the genetics and dynamics presented, the paranoid personality maintains a tenuous and highly ambivalent relationship with the persecutory, narcissistic object and, in fact, cannot give up the manifestly narcissistic and hostile sadomasochistic relationship. The paranoid unconsciously creates this relationship in fantasy, and may seek to be persecuted and to persecute in reality. The paranoid patient evokes hostility and may provoke the "persecution" that is consciously feared.

In emphasizing the complexity of these types of reactions in later life and other associated paranoid phenomena, I also want to insert a cautionary note about reconstruction. The transference patterns in cases of very severe developmental arrest and distortions and in cases of severe ego regression do not revive actual infantile relationships in their original form. It is important for the therapist to reconstruct the general outlines in his own mind of the infantile patterning of the patient's psychological function. The reconstruction is based on the transference repetition, the life history, etc. This is not to say, however, that the transference repeats the real infantile object relations. Analytic reconstruction in these cases is a very complicated effort. Because of projection, denial, splitting, and other infantile defenses, and because of the general invasion of the cognitive process with the primary process, self- and object representations are distorted, not only by the patient's specific psychological disturbance, but by the general characteristics of unconscious transformations. The persecutor, as is well known, may have the attributes of the repressed unconscious, sinister, evil, smelly, devouring, destructive, etc. The object will not correspond to the real mother or, for that matter, to any of the caretaking objects of infancy, or to the patient's own infantile self.

It is well to be reminded here of Abraham's (1924) and Klein's (1932) formulations of paranoia in terms of fixation to the sadism of the late oral and anal phases of development. The child's own sadism and aggression are projected, with fantasies of destroying the object. Murderous paranoid fantasy may take the form of insatiable cannibalism or anal aggressive elimination of the fecal object. The child is also threatened from within, Klein proposed, by reintrojected object and part objects endowed with destructive attributes. Paranoid patients are preoccupied with all manner of sexual and aggressive assault. However, what I want to emphasize is not the instinctual drive fixation so much as the related distortions of object and self representations. This complicates the laborious process that is necessarily involved in reconstruction of the patient's actual development, experience, and object relationships.

The pathogenesis of paranoia is not any simple failure of endowment or of the environment, of the mother's ministrations or empathy, or the child's response. The child has not been persecuted by a malevolent mother, nor has the mother simply been unable to adapt to an "impossible" child. Many different congenital, constitutional, and experiential factors contribute to the etiology of such serious conditions as paranoia. The complemental series and multiple factors Freud described still hold (Niederland, 1974).

Even where there has been a history of continued ambivalent struggles and embattled relationships, the child's distortions of the parent into the equivalent of monsters are distorted exaggerations and elaborations of the parents' and the child's own unacceptable instinctual and exploitative impulses. The disturbed toddler may not be able to utilize affectionate interest, may have temper tantrums and physically and verbally abuse any caretaker, and may fretfully and negativistically oppose every caretaking action. The extremely infantile adult patient may engage in similar behavior while attempting to preserve some relationship with the nurturant, concerned object. While "holding on" to the object, the inconstant object may be both entreated and berated.

At an earlier phase of life, the patient may have been actually exposed to severe traumata and threats to psychic survival (Bak, 1946); (Frosch, 1967). Patients with a history of paranoia have often had childhood paranoid episodes, and the adult paranoid reactions are recapitulations or derivatives of the earlier childhood paranoid episodes and paranoid trends which were present in childhood and in a borderline adolescence (Blum, 1974), (1980). Actual persecution and identification with paranoid or with persecuted objects may be important issues in some cases, but are not essential etiological factors.

I shall now return to the paranoid's peculiar relationship with the "inconstant object," the ambivalently loved object who seems to be both persecutory and needed. The "constant," persecution is also a substitute deviant need satisfaction from a narcissistic object in whom there is "no confidence." I refer to paranoid suspicion, jealousy, and accusations of disloyalty, paranoid scheming, vindictive exploitation, and actual betrayal of individuals, groups, and causes to which they claimed allegiance and fidelity. As Jacobson (1971) noted, these patients might feel an irresistible urge to look for an opposite group while complaining and bearing grudges about their supposedly unjust experiences with their former friends and allies. The urge to betray, and actual acts of betrayal, are often rationalized on the basis of just punishment and revenge. Because of the blurring of boundaries and the lack of object and self constancy, the wish for independence and/or autonomy will be experienced as the betrayal of the deserting object who wants to be separate with his/her own attitudes and interests.

Children are egocentric, "solipsistic," and infantile omnipotence only gradually yields to increasingly realistic appreciation of the object world, with "decentering" of the way the child thinks. Infantile experience is interpreted in terms of psychic reality, a reality transfigured by ego immaturity and defense. The lack of object constancy is an important factor in infantile attitudes of coercion, desertion, rejection, and chronic resentment. A. Freud's (1965) general observations in this area are pertinent to paranoid pathogenesis. "Before the phase of object constancy has been reached, the object, i.e., the mothering person, is not perceived by the child as having an existence of her own; she is perceived only in terms of a role assigned to her within the framework of the child's needs and wishes. Accordingly, whatever happens in or to the object is understood from the aspect of satisfaction or frustration of these wishes. Every preoccupation of the mother, her concerns with other members of the family, with work or outside interests, her depressions, illnesses, absences, even her death, are transformed thereby into experiences of rejection and desertion. On the same basis the birth of a sibling is understood as unfaithfulness of the parents, as dissatisfaction with and criticism of the child's own person—in short, as a hostile act to which the child in his turn answers with hostility and disappointment expressed either in excessive demandingness or in emotional withdrawal with its adverse consequences" (pp. 58–59).

The inconstant object does not or cannot be allowed to have an independent existence, the threat of betrayal and desertion is ever present, and the problem is not simply the closeness of the external object but intrapsychic separation and the attainment of object constancy. In this sense, the constant, hostile persecution is the reciprocal of libidinal object constancy and may be regarded as a desperate effort to preserve an illusory constant object while constantly fearing betrayal and loss. Once the capacity for fantasy repetition of hostility is obtained after eighteen months of age, there can be a constancy of hatred originally toward the preoedipal mother (Blum, 1980); (Sandler, 1972). Some capacity for libidinal attachment persists if object ties are at all maintained. The "all-bad" persecutory object is not recognized as the same caretaking object that nurtures and is simultaneously the mirror image of the projected all-bad despised self. In paranoia, the hated object and hateful self are linked in projective-introjective processes and incomplete separation-individuation. The manifest persecutory object may be heterosexual or homosexual or may be a group representing the implacable family members who are seen as allied against the patient in a projection of his hostility to his family (Bak, 1946).

Fantasied or real and inevitable disappointments in the self and infantile objects are distorted and used to justify and rationalize the feelings of persecution. As in the secondary elaboration of a dream, the conspiracy is made coherent and given a pseudo-plausible construction. The manifest change from friend to enemy, love to hate, is the culmination of the paranoid predisposition to narcissistic rage, hostility, and splitting of representations. Dr. Jekyl becomes Mr. Hyde with the onset of paranoid regression and persecutory transference. Jekyl and Hyde may not consciously recognize their original or their reciprocal relationship, or their "interidentification" and potential refusion. The split may be in the object or self-representation.

Freud (1923) first noted this type of split representation and antithetical affective states of good and evil, "God and Devil." "It does not need much analytic perspicacity to guess that God and the Devil were originally identical— were a single figure which was later split into two figures with opposite attributes. In the earliest ages of religion God himself still possessed all the terrifying features which were afterwards combined to form a counterpart of him" (p. 86).

The negative Oedipus complex, because of its avoidance of rivalry and challenge, is particularly linked to paranoid fears of castration, passivity, and weakness. Homosexuality may mean masochistic submission and victimization (Meissner, 1978), just as masochism may disguise castration and homosexuality. Manifest issues of phallic narcissistic dominance are suffused with preoedipal influences centering around the patient's need to coerce and control, devour and dominate the ambivalently loved and hated, needed and despised narcissistic object. Oedipal homosexuality may be modeled on earlier passive oral and narcissistic object relations; both oedipal defeat and the betrayal of the child by the parents in the child's primal scene may be linked to the paranoid patient's preoedipal inconstancy and narcissistic injury. A dyadic transference may be inferred with the preoedipal issues coexisting with, within, and behind manifest oedipal transference.

The patient may be as confused in his identity as in his object ties, but the need for the object is apparent, a relationship that has to be maintained even at the possible cost of mutual destruction. Since the psychic survival of the self and of the object is not possible in the absence of the relationship, the persecutory object is sought or shadows the paranoiac. The shadowing of the omnipotent preoedipal mother imago, via projection, becomes the patient's being followed, ensnared, and struggling with separation. The split dyadic object-representation still represents the projections and primary identifications of the simultaneous vulnerable and aggrandized self. The persecutory object, whose presence in all or none infantile terms, indicates the absence of the love object, paradoxically also represents that object to whom there has to be some positive attachment. The paranoid is desperately attached and coercively clings to his persecutor and to the constancy of conspiracy.

Beating fantasies, organized as development proceeds, may be conscious in many of these patients in childhood and adolescence and form the core of the adult paranoid fantasy. Later systems of persecution and attack include regressive derivatives and transformations of the childhood beating fantasy (Freud, 1919); (Bak, 1946). The persecution and victimization are erotized in degree and sometimes idealized, as in martyrdom. However, paranoid fantasy tends to be less erotic than aggressive and less representative of internalized conflict than masochistic fantasy. In the paranoid patient, the beating fantasy may be confused with reality or experienced regressively and enacted in terms of primitive narcissistic and sadomasochistic self object relationship. Paranoid regression will selectively involve personality structure and the beating fantasy. The structure of the personality and of the beating fantasy in paranoia is more primitive and more narcissistic than in the masochistic character (Blum, 1980). The patient identifies with and often colludes to form alliances within the family while engaging in a conspiracy against others, so that the underlying fantasies of conspiracy, espionage, and betrayal may have been enacted in various disguised forms during childhood. This becomes part of the kernel of truth in the later fantastic paranoid conspiracies which also condense actual experiences of collusion, mistreatment, and narcissistic injury, trauma, and the hostility engendered by their own suspicion, provocation, exploitation, and disloyalty. The paranoid's role of victim is itself exploited.

Because of the structural regression, arrests, and deficits, the projected superego discerned in paranoia, is not that of mature superego structure and function. The watching, accusing object has regressive overtones of the preoedipal precursors of the superego. It is no simple matter to differentiate projection of aggression and externalization of superego elements. The superego of the paranoid is poorly internalized and remains prone to regression; it is then archaic, punitive, and unable to assert effective control and regulation, or to offer self comfort and tolerance. Lack of superego stability, the continued projective-introjective processes, and poorly integrated, absolute ideals and injunctions leave the paranoid patient prone to acting out and to experiencing humiliation and shame rather than guilt and self-reproach.

The persecutory plot is thus also a misguided and disguised effort, not only to protect the good self and object, but to reestablish the watchful, concerned care that is reliably internalized in true object constancy. The quality of superego internalization and integration and capacity for guilt are important prognostic considerations in paranoia.

It is very difficult for those patients to accept responsibility for their lives, frailties, and feelings. Impulses are temptations to be punished. Blame and shame are also projected, and objects of temptation or of anger are transformed into persecutory objects. Acceptance of illness or help itself threatens their narcissistic "invulnerability." Narcissistic injury is denied and undone, and there may be simultaneous mobilization of narcissistic rage and persecutory beating fantasy. The "need" for the persecutory object and persecution may be associated with breakthrough of the wish to persecute. The grievance and grudge of the paranoid toward the "disloyal" inconstant object should not be underestimated in strength or tenacity, and in fantasy further injury may be avoided by a preemptive strike and prior injury avenged by counterattack.

The degree of hostility and vindictiveness in the paranoid personality depends on ego modulation of affect and impulse, the balance between love and hate and between masochistic attachment and narcissistic rage. Splitting of representations is usually incomplete, and the persecutory object may be erotized anew. However, in some paranoids, there is an implacable, "pure" hatred (e.g., Hitler) expressed in the persecutory system, imbricated in what is presumed to be a precarious narcissistic personality organization. Without object constancy, distrust and suspicion of betrayal are associated with the panic hate-rage affects that are so readily mobilized. Love is a condition for the repression and taming of hatred. The paranoid's predominant hatred may be associated with ambivalence, but with arrested, deficient, and deviant love. Paranoid hatred is part of the disturbed ego and affective state; it is not primarily a reactive disguise for repressed love. The lack of object constancy is related to paranoid suspicion and hostility and may in itself be part of a vicious cycle of unneutralized aggression, projected hatred, and failures of internalization, integration, and libidinal investment of self- and object representations.

There are many possible outcomes to the instability and regressive loss of object constancy. The clinical picture depends on many other factors, including the capacity to reverse regression and to maintain ego integration and reality adaptation. The paranoid personality is particularly prone to narcissistic injury and to impaired consolidation of emotional object constancy and individuality. In paranoia, there is a proclivity to confuse and fuse the hostile object and self representations with attempts to project, eject, and externally control and coerce the unreliable, dangerous narcissistic object. The destructive loss and attempts to regain object constancy are part of the paranoid persecutory struggle. It is a malignant illness when there is an inexorable narcissistic tyranny with constant expectations of malice and betrayal and a constancy of hatred that permeates the personality.

Summary

The persecutory object relationship is a central aspect of paranoia and will have features from all developmental phases. In the psychotic forms of paranoia, the object may be incompletely differentiated from the self or may be a fragmented object with condensation of fragments of self- and object representation. In the paranoid personality, where many areas of the personality remain intact, object relations are more cohesive and integrated, although still unstable and lacking in constancy in the persecutory relationship. The narcissistic system of megalomania and persecutory object relationship attempts to preserve the crucial relationship with the inconstant narcissistic object. The constant inconstancy of the persecutory object is a distortion replacing libidinal object constancy. Expectations or conviction of infidelity, betrayal, and conspiracy are common, with hate and rage directed at the inevitably disappointing, faithless objects or their disguised representations. There is always suspicion and distrust of the object, but a need to search for and be shadowed by the object, to be persecuted by and to persecute the betraying narcissistic object who inflicts injury. The "constant" persecution displays the hatred and may disguise narcissistic and masochistic gratification in the attachment and bondage to the persecutor. Because of instability of boundaries and the lack of object and self-constancy, the wish for autonomy is experienced as betrayal of the deserting object who wants to be separate, and the wish for narcissistic fusion may be defended against and experienced as a dangerous intrusion or invasion and a threat to identity. The "inconstant" object does not and cannot be allowed to have an independent existence, and the threat of betrayal is ever-present along with the need to maintain the relationship at all costs. The paranoid appears to flee but is always followed or follows his dyadic persecutory partner.

In paranoid regression, the manifest change from friend to enemy, love to hate, is the culmination of the paranoid predisposition to narcissistic injury and rage, narcissistic and sadomasochistic object relationship, and the splitting of self and object representations. Narcissistic, preoedipal issues and unresolved problems of separation-individuation may be discerned within and behind oedipal conflict and distortions. Conflict and deficits are subsumed in a widened contemporary perspective of the development and structure of paranoia. In addition to the pervasive narcissism and use of projection, the ambivalent splitting in which hate overrides love, the failure of self-object constancy and malignant mistrust are interrelated and, in varying degree, consequent to developmental arrest, fixation, and regression.

REFERENCES

Abraham, K. (1924). A short study of the development of the libido, viewed in the light of mental disorders In *Selected Papers on Psychoanalysis* New York: Brunner/Mazel, pp. *418–502.*

Bak, R. (1946). Masochism in paranoia. *Psychoanal. Q.15:285–301.*

Blum, H. (1974). The borderline childhood of the Wolf Man. *J. Am. Psychoanal. Assoc. 22:721–742.*

——— (1980). Paranoia and beating fantasy: an inquiry into the psychoanalytic theory of paranoia. *J. Am. Psychoanal. Assoc. 28:331–362.*

Erikson, E. (1963). *Childhood and Society.* New York: Norton..

Freud, A. (1952). A connection between the states of negativism and of emotional surrender *Int. J. Psychoanal.33:265.*

——— (1965). Normality and Pathology in Childhood. *Writings* 6 New York: Int. Univ. Press, 1966.

Freud, S. (1911). Psychoanalytic notes on an autobiographical account of a case of paranoia. *S.E.:12.*

——— (1919). A child is being beaten. *S.E.:17.*

——— (1922). Some neurotic mechanisms in jealousy, paranoia, and homosexuality. *S.E.*:18.

——— (1923). A seventeenth-century demonological neurosis. *S.E.*:19.

——— (1937). Constructions in analysis. *S.E.* 23.

Frosch, J. (1967). Delusional fixity, sense of conviction, and the psychotic conflict. *Int. J. Psychoanal.*48:475–495.

Jacobson, E. (1964). *The Self and the Object World*. New York: Int. Univ. Press.

——— (1971). *Depression*. New York: Int. Univ. Press.

Kanzer, M. (1952). Manic-depressive psychoses with paranoid trends. *Int. J. Psychoanal.*33:34–42.

Kernberg, O. (1975). *Borderline Conditions and Pathological Narcissism*. New York: Aronson.

Klein, M. (1932). *The Psychoanalysis of Children*. New York: Grove Press, 1960.

Kohut, H. (1972). Thoughts on narcissism and narcissistic rage. *Psychoanal. Study Child*27:360–400.

Loewald, H. (1979). The waning of the Oedipus complex. *J. Am. Psychoanal. Assoc.* 27:751–776.

Mahler, M. (1971). A study of the separation-individuation process and its possible application to borderline phenomena in the psychoanalytic situation. *Psychoanal. Study Child* 26:403–424.

Pine, F. & Bergman, A. (1975). *The Psychological Birth of the Human Infant*. New York: Basic Books.

Mcdevitt, J. (1975). Separation-individuation and object constancy. J. *Am. Psychoanal. Assoc.* 23:713–742.

——— (1980). Brill Lecture New York Psychoanalytic Society, November 25, 1980.

Meissner, W. (1978). *The Paranoid Process*. New York: Aronson.

Niederland, W. (1974). *The Schreber Case: Psychoanalytic Profile of a Paranoid Personality*. New York: Quadrangle.

Sandler, J. (1972). In Panel: *Aggression, A.* Lussier, reporter. *Int. J. Psychoanal.*53: 14.

Spruiell, V. (1975). Three strands of narcissism. *Psychoanal. Q.*44:477–595.

Stone, L. (1961). *The Psychoanalytic Situation*. New York: Int. Univ. Press.

Valenstein, A. (1973). On attachment to painful feelings and the negative therapeutic reaction. *Psychoanal. Study Child* *28:365–392.*

Wangh, M. (1964). National Socialism and the genocide of the Jews. *Int. J. Psychoanal.* *45:386–395.*

CHAPTER 12

The Borderline Childhood of the Wolf Man

(1974). *J. Amer. Psychoanal. Assn.* (22):721–742.

Freud's wolf man remains a favorite teaching case, and it is certainly the most detailed, documented, and exciting of his case histories. The analysis, lasting more than four years—1910 to 1914—was a long, detailed, in-depth study for that early period, when very short analyses were customary. The case history is an extraordinary clinical document, recording original discoveries and the solution of complicated enigmas of symptom and character, personality development, and regression. The many layers of meaning are presented vividly and with great clarity and cohesion. The rich data and pioneering formulations have fostered new insights and the appreciation of new problems.

Never again was Freud to provide clinical material of such sweep and depth. He referred to the case in numerous other publications—in one of his last papers, "Analysis Terminable and Interminable" (1937), he critically commented on the Wolf Man's therapeutic result and the need for further periods of treatment. The case touches on a host of questions regarding psychoanalytic theory and technique (the termination of treatment, the limits of analyzability, the importance of the primal scene, the fundamental significance of the infantile neurosis for later adult disturbance, etc.). It is also a fascinating study of Freud at work with a most challenging patient, a patient from a different social, cultural, and language milieu. It was a transcultural analysis with universal relevance.

One has the impression in reading the Wolf Man that the analysis was more enriching for Freud than it was for his famous patient, a reflection of Freud's scientific and literary genius, and possibly also an indication that the analysis was primarily elucidated and organized in the mind of the analyst.

The voluminous data relevant to the Wolf Man span a period of more than 60 years, providing the lengthiest longitudinal-case-study opportunity in psychoanalysis. The case history is complemented and extended by the subsequent analytic report of Ruth Mack Brunswick (1928), the observations of the patient by other analysts, Muriel Gardiner's (1971) long-term follow-ups, and the patient's own comments and recollections.

The case of the Wolf Man has always been approached with diffidence, perhaps because of our reverence for Freud, and certainly because the patient was alive and bore a special status—a ward of psychoanalysis with a unique analytic identity.

When I was a candidate, the case was taught with almost unquestioned acceptance of Freud's formulations and adherence to his established early views (1914) and those of Mack Brunswick (1928). Neither Freud's nor Mack Brunswick's study has ever been up-dated in terms of structural theory and ego psychology, despite the vast growth in psychoanalytic knowledge since this case history was published.

The Wolf Man was not analytically observed or treated during his childhood. Freud derived knowledge of his infantile neurosis from the patient's analysis as an adult. Indeed, he did not, unfortunately, present his patient's adult neurosis, so that we are missing this important set of primary data. The analytic method, of course, was different in those days and this influenced the data obtained. Freud (1918) noted that the patient was far from an ideal case and was cautious "… of the distortion and refurbishing to which a person's own past is subjected when it is looked back upon from a later period" (p. 9). The Wolf Man, at the age of 83, wrote the recollections of his childhood at the urging of Dr. Gardiner. He had previously avoided writing about his adolescence and childhood, despite having written other autobiographical commentary.

With the advantages of hindsight, follow-up, and the perspective of more than half a century of analytic development, the Wolf Man's personality disorder merits further inquiry. Re-examination of the data suggests new connections and hypotheses. There is, of course, also a danger in overexploiting a classic case history. Referring to the classic cases of Freud, Anna Freud reminds us that " … the very familiarity which analysts began to feel with these patients allows the temptation to deal with them in their imagination as if they were their own patients, to wish to know everything about them, to test the interpretations given, to probe beyond the conclusions drawn, or wherever possible to reconstitute once more the original data from which the author's abstractions had been made" (Gardiner, 1971, p. x.). Even though the Wolf Man has been able to cooperate and to provide additional reminiscences and commentary, there are still dangers of speculation about him that must be acknowledged. Freud called his paper "From the History of an Infantile Neurosis," and the infantile disturbance is of special significance. The concepts of infantile neurosis and developmental disturbance were to undergo further differentiation, and exert a compelling influence on later analytic theory.

In this presentation I shall review the Wolf Man's infantile illness and some of its determinants and consequences and will assume the reader's familiarity with the Freud and Mack Brunswick clinical reports. I shall attempt to demonstrate that the Wolf Man's childhood disturbance was a severe borderline disturbance which provided the foundation for a borderline adolescence and for what I regard as his adult borderline personality. "From the History of an Infantile Neurosis" may be viewed as the history of a borderline childhood with episodes of infantile psychosis. Indeed, the case might be described as, "From the History of an Infantile Psychosis." The psychotic states of adult life were regressive revivals of the infantile psychosis (Frosch, 1967). The paranoia was not recapitulated in the original analytic transference to Freud, but was a posttermination regressive decompensation primarily triggered by Freud's illness (and perhaps the illness and infertility of the Wolf Man's wife). The "transference psychosis" did not appear in the regressive analytic situation, but after termination. The borderline case is often unable to terminate and may require continuing periods of therapeutic support to maintain ego integration.

I am using the word borderline to describe a condition close to psychosis, with severe ego impairments but without the irreversible disorganization and structural fragmentation of psychosis (Kernberg, 1967). The borderline case, such as the Wolf Man, may have a tendency to severe regression with psychotic episodes. The borderline case cannot easily be distinguished from mild psychosis with functional recovery and reintegration. Frosch (1967) considered the Wolf Man a probably psychotic character, a designation very close to borderline psychosis.

In 1937, Freud expressed reservations about the outcome of his analysis and noted further illness of a paranoid character. In his initial interview with Freud, the Wolf Man had offered to defecate on his head and participate in rectal intercourse (Jones, 1955). Freud mentioned his previous diagnosis (by Kraeplin and others,) as "manic-depressive insanity." In the analytic situation, Freud (1918) describes him as, " ... for a long time unassailably entrenched behind an attitude of obliging apathy" (p. 11). Freud observed the patient's inveterate narcissism and his intense and constant ambivalence. "The contrast between the patient's agreeable and affable personality, his acute intelligence and his nice-mindedness on the one hand, and his completely unbridled instinctual life on the other, necessitated an excessively long process of preparatory education, and this made a general perspective more difficult" (p. 104). Severe characterological disturbance was observed: "no position of the libido which had once been established was ever completely replaced by a later one. It was rather left in existence side by side with all the others, and this allowed him to maintain an incessant vacillation which proved to be incompatible with the acquisition of a stable character" (p. 27). Serious sado-masochistic trends were observed in his identification with the suffering Christ, in his torture and beating fantasies, and his depressive and masochistic self-reproach. Freud (1919) referred to the Wolf Man in his classic paper "A Child Is Being Beaten." With prophetic insight, he observed, "People who harbour phantasies of this kind develop a special sensitiveness and irritability towards anyone whom they can include in the class of fathers. They are easily offended by a person of this kind, and in that way (to their own sorrow and cost) bring about the realization of the imagined situation of being beaten by their father. I should not be surprised if it were one day possible to prove that the same phantasy is the basis of the delusional litigiousness of paranoia" (p. 195). The paranoid states that subsequently erupted occasionally, the hypochondriasis and life-long depressions, the tendency to act out his fantasies, the lack of ego synthesis and cohesive personality organization, recurrent crises requiring supportive intervention—all point toward a borderline personality. This would be consistent with the preanalytic picture of the totally crippled adult patient, unable even to dress himself, with his later dependence upon continued therapeutic contact and upon the psychoanalytic movement. (There was a possible transformation of his identity into the Wolf Man of psychoanalysis.) On the other hand, he has had sufficient personality resources to benefit from the psychoanalytic and psychotherapeutic help and to demonstrate a functional adaptation far beyond the invalidism that might have left him confined to a mental hospital.

The borderline syndrome or personality had not been conceptualized at the time of the Wolf Man's analysis, nor was there child analysis or detailed observational studies of borderline and psychotic children. The study of the infantile neurosis and childhood disturbance in the Wolf Man case, in fact, did much to stimulate the development of systematic child analytic investigation. Freud elucidated the Wolf Man's childhood problems as the background of the subsequent adult disturbance, and reconstructed the primal scene as an underlying traumatic experience with important developmental consequences.

The Wolf Man presented a broad spectrum of disturbances throughout his childhood and adolescence. The many symptoms and dysfunction in early childhood would be analogous to a later pan-neurosis. There was an infantile anorexia of unknown dimensions and duration. After age three and a half, his personality underwent a transformation, and he became irritable and violent. This sharp transformation occurred after his nurse's castrating reproach for masturbating and his attempt to suppress masturbation. But it is significant that it developed during separation from his parents (Gardiner, 1971, pp. 5, 170). Freud noted the anal-sadistic regression and cruelty that followed the suppression of masturbation, but had not then formulated his theory of ego regression or alteration. The child took offense on every possible occasion, raging and screaming like a savage or lunatic (p. 15). He could not be consoled, was suspicious and distrustful. At his fourth birthday on Christmas, he had his famous anxiety dream of white wolves sitting quite still in a tree outside his window. He awoke in terror lest they eat him. Freud connected this nightmare at age four and the subsequent wolf phobia with his witnessing the primal scene two and a half years earlier and with his repudiated feminine wishes. Prior to the dream, his sister had teased and frightened him by showing him pictures of an upright wolf with claw extended.

He tormented insects and people, had fantasies of being beaten on the penis, and enjoyed beating horses. Yet, if a horse was beaten, he began to scream. At four and a half his wolf phobia was replaced by obsessional symptoms involving intractable praying and ritualistic signs of the cross, kissing of holy pictures, and preoccupation with anal blasphemies. He developed respiratory rituals of inhalation and exhalation, associated with making the sign of the cross. Torturing others and self-tormented, he was fearful of injury and death.

He was both aggressor and victim and constantly feared attack, as he had in his nightmare. He was terrified of the primal scene as an exciting beating and castration and, I believe, as a mutually destructive devouring. He defended against his cruelty and sadism with obsessive piety and masochism. The obsessional symptomatology continued until about age 10, waning during the period of his German tutor. Under the tutor's influence, he gave up his obsessional piety and the last obsession with heaps of dung. The tutor also discouraged him from his cruelties to animals and his continued practice of cutting up caterpillars. The panic, torture, temper, and screaming reactions with uncontrolled, protracted rages are suggestive of a borderline child with the *anlage* of ego deviation (A. Weil, 1953). He resembled the atypical child, described by Geleerd (1958), who easily withdraws into fantasy, is prone to severe tantrums and expectations of attack, and who needs the presence of the love object to hold on to reality.

The Wolf Man's later nightmarish anxiety may be related to the earlier tantrums. Geleerd (1958) described the panic underlying the flooding rages in borderline children. This is traumatic anxiety with ego helplessness. Omnipotent control is sought as salvation from the utter defenselessness of the ego. The screaming is a cry for help and an expression of helplessness.

The borderline or psychotic child may manifest disturbance and dysfunction in a number of areas, rather than the typical symptoms of adult psychosis. The hyperirritability and excitation is a consequence of not only masturbatory excitement, but a general lack of ego modulation of impulses and affects. The borderline has been overstimulated and traumatized, or has a constitutional defect in binding or synthesis which invites traumatization (Weil, 1953); (Bender, 1968).

Freud related the Wolf Man's fear of being eaten to his fear of and unconscious wish for homosexual gratification from his father. I believe his phobia and overwhelming anxiety can now be related to his conflicts over symbiotic fusion and his regressive tendency to global identifications, which involve merger with the object. This is evident in his nightmare state's extending into everyday life, his attacks of visual hallucinosis, and his withdrawal into a veiled state of narcissistic retreat. The impairment of the separation-individuation process is related to the fear of being devoured and overwhelmed by the object. There appears to have been a persistent fixation to the oral triad of devouring, being eaten, and fused sleep (Mahler, 1971); (Lewin, 1950).

Freud (1918) regarded the aftermath of the patient's condition as a defect following on an obsessional neurosis. It is now known that childhood obsessional neurosis often represents severe personality disorder and that many obsessive children become psychotic as adults (A. Freud, 1965, p. 152).

Because the Wolf Man's childhood was characterized by a persistent, constricting, and very severe obsessional neurosis, one wonders if the popular pseudonym for the case in terms of the transient wolf-phobia is at all appropriate. The title "Wolf Man" is overdramatic and misleading in its clinical implications.

I would suggest that in addition to the symptoms and inhibitions, the defect Freud mentioned may be regarded as an ego defect. This patient displayed narcissistic vulnerability and detachment, disturbed object relations and impulse control, apathy and affective impoverishment, and a tendency to severe regressive response. The neurotic and obsessive overlay to the severe personality disturbance did not prevent a rapid recrudescence of symptoms by the time of puberty at age 13. It is questionable whether there was ever a period when he was totally asymptomatic. After the obsessions subsided, at about age 10 there were depressions, with peaks at five o'clock in the afternoon. At 13 he developed a nasal catarrh and acne. Pubertal acne and blushing were exceedingly painful to this hypersensitive patient. He was also very concerned with his nasal discharge—a forerunner of the later concerns with gonorrheal discharge, and then again with his nose, during the paranoid episode and treatment by Ruth Mack Brunswick. Wealthy, privileged, and sensitive, he had always been teased at school. Troubled by acne and blushing, and obsessed with his nose and skin, he stayed away from school. He became more and more seclusive in adolescence and preoccupied with the care of his body and clothes (Mack Brunswick, 1928, p. 287).

There is no question that his pubertal crisis and the childhood period before his nightmare both involved a struggle against masturbation and the dread of castration. However, the severe phallic conflicts both defended against his preoedipal problems and contributed to the failure of more adequate oedipal and adolescent solutions. In turn, the presumed underlying disturbance of separation-individuation interfered with healthy adolescent development—he was a solitary, depressed, and distrustful adolescent. His panic about his nose at 13 reappeared with delusional intensity at age 37. He then looked slovenly and harassed, according to Mack Brunswick (p. 290), " … as if the devil were at his heels as he rushed from one shop window to another to inspect his nose," constantly studying his face and nose in mirrors (p. 302). The gonorrhea revived his fear of phallic damage, earlier displaced upward to fears concerning nasal damage and abnormal nasal discharge. His genital infection and discharge reinforced his hypochondriasis and fantasies of castration. Freud's case begins with a breakdown of the patient following the attack of gonorrhea at age 18.

A psychoanalytic developmental framework was only in its early stages of evolution during Freud's lifetime. An overview of the Wolf Man's earlier childhood and adolescence demonstrates developmental disruption. Between three and four, following what normally should have been the consolidation of object constancy, he was agitated, beset by beating fantasies, was cruel, distrustful, screaming, and raging. His nightmare and phobic anxiety of wolves at age four became a generalized apprehension, extending from wolf pictures to people, with fears of being stared at and teased. This resulted in screaming on feeling stared at, as he had awakened screaming from his nightmare—an *anlage* of later ideas of reference and derivative, also, of the primal scene. The succeeding obsessional neurosis, at approximately ages five to 10, was associated with continued overt sado-masochism and depressions. Depression and hypochondriasis continued into adolescence, with distrust and seclusion. The (preadult) narcissistic disorder and impairment of object and reality relationships are consistent with the borderline syndrome.

Preoedipal influences have molded the oedipal conflicts of the borderline personality. The picture is often confused because of the coexistence of various developmental phases and the fluctuation between symbiotic strivings and more advanced ego interests and achievements. The borderline syndrome may include deviant, regressive, and mature personality traits (Ekstein & Wallerstein, 1954). Separation-individuation has progressed, but is incomplete or deviant (Frijling-Schreuder, 1969). Regressive defense carries the danger of personality disruption, and the untamed omnipotence and aggression threaten the survival of object relationships (Blum, 1971).

The Wolf Man's borderline childhood was the foundation for his vulnerability to uncontrolled regression. His disturbance underwent various changes, but essentially it persisted, with periods of remission and exacerbation, into the patient's adult life. Not every childhood ego disturbance eventuates in a borderline adult personality; the outcome depends on further developmental vicissitudes. A borderline adult personality such as the Wolf Man, however, emerges from a borderline childhood and adolescence. His adolescence did not consolidate a more cohesive personality organization with ego growth, but culminated in severe regression and withdrawal.

The primal scene and castration anxiety are major threads running throughout the patient's disturbance, his symptoms, and his character disorder. Freud, in addition, presented numerous contributing factors (A. Freud, 1971). These included anorexia and fears of being devoured, anal-urethral fixations, experiences of seduction and early castration threats, fears giving way to guilt—which transforms sadism into masochism—and passive homosexuality (with feminine identification in the primal scene).

Mack Brunswick re-emphasized the importance of the primal scene experience for the Wolf Man's subsequent disturbance. His voyeurism-exhibitionism, his fears of looking and being looked at, and his sexual preferences were all related to the primal scene. Mack Brunswick maintained the basic formulation that he had not resolved his hostile fear of his father and his longing for homosexual gratification in identification with his mother in the primal scene. Being stared at as the wolves had stared at him in his nightmare was a projection of his own staring at the primal scene.

Freud recognized the pervasive importance of the primal scene for his patient and even reconstructed its exact setting: the Wolf Man's age, the hour it occurred, as well as the Wolf Man's awakening response of having a bowel movement. The Wolf-Man was 18 months of age, suffering from malaria, and witnessed coitus *a tergo* at five in the afternoon (when fever recurred), the hour at which his subsequent depressions reached their peak. There were five wolves in the Wolf Man's drawing of his dream, although he reported six or seven of them.

In his later years he complained that the world was hidden from him by a veil which was torn only after defecation following an enema. The Wolf Man, born on Christmas in 1886, relived the primal scene with impregnation and his own rebirth when the veil was torn. The veil, as Greenacre (1973) observed, was also a wall of denial. The window in the dream and the veil represented his wish to see and his blinding denial. His envelopment in the veil was also a withdrawal into sleep and symbiosis. Here was a dramatic depiction of the Wolf Man's narcissistic detachment, intolerance of narcissistic frustration, and fantasy of an intrauterine escape to the safety of fusion with his mother. His sense of reality and the structure and organization of his life were threatened from early childhood.

Mack Brunswick denied that any new memories had occurred in her treatment and emphasized remnants of the homosexual father transference to Freud. Harnik (1930), however, pointed out that there were new findings which had not been previously reported. This led to an interesting exchange between Harnik (1930), (1931) and Mack Brunswick (1930–1931),[1] following the first publication (1928) of her five months of analysis with the Wolf Man in 1926.

The Wolf Man told Mack Brunswick that after his nightmare at age four he couldn't bear to be looked at and would scream if he felt a fixed stare. "He would fly into a temper and cry, 'Why do you stare at me like that?' An observant glance would recall the dream to him with all its nightmare qualities" (Mack Brunswick, 1928, p. 289). Harnik suggested it was the recovery of this new memory that was the favorable turning point in his treatment with Mack Brunswick. The diagnostic and prognostic significance of a "childhood paranoia" was not then appreciated by either Harnik or Mack Brunswick. Harnik criticized Mack Brunswick's singular reliance on the primal scene as an explanation of the Wolf Man's symptoms and character, regarding the newly recovered memory as a screen for infantile masturbation. He disputed her insistence that only unresolved transference to Freud was uncovered during her treatment of the Wolf Man's paranoia. Harnik almost recognized the severe childhood regression after the nightmare and, citing the anorexia and insistent wishes to be fed via gifts, postulated on oral fixation.

Although their dialogue seems naïve and incomplete today, Harnik was groping toward preoedipal problems and the Wolf Man's regressively disturbed sense of reality in childhood. The Wolf Man reported to Freud that, following his nightmare, it took quite a long while before he was convinced it had only been a dream. Freud (1918) commented on the particular significance of the sense of reality, stating that the dream related to an occurrence that really took place and was not merely imagined (p. 33). The reality of the occurrence (the primal scene) was strongly emphasized, in Freud's view, in marked contrast to the unreality nightmare experienced had invaded reality. (The Wolf Man's famous dream may not have been an anxiety dream [of REM sleep], but a symptomatic nightmare.) Nightmares, with their pervasive terror of attack and helplessness, are reminiscent of paranoia, especially when the boundaries

---

1 The author expresses his appreciation & gratitude to Dr. Helen C. Meyers for her translation of the Harnik-Mack Brunswick dialogue.

between sleeping and waking, fantasy and reality, have been blurred. The regression of the sleeping nightmare could not be reversed and regulated in the child's waking life.

This childhood syndrome is a template and model of the Wolf Man's adult paranoia. The case may depict a paradigmatic infantile prototype of paranoia, at three and a half to four years of age: "taking offense on every occasion, raging like a lunatic," beating fantasies and sado-masochistic behavior, distrust and ideas of reference, fears of attack with merger of nightmare and reality, fears of helplessness with passive omnipotence and projection of aggression.

The analysis of the nightmare led to the reconstruction of the primal scene. Was this single early primal scene such a traumatic developmental influence for this patient? The patient grew up on a vast estate on which animals copulated and were castrated; impregnation, birth, and death must have been commonplace. The child undoubtedly knew of the gelding of horses and the castration of rams. The deadly danger of infection was known from his own illness, his mother's pelvic complaints, and the lethal inoculations of the vast sheep herds during an epidemic. He observed sheep breeding, and we can assume he was repeatedly exposed to instinctual activity.

There are further problems. Can we at present accept the formulation that an infant of 18 months, suffering from malaria, undoubtedly with fever and severe stress reactions, could record the primal scene? Infants with malaria may be subject to delirium, febrile convulsions, coma, or exhaustion. Just what was the trauma—the malaria, or the primal scene, or an obscure combination of both, along with unknown vectors concerning parental care and complications? The primal scene was a major determinant of the Wolf Man's disorder, but there are issues of vulnerability, phase specificity, and overdetermination, with interrelated causes and effects.

The complications included the lack of parental empathy and appropriate responses, ego immaturity, general overstimulation, malarial fever, and possible swaddling. The Wolf Man assumes he was swaddled, which,[2] if true,

---

2 The author expresses his appreciation and gratitude to Dr. Muriel Gardiner for transmitting his questions to the Wolf Man.

could have been an important developmental influence and have contributed to the motionless figures in his dream. The physical illness and incapacity could have severe traumatic and sado-masochistic implications, which would also influence any concurrent primal scene experience. A serious and extended malaria at 18 months, as opposed to a single primal scene experience, could lead to ego disturbance and the developmental disruption of separation-individuation. The nearly lethal pneumonia at age three months may also have had unknown psychobiological side effects. Certainly the role of malaria and the earlier pneumonia as possible traumatic experiences in their own right was not appreciated. We do not know the severity, duration, or sequelae of the malaria, or the number of attacks or recurrences.

The reconstruction of the primal scene under these complicated circumstances strained Freud's credulity as it does ours today. This early model of reconstruction remains highly controversial.

Perhaps the most famous and detailed reconstruction, it was a major stimulus to later research on analytic reconstruction. Freud himself continued to struggle with the question of reality versus fantasy and retrospective falsification versus retrospective reactivation of the primal scene. He suggested that the remembered primal scene at 18 months became a fresh traumatic experience at the time of the nightmare preceding his patient's fourth birthday on Christmas eve (1918, p. 109). In his final recapitulation (p. 121), Freud left open the possibility that the Wolf Man had retrospectively introduced a fantasy of his parents copulating into his observation of them together at 18 months of age. Certainly, the Wolf Man's statement about having witnessed, at 18 months of age, upon awakening, the primal scene repeated three times, must be viewed with serious reservations. The child's concept of the number three and of a sequence of three distinct experiences develops considerably later than the age of 18 months. Judging from the early scenes of sexual seduction with Grusha (his nursemaid) and his sister and the many servants on the vast Russian estate, as well as opportunities presented by the animals, it would seem that there was early, repetitive exposure to instinctual overstimulation and early castration threats.

The primal scene, sexual seduction, masturbation, and related danger cannot be viewed in isolation from his parents. There is insufficient attention in the case reports to the Wolf Man's sharing a bedroom, first with his old nurse (Nanya) and sister, and then with his Nanya (Gardiner, 1971). The developmental implications of the intimacy and voyeurism-exhibitionism of this sleeping arrangement are not explored. Nor should the child's interpretation of the primal scene be dissociated from other facets of the parent-child relationships and the parent's relation to each other. The reaction to the primal scene would depend upon the child's developmental phase, his psychic structure, and his own ego-edited reaction to the total experience.

Was Freud's reconstruction of this single primal scene a return to a theory of traumatic parental seduction in neurosogenesis? If trauma, with malaria, rather than primal scene in isolation, is emphasized at 18 months, then this is trauma at the time the basic mood develops, substantially deriving from trust or distrust. It is the rapprochement subphase of separation-individuation, when language, secondary process, and other ego functions are rapidly differentiating and vulnerable to injury (Mahler, 1971).

Freud was always aware of the limitations of his theory and technique. With the growth of psychoanalytic knowledge, many early explanations are obsolete and incomplete. The case of the Wolf Man was originally presented in terms of the castration complex and particularly the negative Oedipus complex. The preoedipal factors influence and contribute to the core oedipal problems. The relationship with the father and the fear of his homosexual love for the father are seen as paramount in the patient's conflicts (Freud, 1918, p. 32). The mother-child relation and maternal influence (as in the other Freud case histories) is in the background and is hardly considered. Problems of the two mothers, his peasant Nanya and his hypochondriacal mother, who was only close to him when he was ill, are not developed. His Nanya may even have spoken a different dialect. There were a series of governesses whose impact and consequence were relatively unknown. We know that the patient identified with his hypochondriacal mother, preoccupied with her pelvic and bodily complaints. She was self-absorbed, not involved in the day-to-day child rearing, and unable to exert a healthy, maternal direction of the household.

She apparently knew little of, or did not control, the patient's sister's teasing and attempts to seduce him.

His father was also unable to provide healthy, paternal direction and stimulation, for he suffered from a manic-depressive psychosis. The father was frequently physically away in sanitoria and in all probability committed suicide, as did the patient's sister, before the Wolf Man underwent analysis with Freud. The father was the model of a castrated cripple, represented by the deaf and dumb servant who was unable to communicate because his tongue had been cut out. The patient identified with his psychotic, immobilized father. Was the father mute during periods of depressive psychomotor retardation? Was the father's "affectionate abuse" of the child as innocent as it seemed, along with his oral threats to gobble him up? Did the father's psychosis contribute to the atmosphere of unbridled instinctual life and possible exposure to the primal scene? How sensitive and understanding were these parents, especially when one recalls not only the mother's narcissistic hypochondriasis, but her comments to her son when she took him to the sanitorium to see his psychotic father? "He had not seen his father for many months, when one day his mother said she was going to take the children with her to the town and show them something that would very much please them" (Freud, 1918, p. 67). His father was gravely depressed and the boy found him pathetic. What was the child previously told about his father's absence, illness, and character change?

One of the Wolf Man's earliest memories was of being alone with his nurse at two and a half and witnessing the departure of his parents and sister. There were not only repeated separations from his parents. but a lack of warm parental involvement and participation in his life. These early relationships are of crucial importance for understanding the Wolf Man's later object relations and ego development. The paranoid psychosis of Schreber and the paranoid episodes of the Wolf Man are all too often discussed in their original formulations without reference to infantile ego development and the early mother-child relation. What is stressed is the feminine attitude toward the father, regression from negative oedipal fantasies, and primitive defenses against homosexual wishes. Preoedipal conflicts, ego development, and early self and object relation had not yet received systematic study.

A great deal more would have to be understood about the Wolf Man's narcissistic detachment and feelings of entitlement and insatiable demanding. His being born in a caul; the favorite and only son; his rebirth as a replacement for his Nanya's dead baby, born at Christmas; the Christ child, and Freud's favorite case were narcissistic gratifications, no doubt reinforced by his fame and position in psychoanalytic history and the special interest and support of psychoanalysts. Had the early distrust and detachment, the veiled wall which separated him from the world, been overcome in his years of treatment and support (psychological and economic) by various psychoanalysts?

Nor can the inherited and constitutional predisposition to severe emotional disturbance in his family be overlooked. There is an extraordinary passivity and rigidity that not only appeared in the analysis of the Wolf Man and his later life history, but was already present in what we know of his earlier childhood—e.g., the stillness in his wolf dream and drawing. He clung with tenacity to any position, giving it up only under great duress, and when offered a substitute on which he then became very dependent. This was apparent in his giving up the phobia for the obsessions and later giving up his religious interests for his German tutor. The analysis with Freud did not move until the imposition of a termination date. Freud tells us, "He immediately gave up working in order to avoid any further changes, and in order to remain comfortably in the situation which had been thus established" (1918, p. 11).

At that time Freud thought the patient's resistance and fixation had given way under the inexorable pressure of the termination limit. "All the information, too, which enabled me to understand his infantile neurosis is derived from this last period of work, during which resistance temporarily disappeared and the patient gave an impression of lucidity which is usually attainable only in hypnosis" (p. 18). The hypnotic compliance and apparent ludicidity did not alter the deeper personality deformations and what Freud called the patient's "psychic inertia." Freud also referred to the concept of entropy (p. 116), which, in thermodynamics, tends to make certain physical changes irreversible and which psychologically opposes the undoing of what has already occurred.

If the Wolf Man was swaddled for nine months according to the cultural custom (Erikson, 1963), this may have further contributed to his passivity and masochism, and even his later identification with Christ on the cross. The possible influence (negative and positive) of swaddling on his personality is unknown. His pervasive passivity, however, would appear to be related to constitutional factors and to developmental failures rooted in his early object relations and identifications. His passive beating wishes and masochistic fantasies were considered derivatives of unconscious female identification in the primal scene. These beating fantasies, however, are also indicative of an early sado-masochistic relationship to the mother and a severe disturbance in ego and drive development (Novick & Novick, 1972). The Wolf Man's analysis preceded but also stimulated the formulation and elaboration of the psychoanalytic theory of aggression.

The Wolf Man's fear of helplessness and passivity, his fear of being devoured, were also related to his wish to be devoured into sleep, into a veil of narcissistic withdrawal and symbiotic reunion. His preoedipal conflicts are now apparent in his clinging, ambivalent, masochistic tie to the preoedipal mother. He demonstrates the vulnerability of some borderline patients to severe regression and their rather typical conflict between the wish to fuse and fear of fusion with loss of the object and identity. Freud may very well have been an idealized selfobject (Kohut, 1971) as well as an auxiliary ego. This patient became paranoid when Freud developed cancer. His own devouring aggression and destructive wishes might now destroy the formerly omnipotent object—and himself. Did Freud refer him to a female colleague to reduce the unconscious threat of castration by the therapist or, perhaps, also to encourage the development of supportive, maternal transference?

The nature of the actual object relation and transference relation with Mack Brunswick are not clarified in her terse treatment (five months) and reported "supplement" to the case. The maternal, narcissistic, and symbiotic transferences were neither understood nor identified. Explanations depended upon the homosexual father transference described by Freud. Even though Mack Brunswick was also Freud's patient, the probable sister transference is not elaborated. She mentions his attachment to his preschizophrenic sister in her later analytic treatment of the Wolf Man. Mack Brunswick's insistence to the Wolf Man that he was not Freud's favorite case must have had special significance for these two patients of Freud. She largely ignored his status as Freud's famous case and Freud's financial support of this special patient as well as his presentation to the Wolf Man of a volume containing the patient's immortal case history with a personally inscribed dedication (1919), and additional analysis without fee (1920).

Whom did Freud unconsciously represent for this narcissistic, omnipotent patient, identified with Christ? Was it true that Mack Brunswick was only an extension of and proxy for Freud, God the Father? His referral to Mack Brunswick was doubtless felt as both a rejection and the presentation of a free but poor substitute for Freud, his lost idealized object. The Wolf Man was unable to express his rage at the "rejection" or his gratitude for the bestowal of free further treatment. To him, Mack Brunswick probably represented Freud and the psychoanalytic movement. Her explanations and formulations adhered to Freud's early published views, not an extension of them. She did not reconsider the transference implications of the patient's personality transformation, transfer, and new female therapist. In addition to mother or sister, was Mack Brunswick his Nanya into whose care he was entrusted by his sickly mother; his English governess who supports and controls him with his nurse-wife; or a composite of these infantile objects?

The Wolf Man was fixedly studying his face in the mirror and may well have developed a narcissistic (mirror?) transference (Kohut, 1971) to Mack Brunswick. The threatened loss of Freud had fractured his ego stability with regression to magical mirror self-object ties (Shengold, 1974). His recovery could be related to the formation of a narcissistic object relationship with her, with fantasies of protective omnipotence and an archaic narcissistic transference "cure." A replacement and transfer of the narcissistic transference to Freud and to psychoanalysis can also be inferred.

His withdrawal disguised his insatiable demands for oral-dependent gifts and narcissistic supplies. Mack Brunswick may have intuitively provided empathic mirroring responses, reliability, reality, and a vital auxiliary ego during his psychotic regression. In the psychosis there was probably a fusion of the grandiose self and ideal object and, with narcissistic rage, the persecutory transformation, splitting, and projection of the unintegrated, aggressively devalued self-object. The regressive retreat moved from narcissistic but differentiated object representations to fusion of self and object representation. The Wolf Man's narcissistic transference to Mack Brunswick was determined by his desperate need to re-establish narcissistic equilibrium and symbiotic relationships when faced with Freud's loss. The Wolf Man's relationships to his analyst were determined primarily by his personality disorder rather than the special nature and research goals of his treatment (cf. Offenkrantz & Tobin, 1973). Freud's fascinating technical variations in the treatment of the Wolf Man are beyond the scope of this paper, as are the countertransference issues (Kanzer, 1972). There would, of course, be particular countertransference problems for anyone undertaking the treatment of one of Freud's patients, now "Freud's famous case." The technical problems are also corollary to questions about this patient's ego resources and analyzability.

His rapid improvement with Mack Brunswick's help is reminiscent of the hypnotic lucidity of the terminal phase of treatment with Freud and the brief additional analysis (four months) with Freud in 1920. Freud (1918, p. 118), recapitulating the problems of the case with characteristic foresight, did not focus on the Wolf Man's homosexuality, but drew attention to the patient's pathological narcissism,

He broke down after an organic infection of the genitals had revived his fear of castration, shattered his narcissism, and compelled him to abandon his hope of being personally favoured by destiny. He fell ill, therefore, as the result of a narcissistic 'frustration." This excessive strength of his narcissism was in complete harmony with the other indications of an inhibited sexual development: with the fact that so few of his psychical trends were concentrated in his heterosexual object-choice, in spite of all its energy, and that his homosexual attitude, standing so much nearer to narcissism, persisted in him as an unconscious force with such very great tenacity. Naturally, where disturbances like these are present, psychoanalytic treatment cannot bring about any instantaneous revolution or put matters upon a level with a normal development …

The Wolf Man's narcissistic disorder has been elaborated by Gedo and Goldberg (1973).

Mack Brunswick (1928) corroborated the veiled state of the patient as a womb fantasy and noted, " … throughout the psychosis, the veil of the earlier illness enveloped the patient, nothing penetrated it" (Gardiner, 1971, p. 300).

During the paranoid regression, the primary nature of his feminine identification (in a symbiotic primal scene) became apparent. Mack Brunswick reported (p. 301): "Dr. Wulff, who knew and attended the patient and both his parents … said, 'He no longer plays the mother, he is the mother down to the last detail.'"

This was a global identification based upon and only a step from merging with his maternal object. His use of the mirror represented his merging femininity and protected his identity against re-engulfment. Here, castration anxiety both screened and evoked the anxiety of disintegration. His facial concerns represented the danger of castration and femininity, but also the deeper danger of loss of differentiation of self and object.

In the window of his nightmare, in looking and being looked at in the mirror, he attempted to face his conflicts, to find his narcissistic object, and confirm his identity. The persecutory nightmare was repeated in the adult paranoia and followed by reparative efforts at ego mastery of the dread of borderline regression into narcissistic fusion.

Summary

The case of the Wolf Man has been surveyed in terms of psychoanalytical theoretical developments subsequent to 1918 and 1928. The Wolf Man affords an extraordinary opportunity for longitudinal developmental study. It is suggested that the patient suffered, not from an infantile neurosis, but from a borderline condition with episodes of infantile psychosis. The infantile psychotic episodes recurred in the paranoid states of adult life. The Wolf Man's famous dream is re-examined as a nightmare in terms of ego response and later revival of analogous ego states. Freud's reconstruction of the primal scene at 18 months is reviewed with particular attention to the possible traumatic role of malaria, and the effect of trauma during the rapprochement phase of separation-individuation. Problems of separation-individuation, and narcissistic disorder and regression are emphasized.

REFERENCES

Bender, L. (1968). Childhood schizophrenia: a review. *Internat J. Psychiat.* 5:*211–219.*

Blum, H. (1972). Psychoanalytic understanding and psychotherapy of borderline regression. *Int. J. Psychother.* 1:*46–59.*

Ekstein, R. & Wallerstein, J. (1954). Observations on the psychology of borderline and psychotic children. *The Psychoanal. Study Child* 9:*344–69.*

Erikson, E. (1963). *Childhood and Society.* New York: W. W. Norton.

Freud, A. (1965). Normality and Pathology in Childhood. *Writings* 6.

——— (1971). The infantile neurosis: genetic and dynamic considerations. The *Psychoanal. Study Child* 26:*79–90.*

Freud, S. (1918). From the history of an infantile neurosis .*Standard Edition* 17:*3–122.*

——— (1919) .A child is being beaten. *Standard Edition* 17:*175–204.*

——— (1937). Analysis terminable and interminable. *Standard Edition* 23:*209–253.*

Frijling-Schreuder, E. (1969). Borderline states in children. *The Psychoanal. Study Child* 24:*307–327.*

Frosch, J. (1967). Severe regressive states during analysis. *J. American Psychoanal. Assn.* 15:*491–507.*

Gardiner, M. ed. (1971). *The Wolf-Man by The Wolf-Man.* New York: Basic Books.

Gedo, J. & Goldberg, A. (1973). *Models of the Mind.* Chicago: University of Chicago Press.

Geleerd, E. (1958). Borderline states in childhood and adolescence The *Psychoanal. Study Child* 13:*279–295.*

Greenacre, P. (1973). The primal scene and the sense of reality, *Psychoanal. Q.* 42:*10–41*.

Harnik, J. (1930). *Kritisches über Mack Brunswicks "Nachtrag zu Freud's 'Gesichte einer infantilen neurose'" Internat. Zeitschrift fr Psychoanalyse* 16:*123–127*.

——— (1931). Erwiderung auf *Mack Brunswick's* Entgegnung *Internat. Zeitschrift fr Psychoanalyse.* 17:*400–402*.

Jones, E. (1955). *The Life and Work of Sigmund Freud, Vol. 2.* New York: Basic Books.

Kanzer, M. (1972). Review of The Wolf-Man by the Wolf-Man *Int. J. Psychoanal.* 53:*419–421*.

Kernberg, O. (1967). Borderline personality organization *J. American Psychoanal. Assn.* 15:*641–685*.

Kohut, H. (1971). *The Analysis of The Self.* New York: International Universities Press.

Lewin, B. D. (1950). *The Psychoanalysis of Elation.* New York: W. W. Norton.

Mack Brunswick, R. (1928). A supplement to Freud's "History of an infantile neurosis," in *The Wolf-Man* by The Wolf Maned. M. Gardiner. New York: Basic Books, pp. *263–307*.

Mack Brunswick, R. (1930). Entgegnung *auf Harniks kritische Bemerkungen Internat. Zeitschrift fr Psychoanalyse.* 16:*128–129*.

——— (1931). Schlusswort Internat. Zeitschrift fr *Psychoanalyse*17:*402*

Mahler, M. S. (1971). A study of the separation-individuation process and its possible application to borderline phenomena in the psychoanalytic situation *The Psychoanal. Study Child* 26:*403–24*.

Novick, J. & Novick, K. (1972). Beating fantasies in children. *Int. J. Psychoanal.*53:*237–42*.

Offenkrantz, W. & Tobin, A. (1973). Problems of the therapeutic alliance: Freud and the Wolf-Man *Int. J. Psychoanal.*54:*75–78*.

Shengold, L. (1974). The mirror as metaphor. *J. American Psychoanal. Assn.* 22:*97–115*.

Weil, A. (1953). Certain severe disturbances of ego development in childhood The *Psychoanal. Study Child* 8:*271–287*.

CHAPTER 13

The Development of Autonomy and Superego Precursors

Blum, E. J. & Blum, H. P. (1990). *Int. J. Psychoanal.* 71:585–595.

Introduction

Within the context of pre-oedipal development and separation-individuation, we will address issues of the development of superego precursors, particularly with respect to the development of autonomy. We will particularly focus on the pre-oedipal period, while recognizing from the outset that major superego developmental transformations and accretions occur in subsequent phases. Freud (1923, p. 48), in addition to his usual post-oedipal emphasis, also referred to the pre-oedipal roots of the superego: 'The super-ego owes its special position in the ego, or in relation to the ego, to a factor which must be considered from two sides: on the one hand it was the first identification and one which took place while the ego was still feeble, and on the other hand it is the heir to the Oedipus complex and has thus introduced the most momentous objects into the ego'. From a contemporary perspective, superego precursors emerge prior to the Oedipus complex, with superego development continuing during and after the oedipal phase, crucially interrelated with oedipal resolution.

Autonomy follows a developmental course, intertwined with processes of separation-individuation and affective development. Early autonomous strivings lead to a variety of encounters with the physical environment and with the object. A broad spectrum of responses is elicited, depending on the nature of the infant's behaviour and the specific qualities and concerns of the caregiver. The upsurge of autonomous strivings related to motor and cognitive developments of the second year coincides with the marked wilfulness associated with the rapprochement phase (Mahler et al., 1975). This poses a particular developmental and interpersonal challenge. The way in which these issues are negotiated colours the development of superego precursors. Autonomous strivings take a number of forms, leading not only to curtailment and inhibition, but also to support and encouragement, later internalized as positive aspects of superego.

Autonomy is a term which has several major conceptual and developmental dimensions. Autonomy commonly refers to independence from external control and from instinctual drives, as well as independence as contrasted with dependency. These are different concepts of autonomy from those of Hartmann (1939). For Hartmann, primary autonomy was innate prior to and independent of psychic conflict, and secondary autonomy was achieved consequent to resolution of conflict. As used here autonomy begins with the capacity for dawning awareness of motive and intent, the ability to achieve an intended goal, converging with developing self-regulation.

The young child becomes increasingly aware of its own powers, and its capacity to act upon its self and environment, with greater and more persistent intentionality. This helps to define and reinforce individuality and separateness. Ultimately, however, autonomy must subserve not only individual exploration and innovation, but the regulation of behaviour. Self-control, necessary for avoidance of danger as well as compliance with parental and cultural standards, must become internalized and thus experienced as autonomous.

This discussion of autonomy and the emergence of internalized controls and rules will describe earlier and more complex superego precursors than have generally been emphasized. A focus on approval and positive affect balances sometimes one-sided attention to disapproval and prohibition. We will address issues regarding the development of behavioural control, necessary for survival and socialization, in the face of increasing needs for and pleasure in autonomous behaviour. The intertwining of these needs with the separation-individuation process and their relationship to superego development is crucial. Of particular significance is the question of the negotiation of the conflict inherent in the increasing sense of self as an individual with a will, seeking autonomy, needing to maintain separateness, and the increasing tendencies to come into conflict with the object world, based on psychical and physical development.

Autonomous assertive strivings become evident in the first year, but it is in the second year that these strivings, for a variety of reasons which we will describe, engender increasing conflict as self-assertion becomes an intrinsic component of the separation-individuation process. We will primarily focus on the second year of life. The basic mood and potential for crisis in the rapprochement phase are influenced by the clash of wills with the caregiver concerning rules and limits. The rules and regulations are not only imposed but are negotiated by child and caregiver. This negotiation of rules and limits is a forerunner of and contributant to superego development. Negotiation is a significant, often subtle process, easily overlooked because of the more conspicuously important simple commands and imperatives. Rudimentary internalizations, beginning towards the end of the first year, are followed by an increasingly refined process of learning and identification.

We have not elaborated here anal phase wishes and defences which are so well described in the classical psychoanalytic literature, but in the context of this paper are part of a larger picture which includes ego development and object relations. The development of psychic conflict and of internalized controls is particularly salient to the later phases of separation-individuation. Toilet training is of course an important arena of conflict, and as denoted by the term sphincter morality, fundamental to superego development.

Early Autonomous Strivings

Typically, by the end of the first year the infant's capacities, particularly in the motor sphere, permit physical separateness and increasing interaction with the external environment, with upright locomotion replacing earlier crawling and cruising. Towards the end of the first year the infant's advancing ego capacities permit the infant to act upon the environment with ever greater goal directedness and effectiveness. The cognitive steps that make this possible include beginning development of knowledge of means-end, cause and effect, spatial relations, and beginning mental representation and incipient capacity to delay. Intentionality, anticipation, delay of gratification, and developmental mastery are, to a degree, interdependent. While bringing about an effect has been demonstrated to be pleasurable in the earliest months, by the end of the first year the infant's joy in mastery becomes even more evident. The experience of causing an effect takes on new meaning and is associated with great pleasure, shared and reflected by the caregiver. This has been described by Mahler et al. (1975) as the elated joy of the practising phase, still under the sway of untamed infantile omnipotence. Developing competence and beginning sense of self, the junior toddler's increasing ability to bring about an effect serves to promote individuation, just as mobility towards and away from the caregiver subserves separation and intrapsychic 'separateness'. Perhaps imitation brings special pleasure as the toddler perceives himself/herself as similar to the caregiver, subserving both closeness and separateness.

As the child's behaviour unwittingly threatens his/her own safety, the physical safety of others, and of inanimate objects, the need for behavioural control becomes imperative. The toddler's burgeoning capacity for interaction with this widening world makes almost inevitable increasing interpersonal conflict, and eventually, intrapsychic conflict as well. By the second half of the first year, with crawling and pulling to stand, the infant now has a variety of behaviours, in addition to crying, which demand a parental response. In earliest infancy the caregiver, except under circumstance of unusual parental psychopathology or gross ignorance, does not expect the infant to be capable of control of its behaviours. A constraint on infant behaviour nevertheless becomes evident at about this time; the infant by about seven months begins to demonstrate fear. Checking with the caregiver to evaluate the safety of a novel or unclear situation soon begins, and the infant interprets the caregiver's communication. 'Social referencing' is a reciprocal affecto-motor communication and an incipient form of shared regulation, related to precursors of the superego.

By about eight or nine months of age the infant will inhibit an action begun when the parent says 'no'. While the action may be resumed or repeated, nevertheless, there is beginning comprehension of the vocal communication, particularly the affective context. The parent might say 'no', but there is little expectation that the infant will comply with the beginning limits set by the caregiver and physical intervention is generally necessary. The infant reaches for an electrical socket and is immediately moved from it. Nevertheless, there is the beginning of both behavioural and affective response. Some infants are, in fact, especially sensitive to even subtle parental communications and alter their behaviour accordingly. An infant of about ten months of age, pulling to stand and cruising, crawls to a dangerous area of an unfamiliar kitchen and is bodily turned in another direction with no verbal admonition. The next day, as she approaches the same spot she turns her head and looks at the adult present, as though to ask permission. At this stage most infants rarely react more than momentarily when they are diverted from a goal-directed behaviour; nevertheless, individual differences in persistence and insistence are apparent. One parent reports, many years later, how persistently her infant, at less than one year of age, went to the TV, ultimately breaking the controls. (This child had continuing conflict regarding control and autonomy, manifest for many years in daytime enuresis.)

Second Year Development

Clearly, there is marked variation in the way transition to external compliance and then to internalized regulation is accomplished. Each youngster manifests ambitendencies regarding compliance and rebellion. Differences in drive endowment, pace of physical development, differences in activity and persistence and temperament, as well as differing parental characteristics and concerns influence these processes. Earlier experience and the quality of the parent-child relationship colour the development and negotiation of the interpersonal and intrapsychic conflict in the second year.

Parallel with increased capacities to understand the physical world, in the second year the toddler becomes increasingly capable of understanding the signals of the interpersonal world. Although there has been development of affective communication from the earliest months, there is now the beginning of semantic communication as well. In addition to the capacity to understand and respond to prohibition during the toddler period, there is also the beginning demand for positive compliance, for example, with regard to dressing, changing activity, going to bed, etc.

Upright locomotion brings about an upsurge in the requirement for behavioural limitation, by the beginning of the second year. Not only has walking generally been mastered, but climbing, and by the end of the second year, running as well. Some toddlers are described as getting into everything, often with little sense of danger. Further, as language begins to develop, caregivers' expectations also evolve with the more advanced levels of communication, comprehension, and integration. the infant has become a toddler, with greater capacity for autonomous action, greater persistence, and considerable evidence of evocative memory. The caregiver generally expects a modicum of compliance and co-operation, and semantic communication begins to accompany the affective communication of pitch, pressure and volume of vocalization. Directives as well as prohibitions begin to be expressed and understood.

At about this time babies often begin to balk at being inhibited, and to tease with respect to compliance. Exasperated parents will describe a toddler's playful opening of cabinets, for example, or persistent climbing. Though this increasing parental control of behaviour does not necessarily dampen the child's 'love affair with the world' at this stage, there must certainly be a beginning sense of disapproval of some behaviours. While the increase in intentionality and need to preserve autonomy are often in conflict with needs for behavioural control, there are also developmental thrusts towards socialization, compliance and self-control.

We see during this period growth in positive identifications with parents, tendencies to emulate, expressions of empathy, and other prosocial behaviours, with manifestations of pleasure in co-operativeness and shared activity. Restraints and prohibition may be turned into a game which converts contention to co-operation. The toddler spontaneously manifests imitative identification with adult behaviour. Many complex relatively autonomous behaviours such as self-feeding, co-operation in dressing, etc. are evident, and autonomous strivings in these areas typically elicit parental approval. Social-referencing becomes frequent; the toddler looks to the parent, seeking affirmation and encouragement. Superego precursors develop from positive as well as prohibiting identifications, from internalization of parental approval and support as well as limits and restraint. Positive identifications are doubtless necessary for superego formation and stability.

It is important to note, however, that not all early identifications are ultimately incorporated as superego content. It is with astonishment, for example, that parents often become aware of their identifications with their own parents, as they find themselves enacting with their children their own parents' behaviours. They comment that they are doing exactly what they had vowed they would never perpetrate on their own children. Children identify with despised as well as idealized and beloved aspects of the object. Thus the potential for superego inconsistency and disharmony begins very early.

Many pro-social behaviours are self-initiated, with little threat to autonomy, but result from autonomous actions of the child. For example, toddlers will go to the aid of an injured child, displaying empathic response to the child and identification with the caregiver. The roots of pro-social superego precursors can be seen in empathy, in identification with the mother's ministrations, and her comforting, and consoling (Furer, 1967), as well as in her support for the youngster's helpful and empathic behaviour. The role of aggression has been emphasized in superego development, but identification with the benevolent comforting parent is also significant (Schafer, 1960). This benevolence and appropriate approval is important to the emergence and gradual internalization of superego precursors.

Parental approval and disapproval are conveyed to the toddler in myriad forms and, closely linked to this, a beginning sense of good and bad emerges. This is related as well to the overall affective tone of the relationship. Until there is a firmly established sense of self and considerable capacity for self observation, the toddler cannot distinguish parental disapproval of a particular action from a more global disapproval of the child. Disapproval of a discrete behaviour is experienced as rejection and accretions of these experiences contribute to a primordial good or bad self feeling. This feeling reflects the prevailing parental attitude of approval or disapproval, though influenced by the child's internal state, temperament, and ego development.

The junior toddler's sense of permission or prohibition is dependent on the presence of the object. One infant may furtively throw food off the table, and say 'no'. The prohibition is remembered and partially internalized, but not yet stable and effective. Another toddler (the same child who in the first year was so attentive to the subtlest of direction), when prevented from throwing food from one side of the high chair, with a mischievous look threw the food from the other side. Another toddler at seventeen months crouched under the table and defaecated while saying, when discovered, 'I'm not doing something' and averted her gaze. The child, not yet being toilet trained, but identifying with a slightly older sibling, in the presence of the caregiver enacts impulse, but communicates some understanding of the rules.

Beginning with the middle of the second year, issues of behavioural control become ever more significant. Parental expectations, in concordance with the child's growing capacities, shift; positive compliance becomes expected, in addition to inhibition of forbidden behaviours. There is often a beginning expectation of control over affective expression as well; the toddler is expected to learn to tolerate a modicum of frustration without undue crying. The youngster who is having a tantrum may be further reprimanded. On the other hand the child has become increasingly wilful for a variety of reasons. Contributing to the child's wilfulness is the growth of both representational capacity and capacity for planful behaviour. By about 1½ to 2 years of age the toddler, in play behaviours, demonstrates planfulness, for example, by announcing intentions or searching for a component needed to carry out the play act. Goals are remembered; out of sight is not out of mind any longer.

In Piaget's outline of cognitive development (1947), object permanence has been attained, and the toddler will search and reach for hidden objects retained in memory. Attention is no longer readily diverted. The need for autonomy has also become pressing; as self-representation is developing, the achievement of the goal is no longer desired just for the end in itself, and inhibition often seems to be experienced as an assault on the self. There is a sense that not only is the goal important, but one's capacity to create and carry out a goal is an essential and treasured component of the precarious and still consolidating sense of self. The self as agent encompasses motives, plans, and purposeful, goal-directed behaviour, with wilful persistence. At this stage inhibition of the toddler's intent not only generates crying, but aggressive behaviours towards the caregiver are increasingly evident. The toddler defends both separateness and wilfulness, and is afraid of passive surrender (A. Freud, 1952); (Mahler et al., 1975).

Not only are intentions remembered at this phase of development, but the toddler is capable of remembering what behaviours are encouraged or prohibited. Rules have been generated and partly learned, and parents expect them to be respected; parental attitudes towards violations of rules may be different from those towards prohibitions at earlier phases when the infant is not expected to remember or comply. During the second half of the second year, in addition, the toddler is achieving greater ego competence and language is rapidly expanding in quantity and complexity. Fantasy appears, and the rudiments of intrapsychic conflict emerge (McDevitt, 1987). The environment is ever fascinating and the little explorer can find numerous ways of getting into 'mischief'. The conflict at this stage represents far more than the momentary prohibition or demand, and numerous interpersonal issues are involved in each encounter. Mothers, fathers, and other caregivers elicit different responses to similar demands or prohibitions. The way in which parental expectation and behavioural control are communicated and learned, with evolving internalization, is particularly important during this period. There are conflicting desires for parental approval and needs for autonomy. How these issues are negotiated can be crucial for many aspects of development, particularly precursors of the superego and drive vicissitudes.

Initially the infant cannot differentiate between prohibitions regarding personal danger, prohibitions regarding injury to material things, prohibitions regarding injury to others, or other expression of aggression. In the beginning of the second year there is only beginning discrimination of the difference between biting the care-giver, assaulting another toddler, grabbing a toy, and spilling a cup of milk. Gradually the toddler comes to know that violation of different sorts of rules will have different consequences. The degree to which these distinctions are made is very much dependent on the variations in parental response in different situations, as well as on development of cognitive and communicative capacities.

One can speculate that in the earliest stages of parental limit setting, the child does not yet understand these distinctions. Parental disapproval will, nevertheless, be internalized as a superego precursor even though what is prohibited is unrelated to moral issues. Later in the second year of life the toddler becomes more capable of making distinctions regarding the parental communications that were earlier on impossible. The simple 'no' or bodily removal of the first year has been expanded to more complex admonitions. The youngster also begins to distinguish between parental preferences and strong prohibitions. Growing capacities to communicate and to symbolize are associated with a beginning sense of future and past and understanding of behavioural sequences. Words increasingly amplify affective expression and permit greater specificity of communication.

Because of the child's drives, defences and ego immaturity, however, the superego precursors may be far removed in quality from the external reality of the caregiver's attitudes and intent. Fantasy elaboration is associated with misinterpretation of parental intent. Parens (1979) describes the aggression generated by the frustration of the toddler's early autonomous strivings. The aggression then begets the need for further control, escalating the conflict. Aggression in parent and child is a major factor in the quality of the superego precursors. The toddler's aggression projected onto the parent will predispose toward a harsh punitive superego. Projection of aggression and fantasy elaboration of anticipated disapproval and punishment lead to the 'talion principle', e.g. fears of being abandoned, eaten, etc. The parents' actual attitudes and frustration tolerance, affection, and consistency, etc. remain important for identification and the later taming of shame and guilt.

The toddler who is constantly reprimanded for only minor infractions may experience disapproval in form and intensity which does not promote discrimination of behaviour which is in fact difficult, rebellious, and problematic. Rules and limits are thus confused and readily compromised and the lack of approval with a predominance of reproach may lead to rigid, sadistic, and retaliatory tendencies. The toddler may feel unsupported in normal strivings for autonomy and may not experience the approval necessary for stable identification with parental standards.

Of prime significance in the altering of behaviour and internalization of rules is the parents' affective accompaniment to limit setting; the child's perception and internalization of himself/herself as good or bad, approved of or disapproved of, has to do with broad aspects of object relationships and behaviour, still not with moral issues at this stage. The caregiver's communication of approval or disapproval determines goodness, or badness, right or wrong. This *anlage* of morality did not escape Freud, (1939, p. 119) who observed, 'Later on, when Society and the super-ego have taken the parents' place, what in the child was called "well-behaved" or "naughty" is described as "good" and "evil" or "virtuous" and "vicious"'. Both the prohibitions and restraints, their fantasy elaborations and distortions, and the sense of self as good or bad become internalized. From the perspective of developing superego precursors, disapproval may be experienced as badness, regardless of the meaning and intention of the behaviour. Only much later will these early notions of good and bad develop into moral concepts of good and evil and moral judgements of right and wrong.

Izard (1978) discusses fear and guilt as motivators, stating that both limit behaviour, but we feel only a germinal form of guilt is present. Frequently the infant is in fact seemingly fearless. Although fear is evoked in infants by some perceptions, for example, the visual cliff or the presence of a stranger, in many other instances the concept of danger must be taught by the caregiver, instilling fear. Depending on definition, fear and anxiety cannot yet be differentiated. Stranger anxiety in the presence of the caregiver is influenced by the attitude of the caregiver towards the stranger, and vice-versa.

Shame develops as an affect during the second year of life and becomes a significant reaction. It implies an observer and an observed self, and retains links to both the later ego ideal and superego, to the intrapsychic and the interpersonal. Provence (1978, p. 295) notes that shame can 'mobilize responses that assist the child in the development of impulse control, which in turn enhances the self and self concept'. Izard (1978, p. 398) states 'shame anticipation motivates the development of skills and competence that increase self-worth and decrease the likelihood of experiencing shame'. Similarly the anticipation of any painful affect would motivate the toddler towards behavioural control, and the capacity to anticipate is a crucial step in cognitive development. Shame may, however, flood the ego and severely inhibit. Erikson (1968) emphasizes the antithesis of autonomy versus shame and doubt. Guilt as a specific superego affect is a later acquisition though present as a 'potential' in germinal form (Blum, 1977).

The issue of being good and bad has particular reverbations during the rapprochement phase, with its consolidating internalizations of self and object. Mahler (1975, p. 330) notes that, beginning in the rapprochement period, 'the fear of object loss is partly relieved by internalization, but this is complicated by the introjection of parental demands; this not only indicates the beginning of superego development, but it also expresses itself in the fear of losing the object's love. This fear in turn manifests itself in a highly sensitive reaction to approval and disapproval by the parent'. Rage at the frustrating object may be especially threatening before the integration of good and bad object representations, i.e. before object constancy has been achieved. The toddler's fears of abandonment or retaliation, related to his/her own aggression, are sometimes reinforced by actual parental threats, at times of conflict, and the toddler is threatened, as well, by loss of love and fear of punishment. Mahler (1975) has noted that during rapprochement the toddler is subject to the confluence of the three great anxieties, loss of the object, loss of love, and castration anxiety. The developmental impact of castration anxiety in this pre-oedipal period has been described by Galenson & Roiphe (1971).

Of particular importance at this time, as we have previously indicated, is sensitive negotiation of conflict and appropriate limits, between caregiver and child. Interpersonal conflict now reciprocally influences intrapsychic conflict. The toddler's sense of omnipotence is deflated at this time and a more realistic sense of self is developing. It is important that autonomy be protected rather than violated, that neither child nor parent always win the battle. Neither party is regularly victorious or defeated, but the child must understand those issues as not subject to compromise. Sensitive parents avoid many a battle by setting limits without unduly violating the youngster's need for autonomy. On the other hand parental psychopathology can seriously compromise the process of negotiation and integration of superego precursors.

Case Example

Conflict with respect to setting limits for her 2-year-old child became apparent in the analysis of a previously anorexic mother with depressive tendencies. The area of eating, generally self-regulated according to bodily need with no inherent moral relevance, became, under the influence of parental psychopathology, involved in a power struggle with serious implications regarding adequate development of superego precursors and behavioural control in other areas.

The patient had been concerned about the kind of parent she would become. For many anorexics pregnancy and parenthood precipitate eating disorder and/ or depression because of demands for adult nurturance and caregiver responsibility and fears of depletion (Garfinkel & Garner, 1982). This patient was fearful of insufficient weight gain during pregnancy and of starving her baby in utero. She had been over-concerned during the first year regarding her infant's feeding, while restricting her own diet. The 'overfed baby' and 'starved self' formed a dyad with many meanings. For example, the self-sacrifice and desire to over-feed 'over-compensated' for maternal hostility and reactively defended against unconscious dependent, devouring attitudes. There was a split between the nurturant and withholding self and object representations.

Symptomatically, the previously anorexic mother attempted to induce bulimia in her infant, the anorexia and bulimia representing two sides of the same inner conflict. Her infant was unconsciously regarded as a narcissistic object governed by the mother's fantasies more than the infant's needs in many areas.

In the second year the child defined a separate identity and was more wilful and determined. The mother was sensitive in some areas, but insensitive in others, and she and her child read and misread each other's signals. True feeding battles ensued, possibly precipitated by the child's slight weight loss, during gastroenteritis. This mother again became fearful of her child being 'starved'. She attempted to over-feed, bribed, cajoled, coerced, and tried to trick the child into additional intake. The toddler rejected the food, which this mother experienced as a personal rejection and as a blow to her self-esteem. Her toddler's good eating meant she was a good mother and signified their mutual love. He would not 'swallow' the mother's anxiety and anger, but dawdled over his food, becoming a highly selective and finicky eater. The mother could not say 'no' to herself and stop her 'feeding fight'. She was also unable to say 'yes' to the toddler, permitting him to eat what he wanted. Although overly controlling with respect to her child's intake, she could not say 'no' to his regular protraction and derailing of meals. They had become a pair of 'gluttons for punishment'. The mother became increasingly enmeshed with the child even as he struggled to preserve autonomy through refusal. Feeding was not a matter of hunger and satiety, but rather a power struggle, endowed as well with elements of good and bad—to eat mother's food was generally good and not to eat was bad.

In the second half of the second year and then into the third, these power struggles continued, often escalating into crisis. The struggle was expressed with regard to play as well as eating. The child's separateness and autonomy from his mother was ambivalently wished and feared, ardently avoided and bitterly defended. Thwarted in an area usually governed by self-regulation, impaired regulation intruded into other areas, with inconsistent acceptance of limits. Battling his mother's coerciveness, the youngster was a 'holy terror' in nursery school; refusing to accept teachers' reasonable limits, he banged and broke toys. He 'controlled' the teacher in his infantile mode, refusing instruction and limits, extending the battle at home with his mother.

Gradually the child's impulse control and ability to respond to limits, rules, and regulations improved markedly. This occurred consequent to beneficial oedipal reorganization and to parallel improvement in the mother as a positive effect of her analytic treatment. As she gained insight into her conflicts, she was able to set appropriate limits and permit appropriate autonomy.

Although we have illustrated a particular form of pathological dyadic relationship, resolution of issues of autonomy and control is all too often to some degree problematic. Parents are extremely variable in the ways that they deal with these issues. The infant conveys its own demands and intentions, and then reads and negotiates parental communications about the nature, intensity, and seriousness of parental demands and commands. Parental directives are often mixed messages, and the toddler's compliance is tentative and not reliable. First orders may not be obeyed, and modest bids for the toddler to 'listen', to 'pay attention', may be followed by escalating insistence. The mixed message from the parent may become louder, clearer, and more coercive, or at other times may be forgotten. The toddler learns that mere parental preference is not the same as imperative 'orders from the high command'. The problem of sorting out mixed messages, while not symmetrical in the parent-infant relationship, exists for both parties. When edicts and orders, however, are non-negotiable, the toddler must accept 'no' for an answer and then internalize the 'no'.

Feeling coerced, the toddler at this stage is typically coercive as well, demanding that the parent do his/her bidding. In problematic relationships mixed messages may become double binds or no-win situations. Appropriate compliance is rewarded and reinforced, and defiance is discouraged with disapproval, loss of love, and/or punishment. Empathy on both sides permits feeling the other's distress, adding to and partly deriving from the infant's identification with parental attitudes and admonitions. Empathy with the object's distress, with parents or peers, probably depends on some experience of parental empathy. While empathy may avoid or mitigate a clash of wills, empathy is lost as clash or crisis ensues. Empathy and trial identification are preconditions for more advanced morality and the capacity for remorse and later for apology (Arlow, 1989). As development proceeds, the child can anticipate the parental distress a transgression would cause, furthering internal regulation.

At some point reciprocity emerges, related to higher levels of negotiation. 'If you withdraw this demand or yield on this issue, I'll yield here, or compensate there; if you do this (e.g. get ready for bed), I'll do that' (read you a story). This reciprocity is coincident with increasingly sophisticated monitoring of the self and object, and greater capacity for self-regulatory modulation of behaviour. Internalization of parental rules and regulations proceeds with increasing selfregulation and 'inner direction'.

The difficulties of the rapprochement period can be seen as due not only to issues of separateness, but to the clash of inner and self-determined function and the environmental pressures to comply. The more problematic the limit setting, and the greater the battle for compliance, the more a punitive mother and negative self may be internalized. 'In those children with less than optimal development, the ambivalence conflict is discernible during the rapprochement subphase in rapidly alternating clinging and negativistic behaviours … as "ambitendency"—that is, as long as the contrasting behaviors are not yet fully internalized. This phenomenon may be in some cases a reflection of the fact that the child has split the object world more permanently than is optimal into "good" and "bad" (Mahler et al., 1975, pp. 107–8). Such a split will perforce impede the development of self and object constancy, but also superego development. The battles over separateness and helplessness are complicated by the battles over 'good and bad' and by power struggles.

The toddler's needs to relinquish omnipotence, to begin to tame narcissistic demands, and to control aggression in this phase are matched by the caregiving controls and directives, and emotional attunement and availability. The clash of wills may greatly complicate and contribute to the rapprochement crisis and the negative basic mood. These battles may leave parent and child emotionally exhausted. A battle for control, 'who's boss', and withdrawal of affection may be concurrent with the rapprochement crisis. If these struggles are not successfully negotiated, they may be the forerunner of later psychopathology and character disorder. The admonitions and prohibitions both contribute to and yet threaten separateness and independence. External controls and criticism are directed to a separate entity, and the clash of wills defines self-object boundaries, and yet intrudes across boundaries and may engulf autonomy.

The issues of separateness, identity, and autonomy are intertwined. During this period increasing awareness of self is apparent. The child has begun to use the first person pronoun, referring to himself/herself, and by 2 the possessive 'mine' is typical. Not only is definition of self enhanced in the experience of self as a wilful person, capable of external refusal, but also in saying 'no' not only to others but to one's self (Spitz, 1965), attempting to control one's own behaviour. By the end of the second year there is increasing understanding of expectations and admonitions. While, during this period increasing intent of the child to control his/her behaviour is evident, the presence of the parent or caregiver is generally required. Earlier prohibitions may be remembered and partly internalized, but true internalization of standards of behaviour has not yet taken place and there is only incipient capacity for self-criticism. As Anna Freud noted (1936, p. 119), 'true morality begins when the internalized criticism now embodied in the standard exacted by the superego, coincides with the ego's perceptions of its own fault'.

With the achievement of object and self constancy, there is presumably also stable internal representation of standards of acceptability, of permission, and prohibition. As development proceeds, external control gives way to partially internalized prohibition still permitting enactment, limits depend on the external presence of the object, on the object as conscious internal presence, and finally to internalized representation of authority. With such internalization the child utilizes inner injunctions and directives, and is not simply at the mercy of impulse or afraid of 'getting caught'. In these developmental acquisitions, the role of language and symbolization becomes increasingly important for structuralization and mastery of conflict. The look of approval or disapproval, beaming or berating, is transformed into 'true voice of conscience'.

Internalization is never complete, and the superego is subject to regression and to modification throughout life.

There is wide variation with respect to individual and sub-cultural attitudes regarding obedience and compliance, with different weights and values attached to such aspects of behaviour as appropriate assertiveness, competence, and autonomy, versus conformity and compliance. Some parents feel it's important early on to let the child know who's boss; conflict is confronted head on. Others are so lax or inconsistent regarding limit setting that the youngster feels unprotected as it learns the limits of its competence. As the child emerges from the home environment and parental purview, however, the behavioural standards of the larger subculture must be met. There are marked differences both in the pace of various aspects of development as well as in endowment. Issues of match between parent and child which change with developmental phase are paramount. Ultimately the modulation and transformation of the drives and spontaneous strivings by the object world and superego precursors subserve and facilitate the process of individuation. The individuated toddler can to an increasing degree observe and control his/her own behaviours and affects. The modulation of autonomous strivings requires a degree of individuation and contributes to its further consolidation.

Summary

Superego precursors appear in the latter part of the first year, concomitant with the behavioural control necessitated and made possible by ego development, particularly of intentionality, communication, and mobility. During the second year of life wilful strivings intensify, complicated by the power struggles of the rapprochement crisis. A subtle process of negotiation accompanies the learning of parental rules and regulations, and the infant also learns that some rules and limits are non-negotiable. The development of the superego depends not only on 'identification with the aggressor' and self-directed aggression, but on positive identifications and internalizations of approval.

While the real attitudes of the caregiver are communicated and are important, superego precursors, because of the infant's drives, defences, and ego immaturity, may be far removed from the reality of the caregiver's attitudes and intent. The parents' and infants' inter-identifications and empathy for each other contribute to the capacity for self-criticism, guilt, and remorse, attributes of the developing superego.

REFERENCES

Arlow, J. (1989). Psychoanalysis and the quest for morality. In *The Psychoanalytic Core: Essays in Honor of Leo Rangell,* ed. H. Blum, E. Weinshel. R. Rodman. New York: Int. Univ. Press.

Blum, H. (1977). The prototype of preoedipal reconstruction. *J. Am. Psychoanal. Assoc.* 25:*757–786.*

——— (1985). Superego formation, adolescent transformation, and the adult neurosis .*J. Am. Psychoanal. Assoc.* 33:*887–910.*

Erikson, E.H. (1968). *Identity. Youth and Crisis,* London: Faber Faber.

Freud, A. 1936 The Ego and the Mechanisms of Defence. *Writings II* New York: Int. Univ. Press.

——— (1952). A connexion between the states of negativism and emotional surrender. *Int. J. Psychoanal.*33:*265.*

Freud, S. 1923 The ego and the id .*S.E.* 19.

——— (1939). Moses and monotheism. *S.E.* 23.

Furer, M. 1967 Some developmental aspects of the superego .*Int. J. Psychoanal.* 48:*277–280.*

Galenson, E. & Roiphe, H. (1971). The impact of early sexual discovery on mood, defensive organization, and symbolization. *Psychoanal. Study Child* 26:*195–216.*

Garfinkel, P. & Garner, D. (1982). *Anorexia Nervosa: A Multidimensional Perspective.* New York: Brunner Mazel.

Hartmann, H. (1939). *Ego Psychology and the Problem of Adaptation.* New York: Int. Univ. Press, 1958.

Izard, C. (1978). On the ontogenesis of emotions and emotion-cognition relationships in infancy, In *The Development of Affect,* ed. M. Lewis. L. Rosenbaum. New York: Plenum, pp. *389–413.*

McDevitt, J. (1988). The emergence of intrapsychic conflict during the separation-individuation process. Mahler Symposium Paper, Philadelphia, May 1988.

Mahler, M. (1975). On the current status of the infant neurosis *J. Am. Psychoanal. Assoc.* 23:*327–333.*

——— Pine, F. Bergman, A. (1975). *The Psychological Brith of the Human Infant. New* York: Basic Books.

Parens, H. (1979). *The Development of Aggression in Early Childhood.* New York: Aronson.

Piaget, J. (1947). *The Psychology of Intelligence.* NJ: Littlefield, Adams.

Provence, S. (1978). A clinician's view of affect development in infancy. In *The Development of Affect,* ed. M. Lewis. L. Rosenbaum. New York: Plenum, pp. *293–307.*

Schafer, R. (1960). The loving and beloved superego in Freud's structural theory *Psychoanal. Study Child*15:*163–188.*

Spitz, R. (1965). *The First Year of Life.* New York: Int. Univ. Press.

CHAPTER 14

The Clinical Value of Daydreams and a Note on Their Role in Character Analysis

(1995). In *On Freud's Creative Writers and Day-Dreaming*,
Eds. S. Person, P. Fonagy, & S. Figueira. New Haven,
CT: Yale University Press, pp. 39–52.

The publication of *Creative Writers and Day-dreaming* (Freud, 1908) was a landmark in the application of psychoanalysis to culture. The paper deals with the wish-fulfilling functions of fantasy, and Freud indicated that the wish-fulfilling character of dreams could have been derived from the similarity of dream and daydream. Considering the characteristics of daydreams and how the artist softens the character of his daydreams by altering and disguising them, Freud also introduced the dimension of defense. Daydreams are characterized by conscious wishes and defenses, and the paper may be regarded as an introduction to the study of conflict and compromise formation. The creative writer "bribes us by the purely formal—that is, aesthetic—yield of pleasure which he offers us in the presentation of his phantasies. It may even be that not a little of this effect is due to the writer's enabling us thenceforward to enjoy our own day-dreams without self-reproach or shame" (p. 153).

Freud noted that the source of artistic creation may be found in fantasy, and also that collective or shared fantasies could be found in the common fairy tales of childhood, and in the myths and legends of nations. These fantasies, especially those associated with repressed wishes, could be found in the underlying symptoms and personality disorders of neurotics. Beneath the distortions of dreams, daydreams, and symptoms were the same unconscious wishes and conflicts of childhood.

261

Daydreams usually afford a high yield of pleasure, comparable to the "castles in the air" of the child, and may be regarded as intimate, cherished possessions. Freud noted that the products of fantasy change over time and receive a "date mark" with every fresh impression. The daydream, or conscious fantasy, hovers among three moments of time: that is, it is linked to some current depression, harks back to a childhood experience, and creates a future situation that represents a wish fulfillment. The paper is thus an important contribution not only to the psychology of fantasy but also to aesthetics, as well as to formulations of pathogenesis and psychoanalytic reconstruction.

Freud considered the relationship between daydreams and play, and he observed that the two activities parallel and mirror each other. The child takes his play seriously, and "the opposite of play is not what is serious but what is real" (p. 144). The creative writer is like a child at play, and language preserves the relationship between children's play and drama. Like the daydream, the poem or drama links past and present, fantasy and reality, internal demands and extemal concerns. In the daydream, the individual is relatively awake and conscious of both the daydream and reality and of the daydream as distinct from reality. Freud (1911) later noted that the daydream is dependent upon the development of the sense of reality. He linked the emergence of conscious fantasy, associated with the pleasure principle, with the development of the reality principle. The daydream, or conscious fantasy, was described as a reservation, like Yellowstone Park, which had been reclaimed from the regulation of the reality principle.

In the childhood of psychoanalysis, Freud's pioneering elucidation of daydreams may be regarded as a prototype and paradigm for the later psychoanalytic study of the structure, functions, and meanings of fantasy. There is a spectrum of fantasies arising during altered states of consciousness, such as hypnogogic and hypnopompic fantasies, transference fantasies arising during free association on the couch, and fantasies of the waking state. In the 1908 daydream paper Freud did not discuss the distinctions between different types of conscious fantasy. He did not attempt to distinguish between transient or fleeting fantasies and relatively stereotyped, enduring daydreams that had persisted from childhood or adolescence into adult life. Prior to the consideration of daydreams as a compromise formation among the tripartite psychic structures, they were understood as a compromise not only between wish and defense but also between the repressed past and present interests.

The role of the daydream in artistic sublimation was outlined in Freud's 1908 paper, but not the role of the daydream in adaptation to reality as a form of trial action or rehearsal for and planning for real action, or as a form of experimental object relations. Actually, Freud's prototypical paper on daydreaming could be updated in view of later advances in psychoanalytic theory and knowledge of development. Thus, the daydream is not only to be distinguished from what is real but is also related to the suspension of reality and the leave of absence from reality that are at the heart of pretend play (Waelder, 1932; Peller, 1954). Both fantasy and play were safe from influences in the real world. This would be later understood in terms of freedom not only from reality consequences but also from self-criticism and superego condemnation.

Indeed, the capacity for make-believe occupied an intermediate position between fantasy and reality and allowed for a continuation of infantile omnipotence and magical control in the creation of fantasy and fantasy play (Winnicott, 1971). The daydream as conscious fantasy may be enacted in play, while the daydreams of a later life replace children's play. Much of what Freud said about play also applies to the typical daydreams of children, especially the wish to be big and grown-up, which Freud emphasized as a determining wish of child play. One reason given by Freud for the adult's becoming ashamed of his fantasies is that they are childish. What would later be characterized as the superego attitude toward the daydream is described in terms of the daydreams becoming impermissible.

Freud noted that daydreams occur with equal frequency in both sexes, but that in women they are invariably of an erotic nature, while in men they are either erotic or ambitious. The heroine is thus erotically motivated, but the man's heroic exploits in his daydreams are achieved only to please a woman and to become her favorite among male rivals. These statements betray the date of their composition and no longer represent psychoanalytic thought on the subject. Both sexes may have narcissistic, ambitious, and homosexual daydrearns as well as all other forms of fantasy. Sex and gender tend to influence the dominant daydream themes, as in pregnancy fantasies. The relation of fantasy to ego mastery evolved more slowly, parallel with the development of structural theory and interest in ego function. Fantasy and its enactment in play could serve to turn passive into active and aid in the mastery of traumatic experience through repetition. The repetition itself could be controlled and modulated, and the traumatic experience given a more satisfactory outcome.

In a companion paper, "On Hysterical Fantasies and Their Relation to Bisexuality" (1908b), Freud further commented on daydreams and specifically on the relationship between fantasies and symptoms. It is of interest that Freud (1908b) stated that

"every hysterical attack which I have been able to investigate up to the present has proved to be an involuntary irruption of daydreams.... Our observations no longer leave any room for doubt that such fantasies may be unconscious just as well as conscious; and as soon as the latter have become unconscious they may also become pathogenic.... In favorable circumstances, the subject can still capture an unconscious fantasy of this sort in consciousness" (p. 160).

Despite the importance of daydreams for the understanding of creativity and psychopathology, it is fascinating to note that Freud's 1908 statement that they have received insufficient notice in the literature still holds true today. Daydreams are not regularly described in clinical reports or continuous case seminars, and they have not been explicitly the subject of psychoanalytic panels and symposia. It is dreams that have occupied center stage in psychoanalytic theory, practice, and education. The theory of dreams and the interpretation of dreams are taught in institutes, and in supervision, and are often included in sessions presented for a supervisory conference. The lack of attention to daydreams by analysts as well as patients may be partly responsible for the paucity of discussions of daydreams at analytic meetings and in the analytic literature. Everyone daydreams, and many daydream during meetings and the presentation of papers, but daydreams are neglected in favor of other matters. Except for transference fantasies, typical daydreams have been devalued, while dreams tended to be accorded exceptional significance in analytic work (Greenson, 1970; Blum, 1976; Brenner, 1976).

The daydream cannot really be differentiated from conscious fantasy and has been submerged in broader studies of fantasy. A particular class of daydream, masturbation fantasies, has received special attention, and many daydreams are altered and disguised transformations of masturbation fantasies. Freud (1908) emphasized not so much how the daydream mediates between internal pressures and the demands of reality as how the daydream compensates for unsatisfied internal wishes and reality disappointments. The complex derivation of daydreams and the relation of daydreams or conscious fantasy to unconscious fantasy awaited much later elucidation and a metapsychology of fantasy (Sandler and Nagera, 1963).

Like the dream, the daydream *per se* does not belong to psychopathology. The capacity to fantasize is a developmentally necessary achievement, and aids reality adaptation. However, as Freud and later Winnicott (1971) noted, excessive immersion in fantasy and excessive flight into fantasy or from fantasy may represent pathological tendencies. Today we understand that daydreams may be repetitive, compulsive, and addictive. Some of the early illustrations of daydreams by Freud (1908b) indicate that they may be transient and fleeting or long-lasting and enduring, they may be burdensome or playful, and they may be experienced not only as pleasurable but also as intrusive and unpleasant. Not just erotic fantasies but also narcissistic, aggressive, and punitive fantasies are common. There are daydreams of coercion and enslavement, retaliation and revenge, and rescue fantasies sometimes associated with traumatic assault.

The typical fantasies of the family romance may be understood, as Freud (1908c) described in another companion paper, as compensation for oedipal disappointment and narcissistic injuries. Self-aggrandizement and wishes for idealized parents in an idealized childhood are regularly found in the transformed hero, heroine, and heroic figures of daydreams and fairy tales. With or without verbalization, the daydreams of children may reappear in their play, drawings, and various aspects of behavior. The hero who is threatened by the parent figure almost always emerges victorious; the conscious fantasies—that is, daydreams—were based upon a defense against and revenge for castration threat, so that the adult who threatened castration ends up as castrated. In typical daydreams, the forbidding adult or authority figures are overcome, the hero or heroine finds magical protection and reassurance against all the dangerous situations of development, and injured narcissism and self-esteem are restored.

In other situations, however, as in masochistic, self-punitive, and otherwise dysphoric daydreams, the daydream may be consciously experienced as unpleasant, although there may be hidden unconscious gratifications. In treatment, the daydream always has a transference dimension, and the patient's attitude toward the daydream, the telling of the daydream, and the style of daydreaming, are replete with significance. The form and content of the daydream may prominently indicate defenses and adaptive functions. The vulnerable child becomes the invulnerable hero or irresistible heroine; the child succeeds while under the protection of an omnipotent bodyguard, fairy godmother, or guardian angel.

In her very first paper, "Beating Fantasies and Daydreams," Anna Freud (1922) described the complex developmental vicissitudes of conscious and unconscious masochistic fantasy that Freud (1919) first elucidated in "A Child Is Being Beaten." She showed how masochistic fantasies linked to central masturbation fantasies were gradually tamed in their elements of punishment and torment, shorn of their connection with sexual excitement and masturbation, socialized, and then narrated as "nice stories." The perverse masochism took on a masochistic character without manifest sexual gratification. The transformation and taming of the sadomasochistic and punitive content was associated with what would later be called progressive ego and superego modification and the development of sublimation. "The sword had been beaten into the plowshare," and the author could now share the previously forbidden fantasy with an audience, providing pleasure for both author and audience. This achieved internal approval instead of self-reproach, and additionally provided narcissistic rewards and social recognition.

This type of repetitive, stereotyped, enduring daydream, in this case a masochistic fantasy, is of special interest for purposes of this essay.

Daydreams have been regarded primarily as reflecting suppressed aspects of the personality organization, without consideration of character trends or their possible organizing effect or formative influence on the personality. Daydreams that persist through developmental phases may not only reflect character but may also influence character formation. Character development is vastly overdetermined, but it has long been known that there is a close relationship between unconscious fantasy and specific character traits. In the case of a masochistic character, for example, unconscious beating fantasies may be regularly anticipated, and some masochistic patients have retained conscious beating fantasies.

However, the role of the conscious masochistic daydream persisting from childhood into adult life, with or without accompanying sexual arousal and masturbation, has been little explored for its influence on character formation. Such daydreams have been understood as ego-edited manifestations of the unconscious sadomasochistic fantasy constellation but not as developmentally significant in their own right. The organizing influence on character development has been attributed primarily to the persisting unconscious fantasy. The possible developmental influence of the persisting daydream has only been hinted at, though some patients attempt to live out their daydreams or protect against their worst fantasies as major life themes. Close to self and conscious experience and relinquished only with great difficulty, the persisting daydream with variations on the theme may have its own development influence. Implicated within the personality and a valued, intimate possession of the personality, the enduring stereotypical daydream is linked to elusive but important issues of self, identity, and character.

One of the pioneer case reports in the psychoanalytic literature relevantly deals with the use of daydreams in child analysis and records a prescient, persistent daydream. A latency girl daydreamed of her own death. "I wish I had never come into the world at all; I wish I could die. Sometimes I pretend I do die, and then come back into the world as an animal or a doll. But if I do come back into the world as a doll, I know who I mean to belong to—a little girl that my nurse was with before, who is especially nice and good" (A. Freud, 1946, p. 21). While sibling and oedipal conflicts were elaborated, there appeared to be a childhood depression that was unrecognized or perhaps not interpreted at that early time. This latency girl's sad daydream with its dysphoric affect and defeatist attitudes proved to be representative of underlying depressive psychopathology and predictive of self-destructive tendencies. More than forty years later, under the stresses and conflicts of her middle years, this patient acted out her daydream and committed suicide.

In contemporary analysis, such daydreams would be examined in terms of psychic structure and character structure, changing self and object representations, and tendencies to enact the daydream and its derivatives in the analytic situation, and in life. Daydreams are of a particular type of compromise formation, conscious fantasies that both derive from and have contributed to unconscious fantasy (Sandler and Nagera, 1963). The importance, theoretically and technically, of unconscious fantasy has been described by Arlow (1969, 1985), who prepared the continuous elaboration of fantasy on a topographic continuum. However, it should be noted that conscious daydreams that have become subject to repression and been incorporated into unconscious fantasy are another route for the influence of the daydream on symptom, character, and personality organization.

I should now like to offer an example of contemporary analytic work with a long-persisting daydream that had special subjective significance for the patient. This daydream was very much in character and was a red thread in her psychoanalysis (Neubauer, 1993). The conscious daydream was recalled from her preteen years; she thought it had probably started during her latency, and persisted, with variations, into her adult life, including her psychoanalytic experience.

My patient's daydream was that she was acclaimed by her classmates and that first a teacher and later the student government ordered a choice of student-lover for her. Who was to love her was not a matter of chance, but not entirely her choice either; it was love by decree. She did not actively win the lover's affection, and her low self-regard was implied. When reading what various classmates had written about their achievements after college graduation, she had the fantasy, another related daydream, that her great achievement was to have had several wonderful, exciting extramarital affairs.

This "wonderful" accomplishment was allied with a "new" daydream variant in which she was a woman of irresistible beauty and charm who could compel her chosen lover to show his attraction and affection. Although these daydreams were related to her extramarital affairs and had acquired intense transference meaning, she did not develop an erotized transference to me.

This serial, regularly repeated daydream had the advantage for analysis that the patient had often thought about it and that, unlike other daydreams or dreams, it was not transient and fleeting, alien and readily forgotten. As a conscious link of the unconscious fantasy system, the daydream is also often a transformed, disguised derivative of a masturbation fantasy to which the patient has returned again and again. In this case, the linkage to infantile masturbation fantasy had been severed, but variants of the fantasy were associated with late adolescent and adult masturbation. The daydream appeared to preserve some of the compelling power and pleasure of masturbatory play. The well-organized serial daydream may have served an integrative function in aiding the patient's overall adaptation to realistic disappointments and the frustration of internal demands. As a very personal, private, and privileged drama, it was only partially egosyntonic and could be co-opted for character analysis.

This patient began analysis in her early thirties with symptoms and overt character disorder. Although she suffered from psychosomatic gastritis and spastic colitis, was chronically anxious, and tended to bite and pick at her nails, she gave her symptoms short shrift in the initial interviews. Rather, she presented a seductive, masochistic character, who had had a number of sequential and simultaneous extramarital affairs. She sought help because she was puzzled and troubled by these affairs and wondered if she might be a nymphomaniac. She was in the throes of a marital crisis, since her husband had recently learned that she had an affair with a mutual male friend. She had actually started her affairs shortly after the birth of their child, when her husband was away on business trips. She felt deserted, resentful, lonely, and in need of affection. She had never felt really pretty, popular, or desirable, and quickly agreed to her husband's marriage proposal when she was a college student. Although he did not share her educational and cultural interests, he was some years her senior and seemed sophisticated, wise, and a successful man of the world. It was only after she had difficulties rearing her children, finding herself short-tempered with the children and her husband, and unable to persuade her husband to take her with him on his trips or to be a more ardent lover at home, that she began to become disillusioned about her marriage.

Soon after she started treatment she reported this vivid, recurrent daydream dating from her preadolescence. She did not relate the daydream to her seductive behavior. She had conscious fantasies of being the equivalent of a female Don Juan but denied being aware of prostitution fantasies. She consciously related the daydream and derivative daydreams to immediate realities and recent history. She did not recognize that the daydream also referred to her childhood and her particular family experience. At first she hesitated to report it, lest it be regarded as childish and a humiliation. Subjectively, she was more embarrassed than ashamed, and there was a touch of pride about her fantasy. She was also curious about why it had seemed so gripping and important in her mental life, and was remembered and repeated with such clarity. The daydream was itself brief, and the patient did not indulge in excessive or uncontrolled daydreaming. There were initial hints of the role of the daydream in compensating for early narcissistic injury and painful experience. Bornstein (1951) described a fragment of the analysis of a child's daydream in which denial in fantasy was interpreted. The child reversed shame into glory, and the use of reversal persisted as defense against affect and impulse.

My patient's daydreams were an object of analytic interest and gradual self-inquiry, and facilitated further access to her unconscious conflicts and fantasies. Her seductive style was used to ward off aggression, to maintain omnipotent power and control, and to repair and master infantile and childhood traumata through active manipulation rather than passive victimization (Blum, 1973). Issues of coercion and control rapidly emerged. Behind the seduction were the patient's efforts to coerce her love object's interests, demand affection, and control her own and his affects and impulses and any threat of desertion or rejection. It developed that she felt most in control when she brought her partner to orgasm but she did not have an orgasm. Unconsciously she depleted and castrated the partner, rendering him helpless and impotent and arrogating his phallus and strength. She would frequently cry after orgasm because of the frustration of her unconscious longings, feeling of guilt over her promiscuity, and expectations that the partner would retaliate for her aggression and transgression. She was fearful of real and fantasied disapproval and abandonment. The crying was also a loss of control and symbolic incontinence.

So great were her guilt and grief that she tried for a long time to regain her husband's affection and to ward off the threat of divorce and rejection. In addition, she wanted to make her husband and her lovers jealous of one another with the illusion of their vying for her affection. Her seductive style and affairs seemed clearly related to attempts to overcome the exclusion, overwhelming excitement, and frustration due to primal scene and familial seduction. Her father had exhibited himself nude in front of her throughout her childhood, and both her mother and an older brother would visually and manually check on her breast development. Because of the incestuous character of many of her sexual fantasies and responses, she often had feelings of disgust and guilt when excited. Her fears of being a nymphomaniac were clearly connected to her unconscious enactment of prostitution fantasies that were both incestuous and homosexual. The daydreams were anchored in the reality of childhood seduction, overstimulation, and lack of parental limits and protection. The theme of coercion appeared repeatedly, and she attempted to dictate the frequency and length of sessions and, early in analysis, to control the timing and content of interpretations. The student government, representing her parents and later the analyst, was to coerce her siblings, especially her brother, in the forn of her classmates, to love her and to ensure her victory in oedipal and sibling peer scholastic competition.

One of the primary issues of control was, of course, impulse control. In addition, this was related to the patient's fears that she could not control her thoughts, her feelings, her behavior, and her sphincters. In her daydream, control was achieved and exercised by herself or the authorities, but in her dreams, there was a regular incontinent loss of control. She had unconscious fantasies of uncontrolled vaginal bleeding, recalling an embarrassing episode when a tampon had dropped out of her vagina. Her fantasies of being dirty and in great need of baths and perfume were regressive representations of her feeling guilty, "unclean," and having degraded herself. Afraid of her own aggressive wishes to soil and degrade, she was also afraid of being the object of filthy insults and humiliations. She then revealed that her fear of not having sufficient sphincter control and of being rejected like feces and flatus had sometimes led her to give herself an enema before a date. In this way, she both lost control and assured herself that she would be in control and would invite approval rather than disparagement.

The coercion and incontinence then appeared in a new light concurrent with maternal transference and reconstruction of the mother-daughter relationship of her childhood. Her mother, hitherto described as warm, buxom, cultured, and ambitious for her daughter, was now also seen as coercive, controlling, and intrusive. The patient had been subjected to rigidly timed feedings, rather rigid toilet training, and stringent rules and regulations concerning speech, play, bedtime, and so forth. Her mother had also given her frequent enemas, supposedly because of the patient's gastrointestinal disturbance in childhood. The gastrointestinal disturbance, in retrospect, appeared to be a reaction to the mother 's rigid regulations, intrusive attitudes, and bodily invasion, robbing the child of independence and autonomy of her body functions. The enemas were both exciting and enraging, and were repeated in life as self-administered. Her extramarital seductions could be compared to seduction traumas representing her mother's anal rapes and homosexual seductions in heterosexual guise. The heterosexual "nymphomania" masked and defended against her wishes for, and fears of, homosexual attachment. The severe narcissistic injuries associated with her childhood traumata were compensated in her daydreams of coercive love and irresistible beauty.

Discussion

Within the analytic process, this patient's daydream is closer to the analytic surface and to issues of defense, style, and character than dreams or fantasies during markedly altered states of consciousness. As a siren and seducer of choice, this patient did not appear to be degrading and self-denigrating, and she consciously considered herself far from prostitution. She was not aware of the intensity of her masochism and self-defeating trends. Her narcissistic facade featured her illusory presentation of herself as a desirable, giving, and alluring playmate, and a socially sophisticated companion. She could socially excel, conquer, and temporarily succeed in winning her hero. Her daydream was actually closer to her conscious character and ego style, to her efforts at mastery and sublimation, than her dreams.

The daydream is Janus-faced in its regressive and progressive tendencies. Related to trial action, the daydream may be prelude to actual alterations of reality and behavior that may be irrational or rationally constructive. The daydream may be acted out in the service of wish fulfillment and defense, and it may function as a form of regression in the service of the ego, facilitating artistic and scientific creativity. Although daydreams turn away from and suspend reality, they paradoxically also permit and plan return to reality. Hartmann (1939) particularly indicated the role of fantasy in an adaptation to reality, and in the imaginary, experimental manipulation of reality. Character is closely related to a patient's habitual mode of adaptation to outer reality and consolidated compromise solutions to conflict. Analytic work with this patient's daydream and its variations, especially as they evolved in the course of analysis, contributed to the resolution of her character pathology.

It is not only the pleasure associated with the persisting daydream that makes the daydream a treasured and tenaciously retained possession. It is also the integrative aspect of this type of daydream with its relation to adaptation and character and its closeness to self and conscious experience. Patients do not tend to report their daydreams because they belong to a very private part of the self. Since daydreams are under the patient's conscious control and are conscious creations, the patient feels personally responsible for them, and they are paradoxically both egosyntonic and egodystonic. The egodystonic dimension of the daydream makes it more accessible for analysis than other aspects and expressions of character pathology. This patient's obsessive control and omnipotent coercion were analyzed in the transference and in the reconstruction of her enactment of the daydream in life. Her characteristic daydream became a vehicle for character analysis.

As a childish creation, not fully compatible with adult ideals and values, the daydream is likely to be reported with embarrassment, shame, and humiliation. Unconscious guilt may be inferred, but the feelings exposing private and childish aspects of the secret self usually involve shame and defenses against shame. Shame that is reversed and turned into glorified heroism may be a latent part of the daydream, but it should be borne in mind that the attitude toward the daydream changes with the advancing development phases of life. The adult, as Freud (1908a) noted, is ashamed of his or her childish creation. As a blessing and burden, the daydream allows the patient to turn defeat into victory and to triumph over trauma, while repeatedly experiencing the gap between illusory idealization and ordinary life.

The daydream is a part of this patient's idealized self and could not be relinquished without the renunciation of magical control and infantile omnipotence. Her infantile omnipotence was a dimension of her narcissism and masochism and was fundamentally related to her characterological preoccupation with control and coercion. Her character pathology in its different forms and her persisting, organized, and organizing daydream could not be relinquished without the analytic taming of her infantile omnipotence.

A final word may be said about the complementary daydreams of the analyst. The analyst daydreams about the patient during and after the analysis, which provides valuable sources for his or her self-scrutiny of countertransference and for self-analysis. Calder (1980) noted the closeness of daydream to immediate experience: their being ego-syntonic, their accessibility to self-observation and study, and hence their value for self-analysis. There has also been an analytic group countertransference in the lack of attention and reports about the daydreams of patients and analysts. The analyst's daydreams may be a source of insight about his or her own conflicts as well as those of the patient, and will reflect aspects of his or her character and ego style. The observing ego and the experiencing self are at the conscious center of daydreams. The self is almost always at the center of the daydream drama.

This contributes to defense against exposing the daydream and to renewed awareness of its clinical and theoretical importance.

REFERENCES

Arlow, J. (1969). Unconscious fantasy and disturbance of conscious experience. *Psychoanal. Q.* 38:1–17.

––– (1985). The concept of psychic reality and related problems. *J. Amer. Psychoanal. Assn.*33:521–535.

Blum, H. (1976). The changing use of dreams in psychoanalytic practice: Dreams and free association. *Int. J. Psycho-Anal.* 57:315–324.

Bornstein, B. (1951). On latency. *Psychoanal. Study Child* 6:279–285.

Brenner, C. (1976). Psychoanalytic technique and psychic conflict. New York: International Universities Press.

Calder, K. (1980). An analyst's self-analysis. *J. Amer. Psychoanal. Assn.* 28:5–20.

Freud, A. (1922). Beating fantasies and daydreams. In *Writings* 1:137–57. New York: International Universities Press, 1974.

––– (1946). *The Psycho-analytical Treatment of Children*. London: Imago.

Freud, S. (1908a). Creative writers and day-dreaming. *S.E.* 9.

––– (1908b). Hysterical phantasies and their relation to bisexuality. *S.E.* 9.

––– (1908c). Family romances. *S.E.* 9.

––– (1911). Formulations on the two principles of mental functioning. *S.E.* 12.

––– (1919). A child is being beaten: A contribution to the study of the origin of sexual perversions. *S.E.* 17.

Greenson, R. (1970). The exceptional position of the dream in psychoanalytic practice. *Psychoanal. Q.* 39:519–549.

Hartmann, H. (1939). *Ego Psychology and the Problems of Adaptation*. New York: International Universities Press.

Jones, E. (1955). *The Life and Work of Sigmund Freud*. New York: Basic Books.

Neubauer, P. (1993). The clinical use of the daydream. Presented at the panel: Clinical Value and Utilization of the Daydream, American Psychoanalytic Association, December 1993.

Peller, L. (1954). Libidinal phases, ego development, and play. *Psychoanal. Study Child* 917:178–198.

Sandler, J. & Nagera, H. (1963). The metapsychology of fantasy. *Psychoanal. Study Child* 18:159–96.

Waelder, R. (1932). The psychoanalytic theory of play. In *Psychoanalysis: Observation, Theory, Application: Selected Papers of Robert Waelder,* ed. R. Guttman, 84–100. New York: International Universities Press.

Winnicott, D. (1971). *Playing and Reality.* New York: Basic Books.

CHAPTER 15

The Writing and Interpretation of Dreams

(2000). *Psychoanal. Psychol.*, (17)(4):651–666.

Freud's (1900/1953a) magnum opus, "The Interpretation of Dreams," largely based on the self-analysis of his own dreams, incorporated a wide variety of source material. Concerned about exposure and discretion, he nevertheless published his dreams with many personal associations and revelations. Despite the self-analytic, research, and educational value of his written dreams, Freud paradoxically devalued written dreams in clinical psychoanalysis. Written dreams can be preserved, collected, compared, and reexamined. Writing dreams protects against forgetting the dream with its unconscious representations. Written dreams of patients are not simply resistance or enactments, but analytic communications with transference countertransference significance. A clinical vignette exemplifies use of the written dream in attempted ego mastery of unconscious trauma and conflict.

This is the centenary of Freud's (1900/1953a) "Interpretation of Dreams," in its day a revolutionary treatise, now one of the great books of the ages. The book was a landmark, inaugurating psychoanalysis, as well as a landmark in the history of ideas. Freud, in what is generally regarded as his masterwork, altered the way people understand dreams, themselves, and human nature. The book was also a major contribution to the history of ideas—"We are such stuff as dreams are made on" (Shakespeare, "The Tempest," Act 4). Dreams were reported and deemed to be significant from the beginning of recorded time. The oral and written communication of dreams is part of ancient history as well as the history of psychoanalysis. In antiquity, dreams were given special significance as messengers from the Gods, divine omens with prophetic and clairvoyant powers. The dream as a vivid visual hallucination was endowed with the conviction of reality that sometimes persisted into waking life as a mystical influence.

The first known recorded dream dates from about 2500 BCE in Mesopotamia, and there are also dreams dating from ancient Egypt. The supreme importance attributed to dreams and the idealization of dream interpretation was apparent in ancient Greece. Dreams were brought to the Delphic oracle, the renowned motto of which was "know thyself." Dreams were associated with healing as in the cult of Aesculapius. The Temple of Aesculepius at Epidaurus had votive tablets that described the cure effected by the particular dream. Aristedes, an afflicted devotee of the healing cult of Aesculapius, left a record of 200 dreams. He contacted Aesculapius in a dream and, pertinent to this article, he was ordered to create a journal of dedication: The most important ancient dream book was that of Artemidorus (2nd century CE). This book of dream analysis, to which Freud referred, was also written as instructed in a dream (Kilborne, 1987). Dream interpretation had social, medicinal, prophetic, and religious importance with implications for self-knowledge.

The interpretation of dreams could be used for diagnosis, prognosis, and proper treatment. Thus, although dreams in antiquity were often idealized, they could also be devalued as nonsensical. Aristotle (350 BCE) was among later writers who considered dreams as natural rather than supernatural phenomena. The tendency toward the idealization and devaluation of dreams continued as dreams were considered by many scientists and physicians prior to Freud as being babble, the irrational product of a sleepy mind in a sleeping brain. Since the publication of the "Interpretation of Dreams," which first appeared on November 4, 1899, dreams were given an exceptional position by Freud and the pioneer analysts. The dream in the "id phase," the childhood of psychoanalysis, was the preeminent path to achieving the analytic goal of making the unconscious conscious. Freud, however, would soon caution about the analytic abuse of dreams, writing about dreams as resistance and as an art for art's sake. Many theoretical and technical developments were yet to be formulated. In the recent past the exalted position of dreams would be challenged. In the era of ego psychology, some analysts considered dreams of no more value than any other analytic data, now a time-worn debate (cf. Blum, 1976; Brenner, 1976; Greenson, 1970). Different from other data, dreams often have special access to unconscious fantasy. Unconscious fantasy in general later became a central focus of interpretation (Arlow, 1979).

Freud identified with the biblical Joseph who interpreted dreams of prophetic importance and who was duly elevated and rewarded for his dream analysis. Joseph achieved the prestige and position accorded to analysts in the post World War II era of idealization. Although Freud (1923/1961) later warned against the overvaluation of dreams and their technical misuse, he always returned to dreams as having personal importance to him. It is known that he created a scrapbook of dreams in his childhood and wrote dream fragments on scraps of paper, a process that continued before and after his writing "The Interpretation of Dreams." Freud's early notebooks on dreams were either lost or destroyed, but he kept notes of his own dreams during medical school. Writing to his future bride, Martha Bernays, on July 19, 1883, he mentioned a blissful dream of a landscape, "which according to the private notebook on dreams which I have composed from my experience indicates traveling" (Jones, 1953, pg. 351). About 225 dreams are reported in "The Interpretation of Dreams," of which only about 50 are Freud's. However, it is Freud's dreams that are most intensively and extensively discussed and analyzed. Freud later made this observation:

I soon saw the necessity of carrying out a self-analysis and this I did with the help of a series of my own dreams which led me back through all the events of my childhood and I am still of the opinion today that this kind of analysis may suffice for someone who is a good dreamer and not too abnormal. (Freud, 1914/1957, p. 20).

Freud had reclaimed dreams from popular beliefs, magic, and mysticism. He made the interpretation of dreams a point of differentiation between those who had become or could become psychoanalysts, and those for whom dreams remained incomprehensible. In the preface of the second edition of the dream book (which appeared in 1908), Freud stated, "it has always been the interpretation of dreams that has given me back my certainty" (Freud, 1900/1953a, p. XXI). He later asserted (Freud, 1913/1958a, p. 170) that "dream interpretation is the foundation stone of psychoanalytic work." He referred to the dream as a "sheet-anchor" and stated, "Whenever I began to have doubts of the correctness of my wavering conclusions, successful transformation of a senseless and muddled dream into a logical and intelligible and mental process ... would renew my confidence of being on the right track" (Freud, 1933/1964, p. 7).

Freud may have been in transient altered states of consciousness during his work on the dream book. He wrote to Fliess, "I shall force myself to write the dream in order to come out of it" (Masson, 1985, p. 278). Immersed in writing "The Interpretation of Dreams," Freud wrote to Fliess (Masson, 1985, p. 305), "I can compose the details only in the process of writing." A "writing cure" has been suggested (Mahony, 1994), emphasizing the importance writing had for Freud. Freud attributed writing his dreams to the dictation of the unconscious, although his own inner self-reflection, his vast reading, and his intellectual inquiry are evident throughout the book. "The Interpretation of Dreams" was contemplated for years, was written over more than a year's time, and was subjected to successive later revisions. New material and footnotes were introduced in every new edition; the largest of the additions pertained to symbolism. Unfortunately, the original manuscript of "The Interpretation of Dreams" was discarded, lost to posterity like so many of Freud's manuscripts. Ever passionate about books and publications, Freud did not hesitate to correct page proofs or to demand royalties from the publishers of the subsequent editions of the dream book.

Freud's dreams recalled and his writings of dreams were already a translation of his own memories, self-observation, and inner speech. He had the facility for recalling the dream imagery and for organizing the visual images into meaningful patterns. Freud had been interested in language development and disorder long before—for example, having published "On Aphasia" in 1891 (Freud, 1891/1953b). He had noted that dreams in some respects are closer to hieroglyphics and a rebus than to actual written verbal language. One may conclude that Freud's symbolic processes were especially well endowed in pictorial, iconic, and linguistic intermodal capacities. The interpretation of dreams required the capacity to think and remember pictorially, to understand unconscious symbols and their perceptual referents, and to be able to freely translate from the pictorial to linguistic symbols and back again from linguistic symbolic processes to the visual imagery of the dream. Freud's eidetic, remarkable memory potentiated the synthesis of retrieved, isolated memories and their integration into reconstructions of his childhood.

The writing block Freud experienced as he proceeded with his dream work became an incentive to self-analysis, the inhibition gradually subsiding during further self-analysis. The writing block was overdetermined by a number of unconscious childhood conflicts connected with Freud's need to communicate. This need as well as the capacity to communicate are evident in Freud's voluminous scientific papers and documents and his almost unsurpassed quantity of letters. He abjured dictating to impersonal secretaries and later to the use of the typewriter and preferred writing by hand. His correspondence was answered promptly and meticulously with the use of a ledger. One of his many complaints about America after his 1909 visit to Clark University was that his handwriting had deteriorated. Writing was associated with the flow of body fluids, with procreation, fertility and creativity, and with the conflicts of all developmental phases. His writings were influenced by his real and transference relationship to Fliess, as well as by anxieties connected with writing his dreams and his associations for publication.

As a transference figure, Fliess represented Freud's childhood object representations, especially an initially idealized parent. In reality, Fliess was granted an intimacy and authority to which Freud adapted in degree, the relatively "secret sharer" of his ideas and propositions. Perhaps another transference figure would have been found if the Fliess relationship had never evolved. Yet Freud was his own analyst and patient and progressed with and without Fliess, helped and hindered by the external collaboration (Blum, 1990). As Freud's brainchild, psychoanalysis was a narcissistic object, and this would become a problem for those of his followers who were identified with his person rather than his analyzing functions and his quest for analytic mastery. The idealization of the dream in analysis was also an idealization of Freud.

Editorially influenced by Fliess, "The Interpretation of Dreams" was to be ready for publication on the birthday of Fliess. It was to be a birthday present celebrating the birth of psychoanalysis. Similarly, Freud had referred to his pregnant wife's own birthday celebration in his write-up of the initial specimen dream, now called "The Irma Dream"; Freud identified with the pregnant mother and with creative individuals. Fliess had a paucity of publications, and the dream book would far surpass Freud's previous prolific and influential writings. (Mahony, 1994) All of Freud's teachers are referred to in his dreams, but it is Freud who is there as the teacher, narrator, and explorer of the forbidden and alluring unconscious mind.

In the dream book Freud's life and work coalesce. Why did Freud use his own dreams and exhibit to the world so much of his own private life? One can have only partial answers. It is known from his publications and his private correspondence that the issues of private versus public were highly conflicted. Freud (1900/1953a, p. 104) remarked about the difficulties he had to overcome within himself: "natural hesitation about revealing so many intimate facts." Readers would be initially interested, Freud thought,

> in the indiscretions which I am bound to make…. I am obliged to add however, … that in scarcely any instance have I brought forward the complete interpretation of one of my own dreams, as it is known to me. I have probably been wise in not putting too much faith in my reader's discretion. (Freud, 1900/1953a, p. 105)

So much is concealed, and so much is revealed, and so much continues to be unearthed despite Freud's reluctance and decision against full disclosure. Subsequent generations of analysts and historians have made Freud an icon, an exceptional object of investigation. Freud had already destroyed many of his documents in 1885 and 1907 and again when departing from Vienna in 1938. He indicated that he intended to make things difficult if not impossible for biographers. In contrast to his scientific papers, Freud's correspondence was never intended to be public. In the correspondence, Freud still consciously and unconsciously selected and edited his material.

In the dream book Freud engages his reader, inviting and exciting the reader's curiosity. His own dreams and those of the others in the book are used as teaching tools for the edification of the public and the education of future psychoanalysts. Was Freud's personal exposure a form of self-sacrifice? He had frequent dreams of appearing naked in public. Exhibitionism was sublimated and transformed in his mature desire to disseminate his discoveries and to achieve scientific success, fame, and fortune. He was willing to courageously confront scorn and derision in the service of his scientific and scholarly objectives. although infantile narcissistic motives can be discerned in Freud's wish for his book to be recognized as a stunning achievement and a revolutionary new humanistic psychology, similar motives are present in virtually every revolutionary thinker. Confronting the unconscious and the infantile, "The Interpretation of Dreams" Does in fact remain a masterpiece of education, exposition, clarification, and insight. In 1931, in the preface to the third revised English edition, Freud stated of the dream book, "It contains even according to my present day judgment, the most valuable of all the discoveries that it has been my good fortune to make. Insight such as this falls to one's lot but once in a lifetime" (Freud, 1900/1953a, p. XXXII).

Noting that the same piece of dream content may conceal different meanings in different people in different contexts, Freud was led to his own dreams because they

offer a copious and convenient material, derived from an approximately normal person…. No doubt I shall be met by doubts of the trustworthiness of self-analyses of this kind; and I shall be told that they leave the door open to arbitrary conclusions. (Freud, 1900/1953a, p. 104).

Dreams were found in normal persons; everyone dreamt, although it was not then known that everyone dreams several times during every night. Freud relied more on his own dreams than any other source of material. He was probably more confident in his self-knowledge acquired by his self analysis than he was in the more superficial and shorter analyses of patients prior to his writing the dream book. His own written dreams could be preserved, collated, compared, and later reexamined by himself and others.

Freud's interpretation of his own dreams is sometimes concentrated in one section of the dream book, as in the specimen dream (Irma dream). References to his dreams are scattered throughout the dream book and are used to illustrate different dream mechanisms and meanings. Although the diffusion of comments about his dreams may have served greater anonymity, it also placed a confident Freud throughout his magnum opus. At times Freud later revealed that an anonymous dream was his own, as in the dream that the Pope was dead (Freud, 1900/1953a, p. 232; Grubrich-Simitis, 1996).

Freud's initial work on dreams may also have been facilitated because dreams are relatively ego alien compared with walking thoughts and fantasies. They are perhaps first easier to contend with as foreign phenomena, yet harder to understand as strange, perplexing productions. Many persons feel more responsible for their daydreams than their dreams, and indeed Freud recorded 10 times as many of his dreams as his daydreams. Dealing with more unconscious, primary process derivatives, Freud's self-dissection of his dreams resulted in troubling insights that were lost and found again, isolated and reintegrated (Rangell, 1987).

Freud asked not only the indulgence but also the intense interest of the reader in his dreams and in their dreamer. This made Freud the object of analytic inquiry that he simultaneously disclaimed. He stated

And now I must ask the reader to make my interest his own for quite awhile, and to plunge along with me, into the minutest details of my life; for a transference of this kind is peremptorily demanded by our interest in the hidden meaning of dreams. (Freud, 1900/1953a, pp.105–106).

This invitation was bound to be frustrating because some details were withheld, that is, censored. Even while he lifted the censorship from the meanings of dreams, Freud exercised selective censorship and permitted Fliess to be an external censor and editor. Identifying the readers with himself and his mentors, Freud attempted to overcome doubts and to open the readers' minds and lift the tendency to censor his own and their own fantasy life and unconscious conflicts.

Freud took pride in his own composition, accomplishment, and radical creativity. Like so many artists, he has provided a great self-portrait. As Freud attained an analytic identity, a transformation was also occurring in the history of ideas and in the way people think about their thoughts and feelings. Dreams were used to illustrate the relationship of the dynamic unconscious to consciousness and the unseen relationships between dreams, neuroses, and the structure of the human mind. The manifest content of both dreams and symptoms hid and disguised repressed wishes. Repressed wishful fantasy was further obscured by the primary process mechanisms of condensation, displacement, and symbolization. The surface of dreams is a variably disguised facade, a compromise formation with deeper significance representing wishes and motives derived not from mature adult life but from childhood and infantile life.

Although Freud allowed for a different mechanism for traumatic dreams and nightmares, he generally attempted to subsume the variety of frightening, punitive, and persecutory dreams under the rubric of disguised and prohibited wish fulfillments. He identified with Moses, a prophet presenting a new message and a new method for the comprehension of humans' most primitive impulses, conscious and unconscious moral principles, and cultural values. For Freud, derivates of unconscious fantasy emerged in transference, and pictorially in dreams. One picture could be worth a thousand words. "'The Interpretation of Dreams' is the royal road to a knowledge of the unconscious activities of the mind." (Freud, 1900/1953a, p. 608) The road was not only a path to the exploration of primary relationships and primal scenes, but an unconscious return to or merger with the maternal body, the ineffable navel of the dream. The navel was unfathomable and may also have meant the undifferentiated psyche and the nascent mind. He wrote to Fliess on August 6, 1899 (Masson, 1985, p. 365), "The whole thing is planned on the model of an imaginary walk." The royal road was the great analytic journey through the different phases of development and of life, recapitulated in dreams. The dream represents past and present, childhood and current conflict. The dream itself is a metaphor for the forward journey through adulthood and the analytic as well as regressive journey of the dream back into childhood. The dream book has manifold references to parent and child, adult and infant, birth and death.

Freud's capacity to interpret dreams and his special gift of correlating so many different forms of symbolic processes were probably unique. Even today little is known about such exceptional persons with special endowments, special motivation, and fortuitous development that facilitates originality and creativity. Freud was a visionary, and "The Interpretation of Dreams" his vision. As a dreamer, he has had a profound influence, and psychoanalytic thought has permeated virtually all aspects of culture while becoming the basis of all rational psychotherapies. The dreamers and visionaries who are truly creative are ordinary mortals in life, although immortals in their work. They have to deal with their own conflicts about being so original, with infantile omnipotence supported by reality. They are so different and yet in so many ways ordinary people with ordinary frailties.

The command or urge to write the dream appears to be connected to the search for power, mastery, and significant communication with oneself or others. The written dream was to be read and understood, increasing self knowledge, with psychoanalytic insight eventually replacing the ancients' foresight. The regressive narcissistic omnipotence of the ordinary dreamer could be projected onto the dream or the childhood objects in the dream, transferred to the gods or figures in the external world. Through this process the dream in ancient times acquired a grandiose and divine significance.

A century after Freud, with less narcissistic investment in that first journey into the dream world, it is known there is no royal road without resistance. The dream book itself remains far more complicated and profound than it may superficially appear, even to the informed reader. Current neurophysiology is consistent with much of Freud's dream theory, and it appears that infantile emotional memories may be permanently registered in the brain (Le Doux, 1996). Dreams, despite their more recently elaborated psychology and neurobiology, still retain some of their mystery. "The Interpretation of Dreams" will be periodically reinterpreted and revised in its timeless journey.

Despite its research importance in the development of psychoanalysis, the written dream was soon designated as acting out and as a resistance in the analytic situation. Freud paradoxically adopted a negative attitude toward the written dream in psychoanalytic treatment. Despite his own use of the written dream, and apparently recommending it to Anna Freud, he stated

Even if the substance of a dream is in this way laboriously rescued from oblivion, it is easy enough to convince oneself that nothing has thereby been achieved for the patient. The associations will not come to the test, and the result is the same as if the dream had not been preserved. (Freud, 1911/1958b, p. 96).

Abraham (1913) regarded the patients writing down their dreams as departing from the fundamental rule of psychoanalysis. He emphasized the return of the resistance in attempts to salvage the dream because the writing was either illegible, discarded, or nonproductive of usable associations.

Psychoanalytic writing about written dreams, other than Freud's own, has been sparse. Whitman (1963) dissented from the dismissive attitudes of Freud and Abraham and suggested that for some patients the written recording of dreams is definitely useful in psychoanalytic treatment. He theorized that dream forgetting is due not so much to resistance as to a functional demand that the ego cannot meet. On awakening, the confrontation with reality results in shifts to secondary process thinking, to external perception, and to motor activity that is incompatible with the dream state. According to Whitman, the patient may find it helpful to record a fraction or all of the dream, thereby overcoming the tendency to forget the dream.

In my experience, some patients do not remember dreams or are little attuned to dreams or both. Writing them may be an initial effort to make them available for analytic work. Both dream reporting and the writing down of dreams will be influenced by the analyst directly conveying an interest in dreams or urging the patient to try to recall or to write down the dream. A patient may spontaneously write a dream or dreams just as a patient may spontaneously bring diaries or other personal documents into the analytic work. The analyst need make no specific interdiction against writing, and any written dream can be handled analytically in the context of its spontaneous production. As noted by Lipschutz

(1954), the written dream will prove to have a powerful transference significance. Although any dream may be designed to please or placate, confuse or deceive the analyst, putting the dream in writing may be an attempt to confer upon it special authority and endurance. The fact that the dream has been written and the surrounding circumstances must be considered analytically in addition to the analysis of form, content, and associations. In addition to the function of preventing forgetting, multiple unconscious meanings are associated with the writing of the dream. It should be emphasized that the dream may signify any object, part object, narcissistic object, or body process or product. Thus the written dream may have in addition to its function of protection against loss of the dream the unconscious protection against loss of whatever memories and objects or aspects of the self the dream represents.

As with all dreams, the form, style, content, complexity, length, quantity, and so forth of written dreams are significant. The manifest content may be more or less a translucent envelope, a surface that may reveal, conceal, or both. Some dreams are passively given to the analyst without interest or effort at further inquiry by the patient. The patient's associations, a knowledge of the patient's life, the phase of treatment, the state of the transference, and the particular ability of the patient and the analyst to engage the dream in the context of the analysis are all important considerations. The written dream is not necessarily an impediment but can be addressed as an analytic communication in all its aspects (Blum, 1968).

The conflicting opinions of Freud himself and those of later analysts concerning the written dream indicate the importance of clinical exploration. Using the following clinical vignette, I consider many of the controversial issues regarding the written dream and its meanings in the analytic process. A female patient in her second analysis rarely brought dreams to her analytic sessions. Although she had briefly kept a childhood diary, she had never before in her analysis come with any written material, nor had the analyst ever suggested that she record her dreams. After 3 years she walked in and handed the analyst a piece of paper announcing that she had had a sleep disturbance. She woke recalling the dream, and immediately decided to write it down before it would be forgotten. The written dream was as follows:

Was in house which was attached to other houses almost like apartments. Heard series of blasts—one of which tore down one of my walls. I ran into garage as place of safety. Next running in street—looking for somebody— later thinking it may have been children. I asked policeman what it was all about. Policeman said we were being bombed. Later I didn't recall asking the policeman; I seem to feel I may have imagined loud noises.

She originally told the dream in the morning to her children who were under active consideration for psychotherapy. The children were underachieving in school and manifesting behavioral disturbances.

The patient had an obsessional character, her spastic colitis was active, and in her associations she proceeded to blast friends for being selfish and indifferent to her difficulties. She had argued with her husband about money at breakfast. The analyst interpreted her hidden aggression in the analytic situation and her avoidance of argument with the analyst. The patient immediately recalled that she had intended to bring in the check for analytic payment but had forgotten. She was always angry that she had to pay. The police represented arrest and punishment for attempted robbery as well as protection from her aggression and fear of retaliation. The analyst pointed out that she had written the dream instead of the check, she had brought in the written dream instead of bringing in the forgotten check. Although the dream was an apparent gift, it was covert withholding. Associations further led to the analyst handing her a written piece of paper, the bill, which contributed to this exchange of notes. She had been handed a written bill, and in turn handed the analyst the written dream. Her written dream was therefore also a mocking, hostile identification with the analyst rendering the bill. In writing the dream she guarded against forgetting the dream and turned her hostility into the passive aggressive forgetting of the check.

The patient was actually quite ambivalent to her children, projecting her own infantile demands onto them. After payment of the bill, she was frequently irritable with the children, arguing over extra cookies, unable to be loving and giving. Afterward, guilty over her withholding and provoking, she would overindulge the children. She developed cramping diarrhea and felt empty and depressed with thoughts of "I would rather die than pay." Not acknowledging her own greed, envy, and spiteful withholding, she felt that she was being castrated and robbed of food and body contents. One difference in her second analysis was that she was presented with a written bill, whereas her first analyst had invited her to tally her own sessions and to pay accordingly without receiving a bill. They colluded in avoiding "the fight over the fee." With frequent associations and analytic observations, patterns of withholding and reluctantly giving emerged; she then revealed that her husband had cheated his analyst by continuing to pay a markedly reduced fee long after his income had greatly increased. She was therefore also identifying with her husband. Her husband had urged her not tell her analyst their true income and attempted to financially obstruct the analysis. Having cheated his analyst, her husband's premature ejaculation continued after his analysis possibly as a basic form of cheating and withholding from the partner. While consciously annoyed at her husband's symptomatic dishonesty, she was unconsciously pleased by her feelings of superiority. He represented the men in the family whom she wished to humiliate and have arrested and punished for what she thought was their mistreatment of her.

The communication of the dream to her children was a desire to provide police protection from her aggression toward them as well as to attack them. One child unconsciously represented an ambivalently regarded deceased brother, and the other, herself. By going into treatment, they would create financial difficulties and possibly bomb her out of her own analysis. The bombing and looking for the children is consistent with the written message as an ambivalent gift of feces and baby, also representing doing and undoing, birth and death. She also withheld her infantile aggression and longing for love. Much more could be said about the relationship of this written dream to traumatic experiences of childhood illness and object loss. Suffice it to say that childhood conflict linked to the patient's adult character and symptoms were related to her need to protect and defend against renewed loss and injury and to obtain reparations and revenge for her troubled life.

The writing of the dream obviously defended against forgetting, which could represent loss at all phases of development (Kanzer, 1955, 1959; Lewin, 1953). Her preoccupations with overeating and dieting, constipation and diarrhea, and in analysis with silence and speech were all related to problems of separation individuation with preoedipal issues of receiving and withholding, give and take. Reverberations of separation-individuation conflict could be inferred from the dream. The collapsed wall referred to the patient's anxiety about loss of ego boundaries, separation anxiety, anger, and oscillating between dependent and independent strivings.

During latency the patient's problems gave rise to a learning block and difficulty in doing her homework, in completing writing assignments. Her written dream was therefore also a disguised communication to the analyst concerning the revival and resolution of her learning block in analysis and her ongoing use of analytic reeducation. Perhaps the converse of slips of memory and of the pen, her written dream was a form of homework that took the place of direct analytic work in the analytic situation. She wanted the approval of her parents for completing a homework assignment. Analytic work continued in the session while avoiding the oral report of the manifest dream. The writing of her dream imagery superimposed an advanced form of secondary process thought, and a secondary elaboration of the immediately remembered dream. It could also be understood as an attempt at mastery of trauma, restoring the dreamer's sense of reality, control, and ego organization. The writing externalized on paper her frightening thoughts, feelings, and dream fantasy. In her manifest dream, she "ran into the garage as a place of safety," and in the written dream she took refuge from a fantasized attack and counterattack superficially represented by the analytic "battle of the bill."

Writing her dream may also have represented an ambivalent attachment to the writing analyst who writes papers and discussions, stimulating the patient's admiration, envy, and criticism. The patient wanted and feared to be included in the analyst's writings.

The written dream has aspects of a dream from above (Freud, 1923/1961). It is variously controlled, censored, and communicated in a form that lacks the rich variety of associations and accompanying nonverbal communications of the orally verbalized dream in the analytic situation. It has intense transference and countertransference implications. Any departure from the usual framework invites the analyst's collusion in possibly subverting the analytic process.

In the person with creative endowment, the written dream may become a form of active ego mastery of conflict and trauma that leads to sublimation. Kafka, for example, was a novelist who wrote his dreams, used them as a source of creative inspiration, and wove them into his literary activity. The elaboration and communication of the written dream in literary art permits the sharing of forbidden fantasies with the reader. The writing out of the dream should not be regarded simply as an acting out. It may also serve containment, control, and regulation of tendencies to act out. The written word may suppress and substitute for the concrete deed. A private nightmare can then be converted into socially approved and interesting fiction.

The writing and presentation of the dream is an attempt to preserve object relations and communication. Choosing the written rather than the oral mode of presenting the dream to the analyst has multiple meanings, both conscious (e.g., in order not to forget) and unconscious. The written dream may particularly convey an edited version of earlier conflicts concerning reading and writing, silence and enactment. Written to be read by analyst and analysand, it converts monologue into dialogue and interpretive discourse. Freud's writing "The Interpretation of Dreams" was such a dialogue with the reader.

REFERENCES

Abraham, K. (1913). Should patients write down their dreams? In *Clinical papers and essays on psycho-analysis* (pp. *33-35*). New York: Brunner Mazel.

Arlow, J.A. (1979). The Genesis Of Interpretation. *J. Amer. Psychoanal. Assn.* 27:*193–206*.

Blum, H. (1968). Notes on the written dream. *Journal of Hillside Hospital*, 2 & 3:*67–68*.

——— (1976). The Changing Use of Dreams in Psychoanalytic Practice—Dreams and Free Association. *Int. J. Psycho-Anal.57:315–324*.

——— (1990). Freud, Fliess, and the Parenthood of Psychoanalysis. *Psychoanal Q.* 59:*21–40*.

Brenner, C. (1976). *Psychoanalytic technique and psychic conflict*. New York: International Universities Press.

Freud, S. (1900). The interpretation of dreams, *Standard Edition 4*.

——— (1891). *On aphasia*. London: Imago.

——— (1911). The handling of dream interpretation in psychoanalysis. In *Standard Edition* 12:*89–96*.

——— (1913). The claims of psychoanalysis to scientific interest. *Standard Edition* 13:*163–190*.

——— (1914). On the history of the psychoanalytic movement. In *Standard Edition* 14:*1–66*.

——— (1923). Remarks on the theory and practice of dream interpretation. In *Standard Edition* 19:*109–122*.

——— (1933). New introductory lectures on psychoanalysis. *Standard Edition* 22:*3–182*.

Greenson, R.R. (1970). The Exceptional Position of the Dream in Psychoanalytic Practice. *Psychoanal Q.39:519–549*.

Grubrich-Simitis, I. (1996*). Back to Freud's texts*. New Haven, CT: Yale University Press.

Jones, E. (1953). *The life and work of Sigmund Freud (Vol. 1)*. New York: Basic Books.

Kanzer, M. (1955). The Communicative Function of the Dream. *Int. J. PsychoAnal.36:260–266*.

——— (1959). The forgetting of dreams. *Journal of Hillside Hospital*, 8:*74–85*.

Kilborne, B. (1987). Dreams. In M. Eliade (Ed.), Encyclopedia of religion (Vol. 4:pp. *482–492*). New York: Macmillan.

Le Doux, J. (1996). The emotional brain: The mysterious underpinnings of emotional life. New York: Simon & Schuster.

Lewin, B. (1953). The forgetting of dreams. In R. Lowenstein (Ed.), Drives, affects, behavior (pp. *191–202*). New York: International Universities Press.

Lipschutz, L.S. (1954). The Written Dream. *J. Amer. Psychoanal. Assn.*2: *473–478*.

Mahony, P. (1994). Psychoanalysis–The writing cure. In A. Haynal & E. Falzeder (Eds.), *100 years of psychoanalysis* (pp. *101–120*). London: Karnac.

Masson, J. (Ed.). (1985). The complete letters of Sigmund Freud to Wilhelm Fleiss. Cambridge, MA: Harvard University Press.

Rangell, L. (1987). Historical perspectives and current status of the interpretation of dreams in clinical work. In A. Rothstein (Ed.), *The interpretation of dreams in clinical work* (pp. *3–24*). New York: International Universities Press.

Whitman, R.M. (1963). Remembering and Forgetting Dreams in Psychoanalysis. *J. Amer. Psychoanal. Assn.*11:*752–773*.

CHAPTER 16

The Confusion of Tongues
and Psychic Trauma

(1994). *Int. J. Psychoanal.*, (75):871–882.

ABSTRACT: 'The confusion of tongues' characterized the polarised dimensions of the closing Ferenczi/Freud communication, and extended to problems of psychoanalytic formulation and publication. There were manifest and latent issues which remain of historic importance. Ferenczi was dying and assumed Freud was dying when he wrote this classic essay so relevant to contemporary psychoanalytic thought and controversy. Denying and sometimes acknowledging his progressive, fatal illness, Ferenczi made enduring contributions to the understanding of child abuse and trauma while severely traumatized. Concepts of trauma and countertransference were amplified and expanded. Freud remained remarkably creative while physically declining with oral cancer; Ferenczi manifested progressive and regressive trends, fostering both sublimated innovation and wild analysis. Psychoanalysts tended to avoid, for half a century, confronting the problems of the ill, impaired, and dying analyst. The clarification of 'The confusion of tongues' continues in contemporary psychoanalytic discussion and debate. The paper presaged a widened interest in the analyst's analyzing functions, unconscious communication, countertransference, and the interplay of reality and fantasy inside and outside the psychoanalytic situation.

The history of psychoanalysis illuminates developmental changes within the field and our evolving concepts and controversies. 'The best way of understanding psycho-analysis is still by tracing its origin and development' (Freud, 1923, p. 235). For this special occasion of the 75th Anniversary celebration of the *International Journal of Psycho-Analysis*, I have chosen to focus on one of the most important controversial papers of the past, which continues to have a significant influence on present-day analytic interests and issues. The 'Confusion of tongues' is also an important issue for the *International Journal of Psycho-Analysis* and for all analytic journals. The history of the tumultuous reception of Ferenczi's (1933) paper, 'Confusion of tongues between adults and the child is important in its own right as well as because of its later ramifications in psychoanalytic theory and technique. The original title of the paper was 'The passions of adults and their influence on the sexual and character development of children'.

This relatively brief, impassioned paper aroused a storm of protest and a babble (as well as Babel) of confusion and misunderstanding in its wake. Balint reviewed the tragic circumstances surrounding this newly-reconsidered classic and concluded that, 'The historic event of the disagreement between Freud and Ferenczi acted as a trauma on the psychoanalytic world' (1968, p. 152). 'The confusion of tongues' certainly had a dramatic impact upon Freud, Ferenczi, the 'inner circle', and the wider psychoanalytic community, but I do not believe that the analytic group suffered a mass seduction trauma. The paper did not lead to a new school of psychoanalysis, nor was there a split within the field. Some analysts were afraid of challenge to accepted theory, and felt that any threat to undermine the importance of psychic reality might undermine the safety and security of the psychoanalytic 'movement'. There was, however, confusion and contention about manifest and latent issues which are still significant. Controversy about what is a clinical fact, whether seduction is fact or fantasy, the interrelationship of psychic and material reality, how 'clinical facts' are defined, determined, and validated; how authority, identification, and idealized teachers and texts influence concept formation and transformation; whom is cited or ignored in a given context and culture are all relevant to this symposium. A confusion of tongues and profusion of theories pervade the current psychoanalytic scene.

Exemplifying the importance of the inner state of the analyst, this paper will also address the largely unrecognized, historical significance of illness in the analyst and its subtle effects on creative analytic work and interests, as well as the special clinical problems of the analyst with a fatal illness. Such trauma may influence the formation and fate of psychoanalytic ideas. I refer to the fact that the 'Confusion of tongues' paper was written by a dying analyst to his analyst, whom he considered to be dying, and with whom he was identified. Their dialogue would continue in Freud's last papers such as 'Analysis terminable and interminable' (1937), and would transcend their life and death, with repercussions and reverberations, in the contemporary psychoanalytic literature. The regression of the dying analyst often leads to confusion and disorganization, and/or in exceptional analysts, to sublimation and innovation. There is a constant interplay of reality and fantasy in life and within the psychoanalytic situation.

Ferenczi's 'Confusion of tongues' may be used to discuss the transference as genetically determined or co-created in the 'here-and-now', the influence of past and present trauma, the real relationship, the analyst as new object, and the significance and limitations of the interpersonal, intersubjective aspects of the psychoanalytic situation. For Ferenczi, the psychoanalytic situation could never be divorced from the personality of the analyst and the unconscious communications of analyst and patient. Ferenczi must be considered as one of the great exponents of the analyst's role, reactions, and influence upon the psychoanalytic process. His vision of analysis was a two-person process concurrent with a transference–countertransference intrapsychic field. His contributions to the clinical significance of trauma and the consequences of child abuse have a modern character.

Problems of analytic communication (linguistic, semantic, conceptual, translation, transformation, transference, context, politics, etc.) are particularly relevant to the 'Confusion of tongues' paper and to the historical importance of the *International Journal*. For a variety of reasons, there was opposition to Ferenczi's presentation of the paper at the 1932 IPA Conference at Wiesbaden and to the later publication of the paper. The threatened suppression or imposition of censorship elicits retrospective analytic inquiry. Many leading analysts of the day regarded Ferenczi's paper as apostasy and heresy, or in danger of discrediting analysis and serving no useful purpose, merely increasing confusion. Freud, however, was hardly likely to be seduced or threatened by new or repeated emphasis upon seduction trauma. He had noted, 'Phantasies of being seduced are of particular interest because so often they are not phantasies but real memories' (1917, p. 370), and had stated shortly before the 'Confusion of tongues' paper, 'Actual seduction is common enough' (1931, p. 232).

Freud was both disappointed in Ferenczi, considering his paper 'harmless and dumb', and protective of Ferenczi's work and reputation. Freud wrote to Ferenczi on 2 October 1932,

> *I did not want to abandon the hope that in pursuing further your work you would recognize yourself the technical errors of your technique and the limited validity of your results. (You seem to concede to my demands not to publish.) But, I free you from your promise. I relinquish any influence. I no longer believe that you will correct yourself as I corrected myself a generation ago (Dupont, 1988, p. xvii).*

Reading the history of this paper, one is again struck by the rivalry among the pioneers for Freud's affection, approval, and esteem. This may have contributed to Jones's decision to withhold publication in the *International Journal of Psycho-Analysis* in English, until its publication by Balint in 1949. While Jones may have disparaged Ferenczi as borderline or psychotic, Freud (1933) noted that all analysts were Ferenczi's pupils. Freud was impressed by Ferenczi's ideas when he was shown the clinical diary after Ferenczi's death, and one is reminded of his immediate appreciation of Ferenczi soon after they met in 1908.

It was an immediate affinity, and Ferenczi quickly became an intimate companion, often addressed as 'Dear Son'. Ferenczi was then 35, seventeen years younger than Freud. The following year, in 1909, Freud invited Ferenczi to accompany him and Jung on his voyage to America, and he later noted that it was Ferenczi who, on their walks together, sketched out the lectures which Freud gave at Clark University. They developed a close friendship and collaboration, colored by conflict and disappointment. Freud later described their relationship as a 'community of life, thought, and interests … ', 'And a number of papers that appeared later in the literature under his or my name took their first shape in our talks … ' (1933, pp. 227–228).

In addition to their analytic collaboration, there was probably some mutual analysis aboard the ship carrying them to and from America, and Ferenczi had two episodes of two to three weeks of 'analysis', or rather of analytic encounters, with Freud in 1914 and 1916. Freud assented to Ferenczi's request for double sessions, and requested of Ferenczi that there should be no analytic discussion during lunch with the family. Mentor, monitor, close friends and travelling companions, they also remained in passionate, intense correspondence, analyst and analysand.

The situation was further complicated by Freud's psychological involvement in Ferenczi's love-life. Freud may have hoped that Ferenczi would marry his daughter, Matilda. Freud visited Ferenczi in Hungary, and Ferenczi entertained Anna Freud. Ferenczi fell in love with the daughter of his own mistress and could not decide about marriage between mother and daughter. His mistress had been his patient and subsequently Ferenczi had taken her daughter, Elma, into analysis. There were a series of mutual psychological 'seductions' (Bokanowski, 1992). Struggling with his own neurotic countertransference and vicariously asking for personal analysis, Ferenczi asked Freud to take on her case. For a period of approximately three months, circa 1911 to 1912, Freud analyzed Elma, the daughter, and she then returned to Ferenczi for a brief period of analysis again. Freud had advised Ferenczi to marry the mother, Gizella (a name significant to both Freud and Ferenczi), and this was a further complicating factor. Freud may have inferred that he needed a mothering partner, but this would mean Ferenczi's marriage to an older woman, and his being childless. There were extra-analytic communications and confused roles and relationships. Additional transference significance may have resided in the various names—Ferenczi having an older brother named Sigmund, and an older sister to whom he was erotically attached, named Gizella. Moreover,

Gizella Palos had another daughter who was married to one of Ferenczi's brothers.

Ferenczi's communication and analytic collaboration with Freud was repeatedly strained, beginning with, for example, Ferenczi whining for attention and forbidding Freud to dictate his notes on the Schreber Case to him when they were vacationing together in 1910 in Sicily (24 December 1921, in Dupont et al., 1982). Transference and countertransference reactions surfaced.

Countertransference was then a daring new formulation, and Freud (31 December 1911, in McGuire, 1974, p. 476) cautiously wrote to Jung: 'I believe an article on "countertransference" is sorely needed; of course we could not publish it, we should have to circulate copies among ourselves'. Ferenczi's correspondence with Freud, his clinical diary, and the 'Confusion of tongues' paper are all complementary, but until now could not be read together.

Ferenczi's widow gave his clinical diary to Michael Balint, who wanted to publish the clinical diary and the Freud/Ferenczi correspondence concurrently. The extraordinary correspondence encompassed 1, 236 letters over twenty-five years. Since Anna Freud at that time was unwilling to publish the correspondence in its entirety, and Balint would not agree to an edited selection of the letters, neither the diary nor the correspondence was published. However, Balint also engaged in censorship, omitting several paragraphs of the clinical diary; statements by Ferenczi that were critical of Freud. The problems of idealization, denigration, and fear of being critical of or departing from authority and authorized attitudes all contributed to the confusion.

Freud remained *the* authority and model for analysts during and long after his lifetime. And the trauma that shook the analytic world was not Ferenczi's paper but the development of Freud's cancer and fears of his impending death. Freud wrote to Joan Riviere (8 May 1923),

My 67th birthday was celebrated as if it were the last, which seems, in fact, not to be excluded. I am being frank in this communication because I intend

it only for you, officially a more harmless version will be put out (Hughes, 1992, p. 273).

There was at least official, initial censorship of the possibility that Freud had a malignant neoplasm. But Freud remained extraordinarily creative during his protracted illnesses. Freud would undergo thirty-three operations prior to his death, while making major revisions and original contributions to psychoanalysis. His jaw prosthesis seriously interfered with speech, and he no longer attended Congresses or gave public papers. He also developed unilateral deafness, requiring that he reverse his position in the chair. Freud did not write of the impact of his illness on himself or on his patients, but when the Wolf-Man was threatened with the loss of his omnipotent object, he decompensated with a paranoid regression (Blum, 1974); (Halpert, 1982).

Except for a few remarks to and by individual patients, we know little of the infantile conflicts and fantasies Freud's illness must have aroused, and the inevitable anxiety and guilt, along with genuine concern that his patients must have experienced. In one of his letters to Marie Bonaparte, Freud apologized to her for having allowed his preoccupation with cancer to keep him from recognizing a transference phenomenon in her analysis. Freud admonished Eva Rosenfeld for hiding the fact that Ruth Mack-Brunswick had confided her fears about Freud's condition to her (Schur, 1972, p. 382).

Describing the pleasures in creativity that become possible through sublimation, Freud observed,

this method cannot give complete protection from suffering. It creates no impenetrable armor against the arrows of fortune, and it habitually fails when the source of suffering is a person's own body (1930, p. 80).

Analytic exploration of the analyst's illness and of the problem posed by the severely ill, impaired, or dying analyst had hardly begun. Analysts resisted confrontation with their own infirmity and mortality. Analytic papers on this topic did not appear until a half-century later, although there were previous studies of analysts working with the dying patient (Abend, 1982); (Dewald, 1982); (Eissler, 1977); (Schwartz & Silver, 1990).

Freud's colleagues as well as his patients reacted to his illness. Freud was suffering a great deal from oral cancer, and Ferenczi had also become dangerously ill, far beyond his typical somatic complaints. Ferenczi wrote to Freud on 20 July 1930,

> *Though somewhat sooner than you Professor, I too am preoccupied with the problem of death, naturally in regard to my own destiny … Part of my love for the corporeal me appears to have sublimated itself in scientific interests … That was the path which led me to revive the theory of traumatism, apparently obsolete (or at least temporarily pushed aside) (Dupont, 1988, p. xiv).*

In September 1931 Ferenczi wrote on the research that would culminate in his clinical diary and 'Confusion of tongues'. He was confused and stated, 'I was and still am immersed in extremely difficult internal "clarification work"— internal and external as well as scientific' (Dupont, 1988). Ferenczi's confusion and regression intensified his envy of and rivalry with other analysts for Freud's attention. He wanted Freud as the idealized parent to show unlimited love and approval, which often resulted in Freud's being annoyed and even exasperated with him. Ferenczi could be the adolescent rebel, the *enfant terrible*, and the clinging child.

Ferenczi's dependent needs for nurturance were probably insatiable and were at the basis of or at least closely related to the theme of his *Thalassa*(1924). *Thalassa* deals with a theory of genitality, but a central thesis is the wish for the return to the mother and the womb. Ferenczi and Rank converged in their interest in pre-oedipal development and separation anxiety. Freud is the father and Ferenczi has sometimes been called the mother of psycho-analysis. Actually, the 'Confusion of tongues' between the pre-oedipal and oedipal; real trauma and psychic reality; the interpersonal and the intrapsychic also apply to the personal relationships; the professional, social, and economic relationships between Freud and these closest colleagues. Dazzled by Freud's genius, awed by his personality and creativity, the pioneer analysts competed for the attention and appreciation of their idealized hero and collective ego ideal. The problems of idealization, authority, dependency, and loyalty tended to obscure the scientific issues. Psychoanalytic science was too often subordinated to adherence to the "cause," and understanding could be replaced by rivalry and a contentious confusion of tongues.

When Freud became ill in 1923, the inner circle of his 'paladins' were personally and collectively threatened. Otto Rank wrote *The Trauma of Birth*(1924) at the time he was concerned with the trauma of Freud's cancer. Rank proposed termination of analysis after nine months in a rather concrete 'cutting of the umbilical cord'. The underlying problem was Rank's destabilization after discovering that Freud was ill, as happened to the Wolf Man. He probably became cyclothymic, with a tremendous need to declare separation and independence from Freud, whom he thought to be dying and about to separate from him. Rank had first to separate in both theory and practice. After leaving, returning, asking to be received as the prodigal son, declaring his independence again, he left the fold. The birth trauma was actually a death trauma, and Freud recognized that Rank's theoretical divergences were based upon an unconscious, regressive reaction to Freud's physical illness and cancer. (Rank would develop his theories, and in some ways anticipated Mahler's concepts of separation-individuation.) Ferenczi struggled ambivalently, with a strong desire to remain closely allied to Freud and to have his protection and sustenance while seeking, at the same time, to gain a new independence.

Reacting to his own illness, Ferenczi's clinical diary is a personal manifesto, which, like his correspondence, is part of his personal analysis with Freud and his own self-analysis. It is also a declaration of independence, an attempt to create while he is in the process of being slowly destroyed. It is a message, in some measure, of his mortality and frailty, his desire to find meaningful renewal for his life and work, to resolve his inner confusion, and to be innovative, without fear of loss of love or criticism. His own unorthodox and rather *ad absurdum* experiments went beyond his earlier experimentation with prohibitions and deprivations, followed by experiments with analytic indulgence and gratification.

Ferenczi, though naive about the evidence of actual seduction, noted the hypocrisy, pathological lies, evasions, and silent collusion of the traumatizing adults. He was concerned with the revival of trauma and its repetition, though not simply in the transference. The analyst might traumatize the patient because of countertransference impediments and enactments of the analyst. Ferenczi stressed the object-relations aspects of trauma and the child's relationship to the traumatizing caregivers which continues after the traumatic experience. He explicitly recorded *sequelae* of identification with the aggressor: dissociation, fragmentation, and the split in the child's personality between the observing and comforting self and the dissociated, traumatized self. The child is relatively helpless, desperate for the love and approval of the parent, or surrogates who are abusive. The child cannot protest, and silently submits to authority. 'Tongue-tied', during and after the trauma, the child also introjects or identifies with the parents' unspoken shame and guilt. He recognized the parents' tendency to project blame and guilt on to the child, and that the child is often punished for the parents' misdeeds. He noted the conspiracy of silence, the censorship, blame of the child, and child's self-blame which so often surrounds and follows child abuse. Ferenczi's work anticipated later concepts of strain and cumulative trauma and contemporary concepts of child abuse (Rachman, 1989).

Most remarkably, Ferenczi himself was in a traumatic state when stressing, enlarging, and amplifying the psychoanalytic theory of trauma. Though traumatized with regressive trends, Ferenczi was not mad nor had his mind 'deteriorated'. But it appears that he was both aware and unaware of his illness. With such an illness there is inevitably both knowing and not knowing, splitting of the ego with denial and acknowledgment. Freud did not abandon Ferenczi, and complained that he was withdrawing into isolation. Freud was still hoping that Ferenczi would accept the presidency of the International Psychoanalytical Association, Ferenczi replied:

I must admit quite honestly that when I refer to my present activity in terms of 'a life of dreams', 'day-dreaming', and 'a crisis of puberty', this does not mean that I admit that I am ill. In actual fact I have the feeling that out of the relative confusion many useful things will develop and have already developed (19 May 1932, in Dupont, 1988, p. xvi).

Each of the points about trauma which was discovered in Ferenczi's patients applied to himself and appears simultaneously to acknowledge and defend against the awareness of his own trauma. Many analytic contributions have emerged from the analyst working out his own inner conflicts and traumata, and there is a hidden point-by-point correspondence between Ferenczi's inner traumatization and his fertile analytic investigation of trauma. His regression compromised his ego and was in the service of the ego; his confusion about his own trauma and the patient's trauma was also a spur to his creativity.

We can only surmise Ferenczi's own grief, guilt, anxiety, and rage,

the time will come when [the analyst] will have to repeat with his own hands the act of murder previously perpetrated [by the parent] against the patient (Dupont, 1988, p. 52).

Freud's illness was visible and evident to himself and his patients, but Ferenczi's illness was insidious as it was destructively pernicious. Concerning the conspiracy of silence, we do not know exactly what his doctors told him and his family. Nor do we know with certainty what he actually told his patients of his illness. He wrote his nine-month diary from January to October 1932, while fatally ill. He actually gave up his practice at the end of the year as he developed overt, neurological impairment. He died in May 1933. What did he tell his patients of his life-threatening illness? How did he prepare them for his impending retirement? Was he prepared himself, and how aware was he of his impending death?

Hidden behind the remarkable experimentation, the innovative ideas and formulations, the blind alleys, the blatant errors, and infantile enactments of the *Clinical Diary*, one can infer the feeling of a frantic search for help. He wanted to be rescued, a fantasy he shared with or which he projected on to his patients. He wanted to give them the same love that he desperately wanted; he wanted from them the tenderness and sustenance that he craved, and he denied in his loving and indulgent attitudes his own rage and hate. Ferenczi did not simply give up and resign himself to death, though there is some evidence of an erotization of death. In fantasy, death could be denied, defied, delayed, and romanticized. Death was silently waiting, a silent presence and preoccupation. Ferenczi seemed to have been concerned to have accomplished his goals before it was too late, to create before his life was 'cut short'. Ferenczi was writing an epitaph of transcendent triumph as well as silent victimization and hapless resignation to a malevolent fate. He was partly identified with Dylan Thomas's attitude, 'Do not go gentle into that good night. Rage, rage against the dying of the light'.

The pernicious anemia from which Ferenczi suffered is an illness that progresses over years and involves multiple systems. In addition to fatigue, lethargy, the inability to concentrate—all of which Ferenczi at one time or another complained about—it is perhaps noteworthy that the tongue is frequently inflamed, a telltale glossitis. (He may have denied the significance of the 'traumatized' tongue.) The more serious symptoms involve megaloblastic anemia, wasting, and severe neurological impairments with combined degeneration of the spinal cord. Ferenczi felt abused and assaulted in body and mind. The disease process exerted a chronic regressive pull, an enormous intensification of his fears, and wishes for dependent gratification. His fatal illness incited his final struggles for independence, and his experiments in mutual analysis and self-disclosure of frailties, weaknesses, and errors to patients. In his reversal of roles with the patient, he enacted his wish to be the patient, to be tenderly cared for, and to have psychotherapeutic support. Ferenczi unconsciously confessed his waning powers, for example presenting his 'small-penis complex'; agreeing with patients' complaints about his work (Dupont, 1988, p. 164). His self-criticism increased with his vulnerability and compromised analytic functions and ideals. He struggled with intolerance of patients' aggression towards him and their regressive demands upon him.

The confusion of tongues between adult and child, Ferenczi and his patients, was also evident between Ferenczi and Freud and the rest of the psychoanalytic community. In mutual analysis, he continued his analysis with Freud and self-analytic efforts, with unresolved ambivalence (Aron & Harris, 1993); (GrubrichSimitis, 1986). Ferenczi deeply wished to be rescued by Freud, his colleagues, and patients. However, he dealt with his own current traumatic situation in terms of his fear of retraumatising the patient in the analytic situation. He was aware of problems of mutual analysis and knew that this could deflect attention from the patients' conflicts, that patients would miss treatment, and that confidentiality would be broken if the analyst were to speak of other patients to the patient. He did not write about who paid the fee and set the time. He appears to have been unaware, however, of his own inner confusion, denial, and his magical expectation that the patient could both analyze and supervise the analyst. His illness, and his hiding his illness, contributed to his guilt towards the patient, and his need for confession and absolution by the patient. If he did not inform patients of his illness, he may have felt like the hypocrite condemning hypocrisy, while there was a shared denial of traumatization by both himself and the patient. His need to carry on, indeed, expressed his analytic identity and productive work as resistance to regression. It may have been augmented by economic necessities and a fear of not even having funds for his medical and nursing care. He unconsciously dramatized his own need for treatment, both psychoanalytical and medical, and his magical, regressive expectations that the patients would be able to understand him and sustain him through their dedication to his treatment. His need for his wife's support and care and her actual response to her dying spouse could also have been critically important.

The analyst's judgement of theory and technique can be seriously impaired by the onslaught of illness with its attendant narcissistic and castrating injuries. Serious illness imposes the threat of destabilization, disorganisation, and regression to abject symbiotic dependency. Concentration, listening, and empathy are impaired. The spontaneity of trial identifications with the patient are replaced by emergency identifications which interfere with capacities for objective observation and the maintenance of relative neutrality and an analytic attitude. Ferenczi projected his own traumata, and in an analogue of projective identification, he identified with the illnesses of his patients and acted out issues concerned with abandonment and rescue, trauma and recovery, destruction and creation. His noting that traumatic experience could not be put into words at the time also applied to himself. He acted out what could not be recognized and verbalized.

Even as Ferenczi believed he was rediscovering the pathogenicity of trauma, the traumatic experiences which he was analyzing in patients also served as his own screen trauma. He used his real illness to see himself as the innocent victim, and then his patients as 'innocent victims'. Psychic trauma persists long after episodes of traumatic physical illness, and may influence the analyst's work ego and analytic stance without conscious awareness on the part of the analyst. The repetition and re-enactment of trauma which Freud originally discovered is more likely to occur when it is invited and shared within the analytic situation, anchored in transference/countertransference fantasy enactment. Ferenczi's concerns with retraumatizing the analytic patient were related to his tendencies to countertransference enactments, and it was these tendencies which alarmed Freud. They had apparently discussed Ferenczi's seductive 'indiscretions with patients' in the course of their mutual analytic exchanges years before. Ferenczi introduced the concept of regression to permit a 'new beginning', and began to distinguish between regression and developmental arrest. He aroused analytic concerns about inducing excessive regression. He did not recognize the controversy inherent in the notion of regression to 'rock bottom' as in itself therapeutic or a precondition for new development. To begin anew would reverse a tragic end—regeneration instead of fatality.

Ferenczi had idealized Freud, an idealisation which broke down over Ferenczi's infantile demands, emerging independence, and diverging ideas and concepts.

There had been multiple old and new disappointments which included being denied the presidency of the IPA in favor of Jones; Freud's dismissal of his final paper; and his decline, and anticipated progression of his illness.

Though concerned about Ferenczi's diverging ideas, Freud indicated that Ferenczi's presidency had only been delayed, and that he would hate to die before Ferenczi had the presidential post to which he had long been entitled.

On 17 January 1930, Ferenczi wrote his longstanding complaint to which Freud replied in 'Analysis terminable and interminable'. He described Freud as his 'adored teacher and unobtainable model' while reproaching Freud for not analyzing the negative transference years earlier (Dupont, 1988, p. xiii). Ferenczi had hidden his own fears of retaliation for his own aggression, his cravings for Freud's love, as well as his wish to again be the favorite sibling among the 'ring bearers'. Freud was aware of Ferenczi's cravings and had overindulged him as his dearest, favorite, most admired colleague, and adopted son for many years. Ferenczi was the eighth of twelve children, and Freud understood his feeling that he had never had enough of his mother's love. Ferenczi had also noted that his mother would complain that he would be the death of her.

Having described himself as the *enfant terrible* of psychoanalysis, Ferenczi may have fantasized that he was responsible for Freud's cancer and that Freud retaliated by omnipotently inflicting Ferenczi's fatal illness. Blaming Freud for not analyzing his negative transference denied his tragic decline and his wish for omnipotent cure and salvation. Freud was also ill, could not save him, and he was deprived of the continuity of children. In many respects, the corrective emotional experience which Ferenczi wanted to provide to traumatized patients referred to the repair and restitution of his own previous injuries and traumata. His wish to reverse and undo narcissistic injuries, oedipal defeats, etc. were also linked to his unresolved infantile longing for mother's exclusive affection and nurturance. His well-taken warnings about analytic repetition of the original trauma, did not seem to be reconciled with his need to be the child/patient (Hoffer, 1991).

He correctly surmised that traumatized children who had been seduced and abused might also become 'parentified' by adopting a parental, protective role towards their own parents and the sick part of themselves. This led to the syndrome of the 'wise baby' (Ferenczi, 1933), in which the infantile personality, fragmented and tormented, was hidden behind a precociously mature facade. The wise baby was Ferenczi himself, in a state of confusion. He acted out his countertransference, seemingly unaware of the tremendous, regressive vulnerability of the fatally ill analyst. He confided in Jones that he had pernicious anemia, but could not otherwise disclose his condition. Ferenczi's regression and his experimental induction of regression, his acting out with patients, reminded Freud of these earlier tendencies in Ferenczi. Freud wrote to him on 13 December 1931,

we have hitherto in our technique held to the conclusion that patients are to be refused erotic gratifications … where more extensive gratifications are not to be had, milder caresses very easily take over their role … A number of independent thinkers in matters of technique will say to themselves: 'why stop at a kiss?' …

and soon we shall have accepted in the technique of analysis the whole repertoire of demiviergerie and petting-parties, resulting in an enormous increase of interest in psychoanalysis among both analysts and patients … Father Ferenczi gazing at the lively scene he has created will perhaps say to himself: maybe after all I should have halted in my technique of motherly affection before the kiss (Masson, 1984, p. 159).

Freud pointed out that such behavior would only promote resistances and declared in his penultimate sentence,

According to my memory the tendency for sexual playing about with patients was not foreign to you in pre-analytic times, so that it is possible to bring the new technique into relation with the old misdemeanors (pp. 159–60).

Jones reproduced this letter in his biography of Freud, but deleted this last sentence, probably to protect both Ferenczi and possibly himself from historical reference to erotic enactment with patients.

In this final period, Ferenczi was erratic, engaging in 'wild analysis' while making fertile and enduring contributions to the psychoanalytic understanding of countertransference, trauma, and borderline conditions. This was probably both in spite of and because of his own traumatization and countertransference difficulties. Ferenczi was one of the prime originators of our present view of the analyst as participant/observer rather than solely the observer and interpreter of the free-associating, participating patient. The analyst was not simply a mirror who reflected the patient's unconscious conflicts back to him. Countertransference was not limited to blind spots, but could reside in issues affecting the analyst's tact, empathy, honesty, sensitivity, and acceptance of the patient. Countertransference could pervade any aspect of analysis or the entire process. Furthermore, awareness of countertransference thoughts and feelings could be used to facilitate the analytic process. There were now two participants, two observers, and even two interpreters. Ferenczi emphasized the importance of ongoing analytic self-scrutiny and self-criticism:

> I started to listen to my patients, when, in their attacks, they called me insensitive, cold, even hard and cruel, when they reproached me with being selfish, heartless, conceited ... whether, despite all my conscious good intentions, there might after all be some truth in these accusations (Ferenczi, 1933, p. 157).

Transference does not eliminate the analyst's actual behavior and communications and can be enmeshed in his countertransference reactions (Gill, 1983). Ferenczi did not indicate the difficulty that may ensue in the admixture and differentiation of negative transference and reality.

Ferenczi's notion of the patients being clairvoyant in their knowledge of the analyst's tendencies, expectations and conflicts, was an attribution of infantile omniscience and omnipotence to the patient. And the patient was no more capable of conducting analysis or self-analysis than the 'wise baby'. In this forerunner of the interpersonal and intersubjective formulations of the analytic process, Ferenczi periodically assumes a capacity of the troubled analyst for autonomous, dispassionate observation. He did not take into account his own subjectivity while appearing to himself to being objective. The dying analyst may believe himself to be an objective observer while denying the gravity of his illness and its fatal outcome. He may rationalize that his illness has made him more sensitive and empathic. Furthermore, each patient reacts to the analyst's regressions, errors and enactments in terms of their own personality and transference. One patient might demand more love, another react by becoming furious with the analyst, a third patient might narcissistically gloat and triumph over the analyst's infirmities and frailties, etc. The infantile past, as Freud reminded Ferenczi, lives on in the adult. The transference, for example, of incestuous fantasy, is not intersubjectively cocreated. Incestuous fantasy evolves in childhood, but may be activated, anchored, and validated by the analyst's regressive responses in the analytic situation.

Ferenczi's own childish repetitions confirm the primary source of transference and countertransference in unconscious infantile conflict. His focus upon external trauma defended against attention to intrapsychic conflict and unconscious fantasy (Grunberger, 1980). The transference paradigm is influenced by the analyst, and Ferenczi observed that the analyst affects, and is affected by the patient. His ideas foreshadowed the intrapsychic and interpersonal interrelationship in analytic work, but without a stable intrapsychic focus. What Ferenczi also did not elaborate was the confusion of transference and reality, the blurring of analytic boundaries and roles, and the effect of excessive transference gratification. Unanalyzed countertransference could obstruct the analytic process, although, when scrutinized and analysed, it facilitated analytic empathy and interpretation. However, major parameters and serious technical errors or enactments may not be analyzable.

Ferenczi believed that the patient could be aware of the analyst's whims and wishes, sympathies and antipathies. But the analyst in a state of resistance and regression would not necessarily be able to accept the patient's observations or to utilize a patient's or colleague's 'supervision'. In his formulation of traumatic splitting of the ego, he did not recognize his own split-off tendency to reformulate psychoanalytic theory and technique without universal, unconscious infantile, sexual, and aggressive conflicts. Calling for the avoidance of collusion and total honesty in the analysis of countertransference, Ferenczi may very well have inwardly felt like a silent conspirator as he concealed his illness from colleagues and patients. What was not revealed was of vital significance. He had been shocked that Freud had supposedly stated that he had appeared to be prematurely old and senile, and had in fact remarked that Ferenczi looked older than Freud himself. His passionate plea for the recognition of the reality and frequency of child abuse simultaneously referred to his personal trauma and countertransference.

Freud and Ferenczi did not part with compassionate farewells after Ferenczi read his 'Confusion of tongues' paper to Freud. The paper was presented against opposition and was received with opposition at the 1932 Wiesbaden IPA Congress. Just before this final meeting with Freud, Ferenczi wrote of mutual forgiveness, referring to injuries in their relationship, and to Freud as a judge.

His paper and, unconsciously, his regressive dysfunction, would be judged.

Ferenczi was also asking for reconciliation in anticipation of death. After Ferenczi had read the paper to Freud, he had written a note on shock, and after the Congress he attempted to recuperate. His last Diary note began,

regression to being dead ... Is a new kind of solution ... possible after such sinking into the traumatic? (2 October 1932, Dupont, 1988, p. 257).

The dialogue between Freud and Ferenczi into and beyond death (Haynal, 1993) continued in the ongoing development of psychoanalytic thought. Freud was too ill to attend the Wiesbaden IPA Congress, did not see Ferenczi again, and possibly believed he and Ferenczi would both soon be dead. On 12 September 1932, Freud wrote to Jones,

Unfortunately the regressive intellectual and affective development seems to have had, in his case, a background of physical decline. His clever and good wife conveyed to me that I should think of him as a sick child (Masson, 1984, p. 174).

And in his obituary of Ferenczi, Freud stated,

Signs were slowly revealed in him of a grave organic destructive process which had probably overshadowed his life for many years already. Shortly before completing his sixtieth year he succumbed to pernicious anemia. It is impossible to believe that the history of our science will ever forget him (1933, p. 229).

The regression associated with Ferenczi's progressive, fatal illness may never have been within his full insightful awareness as Freud surmised during Ferenczi's final decline and more clearly after his death. Ferenczi advanced the theory and techniques of countertransference analysis even as he subjectively misunderstood the pivotal fragility of his own life and work. Ferenczi's pre-obituary paper posthumously achieved the analytic influence and recognition he desperately wanted and could not have foreseen. Most importantly, the silence which enveloped the 'Confusion of tongues' has given way to open dialogue and the examination of controversy through theoretical and technical discourse based upon further clinical experience. Ferenczi left a legacy of historical import (Gedo, 1986). His work on trauma can be all the more appreciated in the light of his concurrent inner conflicts and trauma. Attempts to clarify the confusion of tongues have contributed to our contemporary awareness of analytic problems in the selection, organization, communication, conceptualisation, and validation of analytic observations and inferences.

REFERENCES

Abend, S. (1982). Serious illness in the analyst: countertransference considerations *J. Am. Psychoanal. Assoc.* 30:365–379.

Aron, L. Harris, A. (eds.) (1993). *The Legacy of Sandor Ferenczi*. Hillsdale, NJ: Analytic Press.

Balint, M. (ed.) (1949). Sandor Ferenczi number *Int. J. Psychoanal.* 30:4.

——— (ed.) (1968). The disagreement between Freud and Ferenczi, and its repercussions In The Basic Fault New York: Brunner/Mazel pp. 149–156.

Blum, H. (1974). The borderline childhood of the Wolf Man *J. Am. Psychoanal. Assoc.* 22:721–742.

Bokanowski, T. (1992). Ferenczi's transference depression (Unpublished paper).

Dewald, P. (1982). Serious illness in the analyst: transference, countertransference, and reality responses *J. Am. Psychoanal. Assoc.* 30:347–379.

Dupont, J. (ed.) (1988). *The Clinical Diary of Sandor Ferenczi.* Cambridge, MA: Harvard Univ. Press.

——— (ed.) (1994). Freud's analysis of Ferenczi *Int. J. Psychoanal.*75:301–320.

———, et al. (eds.) (1982). *Sandor Ferenczi et Georg Groddeck: Correspondance (1921–1923).* Paris: Payot.

Eissler, K. (1977). On the possible effects of aging on the practice of psychoanalysis. *Psychoanal. Q.*46:182–183.

Ferenczi, S. (1924). *Thalassa: A Theory of Genitality.* London: Karnac, 1984.

——— (1933). Confusion of tongues between adults and the child. In *Final Contributions to the Problems and Methods of Psychoanalysis.* London: Karnac, pp. 156–167.

Freud, S. (1917). Introductory lectures on psychoanalysis *S.E.* 16.

——— (1923). Two encyclopaedia articles *S.E.* 18.

——— (1930). Civilization and its Discontents. *S.E.* 19.

——— (1931). Female sexuality *S.E.* 21.

——— (1933). Sandor Ferenczi *S.E. 22.*

——— (1937). Analysis terminable and interminable *S.E.* 23.

Gedo, J. (1986). *Conceptual Issues in Psychoanalysis* Hillsdale, NJ: Analytic Press.

Gill, M. (1983). *Analysis of Transference, Vol. I. Psychological Issues,* Monograph 53. New York: Int. Univ. Press.

Grubrich-Simitis, I. (1986). Six letters of Sigmund Freud and Sandor Ferenczi on the interrelationship of psychoanalytic theory and technique *Int. J. Psychoanal.* 13:259–277.

Grunberger, B. (1980). From the 'active technique': to the 'confusion of tongues' In *Psychoanalysis in France.* ed. S. Lebovici. D. Widlocher. New York: Int. Univ. Press, pp. 127–152.

Halpert, E. (1982). When the analyst is chronically ill or dying *Psychoanal. Q.*51:372–389.

Haynal, A. (1993). Ferenczi and the origins of psychoanalytic technique In *The Legacy of Sandor Ferenczi.* (eds.) L. Aron. & A. Harris. Hillsdale, NJ: Analytic Press, pp. 53–74.

Hoffer, A. (1991). The Freud/Ferenczi controversy: A living legacy. *Int. J. Psychoanal.* 18:465–472.

Hughes, A. (1992). Letters to Joan Riviere 1921–1939. Int. *J. Psychoanal..* 19:265–284.

Jones, E. (1957). *The Life and Work of Sigmund Freud,* vol. 3. New York: Basic Books.

Masson, J. (1984). *The Assault on Truth.* New York: Farrar, Straus.

Mcguire, W. (ed.) 1974 The Freud/Jung Letters. London: Hogarth Press.

Rachman, A. (1989). Confusion of tongues: The Ferenczian metaphor for childhood seduction and emotional trauma. *J. Amer. Acad. Psychoanal.* 17:181–205.

Rank, O. (1924). *The Trauma of Birth.* New York: Harper Row, 1973.

Schur, M. (1972). *Freud: Living and Dying.* New York: Int. Univ. Press.

Schwartz, H. & Silver, A.S. (1990). *Illness in the Analyst.* New York: Int. Univ. Press.

CHAPTER 17

Anti-Semitism in the Freud Case Histories: A Prologue to the Psychoanalysis of Social Prejudice and Racism

(2010). *The Jewish World of Sigmund Freud*, pp. 78–95; ed. A.D. Richards, Jefferson, NC: McFarland.

ABSTRACT: Rampant in Vienna during Freud's lifetime, the influence of anti-Semitism is present in all of his classic case histories, many other papers, and his personal correspondence. This paper traces the influence of anti-Semitism and related conflicts in each of the case histories. Though not addressed or analyzed, conflicts and ambivalence about Jewish identity are evident in Freud, his patients, and their treatment. Anti-Semitism does not appear in the minutes of the Vienna Psychoanalytic Society, and was little addressed in the early psychoanalytic literature. There was conscious and unconscious avoidance of issues of social and cultural prejudice and racism. The social surround may be observed, yet remain invisible and inaudible. Freud was concerned that psychoanalysis should not be identified with one ethnic group, but that psychoanalysis had universal application. Considerations of anti-Semitism contribute to an enhanced understanding of the cultural dimension of the case histories, the development of psychoanalysis, and Freud biography. Insights into the impact of anti-Semitism are currently applicable to other forms of socio-cultural prejudices and persecution as well as their often silent influence on the analytic process.

In order to understand the influence of their cultural milieu on Freud, his patients, and their treatment, one must consider the intra-psychic and interpersonal effects of anti-Semitism in Vienna. Many of the same considerations would be applicable to other forms of religious, racial, and social prejudice. I shall infer how anti-Semitism and Jewish identity were significant in the Freud case histories, though usually silent and presumably not addressed. Conflicts related to Jewish identity were kept from conscious awareness, or were not the focus of Freud's current clinical interest, or were eliminated from psychoanalytic publication. Freud was acutely aware of conflicts of identity, tradition, conversion, and assimilation, but also had his own resistance and counter-transference to the analysis and self-analysis of these issues. Though not specified in an individual paper, these conflicts infiltrated Freud's correspondence and his published corpus (Frosch, 2005). However, given the analytic and historical limitations of the original case histories, the inferences involve inevitable conjecture and and alternative explanations. Retrospectively it is impossible to know how exploration of anti-Semitism would have affected each of the individual patients.

Freud wanted psychoanalysis to achieve scientific and academic acceptance; "it was only by the Christian Jung's appearance that psychoanalysis escaped the danger of becoming a Jewish national affair" (Freud and Abraham, 1965. Letter to K. Abraham, May 3,1908). Moreover, influenced by the enlightenment and German romanticism, assimilated, cultured Jewish intellectuals commonly held humanitarian ideals and a cosmopolitan outlook regarded as above and beyond their Jewish ethnicity.

In 1867 the Jews were granted full political rights and advanced rapidly in the professions parallel with their increasingly secular education. But in many other areas of life, Jews were restricted; emancipation was never fully realized. Anti-Semitism was an obvious impediment but also a goad to competitive and creative achievement. The Jewish population had dramatically increased in size and prominence, and had rapidly advanced in the business and cultural life of Vienna. Despite legal rights, there were limits; e.g., there was not a single Jewish full professor or judge in Vienna. A new kind of racial anti-Semitism appeared. Previously denigrated as infidels, and apostates, the Jews were now considered as an inferior, despised race. Wilhelm Marr, coined the term "anti-Semitism", promulgated in an infamous pamphlet, "The Conquest of the Jews Over the Germans" (1879). The son of a baptized Jew and exemplifying Jewish anti-Semitism, Marr introduced the pseudo scientific discourse of race. Jews were considered a perverse breed apart, and were regarded as having racial contaminants which could damage the Christian population (Gilman, 1986). There were anti-Semitic myths, jokes and slurs about Jews, their deformed, effeminate person and personality, with images of Jews with horns, predatory teeth, and long curved hooked noses. Stereotyped vilification of Jews was internalized, contributing to Jewish anti-Semitism (Ostow, 1995). Freud, in the meeting of the Vienna Psychoanalytic Society, December 9, 1908,connected a Jewish patient's persecutory delusions about his nose to conflicts about being Jewish and wanting to be baptized in opposition to his Zionist father. Conflict about Jewishness was, in effect, recognized as displaced oedipal conflict. There was, however, no further elaboration by the group about conflict concerning conversion to Christianity or becoming a closet Jew (Nunberg and Federn, 1967).

That Freud was a scion of an Eastern European Jewish family and later a Jewish intellectual of the enlightenment does not do justice to his philo-semitism or to his ambivalence and his conscious and unconscious conflicts about his Jewish identity. Though marginalized at the borders of converging, clashing cultures Freud belonged to the first generation of Viennese Jews who entertained hopes of no longer being disadvantaged, second class citizens. While many Jews avidly wanted to become assimilated Austrians and Germans, the culture was insidiously and perniciously prejudiced against them. Paradoxically, their prejudiced society potentiated the secular education of male Jews who then importantly contributed to cultural development.

No one can completely escape his/her historical time and place; this was true of Freud himself. Freud wrote to Fliess (Freud, S. 1985; 5 November, 1897, p. 277): "One always remains a child of one's age". He wrote "of the increasing importance of the effects of the anti-Semitic movement upon our emotional life," (Freud, 1900, p. 196). Emerging from residues of adolescent shame about Jewishness, with pride in his Jewish heritage, he unconsciously internalized anti-Semitic attitudes that he simultaneously fought against and ultimately analyzed. Freud provided the basic analytic insights into the unconscious conflicts and fantasies, conflicting identifications, internalized aggression, hate, and negative affects associated with the experience of socio-cultural prejudice and persecution. He joined Bnai Brith after his father's death in 1896 where he gave pioneer lectures on psychoanalysis to his Jewish "brothers". Jews were frequently slandered at city council meetings and Carl Lueger, who became Mayor of Vienna in 1897, was rabidly anti-Semitic. Anti-Semitism was overdetermined, with multiple meanings and functions in external reality, in fantasy life, and in the reciprocal influence of psychic and external reality. (Young-Bruehl, 1996; Knafo, 1999).

When Freud finally escaped from Vienna in 1938 to England, one of his first acts was to join the British branch of the Bnai Brith. His final work on Moses and Monotheism (1939) was written during the escalating Nazi persecution of the Jews and while Freud was gradually succumbing to cancer. Freud attempted to understand the origins of anti-Semitism and the character of the Jews, which he thought contributed to anti-Semitism. Here Freud ambivalently implied that the Jews were partly to blame for their own persecution, indicative of negative splitting from the largely philo-Semitic attitudes expressed in the work.

Freud's concerns with anti-Semitism for the most part, however, do not appear in his published scientific writings. Breuer and Freud wrote (Breuer and Freud, 1895, p. 18), that psychoanalysts "were obliged to pay as much attention in their case histories to the purely human and social circumstances of their patient as to the somatic data and the symptoms of the disorder", but the discussion of anti-Semitism which would then have been expected in the case histories were either absent, obscured or disguised. Anti-Semitism does not appear in the index of "Studies on Hysteria" (Breuer and Freud, 1895), in the minutes of the Vienna Psychoanalytic Society, or directly in the case histories, except for a crucial footnote in Little Hans (1909). What was silent or spoken, hinted or implied were all significant considerations. Through unconscious defense, preconscious silent collusion, and conscious avoidance, anti-Semitism for a long time was a neglected topic in the psychoanalytic literature.

Anna O. (Bertha Pappenheim)

The Jewish background of the prototypical case history of Anna O. is nearly invisible and inaudible, and serves as a prelude to the submerged Jewish issues in Freud's later cases. Anna O., now identified as Bertha Pappenheim, was treated by Joseph Breuer between 1880 and 1882. Freud's mentor and senior colleague, Breuer later discussed this now famous patient with Freud, resulting in their joint publication of the case report in Studies on Hysteria (1895). In 1880, when Anna O. was 21 years old, she was delegated to be the nurse of her father, who was very ill with tuberculosis. She was Jewish, very bright, imaginative, and poetic, with penetrating intuition and fluency in many languages. She herself became ill, weak, easily fatigued, with a panoply of motor, sensory, and perceptual symptoms. She fell into somnolent states in the afternoon and her severe widespread symptomatology forced her to give up nursing her father. She would sometimes awaken from this state finding it difficult to speak; she gradually lost the ability to speak and was completely mute for two weeks. After her father died in 1881 her symptoms worsened and her spoken German deteriorated. Able to read French and Italian, she then spoke and responded to English with Breuer, and prayed in English. Breuer, one of the most eminent Jewish Viennese physicians of the day, physician to Brahms and other celebrities, observed that Anna O. was without religion, despite having heard her pray in English. Neither Breuer nor Anna O. questioned her prayer being recited in English. Ordinarily she would have been praying in Hebrew; Hebrew prayers were probably said after her father died, and when he was buried in a Jewish cemetery. Anna O. coined the term "talking cure" in a foreign tongue, English, avoiding German, and Yiddish.

Later in Anna O's life her suppressed and repressed Jewish identity returned with extraordinary intensity. She traveled widely on behalf of Jewish interests, particularly devoted to saving Jewish women who had been forced into sexual slavery. In 1904 she formed the Federation of Jewish Women. She established a shelter for unmarried Jewish mothers and visited the Henry Street Settlement in New York in 1909. At approximately the same time that Freud was lecturing at Clark University, citing the case of Anna O, Bertha Pappehneim was lecturing in America on problems of prostitution. She later translated Jewish folklore from Yiddish into German and wrote a book, "the Jewish Woman," strongly supporting the education and equal rights of women (Ahsen, 1974).

A decade after the end of Anna O's treatment, in 1882, Freud urged Breuer to write up her case for the collaborative work, "Studies in History." (1895). Following her gradual recovery, Jewish issues occupied the remainder of her life but do not appear in the comments or interpretations in the case history. The emancipated Jews largely rejected the Orthodox religion in which many had been reared. Paradoxically, emancipation, which might have promoted expression of their religious and ethnic backgrounds, contributed to the denial and avoidance of Jewish language, culture and customs. Breuer, Freud and Anna O. avoided the Yiddish that was very likely the mother tongue for all three. Nor did they indicate an appreciation of possible psychological and social conflicts involved in the typical celebration of Christmas by Viennese Jews.

It was during Christmas 1881 that Anna O. re-experienced scenes from the previous Christmas. She had at that time relinquished her nursing her father (which would have aroused her own fears of contracting TB). She was symptomatically improved after she recounted the scenes of the prior Christmas, during the subsequent Christmas. Christmas was likely an unnoticed stimulus and spur to their joint therapeutic efforts but not to recognition of her conflicts concerning Christian and Jewish observance.

Dora

The treatment of Dora was published by Freud (1905), "Fragment of an analysis of a case of hysteria". He had "analyzed" her for hysterical symptoms, e.g., aphonia, dyspnea, tussis nervosa, for the last three months of 1900. Anti-Semitism figures in disguised form in the Dora case, which I regard as a contribution to the literature on the pre-history of the Holocaust (Blum, 1994). During Freud's lifetime and until after World War II and the Holocaust, the social, cultural and historical framework of Freud's case histories were little explored. Dora's adolescent phase of life, her female gender, her family's relative affluence and their being Jewish, are all significant to multidimensional understanding of Dora's conflicts and symptoms. The influences of her Jewish and anti-Jewish milieu were important unexplored issues in Dora's personality development and disorder (Decker, 1991). In September 1900, just before Dora started treatment with him, Freud learned that his coveted promotion to Associate Professor from his previous status as a lecturer (privatdozent) had been denied. Freud had regarded his not being promoted as an act of anti-Semitic prejudice.

"Dora," Freud's pseudonym for Ida Bauer, was analyzed for three months from October through December 1900, in turn of the century Vienna. This eighteen-year old girl could not have anticipated that she would become an historical figure in psychoanalytic and feminist literature. Preceding and during Dora's treatment with Freud anti-Semitism was rampant in Europe. Many Jewish establishments were boycotted and vandalized, and there were"blood libel." accusations and prosecutions. The ongoing Dreyfus case in France added fuel to the fire of European anti-Semitism.

When Philip Bauer brought his daughter Ida for treatment, she could hardly have regarded the world as her oyster. She was denied the opportunity for higher education provided for her brother, Otto, who later became the Foreign Minister of Austria. Worldly and bright, with many cultural interests, Dora was oppressed by a society, which limited opportunities for Jews and for women. The body language of her hysterical symptoms probably had determinants that included the prejudice to which Jews and women were subject. Dora's family and friends were all Jewish, as were Freud's family, friends and the initial members of the Wednesday Night Psychoanalytic Society. Dora's parents moved to the South Austrian town of Merano, now in Northern Italy, where she lived from 6 until 16. Although the town was popular as a summer spa resort among Viennese Jews, Dora did not have a secular childhood education.. She was sent to a convent school and exposed to the prevailing disparaging attitudes towards Jews in school and in the town. Christian texts at the time commonly depicted the Jews as villains, betrayers, Christ killers destined for punishment in this world and the next. Her convent schooling, not reported in the published case presumably had great psychological and social significance for Dora and for her Jewish parents. Choosing a Catholic school for their daughter could well have had significance for their daughter's later enactment of the parents' unconscious fantasies and conscious ambivalence regarding Jewish identity.

Freud wanted to demonstrate the clinical use of dreams in psychoanalytic treatment, and the Dora case revolves around two dreams. The first dream that Freud subjected to extensive analysis (Freud, 1905, p. 64), was "A house was on fire. My father was standing beside my bed and woke me up. I dressed quickly. My mother wanted to stop and save her jewel case; but father said: 'I refuse to let myself and my two children be burnt for the sake of your jewel case.' We hurried downstairs, and as soon as I was outside I woke up." Freud's interpretations of this dream have been elaborated by a host of authors. My comments about this dream will be largely restricted to what I regard as hidden issues of Jewish identity. Jewish issues were denied, evaded and avoided by analyst and analysand, consistent with the denial practiced by Dora's family. Her mother denied the affair between her husband and Frau K.; Herr K. denied the affair between Dora's father and Frau K., Dora's parents were in denial about the sexual advances of Herr K. toward their daughter. Dora both denied and affirmed that she was being sacrificed for the secret motives and agendas of her parents and the K.'s. Her father would swap his daughter, a bartered bride, for Herr K's wife. The jewel case represented not only Dora's virginity, but also her pride, honor, and the ideals and values which were being compromised by the adult authority figures in her life. The burning house in the first dream described may also have been the burning house of Jewish factories set afire in the periodic rioting since 1897 in Bohemia where her father's factories were located. (Bauer, Breuer, and Freud had roots in Bohemia). Dora's fleeing a burning house in the dream was over-determined (Blum, 1994). Dora abruptly fled from treatment on December 31, 1900, when she informed Freud that that day was to be their last session. She married three years later in December 1903 at a reformed temple in Vienna. In 1905, her son was born and two months after his birth, Dora fled the house of Israel and left the Jewish community. She was formally baptized with her husband and son into Christianity. She ostensibly attempted to erase the humiliation and racial stigma of being Jewish, probably hoping to provide more advantages and opportunities for her family.

There were harbingers of the same conscious and unconscious conflicts and compromise formations in the second dream. In the second dream … Dora reported: "I was walking in a strange town … I came into a house where I lived, went to my room, and found a letter from my mother lying there. She wrote saying that as I had left home without my parents' knowledge she did not wish to write to me to say that father was ill. Now he is dead and if you like you can come home … I walked into the porter's lodge, and inquired for our flat. The maid opened the door to me and replied that mother and the others were already at the cemetery." The second dream occurred during Christmas, and the maid might well have been Christian. There were only two or three hours left of analysis before Dora's departure; Father Freud and her analysis were about to be buried.

There is an addendum to the second dream, which Dora initially forgot. (Freud, 1905, p. 133-134). She had received a Christmas present, a photograph album sent by a young man, with a picture of the town square that Dora dreamt about. Her dream of being in a strange town reminded Dora of a previous visit to Dresden, when a cousin offered to show her around the famed museum. Dora declined the offer and went alone to the museum where she stood for two hours before Raphael's Madonna. The significance of Christmas, standing before the Madonna for an awesome two hours, did not elicit further reflection or questions. What so possessed her about the picture of the Madonna that she was transfixed? How did this behavior relate to her ten years in a convent school? Who can stand before any picture for hours, and why did not Freud question her reaction? The idealized mother of Christ replaced Dora's denigrated Jewish mother and her own denigrated Jewish self-representation (Blum, 1994; Billig, 1999). Freud noted that identification with the Virgin Mother allowed the teenager to fantasize motherhood without guilt over unacceptable sexual fantasy. Freud remarked on her maternal longings but was seemingly silent about her conflicts about being Jewish and idealizing the Madonna. Dora acted out the second dream by becoming the Christian mother of her baptized infant son. In retrospect Dora may well have been considering conversion to Christianity and burying her Jewish heritage when she reported the second dream.

Conversion had been the subject of discourse of Viennese Jews, but was not popular and deserters from the faith were recorded in "lists of shame." The reaction of Dora's parents to her conversion to Christianity is unknown. It is of interest that Dora's brother, Otto Bauer, who became the foreign minister of Austria, always remained a member of the Jewish community. Yet Otto Bauer later espoused gradual assimilation, advising Jews to marry Christians and to change their speech and manners so as not to alienate Christians. Identifying with the racist attitudes of the aggressor, he proposed that the undesirable features of the Jews had been inherited and could be modified and diluted through generations of intermarriage. Theodore Herzl, the founder of the Zionist state, contemplated Dora's solution before championing an independent Jewish state. Herzl proposed leading the Jews of Austria, except himself and other leaders, in a mass conversion to Christianity (Loewenberg, 1983). In his letter to Fliess of May 7, 1900, just months before Dora's analysis began, Freud described himself as "an old, somewhat shabby Jew" (Masson, 1985, p. 412). Internalizing the insults and denigration of the surround, many Jews harbored self-images of being shabby, seedy, and inferior. Social prejudice contributed to narcissistic injury, shame and humiliation. Dora's Christian identity was revoked after passage of the persecutory, dehumanizing racial laws in Nazi Germany. Both Dora and Sigmund Freud had to flee from Vienna just before emigration was foreclosed.

Little Hans

The case of Little Hans, entitled " The Analysis of a Phobia in a 5 Year Old Boy," (Freud, 1909), may be regarded as the precursor of child psychoanalysis. Freud (1909, p. 6) wanted to use the case to confirm his findings about the importance of infantile sexuality and the Oedipus complex, which he had discovered in adults. Freud stated, (1909, p. 6), "surely there must be a possibility of observing in children at firsthand and with all the freshness of life the sexual impulses and wishes which we dig out so laboriously in adults from among their own debris." Little Hans, with persistent habitual masturbation, directly illustrated childhood sexuality. Little Hans was treated by his father, with Freud's "supervision", from January through May of 1908. Raised by affectionate, and supposedly permissive parents, the case report indicates that his parents could be quite seductive, coercive and punitive. He was threatened by his mother with abandonment, and castration. When he was 3 ½ his mother found him masturbating and warned, "if you do that, I shall send for Dr. A. to cut off your widler" (Freud, 1909, p. 8). Little Hans and his parents were focused on his "widdler", (penis) parallel to Hans' preoccupation with the "widdlers" of his parents, children, horses, and other animals.

Concerns of his parents about being Jewish, about raising their son as a Jew , and the xenophobia encountered by the Jewish minority in Vienna, were not discussed in the case history. In the paper that Max Graf, the father of Little Hans, wrote about his early experience in Freud's Wednesday Night Study Group, Max Graf (1942) referred to this very question. He had asked Sigmund Freud about raising his son as a Christian, and "wondered whether I should not remove him from the prevailing anti-Semitic hatred … "Freud had pointedly counseled his father, "if you do not let your son grow up as a Jew, you will deprive him of the little sources of energy which cannot be replaced by anything else. He will have to struggle as a Jew, and you ought to develop in him all the energy that he will need for that struggle." (Graf, 1942, p. 473). Max Graf, whose father had converted to Christianity, had remained a member of the Jewish community and had married a Jewish woman, Olga Honig, who had been Freud's patient. The caring, hesitant parents of Little Hans must have been willing to follow Freud's advice as it resonated with their own inclinations. Freud had many times been to dinner at the apartment of Max and Olga Graf, and had probably known Little Hans from birth. In the case report there is no reference to parental concern about Jewish identity, ethnicity, or the Jewish male's stamp of circumcision. Freud's counter-transference and ambivalence contributed to the avoidance of Jewish issues (Rudnytski, 1999). However, close reading of Little Hans, reveals that anti-Semitism appears in an almost casual, impersonal footnote. It is an extraordinary footnote, that bridges body and mind, individual and group psychology, unconscious fantasy and cultural attitudes. Here Freud asserts his own Jewish identity and interests as he initiates the psychoanalysis of anti-semitism, and its relevance to little Hans. Freud (1909, p. 36) stated, "I cannot interrupt the discussion so far as to demonstrate the typical character of the unconscious train of thought which I think there is here reason for attributing to Little Hans. The castration complex is the deepest unconscious root of anti-Semitism; for even in the nursery little boys hear that a Jew has something cut off his penis—a piece of his penis, they think—this gives them a right to despise Jews. And there is no stronger unconscious root for the sense of superiority over women … what is common to Jews and women is their relation to the castration complex." Freud presented an entirely new interpretation of circumcision (considered apart from his inaccurate propositions on femininity). Freud (1913, p. 153) later stated, "When our Jewish children come to hear of ritual circumcision they equate it with castration". Circumcision thus elicits castration anxiety in both Jews and Gentiles.

This was the first psychoanalysis of a socio-cultural prejudice and the first psychoanalytic contribution to an understanding of an important unconscious determinant of anti-Semitism. Before Freud no one related circumcision to castration anxiety and then castration anxiety to anti-Semitism. In the case of a boy, avoidance of circumcision could be avoidance of a stigmatizing bodily sign. Pertinently, the girl's clitoris was called "the Jew" in idiomatic slang in Vienna (Gilman, 1993). Although other religions also practiced circumcision, in Vienna at that time, circumcision identified the male as a Jew. This became particularly dangerous when the Nazis came to power.

We know that Freud was circumcised since Sigmund Freud's father noted it in the family bible (Rice, 1990). Questions have been raised, however, about whether Freud circumcised his own sons. Their not being circumcised is particularly hard to believe considering Freud's own Jewish identity, the traditions of his Jewish family who still observed Jewish holidays, and the relatively orthodox Jewish background of his wife, Martha Bernays Freud.

Family and friends would visit after the birth of Freud's sons. Little Hans was born in 1903, not long after the birth of Freud's sons in the early 1890's. Could Freud have hypocritically urged Max Graf to raise his own son as a Jew, to not baptize Little Hans, having failed to raise his own sons as Jews beginning with their circumcision? Some of Freud's dreams and associations refer to his concerns that because of anti-Semitism his children would be deprived of the security of a homeland and the opportunity for successful careers. The Jewish phallus, often displaced to the nose, was associated with the social stereotype of the predatory and perverse character of the Jews. The conflicts associated with Jewish identity would most likely have been present in Little Hans, as they had influenced the lives of his parents and grandparents. Though admired in Europe as an operatic prodigy, Herbert Graf went though a mock baptism in the hope that it would be helpful with the Nazis.

During the years of the case histories, Freud had continued to be concerned with the problems of Jewish identity and anti-Semitism. Detecting anti-Semitism in Jung and other Swiss psychiatrists, he indicated to Abraham that their anti-Semitism had been directed away from himself and toward Abraham. On December 26, 1908, anticipating the publication of "Little Hans," creating an outcry, he wrote to Abraham (Freud and Abraham, 1965), "German ideals threatened again! Our Aryan comrades are really completely indispensable to us, otherwise psychoanalysis would succumb to anti-Semitism. " Just after the termination of the little Hans treatment, and initial international "congress for Freudian psychology" Freud wrote to wrote to Abraham, May 3, 1908, regarding Jung, " his association with us is therefore all the more valuable. ….it was only by his emergence on the scene that psychoanalysis was removed from the danger of becoming a Jewish national affair". Freud's correpondence suggests that he may have consciously sidestepped anti-semitisim in the body of the little Hans case in order to emphasize the universal dynamics of the childhood phobia.

Between Little Hans and the Wolf-Man cases, Jung had confessed to Freud in March 1909, about a scandalous relationship with a patient who soon identified herself to Freud as Sabina Spielrein. She fantasized having a child named Siegfried, representing a harmonious merger of Aryan and

Jew, Freud and Jung, as well as the symbolic marriage and child of herself and Jung. During the Wolf-Man's analysis on August 20, 1912, Freud wrote to Spielrein, "My wish is for you to be cured completely. I must confess, after the event, that your fantasy about the birth of the savior to a mixed union, did not appeal to me at all. The law, in that anti-Jewish period, had him born from the superior Jewish race. But I know these are my prejudices." He later wrote to the pregnant Sabina Spielrein that he was cured of his predilection for the Aryan cause (Carotenuto, 1984, p. 116,120).

The Rat-Man

Ernst Lanzer, tormented by obsessive fantasies, began his analysis with Freud on October 1, 1907. The analysis lasted approximately one year and was thus concurrent with the treatment of Little Hans. Because of the dramatic effect of his fantasy of a lethal torture consisting of a starved rat penetrating the rectum of his father and his future bride, he became known to posterity with the pseudonym of "The Rat-Man". Lanzer used many words with the stem of "rat", such as heirat, hofrat, errat, spielrat, etc. He spoke a "rat language" infused with obsessive thinking and a compulsion to talk. After hearing of the rat torture while in military service, in August 1907, he thought he saw the ground heave, as though there were a rat under it. Seeing a rat while visiting his father's grave, he assumed that the rat had had a meal from his father. As a child he used to bite. The rat had multiple meanings, e.g., feed and greed, lust, aggression, money, feces, penis, and baby.

The meanings of the rat, however, have negative denigrating connotations pertaining to Jews, and thus to the Rat-Man's conflicts about his Jewish identity.

Freud's notes on the Rat-Man are the only surviving summary notes of the analytic process of any of his patients. The original record of the case, rather than the published case, has referents to the Jewish world and words of this patient and Freud. The Rat-Man thought "twenty kronen are enough for the parch", translated in a footnote, as a Jewish term for "a futile person" (p.298). Strachey used the term "Jewish" rather than "Yiddish", and "parch" is now better translated as frugal or penurious. The Rat-man's overt preoccupations regarding the anus, odor, disease, and money were those attributed to Jews by the anti-Semitic culture. The Rat-Man was identified with a miserly mother, a father who was a gambler from a poor family, and he struggled with a family plan to have him marry a wealthy relative for money. He began treatment with a thought about the fee: "for each florin a rat". He reacted compulsively as though trivial debts to a fellow army officer and a post-office lady were matters of life and death. He fantasized that the money lender must be paid or the rat torture will be invoked, an unnoticed analogy to Shylock in "The Merchant of Venice" (Shakespeare, 1595). Freud, 1909. p.288, noted that "rats have a special connection with money ... 'ratten' (rats) meant to him 'raten' (installments; rates ... money and syphilis converge in rats. He pays in rats– rat currency ... Syphilis gnawing and eating reminded him of rats ... " He thought his father and soldiers were syphilitic. The association of Jews with vermin, and with buying and lending on installments were social stereotypes.

On December 23, 1907, preceding Christmas, the Rat-Man recalled the suicide of a rejected women, sleeping through the night of his father's death, and thoughts of immortality. Just after Christmas, on December 27, the Rat-Man recalled a detail from the Spring, 1903 (Freud, 1909, p.301–302). Entering a church "he suddenly fell on his knees, conjured up pious feelings and determined to believe in the next world and immortality. This involved Christianity and going to church after he had called his cousin a whore. His father had never consented to be baptized, but much regretted that his forefathers had not relieved him of this unpleasant business. He had often told the patient he would make no objections if he wanted to become a Christian." Freud remarked that the Rat-Man's kneeling must have been against the scheme to marry him into a wealthy family of observant Jews. But neither Freud nor the Rat-Man wondered about the meaning of Christmas, his kneeling in church, and conflict about Jewishness. Freud's notes record the Rat Man's use of the Yiddish word for whore, which he expected Freud to understand. The rat-man had a pious period of frequent prayers in his teens. He used prayers, magical incantations, and compulsive acts to ward off and undo his murderous, torturing fantasies and his incestuous behavior. The meaning of his religious bent and his conflicts about Jewish identity were not explored though Freud (1907) had already published "Obsessive actions and religious practices". The Rat-man was inconsistently described as having become a free thinker, yet "he made up prayers for himself, which took up more and more time, and eventually lasted for an hour and a half"(Freud, 1909, p.193). His pious phrases, such as "May God protect him" could turn into their opposite—may God <u>not</u> protect him." Hebrew prayers were not referred to in the written account of the treatment.

On December 28, 1907,the next day in Freud's notes of the same Christmas holidays, the Rat-man recalled a story about a military officer's father who had been his own father's commander. The Rat-man's father had provided Jews with spades to clear snow from a market station, a market that Jews were ordinarily forbidden to enter. The commander praised his father, whereupon his father retorted (Freud, 1909 p. 305). "You rotter! You call me old comrade now … but you treated me very differently in the past". Jews were simultaneously prohibited and exploited. The associations are replete with transference-counter-transference implications concerning Jewishness. But in the original case publication Jewish ethnicity and anti-Semitism were not explored and did not have free access to the market place of ideas.

The Wolf-Man

Serge Pankejeff, known to psychoanalytic posterity as The Wolf-Man, is also pertinent to both overt and covert anti-Semitism. Freud's four-year analysis of the Wolf-Man began in February 1910, and lasted four years. Their first meeting, a suggestive sadomasochistic primal scene, anticipated the major conflicts and personality disturbance described in the Wolf-Man's case history. Freud rather casually reported this patient's initial treatment reaction in a letter to Ferenczi, February 13, (Freud and Ferenczi, 1993, 1910, p. 138,) "A rich young Russian, whom I took on because of compulsive tendencies, admitted the following transferences to me after the first session: Jewish swindler, he would like to use me from behind and shit on my head .." Money and privilege were important to the Wolf-Man who encountered Freud with socially acceptable contemptuous anti-Semitic epithets. Even if exaggerated for shock effect, a Russian aristocrat could readily greet a Jew with insult and invective. In Russia and Europe, the Jew was the split –off bad self and object, the universal scapegoat who could be readily and remorselelessly denigrated and despised. Born on Christmas Eve, the Wolf-Man expected to be regularly rewarded with a double set of gifts, birthday gifts, and Christmas gifts. He was entitled, elite, and identified with Christ, dissociated from the lowly Jews on whom he projected and displaced his own unacceptable homosexual and hostile impulses. Having led a dissolute life of the idle rich, he abruptly lost his fortune after the Communist revolution in Russia. Freud then arranged to take up a collection for him, so that Freud in effect gratified his wish to receive bountiful gifts. The Wolf-Man was in retrospect a borderline personality with multiple symptoms including constipation and derealization (Blum, 1973). His feeling isolated from the world, was experienced as being enveloped in a veil. Prior to his analysis, this veil and his constipation were relieved by an enema usually administered by a male attendant. This was the relationship he proposed to repeat with Freud when he offered to have anal intercourse and defecate on his Jewish doctor in a fantasized homosexual rape and robbery. After his analysis with Freud, who had promised him a cure of his constipation, the constipation recurred. Freud re-analyzed him for four months, in 1919, without payment. In 1926 the Wolf-Man was referred for treatment to one of Freud's other patients, Ruth Mack, then in her mid-twenties. This very gifted young woman from an affluent Jewish family was nevertheless a psychoanalytic novice without prior training. Having concealed some funds and jewels that he retained, the Wolf-Man was essentially treated by Ruth Mack without fee. This fortified his expectation of monetary gifts and narcissistic entitlement. He was however, narcissistically injured because he was being treated by the young pupil rather than by the master. The Wolf-Man became enraged at Freud and at her. He subsequently reported the following dream (Mack-Brunswick, 1928, p. 286.):"the patient's father, in the dream a professor, resembling, however, a begging musician known to the patient, sits at a table and warns the others present not to talk about financial matters before the patient. His father's nose is long and hooked, causing the patient to wonder at its change." In the Wolf-Man's associations the musician had tried to sell old music, which the patient refused to buy. The musician looked like Christ and the Wolf-Man's father; the Wolf-Man recalled that his father had been incorrectly called a "sale juif", a dirty Jew. In Russia (and the rest of Europe) Jews were regarded as mercenary and avaricious. The professor-father, that is Freud, is the dirty Jewish psychoanalyst, the swindler, trying to sell him psychoanalysis. His ascribing an avaricious motive to Freud was clearly a social stereotype of the Jews, as well as a projection of his own conflicts. In the Wolf-Man's childhood obsessional neurosis he was compelled to exhale when he saw beggars or cripples, exorcising the evil spirits causing his blasphemous thoughts. Jews were often depicted as evil sprits and predators, and exorcism was analogous to an enema. The beggars and thieves were Jews, like his analysts, after his fecal money. The Wolf-Man felt that Freud had over charged him when he was rich and not protected him, as God the father did not protect his son from the crucifixion God ordained. The divine Christ was also a human who needed to defecate. He resolved this paradox by reasoning that if Christ ate nothing Christ would not have to defecate (no meal, no payment).

The long, hooked nose in his dream invoked the stereotype of the perverse Jew-swindler. He had not relinquished his anti-Semitism in the service of his narcissistic entitlement and rage. The Wolf-Man was preoccupied with his own nose, symbolizing his penis, before and during his analysis. In adolescence he had severe acne and a sebaceous gland infection, which left a tiny hole in his nose. He would study his nose in the mirror, became reclusive and afraid of people. Considering the Wolf-Man's desiring gifts, as if it was always Christmas, Freud suggested instead that the Wolf-Man present a gift to Freud at termination. Reversing roles and requesting a gift, Freud believed this would relieve the Wolf-Man of excessive feelings of obligation toward his analyst. The Wolf-Man chose an Egyptian artifact, which Freud placed on his desk where it remains today. The Wolf-Man was now delegated to donate to Freud, resonating with his initial fantasy of the exploitative Jewish analyst. The gift exchanges did not then halt, extending from their initial transference- countertransference reactions. When the Wolf-Man visited Freud at the end of World

War I, Freud (1918) presented him with a book with a dedication written to the Wolf-Man and containing his own case report "From the History of an Infantile Neurosis".

The Schreber Case

Carl Jung called Freud's attention to Schreber's "Memoir of My Nervous Illness (1955; written in 1900 and published, 1903). Having never met Schreber, Freud (1911) inferred a psychoanalytic interpretation of thi censored memoir shortly before Schreber's demise. The Memoir and Freud's case study illustrate the theme of this paper, so this commentary is included with the prior case histories.

Freud's (1911), "Psychoanalytic notes on an autobiographical case of paranoia" can now also be understood in an expanded context of cultural prejudice and racism. Daniel Paul Schreber (1842-1911) apparently suffered from paranoid schizophrenia with delusions, hallucinations, and suicidal behavior. He believed that God, colluding with the Director of the mental hospital, Dr. Paul Flechsig, had emasculated him, that he was an object of their persecution. In his delusions he was castrated, given a woman's breast and genitals, and would be impregnated by God's rays, giving birth in identification with the Virgin Mary and Christ. He was delusionally transformed into the idealized Madonna, and a degraded strumpet equated with a castrated Jew. (fragmentation, multiple splitting and confusion encompassed polarities of male-female, self-object, phallic-castrated, Madonna-whore, Aryan-Jew, idealized-devalued)

Freud (1911, p.24) noted that Schreber divided God into anterior and posterior realms. "The posterior realms of God were, and still are, divided in a strange manner into two parts, so that a lower God (Ahriman) was differentiated from an upper god (Ormuzd) ... Schreber can tell us no more than that the lower God was more especially attached to the peoples of a dark race (the Semites) and the upper God to those of a fair race (the Aryans)."

Freud did not choose to comment upon the prevalent racial anti-semitism interwoven in Schreber's delusional system.

But Schreber told us much more about prejudice and persecution in his memoir (Gilman, 1993). Schreber's lower Semitic god, Ahriman had rays that emasculate, whereas the rays of the Aryan upper god (Ormuzd) could miraculously restore manhood. Castrated by the Semitic-Jewish God, he imagined that he was further victimized by being deprived of his healthy natural stomach and instead given an inferior Jew's stomach. Schreber lost his genitals, his stomach, his identity, his self-regard, self- definition and self-determination.

Schreber's cruel God could not learn, and misunderstood human beings. Freud (1911, p.25) observed " … God was quite incapable of dealing with living men, and was only accustomed to communicate with corpses." Schreber's delusional system foreshadowed Nazi ideology and the Holocaust (Blum, 1986). The Nazi God (Hitler) preferred corpses. The Nazi division of people into the Aryan superior race and the inferior Semitic race is literally a page out of Schreber, congruent with the prevalent cultural racism manifest in his delusions. Schreber's life experience in an authoritarian, racist society and culture had an inescapable psychological influence, apparently infiltrating his delusions. How could it be otherwise? Schreber's delusions are historically pertinent to later Nazisim. Schreber identified with the aggressor, though predominantly with the castrated, humiliated, powerless victim. As a megalomanic female redeemer, Schreber would give birth to a new race consonant with the order of things. Schreber's fantasies are consonant with the homologous Nazi "new order", with the goal of a supreme Aryan racial purity. In his paranoia he was a victim of physical abuse, sexual abuse, and psychological abuse ("soul murder"). The massive abuse, a harbinger of subsequent Nazi atrocities, was labeled with the euphemism of divine miracles. Paranoia may also predispose to being attuned to real environmental, external threats of abuse, persecution, and destruction. Rather than Schreber's repressed hatred, Freud formulated Schreber's unconscious homosexual love of his father at the root of his paranoia. However, Freud had remarkably wondered whether Schreber's father might have really been an abusive tyrant in a letter to Ferenczi, but not in the published case. Flechsig's lack of psychological comprehension, his actual practice of castration to treat hysteria, and the probable traumatic child abuse of Schreber by his physician father (Niederland, 1984) are beyond the scope of this brief discussion. The anti-Semitism and racism in the Schreber autobiography and Freud's case report, so long overlooked by psychoanalysts, are important analytic, historical, and cultural considerations.

In conclusion, for Freud, especially in the pioneer era of psychoanalytic discovery it was important to present scientific findings and hypotheses not "tainted" by data that might be considered to be uniquely Jewish. He considered psychoanalytic findings and formulations to have universal application, not limited to any ethnic group, race, society, or culture. It was important to have analytic validation of what were then revolutionary findings. However, the affective influence of external and internalized Jewish anti-Semitism is inferred as problematic for Freud and the patients of his published cases. While anti-Semitism was overt or covert in each case history, it was not explored in the case publications. Similar issues may have surfaced a half-century later, when the editors of the original edition of Freud's letters to Fliess expunged Yiddish expressions.

For cross-cultural verification and illustration, Freud chose the non-biblical Greek myths of Oedipus and Narcissus to describe crucial developmental phases and universal fantasies. However, his related writings on the mythical Moses are far more intimate, personal, and ambivalent. Freud's insights are invaluable for all forms and targets of irrational social and cultural denigration and discrimination. Analyst and analysand may share the same fantasies, defenses, and bias, especially if they are culturally syntonic and become relatively ego-syntonic. The influence of the bigoted culture on the personality, and on the analytic process may then be overlooked, dissociated, suppressed, and repressed (Smith, 2006). Freud's insights and oversights can retrospectively be utilized with current analytic concepts to enlarge understanding of unconscious conflicts and fantasies crucially involved in socially sanctioned devaluation and hatred. Finally, these ever fascinating case reports represent the burgeoning early evolution of psychoanalytic theory and therapy with enduring relevance to contemporary psychoanalysis.

REFERENCES

Abraham, H.C. & Freud, E.L., Eds.(1965). *A Psycho-Analytic Dialogue: The Letters of Sigmund Freud and Karl Abraham 1907–1926*. New York: Basic Books.

Ahsen, A. (1974). Anna O—patient or therapist? An eidetic view in: *Women in Therapy,* eds. V. Franks and V. Burtle, New York: Brunner/Mazel, pp.263–283.

Beller, S. (1989). *Vienna and the Jews, 1867–1938*. New York:Cambridge University Press.

Billig, M. (1999). *Freudian Repression*. New York: Cambridge University Press.

Blum, H. (1974). The borderline childhood of the Wolf Man. *J. Amer. Psychoanal. Assn.*, 22:721–742.

——— (1986). On identification and its vicissitudes. *Internat. J. Psychoanal.*, 67:267–276.

——— (1994). Dora's conversion syndrome: a contribution to the prehistory of the holocaust. *Psychoanal. Quart.* 63:518–525.

Breuer, J. & Freud, S. (1895). Studies on hysteria. *S.E.*, 2.

Brunswick, R.M. (1928), In: Gardner, M. ed. (1971). *The Wolf Man. With the case of the Wolf Man by Sigmund Freud, and a supplement by Ruth Mack Brunswick.* New York: Basic Books.

Carontenuto, A. (1984). *A Secret Symmetry*. New York: Pantheon.

Decker, H. (1991). *Freud, Dora, and Vienna*. New York: The Free Press.

Freud, S. (1900). The interpretation of dreams. *S.E.*, 4, 5.

——— (1905). Fragment of an analysis of a case of hysteria. *S.E.*, 7:1–122.

——— (1909a). Analysis of a phobia in a five-year old boy. *S.E.*, 10:3–149.

——— (1909b). Notes upon a case of obsessional neurosis. *S.E.*, 10:153–318.

——— (1911). Psychoanalytic notes on an autobiographical account of a case of pparanoia (dementia paranoids). *S.E.,*12.

——— (1913). Totem and taboo. *S.E.*, 13:1–162.

——— (1918). From the history of an infantile neurosis. *S.E.*, 17:3–122.

——— (1939). Moses and monotheism. *S.E.*, 23:1–137.

——— (1985). *The Complete Letters of Sigmund Freud to Wilhelm Fliess, 1887–1904,* Trans. J. Masson. Cambridge, MA: Harvard University Press.

Freud, S. and Ferenczi, S. (1993). *The Correspondance of Sigmund Freud and Sandor Ferenczi,* vol. 1. eds. E. Falzeder and E. Brabant. Cambridge, MA: Harvard University Press.

Frosch, S. (2005). *Anti-Semitism , Nazism, and Psychoanalysis.* Basingstroke: Palgrave Macmillan.

Gilman, S. (1986) Jewish Self-Hatred. Baltimore, MD:Johns Hopkins University Press.

——— (1993). *Freud, Race, and Gender.* Princeton, NJ: Princeton University Press.

Graf, M. (1942). Reminiscences of Professor Sigmund Freud. *Psychoanal. Q.* 11:465–476.

Knafo, D. (1999). Anti-Semtisim in the clinical setting. *J. Amer. Psychoanal. Assn.* 47:35–64.

Loewenberg, P. (1983). *Decoding the Past.* New York: A. Knopf.

Niederland, W. (1984). *The Schreber Case.* Hillsdale, NJ: The Analytic Press.

Nunberg, H. & Federn, E., eds. (1964). *Minutes of the Vienna Psychoanalytic Society, vol. 2:1908–1910.* New York: International Universities Press.

Ostow, M. (1995). *Myth and Madness: The Psychodynamics of Anti-Semtism.* New Brunswick, NJ: Transaction Publishers.

Rice, E. (1990). *Freud and Moses.* Albany, NY: State University of New York Press.

Rudnytski, P. (1999). Does the professor talk to God? Counter-transference and Jewish identity in the Case of Little Hans. *Psychoanal. And History* 1:175–194.

Schreber, D. (1955). *Memoirs of My Nervous Illness.* Ed. I. Macalpine & R. Hunter. Cambridge, MA: Harvard University Press.

Smith, H. (2006). Invisible racism. *Psychoanal. Quart.* 75:3–19.

Young-Bruehl, E. (1996). *The Anatomy of Prejudices.* Cambridge, MA: Harvard University Press.

CHAPTER 18

The Prototype of Pre-oedipal Reconstruction[1]

(1977). *J. Amer. Psychoanal. Assn.* (25):757–785.

Reconstruction has always been an integral part of psychoanalytic theory and therapy. While usually viewed in terms of a specific technical application, reconstruction has actually been a significant tool in the development of theory as well as a check upon theoretical constructions and formulations.

Emerging from the analytic process, reconstruction and developmental knowledge are mutually explanatory. Reconstruction reciprocally influences understanding and interpretation and may catalyze derivative recollection (Kris, 1956); (Kanzer and Blum, 1967). Reconstructions are tested and remodeled by analyst and patient with increasing refinement of working hypotheses. Greenacre (1975) prefers "construction" to denote the preliminary models of past development and pathogenesis utilized by the analyst, and has elaborated and stressed the importance of reconstruction in psychoanalysis. The careful and continuing evaluation of data and inferences is essential to psychoanalytic investigation and to the elucidation of controversy concerning genetic reconstruction and early development.

This paper focuses upon the early utilization of reconstruction in psychoanalysis and its relation to contemporary preoedipal reconstruction. In addition to conflict and defense, reconstruction now includes archaic ego states and object relations, reaction patterns and developmental consequences.

---

1 This paper was presented for the Margaret S. Mahler Birthday Celebration of the New York Psychoanalytic Society and Institute, May 10, 1977, and was awarded the first Margaret Mahler Literature Prize.

Articulating with and amplified by the developmental concepts of separation individuation (Mahler, 1966); (Mahler et al., 1975), the reconstructions here are particularly relevant to the origins of structuralization, to preoedipal patterns and their later reactivation or persisting influence.

Freud (1937), having wrestled heroically with the problem of reconstruction, compared psychoanalytic work to the work of the archeologist in discerning, rearranging, and creatively synthesizing meaningful patterns out of the maze of piecemeal evidence provided by the patient in the analytic situation. Psychoanalysis may be said to have begun with an incorrect construction when Freud, believing the stories his patients told him of their childhood seduction traumata, assumed that neurosis was caused by parental seduction. The concept of defense was conceptualized at that time as a repressive force designed to keep painful memories of real traumatic experience outside of consciousness. When Freud made the momentous discovery that the fantasies of parental seduction were universal oedipal fantasies, he formulated the concept of the Oedipus complex, and the analysis of the Oedipus complex became the central issue. The libido theory was enunciated with its complex maturational sequences and developmental challenges, with the Oedipus complex emerging out of important preceding developmental phases. Although he also uncovered preoedipal conflicts and related them to character formation, as in such early papers as "Character and Anal Erotism" (Freud, 1908), the preoedipal contribution to and coloring of character was clinically isolated. The short analyses and techniques of the pioneer days did not permit character analysis. Analysis was symptom oriented, and symptoms and conflicts were mainly determined and evaluated in terms of the Oedipus complex. The crucial elucidation of the Oedipus complex overshadowed other discoveries. It is of interest that whereas Freud (1900, p. 245) referred to the preoedipal phase before age three as "the prehistoric period," he incorporated, over the years, the reconstruction of preoedipal reactions and influence, so evident in character, into psychoanalytic theory and technique. Preoedipal determinants and imprints were discerned in psychic structure and oedipal conflict, in the form and content of the infantile neurosis.

But when did preoedipal reconstruction first appear in psychoanalysis and how was it utilized? Most of the preoedipal dimensions of Freud's reconstructions have been overlooked. The extraordinary reconstruction of the primal scene at eighteen months in the Wolf Man case, probably the most famous of psychoanalytic reconstructions, was a preoedipal reconstruction. Freud (1918) gave an extremely detailed reconstruction of this scene, including the age of the Wolf Man, his illness—fever—the time of day, the position of the parents, the child's immediate reaction, and the developmental consequences. Freud regarded this single traumatic experience of the primal scene as a traumatic sexual seduction, but occurring in preoedipal infancy (Blum, 1974).

At that time Freud did not regard the primal scene as immediately significant in the mental life of the eighteen-month-old infant. In the magnificent discovery and documentation of the infantile neurosis, such traumata as a protracted life-threatening malaria and pathological object relation were eclipsed and the focus was upon the primal scene. He then directly linked the primal scene with instinctual overstimulation, which explained the relation of the primal scene to trauma, but not to trauma that seemed to be tied to a later developmental phase. Invoking the concept of delayed trauma as a possible explanation, Freud proposed that the preoedipal primal scene became pathogenic as a phase specific oedipal trauma at the time of the Wolf Man's nightmare on his fourth birthday. This preoedipal reconstruction, so daring in its conception and elucidation, was "reconstructed upward" to the oedipal phase. The preoedipal situation and the mode and timing of the reconstruction are often overlooked because of the phallic content, the shift in the significance of the reconstruction from eighteen months to the phallic phase, and the close relation of the primal scene to Freud's discovery of the oedipal infantile neurosis as the precursor of the adult neurosis.

Freud's thinking encompassed developmental issues and the effects of traumatic overstimulation at different levels of development and on different areas of the personality. The unconscious gratifications and the threat of castration associated with the primal scene were evaluated in terms of oedipal progression and libidinal regression. The primal traumatic event of the single primal scene was reformulated as a universal oedipal configuration. The preoedipal primal scene was linked to pathogenic oedipal conflict (Esman, 1973); (Blum, 1974).

Freud's complex discussion of the primal scene engaged different levels of memory, reconstruction, and personality organization. Freud also questioned whether he had reconstructed a phylogenetic memory, a dream equivalent of memory, a primal fantasy, or an actual experience—an animal or a human primal scene—and whether a reconstruction to eighteen months was a retrospective falsification or whether the Wolf Man's nightmare at 4 years of age reactivated and organized the seduction trauma at eighteen months in terms of the negative Oedipus complex (cf. Eissler, 1966).

The puzzling and vexing problems of such early reconstruction can now be understood also if considered in terms of Freud's simultaneous analysis of himself and his patients. Freud's analysis of the Wolf Man touched upon issues in his self-analysis (Kanzer, 1972) which were in a continuing process of question, investigation, illumination, and extrapolation. In the Wolf Man, and in his self-analysis, Freud uncovered persistent early infantile influences which had profound consequences for later development.

Oedipal and preoedipal reconstructions actually make their appearance simultaneously, and long before the Wolf Man case. They are to be found in Freud's first analysis—his self-analysis—which can be traced in the Fliess correspondence (Freud, 1887–1902). Freud reported his discovery of the Oedipus complex to Fliess in September-October 1897 (letters 69, 70, 71, pp. 218–221) and also reconstructed what would now be regarded as important preoedipal influences; and most of the reconstructions in the Fliess letters are actually preoedipal reconstructions, e.g., Julius Freud, the one-eyed Doctor, the Czech nursemaid. The presence of the first remarkable reconstruction by Freud (letter 70, October 3, 1897) of the period between eighteen and 24 months—during his separation-individuation phase—has been essentially unnoticed in these terms. Freud reconstructed his relationship at this period of life not only to his one-year-older nephew, but to his one-year-younger brother, whom we now know died on April 15, 1858, after having lived for approximately six months. Freud, then, was approximately one and one-half years of age when his brother was born and just under two at his brother's death. Freud's brother Julius was, therefore, alive only during the rapprochement phase of Freud's preoedipal development. Lacking the sophisticated tools of contemporary analysis, Freud's initial reconstruction of his infancy is uncanny in its authenticity, complexity, and correlation with contemporary analytic and developmental observations. Freud, unraveling screen defenses, has given us an immediate and vivid picture of reconstruction to the period of rapprochement, with a rapprochement crisis complicated by the birth and death of his younger brother Julius.

Later, in the *Nonvixit* dream of October, 1898 (Freud, 1900, pp. 421–425), Freud's nephew John reappears as a revenant, an infantile object important in his own right, but also a screen object for his brother Julius, who is not directly mentioned in the associations to the dream, as Grinstein (1968) and Schur (1972) have noted. Freud (1900, p. 483) stated, " … all my friends have in a certain sense been reincarnations of this first figure … they have been *revenants*. My nephew himself re-appeared in my boyhood, and at that time we acted the parts of Caesar and Brutus together. My emotional life has always insisted that I should have an intimate friend and hated enemy." Referring to Brutus's speech of self-justification in Shakespeare's *Julius Caesar*, Freud proceeds to analyze the "Proto transference" to Fliess, representing not only his father, but his brother Julius. Fliess, like Julius, was born in 1858 and thus younger than Freud. Brutus slew Julius Caesar, and Freud noted he was playing the part of Brutus in the dream. Freud and John really did act the roles of Brutus and Caesar during Freud's adolescence when John visited Vienna. Freud was identified with Brutus, and carried the "germ of self-reproach" for his death wishes toward Julius. The dream memorial bore the inscription *Nonvixit*, meaning he didn't live. In the day residue, the monument for the Kaiser Joseph refers to brother Julius (Kaiser = Caesar), father Jacob, and Freud's identification with the Biblical favorite son of Jacob, Joseph the dream interpreter and the other Josephs who were so important in his life.

The dream parapraxis of *Nonvixit*, or not having lived, rather than *Nonvivit*, not being alive, refers to his baby brother Julius, as do Freud's comments (1900, p. 484), "It serves you right if you had to make way for me. Why did you try to push *me* out of the way? I don't need you … "

Freud utilized familial information in his self analysis to help organize and test derivative dream reconstruction. In a scene described to him by his father as occurring when he was not yet two years old, Freud had been fighting with his nephew, John. Freud (1900, p. 425) asserted, "It must have been this scene from my childhood which diverted *'Non vivit'* into *'Non vixit'* for in the language of later childhood the word for to hit is *'wichsen.'*" This is the precise period of the death of Julius, when Freud was not quite two years old (cf. Grinstein, 1968, p. 308). It is the anal phase of psychosexual development with all its problems of sadism, impulse and sphincter control and retention or loss of stool. From an ego orientation, it is also during separation-individuation, the rapprochement subphase, with continuing definition of self and object, animate and inanimate, male and female, with heightened separation anxiety and fears of re-engulfment. The issues of disappearance and reappearance in this preoedipal period of Freud's life might possibly be related to the discovery, loss, and rediscovery of preoedipal influences in the development of psychoanalytic theory.

The enmity toward Julius was associated with the enmity toward his nephew John and his next sibling Anna, who was born December 1858, some eight months after the death of Julius. As we now know (Schur, 1972), sexual relations, birth, and death occurred in the same room during Freud's preoedipal development.

In "The Interpretation of Dreams" Freud's reactions to Julius and John and their parents are revived in an elaborate disguise in which the early sibling preoedipal material is condensed with oedipal fantasies. In a less disguised reconstructive letter to Fliess, Freud (1892–1899, p. 219) reported, " … I welcomed my one-year-younger brother (who died within a few months) with ill wishes and real infantile jealousy, and that his death left the germ of guilt in me. I have long known that my companion in crime between the ages of one and two was a nephew of mine who is a year older than I am and now lives in Manchester; he visited us in Vienna when I was fourteen. We seem occasionally to have treated my niece, who was a year younger, shockingly [cf. Freud, 1899]. My nephew and younger brother determined, not only the neurotic side of all my friendships, but also their depth."

Grinstein (1968, p. 315) has noted the series of deceased figures whom Freud survived with pleasure and guilt, tracing Freud's guilt over his father's death to the guilt over the death of his brother. Both Grinstein and Schur have enriched our understanding of Freud's dreams and the psychobiographical significance of *Nonvixit* and Julius Freud, without, however, a contemporary elucidation of the preoedipal dimension.

Schur (1972, pp. 119, 161, 241) emphasized the "guilt of the survivor" and documented the significance of this theme in Freud's life and work. In a letter to Fliess, Freud (1887–1902, p. 171) interpreted the dream, "You are requested to close the eyes," he had just after his father's death in October 1896. "The dream was thus an outlet for the feeling of self-reproach which a death generally leaves among the survivors." The request to close the eyes refers to denial as well as death wishes and punitive blindness. The *Nonvixit* dream, occurring just two years after his father's death, is a richly overdetermined anniversary dream. On the anniversary of the "request to close the eyes," the object is annihilated with a piercing look and *Nonvixit* words. The oedipal referents are clearly indicated in the associations. Freud has survived Brücke, Paneth, and Fleischl. A memorial had just been unveiled to Fleischl. Fliess, represented by "Fl" whose name was similar to that of the dead Fleischl, had just both celebrated his 40th birthday and confronted serious surgery. The linkage of these figures with the series of Josephs, with whom Freud was also identified, is also clear and includes, ultimately, his father, Jacob, and his brother Julius (Shengold, 1971). Fliess would soon "disappear" as had the others, and Freud recognized the unconscious childhood equation of separation, disappearance, and death. From the recent past of his professional life, Freud leaps to the infantile ghosts who return in the *Nonvixit* dream. In his early life John had not died, but he disappeared along with Julius, Freud's nursemaid, his half-brothers Emanuel and Philipp, and his first home (cf. Schur, 1972, p. 173). However, Freud's reported affective reaction to the birth and death of Julius is not yet superego-derived guilt, but, in his own terminology, "the germ of guilt," or the "seed of self-reproach" (cf. Schur, 1972, p. 164). The phrase "germ of guilt," translated from letter 70 of Freud's letters to Fliess was also translated by M. Schur as "seed of self-reproach." I shall utilize both translations,[2] as complementary, and emphasizing the affective, cognitive, and structural processes consistent with the reconstructed infantile phase. The "germ of guilt" is analogous to a depressively tinged basic mood, and the "seed of self-reproach" to the developing sense of self and to a precursor of the superego. The basic mood and superego precursors develop during the rapprochement subphase of separation-individuation, the developmental period of Freud's *Nonvixit* reconstruction. Julius did not live, and if his brief life was denied and repressed, it would seem he never "existed," "… *people of that kind only existed as long as one liked and could be got rid of if someone else wished it*" (Freud, 1900, p. 421). And in the case of Julius, the wish for his elimination became a reality.

The references in the *Nonvixit* dream to birth, death, and rebirth occur in many forms of appearance and disappearance. The visual annihilation is reminiscent of infantile omnipotence, but also of the archaic primitive superego (Peto, 1969). It is also possible, utilizing the developmental level of the Julius reconstruction, to reconstruct the significance of the visual gaze in terms of eye contact and its maintenance, and to wonder about peek-a-boo games and the denial and acknowledgement of object loss. The greater sense of separateness during rapprochement leads to a heightened sensitivity to object loss. As Mahler (1975) notes, the fear of object loss is then partly relieved by internalization, which includes the beginning internalization of the object's demands and commands. The fear of losing the object's love, now a relatively well-differentiated object, becomes an intensified vulnerability on the part of the rapprochement toddler, which manifests itself in a highly sensitive reaction to the parent's approval and disapproval. By this time the child can already verbally evoke "Mama" during her absence, and can say "byebye" in anticipation of separation from mother. The capacity for delay, anticipation, reality testing, and symbolic substitution develops with object relations, and ego advances and drive development occur in the matrix of adequate object response. The achievement of representational thought and

---

2 I am indebted to Drs. Mark Kanzer and Jules Glenn for indicating that the optimal translation should be "germ of self-reproach." This translation underscores Freud's avoidance of any confusion of the superego and guilt with the precursors of the superego and of guilt and self-reproach.

language is associated with a more enduring, internalized, and stabilized image of the mother, which permits the shift to active separation experiences characterized by volitional approach and detachment or distancing behavior (Mahler et al., 1975); (McDevitt, 1975).

The reconstruction of the "prehistoric period" of childhood via dreams and screen memories is recorded in the Fliess letters for the first time in history. Transference, the return of "revenants," is codiscovered with reconstruction in "The Interpretation of Dreams" in the context of infantile object relations. In the evolution of the psychoanalytic process, this preoedipal reconstruction (of the rapprochement phase) was an object-relations model which actually preceded libido theory, and which returns as an important dimension of development in modern psychoanalysis. The reconstruction of the maturational phases of libidinal psychosexual development in childhood was one of the great achievements of Freud's analytic work with adults. The preoedipal reconstruction of early ego development and object relations was intimately related to libido theory, to the "libidinal object." Freud introduced dynamic formulations with a genetic viewpoint so that both dynamic and genetic viewpoints were interdependent and interrelated in the origins of psychoanalytic theory.

The *Nonvixit* dream is often used to indicate the revival and recapitulation of early object relations without indicating that the infantile object relations were indeed from the second year of life, so that such transference would be a preoedipal transference. Further, Freud's statements about his later relationships being determined by his brother Julius and his nephew John merit re-evaluation, just as does his statement that his nephew was his partner in crime at one year of age. In "The Interpretation of Dreams" only John appears as the "inseparable" friend of his childhood until Freud's third year, and the revenants were said to be a series of reincarnations of this friend (Freud, 1900, p. 485). How important were these companions, his one-year-older nephew and his brother who died at six months, probably even before he was able to sit up, and certainly before he had language and locomotion? Did not his "friend" represent a composite figure, viz., his brother and other close relatives? As with the reconstruction in the Wolf Man case at eighteen months of age, what may be most important would not be the validity of a specific content, but the methodology of reconstruction and the developmental level to which it pertains. The recapture of the infantile object relations in Freud's first reconstruction is associated with enduring preoedipal influences and a basic affective state. The therapeutic importance of reconstruction in the reorganization of memory and self-representation is implicit in Freud's formulation. The "friend" of his infancy becomes a screen memory to be analyzed.

Just as the primal scene, birth, and death fantasies are so significant in the case of the Wolf Man at eighteen months, so were these issues bewildering infantile realities in Freud's self-analysis. The birth and death of his younger brother may have been at least as significant during Freud's rapprochement subphase as his ambivalent relation to play with John. Moreover, to follow Freud's reconstruction in his letter to Fliess, are the most significant relationships of that period of life likely to be the younger brother and the older nephew, or do these two figures really represent the most significant objects in the toddler's life, namely, the parents? (We do not have the data to indicate just how important a mother surrogate and how significant an influence his Czech Catholic nursemaid was, or his half-brothers.) Doubtless, the most important relationship at that period of Freud's life which is not delineated in his 1897 comments or in the analytic literature on his letters or dreams is the (rapprochement) relationship with his mother.

Freud's genius permitted this first reconstruction in psychoanalysis, a preoedipal reconstruction to 18–24 months of age. His "inseparable companion," his partner in life between the ages of one and two was his loving and adoring mother. His relation with his mother remains in the background of the father and brother associations of the *Nonvixit* dream, and, indeed, of Freud's (1900) dreams in "The Interpretation of Dreams." The preoedipal mother in the dream book is hidden behind the pale shadow of his oedipal parent, usually the father. On October 15, 1897, Freud analyzes a haunting memory concerning separation from his nursemaid, also representing his beloved mother. "I was crying my heart out, because my mother was nowhere to be found" (1887–1902, p. 222), is a poignant expression of his separation anxiety and infantile grief.[3] The import of Freud's discoveries is to be seen in all later theoretical developments. His (1917) delineation of the predisposition to and mechanisms of depression, consonant with preoedipal reconstruction, took into account regression to orality and narcissistic object relations and pointed to the precursors and consequences of superego development. The loving and beloved superego (Schafer, 1960) was also anticipated, along with the formulation of subsequent internalized self-criticism, conscience, and self-punishment.

Freud's nephew and younger brother ostensibly determined the depth of all future friendships. This can be reinterpreted, i.e., his parents were the prototype of object relations and object love. Behind and beyond the ambivalent and complex relations to women Freud (1913) described in "The Theme of the Three Caskets," his 1897 remarks presage appreciation of the essential ingredient of a mother's love for the infant's development of "confidence" and "basic trust." (Confidence, basic trust, and self-regard were formally introduced and studied much later in psychoanalysis.) Freud (1917, p. 156) later observed: " … if a man has been his mother's undisputed darling he retains throughout life the triumphant feeling, the confidence in success, which not seldom brings actual success along with it. And Goethe might well have given some such heading to his autobiography as: 'My strength has its roots in my relation to my mother.'" Freud was identified with Goethe and would be awarded the Goethe Prize (1930); the observations apply to Freud as well as Goethe.

When Freud (1900) states that his emotional life requires an intimate friend and a hated enemy, as he does in association to the *Nonvixit* dream, ambivalence is apparent. The ambivalence and tendency toward splitting with displacement of anger and projection of aggression so characteristic of the normative rapprochement crisis can be suggestively discerned in his further associations: " … and it has not infrequently happened that the ideal

---

3 His nursemaid was also used as a probable screen for his mother in the preceding letter (70), where Freud states, "… I shall have to thank the memory of the old woman who provided me at such an early age with the means for living and surviving" (1887-1902, pp. 219-220). Freud, in reconstructing reactions to this obscure preoedipal mother surrogate, also cites her inappropriate mothering and dishonesty (cf. Grigg, 1973).

situation of childhood has been so completely reproduced that friend and enemy have come together in a single individual—though not, of course, both at once or with constant oscillations, as may have been the case in my early childhood" (p. 483). Freud's description and reconstruction to 18–24 months of age anticipates and is consistent with the modern conceptualization of the process of separation individuation and the specific features of the rapprochement subphase. From that point on in development, conflicts with the mother and other objects are no longer transitory, but persistent and ambivalent. The mastery of the conflicts of this period will be particularly observable in the wooing of the parent, and intrapsychically, in terms of more cohesive, integrated self- and object representations with increasing stability and autonomy.

After being "inseparable" until the end of their third year, Freud's independence from his "companion" at that time is fully compatible with the achievement of object constancy (again translating his inseparable companion as his mother). The senior toddler tolerates longer periods away from his mother and demonstrates the capacity to function and play in her absence because of the security of her "constant" mental representation. Julius had a direct influence on Freud, but also on Freud's parents, who reacted to the birth and death of their baby. The birth of a new sibling during rapprochement is not uncommon, and parental reactions impinge upon the toddler just as the toddler also stimulates parental responses.

All development involves challenges and tasks, with normative crises, and progression interrupted by expectable periods of regression. The birth and death of a sibling during rapprochement accentuates and complicates the cardinal conflicts of that period which, as Mahler (1966) delineated, include the additional trauma of toilet training and of the discovery of the anatomical sexual difference. The beginning deflation of the child's impervious narcissism and magic omnipotence is associated with the child's growing awareness of separateness and helplessness, and the beginning of verbal communication. The rapprochement proclivity to a negative affective response and to the feeling of ego helplessness, which Bibring (1953) characterized as the basic cause of depression, is heightened when the mother-child relation is skewed by maternal grief and depression consequent to the illness and death of their baby.

Bibring (1953), consistent with Mahler's formulations, saw the ego helplessness as a narcissistic injury. It is now possible to follow the evolution of affective dispositions during the separation-individuation process, with depression originating during rapprochement and replacing the intoxicated elation associated with the undiminished grandeur of the practicing period. The depressive proclivity may become a structuralized state, which, as Freud implied in his first reconstruction, may be reactivated in later life, depending upon constitution and later development. It is during and after rapprochement that such depressive reactions, differentiated from transitory grief and sadness in infancy, can be structurally related to depression at later ages. Preoedipal disappointments, narcissistic injuries, internalized rage reactions, oral and anal fixations and frustrations were identified in the classical literature on predisposition to depression. The newer formulations of a depressive basic mood proclivity and the development of superego precursors during rapprochement confirm, amplify and suggest phase specificity to the more global preoedipal hypotheses.

The "germ of guilt," which becomes guilt after the later consolidation of superego function, may also refer to the differentiation of other related affects. It is analogous to the depressive proclivity and the negative basic mood of the rapprochement period. The feeling of loss at that level of development, when validated by reality, reinforces the affective responses of helplessness, sadness, grief, and the *Anlage* of depression. The "seed of self-reproach" is indicative of the beginning of internalization, of "identification with the aggressor" with turning aggression on the self as a superego precursor which antedates and contributes to the formation of the superego.

That the guilt and self-reproach are not triggered only by the death of his father in the *Nonvixit* dream, and in the other dreams of the "Interpretation of Dreams," can be discerned in the specimen dream of psychoanalysis, the "Irma" dream which begins the book. This dream, in which Freud pleads not guilty and confesses guilt at the same time for a variety of sexual and aggressive transgressions, occurred on July 24, 1895, before the death of his father (1896). In his associations, Freud reproaches himself for the deaths of Fleischl and a patient with the same name of his eldest daughter, "Mathilde," and the near death of Irma at the hands of Fliess (Schur, 1972). These self-accusations for adult "crimes" conceal the infantile sources of these reactions in his oedipal guilt, and his preoedipal germ of guilt and seed of self-reproach related to his death wishes toward his parents, his sister Anna, and his brother's death.

The death of Julius when Freud was two years old was the only actual death of a love object during his complicated and turbulent early life. The reconstruction of October 1897 is augured in letter 23 of April 1895 (Freud, 1887–1902, p. 119). Preoccupied by the "Psychology for Neurologists," Freud writes to Fliess, "My heart is in the coffin here with Caesar." Later, August 1898, Freud (p. 261) reports the first understanding of a parapraxis, forgetting a name, that of the poet "Julius" Mosen. " … the 'Julius' had not slipped my memory. I was able to prove (i) that I had repressed the name Mosen because of certain associations; (ii) that material from my infancy played a part in the repression … " This example was never published, just as Julius disappeared from Freud's (1900) associations to the *Nonvixit* dream in "The Interpretation of Dreams."

While the birth of his first sister, Anna, when Freud was two and two-thirds years old doubtless triggered more complex "ill wishes and infantile envy," neither Freud's nor his parents' derivative grief reactions would be fully accounted for by reconstructing upward from the earlier dead brother to the later live sister. (This does not overlook the importance of later development and of regressive defense against oedipal conflict.) Reaction to the birth of Anna was not reconstructed, was not within conscious memory as indicated in his paper, "Screen Memories" (1899), and could have been displaced backwards to Julius (Schur, 1972, p. 123). The hostility to Anna may also represent disguised aggression toward the older brother and father figures, and all the dangerous aggression may be displaced onto the younger weaker brother (Shengold, 1971). But the birth and death of Julius, doubtless with traumatic effects, also colored later reactions. The telescoping of traumatic memories was probably associated with interweaving developmental influences on structuralization and oedipal conflict. Nevertheless, the reaction to the birth of another child is not at all identical to the reaction to the death of a child by the parents and the surviving sibling.

The traumatic infantile loss of Julius and his mother's mourning and new pregnancy appear to be significant roots of Freud's concerns with death, and transience (cf. Atkins, 1977). Fearing an untimely death, he repeatedly tried to time his death, and told Jones (1957, p. 279) he thought of death every day of his life. He had the disconcerting parting remarks of "Goodbye, you may never see me again." The theory of a death instinct is most probably linked to these problems. Further confirmation of Freud's preoccupation with separation and specifically with the death of Julius may be found in his symptoms and self-analysis, e.g., the so-called Tilgner episode (Schur, 1972, p. 100).

Months before Freud's father's death on October 23, 1896, Freud had written to Fliess (April 16) of a neurotic fear of death, on that occasion based upon an identification with the dead sculptor Tilgner. Schur has detailed a number of possible correspondences between Tilgner and Freud, including the intense longing of both to visit Italy. Reading the details of Tilgner's life and death in an obituary, and writing to Fliess in a letter conveying his great ambivalence and, it might be added, possibly concerned about his father's health, Freud suffered from the dread of death. What was not noticed, however, was the date of Tilgner's death and Freud's letter. Tilgner died on April 15, the same date as Julius Freud. Thus, the dread of dying on April 15 may be understood as an anniversary reaction, just as the *Nonvixit* dream was dreamt on the anniversary of the death of a love object.

Such "anniversaries" are overdetermined and may also express familial anniversary reactions. Tilgner died before the unveiling of his Mozart statue, and the *Nonvixit* dream associations refer to the monument to the Emperor and the unveiling of the monument to Fleischl, unconsciously to the deaths of Freud's father and his brother Julius. The Rome of Freud's dreams was the Catholic city of the forbidding father and forbidden mother, but also the pre-Catholic city of Julius Caesar. Freud's extraordinary preoedipal reconstruction of the life and death of Julius was instrumental in his self-analysis and led to deepening understanding of his symptoms and inhibitions. An appreciation of formative preoedipal influences was convergent with Freud's discovery of the nuclear Oedipus complex and a cohesive psychoanalytic theory of neurosis.

Jones (1953, p. 317) recorded Freud's different and isolated levels of interpretation of pertinent oedipal and then preoedipal content. However, Jones did not compare and contrast the different levels of interpretation in different sections of the biography. Freud subjected to critical self-analysis his ambivalent relation to Jung, interpreting his fainting spells in Jung's presence in terms of the positive and negative Oedipus complex, as well as his unconscious submission to, rivalry with, and guilty triumph over Jung, Fliess, and his father. It is significant that Freud, having analyzed his fainting, "expressed the opinion that all his attacks could be traced to the effect on him of his young brother's death when he was a year and seven months old" (Jones, 1955, p. 146). Freud's giving this age is an interesting error or slip, for it refers to Freud's approximate age when Julius was born, not when Julius died, when Freud was just under two years of age.

Sibling birth, death, and new pregnancy are inevitably potential developmental disruptions in the mother-child relationship, and impose special challenges during the child's second year of life. The experience of intrapsychic loss is here compounded during rapprochement not only by anal-urethral and continuing oral problems and beginning castration conflicts, but by the real illness and loss of Julius. The proclivity to ambivalence will then be increased with abandonment anxiety and rage at the object, and possible splitting of the object world (Mahler, 1975, p. 108). Hostility toward the mother may also be displaced and projected onto other objects or turned on the self. Fearful of aggression and retaliation, the child "survivor" may display more intense separation reactions, defensive reliance on denial, reparative undoing, restitutive ambition, and reactive goodness. A basic negative mood will be accentuated by the effect on both the mother and her toddler of the new baby's birth and death, and the mother's withdrawal, grief, sadness, etc. Mahler (1966) has noted that a negative-depressive mood may persist or may give way to an unchildlike concern which may indicate a precocity of superego structuralization. Freuds anticipates and forecasts later developmental research, although what was missing from his knowledge of development at that time would be supplied by his own further research and by the pioneering contributions of his students.

The challenges and crises of rapprochement require maternal acceptance of the child's ambivalence and empathic responses to the child's hostile dependence and separation reactions. The child at this time is easily vulnerable to narcissistic injury and ego and drive regression. Freud (1926) formulated the great danger situations of early childhood, i.e., of the preoedipal period, in terms of fear of loss of the object, and fear of loss of the object's love. The abstract "object" was the mother, returned to a pivotal position in psychoanalytic theory. In connection with the infantile separation experience, which he analyzed and reconstructed, Freud pondered the psychology of pain and mourning and observed (1926, pp. 169–170) of the infant: "It cannot as yet distinguish between temporary absence and permanent loss. As soon as it loses sight of its mother it behaves as if it were never going to see her again; and repeated consoling experiences to the contrary are necessary before it learns that her disappearance is usually followed by her re-appearance. Its mother encourages this piece of knowledge which is so vital to it by playing the familiar game of hiding her face from it with her hands and then, to its joy, uncovering it again. In these circumstances it can, as it were, feel longing unaccompanied by despair." This is the first description of the peek-a-boo game in psychoanalysis.

Freud, to buttress and expand his theoretical constructs, utilized and recommended the direct observation of children. Starting from the consideration of traumatic repetitive dreams, he considered the functions of children's play, with the careful scrutiny of his grandson as his research subject. He noted (1900, p. 461) that all the child's toys were used in separation games, for mastery of separation anxiety by turning activity into passivity. These observations were of a child at eighteen months of age, the rapprochement period of his Julius and Wolf Man reconstructions. The child could express the concept of separation with the word "gone," one of his first words.

Representation in thought, and symbolic play indicative of identification with the mother, convey ego-active modes of dealing with separation distress converging in a more differentiated internalized representation of the mother and the capacity for evocative memory.

The separation-individuation process at this time can be correlated with psychosexual phases with regressive and progressive swings. Psychosexual development and separation-individuation are interrelated developmental processes and frameworks having common roots in Freud's earliest observations and formulations. The concepts of oral incorporation and projection of the part object and retention and expulsion of the fecal object (or narcissistic object) were early correlations of libido and object-relations theory.

I would parenthetically add that I do not believe that Freud's addiction to smoking, his lifelong battle against it, and his reliance on incessant smoking, e.g., twenty cigars daily for creative and productive work can be understood mainly in terms of the masturbatory equivalent and father identification he originally implied (Schur, 1972, p. 61), or as a nicotine drug habituation. The preoedipal roots of such a literally oral addiction, which led to Freud's oral carcinoma, are today much more clearly defined. In this respect, beginning with the examination of the oral cavity in the Irma dream, a preoedipal dimension can be inferred but not confirmed in many of his dreams and screen memories. Contemporary evaluation of addictive tendencies would include considerations of oral fixation and regression and archaic ego states, but also of conflicts related to symbiosis and separation-individuation. Such problems, when focal and attenuated, may coexist with many other areas of advanced personality development, and may also spur mastery and sublimation. Freud's unique capacity for developmental mastery and, later, self-analysis, were resources that fostered his insights into both personality formation and psychopathology.

The preoedipal reconstructions in the Fliess letters demonstrate self-analytic reconstructions related predominantly to the period of life before age three. The Freud family left Freiberg when Freud was three, a factor in his designation of the period before age three as "prehistoric," and isolating in time this period of his infancy. His apparent grasp of preoedipal attachment and ambivalence merged with the simultaneous discovery of the Oedipus complex. Freud checked some reconstructions with his mother (1887–1902, pp. 221–222), a source of validation with the original object frequently utilized by contemporary analysands. His preoedipal reconstructions contributed to the development of psychoanalytic drive, ego, and object-relations theory, to formulations of preoedipal character traits and patterns, and to the technique of psychoanalysis as a reconstructive therapy.

Reconstruction was always far more than a simple genetic interpretation of one segment of experience. It was a whole piece of mental life, as Freud illustrated in his letters to Fliess and described in "Constructions in Analysis." This "piece" of mental life can also be considered as a nodal point in development with both important antecedents and certainly significant consequences and ramifications for later development. The early tendency was to understand this in terms of the reconstruction of trauma with pathogenic consequences, but Freud's own reconstruction shows its general importance for the later development of object relations and both affective and character dispositions. What was reconstructed were not simple actual events, but the child's interpretation and reaction to his experience, in other words, the meaning attached to the experience: the ego state and developmental impact became more important than a consideration of actual history.

The historical reconstruction of real experience and of real traumatic episodes remains significant (Greenacre, 1975), without diminishing the importance of unconscious irrational conflicts and fantasies which may never have achieved consciousness. The unrememberable and unforgettable (Frank, 1969) would then continue to influence further development and the meaning attached to further experience. Even though early trauma might be telescoped into the appearance of the single shock episode, and even though earlier disorder might be overlaid with defensive and adaptive maneuvers and could acquire new meaning, it could be possible under favorable circumstances to reconstruct into the "prehistoric period" of separation-individuation. Analytic interpretation, via reconstruction, can be regarded as a reordering of the infant's misinterpretation of internal and external reality.

Freud's masterful use of dreams and screen memories to reconstruct the infantile past were demonstrated in his own self-analysis long before the development of many other areas of psychoanalytic theory and technique.

Prescient of some of the modern debate and controversy about the value and validity of preoedipal reconstruction, Freud (1900, pp. 451–452) further observed, "It was distressing to me to think that some of the premises which underlay my psychological explanations of the psychoneuroses were bound to excite scepticism and laughter when they were first met with. For instance, I had been driven to assume that impressions from the second year of life, and sometimes even from the first, left a lasting trace on the emotional life of those who were later to fall ill, and that these impressions—though distorted and exaggerated in many ways by the memory—Might constitute the first and deepest foundation for hysterical symptoms. Patients, to whom I explained this at some appropriate moment, used to parody this newly-gained knowledge by declaring that they were ready to look for recollections dating from a time *at which they were not yet alive*."

Many analysts were also skeptical, not only of phylogenetic memories or of elaborate fantasy in the first year of life, but of all preoedipal reconstruction. Regarding this controversy, it is clear that tentative preoedipal formulations and converging hypotheses were utilized by Freud and later pioneering analysts in the expansion of psychoanalytic theory. While inferences especially regarding the preverbal period have to be extremely cautious and careful, such efforts are consonant with Freud's own models and with continued efforts to trace pertinent earlier and verbalized memories to those preverbal and nonverbal phenomena that are isomorphic with the verbalizable clinical material (Mahler et al., 1975, p. 14). There have been many important examples of such efforts which in the long run have been richly rewarding to psychoanalytic understanding. Perhaps the most classic example of this kind of reconstruction to the earliest period of life is the Isakower phenomenon. This revival of very early ego states and attitudes was also reflected in the reconstructive studies of Greenacre (1950) on acting out, Lewin (1946) on the dream screen, and Spitz (1955) on the primal cavity to name a few.

Our expanding preoedipal knowledge and research exemplified in the concepts of separation individuation should not be misunderstood to mean that initial psychic development and differentiation is accessible to psychoanalysis, that there are no limits or ambiguities to reconstruction, or that the earliest ego disturbances are reversible. The twin problems of the genetic fallacy about advanced development and adultomorphic myth about infancy have to be kept in mind. Anna Freud (1971, p. 147) expressed reservations about analytic work in the preverbal area of primary repression, but she also stressed the need for both analytic and observational studies (1971, pp. 24-25): "Where the imprint of more highly developed functions is superimposed on the remnants of archaic layers, the original simplicity of the primitive picture cannot but be distorted; this is true in particular where regression proceeds from verbal to preverbal phases … with regard to the study of the first eighteen months of life, direct observation is indispensable as a means to complement, correct, and verify the conclusions drawn from the analyses of later stages."

It is not to be expected that reconstructive efforts should be exactly parallel with the data of analytic child observation, but the two sets of data should be consistent, and accurate reconstruction should fit or articulate with our current knowledge of development. The formulations of separation-individuation which organize data derived from analytic reconstruction do not detract from an appreciation of psychosexual development and the role of the Oedipus complex in adult neurotic disorder. Rather, these studies have enriched our appreciation of the epigenetic sequence of development wherein each phase is dependent upon the preceding phase for its impetus and solution; and at any point problems of irregular, arrested, or deviant development may occur. Our knowledge of the formative influences that impinge upon oedipal development and solutions have been greatly enriched. Analytic work should take into account all oedipal and accessible preoedipal problems that are encountered in a given case, not excluding the influence of later life. The picture, as we know from our own clinical work and from the dilemmas of many analytic students, can be very complicated and confused. Psychoanalysis is not for those who are looking for an easy solution or the use of some neat oedipal or preoedipal formula, or a conventional mold in which the clinical material can be artificially compressed.

The assessment of preoedipal influences and particularly of preoedipal disorder may be especially noted in the area of the patient's relation to the analyst: the transference, the therapeutic alliance, the attunement to reality, and the quality of object relations. In addition to the clinical history, the patient's use of the analytic process and analytic setting provides valuable information about basic personality function. The more serious the early preoedipal disturbance, with possible structural deficit, the less likely that the patient will demonstrate a classical transference neurosis or that there will be a stable therapeutic alliance. Preoedipal development will influence the formation and form of the oedipal infantile neurosis underlying later transference neurosis. I do not think there is an artificial isolation between preoedipal and oedipal analysis. Though an oedipal transference neurosis is central to analytic work, depending upon the personality structure and depth of regression, varying duration and intensity of preoedipal transference may be discerned or inferred. The analysis of a case of obsessional neurosis will eventually deal with symptoms and character traits related to anal-phase conflicts.

There is no reason to expect that any of the later normal developmental phases of life or pathological states will exactly replicate point by point any of the subphases of separation-individuation or psychosexual development. The early phases of development are not literally recapitulated; various consequences are inferred in terms of residue and influences, of forerunners which undergo further developmental vicissitudes, and which are subject to regressive transformations: "Certain configurations persist in transference or acting-out patterns which seem to be the outcome of unresolved conflicts in the separation-individuation process" (Mahler, 1971, p. 415).

In the origins of psychoanalysis, Freud discovered reconstruction and transference, and immediately reconstructed infantile psychological reactions and patterns dating from his second year of life, and returning as "revenants." He returned to these fascinating complexities in his final paper devoted to this topic. In "Constructions in Analysis" (1937, pp. 266–267), Freud concluded "with a few remarks which open up a wider perspective." Referring to hallucinatory experience, he stated, " … sufficient attention has not hitherto been paid that in them something that has been experienced in infancy and then forgotten returns—something that the child has seen or heard at a time when he could still hardly speak and that now forces its way into consciousness, probably distorted and displaced owing to the operation of forces that are opposed to this return."

Psychic history, which for Freud was preserved in its essentials and "present somehow and somewhere," tends to repeat itself. Freud's (1937, p. 261) last paradigm recapitulates his initial 1897 reconstruction: "'Up to your nth year you regarded yourself as the sole and unlimited possessor of your mother; then came another baby and brought you grave disillusionment. Your mother left you for some time, and even after her reappearance she was never again devoted to you exclusively. Your feelings towards your mother became ambivalent, your father gained a new importance for you,' … and so on." Reconstruction to that nth year (taking into account the most common age sequence in siblings) will most often require preoedipal reconstruction consonant with our expanding knowledge of psychological and developmental processes.

Summary

Freud's first reported reconstruction was to the preoedipal period and referred to the psychological meaning and consequences of the birth and death of his younger brother, Julius. In the historical development of psychoanalysis, preoedipal and oedipal reconstruction were simultaneously utilized, and Freud's thinking encompassed preoedipal influences with the Oedipus complex.

Reconstruction was one of the earliest discovered methods in psychoanalytic technique, reciprocally contributing to psychoanalytic theory, the uncovering of infantile amnesia, and awareness of the persistent influence of unconscious infantile conflict. Freud anticipated the importance of object relations in contemporary psychoanalytic theory before formulation of the libido theory. Reconstruction from dreams and screen memories converged in Freud's self-analysis in the discovery of the repression and revival of infantile object relations, leading to the concept of transference. Psychoanalysis was reconstructive, facilitating memory reorganization, and new ego synthesis.

Freud's self-analytic reconstruction concerning Julius, prototypical of preoedipal reconstruction, was to the proto-verbal anal developmental phase, and the rapprochement subphase of separation-individuation. His reconstruction is remarkably consistent with modern knowledge of developmental processes. The integration of psychoanalytic reconstruction and direct child observation promises a deeper understanding of ego development and disturbance, character formation, and preoedipal determinants of oedipal conflict and the infantile neurosis.

REFERENCES

Atkins, N. (1977). The analyst and transcience .Presented to the Psychoanalytic Assoc. of NY as the M. Sperling Lecture, February 1977.

Bibring, E. (1953). The mechanism of depression. In: *Affective Disorders*, ed. P. Greenacre. New York: International Universities Press.

Blum, H. (1974). The borderline childhood of the Wolf Man. *J. American Psychoanal. Assn.* 22:721–742.

Eissler, K. (1966). A note on trauma, dream, anxiety, and schizophrenia. The *Psychoanal. Study Child* 21:17–50.

Esman, A. (1973). The primal scene: A review and reconsideration. *Psychoanal. Study Child* 28:49–82.

Frank, A. (1969). The unrememberable and the unforgettable: Passive primal repression. *Psychoanal. Study Child* 24:48–77.

——— (1971). *The Writings of Anna Freud 7.*

Freud, S. (1887–1902). *The Origins of Psychoanalysis.* New York: Basic Books, 1950.

——— (1899). Screen memories. *Standard Edition* 3:301–322.

——— (1900). The interpretation of dreams. *Standard Edition* 5 339–627.

——— (1908). Character and anal erotism. *Standard Edition* 9:167–176.

——— (1913) The theme of the three caskets. *Standard Edition* 12:291–301.

——— (1917). A childhood recollection from *Dichtung und Wahrheit. Standard Edition* 17:145–156.

———— (1918). From the history of an infantile neurosis. *Standard Edition* 17:3–122.

———— (19260. Inhibitions, symptoms and anxiety. *Standard Edition* 20:77–177.

———— (1937). Constructions in analysis .*Standard Edition* 23:255–270.

Greenacre, P. (1950). General problems of acting out. In: *Trauma, Growth, and Personality.* New York: International Universities Press, 1952 pp. *224–236.*

———— (1975). On reconstruction. *J. American Psychoanal. Assn.* 23: *693–712.*

Grigg, K. (1973). "All roads lead to Rome": The role of the nursemaid in Freud's dreams. J. American Psychoanal. Assn. 21:*108–126.*

Grinstein, A. (1968). *On Sigmund Freud's Dreams.* Detroit: Wayne State University Press.

Jones, E. (1953, 1955, 1957). *The Life and Work of Sigmund Freud,* Volume 1, 2, 3. New York: Basic Books.

Kanzer, M. (1972). Review of the Wolf Man by the Wolf Man. *Int. J. Psychoanal.* 53: *419–421.*

———— & Blum, H. (1967). Classical psychoanalysis since 1939. In: *Psychoanalytic Techniques.*, ed. B. Wolman. New York: Basic Books, pp. *93–146.*

Kris, E. (1956). On some vicissitudes of insight in psychoanalysis. *Int. J. Psychoanal.* 37:445–455.

Lewin, B. (1946). Sleep, the mouth, and the dream screen. In: *Selected Writings.* New York: Psychoanal. Q., Inc., 1973 pp. *87–100.*

Mahler, M. (1966). Notes on the development of basic moods: The depressive affect. In: *Psychoanalysis: A General Psychology,* ed. R. Lowenstein. et al. New York: International Universities Press, pp. *152–168.*

———— (1971). A study of the separation-individuation process and its possible application to borderline phenomena in the psychoanalytic situation. *Psychoanal. Study Child* 26:403–424.

———— (1975). On the current status of the infantile neurosis. *J. American Psychoanal. Assn.* 23:327–333.

———— Bergman, A., & Pine, F. (1975). *The Psychological Birth of the Human Infant.* New York: Basic Books..

McDevitt, J. (1975). Separation-individuation and object constancy. *American Psychoanal. Assn.* 23:713–742.

Peto, A. (1969). Terrifying eyes: A visual superego forerunner. The *Psychoanal. Study Child* 24:*197–212*.

Schafer, R. (1960). The loving and beloved superego in Freud's structural theory. *Psychoanal. Study Child*15:*163–188*.

Schur, M. (1972). *Freud: Living and Dying.* New York: International Universities Press.

Shengold, L. (1971). Freud and Joseph. In: *The Unconscious Today,* ed. M. Kanzer. New York: International Universities Press, pp. *473–494*.

Spitz, R. (1955). The primal cavity: A contribution to the genesis of perception and its role for psychoanalytic theory. *Psychoanal. Study Child* 10:*215–240*.

CHAPTER 19

The Value of Reconstruction in Adult Psychoanalysis

(1980). *Int. J. Psychoanal.* (61):39–52.

Reconstruction has been important in psychoanalytic theory, technique, and therapy. This paper will reaffirm the technical and theoretical value of reconstruction in psychoanalysis, and I shall take the position that reconstruction is clinically valuable for the patient, and the psychoanalytic process may demand it. Reconstruction assists in the analytic restoration of the continuity and cohesion of the personality. But what may be as important or even more important, reconstruction is fundamental for the analyst. The analyst may not be explicitly aware of his use of reconstruction but he will inevitably reconstruct aspects of the patient's infantile life in order to comprehend the patient's personality disorder. The analyst and eventually the patient will want to know how the child became that particular adult and how that adult has remained a disturbed child. How could the analyst understand the case without some utilization of reconstruction? I have in mind, therefore, the regularity of analytic reconstruction and not just in special cases or syndromes or restricted to use by a limited group of ardent analysts. Reconstruction is not only an important technical tool, but is essential for comprehensive psychoanalytic exploration.

Because of a number of changes in psychoanalysis and current interests, reconstruction seemed to be less cited in the literature, less emphasized and utilized in clinical reports and in psychoanalytic education. After reflecting upon the relative decline of reconstruction, I shall reconstruct upwards to the frequent necessity of reconstruction in clinical psychoanalysis, highlighted by contrast with its current loss of prominence and popularity. Reconstructive insight is often achieved and utilized without specifying the method. It may be added that reconstruction is regaining significant analytic interest and attention (Greenacre, 1975); (Blum, 1977). Greenacre's work exemplifies the technical, therapeutic, and research value of reconstruction. She has pioneered in the reconstruction of infantile disturbance in adult analysis and in its application to psychobiography and studies of creativity. The current revival may be related to increasingly fruitful genetic and developmental studies. Increased interest in reconstruction is also related to specific reconstructions concerning borderline and narcissistic disorders.

The terms 'construction and reconstruction' are not only usually merged in meaning with each other but also with a broadened scope of interpretation. Constructions are preliminary and hypothetical, the initial and tentative phase of reconstruction in Greenacre's (1975) terminology. For purposes of this paper I will not sharply distinguish between the two terms following Freud's interchangeable terminology. Beginning with the initial constructs, I want to stress the continuing analytic reshaping of reconstruction. The patient's life, childhood objects, and experience look differently to the analyst and analysand at different phases of treatment. Because of defensive distortion and areas of ego immaturity, accurate reconstruction is a gradual process involving conjoint efforts and analytic collaboration; usually initiated by the analyst, it is more likely to be valid and effective later in treatment. Reconstruction as a process involves remolding by analyst and analysand with approximations that have ever greater cohesion and explanatory power.

In addition to the diffusion of the reconstruction concept, particularly with regard to genetic interpretation, reconstruction has been silently relegated to a less important position now than in pioneer psychoanalysis which stressed the recovery of traumatic childhood memories. Further, the ascendance of ego psychology with its emphasis upon analysis of defense left the recovery and restoration of memories in the background, and the memories themselves, as screen memories, required analysis. Kris (1956a) complained about an overemphasis on defense analysis with memory recovery and reconstruction assuming secondary importance. The shift from analysis of id fantasy to the analysis of unconscious conflict and complex compromise formations also tended to shift interest from reconstruction of sectors of infantile life to the analysis of the current derivatives of unconscious conflict. Here was the most significant move away from and perhaps toward reconstruction again via the transference. The transference, which is a most valuable guide to reconstruction and a further testing of reconstruction, had by virtue of its preeminence partially eclipsed the role of reconstruction in psychoanalytic clinical theory and technique. Dwelling on the reconstruction the past could become an evasion of the here and now of the transference. This would mean that reconstruction of genetic roots would be thought to diminish or replace transference analysis. It was as if attention to reconstruction would detract from the exceptional importance accorded transference interpretation.

The analysis of conflict derivatives could only be effectively accomplished in the here and now of the transference. The transference was a form of remembering, a living revival of the past in the analytic situation. The transference replaced what was forgotten and was itself a remobilized, though still disguised, return of the repressed. Analysis of the transference was central, and its patterns and paradigms were more centrally significant than individual new memories or recall of single shocks and revived traumatic situations. Because of the early association of reconstruction with the paradigm of shock trauma and often with a single shock as in the Wolf Man Case, reconstruction was linked to antiquated analytic techniques (Blum, 1977).

The persistent, repeated transference fantasies and reactions, their direct observation by analyst and patient as they unfold in the analytic situation were more accessible, reliable, and convincing than memories of the past. Transference interpretation seemed more reliable than reconstruction and interpretation of screen memory.

To further complicate the problems of memory recall and reconstruction, the distorting and distorted nature of early memory is well-known (Kris, 1956a), (1956b). No matter how interlaced and buttressed with cohesive detail and other memories, analysts would not again be seduced by memories. Freud had discovered universal fantasies when he treated his patient's memories of parental seduction as manifest content rather than historical truth. Subject to fantasy distortion, memory also tends to be telescoped, to be influenced by the ego organization in which it was registered, and reshaped by subsequent experience (A. Freud, 1951) and regressive, as well as retrospective transformation. Referring to reconstructive problems, Kris (1956a, p. 73) stated, 'the experience is overlaid with its aftermath, the guilt, terror, and thrill elaborated in fantasy, and the defense against these fantasies.' The truth as revealed by recall and reconstruction could turn out to be deceptive fantasy. Reconstruction synthesized memory fragments and 'created' memory and became the target of the same doubts that applied to recall, although reconstruction facilitated defense analysis and uncovering amnesia.

Analytic reconstruction, supplying, supplementing, and substituting for the recovery of lost memories could be confused with a cathartic method of uncovering the buried traumatic past. It was as if ego psychology and careful analysis of defense might mean that reconstruction would by-pass defense rather than a synergism occurring between the analysis of resistance and reconstruction. Diminished resistance favors reconstruction, which in turn facilitates the analysis of recurrent resistance. Moreover, it is important to recognize that reconstruction deals not only with content, but with ego attributes and functions, affect states and object relations (Greenacre, 1975); (Mahler et al., 1975); it deals not only with conflict, but with development and structure formation, with pre-oedipal influences and with arrests and deficits. Reconstruction is thus related to many contemporary issues and controversies. It is well to note here that reconstruction has theoretical and therapeutic limitations. The formation of the personality will not be altogether accessible, and malformations and deficits will not necessarily be reversible. There are ever-present dangers of rewriting history and enlarging legend.

Reconstruction is often demanded by the backward drift of free association and fantasy, the regressive movement in the analytic associations towards the genetic roots of the adult neurosis. The patient learns of neurotic repetition in transference and in life before and during analysis. In analytic work, reconstruction and recall reduce the transference to its origins and determinants. The past is living in the here and now, but has to be separated. from the present in which it continues. The past continues to influence the present; the present and intermediate or recent past may influence the meaning of the remote past. Reconstruction will attempt to take into account the different derivatives of disturbance that belong together in development, as well as the developmental changes which have occurred since the infantile neurotic disposition.

In supplying and substituting for missing memory, reconstruction becomes an integrative force (Kris, 1956a) and a mode of reassembling fantasies, memories, and distorted historical fragments which will, within the analytic process, lead to structural renovation and reorganization. Reconstruction does not automatically proceed from transference analysis and memory recovery, but from integration of the analytic and anamnestic data, and the gaps and inconsistencies in the data. Primitive transferences will appear to be quite different from the reconstructed infantile object relations (Kernberg, 1979).

Reconstruction then becomes more precise as the analytic process unfolds, simultaneously contributing to the analytic work and the widening of insight. Past and present and their cross-correlations with the totality of the patient's life (in fantasy, dreams, screen memories, conflict, character, behavior, etc.) are reintegrated in a way which uniquely fit together. The analytic autobiography which emerges reflects the personality reorganization effected with insight and the enlightenment concerning life which the reconstructed patterns and meanings have brought.

Reconstruction is related to many contemporary issues and controversies, e.g. pre-oedipal influences, the significance of direct child observation, theories of structure formation and malformation, the diagnosis and treatment of developmental deviations and borderline syndromes, etc. Reconstruction has always been part of classical analysis and is a fundamental dimension of the analytic task. This is a reconstructive task which Freud (1937, p. 258) defined, 'What we are in search of is a picture of the patient's forgotten years that shall be alike trustworthy and in all essential respects complete.'

Reconstruction, for Freud, was much broader than genetic interpretation that dealt with simple elements. Genetic interpretation was an element of reconstruction. Reconstruction also was a substitute for missing memories and incomplete memory fragments and sought to reorganize cognitive, affective, and sensory experience on higher levels of development while simultaneously seeking to understand early development and pathogenesis. These interrelated, but different meanings are important in analysis and Freud (1937, p. 266) asserted: 'If the analysis is carried out correctly, an assured conviction of the truth of the construction … achieves the same therapeutic result as recaptured memory.'

I should like now to give an example of adult analytic work, demonstrating not only the value and validity of reconstruction, but the vital nature of reconstruction to the comprehension of the patient's depressive disturbance and the analytic reorganization of the conflicted personality. While the case is one of object loss, or more specifically parent loss in childhood, it is not a discussion of a single traumatic event. It is rather an example of the complexity and overdetermination of the effects of early object loss, and then of object deprivation with developmental disturbance. As is so often the case, the patient knew of the trauma, but did not know of its significance in her life. What is reconstructed is not the historical event of a father's death when the child is of a tender age, but the intrapsychic meaning of the experience, its ramifications and *sequelae*, its traumatic impact, and antecedent and subsequent influences which determine the effect of such a stressful, depleting loss. Reconstruction clarified the child's reactions to parent loss and different levels of development and regression.

The patient was a young mother in her thirties when analyzed. She was an intelligent, thoughtful, attractive woman, with a lively wit, considerable ambition, and many interests and friends. At the same time, she felt separate from people and was very self-conscious and conscious of what people said about her. She tried to fathom what type of impression she created and was very concerned about appearance, approval, and issues of social recognition, self-respect, and self-esteem. Relatives and friends were thought to be jealous of her accomplishments and critical of her aspirations. She was afraid that affection would meet with disappointment or with painful disillusionment.

She reported long-standing feelings of mild depression, associated with feeling inadequate, unnecessary, and in more extreme form, worthless. There were other symptoms of appetite disturbance, weight fluctuation, gagging, urinary and bowel frequency, and palpitations.

I shall limit this brief presentation to the details of the depression which consumed so much of the analytic work. The depression proved to be causally connected to the parent loss, and it developed that the patient had unconsciously arranged her first appointment on the anniversary of the death of her father. Her father died when she was 4-years-old from a slowly, intermittently deteriorating fatal condition. Shortly after the father's death, a related couple moved into the house with their children. Her siblings as well as her cousin's children were all older. She never got along with her cousin, and the relationships she recalled during her latency and adolescent years were all highly ambivalent. The patient tended to idealize her father and excuse her mother, while devaluing the mother's cousin who seemed to represent the embodiment of malice. There were, of course, many complicated conflicts over loyalty, desertion, and shifting alliances.

Guilt, self-punitive fantasy, and identification with the lost parent were prominent. In addition, denial of loss, the idealization of the lost parent, loss with fantasied reunion, the displacement of aggression from the lost parent to the surviving parent and relatives, the jealousies and loyalty conflicts, etc. all led to great personal and familial discord and turmoil. Restoration of cause and effect, action and reaction, requires reconstruction of the total intrapsychic experience with its external co-ordinates.

The reconstruction of this total constellation is far more than the systematic recapture of the infantile memories or the observations of transference regression and progressive resumption of mourning. Without reconstruction, the repeated anniversary depressions and related symptoms before analysis; the depressive equivalents within and outside the analytic situation; the depressive withdrawal of her mother even before her father's death; the unmodulated grief, rage, and anxiety when confronted with unconscious fantasies of abandonment, would not be decisively related to unresolved problems of childhood and the infantile neurosis. Moreover, the components of her childhood, adolescent, and adult depression (e.g. guilt) was by no means the same in form, content, or intensity as at the time of the loss at the age of 4.

The myriad of verbal and non-verbal associations (memories, dreams, actions, etc.) form a mosaic from which interpretations and inferences lead to reconstructions. The patient was told, in effecting reconstruction, that the analytic evidence pointed, for example, to a configuration of fantasies, feelings, and defenses that were elaborated during her father's illness and in response to his death.

While the transference paradigm varied with periods of regression and progression in the analysis, it became clear that the patient was fixated to the second stage of mourning with hypercathexis of the lost object. The anniversary of the father's death triggered depression, not only in the patient, but in her sibling, and quite possibly in the form of depressive equivalents in the mother. Attaining the age of their father at death, the patient became agitated and depressed. Her own birthday introduced the theme of birth, death, and rebirth into the analysis. Anniversary dates involved a rule of nine for both births and deaths. The father's death occurred in the year of marriage, on the day of the month, and at an age which were all multiples of nine. Significantly, she had become engaged on such a date and arranged for her wedding on Father's Day. She believed she was conceived by her father while he was dying of a malignancy. She felt she was a special person, a living continuation of her dead parent, but also someone who might Harbor the disease and pass it on to her own children.

As a mother, she was overprotective and overconcerned about her children's health and illnesses. She arranged for the birth of her children to occur at the same time of year as her father's death, symbolically arranging for unconscious rebirth and restitution. She wanted a transference baby from the analyst, but there were also fantasies of abortion, and she herself was the baby who had no right to live. She was unconsciously guilty of parental murder, but also projected and assigned the hostile and murderous wishes to others in the family, particularly mother and mother's cousin. Separation had to be undone, or actively inflicted on others. She would forget the children's appointments whenever her own analytic hours were cancelled, and would be furious with her husband if he forgot an appointment with her or the children. She could not tolerate aggressive and regressive encounters with the children, and was upset if they indicated rejection or rebellious independence of her. She realized that she had been angry with her husband since he had been away on a trip which she unconsciously interpreted as a desertion. Arguments with members of the family or with the analyst as the transference deepened, terrified her because of her fear of abandonment, retaliation, and mutual murder.

Approximately one year after beginning treatment, this patient who had previously been affable, witty, and socially charming began to look much worse both outside and inside the analytic situation. As the anniversary of her father's death approached, this time within the regressive analytic situation, the patient for the first time began to describe suicidal thinking. Agitated turmoil and suicidal transference fantasy would develop repeatedly, and both patient and analyst were subjected to very trying times. The usual recreational pastimes outside analysis and the fun of discovery and eager participation in the analytic work all disappeared. Depression deepened; the patient became extremely serious and provocative; imploring and demanding in the analysis; lashing out at the analyst and acting out at home with angry outbursts.

She recalled having transient thoughts years ago of jumping out of a hotel window after having been insulted by a girlfriend; referred to past suicidal ideas of certain relatives and friends. Again, with thoughts of death she brought up childbirth, feeling deserted by the obstetrician who left and by her mother, and siblings who were away and unable to visit. She became more depressed, dependent, and fearful of separation and closeness, but especially separation. The ends of the sessions and separations for the week-ends became scenes of agitated depression, anxiety, and later, fury for the patient.

Countertransference problems were intensified with the patient's increasing sense of despair. Tormented and self-deprecating, she also wanted the analyst to suffer, to feel pangs of sorrow and guilt, demanding that the analyst be omnipotent and omniscient while at the same time proving that he was impotent and helpless. Although she developed suicidal thinking during points of transference regression, there were no suicidal gestures during the analysis. It seemed as though she never completely gave up hope, and there were ego resources to continue the analytic and reconstructive work, even under the most trying depressive moods and despondent attitudes. What the analysis made clear was that the anniversary depression which was the presenting clinical picture, had been repeated many times before and was to be variably repeated many times again in the analysis. Moreover, anniversaries were not the only triggers of her depression and were not only precipitants but symptoms of and repeated efforts to master depression.

The important issue was the intrapsychic depressive constellation and the associated unconscious infantile conflicts, not the external anniversary triggers (Pollock, 1970). The patient reacted to separations from the analyst, to silences and feelings of distance in the analytic situation, to separations in life such as when a sibling as surrogate parent went off to college. In her case, the actual separation proved to be a greater threat than the important symbolic separations and transitions described by Fleming (1972) such as graduation from college, getting married, and having children. These initiations into more adult expectations and responsibilities did not result in overt depressions. However, depressive predisposition and depressive equivalents in the form of food and appetite disturbances could be found throughout her childhood and later life.

Recalling a sibling leaving to go to college, she dreamt of herself soliciting on a roof. She could not bear to lose another object and had fantasies of immediate union and replacement. She was clearly guilty about both her sexual and aggressive fantasies, and seductively wanted to unite with the father to recapture the lost object, his love, penis, and baby. Suicide also meant reunion as well as death, and the patient sought her father in the stars, in the heavens, and in the earth. She dreamt of being entombed, and the analytic situation became the tomb, the womb, and the grave from which she would grow up into adult independent life like a transplanted branch saved from a dying plant.

She herself interpreted fantasies in which her mother appeared as a phallic woman. She attempted to restitute for the missing female penis, but her phallic mother was a combination of father and mother. Although she relied upon her siblings and others as surrogate parents, she referred to the mother's sad life and her overwhelming efforts to be both a father and mother.

She thought of herself as destructive and responsible for her father's death and the subsequent unhappiness of the entire family, but there was blame for all. Fantasies that mother had killed father in the primal scene appeared, along with fantasies that mother and cousin were dangerous and devouring objects who withheld love and protection. These fantasies also clearly pointed to the reconstruction of the mother's withdrawal and anticipatory grief as well as the mother's subsequent depression after the death of her father. The danger of the patient's own destructive, devouring impulses seemed to be validated. At first she could not remember the death of her father at 4 years of age. This had to be reconstructed primarily from transference reactions, dreams, and screen memories. One particularly significant dream involved the patient looking down from a high place and seeing a procession of dancers. A series of associations following the dream led to a procession of celebrants, and then to a procession of dancers, and finally of mourners. It was a funeral procession, and the seeming joyous occasion was the type of screen affect she used to turn feelings of depression into states of relative elation and jocularity.

The analysis began to unleash active mourning with the recovery of fragmented and distorted memories of her father's illness and death. The mourning dovetailed with the reconstruction of the entire object loss constellation and her feeling abandoned and helpless in the face of loss of both parents.

It had not been possible really to tolerate parental loss and to mourn as a child (Wolfenstein, 1966); (Furman, 1974). There was simultaneous denial, repression, and efforts at reunion and replacement.

She reported feeling both bereft and betrayed. This was largely confined to the transference situation, although it spilled over, as I have indicated, into real life and into the waiting room. She left many sessions with tears in her eyes, and on one occasion sat weeping in the waiting room for some time, both waiting for the analyst to offer her more time and support and at the same time to tell her to leave and to function independently. She berated the analyst for being cold and impersonal, split the transference with frequent telephone calls to her friend with whom she shared many of her thoughts and feelings. She did not develop a pseudo-independence of the analyst, but repeatedly struggled with her feelings of dependency and rage and her fantasies of replacement, reunion, and revenge upon the analyst as transference object. The active mourning process within the analysis was exemplified by her longing for her lost father, her driving to the analytic session in a funeral procession, her grieving and mourning in the transference, and by actually going to the cemetery, finding her father's grave and weeping at the site.

The entire analysis took on the cast of a prolonged and protracted mourning process. The fixation in her personality development at the pre-loss level at the age of 4, emerged in special clarity. She enacted games of lost and found in which she could again actively search and find what she herself had chosen to lose. She would find misplaced keys and books, read obituaries in the paper, recite prayers for the dead, reflect on biblical themes of death, execution, and resurrection. Could there be a life after death—things living on for generations such as parents living again in their children and grandchildren? Cuneiform tablets and the Dead Sea Scrolls brought ancient civilizations to life again. Analytic interpretations could become magical incantations, and in the analytic transference, as in isolated sections of her life, the pleasure principle and denial held sway and her father was not dead but continued to live in her fantasy life. There were simultaneous denial and acknowledgement of loss, arrested mourning, fixated development with increased dependency and ambivalence toward the surviving parent, tendencies to regress which repeated the regression at the time of the parental loss.

She identified with a friend who was dying and recalled instances of surgery in which amputated parts were sewn back as in the case of a severed finger. Could the castration, organ, and object loss be repaired? Ideas of suicide through an overdose of pills reminded her of drug induced abortion. We again saw her identification with her dying father whose life had been aborted. Children tend to identify globally with the parents and to undergo regressive dedifferentiation in the face of stress, a reaction exemplified in this patient in her regressive merger fantasies. Though this doubtless involved the wished-for fusion with the lost father, in form and content, the fusion fantasy and possibly transient experiences of fusion involved a reactivation of dyadic pre-oedipal relationship with the analyst. The dyadic transference in which the analyst represented pre-oedipal mother was extremely difficult to define in the overdetermined analytic relationship, and it appeared mostly by inference at times of severe transient analytic regression. The revival of pre-oedipal traumata and losses such as the reconstructed anticipatory depressive withdrawal of the mother in the face of her husband's fatal illness could be reconstructively surmised.

This brings me to the relationship to the surviving parent. This is sometimes relatively overlooked in the older literature in comparison with the importance of the pathological relationships and identifications which have taken place at the time of the object loss. Life goes on, and psychic structure and contents are influenced not only by what happened in antecedent phases, but what happens in the phases of life subsequent to the loss and the surrounding stressful situation. I would like to suggest here that the tenacious hypercathexis of the father and the incomplete mourning process are also associated with a tenacious hypercathexis of the surviving parent—in this case the mother. The child's relationship with her mother was intensified with a hostile clinging dependency on both sides. It may be said that for all surviving members of the family, there were indications that each took on attributes of the deceased parent for the other with varying degrees of displacement, projection, and splitting of self and object representations into idealized and devalued sexual and asexual objects. Because the analyst was so predominantly and pervasively the lost father in the transference, it was exceedingly difficult to get a clear picture of the maternal transference and to reconstruct the later relationship with the surviving mother, screened behind the father transference. The figure of the deceased parent was thus a composite representation.

Reconstruction, then, has to be upward into latency and adolescence, as well as backward into the earliest developmental stages in order to understand and work through the patient's loss reactions. Though her father's death was a phase-specific oedipal trauma, the effects of the loss were both to arrest development at the pre-loss level and to be reorganized in varying degree in the subsequent developmental phases. In this case, the traumatic loss for the little girl and for her mother seemed not to immunize, but rather to sensitize her to future disturbance and to marked depressive disposition. Her self-esteem and ego integration remained fragile apart from anniversaries with their attempted working-through by ritual mourning on definite and declared dates. Anniversary depression denies and acknowledges loss with incomplete mourning and with assurance of both remembrance and magic survival (Pollock, 1975). At times the anniversary may be kept out of awareness, isolated from the depression reaction. An underlying depression persisted, and depressive reactions and depressive equivalents could be discerned during the life cycle.

The patient's anniversary reactions are probably indicative of the subliminal perception of time by the unconscious ego (Mintz, 1971). These reactions also have been shared by other relatives in familial inter-identifications. Time is also irrevocably past and gone, like the lost parent, yet subject to illusions of reversal and retrieval. The period of acute grief was preceded by a family constellation and lifestyle which were radically changed afterwards. The anniversary of such a trauma may be marked by regressive reactivation of conflict with personality disturbance or by non-pathological adaptive outcomes. Attenuated anniversary reactions represent self limited and time limited forms of repetitive and reparative anticipation and assimilation of past trauma. Highly variable reactions include anniversary dreams, daydreams, and screen memories which may be valuable paths toward recollection and reconstruction of the anniversary repetition. In depressive patients, anniversaries denote both wishful fantasies of reunion and incomplete mastery of the danger of retribution, and both immortality and living on borrowed time. The anniversary depression (or similar syndromes) links and demarcates past and present; the anniversary may represent separation and a bridge to new objects and experience. Often, because of denial and other defenses, parent loss in childhood is followed by splitting between denial and acknowledgment of loss and splitting of idealized and devalued self and object representations (Jacobson, 1971). The internal split may be modelled after the attitudes of the surviving family as well as the radical change of circumstances and life style that may occur.

The anniversary of the traumatic situation of childhood parent loss and its stressful consequences may mark a great time divide of personal experience and family life before and after. The trauma and developmental disturbance also lead to personality change, to an inner life that is differently organized than the former state which in turn influences the perception and response to external reality and the object world. The feeling of personality and reality discontinuity will persist unless the trauma is mastered and development can proceed after mourning the losses and adapting to the changes that have occurred. The anniversary reaction points to specific repeated events, but also to a temporal and yet internal discontinuity which invites reconstructive coordination and integration. Anniversary reactions acquire additions and editions, so that the reactions and meanings are altered in life, and reconstruction becomes a complex process. The reconstruction involves repetitions and revisions during different development phases, and the personality disposition and influences which favored this form of neurotic or adaptive solution.

This patient, and many others, organized major aspects of life around unconscious anniversaries, such as marriage and motherhood. Acts of atonement, symptomatic acts, and various sublimations may be stimulated by unrecognized anniversaries, as in charitable endeavors or rescuing wayward youth and dying plants.

These problems were linked to the problems and conflicts of the surviving parent. The little girl's depressive reactions were not recognized or acknowledged by her mother, and there was certainly no opportunity to express or to share grief and guilt, sadness and sorrow. She was not allowed to participate in the funeral or mourning ceremonies. Her mother did not provide realistic information about her father's life before he was ill, the nature of his illness, the meaning of death, and the practical consequences of the father's absence for the whole family. After the mother remarried, the family made no references to his earlier existence. It was like a family secret which haunted her, which she knew she was not to question overtly or discuss, and a secret which conjured up intense conflicts of allegiance and silent avoidance. Reconstruction here involved the conspiracy of familial silence, the conversion of parental prohibition to permission to remember (Kestenberg, 1972), and understanding of maternal support and model for the patient's repression and denial. Ostrich-like attitudes in later life were related to the childhood utilization of denial and disavowal.

The need to reconstruct what is denied, as well as why and in what form, demonstrates that the historical reality or external event cannot be artificially separated from the intrapsychic experience. The historical events, insignificant in isolation, mutually illuminate psychic development, as regularly observed in cases of childhood illness, parental seduction, psychosis, loss, etc.

Reconstruction of both psychic and external reality is important in situations of denial or derealization (Rosen, 1955), but also in the common cases where reality has activated or actualized a fantasy or precipitated a dormant neurosis. There are significant differences between primal scene fantasy versus actual exposure, between fantasied desertion and actual object loss. The traumatic event may have to be identified and reconstructed to restore reality testing and judgment (Greenacre, 1956). The patient has to understand her own denial of parent loss, identification with a depressed or psychotic parent, etc. If the delusion cannot be understood without its kernel of truth, neither can true identification without the actual models at different phases of development. Retrieval of the original course of events and experience is probably not possible, and the meaning and intrapsychic experience are vastly altered. The analysis of the transference in the here and now does not preclude the possibility that the childhood roots of the difficulty and decisive connections between past and present will not be thoroughly established and analyzed. The more current derivatives of unconscious childhood conflict may be analyzed without the basic repressions and the pathogenic childhood conflicts being fully available. To put this another way: if the past and present have not been meaningfully interconnected, than in all likelihood the resistance has not been fully overcome, and the basic conflicts have not been subjected to insight and to new ego integration. Reconstruction goes beyond individual memories and fantasies, and is an integrative act. Reconstruction integrates genetic interpretations and converging analytic data. Offering a piece of development and a new understanding of the patient's psychopathology, reconstruction favors further reduction of resistance and recapture of memories. These processes are synergistic with the widening of insight into the patient's personality and pathogenic conflicts. With the capacity to mourn and give up old relationships and infantile self-representations, and in this case with the resolution of the pathogenic attachment to the dead father and depressed mother, the patient can truly form new mature object relationships in conjunction with a reorganized and more integrated self-representation and cohesive life history.

The abuse of reconstruction will lead to analytic myth. However, without proper genetic reconstructions complementing and integrating other interpretations and observations, personal and familial myths will be joined by analytic myth. Current conflict and psychopathology are inexplicable without genetic antecedents. This will mean continued impairment rather than strengthening of the synthetic function of the ego. The compulsion to repeat cannot be tamed without working through from the adult neurosis to earlier intermediate neurotic formations to the pathogenic origins of the disturbance in childhood. Working through applies insight into the unconscious childhood conflicts to the myriad of derivatives and recurrent defenses. Freud stated (1914, p. 151), 'the transference is itself only a piece of repetition, and that the repetition is a transference of a forgotten past not only on to the doctor but also on to all the other aspects of the current situation.' Freud continued, 'This state of illness is brought, piece by piece, within the field and range of operation of the treatment, and while the patient experiences it as something real and contemporary, we have to do our therapeutic work on it, which consists in a large measure in tracing it back to the past' (p. 152). The analyst needs to trace back to the past, and to uncover, synthesize, and reintegrate the past traces which lead to the origins and solution of the patient's psychological problems. These views were reaffirmed by Freud (1937) and are compatible with, and complementary to, the importance of transference in the analytic process.

At an earlier phase in the evolution of technique, Freud was more optimistic about the effective uncovering of infantile amnesia through the analysis of transference and resistance in the present. Stressing the need for memory recovery, he had then remarked (Freud, 1914, p. 154), 'From the repetitive reactions which are exhibited in the transference we are led along the familiar paths to the awakening of memories, which appear without difficulty, as it were, after the resistance has been overcome.'

However, resistance recurred, and memories did not always appear or coalesce. Within just a few years the role of discrete recollection and recall appeared to recede. Freud (1917, p. 444) shifted the focus of analytic work from memories to the transference neurosis, and he commented, 'When the transference has risen to this significance, work upon the patient's memories retreats far into the background.'

These comments require critical comparison and contrast with Freud's simultaneous and continuing emphasis upon the genetic viewpoint and the reconstructive approach. At the same time he wrote of the retreat from work on memories, he observed (Freud, 1917, p. 454), 'In order to resolve the symptoms, we must go back as far as their origin, we must renew the conflict from which they arose, and with the help of motor forces which were not at the patient's disposal in the past, we must guide it to a different outcome. This revision of the process of repression can be accomplished only in part in connection with the memory traces of the processes which led to repression.'

The analyst shifts to and fro, between reality and fantasy, and between past and present and their mutual influence. Both dwelling upon the past or persistent adherence to the present could function as a form of resistance (Kris, 1956a, p. 56). Reconstruction goes beyond the awakening of memories or the reconstitution and reassembly of fragments of the patient's disguised past to detailed integration of interpretive work. The interpretive work is fitted into an appropriate ego and affect state. The childhood conflict, dangers, and object world within a developmental context, establishes an entirely new set of meanings, and causes, consequences, and relationships for the patient. This is a very different order of understanding than the analysis of the transference reactions as they have occurred in the analysis, and the recovery of discrete memories. Transference is not a replication of the past, but a disguised and revised repetition.

The transference does not follow an orderly sequence or developmental path. The later derivatives of the traumatic constellation of parent loss in the analytic situations are by no means identical with the original experiences, either as reproduced or reconstructed. Transference analysis and reconstruction are mutually facilitating (Rangell, 1979), different dimensions of the psychoanalytic process.

Intrapsychic events are overdetermined even before they occur, and during the course of life, new meanings are acquired and there are progressive and regressive transformations of previous experience. Elaborations and alterations of conflicts occur with new compromise formations. Changes in activity or passivity occur with modifications in the psychic apparatus, for example, in the formation of the superego and because of new identifications at later periods of life. Guilt may transform sadism to masochism (Freud, 1919). Kris (1956a, p. 77) pointed out that these processes are repeated throughout childhood and adolescence with molding of personality patterns. The analyst then rarely deals with isolated or single phenomena but patterns, multiple influences and interrelationships. Separation anxiety may be manifest as a sleep disturbance of infancy, travel phobia of childhood, drug dependence in later adolescence, and a component of adult depression.

The ideal of total lucidity is never attained in analysis. Reconstruction explains and organizes the more significant aspects of the pathogenesis and subsequent course of the patient's illness. Freud (1912, p. 108) had this in mind when he stated that the transference does inestimable service in making the patient's hidden and forgotten impulses immediate and manifest, but also simultaneously stating, 'The doctor tries to compel him to fit these emotional impulses into the nexus of the treatment and of his life-history. …' Without reconstruction and attention to the evolution of neurotic patterns in life, there is always the danger that the analysis will remain isolated from life, and that the patient will not acquire any true conviction concerning psychic reality and the infantile conflicts and adaptations which are largely responsible for the psychological disorder of later life.

A word here about the sense of conviction and the necessity for the patient to have this type of ego response for a reconstruction to be truly assimilated and have an ego integrative effect. Freud (1909, p. 181) stated that a 'sense of conviction is only attained after the patient has himself worked over the reclaimed material.' Later, in describing the most famous reconstruction in psychoanalysis, Freud (1918) indicated the difficulties not only for the patient (Wolf Man) in obtaining a sense of conviction concerning the various complexities of the reconstruction, but also for the analyst. He offered a number of reconstructions utilizing the totality of the analytic data and the effort to sort out the best possible reconstruction and the most useful explanatory model. It is this model of the coherence and convergence of innumerable pieces of analytic work and the totality of the analytic data to which I believe the greatest attention must be given concerning the validity of reconstruction. When 'we produce … an assured conviction of the truth of the construction which achieves the same therapeutic result as a recaptured memory …' (Freud, 1937, p. 266), we have to be sure that the conviction is solidly based upon correct analysis and not upon defense, magic, submission to authority, or idealization of the analytic process. Freud offered a number of different guidelines for understanding the patient's negative or positive responses to reconstruction, and in effect, to all analytic interpretation. Summing up the problem, the conviction of the validity of reconstruction (Freud, 1937, p. 265) asserted, 'Only the further course of the analysis enables us to decide whether our constructions are correct or unserviceable. We do not pretend that an individual construction is anything more than a conjecture which awaits examination, confirmation, rejection…. It will all become clear in the course of future developments.' The analytic conviction of the analyst is, of course, quite independent of regressive and resistant attitudes of conviction in the patient.

Every analyst who has worked with a depressive will expect to find the infantile predisposition and likelihood of prior object loss so well described in the literature. The apparent single loss may telescope a related series of childhood losses, disappointments, and narcissistic injuries. The metapsychology of mourning and melancholia was developed from reconstructive studies of adult cases as well as from considerations of such sociological and cultural phenomena as anniversary depressions, funeral rites, and rituals of mourning and transition. Without psychoanalytic reconstruction it would have been impossible to formulate the phases of normal mourning or the features of pathological melancholia.

Reconstruction of the severe stress of loss of the love object in childhood will usually demonstrate a variety of disturbances and of adaptive outcomes which may be traced longitudinally and in states of progression and regression (cf. Pollock, 1970); (Anthony & Benedek, 1975); (Blum, 1978). How parent loss will be experienced depends a great deal upon constitutional factors and preceding development, ego capacities to deal with the object deprivation, the establishment of new object ties, the level of self and object representations achieved, the capacities to reverse regression and for progressive mourning, etc. In addition to the preceding ego strength and state prior to the parent loss, the effects depend, therefore, upon the age at which the loss occurs, the nature of the identifications with the lost and surviving parents, the availability of 'good enough' parenting and new love objects, and subsequent developmental experience (Fleming, 1972); (Furman, 1974). The adult patient brings mature ego capacities and new identifications with the analytic functions and processes which prompt reconstruction. The patient can better understand and assimilate not only the continued, incomplete mourning, but the anticipation of loss, the anniversary reactions to loss, and the threat of the overwhelming revival of the depressive-loss complex and repeated losses.

I should like to emphasize that the reconstruction is not only a new form of remembering, but also a reliving of the past with the analyst under entirely new conditions in the analytic situation (Kanzer, 1979). The fashioning of the reconstruction, its reshaping and remodeling during the analytic process is, therefore, a special form of reliving of the past in a way in which it was never experienced, and could never have been experienced, in childhood because of the child's developmental immaturity. It is this living quality of reconstruction which also adds a sense of conviction and reality to the requisite analytic work and which differentiates past and present while creating a new past and present. Reconstruction then comes alive not only in the transference, but in the dissolution of the transference. Realistic and appropriate response replace infantile repetition and irrational misconstruction. Reconstruction explains what has been continually repeated in the transference and adult neurosis.

Transference reliving is assigned to the past, so that living can proceed without domination by the pathogenic past. This is also valid for the analyst's own analysis of his transference and countertransference to the patient.

Reconstruction will assist the analyst in sorting out his own childish reactions. These forms of countertransference are impediments to analysis until they are analyzed. Countertransference may then be secondarily used to learn about the patient but reconstruction of the analyst's childhood and reconstruction of the patient's childhood are quite separate if at times reciprocal processes. Reconstruction of the genetic antecedents of the patient's transference neurosis will also help to evaluate and disentangle the possible untoward effects of countertransference on the patient's treatment and illness. The form and intensity of neurotic repetitions and derivative disturbance, as in anniversary reactions, may be compared before, during, and after analysis.

The analytic relationships and the influence of countertransference are also more clearly defined in developmental perspective. The analyst may incorrectly assess his own importance and the iatrogenic effects of countertransference without full appreciation of the patient's neurotic exploitation of life and of analysis. The prolonged arduous analytic work with its unique qualities may acquire a 'life of its own' but it cannot be artificially isolated from the totality of life experience. The memories of innumerable reactions in the analytic situation are those of re-experiencing the past, but also those of the analytic process with new levels of meaning, development, and ego mastery. The reconstructions expand in development in life, as the parent-child relationships are reviewed, for example, with parenthood, grandparenthood, positions of authority and responsibility, etc.

Reconstruction during termination of analysis may include reconstruction of the phases of the analysis. The patient and analyst will rediscover and even discover significant features of the mode of referral and choice of treatment, the precipitating factors in the onset of symptomatic disturbance, the presenting clinical picture, and initial responses and resistance. The major conflicts, transference configurations, and insights achieved may be profitably reviewed. This may be timed coincident with the reactivation of earlier conflicts and symptoms in termination. In any case, the earlier analytic situation may have become vague, distorted, and have receded from conscious memory over the years of analysis. This reconstruction of the clinical picture and analytic process will be particularly useful to the analyst and the future analyst. The analyst's limited knowledge and initial lack of understanding or misunderstanding may be clarified; surface phenomena may be contemplated anew in the light of the depth analysis which followed.

Beyond its clinical and technical role, reconstruction establishes a new context and framework (Kennedy, 1971) in which inferences are elicited and from which theoretical hypotheses may be formulated and then tested. Analytic work and analytic knowledge lead to reconstruction which in turn contributes to our analytic work and knowledge. Reconstruction is of special importance in the analytic investigation of earliest mental processes and influences which leave obscure imprints and traces and which are only very indirectly accessible, if at all, because of the overlay and alterations of later development. The combined utilization of analytic reconstruction and direct developmental studies of children holds continued promise to expand and stimulate the growth of psychoanalytic knowledge.

Summary

Reconstruction is clinically valuable for the patient and fundamental for the analyst. The analyst will inevitably use reconstruction in order to comprehend the patient and to understand how that adult has remained a disturbed child with that particular psychopathology. Although not necessarily specified, reconstruction remains a very important dimension of psychoanalytic technique that is regaining analytic attention.

After reviewing reasons for the shift of attention away from reconstruction, the significance of reconstruction is emphasized for restoring personality continuity and cohesion and for explaining neurotic repetition as it has developed in life and in the analytic transference. This utilization of reconstruction is illustrated in a case of anniversary depression, demonstrating the linkage between historical events and their intrapsychic interpretation and response, as well as the linkage between past and present, childhood and adult disorder.

Reconstruction does not always automatically follow from the transference and analytic work. It is an inferential and integrative act which may overcome resistance and amnesia, which synthesizes memories and genetic interpretations in addition to substituting for missing memory and gaps in history. Without reconstruction, the personal and familial myths of the past may be joined by current analytic myth. The reconstructive integration identifies patterns and interrelationships rather than isolated conflicts and experiences, and the intrapsychic configurations, consequences, and developmental influences are far more important than actual historical facts. The past is transformed to new meanings and reorganized on new levels of development.

Reconstruction leads to consideration and investigation of the mental processes of childhood and early infancy. It has had a significant role in the development of psychoanalysis, and reconstruction contributes to the formulation, testing, and validation of psychoanalytic theory. For clinical research, it will be particularly rewarding to reconstruct the different phases of the psychoanalytic process.

REFERENCES

Anthony, E. Benedek, T. (eds.) (1975). *Depression and Human Existence*. Boston: Little Brown.

Blum, H. (1977). The prototype of preoedipal reconstruction. *J. Am. Psychoanal. Assoc.* 25:757–785.

——— (1978). Reconstruction in a case of postpartum depression. *Psychoanal. Study Child* 33.

Fleming, J. (1972). Early object deprivation and transference phenomena: The working alliance. *Psychoanal. Q.* 41:23–49.

Freud, A. (1951). Observations on child development. *Psychoanal. Study Child* 6.

Freud, S. (1909). Notes upon a case of obsessional neurosis S.E. 10.

——— (1912). The dynamics of transference. *S.E. 12.*

——— (1914). Remembering, repeating, and working-through. *S.E. 12.*

——— (1917). Introductory lectures on psychoanalysis. *S.E. 16.*

——— (1918). From the history of an infantile neurosis. *S.E. 17.*

——— (1919). A child is being beaten. *S.E. 17.*

——— (1937). Constructions in analysis. *S.E. 23.*

Furman, E. (1974). *A Child's Parent Dies.* New Haven: Yale Univ. Press.

Greenacre, P. (1956). Re-evaluation of the process of working through. *Int. J. Psychoanal.* 37:439–444.

——— (1975). On reconstruction. *J. Am. Psychoanal. Assoc.* 23:693–712.

Jacobson, E. (1971). *Depression.* New York: Int. Univ. Press.

Kanzer, M. (1979). Developments in psychoanalytic technique. *J. Am. Psychoanal. Assoc.* 27(Supplement).

Kennedy, H. (1971). Problems in reconstruction in child analysis. Psychoanal. Study Child 26.

Kernberg, O. (1979). Some implications of object relations theory for psychoanalytic technique. J. Am. Psychoanal. Assoc. 7(Supplement): 207–240.

Kestenberg, J. (1972). How children remember and parents forget. *Int. J. Psychoanal.* 2:103–123.

Kris, E. (1956a). The recovery of childhood memories in psychoanalysis Psychoanal. Study Child 11.

Kris, E. (1956b). The personal myth. *J. Am. Psychoanal. Assoc.* 4:653–681.

Mahler, M., Pine, F. Bergman, A. (1975). The Psychological Birth of the Human Infant. New York: Basic Books.

Mintz, I. (1971). The anniversary reaction: a response to the unconscious sense of time *J. Am. Psychoanal. Assoc.* 19:720–735.

Pollock, G. (1970). Anniversary reactions, trauma, and mourning. *Psychoanal. Q.* 39:347–371.

Pollock, G. (1975). On anniversary suicide and mourning. In E. Anthony T.

Benedek (eds.), *Depression and Human Existence*. Boston: Little Brown.

Rosen, V. (1955). The reconstruction of a traumatic childhood event in a case of derealization *J. Am. Psychoanal. Assoc.* 3:211–221.

Wolfenstein, M. (1966). How is mourning possible? *Psychoanal. Study Child* 21.

CHAPTER 20

The Reconstruction of Reminiscence

(1999). *J. Amer. Psychoanal. Assn.*, (47)(4):1125–1143.
Originally presented as Brill Lecture, NY Psychoanalytic Society. November 17, 1998).

The lifting of repression and of infantile amnesia was an original aim and goal of clinical psychoanalysis. Memory may be more or less reliable and authentic. However, it tends to be subjective, self-serving, and selective, and there are different memory modalities and systems. The recovery of repressed childhood memory has been largely subsumed under the analysis of unconscious conflict and fantasy. "Hysterics suffer mainly from reminiscences," and these reminiscences interweave with and contribute to reconstruction, which is intrinsic to psychoanalysis. Memory and reconstruction are subject to the influence of special interests, transference, and countertransference. Since open questions remain concerning preoedipal, and particularly preverbal, reconstruction, external confirmation may further both the analytic process and analytic research. The process of reconstruction integrates and transcends memory, facilitating personality reorganization.

Human memory, essential as it is for learning, object relations, and adapting to reality, is extraordinary in both its capacities and its vulnerability. This paper will deal primarily with the psychoanalytic aspects of memory: that is, with the effect of reconstruction on memory, and with the contribution of memory to reconstruction. Reconstruction, the lifting of repression, and insight into unconscious infantile conflict interweave, and cooperatively facilitate the analytic process. I regard reconstruction not as a substitute for memory retrieval, but rather as an analytic remodeling of memory that integrates past and present, and facilitates progressive ego reorganization. The prominence of reconstruction has waxed and waned over the course of the development of the theory of technique, and there has been continuing controversy and debate over how memories are conceived, evaluated, and confirmed extra-analytically. I will comment on these lasting problems also, although they are inevitably isolated to some extent from the other dimensions of the psychoanalytic process.

There is a vast literature on the neuropsychological and neurophysiological aspects of memory, covering its development, registration, storage, and retrieval as well as its encoding systems and contextual organization. It should be noted that memories are no longer regarded as fixed, but fluid; they are considered not unities, but incomplete conglomerates. Different memory systems appear to be involved in recording cognitive, emotional, and temporal aspects of experience. Declarative memory (that is, cognitive, verbal, and symbolically encoded memory) has been ascribed to the neocortex. Sensory and emotional memory has been mainly ascribed to subcortical structures. Musical memory may have its own unique features. Sensation may stimulate memory, and affect influences what is remembered, as well as the organization of the memory. Autobiographical or episodic memory has been distinguished from semantic memory, our storehouse of general information. Implicit memory (for skills, patterns, and language function) is not repressed, but still it lies outside of conscious awareness. These different memory systems are subjectively experienced as merged, and are typically unified in consciousness (Le Doux 1996), though they in fact have different access to consciousness, language, and autobiographical context. Further, memory interacts with the other ego functions, the early developmental phases, and the ongoing experiences of later phases of life. Aging may affect memory for names and recent experiences, for instance, while reminiscence of the more distant past may be expanded and reviewed, as in the writing of a memoir.

Memory is inseparable from its converse, forgetting. Learning without review is followed by a predictable logarithmic curve of forgetting (Ebbinghaus 1885). Conscious memory is influenced by motivation, attention, salience, and unconscious fantasy. Momentary memory problems may subside when conscious effort to recall is relaxed, allowing subsequent recovery of the missing name or word.

Some persons recall events without emotions; others recall only emotions, without context. Pleasant memories are generally more readily remembered than others, and memory tends to be self-serving and self-protective. Memory may be blissful or bitter: it can be an analgesic or sedative, but it can also be anxious, haunting, and tormented. Unpleasant memories are usually the more easily forgotten or lost, though some persons are devoted historians of their pain, grief, and grievances. Some seemingly never forget the smallest slight or insult. Some recall only what was done to them, never what they have done to others. The reaction to memory may merge with the former memory configuration. Screen memories provide extra insurance against the intrusion of traumatic memory into consciousness. Flashbacks, nightmares, fugue states, and behavioral enactments have all been regarded as traumatic memory equivalents.

Even eyewitness memories are accurate only to a degree, and with great individual variation. This is the Rashomon phenomenon, well known to the legal profession, and named after the famed movie that depicted a primal scene of rape-murder through the different memories of different persons. Memories are more or less reliable and authentic. Some correspond closely to the "truth" of actual experience; other memories clearly could not have occurred as reported (Blum 1994). The reporting itself, the gaps, emphases, affects, the variations on the theme, and the context are all important to the reconstruction of reminiscence (Shapiro 1993). Despite the facts that many memories can be shown to be accurate, and that important memories can be confirmed by historical documents and official records, memory is nevertheless subject to fragmentation, modification, selection, and synthesis into a gestalt, a construction. "We are liable to fill in from our imagination the incoherent and disjointed fragments furnished by memory…. we willingly become creative artists" (Freud 1900, p. 47n).

Freud's analytic contributions to the understanding of memory and its problems may well be related to his own remarkable eidetic memory: "When I was a schoolboy I took it as a matter of course that I could repeat by heart the page I had been reading; and shortly before I entered the University I could write down almost verbatim popular lectures on scientific subjects directly after hearing them…. In some subjects I gave the examiners, as though it were automatically, answers which faithfully followed the words of the textbook that I had skimmed through only once in greatest haste" (Freud 1901, p. 135). Freud's autobiographical memory and his storehouse of knowledge of both science and the humanities significantly facilitated the development of psychoanalysis.

Beginning with his work in hypnosis, Freud quickly came to emphasize the recovery of childhood memories and the undoing of infantile amnesia.

Symptoms and other forms of psychological

disturbance could not be understood without taking childhood and infantile neurotic disturbance into account. "Hysterics suffer mainly from reminiscences" (Breuer and Freud 1893-1895, p. 7), a precursor of the genetic principle, was a reference to repressed memories of traumatic experience. This often cited and often misunderstood adage did not mean that these reminiscences were undisguised and unaltered. Rather it meant that the past leaves a living record within the personality, dynamically related to the present, and that studies of pathogenesis inevitably lead to childhood origins. Freud was fond of archaeological metaphors for the analytic process. He compared the uncovering of unconscious childhood traumas to archaeologists' uncovering of the buried past. Repressed traumatic memories were to be recovered, reexamined, and reintegrated by the mature personality. The retrieval of traumatic memory, which is associated with emotional catharsis, still has its place in psychoanalysis and in crisis intervention. Trauma has a special historical and theoretical position in psychoanalysis, but all sorts of significant memories are recovered in every psychoanalysis.

Freud began with self-analytic memories and reconstructions, primarily from his own dreams. He considered dreams, like transference and symptoms, "another kind of remembering…. It is this recurrence in dreams that I regard as the explanation … that patients themselves gradually acquire a profound conviction of the reality of these primal scenes, a conviction which is in no respect inferior to recollection" (Freud 1918, p. 51). Memories, again like dreams, are subject to secondary elaboration. The reconstruction of the Wolf

Man's primal-scene experience was a forerunner of the way reconstruction eventual superseded the recovery of repressed memory. Earlier, Freud's (1910) "Leonardo da Vinci and a Memory of His Childhood" had actually dealt with a screen memory, which Freud reconstructed to illuminate the artist's life and art. (It may be noted that the Leonardo and Wolf Man papers both deal with preoedipal constructions condensed and transmuted into oedipal reconstructions.) Freud (1937) later returned to his study of reconstruction, and proposed that it substituted for and contributed to memory recovery.

Reconstruction has largely replaced the lifting of infantile amnesia in the theory of technique. Originally associated with topographic theory and the technique of catharsis, the concept of reconstruction changed with advancing structural and developmental theory, and contributed in its turn to theoretical development (Ekstein and Rangell 1961). Freud is currently berated both for having believed stories about the sexual seduction of children, and for not having believed the very same reports. The patients' reports, and thus their memories or beliefs, are supposed to have been falsified, either by Freud, by the patients themselves, or by members of their families. These notions are relevant to the controversial issue of true and false memory in analysis, in therapy, and in life (Spence 1982; Brenneis 1997). Where does the truth lie? For the analyst, this problem primarily concerns the validity of reconstruction, but it also raises the question of the differentiation of memory, screen memory, and fantasy (Blum 1996; Good 1998): if even a delusion has a grain of truth, how "true" does a memory have to be in order not to be a false memory or pseudomemory? Reconstruction here is not aimed only at a cohesive narrative of the past or a shared construction, but also at a relative correspondence to past realities (Hanly 1990, 1995).

Considering the often blurred boundary between memory and fantasy, Freud (1899) wondered whether what was remembered was in fact modified, and essentially recreated, in the present. He proposed: "Our childhood memories show us our earliest years, not as they were, but as they appeared at the later periods when the memories were aroused. In these periods of arousal, the childhood memories did not, as people are accustomed to say, emerge; they were formed at that time. And a number of motives, with no concern for historical accuracy, had a part in forming them, as well as in the selection of the memories themselves" (p. 322). The patient's memory is also subject to distortion in the present, and has elements of pseudomemory. Screening memories are common, beyond the more narrowly defined, luminous, seemingly realistic "screen memories." In the case of cumulative trauma, screen phenomena tend to expand to protect the beleaguered ego. Screen memories and related defensive phenomena may contribute to the alteration of personal history and identity (Greenson 1958) and to screen reconstructions (Good 1998).

Freud (1917, p. 370) at times, and inconsistently, proposed that the differentiation of fantasy and reality might not only be impossible, but might not matter. He averred that in neurosis, psychic reality was more important than material reality (1925, p. 34), yet he always maintained the importance of actual experience and its authentic memory or memory equivalents. Actually, Freud (1937) continued to seek historical truth—even in delusions, legends, and myths. His case histories are replete with reports of actual experience. Supervising the first attempted analysis of a child, he stated that "It is one of the commonest things —psychoanalyses are full of such incidents—for children's genitals to be caressed, not only in word but in deed by fond relatives, including even parents themselves" (1909a, p. 23). Reality was repeatedly stressed, as for example when Freud (1917) later observed, "Fantasies of being seduced are of particular interest, because so often they are not fantasies but real memories" (p. 370). Though memory is subjective, relatively objective real memories of real experiences and of childhood and adolescence have always been a dimension of psychoanalytic thought.

Memory is established in early infancy, and progresses from recognition to active retention to recall. Most adults place their earliest conscious memories between two and four. Articulated memories and their temporal sequence seem to be established after self and object constancy have been achieved. These are usually isolated sensory memories that lack continuity, logical context, or strong affect (Piaget and Inhelder 1973). Early childhood memory is especially subject to distortion and suggestion because of ego immaturity, repression, magical thinking, and the dependent position of the child. Freud

(1909a) was aware that memories could be created by parental authorities, in a process analogous to the formation of national legends. It follows that the regressed analytic patient may be particularly vulnerable to iatrogenic influence and the danger/pleasure of shared fantasy. The external authority of the analyst and the patient's unconscious superego may influence the appreciation of reality and fantasy (Oliner 1996). Similar issues are involved in the proposed Munchausen syndrome by proxy, where the caregiver ostensibly instigates and perpetuates a factitious medical illness in the child. Current debate about multiple personality disorder has invoked iatrogenic contributions as well as pathogenic child abuse as causative. Merskey (1992), after researching accounts of MPD, questioned the diagnosis, and wrote of suggestion in "The Manufacture of Personalities" (compare Shopper 1998).

Such problems of reconstruction and recovered memory, and the related issues of suggestion, indoctrination, and distortion, are relevant to all analyses. Analytic conjecture can be misused as reconstruction, cocreating analytic myth, or, in extreme forms, as an analytic folie à deux. As with all interpretation, reconstruction can be distorted by theoretical and technical commitments, cultural biases, and countertransference. No technique, whether it be hypnosis, free association, direct brain stimulation, or a pharmacological "truth serum," can guarantee accurate memory access or valid reconstruction for children or adults (Erdelyi 1996).

Infantile amnesia does not always lift with analytic work, and the retrieval of intact memories does not automatically follow the analysis of defense and resistance. The beautiful archaeological model was oversimplified, and did not do justice to the complexity of memory modification and validation, or to the need to establish or restore meaningful connections and context. In contrast with his earlier views, Freud asserted in 1937 that "The path that starts from the analyst's construction ought to end in the patient's recollection, but it does not always lead us so far…. If the analysis is carried out correctly, we produce … an assured conviction of the truth of the construction which achieves the same therapeutic result as a recaptured memory" (p. 265).

A patient with the capacity and interest in memory of a Freud or a Proust could present a rich reservoir of complex memories. But these memories would still serve multiple functions, and would still be modified and adapted through edited secondary elaboration. Many different memories might be telescoped into one memory, for instance, while a specific memory might be displaced and elaborated into many fantasies, or fragmented into partial memories. It has also been proposed that terrifying trauma may not be symbolically encoded— that it is an experience that cannot be assimilated, and thus leads to dissociated states. A more common concept of dissociation refers to memories that are registered intact, but without context. Dissociated memory is not repressed or horizontally split from conscious awareness, but vertically split off from the rest of the patient's functioning ego. Awareness is restricted, and lacks a distinct sense of memory or reality. Dissociation is now invoked alongside or instead of repression in many instances of traumatic abuse and neglect, but it is not necessarily linked to trauma, or to the accuracy of the encrusted memory (Sandler and Fonagy 1997). Dissociation often involves isolation of affect, and may be more likely to occur in long-standing shock and strain trauma, such as a childhood incestuous relationship that persists into adolescence. The significance of dissociation versus repression and amnesia is an area of current analytic research. But unlike single or infrequent episodes of childhood incest, for example, an incest relationship that persists throughout childhood into adolescence seems not to be subject to repression.

A case of traumatic parent loss in childhood illustrates both the isolation and the clustering of memories. The patient was distressed that he had not looked in his calendar, and had forgotten an important appointment. It "happened" to be the date of his father's death. In this anniversary reaction he both forgot and dramatized a traumatic memory. He dreamt that night of trying to rescue a falling and drowning person. When his father was gravely ill, he had gasped for breath. Although he had not literally died from drowning, he had had lung cancer and pulmonary edema. The patient wanted to undo his father's death, and avoid his own inescapable appointment with death. What had been traumatic and not remembered appeared in relative disguise in the patient's enactments and dreams.

Repetitive acting out, the experience of déjà vu, personal myths, and similar phenomena all refer to such unconscious memory-fantasy configurations.

The personal myth is an autobiographical construction (Kris 1956a) that may modify the sense of self and of reality. Anniversary reactions are a form of reminiscence, and often an attempt at reconstruction. Contemporary evidence indicates that repressed memories of trauma may be processed differently from other memories, and may have neurobiological as well as psychological ramifications. It is not at all certain, however, that memories of trauma may only be accessible in "state dependent" emotional revivals identical to the past trauma, although it is possible that in some cases severe trauma may damage memory systems.

For example, a patient with a history of childhood exfoliating dermatitis was as an adult a voyeur who compulsively watched pornography. He became an exhibitionist, and attempted to shock women by exposing his penis. Through interpretation and reconstruction, memories of traumatic sexual experience became available without revival of the traumatic situation. We learned that as a child he had been traumatized by exposure to his mother's vaginal bleeding and the exhibitionism of both parents. His dermatitis was a somatization related to the childhood trauma. He later identified with the exhibiting, shocking parent while reversing affect to prove that he was not the castrated victim. The patient "suffered from reminiscences" that led first to somatization, and later were incorporated and altered in unconscious fantasy. Kris (1956) challenged the possibility of recovering original memories of events, believing that such memories are merged into dynamic patterns in the course of development. This vignette, however, illustrates that discrete memories can sometimes be recovered, and their patterning reconstructed.

The pendulum in analytic technique gradually swung away from the recovery of childhood memory, and increasingly toward the analysis of the transference. The transference is also a fantasy-memory complex—a regressive expression of childhood conflicts in their unconscious fantasy elaboration (Arlow 1969; Brenner 1982). Transference fantasy is a "new edition," a revision of memory that never photographically reproduces the past. The infantile fantasies and the self and object representations in the transference are hardly realistic.

Paradoxically, the transference has to be reconstructed even while it is itself a primary source of analytic data for reconstruction. The transference cannot actually be understood or resolved without genetic interpretation within a framework of reconstruction. In this connection Freud asserted, "We have to do our therapeutic work on it [transference], which consists in a large measure in tracing it back to the past" (1914, p. 152). Writing on analytic technique, Glover observed, "We are never finished with transference interpretation until it is finally brought home to roost. To establish the existence of a transference fantasy is only half of our work; it must be detached once more and brought into direct association within infantile life" (1955, p. 152).

The long ago and far away of infancy attracts and dismays analysts. How to understand the reconstruction of early impressions, the registration of preverbal experiences, and the subsequent transformation of these in the course of development, has long been a subject of controversy. The literature has many examples of preverbal reconstructions, such as the Isakower (1938) phenomenon, poise (Rangell 1954), smugness (Arlow 1957), and elation and the oral triad (Lewin 1950). A patient given to biting sarcasm, grinding her teeth, and protracted chewing of her food consulted her dentist for temporomandibular joint pain. The dentist looked into her mouth and at once stated that she needed "oral reconstruction." "Body memory," psychosomatic phenomena, primitive affects and moods, dream imagery, narcissistic objects, and the splitting and merger of proto-representations have all been invoked in reconstructions of the preverbal phase. Suffice it to say here that the developmentally earliest phases are the most problematic to reconstruct, and are subject to the most conjecture. Genetic antecedents cannot always be found, and developmental discontinuities may defy reconstruction. However, preverbal reconstruction may provide a temporal, linguistic, cognitive, and affective contextual organization that did not formerly exist. A toddler's efforts to engage a depressed mother may be an affectively meaningful and cogent reconstruction (Valenstein 1989). Reconstruction is not only childhood revisited, but recreated. The past is a paradox; it is not really past, but neither did it ever exist in the present form into which reconstruction organizes it.

Today therapeutic results are thought to depend on conflict analysis with reconstruction, rather than on recaptured memory. Unconscious conflicts, for example in the transference and countertransference, codetermine whether, when, and how events are recalled, as well as the form and content of the recollections, and their meaning or significance. Reconstruction involves analytic inference and integration; it is an interpretive formulation and a template for genetic interpretation. The analyst listens and learns and builds tentative constructions about the patient's life problems and inner conflicts (Greenacre 1975; Blum 1994). Associations form a network of connections that encompasses memories, fantasies, dreams, symptoms, etc. The analytic data converge in a picture of some significant aspect of the patient's childhood that is related to the patient's unconscious conflicts. The analyst comes gradually to understand the conflicts and character of the patient, and how the individual of today developed from the infant and child that the patient once was and in some respects continues to be. The individual analytic data and the analyst's psychoanalytic knowledge will usually strongly support one specific reconstruction among many less cogent or probable alternatives. From their initial constructions, different analysts will likely formulate interrelated and similar, but not identical, reconstructions, and they may make use of their reconstructions differently. (By "construction" I mean here the analyst's early, tentative, private hypothesis about the patient's childhood. "Reconstruction" is based upon cumulative analytic data, is shared with the patient, and gradually includes the patient's expansion and modification. It illuminates pathogenesis and, in favorable circumstances, the genesis of sublimation.) Reconstruction potentiates a more accurate analytic autobiography, and provides historical perspectives that restore the continuity and cohesion of the self.

Reconstruction "beyond a reasonable doubt" may be uncommon without objective validation, but it is analogous to the process a jury uses in coming to a decision based upon evidence and inference. Other analogies might be made: to the reconstruction of the text and context of the Dead Sea scrolls, for instance, or to the reconstruction of an evolutionary fossil series without the aid of DNA analysis. The concept of reconstruction itself has evolved, and may be regarded today as an elastic concept, invoking a particular time and developmental phase in a familial and social context. The persisting past is reviewed and recreated, as it is experienced differently with different objects, in different phases of life, and in different phases of psychoanalysis.

I will now contrast some vignettes of pioneer reconstruction with contemporary examples.

Freud (1909b) reflected on the Rat Man's report that he worked late hours, and that between twelve midnight and one in the morning he would open the door as if expecting his deceased father's ghost. The Rat Man would then expose his penis and observe it in a mirror. By keeping his nose to the grindstone, the Rat Man complied with his father's demand for hard study and dedicated work. But he then defied his father with thinly disguised masturbatory play. Freud recorded the following intervention during the first month of the Rat Man's analysis.

> I ventured to put forward a construction to the effect that when he was a child of under six he had been guilty of some sexual misdemeanor connected with masturbation and had been soundly castigated for it by his father. This punishment, according to my hypothesis, … had put an end to his masturbating, but on the other hand, it left behind an ineradicable grudge against his father and it established him for all time in his role of an interferer with the patient's sexual enjoyment. To my great astonishment the patient then informed me that his mother had repeatedly described to him an occurrence of this time which dated from his earliest childhood and has evidently escaped being forgotten by her on account of its remarkable consequences. He himself, however, had no recollection of it whatever…. It became possible to establish the date more exactly owing to its having coincided with the fatal illness of an elder sister—he had done something naughty for which his father had given him a beating [p. 205].

Freud's rapid reconstruction may have served defensive intellectualization, but it was also a pathfinding effort to help the patient make sense of his life and of his neurosis. It enlisted the Rat Man's interest in a genetic explanation for his irrational behavior, and restored connections between the patient's childhood, his being childish, and his adult disorder. The Rat Man's mother affirmed that the Rat Man had not manifestly been punished for masturbation. He had been beaten by his father because he had bitten someone ("biting like a rat"), and he had continued to expect retaliation for his forbidden impulses. The reconstructed child within was still alive—biting, fighting, and masturbating.

However, the Rat Man reconstruction now appears incomplete and limited, lacking the explanatory reach available today. The rat punishment had many roots. The importance of object loss—in this case the death of a sibling with its guilt-inducing, punitive, and self-punitive responses—had to await later theoretical and technical elaboration. Issues of methodology in reconstruction —its form and content, its timing in the analysis and in the patient's earlier life, and its validation—would emerge later in the theory of technique.

An adult woman entered analysis ostensibly because of a marital crisis, feeling that her husband was a huge headache. Sensitive to rejection, she had always been fearful of illness and injury, and in later childhood had intimidated her parents with threats of self-injury. Before analysis, the patient had not connected her adult disturbance to childhood, and her memory of her childhood was hazy and fragmentary. In her analysis more and more memory fragments emerged, including fragmentary remarks of her parents about her illness. These bits and pieces of memory were used with other analytic data to reconstruct the outlines of her childhood traumatization. This re-established cause and effect, and promoted insight into her core unconscious fantasies and childhood conflicts. Recurrent mastoiditis between ages four and five had necessitated repeated hospitalizations, with tonsillectomy and mastoidectomies. Her illness was unconsciously regarded as retaliation and punishment for her forbidden oedipal wishes; it was a relatively phase-specific oedipal trauma.

The relationship to and identification with caretakers was of critical importance for the traumatized child (Blum 1987). This patient's mother had been frantic about her child's frightening recurrent illnesses, which included fever, pain, confusional states, and the threat of such complications as meningitis and encephalitis. Adolescent rape fantasies were also codetermined by her illness and the medical procedures that resulted. These fantasies were also related to the effects of her illness upon her parents.

In some conscious adolescent fantasies, a female lover held the patient's head against her bosom, stroking her long, beautiful hair. The patient's hair had actually been cut, and her head shaved, at the time of the surgical procedures.

She had later desired to have long full hair to cover the mastoid scars. The scars were also psychological lesions representing her feelings of narcissistic injury, inferiority, mutilation, and castration. During the process of reconstruction she had complained about my having her head in a vise: a transference repetition.

Specifically, I reconstructed the way her parents also had been traumatized by her traumatic illness and nearness to death. Her parents' reactions contributed to her splitting of and identification with aggressor and comforter, cruelty and compassion, and the sadomasochistic interpretation of her illness and medical treatment. Here the process of reconstruction contributed to insight into unconscious infantile conflict and the fantastic nature of archaic intrapsychic representations of self and object.

This reconstruction was far more complex, developed more gradually, and evolved later in analysis than did the reconstructions of the pioneer era. It enveloped crucial aspects of the patient's object relationships and identifications. Many of the details of the reconstruction, for instance the panic of the parents, were confirmed by a relative, who also described the child's withdrawal and sadness (which had not been recalled or reconstructed). The amalgamation of the patient's own memory fragments with what she may later have heard from her parents probably influenced the process of reconstruction. The inferences concerning the parents are analogous to reconstruction in applied analysis: e.g., psychobiography.

The reconstruction of childhood has a historical dimension. An ahistorical purely "here and now" treatment, and a narrative constructed in the present, evade childhood conflicts and avoid a patient's infantile traits and trends. Historical truth is significant, and it makes a difference when a patient's traumatic experience is understood or treated only as screen memory or fantasy. At the same time, experience also involves unconscious motivation and meaning, and unconscious fantasy distortion and elaboration. Analysis discovers and uncovers how unconscious processes organize and represent earlier experiences (Shapiro 1993).

The following clinical vignette concerns the reconstruction of adolescent transformations in the reanalysis of an adult Jewish man who had grown up in the persecutory milieu of Nazi Germany. Despite the patient's several analytic experiences, he continued to have masochistic tendencies and obsessive fears of contamination. Two of his analysts reportedly spoke with German accents similar to his own, but there had never been any discussion of their common mother tongue. One Jewish analyst was experienced as contemptuous of Jewish traditions. There was never any discussion of the war, of the holocaust, or of being a refugee transplanted in this country; there was only silent analytic collusion against memory of the Nazi and refugee experiences of his adolescence.

The patient casually mentioned that he was given the "silent treatment" in school as the class Jew, but he seemed unaware of his traumatic adolescent indoctrination into self-hatred. During the analysis he recalled having been arrested, warned of the dire consequences of racial defilement of an Aryan, and lectured on Jewish immorality. Adolescent sexual curiosity and masturbation were filled with dread and guilt. It took considerable analytic effort for the patient to realize how numbed has affective responses had been, how he had swallowed any anger, stifled protest, and silently submitted to abuse in an atmosphere of contagious fear and hate. The patient had continued to be passively complaint in his analyses, accepting the insults of his "wild analyst," hardly questioning an interpretation.

The patient recalled that his parents had suffered in silence, unable to protect themselves or their son. At seventeen the patient had managed to escape, becoming an outcast in a new country. He was deprived of benevolent peer experience, and he felt guilty that his family remained ever more vulnerable to escalating peril.

Unconscious identification with the aggressor emerged as a core determinant of the patient's adolescent development and disorder. Feeling inferior and filled with self-hate, he admired the power elite: "If you can't beat them, join them." He had a vague memory of imagining saying "Heil Hitler" and giving the Nazi salute practiced by his classmates, but this was an adult fantasy as well. During the analysis, the patient in a dream about the Mafia held a knife, which he turned toward his own throat. He alternately identified the analyst and himself with both the Mafia (Nazi) murderer and the murdered victims.

Sadomasochistic fantasy was anchored in reality; strain trauma and narcissistic injury were regular features of his life.

During the analytic reconstruction of the patient's traumatic adolescence, an extraordinary event occurred. The reconstruction was confirmed and expanded by the arrival of one of the patient's former classmates. The former tormentor had sought him out in a search for absolution and self-justification. He added details of the abuse the patient had undergone, the painful memories of which had been buried. The knife in the patient's dream was unconsciously connected with circumcision and castration. The patient had recalled being taunted about his circumcised penis, but his classmate reminded him that a group had threatened to "pull it off." Although the patient had not remembered it previously, this castration threat was real, and in reconstruction it was linked to memories of a Nazi teacher's ceremonial sword, and to Nazi songs of knives and Jewish blood. He inferred that his classmates had felt threatened by his circumcision. Aware that circumcision identified him as a Jew, he had not been aware of castration anxiety and castrating impulses. In analysis he became aware of his murderous rage toward the classmate, which he had hidden behind a polite veneer. The class scapegoat, he had hated his classmates and teachers, and he could not forgive his peers, his parents, or himself.

Reconstruction contributed to the working through of shame and guilt, and to the closure of major gaps in the patient's self-awareness and memory. The reconstruction of silent collusion and internalized prohibition against memory and inquiry was of particular importance in this analysis. The recent traumatic past was overburdened by silence and the social suppression of memory. A command to remember may supplant a command to forget, both relieving and reviving guilt and shame.

Patients' interest in revisiting the past may represent efforts to correct and complete or to resist and refute reconstruction, just as it can be a flight from current transference issues. External confirmation certainly contributes to patient's feelings of confidence and conviction in the process and content of reconstruction. How much weight should be given to external evidence for reconstruction? This issue has recently been submerged in objective research on analytic outcome. Although external validation may not be sought or suggested by the analyst or required by the analytic process, many patients spontaneously seek external confirmation: they look at old diaries, letters, home movies, visit old homes and graves, and discuss their childhoods with close relatives. Formerly such investigations were treated either with haughty indifference or as acting out, or, conversely, they were recommended (Novey 1968). However, they may also be seen as part of working through and reclaiming lost childhood. Of course, relatives and friends may give self-serving, distorted, or fabricated accounts. Thus the contributions of the relatives may be constructive or may be an impediment. However, when confirmation does occur, it is welcome as well as useful for checking alternative reconstructions and for articulation with theory and child development research (Good 1998). As a template for interpretation, the accuracy and precise fit of reconstruction may influence the analytic process, sometimes in undetected form.

Reconstruction usually strengthens analytic conviction even about such things as repeated parental denials or fabrications: I have in mind, for instance, a situation where a parent fabricated a noble birth. Validation may confirm parts of a reconstruction, as in the Rat Man case, while clarifying, modifying, and expanding other areas. Freud checked the reconstructions in his own self-analysis with his mother. It was once implied to Freud (scandalously, in those times) that he had been conceived out of wedlock. When his interlocutor asked how he knew his real birthday, he replied that his mother had told him, and that she ought to know! Subsequent patients have been impelled to do the same while checking their own analysts' reconstructions. "Just as our construction is only effective because it recovers a fragment of lost experience, so the delusion owes its convincing power to the element of historic truth which it inserts in the place of rejected reality. In this way a proposition which I originally asserted only of hysteria would also apply to delusions—namely, that those who are subject to them are suffering from their own (reminiscences) recollections" (Freud 1937, p. 285). Freud thus traversed the pathway from reminiscence to reconstruction, and explored their interrelationship.

Contemporary reconstruction takes into account the interaction of psychic and external reality in unconscious fantasy, in developmental transformations and discontinuities, and in historical and cultural context. A new vision of past and present is forged, with new ego integration. This new integration emerges in the literary landscape and dreamy vistas of Marcel Proust's *Remembrance of Things Past*:

> *When from a long distant past nothing subsists, after the people are dead, after the things are broken and scattered, still, alone, more fragile, but with more vitality, more unsubstantial, more persistent, more faithful, the smell and taste of things remain poised a long time, like souls, ready to remind us, waiting and hoping for their moment, amid the ruins of all the rest; and bear unfaltering, in the tiny and almost impalpable drop of their essence, the vast structure of recollection [Swann's Way, p. 148].*

The artist's intuitive composition is reminiscent of the process of reconstruction, integral to psychoanalysis.

REFERENCES

Arlow, J.A. (1957). On Smugness. *Int. J. Psycho-Anal.* 38:1–8.

——— (1961). Ego psychology and the study of mythology. *J. Amer. Psychoanal. Assn.* 9:371–393.

Blum, H.P. (1978). Psychoanalytic study of an unusual perversion—Discussion. *J. Amer. Psychoanal. Assn.* 26:785–792.

——— (1987). The Role of Identification in the Resolution of Trauma: The Anna Freud Memorial Lecture. *Psychoanal Q.* 56:609–627.

——— (1994). *Reconstruction in Psychoanalysis: Childhood Revisited and Recreated.* New York: International Universities Press.

——— (1996). Seduction trauma: representation, deferred action, and pathogenic development. *J. Amer. Psychoanal. Assn.* 44:1147–116.

Brenneis, C. B. (1997). *Recovered Memories of Trauma.* New York: International Universities Press.

Brenner, C. (1982). *The Mind in Conflict.* New York: International Universities Press.

Breuer, J., & Freud, S. (1893–1895). Studies on hysteria. *Standard Edition* 2.

Davies, J., & Frawley, M. (1994). *Treating the Adult Survivors of Childhood Sexual Abuse.* New York: Basic Books.

Ebbinghaus, H. (1885). *Memory.* New York: Dover, 1964.

Ekstein, R. & Rangell, L. (1961). reconstruction and theory formation. *J. Amer. Psychoanal. Assn.*9:684–697.

Erdelyi, M. (1996). *The Recovery of Unconscious Memories.* Chicago: University of Chicago Press.

Freud, S., (1899). Screen memories. *Standard Edition* 3:301–322.

——— (1900). The interpretation of dreams. *Standard Edition* 4/5.

——— (1901). The psychopathology of everyday life. *Standard Edition* 6.

——— (1909a). Analysis of a phobia in a five-year-old boy. *Standard Edition* 10:3–149.

——— (1909b). Notes upon a case of obsessional neurosis. *Standard Edition* 10:153–318.

——— (1910). Leonardo da Vinci and a memory of his childhood. *Standard Edition* 11:59–137.

——— (1913). Totem and taboo. *Standard Edition* 13:1–161.

——— (1914). Remembering, repeating, and working-through. *Standard Edition* 12:145–156.

——— (1917). Introductory lectures on psychoanalysis. *Standard Edition* 16:243–263.

——— (1918). From the history of an infantile neurosis. *Standard Edition* 17:3–123.

——— (1925). An autobiographical study. *Standard Edition* 20:3–74.

——— (1937). Construction in analysis. *Standard Edition* 23:256–269.

Glover, E. (1955). *The Technique of Psycho-Analysis.* New York: International Universities Press.

Good, M. I. (1998). Screen Reconstructions: Traumatic Memory, Conviction, and the Problem of Verification *J. Amer. Psychoanal. Assn.* 46:149–183.

Greenacre, P. (1975). On Reconstruction. *J. Amer. Psychoanal. Assn.* 23:693–712.

Greenson, R.R. (1958). On Screen Defenses, Screen Hunger and Screen Identity. *J. Amer. Psychoanal. Assn.* 6:242–262.

Hanly, C. (1990). The Concept of Truth in Psychoanalysis. *Int. J. Psycho-Anal.* 71:*375–383*.

——— (1995). On Facts and Ideas In Psychoanalysis. *Int. J. Psycho-Anal.* 76:*901–908*.

Isakower, O. (1938). A contribution to the patho-psychology of phenomena associated with falling asleep. *Int. J. Psycho-Anal.* 38:*331–345*.

Kris, E. (1956a). The personal myth. In *Selected Papers of Ernst Kris*. New Haven: Yale University Press, 1975, pp. *272–300*.

——— (1956b). The recovery of childhood memories in psychoanalysis. In *Selected Papers of Ernst Kris,* New Haven: Yale University Press, 1975, pp. *301–340*.

Lewin, B. (1950). *The Psychoanalysis of Elation*. New York: Norton.

Merskey, M. (1992). The manufacture of personalities: The production of multiple personality. *British Journal of Psychiatry* 160:*327–340*.

Novey, S. (1968). *The Second Look*. Baltimore: Johns Hopkins University Press.

Oliner, M.M. (1996). External Reality: The elusive dimension of psychoanalysis. *Psychoanal Q.* 65:*267–300*.

Piaget, J., & Inhelder, B. (1973). *Memory and Intelligence*. New York: Basic Books.

Proust, M. (1913–1926). *Remembrance of Things Past: Swann's Way*. New York: Random House, 1934.

Rangell, L. (1954). The psychology of poise—with a special elaboration on the psychic significance of the snout or perioral region. *Int. J. Psycho-Anal.* 35: *313–332*.

Sachs, O. (1967). distinctions between fantasy and reality elements in memory and reconstruction. *Int. J. Psycho-Anal.* 48:*416–423*.

Sandler, J., & Fonagy, P., Eds. (1997). Recovered Memories of Abuse. New York: International Universities Press.

Shapiro, T. (1993). On reminiscences. *J. Amer. Psychoanal. Assn.* 41:*395–421*.

Shopper, M. (1997). The creation of memories. Paper presented to the New Directions Program, Washington Psychoanalytic Foundation.

Spence, D. (1982). *Narrative Truth and Historical Truth: Meaning and Interpretation in Psychoanalysis*. New York: Norton.

Valenstein, A. F. (1989). Pre-Oedipal Reconstructions in Psychoanalysis. *Int. J. Psycho-Anal.* 70:*433–442*.

CHAPTER 21

Psychoanalytic Reconstruction and Reintegration

(2005). *Psychoanal. Study Child,* (60):295–311.[1]

Psychoanalytic reconstruction has declined in theoretical and clinical interest as greater attention has been directed to the here and now of the transference—counter-transference field and inter-subjectivity. Transference, however, is based upon childhood fantasy, and is a new edition of unconscious intrapsychic representation and relationships. In this paper transference is viewed as a guide to reconstruction, but transference itself is also an object of reconstruction. Reconstruction is a complementary agent of change, which integrates genetic interpretations and restores the continuity of the self. The patient's childish traits, features, fixations, and irrational childish fantasies and behavior point to the necessity for reconstruction. Reconstruction organizes dissociated, fragmented memories, potentiating the further retrieval of repressed memories. Reconstruction is essential to the working through and attenuation of early traumatic experience. Recapture of the past is necessary to demonstrate and diminish the persistent influence of the past in the present, and to meaningfully connect past and present. A case is presented in which reconstruction had a central, vital role in the analytic process.

In its second century, psychoanalysis has moved in many new directions, often with increasing distance from its origins and core formulations.

---

1 Given as the Freud Lecture, Germany, November 1, 2002, and originally published in German under the title "Psychoanalytische Rekonstruktion und Reintegration" in "Zeitschrift fur Psychoanalytische Theorie und Praxis/Journal for Psychoanalytic Theory and Practice" 2/2003 (XVIII) © 2003 Stroemfeld Verlag, Frankfurt am Main/ Basel, published here in English with the permission of Stroemfeld Verlag.

Psychoanalytic reconstruction has been treated either with neglect or declining interest as attention has turned to other psychoanalytic issues and agents of change. Psychoanalysis itself is not regarded as particularly popular in many parts of the world today, and reconstruction has particularly fallen out of favor as there has been more immediate attention and emphasis on the here and now, inside and outside psychoanalysis. Actually, analysts and patients have pondered the question of where the patient was coming from, and how he or she got there. It is not only the adopted child who is curious about his/her origins, but all persons and peoples. Nations have legends about their origins, which are constructions compounded of fact and fantasy. Freud (1919, p. 83) asserted: "analytic work deserves to be recognized as genuine psychoanalysis only when it has succeeded in removing the amnesia which conceals from the adult his knowledge of his childhood … This cannot be said among analysts too emphatically or repeated too often … anyone who neglects childhood analysis is bound to fall into the most disastrous errors. The emphasis which is laid here upon the importance of the earliest experiences does not imply any under-estimation of the influence of later ones." Extending my previous work on the theoretical and therapeutic value of reconstruction (Blum, 1980, 1994, 2000), this paper supports reconstruction as inherent to the psychoanalytic point of view and virtually all clinical work. In my view, reconstruction is not only reciprocal to transference interpretation in the present, but it is a complementary agent which guides and integrates interpretations and reorganizes and restores the continuity of the personality.

Reconstruction for Freud was both a technique, a means toward the goal, and a goal of psychoanalysis. Experience such as the birth or death of a sibling had an impact on the patient's life, permanently influencing the personality. Freud (1937, p. 26) illustrated such a prototypical reconstruction, "Up to your nth year you regarded yourself as the sole and unlimited possessor of your mother; then came another baby and brought you grave disillusionment. Your mother left you for some time; and even after her reappearance she was never devoted to you exclusively. Your feelings toward your mother became ambivalent, your father gained a new importance for you … and so on."

A genetic interpretation shows that a current symptom, behavior, thought, feeling, or trait is derived in some way from childhood. It is specific and focal, and it traces, for example adult obesity, to childhood conflicts concerning feeding and object loss. Genetic interpretations are fostered by the regressive character of free association and transference. Reconstruction would encompass broader considerations, e.g. of dependent relationships, concurrent parental regression, inability to mourn and accept loss, identification with the lost object, etc.

Reduction of the transference to its childhood roots and the accumulated analytic data converge in a reconstruction, which in turn furthers the analytic process. Contrary to the current position in some analytic quarters, that such genetic data are co-determined by the analyst's suggestion or countertransference, the childish character of the transference, the patient's childish traits, features, fixations, and irrational childish fantasies point to the childhood locus of pathogenesis and the patient's psychopathology. Although analytic work requires the reconstruction of childhood (Freud, 1937), this does not mean that any two reconstructions by two different analysts will be identical. Each analyst will select, organize, and interpret the data with some degree of theoretical and personal preference. The analyst's countertransference may make it difficult to analyze the transference, or from another point of view, it may provide further insight into the patient's conflicts, the transference, and the patient's resistance in the analytic process. The analyst's analytic attitude, self analysis, education, and experience should contain and limit the analyst's human subjectivity, retaining "good enough objectivity."

Analytic theory does not derive entirely from adult regressive states, which do not reproduce earlier states unaltered, but has long been complemented by infant observational research and child analysis. The reconstruction of childhood takes into account affective, cognitive, and moral development. Reconstruction considers the overlap and sequence of developmental phases, and the unique quality of individual endowment and experience. Because of the theoretical implications of reconstruction, it has been used from the beginnings of psychoanalysis to propose, confirm, or challenge a theoretical or developmental hypothesis.

As analysis proceeds, the wealth of associations, memories, transference reactions, etc. provide a foundation for the process of reconstruction. Usually there are a number and variety of reconstructions rather than one grand encompassing reconstruction. Like interpretation, reconstruction is neither arbitrary nor capricious nor dogmatic. All too often what is depicted as analysis in popular distortions and misconceptions is a parody of the psychoanalytic process. A caricature of the psychoanalyst as insensitive, insistent, robotic, and self-serving is deployed to defend against the authentic yet disturbing nature of analytic insights. Self-protection is preferred to self-knowledge. When a reconstruction is offered to the patient, it is a product of prior analytic work, tentative and always an approximation. Psychoanalysis and the process of reconstruction are not based on faith, dogma, or conjecture, but on evidence, inference, and further confirmation or alteration with new data. Fragmented, dissociated, and repressed memories emerge and have to be differentiated from screen memories and pseudo-memories. Screen memories are often similar to the patient's constructions.

Our knowledge of memory has significantly advanced in the recent decade. Bridges are under construction between psychoanalysis and neuroscience, and both disciplines should benefit. Several memory systems are now recognized. These systems appear to have their respective modes of registration, storage, and retrieval with interrelated functions and controls. Autobiographical memory is closely connected to declarative, explicit, usually conscious verbal memory for persons and places and general knowledge. Procedural, implicit memory for skills, e.g. riding a bicycle, playing the piano, is not conscious, though not repressed, and is not modified as a consequence of psychoanalysis. At this time the dynamic unconscious has not been definitely delineated within any specific memory system or configuration. Traumatic memory is an exception, however, and appears to be processed differently from other memory. Severe trauma alters the structure and the memory function of the hippocampus. Unconscious traumatic memory is essentially formed in the amygdala (LeDoux, 2002), which appears to instigate automatic fight-flight reactions to stress. These findings illuminate the complexity of memory and the necessity of reconstruction superseding the limitations of discrete memory.

Patients sometimes offer reconstructions before the analyst. In any case, reconstruction will be invoked in analysis unless the past continues to be resisted and avoided. If the past and present have not been meaningfully interconnected, then the patient's defenses have not been sufficiently diminished. The past will continue to influence the present, but the past may also defend against the present. A patient, for example, preferred to reconstruct her childhood strife with her mother, rather than scrutinize her derivative overprotection and over-indulgence of her daughter. Any confrontation with her daughter was to be strenuously avoided. The present as well as the childhood past may be viewed through a glass darkly.

Before the reconstruction is verbalized and offered to the patient, the psychoanalyst has been building a mental construction of the patient's childhood. Based on the patient's presenting symptoms and character, the life history described by the patient, and the initial transference reactions of the patient along with the analyst's counter-transference responses, construction evolves. Construction is an initial preliminary formulation, which goes on silently in the analyst's mind, particularly concerning the nature of the patient's psychopathology and its relationship to pathogenesis. Construction is thus an initial set of hypotheses about the patient's unconscious conflicts and character structure which is not shared with the patient and which develops during the opening phase of psychoanalysis (Greenacre, 1975; Blum, 1994). Differentiated here from construction, reconstruction is generally formulated after the opening phase of analysis and is shared and shaped with the patient.

In the material that follows I shall focus primarily on reconstruction. This will allow a deeper understanding of the significance of the child that lives on within the adult, the persistence of childish features and fixations within the adult personality, and the revival of childhood in the patient's regressive responses. This is not to say that the child in the adult is ever revived as he/she actually existed in childhood. Childish reactions in the adult may or may not serve their original defensive and adaptive functions, and there may have been developmental transformation of meaning and function. The adult's present personality and life situation influences the form and content of childhood revivals. Reconstruction of the patient's past is necessary to demonstrate the persistent influence of the childhood past in the present, but contemporary reconstruction also demonstrates the influence of the present in the way the past is revived, re-experienced, and understood. The archeological metaphor which Freud originally used in his description of reconstruction as reclaiming the buried past is still apt in many respects. "His work of construction, or if it is preferred, of reconstruction, resembles to a great extent an archeologist's excavation of some dwelling-place that has been destroyed and buried or of some ancient edifice…. except that the analyst works under better conditions and has more material at his command to assist him, since what he is dealing with is not something destroyed but something that is still alive …" (Freud, 1937, p. 259). Patient and analyst develop rational conviction about a reconstruction based upon analytic knowledge, observations, inferences and their cohesive integration. Reconstructions have transference and countertransference meaning, however, so a patient's reaction to reconstruction becomes part of the analytic process.

Some of the main features of clinical reconstruction will be illustrated in the following clinical material. The primary case report is that of the analysis of a white male in his thirties who held an academic position. He was gaining increasing recognition and was developing a consulting practice, which made private psychoanalysis possible. He sought treatment because he suffered from intermittent depression with feelings of poor self-esteem. He was quite conflicted and indecisive with respect to their relationship. He felt that the analysis was necessary, and he anticipated it would be painful to expose his vulnerabilities. He hoped to develop a more positive confident self-image, and greater self-esteem and to become more successful in his life goals. He was completely naïve about analysis and at the same time, seemed to have an intuitive grasp of what was expected of him. He was fascinated with the idea of "everything means something."

During the first half year the patient remained interested, enthusiastic, and motivated. He was very intelligent and seemed very cooperative. This honeymoon period did not last and what then emerged was a person who expressed himself in two different ways, almost as if he were two different people. Frequently his language was crude, with poor grammar and frequent curses and obscenities. On the other hand, he would make frequent literary allusions, quoting Shakespeare, Proust, Joyce, and other authors. He was capable of using a very large excellent vocabulary and subtle expressions, just as he was capable of using crude language riddled with profanity. He alternated between curiosity and indifference regarding his two contrasting language styles. He also had two different ways of relating to the analyst, and similar expectations of how the analyst would relate to him. He expected his analyst to be in either a crude and uncontrolled dangerous closeness, or to be more distant and cultivated. He indicated that he was afraid he would become too dependent on the analyst and analytic process. The analysis had become one of the most important things in his life.

The patient then revealed a secret, which he had withheld at the beginning of analysis. He not only had two languages, but there were two women in his life. While living with his girlfriend, presumably exclusively, he actually saw other women, primarily his ex-fiancee. His lover had resumed sexual relations with the patient during the time that he was living with his present girlfriend. He actually became closer to his former fiancee whom he began to visit regularly.

He was afraid to reveal this to his girlfriend for fear that she would reject him. He was divided between his two conscious loves, his present and former girlfriend. This had now become intolerable. His divided love and loyalties, and his guilt toward these women, were major reasons for his seeking psychoanalysis.

When his girlfriend learned about his "affair" with his former fiancee, she repeatedly told the patient that had hurt her deeply, and then she broke off all contact with him. Separation reactions activated in the transference. He was reluctant to leave sessions, and on Friday would cheerfully state, "have a nice weekend."

The intrigues in his personal life entered the analytic situation. He confessed guilt about reading a magazine report about a mass murder in the waiting room. Although he was afraid of getting caught, he had somehow left the magazine open to that page. He then recalled that in adolescence he had found his father's pornographic pictures. Disgusted, but excited, he masturbated with these pictures. He was so afraid of being discovered that he replaced them exactly as he found them. He thought his parents were shameful hypocrites. When he had asked for the analyst's card, he was unconsciously referring to his father's pornography, wondering if the analyst were trustworthy or a lascivious hypocrite.

This led to feelings about morality and specifically religion. He wondered if the analyst were Jewish. He had grown up in an anti-Semitic milieu with contempt of Jews. In a Catholic college he had told a fellow that he had no use for any Jews and this person declared, "I'm Jewish." The patient was stunned and mortified. In his view, though weaklings, Jews could be ruthless and they did the dirty work (like servants). Later he began to examine the many stereotypes of his childhood. He was unconsciously afraid that the possibly Jewish psychoanalyst would encourage immoral thoughts and acts. On the couch he was vulnerable; he felt feminine and was homophobic. The patient was dimly aware of his fear of all women and preferred to think of them as asexual Madonnas. As a child he had wondered about sounds coming from the thin partition of his parents' bedroom, and as an adolescent he audited their sexual relations and was sexually aroused. His adolescence was burdened by guilt and fears of punishment.

At this point the analyst could reconstruct the patient's reactivated primal scene fantasy and sibling experience during his childhood and adolescence, which reflected in all his current relationships. He had slept in the same room as a sister until puberty, undressing together. His removal from their bedroom at puberty convinced him of his sinfulness and motivated his urge to confession in church and later in analysis. His masturbation while looking at the parental pornography was unconsciously incestuous, and he was fearful of the incestuous voyeurism, exhibitionism, and sibling sex play. He was guilty and anticipated punishment for his incestuous fantasies. The secret of his affair was tied to the secrecy of the primal scene, his sibling experience, and his unconscious fantasy of impregnating sister and mother. After this reconstruction he could understand his fear of intimacy. The patient spoke again of the hypocrisy of his parents, their own crude behavior, their not setting limits, and their implicit condoning of inappropriate sibling intimacy. His attention turned to his irrational fear of the analyst's cruel and dirty impulses and then to recollections of parochial school. The priests and nuns were supposed to be kindly but they were frequently cruel. They too were unreliable hypocrites. He then described physical abuse, endless repetitions of prayers, and penance for minor infractions. He had despised the Jews in part as a defense against his ambivalence toward the Christian authorities of his childhood and adolescence.

The analysis deepened in its middle phase after a vacation. The idealization of wealth was introduced when the patient had difficulty in paying the analyst, ostensibly because he did not have an envelope in which to enclose the check. The bare check would be nude, not proper, but pornographic. Payment led to associations about dirty money, greed, and the analyst becoming enriched through the patient's efforts and expense. A very important childhood theme then affectively emerged in the center of analytic work. The patient had grown up in New England, mostly on large estates in which his parents worked as servants. He was the son of servants, within a socioeconomic class system. The analyst reconstructed the influence of the servant experience on his fear of being compliant and dependent, his fragile self-esteem and compensatory striving for social status and affluence. His father was a tyrant at home but deferential and subservient toward his rich employers. The patient too had to know his place. He recalled with humiliation and rage how his father made him walk to the back door, the servant's entrance, and how he hated being a caddy, carrying golf clubs for affluent adults to earn extra money. The patient had played with a Jewish employer's son, but they were not allowed to eat together in the main dining room, nor did he know proper etiquette. The primary house of his childhood was actually a cottage on an estate, servant's quarters. He realized this accounted for the lack of boundaries and privacy since the few small rooms had flimsy walls. The two different styles of language and manners, which had appeared in the transference, could now be reconstructed as related to his early experience, that of observing two classes, his parents and the estate owners with different styles of language and dress.

He identified with his parents of the servant class and also with the aristocratic parents. He had not been aware of his dual identifications, languages, and ambivalent attachments. He had lived in two worlds which were dissociated; ego integration was possible only after reconstruction of his childhood.

Reconstruction elaborated how he and his family were filled with awe, envy, and resentment of the aristocrats. The "have-nots" attempted to devalue what they did not have. He should have been rich, and what a better life he would have if he were the son or adopted son of the nobility. Yet his identification with the cultivated, educated, refined aristocrats proved to be a very important factor in the patient seeking higher education and developing many cultural interests. He displayed the superficial accoutrements of affluence, and elegance but he knew that deep inside he had a servant mentality. Secrecy had also referred to the social devaluation of servants, which he regarded with shame and humiliation. Moreover, servants knew some of their employers' secrets, and could know too much.

Acting servile and submissive was unconsciously associated with being feminine, with being Jewish. Anything that reminded him, or was suggestive of being submissive or subjugated, enraged and frightened the patient. He transiently thought of quitting analysis rather than lying compliantly on the couch. He needed to be clean and neat, not only because of his guilt, but because of the dirty work of his parents. His father had done manual labor, and his mother probably served as a maid. He felt compassion and pity, but also contempt, for manual laborers and for the lower class. He identified not only with the values of the aristocracy but also with their condescending, haughty superiority toward their servants. He admired and idealized their prestige and power. He wanted to realize grandiose omnipotent fantasies and to never again be subjected to being humble and humiliated.

A flood of painful memories returned, integrated in the reconstruction of the patient's childhood as the son of servants. The wealthy estate owners had referred to his parents by their first names or without a name. The patient saw this as a lack of respect, treating his belittled parents as if they were children. He thought that one of the reasons they worked on different estates was that his parents had been summarily dismissed from some of their jobs. Apparently some of the estates were owned by descendents of the "Robber Barons," influential individuals who inherited great wealth from the financial manipulations of their forebears. The estate owners, partially through projection, feared that their servants would engage in theft. The patient had fantasies of acquiring great wealth by defrauding the rich. In the analysis he wondered about concealing his still rising income so that he would not have to raise the fee. In fantasy he was the greedy thief, the Robber Baron, a role formerly assigned to his analyst and Jews. He realized that he, his parents, and the aristocrats all had a common religion—they worshiped wealth.

These various associations and interpretations were followed by further enlarged reconstruction to which the patient contributed. The analysis then veered further into the arena of shame, guilt, and humiliation. The analyst pointed out that the patient's view of his servant parents was that they had to swallow their pride. As servants they had been fed and swallowed a steady diet of denigration. The patient had a fleeting coprophagic fantasy; he identified with his degraded parents, but also was hungry for money and its power. On one level he regarded his parents as shameless, but he identified with their silent compliant acceptance of shame and humiliation. The patient wanted to erase, reverse, and revenge the humiliations. The analyst reconstructed the patient's organizing his life around overcoming any narcissistic injury, obtaining narcissistic supplies, and becoming an aggrandized aristocrat. As a consequence of the reconstruction, many of his disconnected thoughts, memories, and feelings were organized into a cohesive, coherent, meaningful constellation. He could reflect on the family life of servants. He had fantasized that he was not the child of the servants, but the masters. He was of, or destined to be, the nobility. The reconstruction unified what had been a double identity, prince and pauper, servant and master. He had two languages, two sets of parents, two women, and two polarized sets of attitudes toward people and society. His self and object world had been split between idealized and denigrated childish representations. In a parallel reconstruction, he had taken upon himself or had been delegated by his parents to redress their narcissistic mortification, to overcome the family shame, and turn humiliation into pride and glory. He rebelled against any idea of being subservient toward his analyst.

He would not be treated with contempt by his analyst or any authority, but would rise to the superior status to which he was entitled, like the landed aristocracy.

The patient could see that some memories defended against much more disturbing memories of his adolescence and childhood. The secrecy of his exwife's illegitimate child, the secrecy of sibling sex play, the secrecy of the primal scene were associated with the child's secrecy and confusion concerning his parents' denigrated status. Why their job dismissals and moves? Servants had no job security and no status. Were they actually fired because they committed robberies? Frequently paid in cash, they avoided income tax. Did they deserve punishment? Were they without self-respect, and/or secretly enjoying humiliation? What had led to their becoming servants? Did his parents also idealize and identify with the aristocracy, basking in their reflected glory, while denying their own devaluation? Did they wish to be adopted as he did by the estate owners and analyst in a familial family romance just as he had, now manifest in wishes to be adopted by the analyst (Freud, 1909; Frosch, 1959)? The reconstruction gave him insight into his thoughts and feelings about the past and his plans for the future. It allowed greater access to the negative feelings of guilt, shame, and humiliation, his low self-esteem, his fear of failure, and his drive for success.

The reconstruction elucidated to the patient's intrapsychic fantasies and responses to his pre-adult experiences. He was less confused by his pendulumlike swings between his feeling affluent and indigent, aristocrat and servant, master and slave. The reconstruction did not compete with nor defend against transference interpretation, but advanced understanding of both transference and genetic interpretation. The recovery of dissociated, forgotten, and repressed memories reciprocally facilitated reconstruction.

Although Freud noted that reconstruction may serve as a convincing surrogate for a memory that could not be retrieved from repression, his basic premise was developmental and dealt with a forgotten piece of childhood. Freud reconstructed a part of the analysand's development, with pathogenic or progressive ramifications. Freud's (1937) formulation went far beyond a single memory or element: "What we are in search of is a picture of the patient's forgotten years that shall be alike trustworthy and in all essential respects complete" (p. 258). Freud added that the task of the analyst "is to make out what has been forgotten from the traces which it has left behind, or more correctly, to construct it." Freud (1920) anticipated the contemporary developmental issues in reconstruction, and early differentiated between genetic and developmental perspectives.

> *So long as we trace the development from its final outcome backwards, the chain of events appears continuous and we feel we have gained in insight, which is completely satisfactory or even exhaustive. But if we proceed the reverse way, if we start from the premises inferred from the analysis and try to follow these up to the final result, then we no longer get the impression of an inevitable sequence of events, which could not have been otherwise determined. We notice at once that there might have been another result, and that we might have been just as well able to understand and explain the latter. The synthesis is thus not so satisfactory as the analysis (p. 167).*

The problem of reconstructing developmental steps and sequences, of tracing the over-determined numerous factors of pathogenesis both evokes and challenges reconstruction. The issues of genetic fallacy and adultomorphic myth are further complicated by the possible confusion of pathological regression, normal development, and deviant development; by the number of factors and varied strength of forces involved; and by the discontinuities which have to be bridged. Reconstruction is made possible by the wealth of information provided by the analysis. But it is never a singular, veridical "red thread" of connections. The reconstructive inferences depend upon the totality of analytic data, and not just the transference alone, on the elaboration and remodeling of the reconstruction in the crucible of the analytic process. How could this patient understand his master-slave fantasies, his feelings of emasculation and inferiority, his overall preoccupation with narcissistic injury and self-aggrandizement without the affective reconstruction of his childhood?

Some of the unresolved analytic issues in this case are of great interest. The genetic interpretations, and the reconstruction to which they were attached, did not fully explain the patient's psychopathology. So far the classical explanation of the patient's disorder was in terms of oedipal conflict. Were there not also primary narcissistic and pre-oedipal issues, which were important antecedents of later conflict? Of course the further back into the preoedipal period a reconstruction is attempted, the more speculative it inevitably becomes. The earlier the level of reconstruction, the greater the level of conjecture. What was his early experience with his mother? She was stoic in her menial work of cleaning and laundering. Some of the ambivalence toward his father may have been transferred and displaced from his mother. She was not described in warm terms and was regarded as rigid and unempathic. She was quite possibly depressed during his early childhood, hardly playful. It is likely that his feeding, sleeping, and toilet training were rigidly controlled. Was his mother the prototype of the rigid, insensitive, callous nun? Mother could be a Madonna-like figure who protected him from his own impulses, but also an exciting and emasculating prostitute. He stated, "I'm uncomfortable with cracks in the edifice I have created." Women were cracked, tempting, and dangerous; they were split into degraded pairs of prostitutes and nuns. Only after more analysis could he admit that some of the clergy were dedicated and effective educators. There were few if any parties in his childhood, and holidays were not celebrated. He had never had a birthday party, though the patient was aware that the aristocrat's children on the estate had such parties. His father was not sure about his son's birthday.

The atmosphere of home was somber. His parents' relationship was not marked by overt affection and friendship, and they were little interested in their children's feelings. If he did not like the food he was offered, he was expected to eat it without complaint, so that his preferences were largely ignored. In later childhood he was painfully ashamed of his parents and strenuously defended against feelings of shame. His parents conveyed their feelings of denigration to their son, but they and the aristocrats encouraged both his later achievement and entitlement.

Transference analysis and reconstruction were synergistic rather than competitive or adversarial. The reconstruction was regarded as mutative, "making a decisive difference in clinical analysis … the past within the present is

426

transformed forging a new vision of reality" (Blum, 1994, p. 150). In the process of reconstruction, self-representations as well as object representations from various phases of life are re-evaluated and reintegrated into new and more realistic representations. Not only were the defenses modified, but also the patient's apperception of his/her inner and outer world.

In clinical situations where there has been massive psychic trauma, there may be ego regression and damage to cognitive and affective processes. What the patient cannot remember and articulate has to be laboriously reconstructed. Somatization reactions and non-verbal communication may be at least initially of great importance. Reconstruction may contribute to the retrieval and reorganization of fragmented, distorted, memories, as well as filling in memory gaps. Without the reconstruction of memory what is indescribable and ineffable may be somatized, enacted, or acted-out through the children, the next generation. To avoid a collusion of silent avoidance, reconstruction is required of the trauma, terror, and panic, of the feelings of helplessness, and of the void of protecting or rescuing objects (Grubrich-Simitis, 1981; Krystal, 1991; Blum, 1994). An attempt is made to clarify the details of the traumatic situations, and when necessary, to uncover the intergenerational transmission of trauma, with analytic awareness of inevitable unknowns and ambiguities. Only then can traumatic reality and its fantasy elaboration be integrated into the relatively intact personality. The verbal reconstruction coalesces with step-by-step working-through of trauma and terror. This permits the massive trauma of the past, recalled and reconstructed, to belong to the past rather than the ever present. Further analytic reconstruction may encompass prior and subsequent traumatic experience, telescoped into the maelstrom of massive trauma.

I shall now turn to the early facilitating value and integrative effects of reconstruction in psychoanalysis and in insight oriented psychoanalytic psychotherapy. While it is true that reconstruction is not necessarily a part of psychotherapy as it is in psychoanalysis, reconstruction is often utilized to help the patient become aware of the power and persistence of childhood fantasy and experience into their adult lives. Transference and current reality may take precedence, but at the same time, reconstruction may be necessary to illuminate the transference and the current reality situation, which the patient has helped to create. A borderline patient, who is bitterly critical and contemptuous of the analyst, may not respond to the analyst's attempts to show the patient that the attacks on the analyst are irrational and unjustified. The psychoanalyst regards the patient's criticism as part of transference fantasy, whereas the patient believes that the analyst truly merits criticism. The analyst has a negative counter-transference, about which he is inwardly conflicted. The patient has succeeded in eliciting the psychotherapist's hostility, justifying in his mind his criticism of the analyst. A transference-countertransference stalemate might ensue.

There are different approaches to such thorny problems, but early reconstruction can be very helpful, to the psychoanalyst as well as to the patient. This is a departure from the general use of reconstruction after the initial phase of therapy. The exception here is not meant to detract from Freud's (1940) counsel, "we never fail to make a distinction between our knowledge and his knowledge. We avoid telling him at once things we have often discovered at an early stage, and we avoid telling him the whole of what we think we have discovered. We reflect carefully over when we shall impart the knowledge of one of our constructions to him … which is not always easy to decide" (p. 178).

Where the patient has experienced a pathogenic relationship with a parent involving regular overdoses of criticism, contempt, and disparagement, the therapist could point out that the patient had experienced withering criticism long before his treatment. His feelings of mistreatment derived not from the present, but predominantly from the past with his parent. The patient has identified with the aggressor and was treating the therapist to the same disparagement to which he was subjected. The patient had become the critical parent and the analyst is treated as the child whom the parent holds in contempt of court. Without this reconstruction of a piece of the patient's childhood, it may not be possible for an ego impaired patient to distance himself from the transference as well as to understand and accept transference interpretation. Furthermore, the reality of a patient being contemptuous and insulting toward others in his life situation, may still be readily subjected to projection and rationalization that the others deserved his animosity.

The adult woman who is seductive and exhibitionistic in an erotic transference may have similar dynamics. Seduced by an older brother into sibling sex play, she is now the active seducer. This would be a specific genetic interpretation. She gains control over the analyst in fantasy and unconsciously seeks not so much his falling in love with her, but his downfall. In this case the erotic transference recapitulates the sibling relationship, and defends against an underlying hostile fantasy of emasculating the analyst and destroying his reputation. The reconstruction integrates and explains her seductive behavior as repetition and revenge, weapon and defense, in analysis and in life.

Is reconstruction important in the contemporary analytic process as Freud (1937) had earlier proposed? To my mind the reconstructions presented here were essential to the analytic and the therapeutic process and progress. It is difficult to understand how analytic experience without the insights enriched by reconstruction would significantly alter unconscious, unrealistic self and object representations, as proposed by inter-subjective theorists. An emphasis on the mutative effect of the here and now analytic experience takes account of the influence and effect of the analyst's counter-transference and subjectivity, but with loss of balanced focus on childhood, and patient's infantile neurotic fantasies and features. The analyst also engages in reciprocal self-examination and counter-transference analysis. The value of reconstruction is exemplified in the clinical material in which the past so prominently influences the present and impinges on the future. Without reconstruction, psychoanalysis tends to become a-historic, dissociated from the infantile unconscious, and the context and shaping of life experience. Reconstruction restores the continuity and cohesion of personal history, correcting personal myths while simultaneously fostering greater and more realistic self-awareness, knowledge, and insight.

Spanning life experience, reconstruction integrates past and present, fantasy and reality, cause and effect.

Reconstructions are selected from their alternatives on the basis of the convergence of analytic data and of the patient's response to the reconstruction.

Individual fantasy and experience may coalesce with universal fantasies and the universals of life experience, but there are always individual variations. This is exemplified in the family romance of the son of servants. A reconstruction should be internally consistent and cohesive, logical and lucid, and closely linked to the prevailing unconscious conflicts and analytic issues. While it may replace gaps in memory, reconstruction has a different contemporary position in the theory of technique, deriving from and applying the genetic and developmental points of view in clinical psychoanalysis. In contemporary psychoanalysis, reconstruction has largely supplanted reliance on the recovery of repressed memory. Patterns are more important in general than are single memories, with the major exception of shock trauma. Reconstruction also has an important current research dimension, testing and potentially integrating analytic data with the findings of infant developmental studies.

Validation and conviction are not necessarily achieved. Either analyst, analysand, or researcher may be much more convinced of the validity of a reconstruction than the other persons. While Freud at times shifted positions concerning the relative importance of fantasy and real experience, he never relinquished the importance of trauma. Freud (1926) referred to the sometimes "irrefutable evidence that these occurrences which we inferred really did take place" and he then stated, "The correct reconstruction, you must know, of such forgotten experiences of childhood always has a great therapeutic effect, whether they permit of objective confirmation or not" (p. 216). Unlike the past when non-analytic data tended to be dismissed or scorned as impediments or contaminants in the analytic process, such concerns are no longer regarded as entirely appropriate. External confirmation can be analytically useful and contribute to rational validation and conviction of correct reconstruction (Good, 1998). Patients are stimulated to check and correct reconstructions whenever possible through objective evidence, e.g. of documents and the reports of relatives and witnesses. It is remarkable how often psychoanalytic reconstructions are confirmed and expanded with extra-analytic evidence. However, no source or selection of data is inherently free of distortion. The legal system has painfully learned that eyewitness reports may not be reliable.

The past is not only rediscovered but is recreated in clinical psychoanalysis. Memory is remodeled. The past has taken on elaborate new meanings, which did not exist in childhood. Moreover, developmental transformations may not be retrievable in their pristine form. The "second look" (Novey, 1968) at childhood is through analytic eyes with the refraction of an adult lens. Though the analytic autobiography is further illuminated and integrated by a particular reconstruction, there are no guarantees in analysis of valid reconstruction or interpretation. Psychoanalysis requires tolerance and evaluation of alternative considerations. Ambiguity and perplexity are part of psychoanalytic work and the quest for greater insight. In addition to Freud's (1911) two principles of mental function, the pleasure and reality principles, we live and work with the uncertainty principle (Heisenberg, 1958).

REFERENCES

Blum, H. (1980). The value of reconstruction in adult psychoanalysis. *Internat. Psychoanal.*, 61:39–54.

——— (1994). Reconstruction in Psychoanalysis. Childhood Revisited and Recreated. New York: International Universities Press.

——— (2000). The reconstruction of reminiscence. *J. Amer. Psychoanal. Assn.*, 47:1125–1144.

Freud, S. (1909). Family romances. *S.E.*, 9.

——— (1919). A child is being beaten. *S.E.*, 17.

——— (1920). The psychogenesis of a case of homosexuality in a woman. *S.E.*, 18.

——— (1937). Constructions in analysis. *S.E.*, 23.

——— (1940). An outline of psychoanalysis. *S.E.*, 23.

Frosch, J. (1959). Transference derivatives of the family romance. *J. Amer. Psychoanal. Assn.*, 7:503–520.

Good, M. (1998). Screen reconstructions: Traumatic memory, conviction, and the problem of verification. *J. Amer. Psychoanal. Assn.*, 46:149–183.

Greenacre, P. (1975). On reconstruction. *J. Amer. Psychoanal. Assn.*, 23:693–771.

GrubrichSimitis, I. (1981). Extreme traumatization as cumulative trauma: Psychoanalytic investigations of the effects of concentration camp experiences on survivors and their children. *Psychoanal. St. Child*, 36:415–450.

Heisenberg, W. (1958). Physics and Philosophy. New York: Harper.

Krystal, H. (1991). Integration and self-healing in post-traumatic states: A ten year retrospective. *Amer. Imago*, 48:93–118.

Laub, D. (1998). The empty circle: Children of survivors and the limits of reconstruction. *J. Amer. Psychoanal. Assn.*, 46:508–529.

Ledoux, J. (2002). Synaptic Self: How Our Brains Become Who We Are. New York: Viking.

Novey, S. (1968). The Second Look. Baltimore: Johns Hopkins University Press.

CHAPTER 22

Reconstructing Freud's Prototype Reconstructions

(2015). *Int. Forum Psychoanal.*, (24)(1):47–56.

Although at age 75, Freud asserted "deep within me there continues to be the happy child of Freiberg" (Příbor), his statement may now be regarded as an idealized version of his infancy and early childhood, devoid of trauma and stress. His reconstructions of his first three years of life, reported in his letters of October 1897 to Wilhelm Fliess, are subject to their own reconstruction. He had just repudiated seduction trauma as an exclusive etiology of psychopathology. Freud was then in the throes of an intense transference-countertransference relationship with Fliess, with reactivated unconscious conflict and developmental challenge. The reconstructions of his nursemaid, of his reactions to the birth and death of his first sibling, and of seeing his mother "*nudam*" require re-evaluation and revision in the context of contemporary psychoanalytic theory and new knowledge. While the specific reconstructions are of continuing interest, the methodology of analytic inquiry into early childhood and parenting transcends the inevitable limitations of the infancy of psychoanalysis. The concept of reconstruction potentiated the development of psychoanalytic thought, although with recurrent controversy, especially concerning retrospective meaning, psychic reality, and historical reality.

In October 1931, Freud wrote to the Mayor of Příbor "Deep within me, although overlaid, there continues to live the happy child of Příbor … who received from this air, from the soil, the first indelible impressions" (Gay, 1988, p. 575). Freud's childhood, however, was more complicated and conflicted than his statement suggests. His infancy was also characterized by trauma, stress, interpersonal conflict, and burgeoning intrapsychic conflict. The happy child he described in 1931 may be compared with an idealized screen memory. Freud actually wrote in somber terms about his childhood in Příbor in his initially anonymous paper "Screen memories" (1899). Little Sigmund's early childhood involved a series of losses, a familial upheaval, and a socioeconomic crisis. Freud later indicated that his life in Příbor had a catastrophic end.

Much of Freud's initial reconstructions, the main focus of this paper, concerned his first three years of life in Příbor, in the Czech Republic, then within the Austro-Hungarian Empire. Astounding for their brilliance, complexity, and depth, these reconstructions were related to Fliess (Freud, 1985) in a series of letters during the very brief period of the month of October 1897. They pertained to his infant brother, Julius, his mother, his nursemaid(s), and his relationship with his nephew, John. The Oedipus complex was first formulated, and simultaneously antecedents of the Oedipus complex were reconstructed and given importance in their own right. The social, cultural context of life in Příbor (Burianek, in press; Mahler, this issue; Papiasvili, this issue), the intersection of Freud's internal and external worlds, historical facts, our imagination, and our transference and countertransference to Freud will all influence the process of reconstruction and reinterpretation.

Reconstructions of early childhood had never before been systematically attempted, nor had early object relationships been considered as forerunners of adult object relations and adult personality. Freud glimpsed his own infantile life and fantasy life largely from dreams, as well as memory fragments and screen memories. Without a well-defined methodology, skeptical of his own findings, he checked his reconstructions and distorted memory fragments with his mother. Asking her for factual correction and validation, he struggled to differentiate fact from fantasy, historical reality from psychic reality, the interpersonal and the intrapsychic. These issues, which concerned Freud for a lifetime, have recurred as controversial subjects up to the present.

Reconstruction was an entirely new approach to the understanding of infancy and early child development beyond the reach of conscious adult memory. These initial reconstructions, dazzling in their day, require modification and updating in the light of contemporary theory and new knowledge. They are nevertheless landmarks in the evolution of psychoanalysis; the process of reconstruction transcends the content.

Freud did not appear to be aware of his own motivations for these reconstructions, nor did he comment on his own vacillation at that time regarding seduction trauma, a misleading term for child abuse. He did not link his pioneer reconstructions in the very brief period of October 1897, which reinstated the seduction trauma (child abuse) of pathogenesis, after his just having repudiated it (September 1897). This repudiation had exonerated his father, whom he had previously accused of abusing his siblings. He did not refer to the first anniversary of his father's death in October 1896, and was not then aware of the significance of his own fatherhood. He was apparently not cognizant at this time of his ambivalent transference relationship with Fliess, nor of the possibility that, at 41 years of age, he may have been experiencing a mid-life crisis (Anzieu, 1986). Freud was motivated toward his work on dreams from an early age, but the first anniversary of the death of his father, the replacement of Breuer by Fliess, and his burgeoning inner struggle to emancipate himself from dependency on Fliess were all determinants of his seemingly sudden burst of insight in October 1897.

Life in one room in Příbor

Little Sigmund was domiciled for his first three years and four months in one small room in which he lived with his parents. This was on the second floor of a building above a locksmith's shop. The locksmith lived in the other second-floor room. In the framework of the one room, little Sigmund would have been exposed to the sights, sounds, smells, movements, vibrations, and emotional resonances of that confined space. There was no running water, plumbing, heating, toilet, or kitchen. There were temperature extremes of freezing winters and burning hot summers. Freud's very likely exposure to the primal scene in the one room with his parents in Příbor has been frequently emphasized in psychobiographical discourse. Freud's later reconstructions of the primal scene are related to his early experience in Příbor. His case of the

Wolfman (Freud, 1918) in particular, centered on the reconstruction of the patient's primal scene experience, may be understood as having a parallel in Freud's own primal scene reconstruction. Besides the primal scenes disguised in his Specimen Irma dream and others in the "Interpretation of dreams," he urged analysts to send him clinical reports of primal scenes. However, a singular focus on the primal scene will be blind to the complexity of family life in the framework of the one small room.

Freud's first exposure to language in the Freud's room would have been Yiddish, spoken between his parents and to him. German and Czech and other dialects would have been first encountered in the world external to this room. Communication within the room, the private life and the secrets of the parental couple, would have been very different from their public persona, language, and behavior; different from the external cultural, linguistic, and religious milieu. Parental harmony or discord, the obvious as well as the more subtle affective reactions of the parental couple, would have been conveyed to little Sigmund, and his every cry or laugh, and so on, heard by Amalia. The intimate scenes may have greatly stimulated rather than inhibited the curiosity of an infant with Freud's endowment.

In the one small room, Freud also would have been exposed to his mother's pregnancy with Julius and accompanying bodily changes, her nursing of Julius, and Julius's fatal gastrointestinal illness. Probably born in October 1857, Julius would have been conceived when Freud was about nine months of age. Freud may have been exposed to the home birth of Julius when Freud was 18 months of age. Considering the amenorrhea of lactation, a natural form of contraception, Freud was likely to have been nursed for no more than seven months. The oral-maternal deprivation coincident with the life and death of Julius may have been an important determinant of Freud's oral addiction to cigars, and his later oral cancer.

Play within the room would have been limited and close to or with Amalia. Play with his nephew John in the fields would have been an important developmental experience for little Sigmund, with wild space for experiment and exploration of reality (Winnicott, 1971). The lack of privacy, the probable difficulty of maintaining personal boundaries, and the enclosure without personal space can be stifling and deeply disturbing. However, a crowded room was then the way of life of most people in little towns like Příbor, and indeed is currently so in many areas of the world. Issues of space, suffocation, and separation abound.

Before her marriage, Freud's mother, Amalia, had been living in Vienna with her parents, Jacob and Sara Nathansohn ("Amalia" is derived from her Hebrew name, Malka, meaning queen). She was born in Brody, Jewish Galicia. At 20 years of age, she moved to Příbor with her new husband, like her father named Jacob, and twice her age. Jacob Freud had two grown sons living in Příbor from his first marriage in Tysmenitz, Galicia: Emanuel, age 24, and Philip, age 20. How did Amalia psychologically adapt, so far removed from her family and friends, with no relatives in Příbor, except for her husband, his sons, and Emanuel's wife? Her experience would have been similar to that of a recent immigrant.

Now in a different sociocultural and linguistic surround, she quickly became pregnant with Sigmund, born nine months after her marriage. Her pregnancy with Julius, and his birth and death, were followed by the birth of Freud's five sisters and his brother, Alexander, all before Freud was 10 years old. Jacob Freud had lost his father, Shlomo, for whom Freud was named, six months before Freud's birth. Although named Shlomo Sigismund Freud, neither Shlomo nor Solomon was used as his first name. Freud changed his first name from Sigismund to Sigmund in connection with his shifting adolescent identity.

Amalia lost her brother Julius one month before the birth of her son Julius, probably named for his deceased uncle. While Amalia's health and state of mind during her pregnancy with Sigmund and then with Julius are not recorded, object loss, mourning, and possible maternal depression would all have influenced her relationship with infant Sigmund. Freud's mother, conspicuous by her absence, is hidden behind a defensive barricade; there are many more references to his father in "The interpretation of dreams" (Freud, 1900), and in his case histories. Off limits for published discussion, Amalia, was alive until 1930, age 95. Amalia was supposedly the only woman Freud kissed in public.

The Freud family in the Příbor area

Born in Brody, Galicia, a town with an 88% Jewish population, Freud's mother initially spoke Yiddish. Having moved with her parents to Vienna, she acquired some degree of fluency in colloquial German. Upon arrival in Příbor, she presumably had to learn a rudimentary Czech language. Freud's father conducted his business in Czech and in German, could read and write Hebrew, and would have known Polish from being reared in Tysmenitz. Brody and Tysmenitz were centers of Jewish religious and cultural life in Galicia, Poland, now part of the Ukraine. Both orthodox and more assimilated Jews were to be found in Tysmenitz (Krull, 1986). Although in business with his orthodox Jewish grandfather, Jacob Freud was exposed to the wider world as a traveling merchant before settling in Příbor. Assimilated, Freud's parents were married by a non-orthodox Rabbi.

There are no Jews lefts in Tysmenitz or Brody; virtually all the resident Jews were murdered in the Holocaust. Sigmund Freud never visited Tysmentiz or Brody. In Příbor, Jacob Freud was a "tolerated Jew," requiring that his business permit be renewed about every six months. Jacob also told Sigmund at about age 10 the humiliating tale of his having had his hat knocked off and being forced into the gutter in Příbor by an anti-Semite who hurled the insult "Jew, get off the pavement." To add insult to injury, Jacob had donated funds beyond the tax for pave the walk (Burianek, in press). The gutter was littered with animal droppings and sewage, so Jacob's humiliation was meant to be severe and public. Jacob would have to watch his step; Jews would have to keep a low profile.

Wider meanings of Jacob's report to Sigmund at age nine or 10 may be inferred (Freud, 1900). His father may have unconsciously conveyed his fantasy of his son avenging his humiliation or compensating for his humiliation through high achievement. Jacob may have indicated that Jewish life in Vienna was superior to that of Příbor six years prior, that paths and opportunities were open to enterprising Jews. At the same time, Jacob devalued himself in front of Sigmund in his depiction of abject submission to bigotry. Jacob failed in business and could not support his family. He may have symbolically ceded his paternal authority to Sigmund, who would then have to resolve his guilt over his Oedipal victory in developing psychoanalysis. Sigmund then identified with Hannibal and other military heroes who would be victors rather than victims, and who could reverse defeat and masochistic submission. A 3% minority in Catholic Příbor, a village with a population of 4500, the Jewish families were insecure and aware of anti-Semitic diatribes, uprisings, and a history of violent persecution. Jews in Příbor were accepted, yet foreign, outsiders in a xenophobic land (Mahler, this issue; Papiasvili, this issue; Robert, 1975).

Pregnant with Julius, Amalia stayed at the Spa at Roznau, 10 miles south of Příbor, with Sigmund and one of his nursemaids, Resi Wittek, for several months. She was separated from her husband, his relatives, and friends such as the Fluss family. According to their records, babies were born at the Spa, possibly including Julius Freud. The Spa "cure" was primarily mineral baths, rich in sulfur, with rest in the sun for the treatment of pulmonary disorders. Since the Freud family lived a poor, spartan life in one room in Příbor, how could Amalia afford the prolonged stay at the Spa? If Amalia had tuberculosis like her deceased brother Julius, her delicate physical and or psychological condition could have justified the stay. Jacob and his sons or Amalia's family of origin would have somehow defrayed the cost. Amalia appears to have been indulged in frequent visits to the Roznau Spa even after she had moved to Vienna. She visited Roznau 24 times for stays of variable length while living in poor circumstances in Vienna. It does not appear that she ever visited Příbor again, even though it was very close to the spa. Twice she was accompanied to Roznau by Sigmund and a sibling. Were the stresses of closely repeated pregnancies, nursing, and nurturing relevant to her spa retreats? Had she been worried about her own health? Was she concerned about the transmission of disease to her children, especially after the illness and death of her infant Julius? Mourning and depressed after his loss, the spa might also have been viewed as a physical and psychological place for her to recover. If she had been depressed, the availability of the nursemaid (Resi) at the Spa takes on greater meaning (Green, 1986; Guntrip, 1975; Kardiner, 1977).

The nursemaids

Freud's references to his nursemaid in his early reconstructions are fascinating, contradictory, and enigmatic, both revealing and concealing. Many prior analytic contributions have elaborated the significance of Freud's nursemaid(s) (Grigg, 1973; Hardin, 1987, 1988; Swan, 1974). Condensed into one figure in Freud's letters, three nursemaids have now, however, been documented. Two of the three nursemaids, Monica Zajic and Magdalena Kabatova were in their 20s, similar in age to Amalia and Maria, Emanuel's wife. Monica was the daughter of the locksmith, the family's landlord, although both she and Magdalena were listed as residing in Emanuel's home. They may have shared functions as housemaid and nanny for the children of Amalie and Marie. Magdalena is the only one referred to in the historical records as a nanny, and, of interest, also as a wet nurse. Did she function as a wet nurse for any of the Freud family's children? Was there a brief period of Sigmund having had a wet nurse when Amalia was pregnant with Julius? While there are retrieved records of two nursemaids having resided in Příbor, the third, Resi Wittek, is mentioned only as having accompanied Amalia to the spa; her name appears on the guest list of the Roznau Spa as a servant of Amalia Freud in June 1857. That there were three nursemaids might have added to little Sigmund's bewilderment about their relationship to him. Three nursemaids with different temperaments and attitudes might also have been a spur to Sigmund's adapting and attuning to a world of different languages, cultures, and religions.

Freud alleged that the nursemaid had been his teacher in sexual matters, implying sexual abuse (letter to Fliess, October 4, 1897). Freud stated, "She washed me in reddish water in which she had previously washed herself [The interpretation is not difficult … (i.e., he had been washed in her menstrual blood. I find nothing like this in the chain of my memories so I regard it as a genuine ancient discovery.)]."

Freud thought the nurse had induced him to steal coins for her, corrected in the next letter to Fliess, on October 15, 1897. His nurse was the direct thief, discovered by his half-brother Philip, and was arrested by the police during Amalia's confinement with Freud's first sister, Anna, born December 31, 1858.

Freud's mother validated the reality of his reconstruction, adding that the nurse was imprisoned for 10 months. No record of her arrest or imprisonment has yet been found, but she could have been immediately dismissed and disappeared, or the prison records lost. Freud would ever more grapple with the issues of reality or fantasy, historical reality or psychic reality, memory or screen memory or pseudo-memory.

Freud's ambivalence to his nursemaid(s) is marked in the letters of October 3 and 4; he briefly referred to the "prime originator" (the nursemaid) as the source of his neurotic conflicts. The nursemaid(s) was seen as the perpetrator of seduction trauma, which was then reinstated as a source of psychopathology. However, seduction trauma was no longer the virtually exclusive etiology. In the October 3, 1897 reconstruction, the "prime originator" was:

> an ugly, elderly, but clever woman who told me a great deal about God almighty and Hell, and who instilled in me a high opinion of my own capacities ... If I am successful in resolving my own hysteria, then I shall be grateful to the memory of the old woman who provided me at such an early age with the means for living and going on living.

Freud's ambivalently loved nursemaid was depicted as both a protective, supportive mother surrogate and, in contradiction, also as a corrupt perpetrator of seduction, abuse, and delinquency. Was this ambivalence to a nursemaid an example of splitting or a reaction to different nursemaids? Did any of the nursemaids have a living child of her own? Had any of the nursemaids had a recent miscarriage or a deceased infant? A nursemaid who did not produce sibling rivals could have been safely dissociated from a disappearing mother. The nanny could have been a displacement for his mother, and the mother a displacement for the nanny (Colombo, 2010).

Why did Freud consider his nursemaid rather than his mother as bolstering his self-esteem and providing "the means for living"? I believe his mother was always more important, more influential in his life than any one nanny. The relationships of the nursemaids to Freud's mother, to each other, and to their shared care of little Sigmund are obscure. The nursemaids were Christian; as paid servants they could be dismissed at any time. Moreover, the existence of three nursemaids suggests that an attachment to any one of them would have been limited. Freud's mother's initial reference to the nursemaid as ugly and old suggests an emotional dislike, rather than merely a comment about her physical appearance. This shifting displacement among the main women in Freud's life would not have been unique at that time. In his letter to Fliess on February 9, 1898, Freud mentioned, "Had a delightful dream … which unfortunately cannot be published … its second meaning shifts back and forth between my nurse, my mother!, and my wife and one cannot really publicly subject one's wife to reproaches of this sort." The figure of the nursemaid was recurrent in Freud's dreams and thoughts. Freud's references to the nursemaid or nanny far exceed in number the rare references to his mother in the Fliess letters and in "The interpretation of dreams."

At the time the Freuds were in Příbor, and subsequently in Vienna, Jews were periodically accused of the mythical crime of killing Christian children to use their blood in the ritual Passover meal. These accusations and occasional arrests caused widespread fear among European Jews. In what was then a famous case, the nanny of a Jewish child claimed she had secretly baptized him, taking him to church as an infant. The Catholic Church proclaimed that no Christian child could be raised in a Jewish family. Forcibly taken from his distraught parents in June 1858, the child, Edgardo Mortara, became a ward of the Pope; later he became an evangelical priest encouraging Jews to convert (Kertzer, 1997). International protests against the Jewish child's kidnapping may well have reached Příbor when Freud was two years old. (I wrote to the Vatican many years ago to inquire if there was any record of Sigmund Freud having been baptized, but received no reply.) Despite this atmosphere, Freud's parents were not alarmed by the nanny taking their toddler to church, or afterwards by Freud's preaching like a priest. Did his parents want privacy and time without their child? Amalia may have been more relieved than alarmed about Sigmund being taken to church.

The "reddish water" reconstruction may have been further overdetermined, including Freud's experience with his nursemaid in church. Freud possibly confused a reference in church to being "washed in the blood of the lamb" with the nursemaid's washing him (Vitz, 1993). An observant toddler, Freud might have noticed the bloodstained garments of mother or nursemaid being washed, conflated with his own bath. (Sanitary napkins and tampons were not available until 1890.) Freud might possibly have confused bloody water from the nearby slaughter of animals or from reddish colored water in a close stream (Burianek, in press). If, as Freud was convinced, he had really been bathed in bloody water, might he also have been abused in other ways? Was he subjected to harsh treatment, for example in bathing or dressing or after urination or defecation? Washing Freud in the nursemaid's menstrual blood could have been the enactment of her fantasy that he was born from her womb, her biological child. The nursemaid appears without further genetic analysis in other of Freud's (1900) dreams, for example in his dream of "running up the stairs," and in "my son, the myops" (Anzieu, 1986).

Julius

Freud (in a letter to Fliess dated October 3, 1897), reconstructing his reactions to the birth of his brother Julius and his rivalry with him, Freud stated, "I greeted my one year younger brother (who died after a few months) with adverse wishes and genuine childhood jealousy; and that his death left a germ of self reproaches in me." (While Julius's death certificate exists, no documentation of the date and location of Julius's birth has as yet surfaced.) Infant mortality, then about 33%, deeply influenced parent–child relationships and social attitudes towards children. Freud's reconstruction of his reaction to the birth of Julius and to the death of Julius at six months of age when Freud was just 23–24 months of age was remarkable (Blum, 1977). Without any overt acknowledgement of his prior (1897) Julius reconstruction, Freud (1931, pp. 132–133) elaborated and generalized on reactions to new siblings:

This jealousy is constantly receiving fresh nourishment in the later years of childhood and the whole shock is repeated with the birth of each new brother or sister. Nor does it make a difference if the older child remains the mother's preferred favorite. A child's demands for love are immoderate. They make exclusive claims and tolerate no sharing of their mother.

Note that this essay, written soon after his mother's death (1930), still avoids the mother's reactions to her pregnancies, the death of Julius, and to having additional children. Did Freud unconsciously blame his mother as well as himself for the loss of Julius and the concurrent disappearance of a nursemaid? He also lost his mother to his sister Anna. There is an implication that he unconsciously fantasized that his mother had been impregnated by his halfbrother Philip rather than his own father. An increase in size of the family alters the relationship of the parents to their first child, the parents to each other, and each sibling's relation to each parent and to each other. In this connection, Freud (1914) once designated the Oedipus complex as a family complex without further explanation. The term "Oedipus complex" in its schematic form, however, did not at first address the negative Oedipus complex, or the "family complex" in which there is more than one child (Blum, 2011). Related to the discovery of the Oedipus complex, his father and his halfbrother Emanuel were building their families at the same time in Příbor, very likely with Oedipal conflict.

Freud's infantile jealously of his first sibling, his brother Julius, can be interpreted in relation to his unconscious infantile rivalry and envy of Fliess. Fliess was two years younger than Freud and could represent Julius as well as Freud's parents. His rivalry with Fliess for scientific discovery, underneath their friendly collaboration, was another powerful incentive for Freud's own discoveries. Freud's and Fliess's wives had been pregnant concurrently, and Freud was pregnant in conscious fantasy, gestating psychoanalysis: "After the frightful labor pains of the last few weeks, I gave birth to a new form of knowledge." His allusions to being pregnant disappear after the Fliess relationship had terminated and Freud had analyzed his feminine identification in their relationship, and bisexual identification in the primal scene (Blum, 1990; Newton, 1995).

Travel phobia

In his October 3, 1897 letter to Fliess, Freud noted that his travel phobia was at its height. Related to his travel phobia and his father having been forced off the pavement, Sigmund Freud analyzed the myth of Oedipus dramatized by Sophocles. Oedipus did not permit his father to travel beyond where the three roads met, unknowingly killing his biological father. Freud could not enter Rome until sufficient progress had been made in his self-analysis in 1901. Similar unconscious conflicts were reactivated in 1904 when Freud experienced depersonalization and de-realization on the Acropolis (Robert, 1975).

Freud had observed that two great universal questions of children are "where do babies come from?" and "what are the anatomical differences between the sexes?" In this same letter as the reconstruction of his reactions to Julius (October 3, 1897), Freud recounts an experience of seeing his mother *"nudam"* on the train journey from Leipzig to Vienna when he was between two and two and a half years of age. Freud was actually closer to three and a half or four years of age at the time of that train trip. By using Latin and dating the exposure to his nude mother at an earlier age, Freud may have been defending against his dawning awareness of incestuous overstimulation and Oedipal guilt. The letter gives the impression of a first and single exposure to his naked mother. A contemporary deconstruction of his reconstruction of *"matrem nudam"* suggests that repeated exposure to his mother's body and to the primal scene in the one room in Příbor seems far more probable. Freud might have seen his mother dress and undress, and he had to have observed changes in her body during and after her pregnancy with Julius (Balsam, 2012). Amalia was probably pregnant again during the train ride to Leipzig, since Freud's second sister, Rosa, was born on March 22, 1860 in Vienna. The train ride with his mother, apparently without the presence of his father, might have condensed into the single incident previous frequent exposures and intimate excitement. Freud's exposure to his pregnant *matrem nudam* was probably a further contribution to the pathogenesis of Freud's travel phobia. His travel phobia may have been related to conflicts regarding both seeing his mother nude as well as not seeing her and experiencing separation anxiety.

Reconstruction and screen memory

In a letter to Fliess of October 15, 1897 Freud wrote, "a scene occurred to me which in the course of 25 years has occasionally emerged in my conscious memory without my understanding it." Screen memories are enduring, vivid, visual, and usually isolated or encapsulated. Bernfeld (1947) realized that Freud's early years in Příbor were referred to in this letter, later disguised as the report of a patient in Freud's paper "Screen memories" (1899). The subjects remained anonymous because of the autobiographical character of the content.

A compromise formation, Freud's screen memory has been described as unusual, an adolescent memory projected backward in time to early childhood. Freud's screen memory, however, concerns both his adolescence and his early childhood in Příbor and a constellation of memories and fantasies (La Farge, 2012). Freud did not connect his adolescent fantasy to his father having fathered his half-brother when his father was an adolescent. Fantasy and memory may have been reactivated when Freud's father and his half-brother Emanuel were concurrently fathering children in Příbor. The Oedipus complex had many roots and offshoots in its initial construction in October 1897.

In the "Screen memories" paper, the disguised subject (Freud) and his nephew (John) snatched a bouquet of yellow flowers (dandelions) from his niece, Pauline. Without identifying the Příbor setting, Freud (1899) quoted the presumed patient:

At the top end of the meadow there is a cottage … in front of the cottage door two women are standing, a peasant woman with a handkerchief on her head and a children's nurse. Three children are playing … one of them is myself (between the ages of two and three)… the two others are my boy cousin who is a year older than me, and his sister who is almost the exact age as I am. We are picking the yellow flowers (dandelions)… The little girl has the best bunch … we the two boys—fall on her and snatch away her flowers. She runs up the meadow in tears and as a consolation the peasant woman gives her a big piece of black bread … we throw the flowers away … ask to be given some bread too. And we are … given some.

The scene would have taken place in 1859, in April or May when dandelions bloom; Sigmund was about three years old, John (born, August 13, 1855) three and three quarters, and Pauline, two and a half. The peasant woman might have represented Marie, Emanuel's wife; the nurse could have represented any or all of Freud's nursemaids (Krull, 1986).

In the same "Screen memory" paper (1899), an adolescent girl wore a yellow dress, as had Gisela Fluss, the object of Freud's adolescent crush, when he visited Příbor. This dress appears to be linked to the yellow flowers stolen from Pauline. In the paper, Freud related a fantasy of deflowering a bride, apparently a conscious adolescent masturbation fantasy. The flowers are significant in Freud's 1898 dream of the botanical monograph with associations referring to screen memories (Anzieu, 1986). We now know that Freud was passionately admiring not only of Gisela, but also of her mother (Clark, 1980). His screen memory overlay his unconscious incestuous fantasies concerning Gisela's mother and ultimately his own mother. His adolescent fantasy concerning Gisela may be regarded as a reactivation of the childhood scenes with his playmates. Freud also very likely would have been aware that his father was an adolescent when he fathered Sigmund's half-brothers.

Freud regarded his playmates as highly significant in his reconstruction at the time, and as a prototype of his later object relations. Following his reconstruction of his affective response to the birth and death of Julius, Freud (in a letter to Fliess dated October 3, 1897) stated:

I have also long known the companion of my misdeeds between the age of one and two years is my nephew, a year older than myself, … who visited us in Vienna when I was fourteen years old. The two of us seem occasionally to have behaved cruelly to my niece, who was a year younger. This nephew and this younger brother have determined, then, what is neurotic, but also what is intense in all my relationships.

The nature of their collusion in crime against Pauline or possibly also with each other is obscure. Did they play sexual games, or rudely undress Pauline and inspect or touch her genitals? Were they cruel to Pauline in rough and tumble play as well as filching her little bunch of flowers? These reconstructions of the childhood past and the "Screen memory" paper (1899) may have significant connections to Freud's conflicts during October 1897. Freud may have been struggling with his guilt over having recommended the botched surgery Fliess performed on Emma Eckstein. Freud unconsciously then regarded Fliess as his companion in crime, since Emma nearly died of the surgery (Krull, 1986).

John

Freud (1900) repeated the formulation of the roots of his relationships in "The interpretation of dreams" (1900) with some elaboration. He referred to his nephew John as his earliest friend and opponent. They came to blows, and despite the fact that Freud, on dream evidence, assumed he was physically stronger, although in the wrong, "might prevailed over right." Freud stated (1900, p. 483) that:

> my warm friendships as well as my enmities with contemporaries went back to my relations in childhood with a nephew … all my friends have in a certain sense been reincarnations of this figure … my emotional life has always insisted that I should have an intimate friend and a hated enemy. I have always been able to provide myself afresh with both, and it has not infrequently happened that the ideal situation of childhood has been so completely reproduced that friend and enemy have come together in a single individual—though not of course, both at once or with constant oscillations, as may have been the case in my early childhood."

Dependent friendships followed by animosity would characterize Freud's relationships with Breuer, Fliess, and Jung. Dazzling in their day, reconstructions of his relationship with John should no longer be accepted without modification. Are these ambivalent relationships with John stereotypes for all of Freud's subsequent object relations, particularly with men? The splitting of the figure of John into friend and enemy, and the following integration into one person, strikingly foreshadows the developmental concepts of Klein (1957) and Mahler, Pine, and Bergman (1975). Freud's remarks also anticipate a failure to unify split loved and hated self and object representations in severe personality disorders (Kernberg, 1984). In his initial reconstruction, Freud proposed a theory of internalized object relations and implied object representations before the elucidation of drive theory. Aggression and hostility were noted before the introduction of a separate aggressive drive. Freud's nephew could hardly have had the vital influence on his object relations of Freud's mother or father. Little John lacked authority over parental figures, nor does it now seem possible for John to have been an exclusive prototype for Freud's later object relationships. However, John could have been a significant determinant of Freud's ambivalent peer relationships.

John may also be seen as a displacement from Amalia, who was then not clearly within Freud's theoretical framework and is little evident in the reconstruction. Dear friend and hated enemy, John prefigures Freud's Oedipal relationship to his own father (John's grandfather) and on a deeper level his mother. Fighting with John for possession of the field or toys side-steps the trenchant issue of exclusive possession of the mother. Freud's later emphasis would be the rivalry with the father for the mother, with the Oedipal fantasy of parricide. John Freud may well have been a safe substitute target for Freud's hostility toward his parents. That John is revived in Freud's fantasy life testifies to his having been a meaningful figure, deconstructed here also as a composite of parents and siblings.

Considering the mother–son relationship, Freud mainly interpreted erotic rather than both erotic and hostile fantasy. Even in his later years, Freud (1933) regarded the mother–son relationship as the most perfect of human relationships, free from ambivalence. But in the one dream, Freud (1900) recalled from his childhood at about age nine, his mother was carried by birdbeaked figures as though dead. Matricidal fantasy was not interpreted.

Similarly, it may be noted that Freud did not directly confront the mother's possible hostility, jealousy, and destructive attitude toward her baby.

Without reference to his reconstructions in the origins of psychoanalysis, Freud, in his final paper (1940, p. 188) placed the mother figure front and central in his initial reconstruction of pre-Oedipal object relations in his final outline:

> *A child's first erotic object is the mother's breast, that nourishes it; love has its origins in attachment to the satisfied need … This first object is later completed into the person of the child's mother … the root of a mother's importance, unique, without parallel, established unalterably for a whole lifetime as the first and strongest love-object, and as the prototype of all later love relations—for both sexes.*

Discussion

Freud's capacity to trace his psychic life back to its first roots is amazing and still mysterious. Was his rejection of seduction trauma as the crucial determinant of pathogenesis the key to his immediate theoretical advance? Or had these reconstructions been percolating in his unconscious? Recognizing the gulf between hypothesis and the validation of his reconstructions, Freud (in a letter to Fliess, October 3, 1897) wrote, "My self-analysis which I consider indispensable for the clarification of the whole problem has continued in dreams and has presented me with the most valuable elucidations and clues." In the throes of resistance to insight and growing insight into resistance, Freud (in a letter dated October 27, 1897) wrote, "I live only for the 'inner work'. I am gripped and pulled through ancient times … my moods change like a traveler from a train … Many a sad secret of life is here followed back to its first roots." Shortly afterward (in his letter to Fliess of November 14, 1897), Freud incisively asserted, "True self analysis is impossible."

Freud introduced the Oedipus complex in the same burst of creativity as his analytic approach to his brother Julius and nephew John. Oedipal conflict and sibling conflict virtually coalesce in Freud's monumental initial reconstructions, which also encompassed interpretations of *Oedipus Rex* and *Hamlet*. The germ of guilt that Freud mentioned in connection with the death of Julius foreshadows the later significance of Oedipal guilt, and the guilt of the survivor. The differentiation of developmental phases and the awareness of countertransference, subjectivity, and cultural context awaited later conceptualization. The formulation that early object relations are forerunners of later object relations, however, was novel and fundamental. Reconstruction may have diminished resistance to incipient insight, and affectively appropriate insight reciprocally fostered reconstruction.

Freud's (1900) continued genetic interpretation of his dreams led to reconstructions and a working-through of his fratricidal and parricidal conflicts, evident in his 1898 *"non-vixit"* dream. In that dream, the revenants of ghosts of past persons can magically be made to reappear and disappear. Fliess could be annihilated in the present transference, as, in the buried past, Julius had similarly disappeared. Freud would later attribute fainting in Munich 1912 in Jung's presence to unconscious conflict regarding the death of Julius. Freud then said how sweet it is to die (Schur, 1972). Bringing back lost objects in reconstruction and memory may have served undoing, reparation, and atonement Freud, in his reconstructions, searched from the start for correspondence to historical facts, to reality, rather than only to fantasy or what was merely a coherent or plausible narrative. An archeologist of the mind, he sought to reconstruct the buried past. For a long time, he was only irregularly aware of his own countertransference, including counteridentification. There was then, and continues to be, no definite boundary between clarification, interpretation, and reconstruction. The genetic interpretation of dreams, daydreams, and transference may merge with reconstruction. Analysts and patients regularly engage in reconstruction even when this dimension of analytic work is not formally identified. Like the founder of psychoanalysis, current patients are stimulated to consult relatives, memoirs, diaries, home movies, and so on. Despite rigid injunctions by some analysts to rely only on analytic data, I believe it is valuable for rational conviction and analytic research to have reconstruction validated in external reality.

An integration of various strands of analytic work, reconstruction is today understood in a wider context than filling in a missing gap in memory (Blum, 2005; Green, 2012). The retrieval of repressed and dissociated memory is still therapeutically valuable, although screen memories, memory distortions, and fragmentation require reconstruction. Currently, reconstruction complements and often supplants memory retrieval. There is a kernel of truth in the past and present, in the transference–countertransference field (Hinz, 2012). Reconstruction provides a genetic framework for transference interpretation, loosens defenses, and helps to restore the continuity of the self. Pointing from the past to the future, with increasing self-knowledge, reconstruction fosters intrapsychic interpersonal and intergenerational integration on higher levels and greater complexity than was possible in childhood (Faimberg, 2006). Freud's reconstructions are in the realm of autobiographical memory and do not address current propositions regarding ego deficits, procedural memory, presymbolic thought, and somatic imprints.

So appropriate to the postmodern remodeling of the psychoanalytic edifice, Freud (1937, p. 265) soberly cautioned, "We do not pretend that an individual construction is anything more than a conjecture which awaits examination, confirmation, or rejection." Despite the inherent limitations of Freud's first reconstructions, there is on occasion in analysis resonance with Freud's wistful statement to an uncomprehending Fliess, in a letter dated October 3, 1897: "I cannot convey to you any idea of the intellectual beauty of the work."

REFERENCES

Anzieu, D. (1986). *Freud's Self-Analysis*. Madison, CT: International Universities Press.

Balsam, R. (2012). *Women's Bodies in Psychoanalysis*. New York, NY: Routledge.

Bernfeld, S. (1947). An unknown autobiographical fragment by Freud. *American Imago 7:162–196.*

Blum, H. (1977). The prototype of pre-oedipal reconstruction. *Journal of the American Psychoanalytic Association*, 25, *757–785*; DOI: 10.1177/000306517702500401.

——— (1990). Freud, Fliess, and the parenthood of psychoanalysis. *Psychoanalytic Quarterly 59:21–39.*

——— (2005). Psychoanalytic reconstruction and reintegration. *Psychoanalytic Study of the Child 60:295–311.*

——— (2011). Adolescent trauma and the Oedipus complex. *Psychoanalytic Inquiry*, 30, *548–556*; DOI: 10.1080/07351690.2010.518545.

Burianek, V. (2015). Paradise lost and trauma mastered. *Psychoanalytic Forum 25:22–28.*

Clark, R. (1980). *Freud, the Man and the Cause.* New York, NY: Random House.

Colombo, D. (2010). "Worthless female material." Nursemaids and governesses in Freud's cases. *Journal of the American Psychoanalytic Association 58:83–85; DOI:* 10.1177/0003065110390212.

Faimberg, H. (2006). *The Telescoping of Generations.* London: Routledge.

Freud, S. (1899). Screen memories. *SE 3: 303–322*

——— (1900). The interpretation of dreams. *SE 4–5.*

——— (1914). On the history of the psycho-analytic movement. *SE 14:7–66.*

——— (1918). From the history of an infantile neurosis. *SE 17:3–122.*

——— (1931). Female sexuality. *SE 21:223–243.*

——— (1933). On femininity. *SE 22:112–134.*

——— (1937). Construction in analysis. *SE 23: 255–269*

——— (1940). An outline of psychoanalysis. *SE 23: 139–207.*

——— (1985). *The complete letters of Sigmund Freud to Wilhelm Fliess, 1887–1904* (J. Masson, ed.). Cambridge, MA: Harvard University Press.

Gay, P. (1988). *Freud, a Life for our Time.* New York, NY: Norton.

Green, A. (1986). The dead mother. In: *On Private Madness,* pp. *142–173.* London: Hogarth Press.

——— (2012). On construction in Freud's work. *International Journal of Psychoanalysis 93:1238–1248.*

Grigg, K. (1973). All roads lead to Rome: The role of the nursemaid in Freud's dreams. *Journal of the American Psychoanalytic Association,* 21:*108–126.*

Guntrip, H. (1975). My experience of analysis with Fairbairn and Winnicott. *International Review of Psychoanalysis, 2:145–156.* (Reprinted 1996, *International Journal of Psychoanalysis, 77,* 737–754).

Hardin, H. (1987). On the vicissitudes of Freud's early mothering. *Psychoanalytic Quarterly, 56, 628–644.*

——— (1988). Alienation from the biological mother. Freiberg, Screen memories and loss. *Psychoanalytic Quarterly, 57:72–86;* 209–223.

Hinz, H. (2012). Constructions in psychoanalysis: On the assured conviction of the truth of a construction. *International Journal of Psychoanalysis, 93:1266–1283.*

Kardiner, A. (1977). *My Analysis with Freud.* New York, NY: Norton.

Kernberg, O.F. (1984). *Severe Personality Disorders.* New Haven, CT: Yale University Press.

Kertzer, D. (1997). *The kidnapping of Edgardo Mortara.* New York, NY: Knopf.

Klein, M. (1957). *Envy and Gratitude.* New York, NY: Basic Books.

Krull, M. (1986). *Freud and His Father.* New York, NY: Norton.

La Farge, L. (2012). The screen memory and the act of remembering. *International Journal of Psychoanalysis, 93:1249–1265.*

Mahler, M., Pine, F., & Bergman, A. (1975). *The Psychological Birth of the Human Infant.* New York, NY: Basic Books.

Newton, P. (1995). *Freud: From Youthful Dream to Mid-life Crisis.* New York, NY: Guilford Press.

Robert, M. (1975). *From Oedipus to Moses—Freud's Jewish* identity. New York, NY: Doubleday.

Schur, M. (1972). *Freud: Living and Dying.* New York, NY: International Universities Press.

Swan, J. (1974). Mater and Nannie: Freud's two mothers and the discovery of the Oedipus complex. *American Imago, 31:1–64.*

Vitz, P. (1993). *Sigmund Freud's Christian Unconscious.* New York, NY: Gracewing.

Winnicott, D. (1971). *Playing and Reality.* New York, NY: Basic Books.

CHAPTER 23

Reconstruction in the Present Two-Person Process, The Wolf Man Case Reconstructed

(2018). *J. Amer. Psychoanal. Assn.*, 66(3):479–492.

We practice in an era of psychoanalytic diversity, occasioning concerns about confusion and diffusion, but also reevaluation and creative change. New ideas regarding the two-person analytic process, preoedipal development, self- and object relations, narcissism, and inquiry into analytic outcome have influenced the ongoing evolution of psychoanalytic thought. Transference and countertransference are now understood as complex compromise formations with interpersonal/intersubjective as well as traditional intrapsychic determinants (Racker 1968). The techniques of genetic interpretation and reconstruction were influenced from outside traditional/classical psychoanalysis by the concept of the analyst as "participant observer" (Sullivan 1953) and from within traditional analysis by Loewald (1960) and others who considered the analyst a real and new object. Transference and countertransference may to a degree be co-created compromise formations. However, there are limits to dyadic co-creation, in my opinion, since each person brings to treatment a unique personality that is not entirely malleable. Adult character, in particular, is relatively stable, enduring, and resistant to change (Baudry 1989). Although technical approaches to genetic interpretation and reconstruction have been modified over time, both remain important to clinical work and analytic theory. Even if the analyst does not engage in explicit reconstruction, it is an implicit aspect of the traditional analyst's clinical work. Reconstruction is prominent in Freud's case of the Wolf Man (Sergei Pankejeff, 1886–1979), reported in 1918, and figures in all his case histories, his applied analytic papers, and his 1937 paper devoted to the topic. As valuable as reconstruction is, however, the validity of particular reconstructions must always be critically considered.

In a conference comparing the views of object relations analysts with those of more traditional Freudians, my late colleague and friend Richard Gottlieb (2009) observed that object relations analysts did not refer to repression, unconscious conflict, and childhood fantasy in their clinical discourse. Instead they spoke of negotiation, dissociation, and unformulated experience. Reversing his traditional psychoanalytic perspective on the infantile unconscious, Gottlieb (2017) later viewed clinical psycho-analysis as a two-person process involving interpersonal events in the analytic present, as well as intrapsychic perspectives. He questioned the value and validity of reconstruction of the distant past, a procedure exemplified in Freud's Wolf Man case (1918). In Gottlieb's review of that case, he stated that it may have been more about the present than the past.

How timely and appropriate, then, to reconsider the Wolf Man case on the centennial of its publication. The past, clearly, is privileged in Freud's title: "From the History of an Infantile Neurosis." Freud in this case report was not concerned with the interpersonal present. While I agree regarding the significance of the present, inside and outside the psychoanalytic situation, I still consider developmental phases and childhood psychopathology as vitally important in psychoanalytic theory and practice. In my view, some of the conclusions Gottlieb drew from the Wolf Man case, depreciating the value of reconstruction, are not well supported by the clinical data. Nor should the critique of reconstruction in the Wolf Man case, though in part justified, be generalized to other cases. Unfortunately we do not have Freud's clinical notes on the case, as we have for the Rat Man, but the history conveys a wealth of analytic data attesting to the overwhelming importance of the Wolf Man's psychopathology in childhood and adolescence, well before he entered analysis. This case history is the most extensive, detailed, and complex of Freud's four reports on the analyses of his patients.

The Wolf Man's case history, with its detailed first reconstruction of a primal scene, was prepared to refute the theoretical critiques of Adler and Jung. For Freud they may have been like wolves preying on the youthful, rapidly developing science of psychoanalysis. Devaluing the significance of unconscious childhood fantasy and childhood trauma, as well as the regressive revival of infantile mental life in dreams, Freud's critics denied the importance of the primal scene and early childhood more generally. The Wolf Man stated that his famous dream was central among his childhood dreams:

> I dreamt that it was night and that I was lying in bed. (My bed stood with its foot towards the window; in front of the window there was a row of old walnut trees. I know it was winter when I had the dream, and night-time.) Suddenly the window opened of its own accord, and I was terrified to see that some white wolves were sitting on the big walnut tree in front of the window. There were six or seven of them. The wolves were quite white, and looked more like foxes or sheep-dogs, for they had big tails like foxes and they had their ears pricked like dogs when they pay attention to something. In great terror, evidently of being eaten up by the wolves, I screamed and woke up. My nurse hurried to my bed, to see what had happened to me. It took quite a long while before I was convinced that it had only been a dream; I had had such a clear and life-like picture of the window opening and the wolves sitting on the tree. At last I grew quieter, felt as though I had escaped from some danger, and went to sleep again [Freud 1918, p. 29].

Freud's analysis of the Wolf Man's childhood nightmare was crucial to his reconstruction of the primal scene and its sequelae. Freud's critics regarded the Wolf Man case as a fairy tale, like the fairy tales the Wolf Man recalled from his childhood. Freud (1918) declared that "either the analysis based on the neurosis in his childhood is all a piece of nonsense from start to finish or everything took place just as I described it" (p. 199). The analysis of the Wolf Man's dream and the reconstruction of his childhood deriving from the dream, and from memories and associations, has hardly ever lacked controversy. Questions also followed from the Wolf Man's further analysis by Ruth Mack Brunswick (1928) and sporadic psychotherapy, as well as from observations and interviews during his lifetime. He is the only analytic patient known to have been subjected to analytic inquiry from infancy to old age. Thus, the

Wolf Man case might metaphorically be described as a multi-person process with our longest follow-up, including his own memoir. Later clinical, historical, and cultural data, integrated in the context of contemporary psychoanalytic thought, have invited reevaluation of the case by many authors, myself included, representing different schools and disciplines.

When Freud first met the Wolf Man, he rebuked Freud as a Jew-swindler and proposed to shit on Freud's head and penetrate his anus. He feared and wished both to be penetrated and to penetrate Freud. On the surface, the Wolf Man was expressing the stereotypical vilification of a Jew, typical of European society at that time. The wealthy Wolf Man had arrived in Vienna with a personal physician and a male nurse, who in reality anally penetrated the Wolf Man with a daily enema. Presumably, Freud initially inferred an infantile primal scene and homosexual seduction. The Wolf Man's famous dream, recalled from his fourth birthday, was reported early in his analysis and was repeated with numerous variations. His dream imagery of motionless animals is consistent with the dreams of four-year-olds generally; he gave verbal associations to the dream in adult analysis. The Wolf Man's drawing of the dream added associations of visual imagery. Freud (1900) recalled and wrote of only one dream from his own childhood that had elements of the primal scene, birth, and death (p. 583). Analytic work on a recalled childhood dream was in itself related to clinical reconstruction.

The case history of the four-year treatment (1910-1914), conducted six times weekly, is replete with details of the Wolf Man's interpersonal life, as well as his fantasy life. Born on Christmas Eve, 1886, he received double gifts for his birthday and Christmas. The tree in the dream was reported as a Christmas tree in which the gratifying gifts, hung on the branches, turned into terrifying, devouring wolves. Suffering from a panoply of symptoms, he had a wolf phobia (his analytic name derived from the dream) and obsessions. These included beating fantasies, kissing holy pictures, and cruelty to animals (e.g., he cut up caterpillars). He had had anorexia in infancy and contracted severe malaria at eighteen months. At age three he was seduced by his sister, two and a half years older, who had played with his penis, a seduction trauma the Wolf Man related in his old age as more disturbing than the primal scene. His

Nanya (the nursemaid) had threatened a castrating genital wound if he did not cease his childhood masturbation. She was an ambivalently loved parental surrogate for whose deceased child he served as a replacement. The Wolf Man's mother was hypochondriacal and had little contact with her son; his father was manic-depressive; his sister committed suicide in 1906, his father the next year. The Wolf Man became depressed and severely dysfunctional three years before he sought treatment by Freud. The synthesis of the disparate data, including isolated memories and fantasies and symptoms of severe childhood psychopathology, is especially important for the Wolf Man, but this is true for all of Freud's case histories.

Concepts of infantile neurosis and linear development have been altered in current psychoanalytic theory, but virtually all psychoanalysts today agree about the significance of childhood in all its aspects for the later personality. All too often, however, the pioneer analysts' idealization of Freud and their closing ranks against foes precluded their criticizing, modifying, or adding to the Wolf Man's original case history. The reconstruction of the Wolf Man's primal scene exposure at eighteen months is fanciful by today's standards and developmental knowledge. My own work (Blum 1974, 1994) and that of Mahoney (1984) has shown that the Wolf Man could not have observed the primal scene as Freud reconstructed it. Freud proposed a possible phylogenetic innate schema of the primal scene. A more compelling explanation, however, was his alternative reconstruction of the Wolf Man's having transposed observation of animals mating to his parents' mode of copulation. Living on a vast estate with farm animals, horses, dogs, foxes, and other creatures, the Wolf Man would surely have observed many instances of rear-mounting animal copulation. When interviewed by a journalist in old age, the Wolf Man dissented from Freud's account of his supposed primal scene experience. He asserted that a child of wealthy aristocrats would ordinarily not have slept with his parents and that in fact he had slept with his Nanya (Obholzer 1982). His comment is consonant with his dream report that he screamed and woke up: "My nurse hurried to my bed, to see what had happened to me." His Nanya, not his mother, was the caregiver when the Wolf Man awoke terrified. She hurried to his bed, which was likely in her bedroom. But if the Wolf Man knew that he in all probability had not witnessed parental copulation, why did he not object to the reconstruction during his analysis? Was protest stifled in the two-person transference-countertransference interaction? Did the Wolf Man's projective identification contribute to that interaction and to Freud's reconstruction? His passive-submissive attitude and position in the real or imagined primal scene might suggest a transference of obliging submission, desiring Freud's approval, and fear of his aggression toward Freud.

Freud's introduction of the concept of deferred action (*aprés-coup, Nachträglichkeit*) and its classic example in the Wolf Man case led to additional controversy. The primal scene experience at eighteen months becoming traumatic at four years is reminiscent of the pre-analytic seduction theory of pathogenesis. In the case history, trauma at eighteen months was displaced to the oedipal phase, on the Wolf Man's fourth birthday. Thus Freud seized on an oedipal phase trauma in his interpretation and reconstruction. Any preoedipal disturbance, such as the nearly fatal malaria, was deemed peripheral; at the time it was often regarded as regression and defense against oedipal conflict and trauma. Is deferred action better understood as developmental transformation of a revived trauma, modified in the intrapsychic present? Often a precipitating circumstance has revived the trauma, which may be further revised in the verbal report of the visual dream. In his disguised autobiographical paper, "Screen Memories," Freud (1899) referred to the defensive function of a less disturbing substitute memory and went so far as to question "whether we have any memories at all from our childhood: memories relating to our childhood may be all that we possess" (p. 322). This early paper on the editing and changing of memory indicated the necessity for reconstruction, beyond the retrieval of repressed and dissociated memories that are never recaptured and registered in their pristine form. Might après-coup be compatible with the neuroscientific concept of the reconsolidation of memory?

Freud's controversial reconstruction, decades later, of the primal scene at eighteen months could be overgeneralized, bringing into question the value of reconstruction in psychoanalytic technique. Of course, the Wolf Man case preceded modern methical studies of ego development. Reconstruction is no longer so important as a substitute for repressed or forgotten memory.

Transference has in large measure supplanted the emphasis on memory retrieval as a substitute for distorted or fragmented memory. Transference, dream analysis, and reconstruction are complementary, enlarging meaning and analytic comprehension (Greenacre 1981). Memory is not static but may be modified and edited in the course of life. However, recalled memories, such as the Wolf Man's childhood nightmare, and screen memories can initially be valuable analytic data. The Wolf Man's beating fantasy figures in "A Child Is Being Beaten," published in 1919, a year after the case history. There Freud unravels three layers of a childhood beating fantasy, of which the second phase "is never remembered, it has never succeeded in becoming conscious. It is a construction of analysis" (p. 185).

Current reconstruction aims at restoring severed connections and establishing new ones between past and present, fantasy and reality, affect and cognition, and self- and object representations. Aided by developmental knowledge, reconstruction uses the analyst's unconscious affective resonance, empathy, and intuition. Formulation of the reconstruction is a shared endeavor of patient and analyst. Psychoanalytic reconstruction fosters ego integration of repressed and dissociated traumata, the patient becoming the author and critic of his or her life history, facilitating cohesion and continuity of the personality (Blum 1994, 2005).

The elaborate reconstruction of the traumatic primal scene experience (or fantasy) of the Wolf Man brought the concept of the primal scene into general clinical psychoanalysis. Freud asked his fellow analysts for reports of primal scenes in their clinical work and they eagerly obliged. Reconstruction of the primal scene appears to have been Freud's preoccupation, with less attention devoted to other aspects of the Wolf Man's analysis. In his countertransference, Freud was simultaneously attempting to reconstruct his own primal scene experience and unconscious bisexual fantasies (Davis 1996). Freud lived with his parents in their one-room home until he was three and a quarter years old. It is highly probable that he was exposed to parental nudity and the primal scene. The opening of the window in the Wolf Man's dream was thus patient and analyst awakening to witness the primal scene. Freud was also intimately aware of the birth, illness, and death of his brother Julius. His interpretation of the Wolf Man's dream imagery (Teitelbaum 2016) now appears to have been strongly influenced by his countertransference, as well as by theoretical and organizational considerations. Freud's concerns regarding the newly founded IPA shortly before the Wolf Man's analysis began could well have influenced his approach to the case, without diminishing for him the significance of the Wolf Man's infancy-through-adolescence psychopathology. The Wolf Man's initial verbal assault on Freud was not then regarded as evidence of nonneurotic disorder. It can be understood as having tested Freud's tolerance of the Wolf Man's aggression and homosexual tendencies. Moreover, the suicides of the Wolf Man's sister (1906) and father (1907) may have activated unconscious guilt and grief without his being able to mourn their loss. Their relatively recent suicides probably contributed to his emotionally charged initial encounter with Freud. The double object loss would also have been determinants of his depression, constipation, and separation conflicts. Soon after these deaths, in 1908, he fell in love with his future wife, a sanatorium nurse, an unconscious replacement. His severe adult disturbance was later gradually understood in terms of a borderline childhood and traumatic experiences.

The external world of the Wolf Man was blurred, behind a fantasy veil that was removed by a daily enema. He repeatedly acted out his fantasy of anal impregnation and his aggrandizement of his birth, having been born in a caul on Christmas Eve. However, the blurring of external reality was representative of his impaired ego and object relations. Before his analysis people seemed unreal, like marionettes. His nightmare at age four invaded his waking life, and he felt the dream persisting as an invasive hangover, a daymare. He afterwards would scream like a lunatic if shown, say, a picture of a wolf or if he had ideas of reference that people were staring at him. The wolves in his dream could readily represent forbidden impulses; their static pose defended against loss of impulse control and affect regulation. In contrast to the menacing wolves, the sheep dogs directed and protected the flock on his parents' estate. The sheep dogs might have symbolized protective parental figures and his analyst with his faithful dog.

Although the Wolf Man had been diagnosed as manic-depressive during his hospitalization before seeing Freud, current evaluation indicates a diagnosis of borderline personality with pronounced narcissistic features. The Wolf Man's borderline childhood and adolescent borderline psychotic tendencies were repeated in his adult transference psychosis during the Wolf Man's subsequent analysis with Mack Brunswick (1928). Lacan (1966) considered the Wolf Man's childhood hallucination of his finger having been amputated as indicating an episode of childhood psychosis that would be consistent with borderline regression. The Wolf Man had difficulty differentiating dream, daydream, and reality. His borderline personality (Blum 1974, 2013) has been confirmed by new interpretations of a Rorschach test administered to him in middle age (Blum 2013; Schafer 2013; Woods 2013). For these interpretations I arranged that one interpretation should be of an anonymous male, using only the test data. The Wolf Man's impaired sense of reality, identity, lack of self-cohesion, and self-reliance (Magid 1993), his splitting of self- and object representations, and disturbed, highly ambivalent object relations were noted in the largely convergent test reports.

The Wolf Man's adult borderline personality and its development cannot be understood on the basis of his interpersonal, intersubjective analytic experience with Freud and Mack Brunswick. His infantile unconscious conflicts and trauma are fundamental in Freud's case history. However, his adult analyses would surely have been influenced by the interpersonal dimension of the two-person analytic process. Baranger and Baranger (1969) long ago proposed a bipersonal transference-countertransference field. In this two-person perspective, the most salient features of the Wolf Man's personality development and disorder persisted and could still be reconstructed, though shaped by both partners of the analytic dyad. The concept of a two-person analytic process in which the interpersonal and the intrapsychic interact is essentially compatible with current concepts of genetic interpretation and reconstruction. Conscious and unconscious fantasy and interpersonal influence in the analytic dyad preclude the possibility of complete analytic neutrality and objectivity. The analyst has never been a blank screen. All analytic data is to some degree modified by the analyst's listening, selection, transference-countertransference, theoretical preferences, culture, and real personality. The Wolf Man's mother tongue was Russian, so surely his analysis in German had linguistic and cultural impingements. In some severely disturbed cases the interpersonal present may be clinically paramount, with infantile mental life unavailable or purposely maintained at the periphery of interpretation and reconstruction while defenses are strengthened.

Debate about present versus past in the Wolf Man case, revived by Gottlieb (2017), is part of analytic history. In 1926 Rank (see Mahoney 1984, p. 138) claimed that the Wolf Man's dream was not recalled from childhood but was a current transference image. According to Rank, the wolves in the tree represented Freud's close colleagues, including Rank himself, in photographs in Freud's office; further, the six wolves were Freud's six children and the childhood bed was Freud's couch. Rank had joined Freud's detractors, who regarded the case as a fairy tale and an opportunity for Rank to outwit and devalue his formerly idealized master. For Rank, Freud's interpretations and reconstruction of the repressed and forgotten past should have been about the here-and-now transference present, not the patient's remote childhood dream. Rank dismissed the Wolf Man's observations and associations regarding the dream, as well as Freud's statements that it was indeed the Wolf Man's childhood dream. The Wolf Man later reaffirmed that the dream occurred on his fourth birthday and was recalled as originally reported to Freud. As for the Wolf Man's imposed termination after four years of analysis, Rank asserted that the Wolf Man's birth trauma would have required only nine months of analysis. Freud (1937a) refuted Rank in "Analysis Terminable and Interminable" and indirectly in "Constructions in Analysis" (1937b). It is difficult to entirely accept Gottlieb's proposal (2017) that Freud's imposition of a termination date was a dyadic enactment representing the Wolf Man's masochistic submission in the primal scene experience. Having initially interdicted sexual relations with his mistress, at termination Freud approved his marriage to her. Thus, termination signaled liberation from analytic prohibition and regression and represented a thrust toward independent adulthood. Freud regarded the Wolf Man as having settled into obliging apathy and the analysis as stalemated. Could Freud have predicted that setting a termination date would facilitate the analysis, resulting in remarkable progress and clarity? Though the idea was foreshadowed by

Freud, termination was not recognized as a regular phase of psychoanalysis until after Freud's death and World War II.

From a contemporary perspective, the Wolf Man can be understood as a borderline child, evolving into an adult borderline personality disorder with pronounced infantile narcissistic and paranoid features (Blum 1974). The primal scene was prominent, but not exclusive in Freud's overall reconstruction of the Wolf Man's childhood. In a prescient summary statement, Freud (1918) concluded that the Wolf Man "broke down after an organic affection of the genitals had revived his fear of castration, shattered his narcissism, and compelled him to abandon his hope of being personally favored by destiny. He fell ill, therefore, as a result of 'narcissistic frustration'" (p. 235). Freud's summary statement focused not on primal scene trauma per se, but on castration anxiety, narcissistic entitlement, and fragility. Considering both the intrapsychic and the interpersonal in the analytic situation, we can surmise that the Wolf Man's therapeutic benefit came substantially from his narcissistic transference to Freud as an omnipotent God, with himself cast as the glorified Christ child. Freud was also a benevolent new object, functioning as a dedicated caregiver with a positive countertransference. The Wolf Man benefited from the power of Freud's intellect, insight, and integration and his functioning as an auxiliary ego and organizing object. "The specific person of the analyst, in his or her unique subjectivity, becomes a lasting presence in the postanalytic world of the analyst" (Mitchell 1998, p. 23). The specific analyst was Freud, followed by the Wolf Man's later analytic psychotherapists. While the Wolf Man was unable to reliably internalize analytic functions after his analysis, he never again required hospitalization, returned to a sanatorium, or withdrew from social relationships. Having in some measure worked through old patterns of depressive helplessness, he was able to function in the interpersonal world and could maintain employment. Although he made a surface social recovery, his deep-seated personality disorder was revealed in his therapy and in his Rorschach test. He acquired an analytic identity and answered the telephone "Wolf Man speaking"—ironic, yet indicative that psychoanalysis had contributed to his self-cohesion and to stabilizing his identity.

From the perspective of the two-person process emphasized in the present by, among others, Gill (1994) and Gottlieb (1917), many countertransference and interpersonal enactments were later recounted by the Wolf Man and Mack Brunswick. The Wolf Man's analyses were influenced by the unconscious conflicts, fantasies, and traumas of the analytic dyad but without discounting the reconstruction of the patient's childhood. For Freud the wolf was primarily the oedipal father. For the Wolf Man Freud would have represented a condensation of oedipal and preoedipal parental representations.

In 1918, after the Russian revolution, the once wealthy aristocrat returned to Vienna from his homeland. Now an indigent refugee, the narcissistically entitled Wolf Man, who as a child expected double presents for Christmas and his birthday, inspired an extraordinary transference-countertransference enactment. Impressed by the Wolf Man's shattered narcissism and his loss of socioeconomic status, Freud encouraged analysts to contribute funds for the Wolf Man's material support. A fundraiser for the former aristocrat, Freud presented the Wolf Man with an annual financial gift; it continued for six years, until Freud's surgery for oral cancer. The cancer undermined the Wolf Man's fantasy of Freud's omnipotent support and threatened the loss of an idealized object. The Wolf Man reacted with paranoid hypochondriacal regression and emergent rage at Freud and Mack Brunswick, which had been repressed and dissociated. Is Freud's "feeding" the Wolf Man with funds reminiscent of his literal feeding of the hungry Rat Man? This collective transference enactment of the psychoanalytic community was fostered by the humanitarian values of Freud and psychoanalysis. Relevant to the termination of his analysis in 1914, the Wolf Man recounted that Freud had proposed that the Wolf Man present him a gift, ostensibly to resolve his dependent neediness. Freud thus implied that the interpersonal enactment would be therapeutic. The Wolf Man complied with the gift of an Egyptian female figure with a miter, the gift still in a prominent place on Freud's desk in London's Freud Museum. When the Wolf Man visited Freud in 1919, Freud presented him with a volume of his short writings, including his case history, with a personally signed dedication. Patient and analyst had exchanged gifts at termination and reunion.

The Wolf Man case represents a dyadic interweaving of the intrapsychic and interpersonal aspects of clinical psychoanalysis. Recognition of the interpersonal dimension of the analytic process should not relegate the Wolf Man's childhood and infantile psychopathology to the periphery. The case history is now a museum piece, displaying the discovery, recovery, and reconstruction of the Wolf Man's unconscious mental life. The case history was organized primarily in the mind of the analyst rather than in the patient's. Analysis of the Wolf Man's transference to Freud as an omnipotent parent, a condensation of the oedipal father and preoedipal mother, was not possible in depth, given the limited analytic theory of the time. In 1937 Freud referred to the Wolf Man and formulated a fundamental dimension of borderline states: "every normal person is only approximately normal: his ego resembles that of the psychotic in some point or other and to a greater or lesser extent" (1937a, p. 236). The fusion and confusion of borderline disorders and neurosis, of oedipal castration anxiety and preoedipal separation anxiety, was not recognized in the pioneering era of Freud's case histories. Currently, preoedipal reconstruction (Blum 1977) and, more recently, preverbal reconstruction (Botella and Botella 2005) are highlighted by analysts. Confirmation of the validity of preverbal reconstruction (e.g., of the patient's oral phase, attachment, and initial phases of separation-individuation) may vary with each case. Generalizations about preverbal and pre-representational reconstruction will require further analytic research.

Freud's admonition remains pertinent to current two-person psychoanalysis: "anyone who neglects childhood analysis is bound to fall into the most disastrous errors. The emphasis which is laid here on the importance of the earliest experiences does not imply any underestimation of the influence of later ones" (1919, p. 185).

Richard Gottlieb has reawakened interest in exploring the Wolf Man case and reconstruction more generally in the context of the intertwined interpersonal and intrapsychic dimensions of clinical psychoanalysis. We are indebted to him for his many psychoanalytic gifts to us. His perceptive inquiries, insights, and innovation remain an enriching legacy.

REFERENCES

Baranger, M., & Baranger, W. (1969). The analytic situation as a dynamic field. *International Journal of Psychoanalysis 89:795–826*, 2008.

Baudry, F. (1989). Character, character type, and character organization. *Journal of the American Psychoanalytic Association 37:655–686*.

Blum, H.P. (1974). The borderline childhood of the Wolf Man. *Journal of the American Psychoanalytic Association 22:721–742*.

——— (1977). The prototype of preoedipal reconstruction. *Journal of the American Psychoanalytic Association 25:737–785*.

——— (1994). Reconstruction in Psychoanalysis: Childhood Revisited and Recreated. New York: International Universities Press.

——— (2005). Psychoanalytic reconstruction and reintegration. *Psychoanalytic Study of the Child 60:295–311*.

——— (2013). Rorschach interpretation of Freud's Wolf Man at age 69. *International Journal of Psychoanalysis94:955–957, 963–966*.

Botella, C., & Botella, S. (2005). The Work of Psychic Figurability: Mental States without Representation, transl. A. Weller. London: Routledge.

Davis, W. (1996). Sigmund Freud's drawing of the dream of the wolves. In Replications: Archaeology, Art History, Psychoanalysis. University Park: Pennsylvania State University Press, pp. *286–317*.

Freud, S. (1899). Screen memories. *S.E. 3:303–322*.

——— (1900). The interpretation of dreams. *S.E. 4/5*.

——— (918). From the history of an infantile neurosis. S.E. 17:*7–122*.

——— (1919). "A child is being beaten": A contribution to the study of the origin of sexual perversions. *S.E.* 17:179–204.

——— (1937a). Analysis terminable and interminable. *S.E.* 23:*216–253*.

——— (1937b). Constructions in analysis. *S.E.* 23:*257–269*.

Gardiner, M., ed. (1971). The Wolf-Man by the Wolf-Man. New York: Basic Books.

Gill, M.M. (1994). Psychoanalysis in Transition. Hillsdale, NJ: Analytic Press.

Gottlieb, R.M. (2009). Coke or Pepsi? Reflections on Freudian and relational psychoanalysis in dialogue. *Contemporary Psychoanalysis6:87–100*.

——— (2017). Reconstruction in a two-person world may be more about the present than the past: Freud and the Wolf Man, an illustration. *Journal of the American Psychoanalytic Association* 65:305–316.

Greenacre, P. (1981). Reconstruction: Its nature and therapeutic value. *Journal of the American Psychoanalytic Association*29:27–46.

Lacan, J. (1966). **Écrits**. Paris: Éditions du Seil.

Loewald, H.W. (1960). On the therapeutic action of psychoanalysis. *International Journal of Psychoanalysis* 58:463–472.

Mack B.R. (1928). A supplement to Freud's 'History of an infantile neurosis.' *International Journal of Psychoanalysis.* 9:439–476.

Magid, B. (1993). *Self psychology Meets the Wolf Man. In Freud's Case Studies: Self-Psychological Perspectives*, ed. B. Magid. New York: Routledge, pp. *157–188.*

Mahoney, P. (1984). Cries of the Wolf Man. New York: International Universities Press.

Mitchell, S.A. (1998). The analyst's knowledge and authority. *Psychoanalytic Quarterly 67:1–31.*

Obholzer, K. (1982). The Wolf-Man Sixty Years Later. New York: Continuum.

Racker, H. (1968). Transference and Countertransference. New York: International Universities Press.

Schafer, R. (2013). Rorschach interpretation of Freud's "Wolf Man" at age 69. *International Journal of Psychoanalysis* 94:955–957.

Sullivan, H.S. (1953). The Interpersonal Theory of Psychiatry New York: Norton.

Teitelbaum, S. (2016). Do I have to draw you a picture? Sigmund Freud, imagery, and the Wolf-Man's drawing. *Psychoanalytic Inquiry 36:633–643.*

Woods, J.M. (2013). On the Rorschach protocol. *International Journal of Psychoanalysis 94:959–961.*

CHAPTER 24

Masochism, The Ego Ideal, and The Psychology of Women

(1976). *JAPA* (24)(Supplement):157–191.

Models of female development can be surveyed from a number of vantage points, e.g., masochism, passivity, penis envy. I have chosen masochism, proposed as an important dimension of feminine character in the early psychoanalytic literature, as a route to exploring the psychology of women. Special attention to the role of masochism in femininity will lead to reconsideration of psychoanalytic propositions concerning female personality development and structure, and feminine attitudes and values.

Is masochism the normal biopsychological destiny of the human female, or is "feminine masochism" determined primarily by various developmental and sociocultural forces? Are masochistic trends normally synergistic with the female ego ideal? Has the concept of feminine masochism influenced the early psychoanalytic model of female personality development? The answers to these questions depend upon concepts of femininity and masochism. I shall not attempt to elaborate here on the many dimensions of femininity, or on the relationships between masochism and female narcissism or passivity. Masochism is not easily distinguished from passive aggression or self-punishment, and always appears in combination with sadism. Theoretically, one can only speak of sadomasochism, though either masochism or sadism may predominate.

Masochism as used here will refer to pleasure associated with suffering, which is usually a derivative of heightened sexual excitement linked to pain or unpleasure. Masochistic gratifications need not be directly connected with physical pain, but can be associated with mental torture, debasement, or humiliation, or pleasure derived from the induction of anxiety or guilt. The phenomenological description of masochism is on a different level of abstraction from metapsychological formulations and explanations, which relate masochism to the internalization of aggression or the turning around of sadism upon the subject's self, the preservation of the object, libidinization of anxiety, or the erotization of pain. In the masochistic character, as distinct from the overt perversion, the goal of suffering may not be associated with conscious awareness of pleasure or gratification.

Freud's Early Propositions

Freud (1924a) saw masochism and sadism as ubiquitous in man, but presumed the female to have drives with preference for passive aims. He categorized masochism as erotogenic, feminine, and moral. He described masochism as an expression of the feminine nature, stating,

Feminine masochism … is the one that is most accessible to our observation and least problematical, and it can be surveyed in all its relations

(p. 161). After introducing the concept, he stated:

This feminine masochism which we have been describing is entirely based on the primary, erotogenic masochism, on pleasure in pain (p. 162).

Freud regarded the tendency toward the internalization of aggression as a biological basis for feminine masochism. He wrote (1933, p. 116):

The suppression of women's aggressiveness which is prescribed for them constitutionally and imposed on them socially favours the development of powerful masochistic impulses, which succeed, as we know, in binding erotically the destructive trends which have been diverted inwards. Thus masochism, as people say, is truly feminine. But if, as happens so often, you meet with masochism in men, what is left to you but to say that these men exhibit very plain feminine traits?

Freud uncovered the continuum between the normal and the neurotic and the mutual influences of endowment and environment. Nevertheless, during the early emphasis on the biological and instinctual, there was little focus on the relation between the innate and the acquired, nature and nurture. During early phases of psychoanalytic theory, object relations, the role of reality, the influence of culture and society tended to be in the background, though never entirely overlooked (Schafer, 1974).

During Freud's lifetime, psychoanalytic developmental psychology was in its childhood. Lines of normal and pathological development were incomplete and were sometimes not clearly delineated. Freud's appreciation and understanding of maturation, ego development, and sublimation was not always evenly represented in his own work and was not easily applied and integrated into the thinking of the psychoanalytic pioneers. Primitive fantasies were sometimes related directly to derivative adult character traits, by-passing complex developmental transformations. In addition to the genetic fallacy, which confused mature personality trends and their genetic antecedents, incomplete developmental models tended to influence subsequent theory.

Psychoanalytic considerations of the female personality began with the inception of psychoanalysis. Apart from Freud's self-analysis, his earliest patients, starting with Anna O., were female. Freud, despite increasing experience, remained cautious and uncertain about female psychosexual development. He repeatedly indicated his groping and lack of understanding of femininity, stating,

It must be admitted, however, that in general our insight into these developmental processes in girls is unsatisfactory, incomplete and vague [1924b, p. 179].

He referred the psychology of adult female sexuality as a *"dark continent"* (1926, p. 212), and his continued perplexity was manifest in his famous question, *"What does a woman want?"* (Jones, 1955, p. 421).

Freud was not dogmatic about his speculations or theoretical propositions, and he set an example of changing theory in accordance with new data and insights. His principal findings remain the fundamental core of analytic theory and the foundation for later research and development.

The very complexity of Freud's thinking makes it difficult to dissect separate strands for independent study or to synthesize a detailed overview of his many ideas and coordinate propositions. His changing and evolving concepts can be seen in the shift from the claim (1923) that the dissolution of the Oedipus complex is precisely analogous in girls and boys to a different developmental line described in: *Some Psychical Consequences of the Anatomical Distinction between the Sexes* (1925).

The early Freudian developmental line of femininity is more complicated and difficult than for the male, and perhaps never fully traversed. The early theory viewed femininity as first emerging from oedipal and castration conflicts rather than as a preoedipal formation or a primary developmental tendency. The girl's recognition of castration *forces her away from masculinity and masculine masturbation* [Freud, 1925, p. 256].

What was emphasized was the little girl's disappointments, her defeats, and her deprivation. She was deprived of a penis, disappointed in herself and her mother, as castrated, and again disappointed in her oedipal strivings for her father's love, penis, and child. She was defeated by her oedipal rival, her ambivalently loved mother. These major disappointments and feelings of damage led to her need to accept her feelings of bodily and personal inferiority. Her feelings of bodily injury and loss and the influence of castration fantasies produced resentment and penis envy as well as compensatory restitutional longing for a child. Castration shock was linked to the girl's earlier losses, narcissistic wounds, and envious reactions.

In the over-all perspective, the girl's penis envy and masochistic resignation had their male counterpart in the male's castration anxiety, breast and womb envy, and repudiated feminine identification. However, the early theory did not elucidate either a primary or a positive femininity. The girl's discovery that she was castrated pushed her into the Oedipus complex where she experienced passionate conflict with her parents, wanted impregnation and babies, but was also resigned to future motherhood as a consolation for phallic deficiency.

This view of female development did not by any means meet with monolithic acceptance. Jones (1935, p. 495), for example, objected:

To my mind, on the contrary, her femininity develops progressively from the inner promptings of an instinctual constitution. In short, I do not see a woman—as an 'homme manque'—as a permanently disappointed creature struggling to console herself with secondary substitutes alien to her true nature.

Positive gratifying experiences and positive identifications with the mother and nurturant mothering were not elaborated. Nor was the importance of the father, not only in frustrating oedipal wishes, but in confirming his daughter's feminine identity and benevolently supporting the formation of a maternal ego ideal.

The riddle of femininity was compounded by the utilization of, as well as the contrast with, the better-understood male developmental model. Freud (1924a) initially depicted feminine masochism as observed in the male. Here Freud departed from his usual emphasis on constitutional factors, and aberrant male development was an introductory specimen of female masochism. Freud noted that the masochist wants to be treated like a small and helpless child, but particularly like a naughty child.

But if one has an opportunity of studying cases in which the masochistic phantasies have been especially richly elaborated, one quickly discovers that they place the subject in a characteristically female situation; they signify, that is, being castrated, or copulated with, or giving birth to a baby. For this reason I have called this form of masochism, a potiori as it were (i.e., on the basis of its extreme examples), the feminine form, although so many of its features point to infantile life [1924a, p. 162].

It is remarkable that Freud introduced feminine masochism with a male caricature of femininity. The male homosexual specimen of femininity was at the same time a daring and fascinating investigation of femininity in males with excessive bisexuality and feminine identification. Freud, of course, recognized the universality and ubiquity of masculine and feminine trends in all individuals, and he believed in a constitutional bisexuality:

… all human individuals, as a result of their bisexual disposition and of cross-inheritance, combine in themselves both masculine and feminine characteristics, so that pure masculinity and femininity remain theoretical constructions of uncertain content [1925, p. 258].

He later (1933, p. 114) additionally commented on bisexuality, "*… an individual is not a man or a woman but always both—merely a certain amount more the one than the other.*"

Development for both sexes included evolutionary-biological considerations, especially of bisexuality, and could be consistent with an earliest undifferentiated sexuality and one dominant trend and developmental line. Yet, despite the adherence to innate bisexuality, traditional analytic theory before ego psychology presented a biphasic development of femininity. Female development was originally masculine rather than undifferentiated, mixed, or inherently feminine. Freud (1931, p. 228) observed of girls,

Their sexual life is regularly divided into two phases, of which the first has a masculine character, while only the second is specifically feminine.

The little girl's vagina was undiscovered, her clitoris was phallic, and clitoral masturbation was masculine (Freud, 1925, p. 255). This theme appeared in terms of the quality of instinctual energy. Freud (1905, p. 219) initially regarded libido as masculine, and he supported a male developmental model for both sexes. (This was consistent with his views of a primary masculinity, clitoral maleness, prominent derivation of feminine character, and maternal wishes from penis envy.)

And if libido is masculine, according to Freud, women are also characterized by a weaker sexual instinct as well as a more complicated and difficult sexual development (1908, p. 192). This weaker sexual constitution is amplified by Bonaparte (1953, p. 66),

The female organism quantitatively speaking, is in general more poorly endowed with libido than the male.

(Today, parallel questions concern whether the female is endowed with less aggression, and her apparently more variable and greater orgastic capacity.) Freud (1933, p. 118), referring to female entry into the phallic phase, observed: *"We are now obliged to recognize that the little girl is a little man,"* but he modified his view of (masculine) libido. Refining his earlier association of drive activity and masculinity, he stated (p. 131),

There is only one libido, which serves both the masculine and the feminine sexual functions. To it itself we cannot assign any sex; if, following the conventional equation of activity and masculinity, we are inclined to describe it as masculine, we must not forget that it also covers trends with a passive aim. Nevertheless the juxtaposition 'feminine libido' is without any justification. Furthermore, it is our impression that more constraint has been applied to the libido when it is pressed into the service of the feminine function, and that—to speak teleologically—Nature takes less careful account of its demands than in the case of masculinity.[1]

---

1 *The idea of female developmental vulnerability may appear in an early observation of Freud's (1905, p. 191): "In this respect, children behave in the same kind of way as an average uncultivated woman in whom the same polymorphously perverse disposition exists." At the same time, Freud (p. 151) noted the stunting effect of civilized conditions on female erotic life.*

The great constraints and complications of female development also referred to Freud's (1933, p. 119) view of the girl's special burdens:

In the course of time, therefore, the girl has to change her erotogenic zone and her object—both of which a boy retains.

For Freud, "femininity" decisively emerged with the discovery of the vagina at puberty.

Freud's early and tentative theory allowed little opportunity for developmental mastery of infantile conflicts and attitudes in the female. While he scientifically illuminated the profound civilizing and developmental influence of motherhood, he paradoxically observed that women had little capacity for the sublimation of their instinctual impulses (Freud, 1908, p. 195). Suggesting that women impede cultural development, Freud remarked (1930, p. 103),

Furthermore, women soon came into opposition to civilization and display their retarding and restraining influence—those very women who, in the beginning, laid the foundations of civilization by the claims of their love. Women represent the interests of the family and sexual life. The work of civilization has become increasingly the business of men, it confronts them with ever more difficult tasks and compels them to carry out instinctual sublimations of which women are little capable.

This theme was to be repeated and coupled with a supposition of early feminine psychic rigidity (which implied diminished possibility for adaptive transformation). Freud stated,

We also regard women as weaker in their social interests and as having less capacity for sublimating their instincts than men.... A man of about thirty strikes us as a youthful, somewhat unformed individual, whom we expect to make powerful use of the possibilities for development opened up to him by analysis. A woman of the same age, however, often frightens us by her psychical rigidity and unchangeability. Her libido has taken up final positions and seems incapable of exchanging them for others. There are no paths open to further development; it is as though the whole process has already run its course and remains thenceforward insusceptible to influence—as though, indeed, the difficult development to femininity has exhausted the possibilities of the person concerned [1993, pp. 134–135].

Freud noted that the female's preoedipal attachment to and her later oedipal rivalry with her mother are intrinsic to her developmental problems; that woman's particularly intense attachment to her father may have been preceded by a phase of exclusive attachment to her mother (1931, p. 225). The preoedipal phase was at first in the prehistoric past of development and confused, in the girl, with the attachment to the maternal love object of the negative Oedipus complex. Freud's (1933, p. 134) observations of these problems included reference to the preoedipal and oedipal phase of maternal identification:

We are no doubt justified in saying that much of both of them is left over for the future and that neither of them is adequately surmounted in the course of development. But the phase of the affectionate preOedipus attachment is the decisive one for a woman's future: during it preparations are made for the acquisition of the characteristics with which she will later fulfil her role in the sexual function and perform her invaluable social tasks."

Though Freud noted tendencies toward female oedipal and preoedipal fixation or developmental arrest, this is a very different emphasis from a "first masculine phase,"

or lack of capacity for sublimation. It augurs the modern formulation of preoedipal determinants of femininity preceding the castration complex of the phallic phase and the relatively conflict-free sources of femininity in the preverbal period. Recent contributions emphasize primary feminine identification with the mother and the important emergence of feminine identity during separation-individuation (Mahler, 1974); (Stoller, 1968); (Panel, 1970).

In the earlier developmental model, femininity was first discovered to be related to unconscious irrational fantasies of defect and reparation, and disappointment, renunciation, and envy of masculinity. Though the significance of the negative female Oedipus complex and double identification in the primal scene was also stressed, feminine oedipal identification was with a devalued and castrated mother. These unconscious identifications and the female's biological role, anticipation of, as well as experience in menstruation, defloration, penetration, and parturition, all served to excite and structure masochistic fantasies. Actual genital bleeding at puberty confirmed the girl's feelings of injury and inferiority. But the acceptance of menstruation also offered the opportunity of compensatory motherhood and children. (It should be noted that the female experience of genital bleeding and pain is all post-pubertal and not part of the formative experience of childhood. This does not diminish the importance of the child's fantasies, expectations, and whatever knowledge she may have of adult female sexual function [and also the positive meaning of menstruation for fertility and femininity].)

The discovery of the girl's fantasies of mutilation and her subsequent oedipal conflicts, her reactions of denial, envy, shame, modesty, compensatory concern for bodily beauty, her masochistic acceptance of her "inferiority state," or sadistic revenge for her deprivation, etc., were of extraordinary importance in the first scientific unraveling of the eternal enigma of femininity. There was increasing understanding of the admiration and envy of the mother and her maternal role, continuing and coexisting with "penis envy." The theory not only had great explanatory value, but with the gradual integration of new findings, had increasingly important and expanding clinical applications. The theory was always correlated with clinical observation, enlarged with avowed inference and conjecture. Freud (1933, p. 135) concluded his lecture on femininity: *It is certainly incomplete and fragmentary and does not always sound friendly.*

Feminine masochism, an integral part of the early incomplete analytic theory of female personality development, was a consequence of drive endowment, of anatomical-physiological sex differences, developmental vicissitudes, and the influence of oedipal fantasies. Insofar as Freud and many of his followers and students emphasized feminine masochism, it must have been prevalent in their patients' fantasies. Fantasies of rape, of being masochistically abused while excited, of sexual enslavement and surrender with mounting excitement are not uncommon in females' conscious erotic daydreams. Furthermore, the superego of the female adolescent also contributes to these fantasies, which simultaneously represent sexual prohibition and punishment for forbidden temptation. Rape fantasies evade guilt over instinctual wishes. Some of these conscious fantasies are derivatives of infantile beating fantasies. Strachey (in Freud, 1919, p. 245) observes that Freud's *"study of beating phantasies was especially concerned with the infantile sexual development of girls."*

Masochistic masturbation fantasies inevitably also reveal pre-phallic components represented in helpless passivity and omnipotent control, abject submission, and tyrannical power, shameful humiliation and glorified conquest.

In addition to the regressive expression of incestuous love and guilt in the "feminine" beating fantasies of girls, Freud (1919) also noted disguised masculine wishes. That the object of the beating was typically a boy additionally represented the girl's penis envy and wish to be a boy. Freud recognized the influence of specific traumatic factors as well as the ubiquity of beating fantasies in both sexes. Uneasy about the comprehension of these masochistic daydreams, Freud (1919, p. 183) further observed,

> ... *to a great extent these fantasies subsist apart from the rest of the content of a neurosis, and find no proper place in its structure.*

It is problematic whether these unconscious masochistic fantasies of young females are evidence of greater innate masochism than is found in men, where the masochism is generally more disguised and far less ego-syntonic in the manifest content of fantasy. Masochistic perversions are probably more common in males, representing deviant psychopathology. Questions include the defensive role of masochistic fantasies in feminine development and cultural adaptation. Observations of little girls did not record strivings for unpleasure or a greater constitutional masochism in infancy. Freud (1933, p. 118) acknowledged no lag in aggressiveness in the early phases of female drive development, stating:

Analysis of children's play has shown our women analysts that the aggressive impulses of little girls leave nothing to be desired in the way of abundance and violence.

The roots of later sadomasochism have now been traced not only to pregenital libidinal conflicts, but to heightened aggression associated with infantile trauma and disturbed infantile object relations (Panel, 1956).

It is well to note here that one of Freud's major influences upon the "sexual revolution," a social phenomena that continues to evolve to the present day, was to insist upon the capacity of the female for psychosexual fulfillment (and analytic mastery of infantile conflict).

Freud encouraged in their careers his early female students and collaborators, including his daughter, who became extremely prominent teachers and contributors in psychoanalysis. In no other scientific field has there been such outstanding accomplishment and leadership with the fullest recognition and prestige accorded to female colleagues.

Freud's discovery of the castration complex was an extraordinary event in the history of ideas, and an extremely important discovery for the "liberated" sexual and social role of women. For the first time there was a scientific understanding of the contempt and derision toward women based upon overdetermined irrational, unconscious fantasies. Both boys and girls and their parents unconsciously regarded the female as castrated and, therefore, inferior. The female was not simply oppressed by a male chauvinist society, but was unconsciously identified with her own "damaged and defective" genitourinary apparatus. The disparagement and devaluation of women coexisted with an overidealization and chivalrous overprotection, which was seen as an unconscious psychological consequence of the pitiable injury and castrated state of women. Freud uncovered and brought to the attention of the world the utterly irrational nature of this phallic contempt and derision of women.

Freud's discoveries, so important for the liberation of women and men from the tyranny of unconscious forces, coexisted with other of his ideas which paradoxically outlined a masochistic and incomplete feminine personality. Those particular propositions of a diminished and deficient female psyche will bear fresh scrutiny. The female was then viewed as having a diminished and constrained libido, a weaker and masochistic sexual constitution, an ego with an incapacity to sublimate and a tendency toward early arrest and rigidity, a relatively defective superego, and incomplete oedipal and postoedipal development.

Since Freud regarded the major motive for the formation of the superego as castration anxiety, and the girl was already castrated, she was considered to be lacking in the necessary castration anxiety for autonomous superego formation. Freud stated of women, (1925, pp. 257–258),

Their superego is never so inexorable, so impersonal, so independent of its emotional origins as we require it to be in men. Character-traits which critics of every epoch have brought up against women—that they show less sense of justice than men, that they are less ready to submit to the great exigencies of life, that they are more often influenced in their judgements by feelings of affection or hostility—all these would be amply accounted for by the modification in the formation of their superego….

Freud (1933, p. 129) further remarked on this consequence of the girl's incomplete oedipal resolution:

In the absence of fear of castration the chief motive is lacking which leads boys to surmount the Oedipus complex. Girls remain in it for an indeterminate length of time; they demolish it late and, even so, incompletely. In these circumstances the formation of the super-ego must suffer; it cannot attain the strength and independence which give it its cultural significance …

Is this an accurate scientific picture of feminine psychic structure relative to masculine psychic structure, an inescapable aspect of the difference between the sexes? Or is this a masochistic model of female personality development? Did the universal myth of the castrated female influence the theoretical conception of feminine psychic structure? Did the analyzed myth reappear as analytic myth? These formulations would not account for the development of feminine pride, self-esteem, self-confidence, and independence.

Freud's genius uncovered the universal unconscious fantasy of men and women that women are castrated. This fantasy pervades institutions and social attitudes and becomes a ubiquitous myth structuralized as a "cultural force." Freud first analyzed the fantasy, but did not discuss in depth the sociocultural influence exerted by the fantasy of a castrated, inferior female. The probable cultural and developmental influences on Freud's ideas are outside the scope of this paper. His view of women may also be based on a different female population. The women of his time and culture might well have had a different character structure and superego from that of contemporary Western women. Kohut (1959), who affirmed that femaleness cannot possibly be explained as a retreat from disappointed maleness, attributed Freud's views to reliance on the clinical evidence than available rather than to patriarchal bias. Jacobson (1937) proposed that Freud's idea of deficient female superego derived from the study of women prior to female emancipation.

Recent Contributions and Re-evaluation of Female Development

There are essential differences in psychic structure between male and female just as there are in anatomical structure, in biological endowment, and in environmental response. The early psychoanalytic propositions of a diminished and deficient female psychic structure were tentative and are unsubstantiated by current psychoanalytic data. I would reiterate that they belong to an early phase of psychoanalysis, a historical period when the role of culture was eclipsed by biological considerations, when an understanding of preoedipal and postoedipal development was barely in initial outline, and the appreciation of the mother-child relation and the importance of sublimated maternal responsibility and adaptability were insufficiently appreciated.

The preoedipal development of cohesive self- and object representations, of identity and gender identity, and the postoedipal evolution of a feminine and maternal ego ideal are modern perspectives for female personality development. Prephallic genital exploration and masturbation also may contribute to the female body image. The clitoris is probably discovered in infancy, at eighteen months, as an organ of sexual excitement with intentional arousal through apparent repeated self-stimulation (Kleeman, 1975); (Galenson and Roiphe, 1976). Clitoral and other genital perception and sensation contribute to feminine body experience and to affective reactions in the little girl and her observing parents. The female body image is also defined by contrast with the male and through maternal identification and education. Contrary to previous theory (Freud, 1925, p. 255), the clitoris cannot be described as masculine, though t may become invested with bisexual meaning.[2]Within the adult psychosexual organization of genital primacy and the goal of heterosexual union, the clitoris does not "hand over its sensitivity" (cf. Freud, 1933, p. 118), but forms a functional unit with other genital structures. It is questionable whether renunciation of clitoral masturbation is either necessary or desirable for feminine development. The clitoris as a specifically erotic female organ is integrated into mature female sexuality. Some vulva-vaginal sensation and awareness may begin early in life, associated with physical care, infantile masturbation, and possibly nursing and the REM-sleep cycle. Infantile vaginal awareness and sensation might well be repressed before puberty rather than undiscovered (Barnett, 1968).

If the girl has an orgastic potential not found in the boy until puberty, this may have unknown developmental consequences. When does female capacity for orgasm develop? Does earlier puberty, and perhaps an earlier orgastic potential lead to greater defense against female sexual arousal (Fraiberg, 1972)?

---

2 Freud (1925, p. 254) noted what might be regarded as a feminine-oriented clitoral masturbation, "The child which is being beaten (or caressed) may ultimately be nothing more or less than the clitoris itself ..."

The inhibition of female masturbation is by no means as frequent in latency as formerly believed, nor does it seem likely that such inhibition is explained entirely in terms of castration feelings and penis envy, which are also found in girls who continue masturbation (Clower, 1976). Constitutional, cultural, and parental influences certainly codetermine the fate of infantile masturbation. In older girls, the often-associated feelings of severe anxiety and guilt are indicative of the powerful influence of the superego.

There is evidence of infantile penis envy and castration anxiety, or precursors of these later reactions, fused with separation anxiety and anal-urethral conflicts at eighteen months of age (Galenson and Roiphe, 1976). However, the preoedipal danger situations with phase dominance are those described by Freud: loss of the object and the object's love. These infantile dangers are associated with parallel fears of dissolution of the body ego and emergent self. The period of life at about eighteen months may represent a developmental nodal point in which there is a confluence of rapprochement crisis, discovery of sex differences, nascent gender identity, and personal identity with use of the pronouns "I" and "me." Between eighteen months and three years the little girl develops and consolidates a relatively irreversible gender identity and a feminine self representation (Stoller, 1976). It is probable that the girl emerges from sepaation individuation with a femininity that contributes to the shape and solution of her crucial oedipal conflicts (Mahler, 1974). Global maternal identifications before the phallic phase are associated with wishes to be a mother, baby, and to have babies. The identifications are fostered by biological role, gender identity, and the childrearing and socialization process. With ongoing development the toddler's femininity is not that of the oedipal phase or of the adolescent or adult female.

The mother's identification with the little girl and the girl's with her, and the relation with the preoedipal mother are further defined in the expanding relation to the preoedipal father and to the family. The contribution preoedipal femininity makes to the onset and outcome of the oedipal phase has not yet been sufficiently explored. Parental, especially maternal, sex assignment and rearing practices are overriding influences in the formation of gender identity (Stoller, 1968). The child's innate disposition, her body experience and image, parental influence, and social learning, all contribute to the development of a feminine self-representation. Female sex- and gender identity and self-representation in turn predispose toward later female identifications. In normal development, both parents foster and orient the feminine individuation of their daughter, and the love and approval of both mother and father confirm a positive feminine identity, body image and ego ideal.

The Ego Ideal and the Female Superego

Freud's concept of the female superego should not be isolated from his over-all view of the female psyche. The weak superego he postulated for the female was perhaps foreshadowed in his theory of the origin of civilized morality (1913). The theory of the primal deed of patricide by the primal horde of brothers led to guilt and morality without accounting for the origin of morality in women (Muslin, 1972). It is not based upon current clinical observations, nor is it typical of masochism or female depression, usually associated with a sadistic superego. The latency girl shows no lack of superego functioning in prohibition of masturbation and aggressive activity, in demanding social conformity and self-control, in the induction of guilt, shame, and the need for punishment, in industrious work and sublimation.

To explain the girl's entry into the oedipal phase on the basis of castration shock and to explain her deficient superego on the basis of her diminished castration anxiety may constitute an analytic paradox. There is clinical evidence for castration anxiety in women, and that castration anxiety does contribute to, but not singularly initiate, female oedipal development. Oedipal resolution is incomplete in both sexes, with varying effects on superego formation. Girls having felt hurt and disappointed, might well fear new injury. Greenacre (1948) depicted girls as worrisome, already punished for masturbation via castration. Fantasies of castration often coexist with illusory-phallus fantasies. The girl has castration anxiety, but even if she has greater fear of loss of love, the different motives for oedipal renunciation do not predetermine the final superego identifications or the strength of the superego.

It is important to distinguish between superego origins, function, structure, and content. Differences between male and female superego systems are related to biological, cultural, and developmental factors. However, different contents of precepts and values should not be confused with inferior intrapsychic structure or function. If the superego incorporates a cultural ideal of docility and dependency, the strong superego will assert and enforce such values. "Weakness" or compliance could represent a feminine value rather than a deficient structure. Whereas early analytic theory depreciated the female superego, I believe the female superego and maternal ego ideal can now be appreciated as of inestimable importance in the direction and determination of feminine character and interests.

The girl's fear of loss of love is itself a powerful force for superego internalization, related to the subsequent importance of the love and approval of the superego. The bestowal of external and internal approval may reward and foster such "feminine" attitudes as modesty and docility. The postulated rejection of the castrated mother would lead to her possibly being internalized, not only in a defective self-representation, but in an unforgiving, attacking superego. The girl turns to her phallic father from her devalued castrated mother, but also in identification with her loved, admired, and envied mother, and with her mother as aggressor and rival. Actually, the motives and identifications of the little girl and her crucial, continuing relation with her mother need much more detailed elucidation. Girls and boys are both subject to superego precursors, such as sphincter morality, to oedipal rivalry and disappointment, to an elaborate constellation of demands and directives, rewards and punishments; and both identify with the superego of the two parents, and with the ideals of the idealized parents. Jacobson (1964, pp. 112–114) described an earlier nucleus of the ego ideal in the girl than in the boy, which, although vulnerable to regression, could lead to the eventual constitution of a mature maternal ego ideal and autonomous superego. The formation of a feminine ego ideal initiates feminine latency and, with later remodeling, becomes a regulator of feminine interests and aspirations. The female superego is different from the male, but not inferior, even if less rigid and punitive; and feminine values and ideals and masculine precepts are not identical (Schafer, 1974); (Jacobson, 1964). An inconsistent or excessively harsh, punitive superego will undermine ego functioning in both sexes. A punitive female superego will inhibit femininity and abort maternal fulfillment, and a "bad mother" introject will interfere with the formation and function of the maternal ego ideal. The maternal ego ideal is an important organization within the female ego ideal, which is a more inclusive and broader structure and value system. The female ego ideal has a maternal core in origin and function, but includes valued representations of all aspects of the mother—active, cognitive, nurturant, sexual, etc.—as well as selected paternal identifications and elements of the ideal self.

Benedek, (1970, p. 139) has described psychological striving for motherhood, first considered in evolutionary perspective as female destiny and role, as rooted in the central organization of receptive and retentive tendencies of the female reproductive drive. Motherhood is, then, a core feminine wish and not secondary or compensatory, but I would emphasize the importance and influence of the maternal ego ideal for maternal wishes and attitudes. More than an id wish, a narcissistic gratification, or a consolation for fantasied castration, motherhood is a most coveted aspiration of the maternal ego ideal.

Wishful fantasies of being a mother are normally organized and integrated at later developmental levels. In latency, the overdetermined maternal attributes are consolidated in the maternal ego ideal. In adult life, the child not only reproduces the archaic self and objects, but represents the bond between the parents and a realization of the mature maternal ego ideal. Maternal ideals and aspirations are deeply rooted in the unconscious feminine superego and contribute to humanitarian concerns and caring responsibility, and the development of discipline and ethics in the succeeding generation.

Internalization of the ideal mother is linked to wishes for an ideal family. More than the desire for motherhood, the vital capacity for motherliness depends upon the psychosexual maturity of the total personality (Benedek, 1970, pp. 157–160), but especially upon the maternal identifications. Cultural attitudes toward motherhood may be in conflict with powerful unconscious maternal strivings. In addition to the familiar prostitution fantasies, the clash of infanticidal wishes and maternal ideals is among the deepest unconscious conflicts of women. Infanticidal conflicts are core conflicts in women with histories of postpartum depression, child abuse, deviant maternal and child development, etc. Full feminine development usually demands motherhood, but this will depend upon the maternal ego ideal, ego interests, and the capacities for sublimation and substitution. The maternal ego ideal has a fundamental regulatory role in motherhood and maternal sublimation.

Masochism and Further Developmental Considerations

The early theory of feminine masochism was buttressed by observable masochistic phenomena in women and by the clinical and theoretical discussions of students of female psychology, e.g., H. Deutsch (1944) and M. Bonaparte (1953). Deutsch, in her many important contributions to the psychology of women, modified some of Freud's hypotheses. She postulated a gradual detachment from the mother rather than a hateful rejection based upon devaluation and envy, as had been earlier proposed (cf. Freud, 1933, p. 121, 127). Deutsch (1944, p. 253) observed: "… in favorable cases the process ends with a positive, tender, and forgiving relation to the mother - and such a relation is one of the most important prerequisites for psychologic harmony in later femininity." Deutsch, (1944, p. xiii) however, regarded narcissism, passivity, and masochism as the three essental traits of femininity. She enlarged and emphasized *"feminine masochism,"* toward the father, men, and life as a whole (1944, pp. 239–278, 254). Feminine sexuality involved submissive wishes to be castrated and raped by the father.

Deutsch (1945, Vol. II, p. 247) wrote,

… and some degree of gratification of that primary feminine quality that assigns pain a place among pleasure experiences in the psychic economy, are precious components of motherhood.

The conscious erotic desires of women were masochistic expressions of suffering for the lover, of rape, enslavement, and humiliation. Deutsch (1944, pp. 191, 241) also distinguished feminine masochism from the cruelty and suffering of neuroses and perversions, but she believed that masochism was not only normal but desirable and necessary for female adjustment to reality (1944, pp. 276–277).

Excessive masochism could cause women to defend or avoid their femininity, but Deutsch did not clearly distinguish between enduring suffering as the price of love, or in the service of an ego interest or ego ideal, versus masochistic goals. There is a difference between enduring or enjoying suffering—between the goal of motherhood or the goal of labor pains. Persistent fantasies of the primal scene and its masochistic interpretation were regarded as normal rather than neurotic adult female attitudes, although persistent sadistic and castrating attitudes in men were not normally mature. Nor does it follow that girls with fantasied castration would normally seek and enjoy further injury. Deutsch did not question the relative influence of a feminine cultural ideal of devoted sacrifice, that a "mature woman" should assume a masochistic position with contentment and fortitude. Clinically, feminine acceptance of hurts and humiliation might be considered normal rather than neurotic and needing analyss. Further, the masochistic disposition and its transformations and different implications for sexual functioning and for maternal functioning were not explored. I believe there are different developmental lines, though interrelated, for heterosexual partnership, nurturant motherhood, and feminine social roles. The goals of sexual attraction and nurturant mothering are not identical and may be antithetical. Being sexually receptive or nurturant is not equivalent to masochistic submission.

Feminine masochism, in Deutsch's view, was governed especially by feminine narcissism (1944, p. 188). She (1944, pp. 272, 280) also indicated the opportunity for sublimation of feminine masochism, but paradoxically depreciated female intellectual sublimation. She departed from Freud's (1933, p. 117) developmental observation:

One gets an impression, too, that little girls are more intelligent and livelier than boys of the same age; they go out more to meet the external world and at the same time form stronger object-cathexes.

(Freud's observations here contrast sharply with his comments on female narcissism and passivity.) For Deutsch, empathy and intuition were feminine, but not intellectual activity and exploration, which she regarded as expressive of active-aggressive strivings. Deutsch asserted (1944, pp. 290–291),

> Woman's intellectuality is to a large extent paid for by the loss of valuable feminine qualities: it feeds on the sap of the affective life and results in impoverishment of this life either as a whole or in specific emotional qualities…. Everything relating to exploration and cognition, all the forms and kinds of human cultural aspiration that require a strictly objective approach, are with few exceptions the domain of the masculine intellect, of man's spiritual power, against which woman can rarely compete. All observations point to the fact that the intellectual woman is masculinized; in her, warm intuitive knowledge has yielded to cold unproductive thinking.

The masochistic orientation Deutsch depicted as feminine included the renunciation of intellectuality. Yet, surely the analytic gifts and scholarly contributions of Helene Deutsch contradict her own words.

Gardiner (1955), in a very significant paper, took sharp issue with these views of Deutsch and similar formulations. She argued that except for defloration, intercourse is normally without pain and quite pleasurable for the female; that it could be a passive satisfaction without being a masochistic gratification. The feminine wish for a penis and a child from her love object was not a wish for hurt and humiliation. Gardiner agreed with Bonaparte (1953) that a mature woman must have rid herself of the infantile fear originating in the sadomasochistic conception of coitus and the defensive reactions against sexuality. But whereas Deutsch emphasized masochistic development of the female Oedipus complex, masochism, in Gardiner's view, was a component instinct which became fused with other partial instincts under genital primacy. Regression from the genital phase was more likely to lead to masochism in the girl than in the boy. Gardiner differentiated feminine passivity from masochism, rejected normal masochism in mature femininity, but felt that the feminine personality permitted a greater degree of masochistic expression with safety than was possible in the male. She did not regard masochism as necessary for adult feminine sexual fulfillment; the presence of masochistic fantasies or behavior was indicative of unresoved infantile conflicts and fixations. In a panel on masochism (Panel, 1956, p. 536) these ideas were, in effect, supported by Bak who remarked that the masochistic woman was not truly feminine, and by Waelder who commented that masochism was a caricature of femininity. Brenner (1959) depicted masochism as a normal personality component and did not invoke "feminine masochism." Masochistic traits and fantasies are a legacy of infantile, principally oedipal conflicts, with varying importance of the danger situations of early childhood. It would follow from these fomulations that whether sexual relations and penetration are regarded as an injurious invasion or a loving union would depend upon psychosexual maturity and object love. The level of object relationship is reflected in the psychological meaning of intercourse and orgasm (Moore, 1968), and intense sadomasochistic fantasy is usually associated with impaired object relations.

The views of female sexual development promulagated by Freud, Deutsch, and Bonaparte were partially rejected by Horney, Jones, Fenichel, and others (Fliegel, 1973). The discussions of feminine masochism and its role in normal and abnormal feminine personality development indicated the lack of analytic dogma. Person (1974) has pointed to the confusion of meaning of clinical themes with developmental causality in the construct of feminine masochism as an inevitable consequence of the anatomical difference between the sexes.

Early dichotomous views of femininity centered, on the one hand, on an emphasis on biological and instinctual forces, and, on the other, on sociocultural factors. Instinctually, the male was predisposed toward sadism, the female toward masochism. The culturalists disregarded biology and unconscious determinants, attributing the masochism and inferiority feelings of the female to adverse environmental processes. They basically disregarded Freud's view of the complemental and interrelated effects of endowment and environment. Horney (1935) and Thompson (1942) attempted to explain female envy of the male and masochism only on the basis of the socioeconomic inferiority of women and as the consequence of their restricted life. Frustration of adult self-realization led to increased dependence, with ambivalently heightened vicarious living through love objects.

With increasing understanding of the importance of early development and of the "facilitating environment," the analysts paid increasing attention to the differences in the rearing of female children and in their socialization. Man's greater size and strength and his visible phallic prowess, which must have figured so importantly in early civilizations, had also been realized in many societies as superior power and prestige. Tendencies toward feminine masochism and penis envy could be reinforced in a reality which favored the prerogatives and privileges of the male. Masochism was the "weapon of the weak," and used for the "seduction of the aggressor." A masochistic and subjugated mother could represent a feminine model of passive self-effacement. The actual relationship between the parents, the position of her mother in the family and society significantly influences the child's later identifications and masculine-feminine attitudes. The psychoanalytic consideration of masochism includes more than drves; it also includes defensive and adaptive functions (Brenner, 1959).

Freud was aware of these problems, observed (1933, p. 116) the social imposition of masochistic attitudes, and warned against underestimating the influence of social customs that force women into passive situations. Freud did not overlook the anchoring of feminine masochism in historical actuality. One of the significant measures of the advance of civilization has been the gradually improved situation of women and children. History was indeed largely his-story and even where women were the power behind the throne, they lacked full authority and responsibility. At the same time, as Freud remarked, women had made few contributions to the discoveries and inventions of civilization. The virtual absence of great female artists and scientists is a fact which appears to have influenced Freud's judgement of their inability to sublimate. Greenacre (1960) has discussed problems of feminine achievement and creativity.

In addition to fundamental biopsychological forces, cultural factors are involved in creativity. The relative lack of great female cultural contributions can be related to questions of a masochistic disposition and to fear of success, as well as failure in competitive situations (Horner, 1972). The girl may be afraid to compete and excel if this is in conflict with feminine goals and ideals. Female education and cultural pursuits were often denigrated. The potential of women for artistic and intellectual sublimation was not always fully admitted or encouraged. Actually, much of woman's creativity may find expression in motherhood, *"Certainly there is superb artistic creativity involved in the sound rearing of a child"* (Greenacre, 1960, p. 577).

Impetus for man's creativity and "brain children" may be partially derived from his awe, envy, and identification with the active and fertile mother. The full potential of woman's creativity remains to be further evaluated and realized in other disciplines, and compared to their creative contributions to psychoanalysis. (Analyzed women may be especially creative.) The age period of peak maternal responsibility may coincide and compete with certain other forms of creativity which tend to peak at the same age period. With unparalleled educational and social opportunities and encouragement, with freedom from the dangers of uncontrolled, protracted reproduction, there may be new pathways of feminine fulfillment, as well as new conflicts and problems.

It should be noted that the sorrowful, suffering, and martyred mother, the "mater dolorosa," was formerly validated by everyday reality. The young woman of several generations past had experienced the loss of many close female relatives and siblings during her own childhood and could anticipate losses of her own children and possibly of her own health or life in childbirth. Masochistic fantasies and identifications were also based on reality. The early masochistic fantasies of the primal scene and the association of sex and danger are no longer typically validated, nor is there expectation of sick and unwanted children.

The concerned care of children represents both an outlet and a possible impediment for different kinds of feminine creativity. Motherhood need not represent masochistic renunciation, but loving perseverance and the fostering of development in the service of the maternal ego ideal. Commitment to children, despite frustration or deprivation, is not equivalent to masochism or self punishment. Maternal devotion should not be confused with masochistic enslavement or preservation of the object from aggression. Masochism may actually interfere with feminine empathy and predispose toward malformations and pathogenic mother-child conflicts. The child may identify with the mother's masochistic tendencies or may yield to the mother's masochistic provocations with sadistic response or excessive reaction formations and guilt. Maternal selfsacrifice out of consideration and care for the child is not masochism, nor is masochistic provocation of the child mature maternal love. If maternal ambitions and aspirationsare masochistic or narcissistic, they will lead the mother to misread the child's cues and will interfere with the child's development through inappropriate gratifications, restrictions, and demands. Mature mothering requires remarkable sublimation and promotes sublimation and mastery in her child. It is impossible to derive maternal devotion and empathy from masochism, narcissism, and penis envy.

Children receive many parental cues for the development of their ambitions and interests, often with major differences for boys and girls. Parental expectations can become internalized, eventuating in self-fulfilling prophecies. Freud assumed parental preference for sons rather than daughters. He stated (1933, p. 133), "a mother is only brought unlimited satisfaction by her relation to a son; this is altogether the most perfect, the most free from ambivalence of all human relationships." Indeed, if control were completely achieved over the choice of the sex of children, would there be a shortage of girls because most couples would prefer boys? The greater love for a son could foster masochism and envy of the male in the daughter. This view of maternal favor of sons was challenged by Deutsch (1944) and Benedek (1970) who called attention to the mother's desire to perpetuate herself and her own mother in her wish for a daughter. Although Freud (1937, p. 252) suggested that repudiation of femininity in both sexes was biological bedrock, his other writings indicated or implied the importance of early developmental influences and the developmental impact of unconscious fantasies and expectations.

The mother is in relative eclipse in Freud's great case histories, both in terms of developmental vicissitudes and their possible repetition in maternal transference. The developmental research that Freud sought and stimulated has now provided new data about early development. Mothers stimulate and respond differently to different children and to children of different sex.

Female infants may respond to different kinds of stimulation and may elicit different parental responses (Murphy, 1962). The bedrock of biology precedes the oedipal phase and unfolds in a matrix of object relations. Parental attitudes and fantasies impose a gender identity that may not even be congruent with anatomical and physiological sex (Stoller, 1968). Biology strongly influences, but does not by itself determine, destiny or psychic reality, just as the actual configuration of the body does not necessarily determine the body image.

The vagueness of the female genital area was associated with vague feminine ambitions (Greenacre, 1948) and to problems in abstraction and analytic thinking based upon incomplete body image. Psychoanalytic data confirmed the influence of body image on ego style and ego interests (Keiser, 1956). This is illustrated by Erikson's (1964) concept of "inner space" in femininity and Kestenberg's (1968) concept of the "inner genital." The body ego and biological role of the female indicate the metaphorical significance of both inner space and periodic time. The physiological periodicity represented by the menstrual hormonal-fertility cycle influences fantasy and personality function (cf. Benedek, 1963). Rhythmicity may be a special component of the feminine personality, especially after puberty. The menstrual cycle, pregnancy and maternity impose unique developental tasks and are instinsic to the psychobiology of femininity.

The vague and confused external genitals and the invisible internal genitals of the girl are nevertheless also associated with a visible well-defined, and fundamental maternal reproductive role. The uncertain ambitions and goals of the girl may be correlated with her body image and illusory-phallus fantasies, as well as with parental attitudes, sociocultural expectations, and the illusory or real achievements and opportunities in life. Boys and girls show tendencies to have different styles, strengths, and weaknesses, but there is no present scientific basis for any value judgment of a superior sex. Idealization of either parent or either sex, their capacities, functions, or organs is irrational.

Psychoanalytic concepts such as masochism or penis envy should not be invoked or utilized in a simplistic reductionism. Penis awe, penis envy, and the unconscious depreciation of the female are vastly overdetermined. Penis envy is not a simple biological force or id wish, but a developmental concept related to object relations and identifications. It should not be used as an explanatory platitude isolated from ego considerations, e.g., of the meaning of the penis and of envy, and from earlier preoedipal and narcissistic conflicts. Narcissistic injury and envy may be expressed in terms of phallic narcissism and oedipal disappointment and jealousy. Penis envy is not only a primary development but may also be defensive, and reactive, as noted in the past (Chasseguet-Smirgel, 1970); (Horney, 1924). Intractable penis envy may derive from and defend against envy of the preoedipal and oedipal mother. Penis envy is also found in boys and may be discerned in the boy's envy of the larger penetrating and impregnating paternal phallus.

It is necessary to theoretically distinguish between penis envy as a dynamic issue and as a developmental influence. Though very important and ubiquitous, penis envy can no longer be regarded, if it ever was, as the major organizer of femininity. Instead, penis envy might be regarded as the developmental organizer of female masculinity. To derive femininity mainly from penis envy would be developmental distortion and reductionism (although penis envy contributes to feminine character). A feminine identity and self-representation has other important roots. Penis envy may indirectly and adaptively foster a heterosexual feminine orientation, but penis envy is commonly an impediment to femininity.

The feminine superego, including the maternal ego ideal, directs and regulates later feminine trends and interests. Feminine identifications and the ego ideal are of transcendent importance for feminine personality organization.

The awe and admiration of the mother and the cultural expressions of feminine identification may be discerned in such diverse phenomena as initiation rites and *couvade*. The wish to possess, dominate, and control the mother may have become embodied in certain attitudes toward feminine development. The early fantasy of the omnipotent mother (good and evil) and the dominating phallic mother was covered by the devalued image of the incompetent masochistic woman. This can also be viewed as a reversal of the childhood domination and discipline by the mother, the child's first teacher, and the domination by female teachers during the early years of school. In both sexes, repudiated infantile fears of dependency and symbiosis are additional unconscious factors in the devaluation of women. The circular relationship between unconscious fantasies and sociocultural institutions and interests is related to cultural myths about men and women.

There is no evidence that the human female has a greater endowment to derive pleasure from pain or a lesser capacity for neutralization and secondary autonomy. Masochism is not identical with being passive or receptive, and while it is possible that the human female is more predisposed toward masochism than the male, there are ample, if not necessarily equal, sadomasochistic trends in both sexes. The female's earliest identifications and object relations are of crucial importance for her later sexual identity, feminine role, and maternal attitudes. Not masochism, but a mature maternal ego ideal is indispensable for "good-enough mothering." Masochism invites sadism and suffering, impedes maternal care and empathy, and distorts object love. Sadomasochism is universal in humanity, but I would not regard masochism as an essential or organizing attribute of mature femininity. Hypotheses in which femininity was secondary (to masculinity) in derivation and function were allied to a masochistic developmentalmodel. These antiquated formulations were based on limited analytic data, constructions, and developmental knowledge. The repudiation of femininity is not biological or psychological bedrock, and normal femininity has its own primary developmental lines with its own valued and gratifying features. In both sexes bisexuality not only produces conflicts but contributes to personality organization, and personality harmony requires the integration of bisexual trends. The female superego contributes to this harmonious integration with dominant femininity regulated and supported by injunctions and admonitions, values and ideals.

Summary

Psychoanalytic advances have led to refinement and reformulation of early models of female personality development. Masochism was taken as a point of departure for a study of the psychology of women and earlier hypotheses of a masochistic and inferior female psychic structure. Masochism is a residue of unresolved infantile conflict and is neither essentially feminine nor a valuable component of mature female function and character. Though the female might be more predisposed to masochism, there is no evidence of particular female pleasure in pain. It is important to distinguish between masochistic suffering as a goal in itself, and tolerance for a discomfort or deprivation in the service of the ego or ego ideal.

Initial hypotheses of a diminished female libido, ego tendencies toward arrest and rigidity, relative inability to sublimate, and a deficient superego are imcomplete and obsolete theoretical propositions. The female ego and superego are different from but not inferior to the male.

Female development cannot be described in a simple reductionism and overgeneralization. Femininity cannot be predominantly derived from a primary masculinity, disappointed maleness, masochistic resignation to fantasied inferiority, or compensation for fantasied castration and narcissistic injury. Castration reactions and penis envy contribute to feminine character, but penis envy is not the major determinant of femininity. Penis envy variously impedes and fosters femininity but penis envy is more closely related to the girl's bisexual masculinity.

The female Oedipus complex is central to feminine development, but has significant normative roots in primary and positive feminine identifications and individuation. Contemporary contributions to the psychology of women have emphasized concepts of gender and sexual identity, body image and self-representation, psychosexual response and empathic motherliness, etc. The female superego includes an ego ideal with feminine ideals and values and regulates feminine interests. The maternal ego ideal consolidates overdetermined maternal attitudes, guides the formation and integration of maternal attitudes, and directs the developmental achievement of "the ordinary devoted mother." Conflicts between the maternal ego ideal and infanticidal impulses are ubiquitous and clinically significant.

Current theoretical amendments conceptualize mature female autonomy, pride, and self-esteem. Female creativity may be exemplified in many and new forms in addition to motherhood. The capacity to sublimate and to foster sublimation in children is a prerequisite for normal motherhood. Femininity evolves under the influence of parents and culture, with unique developmental challenges and transformations, and a universal psychobiological core linked to functions and roles that should be neither idealized nor devalued.

REFERENCES

Barnett, M. (1968). "I can't" versus "he won't": Further considerations of the psychical consequences of the anatomic and physiological differences between the sexes. *J. Am. Psychoanal. Assoc.*, 16:588–600.

Benedek, T. (1963). An investigation of the sexual cycle in women: methodologic considerations. *Arch. Gen. Psychiat.*, 8:311–322.

——— (1970). Motherhood and nurturing. In: *Parenthood: Its Psychology and Psychopathology,* ed. E. Anthony, T. Benedek. Boston: Little, Brown pp. 153–166.

——— Rubenstein, B.B. (1939). The correlations between ovarian activity psychodynamic process. In: *Psychoanalytic Investigations* New York: Quandrangle, 1973 pp. 129–223.

Bonaparte, M. (1953). *Female Sexuality* New York: International Universities Press

Brenner, C. (1959). The masochistic character: genesis and treatment. *J. Am. Psychoanal. Assoc.*, 7:197–226.

Chasseguet-Smirgel, J., ed. (1970). *Female Sexuality* Ann Arbor: The University of Michigan Press.

Clower, V. (1975). Significance of masturbation in female sexual development and function. In: *Masturbation: From Infancy to Senescence.* ed. I. Marcus. J. Francis. New York: International Universities Press pp. 107–143.

——— (1976). Theoretical implications in current views of masturbation in latency girls. *J. Am. Psychoanal. Assoc.*, 24(Suppl):109–125.

Deutsch, H. (1944, 1945). The Psychology of Women, Vols. I, II: New York: Grune Stratton

Erikson, E. (1964). Womanhood and the inner space. In: Identity, Youth and Crisis New York: Norton, 1968 pp. 261–294.

Fliegel, Z. (1973). Feminine psychosexual development in Freudian theory: A historical reconstruction.*Psychoanal. Quart.*, 42:364–384.

Fraiberg, S. (1972). Some characteristics of genital arousal and discharge in latency girls.The *Psychoanal. Study Child*, 27:439–475. New York: Quandrangle Books.

Freud, S. (1905). Three essays on the theory of sexuality. *Standard Edition*, 7:125–243.

——— (1908). "Civilized" sexual ethics and modern nervous sick. *Standard Edition*, 9:179–204, 1959.

Freud, S. (1913). Totem and taboo. *Standard Edition*, 13:1–161, 1955.

——— (1919). A child is being beaten. *Standard Edition*, 17:177–204.

, 1955

——— (1923). The ego and the id. *Standard Edition*, 19:3–66, 1961

——— (1924a). The economic problem of masochism. *Standard Edition*, 19:157–170, 1961

——— (1924b). The dissolution of the Oedipus Complex. *Standard Edition*, 19:173–179, 1961.

——— (1925). Some psychical consequences of the anatomical distinction between the sexes. *Standard Edition*, 19:243–258, 1961.

——— (1926). The question of lay analysis. *Standard Edition*, 20:179–258,1959.

——— (1930). Civilization and its discontents. *Standard Edition*, 21:59–145, 1961.

——— (1931). Female sexuality. *Standard Edition*, 21:223–243, 1961.

——— (1933). Femininity. *Standard Edition*, 22:112–185, 1964.

——— (1937). Analysis terminable and interminable. *Standard Edition*, 23:216–254. 1964.

Galenson, E., & Roiphe, H. (1976). Some suggested revisions concerning early female development. *J. Am. Psychoanal. Assoc.*, 24(Suppl):29–57.

Gardiner, M. (1955). Feminine masochism and passivity. *Bull. Phila. Assn. Psychoanal.*, 5:74–59.

Greenacre, P. (1948). Anatomical structure and superego development. In: Trauma, Growth, and Personality New York: International Universities Press, 1969 pp. 149–164.

——— (1960). Woman as artist. In: Emotional Growth New York: International Universities Press, 1971.pp. 575–591.

Horner, M. (1972). Toward an understanding of achievement-related conflicts in women. *J. Social Issues,* 28:157–175.

Horney, K. (1924). On the genesis of the castration complex in women. In: *Feminine Psychology.* ed. H. Kelman. New York: Norton pp. 37–53.

——— (1935). The problem of feminine masochism. In: *Feminine Psychology.* ed. H. Kalman. New York: Norton, 1967 pp. 214–233.

Jacobson, E. (1937). Wege der weiblichen Uber-Ich-Bildung. *Internat. Zeitschr. Psychoanal.,*23: 402–412.

——— (1964). *The Self and the Object World.* New York: International Universities Press.

Jones, E. (1935). Early female sexuality. *Int. J. Psychoanal.,* 16:263–273.

——— (1955). *The Life and Work of Sigmund Freud,* Vol. II: New York: Basic Books.

Keiser, S. (1956). Female sexuality. *J. Am. Psychoanal. Assoc.,* 4:563–574.

Kestenberg, J. (1968). Outside and inside, male and female. *J. Am. Psychoanal. Assoc.,* 16:457–520.Ž

Kleeman, J. (1975). Genital self-stimulation in infant and toddler girls. In:

Masturbation: From Infancy to Senescenceed. I. Marcus. J. Francis. New York: International Universities Press pp. *77–106.*

Kohut, H. (1959). Introspection, empathy, and psychoanalysis. *J. Am. Psychoanal. Assoc.,* 7:459–483.

Mahler, M. (1974). Symbiosis and individuation: the psychological birth of the human infant.The *Psychoanal. Study Child,* 29:89–106. New Haven: Yale University PressŽ

Moore, B. (1968). Psychoanalytic reflections on the implications of recent physiological studies of female orgasm. *J. Am. Psychoanal. Assoc.,* 16: 569–587.

Murphy, L. (1962). The Widening World of Childhood New York: Basic Books

Muslin, H. (1972). The superego in women. In: Moral Values and the Superego Concept in Psychoanalysised. S. Post. New York: International Universities Press pp. *101–125.*

Panel (1956). The Problem of Masochism in the Theory and Technique of Psychoanalysis, M. Stein, reporter. *J. Am. Psychoanal. Assoc.*, 4:526–538.

Panel (1970). The Development of the Child's Sense of His Sexual Identity, V.L. Clower, reporter. *J. Am. Psychoanal. Assoc.*, 18:165–176.

Person, E. (1974). Some new observations on the origins of femininity. In: *Women and Analysis. ed.* J. Strouse. New York: Grossman1974. pp. 250–261.

Schafer, R. (1974). Problems in Freud's psychology of women. *J. Am. Psychoanal. Assoc.*, 22:459–485.

Stoller, R. (1968). The sense of femaleness. *Psychoanal. Q.*, 37:42–55.

——— (1976). Primary femininity. *J. Am. Psychoanal. Assoc.*, 25(4):59–78.

Thompson, C. (1942). Cultural pressures in the psychology of women. *Psychiatry*, 4:331–339.

CHAPTER 25

The Curative and Creative Aspects of Insight

(1979). *JAPA*, (27)(Supplement):41–70.

My focus here is upon the vital importance of insight for psychoanalytic therapy, theory, and technique. In affirming the curative and creative roles of insight, I am not subscribing to its idealization or assigning to it magical qualities. In analysis, insight is the one element that is never in excess and yet is never complete. I shall maintain that insight propels the psychoanalytic process forward and is a condition, catalyst, and consequence of the psychoanalytic process. There is a circular interaction between the development of insight and productive analytic work leading to structural change.

Obtaining insights, of course, is not confined to psychoanalytic situations. Artists and poets, more in contact with the unconscious, probed and provided insights into the human mind that preceded and probably facilitated psychoanalytic discoveries. If such insights did not necessarily have therapeutic effects, creative persons such as Sophocles and Shakespeare achieved extraordinary understanding of normal fantasy, psychic conflict, and character disorder that continue to inspire psychoanalytic study.

Despite the punitive expulsion from paradise for gaining forbidden knowledge, the quest for insight has always paralleled the "bliss of ignorance." The hero of the oedipal myth moves and wavers between insight and blindness. Oedipus seeks the truth while asserting innocence of his guilt and ignorance of his identity. Analogous to the analytic process, the oedipal myth depicts the struggle between insight and resistance to insight. Oedipus attempts to evade and avoid the very clues and evidence for which he searches, and resistance is relinquished with the incontrovertible evidence that brings coherence and conviction.

Allied to the poetic and Biblical maxims, "This above all: to thine own self be true," and "the truth shall make you free," Freud (1937, p. 148) asserted:

> ... the analytic relationship is based on a love of truth ...

He had also stated (1933, p. 156),

> I have told you that psycho-analysis began as a method of treatment; but I did not want to commend it to your interest as a method of treatment but on account of the truths it contains, on account of the information it gives us about what concerns human beings most of all—their own nature—and on account of the connections it discloses between the most different of their activities. As a method of treatment it is one among many, though, to be sure, primus inter pares. If it was without therapeutic value it would not have been discovered, as it was, in connection with sick people and would not have gone on developing ...

These comments are closely related to Freud's (1933, p. 80) definition of the analytic goal,

> ... to strengthen the ego ... to widen its field of perception and enlarge its organization.... Where id was, there ego shall be.

Insight may also be achieved in psychotherapy, but is more limited, circumscribed, and superficial, often confined to current derivatives of unconscious conflict in one sector of the personality. In supportive or suppressive psychotherapy, as opposed to expressive or uncovering psychotherapy, the therapist may deliberately eschew insight as a goal. In psychotherapy, resistance may be selectively analyzed or reinforced. In some respects, the role of insight might be conceptualized as on a continuum in psychoanalysis and analytic therapy, but there are critical contrasts between the two forms of therapy which involve the concept of psychoanalytic insight. Psychoanalytic insight reaches and resolves unconscious conflict and is, by far, more pervasive, influential, and enduring than in nonanalytic therapy. Even in analytic psychotherapy, attaining some insight is far more likely to have enduring benefit than purely supportive treatment (Kernberg, 1972).

The limitations of psychotherapeutic goals and methods leaves significant transference and resistance unanalyzed, and rapid benefits frequently derive from forms of "transference cure" and positive changes in symptoms or defense. Psychotherapy depends heavily upon other therapeutic elements that are peripheral to insight in psychoanalysis. Abreaction and verbalization and the analyst's clarifications and confrontations are attuned to the preconscious, but are preparatory and corollary to analytic interpretation (Bibring, 1954).

Interpretation leading to insight is the specific and most powerful agent of the psychoanalytic curative process. The type of insight into preconscious problems achieved from clarification and education is not comparable to analytic insight. Solutions to preconscious problems are ancillary to interpretation of unconscious conflict and its pathogenesis. In analysis, systematic interpretation deals with renewed resistance and is followed by working through, continued analytic work, and continued application and extension of insight. Assimilation of insight is usually gradual, piecemeal, and tenuous until the patient "makes it his own." Analytic insight is confirmed and recreated in the wealth of interlacing, convergent analytic data. The limits of the analytic method, of course, the depth to which interpretation and reconstruction can reach, the lack of personality change despite apparent insight are salient and significant problems for other lines of inquiry.

The psychoanalytic process represents an altogether unique form of investigation and treatment. The process is classically defined in terms of transference and resistance and their vicissitudes and interpretation. Correct interpretation and reconstruction depends upon and conveys insight, so that insight may be stated to be a *sine qua non* of psychoanalysis. Indeed, the psychoanalytic process can be differentiated from psychotherapies because it is a definable process requiring free association and interpretation and leads to insight. An analytic process depends upon correct analytic technique. In psychoanalysis, an opening phase is followed by the development of the transference neurosis, interpretation and working through of remobilized unconscious conflicts, resolution, if not dissolution, of the transference neurosis, and analytic termination with its own phase characteristics.

The analyst's insight, often enriched and advanced by creative patients, should be distinguished from the patient's insight. The analyst must have insight into the patient's defenses, conflicts, and character. The analyst's insight is neither symmetrical nor synchronous with that of the patient, and both precedes and permits proper interpretation and reconstruction. Analytic insight is necessary for the conduct of clinical analysis and resolution of countertransference. The analyst's surpassing insight and special knowledge may be of great preventive value, e.g., regarding parenting and child guidance. Optimally, the insight should emerge from and be part of the analytic process without resort to direct educational measures or advisory parameters. Analysis aims to minimize non-insightful influences and maximize the development of insight. It is not always easy to disentangle the effect of analytic insight from other therapeutic influences, or what appears to be the failure of insight to be effective from other problems of the analytic process, analyzability, and technique. Incomplete, unaccepted, and pseudo insight are everyday problems of analytic work, and countertransference may impede or not heed the patient's insight. The analyst may tactlessly misuse insight for narcissistic or sadistic purposes, disrupting treatment (Bird, 1957).

The analytic process proceeds with the patient's achieving increasing insight into the unconscious pathogenic childhood conflicts and their later derivatives and effects. Kris (1956), in his most illuminating discussion of vicissitudes of insight, referred to its use and abuse, to its gradual acquisition and assimilation, its loss and reappearance. Noting that apparent insight could be subverted for purposes of defense or infantile gratification, he described id aspects and infantile prototypes of insight, e.g., in oral incorporation and tactile grasp. That insight may represent a fecal gift or phallus, magic power, penetration, impregnation, etc. is now common knowledge. Kris pointed particularly to the proliferation of intellectualization as pseudo insight. Some "good hours" are then too good to be true.

Analytic advance proceeds from effective analytic work and increasing ego dominance. The "good hour" has been "prepared" for unconsciously by the preceding analytic work and culminates in new autonomous insight. The neutralized insight that is achieved is ego-integrated into the personality largely out of awareness and contributes to the autonomy of other ego functions. The therapeutic alliance and reality ego are strengthened, and the dynamic processes that lead to insight are beneficially effected by insight in circular processes. Insight, for example, overcomes barriers to curiosity, stimulates inquiry, and facilitates introspection and self-observation which may, in turn, widen insight (Hatcher, 1973). Changes in defense, memory, integration, and other ego functions result from and contribute to insight.

Different levels and availability of insight may be followed and contrasted before, during, and after analysis. For example, insight into a patient's character and symptoms will illuminate and connect genetic, dynamic, structural, and adaptive considerations of the case.

Kris (1956, p. 270) further remarked,

Without other dynamic changes insight would not come about but without insight and the ego's achievement which lead to insight, therapy itself remains limited and does not retain the character of psychoanalysis.

Loewenstein (1956) virtually echoed these remarks. He pointed out that the ability to distinguish between the transferred past and present reality of experience was a function of insight and crucial to the therapeutic effects of psychoanalysis. He regarded enlarging insight as "decisive for the outcome of psychoanalytic work."

Though there is no classical paradigm of technique to which all analysts subscribe, the goal of analysis remains insight, achieved largely through interpretation. In Eissler's (1953) model, any technical deviation from insight via interpretation was a complicating parameter. Technical parameters have often involved attitudes toward transference.

One of the challenges to the psychoanalytic theory of therapy that has periodically resurfaced in different guises was proposed by Alexander

(Alexander, French, et al., 1946). The crux of his therapy was not insight, but a corrective emotional experience. According to Alexander, the transference neurosis could become a regressive evasion, and the analyst should play a benevolent role, antithetical to the threatening role assigned to him in the patient's transference fantasy.

Even today, considerable numbers of psychotherapists regard the analytic situation as too regressively satisfying or as too depriving and too remote from the present and from reality. Various alterations of the psychoanalytic method and conversions to forms of psychotherapy are thus rationalized and justified in terms of transference avoidance, gratification, or manipulation. Unanalyzed transference may be utilized for magical reassurance, suggestion, direction, supportive care, etc.

Psychoanalytic technique has evolved in coordination with psychoanalytic theory. New perspectives have been both enlightening and confusing, and bear on the relative importance of insight in clinical psychoanalysis. The nontransference relationship and the most mature and primitive layers of transference have been carefully dissected (Stone, 1967); (Greenson, 1967); (Loewald, 1978). The analyst was also encountered as a real, new, and consistently mature object, a model for identification. Such identifications were related to the patients' taking over analytic aims, functions, and goals (Sterba, 1934) and to ego and superego development. Mature selective identifications are synergistic with insight, and the role of insight has to be considered with internalization and integrative processes. Many factors in analysis contribute to insight and personality growth, but are subordinate to insight. Insight is complemented by the analysts usually silent auxiliary ego functions, but insight has priority and independently affects the analytic process and positive analytic development. Analytic "cure" is primarily effected through insight and not through empathy, acceptance, tolerance, etc. Serious questions arise, to which I shall later return, concerning the structural development necessary to achieve, use, and retain insight. How much analytic ego growth might occur preceding, permitting, and perhaps by-passing the effects of insight? Can the analytic method really stimulate ego growth without benefit of insight and conflict resolution? Are there technical additions or modifications that could promote ego growth without compromising and distorting the psychoanalytic process? There are also parallel questions concerning the value and validity of verbal insight into the early preverbal phase and its special problems (Blum, 1977); (Loewald, 1978).

In general, there is more contemporary emphasis upon developmental tendencies mobilized by analysis than upon regression and repetition compulsion. The ego attempts to be active where it was passive or helpless (Freud, 1926), and this point of view has long been part of analytic theory. Ego synthesis, the domination of the primary process by the secondary process, the striving toward active ego mastery of trauma (Freud, 1926), the urge to complete development (Bibring, 1937); (A. Freud, 1965, p. 28) support the effects of insight and blend with insight in personality reorganization and structural change.

Because of various needs, the patient may select from the array of therapeutic elements offered by psychoanalysis those less or not connected with insight. Elements of authority and suggestion, for example, are unintended yet unavoidable. What the patient selects and utilizes in the psychoanalytic situation will further the analyst's insight into the patient's ego strengths and psychopathology, just as parameters selected by or forced upon the analyst should be concordant with understanding of the patient's structural fragility or deficit (Eissler, 1953); (A. Freud, 1965, p. 229).

Freud's final views of the analyst's multiple functions ranged beyond interpretation and insight, and envisioned the developmental and technical issues so relevant to contemporary controversy on the widened scope of analyzability and the analysis of ego distortions and deficits. Freud (1940, p. 181) asserted:

We serve the patient in various functions, as an authority and a substitute for his parents, as a teacher and educator; and we have done the best for him if, as analysts, we raise the mental processes in his ego to a normal level, transform what has become unconscious and repressed into preconscious material and thus return it once more to the possession of his ego.

His discussion also included caution against abuse of the opportunity for "after education" afforded by the parental transference and "new superego." He wrote:

In all his attempts at improving and educating the patient the analyst should respect his individuality. The amount of influence which he may legitimately allow himself will be determined by the degree of developmental inhibition present in the patient. Some neurotics have remained so infantile that in analysis too they can only be treated as children

(p. 175). These remarks are important considerations in child analysis, with infantile characters, borderline types, and cases of developmental arrest and deviation, but they remain pertinent to the general theory of therapy, i.e., the analytic process.

Surprisingly, and rather paradoxically, the origins and evolution of the psychoanalytic concept of insight have been relatively obscure. Zilboorg's (1952) statement remains a challenge for contemporary psychoanalytic thought:

Among the unclarities which are of utmost clinical importance and which cause utmost confusion is the term insight. It came from nowhere, so to speak. No one knows who employed it first, and in what sense [p. 2] ...

These reflections are related to perennial questions about the nature of insight, what it is, how it develops, why it works, etc.

The usual attribution (Sandler et al., 1973) ascribes insight to a term borrowed from psychiatry. Patients who do not recognize their own mental dysfunction or abnormality lack "insight," as in children and some cases of adult psychosis or alcoholism. Disturbance might be recognized, but only minimally, and even ascribed to external causes rather than internal difficulty. This type of insight (or its lack) is only superficially related to analytic insight which is much closer to the dictionary definition. Webster defines insight as penetrating and understanding the inner nature of things, a definition in accord with Freud's own use of the term. Freud's reference to creative insight has been overlooked in tracing the origins of the concept.

However, in Freud's Preface to the third English edition of "The Interpretation of Dreams" he made the following observation (1900, p. xxxii):

> [This work] contains, even according to my present-day judgement, the most valuable of all the discoveries it has been my good fortune to make. Insight such as this falls to one's lot but once in a lifetime.

It is clear that Freud was talking here about insight in its widest sense; the general meaning of insight into the nature of human mental processes, normal development and pathogenesis, as well as specific insight into a person's conflicts, character, temperament, and values, etc. Freud's insight was a special quality of his genius and capacity for ego mastery (the relationship between Freud's insight and his self-analysis will be discussed later in this paper). Theoretical and clinical insight are closely connected, though the present discussion is oriented toward insight in the analytic process where it gains life.

Psychoanalytic insight is different from but probably related to the type of insight associated with the solution to problems and to creative struggles. If we knew more, we might be able to categorize different forms of insight.

In a broad sense, resistance refers to resistance to insight. Psychoanalytic insight specifically follows the overcoming of resistance through interpretation. In turn, insight may overcome or elicit resistance. The correct interpretation of resistance results in the patient's coming to grips with the origin and genetic developmental history of the resistance, the functions it serves, the nature of the danger situation that is being warded off, and the secondary gains derived from the associated infantile fixations and regressive adaptations, and the external rewards obtained from inhibitions and symptoms.

The patient becomes acquainted in an entirely new way with the unconscious danger situation as it presents itself in the analytic situation and as it is worked through with the help of analytic interpretation. Working through leads to the assimilation of insight and the progressive resolution of resistance to insight, leading to change (Greenson, 1967, p. 42). Danger is mastered by a mature ego rather than the weak infantile ego of the past. The history of the patient's reactions to danger, with its attendant anxiety and guilt, and the achievement of full conscious awareness of defensive maneuvers and forbidden unconscious impulses are intrinsic to the concept of psychoanalytic insight. Irrational evaluations and patterns of reaction are modified and mastered with development of insight. This can happen outside of psychoanalysis, but under those circumstances is, as I indicated earlier, likely to be sporadic and incomplete. Freud (1926, p. 153) stated: "The ego may occasionally manage to break down the barriers of repression which it has itself put up and to recover its influence over the instinctual impulse and direct the course of a new impulse in accordance with the changed danger-situation. But in point of fact, the ego very seldom succeeds in doing this: it cannot undo its repressions. It is possible that the way the struggle will go depends upon quantitative relations." We can add, with Freud as an example, that it also depends upon special ego endowment and qualities.

Insight is intrinsic to "seeing oneself" and gaining self-knowledge. It is immediate in the here and now of the transference, but it applies to the patient's entire life, and knowledge of the human condition. The transference is the principal but not the only locus of interpretation and source of insight. During intense resistance and a faltering therapeutic alliance, a correct interpretation may do wonders for continued analytic work. Insight may appear as a bolt from the blue, a gift of the gods, but is more likely to endure and enlarge with analysis of previous and subsequent resistance. The patient cooperates and participates in the analytic work, identifying with the search for insight and sometimes arriving at insights before the analyst. Beyond the relief of symptoms and inhibitions, insight becomes an ego aim and ego ideal, a motivation for further analysis. In theory and therapy, psychoanalysis is never without a goal - the goal of insight. Insight, the agency and goal of the analytic process, ideally becomes the patient's goal (Wallerstein, 1965) as well as the need and value of the analyst. Analytic insight extends to the widest understanding of the treatment process, relationship, and situation.

Making the unconscious conscious in a language that communicates the understanding achieved between analyst and patient contributes greatly to insight. But insight does more than make conscious; it establishes causes, meanings, and connections. The concept of insight changed with structural theory and ego psychology. Remembering and recalling, the lifting of infantile amnesia, had to be understood not as specific, isolated, often traumatic memories but against a whole psychological background and organization (Kanzer and Blum, 1967). Autobiography and life experience are reinterpreted (Kris, 1956), relived, and newly revised in analysis.

The patient's insights in analysis will have been brought into full consciousness and verbalized. However, the search for insight and the spread of insight also proceeds in silence and may recede from awareness. Past insight may be regressively lost or may become an intrinsic part of the ego reorganization and growth facilitated by the new insightful integration. The relationship of insight to consciousness and to verbalization or imagery needs further inquiry, including study of insight formation outside of awareness. Insight is not confined to verbal expression and may be communicated in other forms, as in play or art. The intuitive insight of creative artists and analysts are often preconscious, probably with unconscious determinants and contributions (Noy, 1972). Poetic insight, for example, may never achieve conscious reflective awareness. (I shall shortly give an example of Freud's extraordinary insight.) The acquisition and development of insight utilizes unconscious and preconscious ego functions, but "analytic insight" at least is crystallized and organized in its conscious creation.

Insight leads to reintegration by the rational ego. This is not a pale pseudointellectual, cognitive development, but is always associated with enrichment of the inner life (Pressman, 1969); (Valenstein, 1962). The patient can then better recognize, express, and regulate emotions and mood states. Various grades of insight, such as intellectual, affective, dynamic, volitional, or neutral versus emotional, experiential versus descriptive (Reid and Finesinger, 1952); (Richfield, 1954), are components of a holistic concept. Insight may be described as a complex, integrative, ego attribute (Zilboorg, 1952). Consideration of a number of interacting ego functions are necessary to describe the type of insight that leads to a sense of conviction and ultimately to structural change. Past and present, thought and feeling, cause and effect are reintegrated. The development of rational understanding, signal affect, and emotional sensitivity in relating unconscious conflict to various derivatives and experiences in the transference and in life is an essential ingredient of what we understand by insight (Kubie, 1950); (Myerson, 1960). Insights are often disturbing if not painful. The greater equanimity and emotional equilibrium that comes with insight is associated with an appreciation of life's inevitable disappointments and renunciations. Ego assimilation of insight leads to control of impulses and action and capacity for adaptive action and appropriate behavior (Valenstein, 1962).

Insight brings with it intrapsychic and adaptive change. The obsessive patient's sadism is understood in a variety of contexts, particularly as it was manifested in the analytic transference and associated with reaction formation, undoing, and expiation. The isolated anger has been connected to the hostility and sadistic, spiteful attitudes. The unending doubting and counting have been related to the counting of money, possessions, and persons; the counting of one's love objects to insure their existence, and the inability to end the counting without ending their existence and the patient's own security. The origins of the counting will have been explored, and the sublimations of the conflicts and symptoms associated with the obsessive counting will have been recounted, revised, and extended in many directions in the course of the analysis. The patient will have a new appreciation of himself and his family and will not be driven by obsessive thought and attempts to undo his sadistic wishes.

I should like to give a vignette of the emergence of insight in the analytic situation in a setting of considerable transference tension and turbulence. The patient is a highly educated male businessman, proud of his family and his socioeconomic success but disturbed by his continuing difficulties in relation to his wife and children. He has often commented about varying degrees of irritability and bickering and associated to a scene at the dinner table in which there was considerable regressive behavior by the children, characterized by giggling, being ill-mannered, and not listening to their parents. When his daughter reached across the table to grab some favorite food he automatically slapped her hand. He knows that sometimes he is excessively provoked and ill-tempered.

There are things that are difficult to tell me. He would like to present a more admirable picture of himself to himself and to me. He sadly thinks of his parents shopping very carefully for food, watching every penny, and walking distances for opportunities for small sales and savings. He is ashamed to think of incidents where he has been dishonest and, in fact, a cheat. In order to earn extra money when he was a teenager, he had worked as a waiter. Soon becoming proficient, he was given the opportunity to collect the tips of the other waiters, and then began a dishonest scheme. He pocketed some of the tips that belonged to the others. He remembers a particular customer who wanted his bill reduced and indicated as much with an ingenious minimum of words and facial expression. A rapid collusive understanding developed in which the patient reduced the bill in order to gain a larger tip. He went on to describe how mortified and humiliated he was at an early experience when he was caught as a child stealing a chocolate bar.

I pointed out to him that he was describing incidents in which he had been greedily grabbing what didn't belong to him, and that he had started the session by describing the scene at the table in which he had slapped his daughter for grabbing food. The patient himself then recognized that his daughter had been punished for his own guilty deeds, that he had scapegoated her for a conflict externalized onto her which relieved him of blame. At the dinner table and in the scene at the restaurant table, he had wanted some extra food and a large tip. He identified with the customer's entitlement in wanting a lower bill, and then made the connection to the anticipation of receiving the bill from the analyst (his waiter) that session. He had not consciously thought about it or been aware of the anticipation of the bill either at home or, up to that point, in the session. But he wanted a tip of more time and, unconsciously, a "doctored" bill.

Many dynamics and genetics are suggested in this little vignette. The patient (and analyst) dealt with extra-analytic material before the transference fully emerged in the session, and he was able to integrate his conflicts both in the analytic situation and as they were in effect externalized and lived out in the family situation. The guilty culprit who unconsciously wishes to cheat the analyst and receive a doctored bill becomes the punitive parent who mistreats his "mischievous" child.

The analytic work and integrated efforts continued after the session and into the next hour. He realized upon leaving that he had not mentioned his reactions to his clients and partners. He refuses requests of clients to falsify records and bills, but he had forgotten a current temptation. Charged with responsibility for depositing the firm's receipts, he had fantasied, indeed, he had been momentarily tempted to take some of the money for himself. The past scene of taking his co-waiters' tips was very much alive, and he became more aware of tendencies to repeat in different forms and disguise. He could be generous with family and friends, but he began to recognize that he was also engaged in acts of undoing and restitution. Analytic insight developing in the analytic situation was being extended in many different areas and directions.

Insight promotes structural change and then reflects that change. I do not think that the reverse sequence of structural change causing insight is reliable, and would not assign insight a secondary role in the analytic process. The personality reorganization and ego development that occur in analysis require insight. As a "developmental process," analysis has prerequisites of a capacity to participate in an analytic process, secondary process, and sufficient preexisting development to provide for controlled regression, signal anxiety, differentiation of fantasy and reality and of past and present, thought and action, the development of self and object constancy, language, self-observation, and self-criticism are clearly required. It is probably true that some patients become analyzable in the process of analysis, but such difficult patients probably have hidden ego strengths, can eventually attain and retain insight, and primarily recover from regression rather than major developmental arrest and defect. Children who never reached object constancy were unable to establish firm enduring treatment alliances with their analysts (A. Freud, 1965, p. 41), and I believe that this applies with rare exceptions to adult patients as well. The achievement of self- and object constancy is conditional upon cognitive and affective development, ego discrimination, and synthesis, and is necessary for further ego development. In assessing the limits of clinical insight, we have to consider the developmental level and stability of these basic ego functions in addition to the defenses. Kris (1956, p. 270) stated:

> … *the complexity of the ego functions which participate in the process of gaining and using insight may well account for the wide variations of the impact of insight on individual cases.*

The nature of insight itself undergoes development. Insight into unconscious conflicts and processes is not an expectable part of normal development, and much of analytic insight into, e.g., a patient's cannibalistic impulses or incestuous passions, were never conscious in childhood. Structural development in childhood proceeds with "normal" repression, with adaptive as well as pathogenic uses of defense. The normal, adaptive formation of the superego represents a new level of structure and integration, which occurs without insight into the unconscious origins, content, and function of the superego. Analytic insight into structure formation does not mean that structural malformations or arrest are necessarily analyzable or reversible.

How much development is necessary for the most limited insight? The child must have negotiated separation-individuation (Mahler et al., 1975) and have some advanced structurization and critical ego functions, as previously noted. Contrasting the problems that preoedipal trends introduce into the transference relationship, A. Freud (1965, p. 40) referred to "the beneficial elements contributed by the appearance in the transference of object constancy and the attitudes belonging to the positive and negative oedipus complex with the coordinated ego achievements of self-observation, insight, and secondary process functioning." That the limits of insight depend upon developmental achievements is also related to the emphasis upon the resumption of development at the termination of child analysis (A. Freud, 1970); (Van Dam et al., 1975). The insight of children and of infantile adults is developmentally restricted. Comparisons of reconstructions in adult and child analysis should provide valuable information on insight and development and, in turn, should facilitate increasingly accurate reconstructive insight. Studies of insight in children at different developmental levels and of adults with developmental deficits and deviations will delimit those patients who can optimally or minimally use insight, and those who might benefit from preparatory psychotherapy and then analysis.

The breadth and depth of insight varies with the phase of analysis, the resolution of the transference, and the patient's ego development and resources. It is well to add here that the types of insight that are communicated to patients today are by no means identical with what was analytically interpreted in the pioneer days of psychoanalysis (Blum, 1976), (1977). The difference in the range, type, and depth of our interpretations can by no means be entirely attributed to changes in the patient population. (Our technique influences the analytic data obtained, which in turn is the source of theory. Proper technique is molded to theory, so that theory cannot be divorced or discarded from analytic work.)

Our insights into the roots of the personality are much greater today, and we have benefited from the contributions of ego psychology, structural theory, and developmental knowledge. We know more and convey greater insight in longer analyses than in the pioneer days. Greater knowledge of the preoedipal period and its influence on the Oedipus complex and later personality is exemplified in the recent concepts of developmental lines (A. Freud, 1965) and separation/individuation (Mahler et al., 1975).

Similarly, our understanding of later phases of life—for example, latency, adolescence, and young adulthood with the stresses and developmental challenges of parenthood—are also available for a more complete interpretation. The infantile neurosis is the core of the transference neurosis, but we know much more about its complex web of origins (Rangell, 1975), about its antecedents and developmental transformation, and the powerful influence for better and worse of the earlier and later phases of life. Traumatic experience and pathogenic reality situations are better understood, especially in terms of strain patterns rather than isolated single shocks.

What about the fate of insight after psychoanalysis? The maintenance and even expansion of insight post-termination is in need of study in follow-up research and reanalysis. Having learned to free associate, observe, and interpret by the end of analysis, few patients are able to sustain independently the type of ongoing analytic process that Freud (1937, p. 249) described as the appropriate result of training analysis:

> … *we reckon on the stimuli that he has received in his own analysis not ceasing when it ends and on the processes of remodeling the ego continuing spontaneously in the analysed subject and making use of all subsequent experiences in the newly-acquired sense. This does in fact happen, and in so far as it happens, makes the analysed subject qualified to be an analyst himself …*

Reflecting upon the wide variations of the impact of insight in individuals, Kris (1956, p. 270) observed:

> *With some individuals the result of analysis seems to be connected with a lasting awareness of their own problems, a higher degree of ability to view themselves; with others this is not so—and yet the two groups of patients cannot be distinguished according to the range of therapeutic effects. This possibly finds a parallel in the study of what patients retain in memory of the course of analysis, a problem frequently accessible in repeated analyses. It is well known that the variations are extraordinarily wide. It seems that insight with some individuals remains only a transient experience, one to be obliterated again in the course of life by one of the defenses they are wont to use. And it is not my impression that these individuals are more predisposed to future illness than others. This might well remind us how much remains unknown about the conditions under which the ego does its silent work.*

Myerson (1960), (1965) discussed similar problems and described different modes of insight with different ego reactions and depth. Full post-analytic insight into intrapsychic conflict represented an internalization of the analytic process.

Insight may have self-propelling and compelling effects, as Freud noted. Following the principle of multiple function, it tends to catalyze further insight with creative stimulation of comprehension, connection, and new levels of integration. This, of course, does not occur in any straight line, and as indicated previously, new insights are often followed by renewed resistance and regressive retreat. Interpretation must be repeated and insights tested and contested. Insight in one area may be exploited for resistance to insight in another area. A patient may understand his phallic-urethral strivings but not his narcissistic need for unlimited power and prestige. In predisposed patients, insights may trigger negative therapeutic reactions or may be victoriously attained only after the rival analyst has been vanquished.

Without overlooking the possible subversion or loss of insight, the impact and influence of insight may be quite silent yet very significant for personality development and ego dominance. Freud (1927, p. 53) referred to the broad civilizing influence of insight in humans driven by instinct and irrational illusions when he stated, "The voice of the intellect is a soft one, but it does not rest till it has gained a hearing. Finally, after a countless succession of rebuffs, it succeeds. This is one of the few points on which one may be optimistic about the future of mankind…."

Insight is related to the mastery of conflict and regression, but also to creative solutions and to the creation of new organization and structure. There is a creative dimension to insight and its achievement and consequences (Noy, 1978). Analysis diminishes the compulsion to repeat and liberates integrative functions. The reorganization of the personality on new levels of development is clearly more than a recovery of lost memories and past relationships. Causes and connections are established which never existed in the same way with cognitive and affective changes. Insight surpasses the recapture of lost connections, resources, and abilities, and proceeds to the creation of new meaning, modes of understanding, and new adaptive possibilities and opportunities. The reciprocal insight, imagination, and integration of analyst and patient has an artistic, aesthetic quality. Referring to the correspondence between creativity and the insight of the analytic patient, Anna Freud (1957,

p. 491) stated, "What we wish him to achieve is the creation of new attitudes and relationships on the basis of the newly created powers of insight into his inner world."

We know very little about the creative genius responsible for the discovery of psychoanalysis and the seemingly spontaneous insights that characterized his self-analysis and his applications of analytic thought. The burgeoning of Freud's insight has been ascribed to his self-analysis and was in many respects an essential product of his self-analysis. His systematic self-analysis usually is said to differentiate Freud's pre-analytic period and the emergence of psychoanalysis; and his earliest analytic investigations foreshadowed his later conceptualizations.

But where did his self-analytic ability come from? It was not the result of a protracted analytic process, but the creation of the analytic method simultaneous with insights into himself and others. In some ways this occurred preceding deliberate self-analysis. The creative leaps of the imagination were often "quantum leaps," in which insight spontaneously emerged as well as appearing after long preparation and the culmination of inner struggle, experiment, and study. The interweaving of primary-process regression, interpretive self-observation, and secondary-process integration became for Freud a creative process of insight and discovery. The analytic process deliberately fosters both regression and reintegration, and new insights have creative elements and novel configurations. It follows that insight is in many respects related to creativity, and promotes rather than impairs creative discovery and expression. Insight and creativity are complementary, and it is not insight but the absence or deficit of insight that threatens ego flexibility and creativity. All patients, and creative personalities in particular, stand to benefit from stimulation and enhancement of creativity in clinical psychoanalysis with expanding insight. Freud's self-analytic discoveries exemplify how naïve is the notion that psychoanalysis endangers creativity.

Freud, with his uncanny capacity to learn from his experimental efforts, his trials and errors, soon found the roots of hypnosis in unconscious predispositions. Of hypnosis, Freud (1917, p. 462) declared,

We psycho-analysts may claim to be its legitimate heirs and we do not forget how much encouragement and theoretical clarification we owe to it.

Relevant to problems of parenthood and creativity, I should like to call attention to a virtually unknown gem of the Freudian literature. It is in the pre-psychoanalytic publications and is called: *A Case of Successful Treatment by Hypnotism.* (Freud, 1893).

We can observe the father of psychoanalysis arriving at the most extraordinary insights into the psychology of motherhood before his own self-analysis, and long before he had turned particular attention to the study of mothering and the mother-child relationship (Blum, 1978).

The paper was published at the same time as Breuer and Freud's (1893) "Preliminary Communication," and recounts the daring therapeutic intervention of a young Viennese physician. Here is Freud on a house call, confronting an acute emotional crisis. It was the case of a mother with postpartum depression who was unable to feed her newborn baby. Freud's account is precious and timeless, and significant for the history of psychoanalysis. Clinical observation and theoretical construct followed one upon the other. His remarks on the constitutional predisposition are still the open question he pondered.

The patient was a young woman between twenty and thirty years of age with whom he had been acquainted since childhood. She had an apparently happy marriage and had intended to nurse her first child. Freud (1893, pp. 118–120) describes what happened on that occasion:

The delivery was not more difficult than is usual with a primiparous mother....There was a poor flow of milk, pains were brought on when the baby was put to the breast, the mother lost appetite and showed an alarming unwillingness to take nourishment, her nights were agitated and sleepless. At last, after a fortnight, in order to avoid any further risk to the mother and infant, the attempt was abandoned as a failure and the child was transferred to a wet-nurse. Thereupon all the mother's troubles immediately cleared up.

This was, of course, in a society and culture in which there were no sterile formulas and milk substitutes. So, without a wet-nurse, a mother's refusal to feed her newborn was tantamount to infanticidal threat.

Freud was called in three years later when a second baby was born, but

"… the mother's attempts at feeding the child herself seemed even less successful and to provoke even more distressing symptoms than the first time. She vomited all her food, became agitated when it was brought to her bedside and was completely unable to sleep. She became so much depressed at her incapacity that her two family doctors—… Dr. Breuer and Dr. Lut—would not hear of any prolonged attempt being made on this occasion."

A final therapeutic effort was to be made. When Freud was called in, he found the patient on the evening of the fourth day lying in bed,

… furious at her inability to feed the baby—an inability which increased at every attempt, but against which she struggled with all her strength. In order to avoid the vomiting, she had taken no nourishment the whole day…. Far from being welcomed as a saviour in the hour of need, I was obviously being received with a bad grace and I could not count on the patient having much confidence in me.

Undaunted, Freud promptly hypnotized his patient and reported the following hypnotic suggestion: "Have no fear! You will make an excellent nurse and the baby will thrive. Your stomach is perfectly quiet, your appetite is excellent, you are looking forward to your next meal, etc." He then tells us that the patient slept peacefully, took nourishment herself, "and fed the baby irreproachably." However, later the next day her vomiting returned. "It was impossible to put the child to her breast …" Freud now acted with "greater energy," and induced a second hypnosis, reporting the following extraordinary intervention:

I told the patient that five minutes after my departure she would break out against her family with some acrimony: what had happened to her dinner? Did they mean to let her starve? How could she feed the baby if she had nothing to eat herself? and so on.

When he returned on the third evening, the patient refused further treatment, saying she had an excellent appetite, plenty of milk for the baby, and had no difficulty in feeding her child. Freud further stated, "I had many opportunities of satisfying myself in a friendly way that (mother and child) were both doing well. I found it hard to understand, however, as well as annoying, that no reference was ever made to my remarkable achievement." (Did Freud also wish to be fed?)

A year later when a third child was born, the patient succumbed to the same postpartum depression and responded again to the same hypnotic psychotherapy. Freud then proceeded to a discussion of the case, which included the observation that the mother behaved as though it was her will not to feed the child on any account. Although the mother wanted to carry out her intentions to nurture the child, she was unaware of the "counter-will," the forerunner of the formulation of unconscious intrapsychic conflict. The case, as Freud described,

… is a typical one and throws light upon a large number of other cases in which breast-feeding or some similar function is prevented by neurotic influences [1893, p. 123].

Here we see Freud's genius at work—his immediate empathy and insight in a classic case of crisis intervention. I do not believe that we can find a better example of the intuitive application of psychoanalytic insight to a psychological crisis situation than Freud's second intervention. This intervention is by no means hypnotic suggestion. In fact, it is a break with the entire tradition of hypnotic suggestion and may be stated to represent an extraordinary early psychoanalytic interpretation. Hypnotic magic has been replaced by psychoanalytic insight. It is as if Freud recognized that hypnotic suggestion and pure wishful denial only increased the resistance and tendency to regression. Disappointed with hypnotic suggestion, he gave the patient an awareness of her inner conflict. She was offered the opportunity to deal with it in an entirely new way, and permission to recognize and express her inner feelings and attitudes. Her inner conflicts were objectionable not only to her but to her entire family and probably to the family doctors.

Freud's interpretation conveyed his awareness of both her wish to feed the baby in accordance with her mature conscious personality inclinations and her unconscious infantile wishes to be fed. He recognized and accepted her anger and indirectly interpreted her oral aggression and regression. In authorizing her to awaken "crying" to be fed, comforted, and cared for, he implicitly identified her envious identification with her infant, her dependent longings, and her rage over her own unsatisfied infantile hunger. Unlike the first hypnotic intervention, and unlike all preceding hypnotic and psychotherapeutic interventions, Freud told the patient, who was in an agitated depression, that she would wake up angry. How did he know that a depressed patient was angry at not being fed? He realized that the patient needed to express the anger in conjunction with her depressive conflicts. He appeared to recognize the presence of universal oral fantasies at the very root of postpartum depression. His seemingly spontaneous understanding of the core conflicts in the situation and his innovative interpretation defy explanation. The case report represents a confluence of Freud's burgeoning insight into the development of the origins of depression and into a very important dimension of female psychology. In addition to the dynamic appreciation of conflict and symptom formation, the genetic principle emerged. The helpless dependence and orality of her newborn have revived the mother's own infantile wishes. Her own needs for nurturance are reactivated under the demands of nurturant motherhood. This mother could accept neither her own infantile demands nor those of her infant. Her (unconscious) rage at her own infant and at her mother, represented by the family, who should feed her was turned on herself. In pursuing and conveying a more insightful understanding of the patient's postpartum problems, Freud again broke with Breuer (the family doctor) who was reluctant to proceed in this direction.

As a lucid example of brief psychotherapy using psychoanalytic insight, Freud's intervention could be a paradigm for similar application of psychoanalytic knowledge. Psychoanalytic psychotherapy applies psychoanalytic understanding in very helpful ways to a wide scope of disturbances and can be geared toward insight or auxiliary ego support. Observations and inferences derived from the psychoanalytic psychotherapy of psychotics, borderlines, etc. have also provided valuable theoretical insights.

Even in brief psychotherapy, a little insight may go a long way. The flicker of illumination in the dark may lead to light at the end of the tunnel. The tenuous insight may be assimilated in a working through in life. In my opinion, psychoanalysis will continue to be the source of scientific psychological treatment, guiding psychotherapy with its unique insights. While differing in process, technique, and goals, psychoanalysis is the foundation of derivative psychotherapy in providing psychoanalytic understanding of both the psychopathology and the psychotherapy.

Summary

Insight is a *sine qua non* of the psychoanalytic process and is a condition, catalyst, and consequence of the psychoanalytic process. Analytic insight is defined and differentiated from other types of self-knowledge and awareness and from pseudo insight; there are different levels and underlying processes in the development of insight. The importance of insight is delineated in theory and therapy, in analyst and patient, and in psychoanalysis and psychotherapy. Psychoanalysis aims to minimize non-insightful influences and to maximize insight leading to structural change. Psychoanalysis is not without a goal, but has the inexorable goal of expanded insight. Clinical limitations to gaining and retaining insight are recognized. Stress is placed on the acquisition and creation of insight and its relation to ego development, analytic progress, and adaptive mastery. Insight and creativity are complementary, and insight has creative and novel configurations. Although it is organized and consolidated in conscious verbalization, insight may proceed outside awareness. An unnoticed case of Freud's provides an example of creative insight. The achievement of insight effects and reflects structural change. Clinical psychoanalysis maximizes insight and minimizes other therapeutic influences.

REFERENCES

Alexander, F., French, T., et al. (1946). *Psychoanalytic Therapy: Principles and Applications*. New York: Ronald Press.

Bibring, E. (1937). On the theory of the results of psycho-analysis. *Int. Rev. Psychoanal.*, 18:170–189.

——— (1954). Psychoanalysis and the dynamic psychotherapies. *J. Am. Psychoanal. Assoc.*, 2:745–770.

Bird, B. (1957). The curse of insight. *Bull. Phila. Assn. Psychoanal.*,7:101–104.

Blum, H. (1976). The changing use of dreams in psychoanalytic practice: Dreams and free association. *Int. J. Psychoanal.*, 57:315–324.

——— (1977). The prototype of preoedipal reconstruction. *JAPA*, 25:757–785.

——— (1978). Reconstruction in a case of postpartum depression. *The Psychoanal. Study Child*, 33:335–362. New Haven: Yale University Press.

Breuer, J. & Freud, S. (1893–1895). Studies on hysteria. *Standard Edition*, 2.

Eissler, K. (1953). The effect of the structure of the ego on psychoanalytic technique. *JAPA*, 1:104–143.

Freud, A. (1957). Foreword to Marion Milner's *on not being able to paint. Writings*, 5:488–492. New York: International Universities Press1969.

——— (1965). *Normality and Pathology in Childhood. Writings*, 6. New York: International Universities Press 1966.

——— (1970). Problems of termination in child analysis. Writings, 7:3–21. New York: International Universities Press 1971.

Freud, S. (1893). A case of successful treatment of hypnotism. *Standard Edition*, 1:116–128.

——— (1900). The interpretation of dreams. *Standard Edition* 4.

——— (1917). Introductory lectures on psycho-analysis, lecture 28. *Standard Edition*, 16:448–463.

——— (1926). Inhibitions, symptoms and anxiety. *Standard Edition*, 20:77–175.

——— (1927). The future of an illusion. *Standard Edition*, 21:3–56.

——— (1933). New introductory lectures on psycho-analysis. *Standard Edition*, 22:3–182.

——— (1937). Analysis terminable and interminable. *Standard Edition*, 23:211–253.

——— (1940). An outline of psycho-analysis. *Standard Edition*, 23:141–207.

Greenson, R. (1967). *The Technique and Practice of Psychoanalysis*. New York: International Universities Press.

Hatcher, R. (1973). Insight and self-observation. *JAPA*, 21:377–398.Ž

Kanzer, M. Blum, H. (1967). Classical psychoanalysis since 1939. In: *Psychoanalytic Techniques*. ed. B. Wolman. New York: Basic Books pp. 93–146.

Kernberg, O. et al. (1972). Psychotherapy and psychoanalysis. Final report of the psychotherapy research project of the Menninger Foundation. *Bull. Mennin. Clinic,*36:12.

Kris, E. (1956). On some vicissitudes of insight in psychoanalysis. In: Selected Papers New Haven: Yale University Press pp. *252–271*.

Kubie, L. (1950). Practical and Theoretical Aspects of Psychoanalysis New York: International Universities Press

Loewald, H. (1979) The waning of the Oedipus complex. *JAPA*, 27(4):751–775.

Loewenstein, R. (1956). Some remarks on the role of speech in psycho-analytic technique. *Int. J. Psychoanal.*, 37:460–468.

Mahler, M, Pine, F., Bergman, A. (1975). The Psychological Birth of the Human Infant New York: Basic Books

Myerson, P. (1960). Awareness and stress: Post psycho-analytic utilization of insight. *Int. J. Psychoanal.*, 41:147–156.

——— (1965). Modes of insight. *JAPA*, 13:771–792.

Noy, P. (1978). Insight and creativity. *JAPA*, 26:717–748.

Pressman, M. (1969). The cognitive function of the ego in psycho-analysis. II, Repression, incognizance, and insight formation. *Int. J. Psychoanal.*, 50:345–351.

Rangell, L. (1975). Psychoanalysis and the process of change: An essay on the past, present, and future. *Int. J. Psychoanal.*, 32:167–177.

Reid, J. Finesinger, J. (1952). The role of insight in psychotherapy. *Amer. J. Psychiat.*,108:726–734.

Richfield, J. (1954). An analysis of the concept of insight. *Psychoanal. Q.*, 23: 390–408.

Sandler, J., Holder, A., Dare, C. (1973). *The Patient and the Analyst.* New York: International Universities Press.

Sterba, R. (1934). The fate of the ego in analytic therapy. *Int. J. Psychoanal.*, 15:117–126.

Stone, L. (1961). The *Psychoanalytic Situation.* New York: International Universities Press.

Valenstein, A. (1962). The psychoanalytic situation: Affects, emotional reliving, and insight in the psychoanalytic process. *Int. J. Psychoanal.*, 43:315–324.

Van Dam, H. Heinicke, C.M., & Shane M. (1975). On termination of child analysis. The *Psychoanal. Study Child*, 30:443–474. New Haven: Yale University Press.

Wallerstein, R. (1965). The goals of psychoanalysis: A survey of analytic viewpoints. *JAPA*, 13:748–770.

Zilboorg, G. (1952). The emotional problem and the therapeutic role of insight. *Psychoanal. Q.*, 21:1–24.

CHAPTER 26

The Position and Value of Extratransference Interpretation

(1983). *J. Amer. Psychoanal. Assn.*, (31):587–617.

Extratransference interpretation in psychoanalysis seems to have been relegated to a psychoanalytic limbo in discussions of the theory and practice of psychoanalysis. The theory of technique has appropriately centered on the transference, and our technical precepts have not, for the most part, explicitly engaged analytic work outside the transference. Numerous panels have been held on the subject of transference and transference neurosis while, to my knowledge, there has been no specific panel discussion of extratransference interpretation. Similarly, in teaching and supervision, the focus is very likely to be on transference and transference resistance, which remain at the heart of psychoanalysis. Little attention is given to distinguishing interventions and interpretive efforts directed outside the orbit of the transference. Books on clinical psychoanalysis and psychoanalytic technique have extensive discussions of transference and transference interpretation but devote scant attention to the special problems of extratransference interpretation. The problems and indications, value and validity of extratransference interpretation have been insufficiently explored.

The nontransference sphere of analytic relationship has received increasing attention over the years, particularly with respect to select areas such as the "real relationship" and the analytic pact (Freud, 1940) and alliance. However, the understanding of the patient's object relations and reality outside the analytic situation is a very complex part of psychoanalysis. External reality is never entirely objective and absolute; it is jointly and gradually defined and redefined by analysts and patients.

The nontransference sphere, like the patient's conscious history, has also been viewed in terms of defense and personal myth. The patient's history and object relations are subject to defensive distortions, fantasy falsifications, and rationalized revisions. Analysts are careful not to be seduced again by the patient's subjective reports of seduction and victimization. After all, we know the patient through the analytic situation. This is the microcosm from which we build models of the patient's present and past. Analysis was first defined by Freud (1914c) in terms of transference and resistance, and nontransference interpretation might have seemed nonanalytic. To not always deal with the transference might seem to be a technical error or counterresistance. Tacitly, nontransference interpretation might seem to be a poor relation and preparatory, subordinate, and supplementary to transference interpretation.

The transference is paradoxically the carrying vehicle and dynamism of the analytic process, while simultaneously a center of resistance. Clinical psychoanalysis depends essentially on the analytic formation and resolution of an artificial treatment illness, the transference neurosis. However, the analytic process deals with the patient's unconscious intrapsychic conflicts and neurotic problems as they manifest themselves anew in the transference neurosis, but also in extratransference phenomena. Derivatives of unconscious conflict (and their interpretation) are not limited to transference. Transference analysis can become exclusive, all-inclusive, and overidealized.

The formulation of the transference neurosis is an ideal construct: "when … the treatment has obtained mastery over the patient … the whole of his illness's new production is concentrated upon a single point—his relation to the doctor… All the patient's symptoms have abandoned their original meaning and have taken on a new sense which lies in relation to the transference; or only such symptoms have persisted as are capable of undergoing such a transformation" (Freud, 1916–1917, p. 444). This ideal construction is quite removed from clinical transference neurosis as it actually appears both alongside and as a transformation of the adult neurosis. Freud abandoned the term "transference neurosis" after 1922, possibly because of the disparity between the ideal construct and the complex nature of transference-neurotic phenomena and continuation of extratransference manifestations of unconscious intrapsychic conflict.

Correlated to the ideal illness of the transference neurosis and preceding the ideal technique of "interpretation only" (Eissler, 1953), Strachey (1934) delineated an ideal interpretation, namely, transference interpretation. For Strachey, the only mutative interpretation was a transference interpretation.

This meant that only transference interpretation could produce authentic analytic insight leading to structural change and new integration of what was hitherto unavailable to the ego because of defense. Certain tendencies toward idealization (and conversely toward denigration of opposite trends) develop within our formulations and models of psychoanalytic technique. The transference (succeeding the dream) became the "royal road" to clinical interpretation. These developments have great value; they represent the distilled experience of analysts who, along with patients, may have gained their greatest conviction about the significance of unconscious conflict in the human condition in their daily work with transference and countertransference.

At this point, however, a number of problems arise. Concepts of the transference neurosis and its link to the present and to the infantile neurosis have changed over the years (Blum, 1971). The nature of the transference as Freud (1937) noted, is determined by the repetition of the past, a "return" of repressed conflicts which are active in the immediate present. Not all conflicts may be expressed in any one transference situation at a given point in the analysis and in the patient's life. Personality structure and intrapsychic conflict may have undergone various developmental transformations. Present events may have special significance, or the present life situation may provide special support or stress which may obscure their full significance from the analyst or which only would be understandable as the contemporary life of the patient is reconstructed in relation to the transference (Kanzer, 1953). This is how we understand the current influence of birth and death, success or failure, the onset of postpartum depression or fate neurosis. The reality changes need not be dramatic, and their relation to unconscious fantasy and danger situations may be very subtle and highly disguised.

535

The manifestations of certain conflicts may appear in transference but may evade analytic understanding based only on transference. Conversely, certain conflicts may be sharply reactivated, as in the case of separation anxiety and depression, during termination of analysis or following a divorce or a death in the family. Relatives may resist or assist the patient's analysis, and familial change may provide secondary gain or mature gratification. Each patient reacts to the significant real events of life in his own particular fashion, based on his total personality, and some ego-syntonic character patterns may remain distant from transference conflict and analysis.

The analytic process reflects the past, repeats the past, and reviews a past that is given new meaning and definition in the present; the transference itself becomes a major vehicle for reconstructing the past. The task of analysis, Freud (1937) stated, is to reconstruct the patient's childhood from its traces, and in analysis we reconstruct a past no longer directly accessible in the immediate present and that never existed in the way it is reconstructed in analysis. We use the technique of extratransference reconstruction to understand the sources and determinants of the transference, to aid in the resolution of the transference, just as we use the transference itself as our main guide to the patient's childhood conflicts and pathogenic patterns. Transference and extratransference interpretation can be complementary and synergistic. In a broad sense, all interpretation involves transference since there is a transference dimension to all analytic process and all analytic data. Without transference attachment, there could be no analytic alliance and acceptance of interpretation.

Transference is omnipresent, and what appears to be extratransference material is nevertheless invested with transference meaning. As with the patient's associations and symptoms, the analyst's interpretations themselves acquire transference meaning. Interpretations may mean feeding, attention, competition with or penetration of the patient. The patient's mode, manner, timing, and content of reported memories and the concomitant feelings themselves are all subject to transference. The transference is probably never missing, only defended against and unrecognized in varying degree.

This position should not be used to obscure what it is meant to clarify. All attitudes and reactions are subject to the principle of multiple function. Transference does not subsume object relations, but current objects are misperceived and reacted to in terms of fantasied infantile object relationships. All relationships are admixtures of the new and the old, of transference and reality. Freud (1914a) illustrated this particular point when he showed the close relation between transference love and actual object love in ordinary life. Indeed, Freud (1926) noted that transference occurs outside the analytic situation and could dominate the whole of a patient's relation to the environment. The transference is obscured in ordinary object relations, but not absent. Extratransference interpretation is not necessarily nontransference, but it does not deal with the transference to the analyst. Extratransference interpretation may include transference to objects other than the analyst, the real relationship to the analyst or other objects, or may refer to the sphere of external reality rather than the psychic reality of transference fantasy. The extratransference sphere is different from but clinically often amalgamated with the acting out, displacement, and splitting of transference outside the analytic situation. The realities of the patient's life and of the analytic situation are of course invested with transference, but they may also influence the transference as well as reality importance. Strictly speaking, transference and reality, past and present, also determine, define, and interpret each other's domain. In addition to concurrent and mutual influences, it is well to consider that all current associations and reactions of the patient are not necessarily primarily transference, that other forms of neurotic repetition coexist with analytic transference, and that transference is not the sole source of analytic insight or locus of analytic work (which includes, e.g., reconstruction of the past).

Analytic patients have some capacity to free-associate. Their associations will, of necessity, include their thoughts, feelings, and fantasies, their interests and activities, so that we will get to know them as people and form a picture of their day-to-day lives as well as their functioning in the analytic situation. Analysis depends not only on free association, but on a capacity to observe, report, test, and adapt to reality, to assimilate interpretation, and other critical ego functions. When patients tell us about their mothers, fathers, and siblings; whether they are married or divorced; the age, number, sex of their children; the basic facts of their family life and work; we expect there to be a certain veridical statement in the framework from which we can begin to detect omissions, distortions, and inconsistencies. These omissions and distortions become part of the work of defense analysis and are eventually seen in connection with the unraveling of the transference resistance. Self and object representations become more coherent, consistent, and realistic. The analyst will point out a variety of contexts in which the patient has denied reality or isolated affect or has been timid and fearful, just as the patient now deals with the analyst. The patient who is dependent on his mother and then his wife may become similarly dependent on the analyst. He wants the analyst to make decisions for him, complains about the frequency of sessions, becomes angry when there are interruptions in treatment. How can such a patient benefit fully from analytic treatment without connecting the dependent transference to the reliance on his wife?

The extratransference interpretation not only drives home transference interpretation, but often the two are organically connected and deal with different manifestations and localizations of the same unconscious conflict constellations. Either form of interpretation may support resistance or analytic progress, or may maintain or violate analytic neutrality. So-called extratransference interpretation should not be a disguised form of transference manipulation of the patient, directive therapy, or judgment of the patient's life and love objects.

Though transference is of inestimable value, analytic technique, as represented in all of Freud's cases, always includes an extratransference dimension. The present and past life, the familial and cultural background, the social setting, developmental phase, and constitutional endowments are all taken into account. To further understand the transference neurosis, to empathize with patients in all the different areas of their psychological problems and conflicts, requires continued attention to the interface between fantasy and reality, past and present, conscious and unconscious, and recall and repression. The adult neurosis is never entirely within the transference;

conflict derivatives and important compromise formations also appear outside the transference. Elements of the transference neurosis may be displaced, split off, or enacted outside the analytic situation, and the blending or condensation of transference and nontransference derivatives may be exceedingly difficult to disentangle.

Analysts are not immune to idealization which historically occurred, for example, in the idealization of dream interpretation and the early conceptualization of the transference neurosis in the analytic process. Strachey's (1934) formulation of the "mutative interpretation" was a very valuable, stimulating, and incisive idealization which was, nevertheless, misleading in its sweeping charismatic absolutism. Although Strachey's influence has been pervasive, it should not and probably has not dominated technical theory and practice. "All transference" analysis with only transference interpretation has probably been more honored in the breach than the observance. It is, in essence, impossible to do analysis purely on the basis of transference without attention to current conflicts and realities and without reconstruction of the past in which the transference is rooted. Transference analysis only is an ideal fiction like the normal ego and would leave the analysis quite isolated from reality, with danger that the reality principle would not be strengthened but, in the long run, undermined. The analysis might be encapsulated without awareness of its severe limitations. Not all patients are able to translate the transference model of their neurosis into their everyday conflicts. Interpretation, as Loewenstein (1957) indicated, usually moves from conflicts expressed in relation to the analyst, to an understanding of conflicts and symptoms in current life, to their derivation from the infantile neurosis. Freud (1905) understood Dora's unconscious identifications in her hysterical symptoms of aphonia and tussis nervosa and her own seduction and collusion with her parents and the K.'s. Transference could not be fully understood without elucidation of the whole network of shared fantasies and activities and inferences about her object relations and identifications. Dora's "real" life situation became clear concurrent with the discovery of transference and its genetic sources. Freud later scrutinized the influence of the analyst's own conflicts and interventions on the analytic process, so evident now from the

Dora case in his early, rapid interpretation and his prior treatment of Dora's father.

I shall return to the realities of the analytic situation and to the activation and validation, gratification or frustration, clarification or contamination of transference fantasies at a later point. Here I want to emphasize that transference conflicts and fantasies can never be isolated or segregated entirely from other realities and from conflict expression that is not primarily transference.

Strachey's extreme position on "the mutative interpretation" was not directly challenged at the time. Strachey was influenced by the prevailing technical approach of his day, but in his only and major contribution to the psychoanalytic literature he left an enduring influence in an essay which has become a classic. Strachey's views were certainly derived from Freud's early statement that the struggle between doctor and patient is waged in the transference and that "It is on that field that the victory must be won... For when all is said and done, it is impossible to destroy anyone *in absentia* or in *effigie*" (Freud, 1912, p. 108). However, in the very same paragraph, what often goes unnoticed is Freud's attention to the entire psychic field and to considerations that utilized the transference and went beyond it. Freud noted that although the patient regarded the products of "the awakening of his unconscious impulses as contemporaneous and real... The doctor tries to compel him to fit these emotional impulses into the nexus of the treatment and of his life-history..." (p. 108). Freud (1914b, p. 152) called attention to the importance of the patient coming to grips with his illness so that it is not denied or despised, and so that its true importance for his life can be assayed. It was in connection with the phenomena of illness to which the patient must attend (rather than deny) that he then stated: "one cannot overcome an enemy who is absent." His recommendations included construction of the conditions under which symptoms such as a phobia were precipitated in life. He advised mastery of phobia in the life situation as part of the final process of working through. Rather than relying solely on the transference, Freud suggested that unless the patient confronts the phobic situation in life, "He will never ... bring into the analysis the material indispensable for a convincing resolution of the phobia" (Freud, 1919, pp. 165-166). Surveying the nature of analytic work long after the publication of the technical papers, Freud (1937) referred to the significant material the patient puts at the analyst's disposal, and he included "hints of repetitions of … the repressed material to be found in actions performed by the patient … both inside and outside the analytic situation" (p. 258). "The analyst … has at his disposal material which can have no counterpart in excavations, such as the repetitions of reactions dating from infancy and all that is indicated by the transference in connection with these repetitions" (p. 259). These remarks appeared after Strachey's paper, and Strachey's position was not affirmed by Freud (who particularly emphasized the importance of reconstruction).

In psychoanalysis, the transference has the indispensable value of being immediate and manifest, of what we today call "the here-and-now." Transference interpretation by the object of transference strips transference illusion from that object (Stone, 1967) and separates the infantile from current object in a permissive, meaningful experience (cf. Strachey, 1934). In psychoanalysis, the here-and-now distortions of the doctor-patient relationship, the regressive personality alterations and symptoms, need to be linked to related patterns in life and traced to their childhood roots by a circuitous route which takes into account developmental changes in both the neurotic and healthy portions of the patient's personality. Genetic interpretation and reconstruction restore and establish connections between past and present, concurrent with finding new solutions to hitherto unresolved infantile pathogenic conflicts. A purely here-and-now approach would become a form of "new encounter," an existential or experiential psychotherapy. This approach would not permit full contact with the childish fantasies and feelings which continue to excessively influence or even dominate the patient's reactions, as in transference. The childhood origin and childish character of transference would remain unexplained (Blum, 1980).

Analysis of the patient's central conflicts may be furthered by extratransference interpretation. Not everything in analysis is transference, and the transference is not always the most salient point of interpretation (Leites,

1977). This point of view was actually espoused by Stone (1961), who stated that although the most effective interpretations would be related to transference conflicts, "… interpretations other than those directly and demonstrably impinging on the transference can be significant and effective" (p. 141n.). Stone (1967) later remarked, "the extra-analytic life of the patient often provides indispensable data for the understanding of detailed complexities of his psychic functioning, because of the sheer variety of its references, some of which cannot be reproduced in the relationship to the analyst … extratransference interpretations cannot be set aside or underestimated in importance" (pp. 34–35). The subtle and multiform expressions of the total personality are not always reproduced in the transference and may be altered in the transference regression. Nontransference observations may enlarge and correct analytic transference perspectives.

Brenner (1976, p. 128) also recognized the appropriate use of extratransference interpretation. He observed, "It seems unlikely that it is either correct or useful to take the extreme position that Strachey advocated." He went on to state, "Transference should be neither ignored nor focused on to the exclusion of all else; it should be neither excluded from the analytic work nor dragged in by the heels… Its influence often is greater even than one assumed it to be… Nevertheless, it remains but one factor among many in any analytic situation. An analyst has always the task of deciding as best he can from the available evidence which factors are the most important at a particular time in the analysis. If his conjecture … is that something other than transference is most important at the moment, he will interpret whatever the 'something other' may be" (p. 128). I would emphasize the importance of the appropriate "surface" area of interpretation, not including all material as transference or excluding nontransference considerations.

A "pure transference" position in analytic work will lead to distortions of analytic process and explanation. Such a position of only valuing transference interpretation will tend to become "all transference" and mold or artificially force all material into the transference, leading to inappropriate, excessive transference interpretation. Surveying contemporary issues in the theory of therapy, Rangell (1979) called attention to the fact that transference analysis, though indispensable, has also been overdone. "The analysis of transference over a period of some years and prominently today, is often allowed to obscure all other important and necessary elements of the analytic process. A good thing has become hypertrophied and the source of complications" (p. 84). Rangell noted the era of the transference becoming the end rather than the means, with the result that antecedents and genetic roots not only are out of reach but regarded as unnecessary or of ancillary importance. Rangell referred to Fenichel's earlier position that transference and extratransference analysis both go on and are necessary, and that patients may comply with what Fenichel called a monomania of the analyst where an exclusive focus of interpretations is utilized for defensive purposes.

Leites (1977) reviewed the literature on "transference interpretations" only, and noted that many authors were critical of such an extreme position but that their objections took the form of very concise, constricted, and inhibited commentary. Anna Freud (1965, p. 37) noted the exclusive role given to the transference as one of the subjects of controversy in psychoanalysis, warning against the analyst's overinvolvement with the transference. Her statement of the controversy was not taken up by her or other authors in relation to her work on defense analysis. In relation to defense, "transference only" may foster isolation of analysis from life, denial of areas of reality, and continuation of infantile amnesia.

Gray (1973) described the analyst's intrapsychic perspective, the need for continual scrutiny of the patient's psychic reality, and the roles in which the events and experiences the patient reports are given unconscious meaning, in the immediacy of the analytic situation. Excessive concern with reality, traditional in the obsessional preoccupation with trivial and insignificant details of life, is a defensive function and may disguise underlying transference fantasies. Put another way, the day residue is a point of attachment for the latent content of the dream, and excessive attention to the day residue may diminish appreciation of the latent unconscious childhood conflicts. Manifest dream and transference fantasy are compromise formations that disguise the return of the repressed past. Gray, I believe, would give transference priority to other considerations; he recommends an analytic focus "to observe data limited essentially to inside the analytic situation" (p. 492). However, this is not necessarily a priority to working from the surface since the surface and "point of urgency" (Strachey, 1934) are not always transference. The "point of urgency" may be denial of current illness or failure, genetic interpretation of denial of a parent's alcoholism, reconstruction of a parent's psychosis and the patient's identification with the psychotic parent, etc.

Psychoanalytic technique has not abandoned the goal of lifting infantile amnesia and recovering childhood memories (Kris, 1956). The memories often turn out to be screen memories, and the discrete memories in themselves are of less importance than the transference patterns in which they become imbricated. Nonetheless, as in overeating, there can be too much of a good thing; and an exclusive preoccupation with the transference and analytic relationship may actually lead to the omission of significant material or connections from the patient's life that will diminish and distort rather than enrich and deepen the analysis.

Not all conflicts are represented solely, wholly, or primarily at any one point in the transference; and the transference representation may be diminished in intensity and fragmented when one of the important parts of the configuration is lived out. The living out (or acting out) of fantasies may have occurred before the analysis with the pattern continuing and gradually acquiring transference meaning only as the analysis takes effect. Insight may be gained and consolidated in shared analytic work on extratransference issues, such as the patient's reactions not only to the analyst, but to his spouse and children. Consider a female analysand with a persistent central fantasy of performing fellatio on the analyst, a fantasy linked to a childhood seduction experience and to unconscious incestuous conflicts (Dewald, 1972). This patient was also a new mother, caring for a neonate who barely appears in the associations. The transference paradigm of seduction is also a transference resistance against other very important transference and extratransference considerations. The baby who is conspicuously absent probably is partially represented via identification and replacement in the mother's oral demands in the transference. The fantasy replaces the realities of nurturant motherhood, the demands of her own infant, the patient's need to be nurtured in order to be nurturant. New motherhood has revived the mother's own oral-maternal conflicts and has altered familial relationships and psychic equilibrium. That her associations do not include the emotional investment in her infant, reactions to the baby's sex, appearance, temperament, etc., whether mother and child are doing well, or are up all night, even whether the baby was wanted by both parents, leaves such crucial issues conspicuous by their absence. The transference cannot be understood without knowledge of the nontransference reality spheres and their transference implications. Both transference and extratransference interpretation of her maternal conflicts, envy of and identification with her infant, etc., would be necessary and complementary. Extratransference interpretation could focus directly on her ambivalent attitudes and feelings toward her infant (rather than only on the transference to the analyst), loosening defenses against the unconscious dangers associated with mothering and furthering analytic work and understanding of the patient's conflicts.

Childhood patterns of collusive denial and avoidance of reality tend to be continued in later life. It is necessary to interpret the collusion as a defense as well as a hidden gratification, and the anxiety and guilt associated with a conspiracy of silence. Such collusion may be unwittingly repeated in the analytic situation. In analysis there is a continuous reciprocal understanding of the transference and resistance, current extratransference influences and manifestations of neurotic patterns, and reconstruction of the past. The study of neurotic patterns and of character traits in the transference and in life is an important arena of analytic clarification and of complementary types of interpretation. A patient's pattern of passivity and impotence in life, leading to psychoanalysis, will be related to blocking in free association, fear of transference regression, and eventually to the underlying intrapsychic conflicts related to both the passive character and sexual symptom. Some of the extratransference interpretations may be regarded as confirmations and extensions of the transference; other extratransference interventions are preparatory steps which culminate in a transference interpretation; and extratransference interpretation may be necessary and valuable in its own effect on the analytic process. The transference interpretation may usually be our most valuable tool, but it is supplemented, complemented, and regularly used in conjunction with other technical agents, and with the here-and-now of the patient's life and continuing childish reactions.

It is true that attention away from the transference may serve resistance, but exclusive transference interpretation will also serve resistance. Nontransference interpretation may pave the way for analyzing resistance and for conviction about the meaning of symptoms, e.g., predisposition, precipitation, anniversary reactions, etc., before and during analysis (Arlow, 1963). A patient's sleep disturbance and depression were precipitated by the anniversary of his father's death. These problems can be correlated with his denial and fetishistic use of pornography, his fears of death and concern for the analyst's health, his need to expiate his guilt by an act of charity while demanding immediate restitution and reparation for loss through fiscal manipulation.

Extratransference interpretation also concerns the repression of real traumatic experience so often seen in anniversary reactions. Traumatic experience tends to be repeated not only in transference, but in dreams, screen memories, symptoms, and neurotic behavior. The anniversary reactions precede analysis and continue during analysis. We are concerned with the patient's intrapsychic experience, the coordination between fantasy and reality, and the effects of the patient's adult and infantile traumata on conflict, structure, and subsequent development. Each patient defends and adapts in his own way. Some patients who abuse, overstimulate, and seduce their children are repeating the aggressive and sexual abuse they experienced with their own parents. These patterns appear in the transference, and the patient may attempt to use the transference in terms of active mastery of the passively experienced childhood traumata. Nonetheless, the behavior of parents (in analysis) with their children is inundated with meaning and has also to be seen in terms of the meaning, not only of the analyst, but of the child for that particular parent. The past is repeated with their own children before and during the analysis. Of course, the analyst cannot represent all transference figures at any one time and represents more than one object because of condensation and overdetermination. The analyst might represent a parent and the child, an ambivalently loved sibling. The adult parent patient has to see the relation between the transference manifestations during the analysis and the repetitive patterns which have gone on during his own childhood and which are now continued in derivative form with his own children. Sometimes what appears to be a revival of infantile object relations in the transference may not be a simple revival at all. Pathological familial patterns may have been continued throughout life with provocations and seductions going on during family contacts and visits, telephone calls, etc.

If a crucial part of a pathological constellation is acted out, the complete pattern may not be available for analysis. A patient may be defensively masochistic in analysis and a sadistic tyrant at home. Moreover, certain forms of acting out may have serious consequences and sequelae as in the accident-prone patient. With an accident-prone patient, the analyst must understand the form and content of the prior and repeated accidents, what is enacted outside rather than recalled and verbalized in the analytic situation, and the relation between unconscious fantasies of transgression and actual self-punishment. The primal scene may be evoked by transference revival, but may also be stimulated by visits of parents or children, overnight guests, dances, analytic lectures, and publications.

In training analysis, for example, real contacts with the analyst and information about the analyst from the analytic scene in which both analyst and analysand are immersed lead to activation, reinforcement, contamination, and diffusion of certain transference fantasies. The metaphor of the training analysis being conducted in a goldfish bowl applies to the *entire* range of interplay between fantasy and reality and the necessity to ferret out the grains of truth around which transference fantasies (like delusions) tend to crystallize. Reality, transference, and countertransference have to be differentiated in the analysis and professional life of a candidate with recognition that the training analyst may be a real authority for a candidate. The analytic situation is influenced by the complexities of institutionalization, e.g., extra-analytic contact and information; the process of selection, progression, and supervision; the goal of graduation, etc., and these factors all have transference repercussions. Additionally, the negative transference in training analysis may be less available than extratransference hostility. The candidate's countertransference problems to his own patients are not simply reflections of his transference to his training analyst, but are additional areas of analytic work and potential insight.

What about those times where the transference may be superseded in significance at a given moment by attention to extratransference material? Again, it is not a matter of either transference or extratransference, that is, of either-or, but of balance and of what seems to be the optimal choice. The patient's material is always overdetermined, subject to the principle of multiple function, and there is often a layering of potential interpretations with no easy solutions and no simple technical choices. Consider a mother who manages to be provocative, with behavior inappropriate to her children's needs. Her conscious devotion expresses her love, but it is also a reaction formation occasionally breached by her sadistic impulses. She reported that her child was getting out of the car, when she had failed to bring the car to a full stop. The analyst interpreted this mother's murderous conflicts involving her child, an interpretation that had a very favorable effect on the course of the analysis. Notice that the analyst did not say to the patient that the patient wanted to kill the analyst or that the patient wanted the analyst to throw her out of treatment prematurely, or that the patient was identified with the child and wished to leave impulsively before the hour was over, or any number of other possible transference interpretations. What was meaningful to the patient at this particular moment was in the area of the parent-child relationship. This could then be related to the transference and to the genetic determinants which led to such neurotic attitudes and behavior inside and outside the analysis.[11]

An analysis of this patient's superego would also entail a study of the patient's identifications. Any attempt to understand a patient's superego structure and function will require investigation of the genetic origins of the superego. Superego regression and progression can be clearly seen in dreams and transference, but the understanding also depends on reconstruction of the patient's infantile object relations and crucial identifications with his objects.

Another possible effect of failure of analytic attention to both the patient's current and past experience is to have the analysis in isolation from all else. The

---

1   I am indebted to Dr. Jacob A. Arlow for this clinical illustration.

analysis is in danger of becoming an empty ritual, an artificial dramatization, or a narcissistic system, the particular configuration depending on the dominant transference.

Lampl-de Groot (1976) commented that extreme devotion to analytic transference interpretation could support hidden analytic grandiosity. The analyst could seriously overestimate his importance to the patient. If the analyst pays no attention to reality and to the patient's extratransference relations, the implication is that only the analyst, the analytic process, and the patient as analysand are of importance. Analysis is aggrandized and external life belittled. Analysis could unwittingly become a *Folie à deux*. A. Freud (1965) observed that the adult analyst may overemphasize psychic as opposed to external reality. She stated, "If anything he is too eager to see during his therapeutic work all current happenings in terms of transference and of resistance, and thereby to discount their value in reality" (p. 50). It is of historical significance that Fenichel (1942) had noted, "But the patient's life does not consist in transference alone, and often the analyst's resistance is shown in his neglect of the patient's life outside the transference. The patient who responded to a transference interpretation with the words, 'But doctor, you are conceited—everything I say you refer to yourself only!' sometimes may be correct" (p. 31).[2]

The patient's external life is not simply displaced or extended transference. The invaluable formation of the transference neurosis still leaves aspects of character, symptoms, and action not then available in transference in the same form or intensity. Neither the neurosis nor the healthy personality may be completely expressed in the transference in the analytic situation.

Exclusive focus on transference with a tendency to belittle external life is an analytic position communicated to the patient. This may have subtle effects on free association; the compliant patient may produce profuse transference fantasies, like the patient who provides dreams for the analyst who especially favors and savors dream work. This is a special form of transference resistance which may also be related to flight into fantasy. Some borderline patients may

---

2 I am indebted to Dr. Eugene Halpert for this citation.

too readily regress into archaic transference fantasy, and may derive excessive gratification from the analysis compared to their meager gratifications in life. Such patients may attempt to use the analysis to defend against reality disappointments and injuries.

Still another problem engendered by the isolation of analysis from external reality concerns the working through of conflicts in life. This occurs in conjunction with working through in analysis and in the wider application of analytic insight in life during and after analysis. I have already alluded to Freud's comments about the necessity of working through phobia in life; similar considerations apply to other symptoms and character disorder. The working through of the denial of a parent's psychosis or alcoholism, the need to see a spouse as distant and unloving in order to defend against incestuously tinged cravings for love, lead to the appreciation of object relations in a more rational and mature perspective. The analytic picture of the patient's life newly being constructed, which transforms the personal and familial mythical distortions (Kris, 1956), emerges from the transference analysis, but also from extratransference illustrations which show the patient what is being repeated, how it is a repetition, and what elements of the pattern are not repeated but have been developmentally transformed. Neurotic patterns have often undergone transformations during development. Early separation anxiety, for example, may be manifest in an infantile sleep disturbance, a childhood travel phobia, adult insomnia and fears of death. Patients can then apply insight to their life, and psychologically minded patients will begin to show greater awareness, empathy, and even insight in their personal and familial relationships. Patients should understand their adaptation to the various facets of life. As parents, they should gain insight into neurotic reactions with each other and their children. As patients, their appreciation of the real qualities of the analyst should grow so that at termination the real or nontransference relationship is relatively undistorted by transference-neurotic fantasy (E. Ticho, 1972).

An important by-product of analysis is not only more successful but more insightful adaptation to life. One patient brought increasingly clear derivatives of primal-scene fantasy and experience into the analysis. She was very shy, socially and sexually inhibited, had rather puritanical attitudes toward life with an emphasis on decorum and propriety in dress, speech, manner, and behavior. She was defending herself against primal-scene excitement and experience extending through her childhood. Her curiosity was inhibited, she was afraid to explore, and was in constant danger of being seen in and outside the analysis as exposed. Dreams and transference fantasies of erotic nudity in the analysis, the public library, the concert hall, etc., emerged with associated shame and guilt. Her interest in clothes and what was underneath clothes appeared with increasing clarity. The patient then began to discuss how she had dressed her children and the mode of dress and undress within the family. She would want the children, particularly her daughters, to be nicely and neatly dressed and to stand, sit, and carry themselves like ladies. These values did not apply in the same way to her husband, whose own style was what he considered to be relaxed informality at home. He was fond of going into his daughters' room in his underwear, inviting the children into the bedroom when they were partially undressed or in night clothes, and still later, we learned that her husband insisted on keeping the door to the parental bedroom open at night. As the analysis progressed, her husband's behavior led to serious marital discord. He resented her imposing her values on him, unfairly interfering with his lifestyle, and he resented her analysis.

The patient began to understand the implications of the seduction of her own children by their parents in which she was a passive participant. She unconsciously assigned responsibility and guilt to her husband. The primal scene was continued from the past into the present and was actually being enacted in her adult life before and during her analysis. As her own incestuous attachments were clarified, she understood her husband's behavior in an entirely new way and attempted to shift the whole family interaction to what she considered to be a constructive direction. She was able to use the analytic work to show her husband that his discussion of the sexual abuse of patients by dentists and doctors was connected to an unrecognized abuse of his children. Having tried to insist that the door be open during their nocturnal sexual relations, he had, the next day, exploded at their daughter for having gone out of the house into the cold without a coat. She came to understand that he attempted to make the daughter feel guilty about exposure rather than himself, choosing to present himself as offering guidance and concern rather than abuse and exploitation. The mother's resources and strength in being able to confront these conflicts had positive effects on her children's development, and in the long run upon her husband's functioning as well. Interpretations have multiple appeal which extends beyond the transference situation and personality reorganization to the wider spheres of life. Such effects can be detrimental if extratransference interpretation is abused by patients who then engage in wild analysis of family and friends. Patients may evade self-scrutiny by shifting analytic inquiry to the unconscious motivation of others (Greenacre, 1959). Authentic understanding and insight tend to be applied in life as beneficial intrafamilial influences rather than in the service of regression or provocation.

A pure transference position tends to treat extratransference relations as those "objectionable others" (Anthony, 1980) who figure so importantly in our patients' lives in adult and child analysis. It would be interesting to know if child analysts are more comfortable, more at ease with extratransference interpretations and if this technical position complements or competes with essential analysis of the transference. Child analysis has helped to elucidate different dimensions of the analytic relationship and to understand the child in his own developmental phase as well as in his family, social, and cultural setting. Current conflicts are introduced into the analytic situation just as revived unconscious conflicts tend to be reenacted with the original objects at home. Past and present meet and interact in the interpretation of transference and in reconstruction. Within the zone of interaction, there is a redefinition of the past as presently understood and of the present shadowed and shaped by the living past. The past may be used as a defense against the present and the present may be used as a defense against the past (Kris, 1956).

The relationship of transference to the realities of the analytic situation is significant and of particular contemporary interest. The patient reacts to all features, cues, and communications in the analytic situation and process. I refer here to the realities of the analytic situation and the real attributes, style, and function as well as possible malfunction of the analyst (Blum, 1971). This includes the analyst's age, sex, character, attitude, silence, and the whole range of accurate, inexact, and erroneous interpretations. There are scattered references to these issues in the literature. Greenson (1972) explored the nontransference relationship and pointed to the patient's realistic perception of the analyst's style, taste, temperament, and technique. He offered suggestions about the mutual recognition and management of the analyst's technical errors. This is no place to explore, in depth, Greenson's challenging, controversial formulations, but I do not believe that the issues are beyond interpretation. They are beyond pure transference interpretation.

The analyst is a participant observer and not a pure receiving and reflecting mirror. There are transference reactions to his real personality and his unconscious cues and his interventions which should be understood. Gill (1979), giving early and top priority to transference interpretation, emphasizes the "analytic situation residue" as a current stimulus for transference. The analyst's real behavior might make the irrational transference seem plausible, and this should also apply to premature and exclusive transference interpretation. To my mind, if the "analytic situation residue" were truly plausible, it would tend to obscure, contaminate, or validate the transference. Transference repetition of the past would remain confused with the present. Reality inside and outside the analytic situation may provide an important anchor, a "grain of truth," for transference fantasy. Clinic analysis, supervision, insurance payment, etc., all tend to activate or lend reality to transference fantasy and transference gratifications. The patient consciously and unconsciously perceives the analytic situation realities—which are not transference distortions. These realities may influence the transference and its full analysis. In contrast to transference displacement, these realities may be displaced so that the patient's distortions of other objects may contain accurate referents to the analyst.

These current or "day residue" influences on the activation of the transference are not restricted to analytic situation residues (nor do such residues "explain" transference fantasy or repetition). They can be compared to a dream "from above" (Freud, 1923) where the dream is interpreted with the link between the current stimulus and its reinforcement from the unconscious latent content. In analysis, the current stimulus may or may not be of great significance, but the transference issues are always significant (Stone, 1981). The transference, however, is not in its core externally or iatrogenically determined, and the patient is responsible for his transference as for his neurosis.

The realities of the analytic situation cannot be "analyzed away," but the linked transference meanings and reactions, rooted in the past, should be ascertained insofar as possible. The transference meanings will be shown to be childish and ultimately reduced to their genetic origins. The effects of countertransference —parameters, errors, supervision—will be present, but may not be fully analyzable. The realities of the analytic situation should not be denied or overlooked in their possible influence on the analytic process. Not all that a patient thinks or feels about his analyst or analysis is due to transference (Heimann, 1950).

It does make a difference if the analyst is anxious or angry, humorous or serious. If the analyst tends to be caustic and critical, the patient's fears of disapproval and punishment in the transference cannot be analyzed in depth without recognition of the reality which tends to validate the transference fantasy. The transference may be obscured or "contaminated." The patient's fears of disapproval, criticism, punishment, insofar as they are transference, stem from the past and from his own superego. Each patient reacts to the same analyst in his own way. A sadomasochistic patient might enjoy the opportunity for battle; a guilty patient might exploit the analytic situation for self-punitive purposes.

Reciprocal provocations inside the analytic situation may promote acting out. Some analysts may instigate, encourage, or enjoy the patient's acting-out tendencies. If an analyst forgets to unlock the waiting-room door, leaving the patient locked out of a session, we are not surprised to hear, in the next session, about an insolent waiter who kept the patient waiting for the meal and provided terrible service. The patient vowed never to return to the restaurant but returned to the analytic session, without any direct reference to the lockout. The patient was afraid of her intense disappointment and rage and could not discuss her thoughts of quitting or her fears of being thrown out by the analyst. A different patient might not have so defended her own feelings toward the analyst and might have reacted with overt outrage; yet another patient might have reacted with glee over the analyst's fallibility. This masochistically provocative patient elicited a sadomasochistic countertransference. The patient's final quitting of treatment was overdetermined, but it included an element of acting out of the countertransference fantasy, like a child who tends to act out the unconscious fantasies of the parents. A malignant cycle of unresolved transference-countertransference issues may supervene with mutual negative feedback. The hypercritical analysand may fear, invite, and finally incite analytic criticism. Efforts at mastery of these complicated problems are immeasurably assisted by their clarification and insightful interpretation (Kanzer, 1953); (Brenner, 1976). This requires an understanding of the entire psychic field, including the "reality" inside and outside the analytic situation.

The problem of the analyst who abuses interpretation for shock effect or to compete, criticize, erotize, etc., is not resolved by compounding problems with parameters. The analytic solution is still one of interpretation which has to include the countertransference. We may distinguish here among the analyst's protracted countertransference, e.g., critical of a particular patient; countertransference at a particular point, as in response to a patient's criticism; and the analyst's character, e.g., a generally exacting, critical attitude with all patients. The countertransference belongs to the nontransference sphere and, though they interact, should not be confused with the transference. The transference cannot be analyzed through the countertransference any more than self-analysis can substitute for analysis of the patient.

That the countertransference may be constructively analyzed and utilized for the benefit of both the analyst and the patient (Heimann, 1950); (Kernberg, 1965) does not mean that countertransference will not have its own transference consequences. The patient's unconscious response to the countertransference is likely to be missed (Little, 1951). A particular countertransference may obscure, resist, or reinforce certain transference constellations, may provide hidden transference gratifications, and may elicit certain transference reactions. The analyst should be able to recognize his own contribution to the patient's particular transference response; it is now readily noted in case of a change in fee, time, or office situation. Patient and analyst are likely to have exquisitely sensitive transference-countertransference reactions to the analyst's illness (Dewald, 1982), injury, bereavement, etc.

Analytic problems cannot be solved by a blurring of boundaries between psychic and external reality, between transference and nontransference reactions of analyst and patient. In this connection, A. Freud (1954) noted that analyst and patient are of equal adult status in a real personal relationship, and that neglect of this reality may be responsible for hostile reactions from patients which are ascribed only to transference. Reality is usually invoked to avoid recognition of transference, but transference can also be used to evade reality. The sleeping analyst of the sardonic joke, awakened, attributes the patient's negative transference and indignation to the patient's narcissistic need for constant attention.

Compared to countertransference, little has been said about the patient's unconscious response to the analyst's personality. It would be helpful for both analyst and patient to delineate the more subtle transference response to an analyst's ego-syntonic character trends, e.g., his precision of speech and the careful arrangement of his desk and office decor, or tendencies to be sarcastic or witty. The analyst's character and style, his own variations within correct analytic technique, are often overlooked as influencing the analytic process or treated as part of the analytic frame or atmosphere. Because of differences, however subtle, in the patient's reactions to the analyst's age and sex, character, style, and temperament (Blum, 1971), each analytic "match" could influence the analytic process. It might make a difference if the analyst is an ordinary clinician or an authority, married or divorced, parent or childless. The patient will react to the candidate's supervision, or to the status of the senior analyst, with fear of murderous aggression against the latter. Analysts could treat a wide range of patients with similar but not necessarily identical findings and results.

Strachey (1934), toward the end of his paper, tended to retreat from and correct his rather extreme position. He noted that by giving extratransference interpretations the analyst might prepare for a "mutative interpretation." His concluding comments concerning extratransference interpretation are surprisingly little known: "It must not be supposed that because I am attributing these special qualities to transference interpretation I am, therefore, maintaining that no others should be made. On the contrary, it is possible that a large majority of our interpretations are outside the transference—though it should be added that it often happens that when one is ostensibly given extratransference interpretation one is implicitly given a transference one. A cake cannot be made of nothing but currants; and, though it is true that extratransference interpretations are not for the most part mutative, and do not themselves bring about the crucial result … they are nonetheless essential. If I may take an analogy from trench warfare, the acceptance of the transference interpretation corresponds to the capture of a key position, while extratransference interpretation corresponds to the general advance… An oscillation of this kind between transference and extratransference interpretations will represent the normal course of events in analysis" (p. 125).

What is analytically indicated is a consistent analytic attitude with a balanced, holistic process of interpretation. Transference analysis is central and essential, but extratransference interpretation, including genetic interpretation and reconstruction, is also necessary and complementary. Reconstruction of the past and transference analysis in the "here-and-now" are mutually explanatory, circular, and synergistic. Analysis progresses beyond interpretation of transference distortions of the doctor-patient relationship and requires genetic interpretation to fully differentiate transference and reality, past and present, as Freud (1940) indicated, to show the patient "… again and again that what he takes to be new real life is a reflection of the past" (p. 177). Extratransference interpretation is not reducible to resistance, to transference, or a poor relation of and replacement for transference interpretation.

I conclude there is no royal road to analytic interpretation. The transference is the main road but not the only road to mutative interpretation, and we do not analyze just transference or dreams, we analyze the patient.

Summary

The role of extratransference interpretation in the theory of technique has been insufficiently defined and only tangentially discussed. Extratransference interpretation refers to interpretation that is relatively outside the analytic transference relationship. Although interpretive resolution of the transference neurosis is the central area of analytic work, transference is not the sole or whole focus of interpretation, or the only effective "mutative" interpretation, or always the most significant interpretation. Extratransference interpretation has a position and value which is not simply ancillary, preparatory, and supplementary to transference interpretation. Transference analysis is essential, but extratransference interpretation, including genetic interpretation and reconstruction, is also necessary, complementary, and synergistic. Transference is a repetition that requires analysis of its genetic sources in childhood conflict and fixation. Transference and reality, past and present, are newly defined, understood, and integrated in the analytic process.

Transference fantasy cannot be clarified without understanding the "grains of truth" to which it may be anchored in reality inside and outside the analytic situation. The analyst's real attitudes and attributes may influence the transference and transference analysis. Countertransference also tends to evoke transference reactions which are unique to each patient, so that there are contributions from both parties to the analytic process and the analytic data. Analytic understanding should encompass the overlapping transference and extratransference spheres, fantasy and reality, past and present. A "transference only" position is theoretically untenable and could lead to an artificial reduction of all associations and interpretations into a transference mold and to an idealized *Folie à deux*.

REFERENCES

Anthony, E.J. (1980). The family and the psychoanalytic process in children *Psychoanal. Study Child* 35:3–34.

Arlow, J.A. (1963). Conflict regression and symptom formation *Int. J. Psychoanal.* 44:12–22.

Blum, H.P. (1971). On the conception and development of the transference neurosis *J. Am. Psychoanal. Assoc.* 19:41–53.

———— (1980). The value of reconstruction in adult psychoanalysis *Int. J. Psychoanal.*61:39–52.

Brenner, C. (1976). Psychoanalytic Technique and Psychic Conflict New York: Int. Univ. Press.

Dewald, P. (1972). *The Psychoanalytic Process*. New York: Basic Books.

———— (1982). Serious illness in the analyst: transference, countertransference, and reality responses *J. Am. Psychoanal. Assoc.* 30:347–363.

Eissler K.R. (1953). The effect of the structure of the ego on psychoanalytic technique *J. Am. Psychoanal. Assoc.* 1:104–143.

Fenichel O. (1942). Theoretical implications of the didactic analysis *Annual Psychoanal.* 8:21–35, 1980.

Freud, A. (1954). The widening scope of indications for psychoanalysis: discussion *J. Am. Psychoanal. Assoc.* 2:607–620.

———— (1965). Normality and Pathology in Childhood: Assessments of Development. *Writings* 6 New York: Int. Univ. Press.

Freud, S. 1905 Fragment of an analysis of a case of hysteria *S.E.* 7.

———— (1912). The dynamics of transference *S.E.* 12.

———— (1914a). Observations on transference love *S.E.* 12

———— (1914b) Remembering, repeating and working-through *S.E.* 12

———— (1914c). On the history of the psychoanalytic movement *S.E.* 14

———— (1916–1917). Introductory lectures on psychoanalysis *S.E.* 15 & 16.

———— (1919). Lines of advance in psychoanalytic therapy *S.E.* 17.

———— (1923). Remarks on the theory and practice of dream-interpretation *S.E.* 19.

———— (1926). An autobiographical study *S.E.* 20.

———— (1937). Constructions in analysis *S.E.* 23.

———— (1940). An outline of psychoanalysis *S.E.* 23.

Gill, M. (1979). The analysis of the transference *J. Am. Psychoanal. Assoc.* 27 (Suppl.): 263–288.

Gray P. (1973). Psychoanalytic technique and the ego's capacity for viewing intrapsychic activity *J. Am. Psychoanal. Assoc.* 21:474–494.

Greenacre P. (1959). Certain technical problems in the transference relationship *J. Am. Psychoanal Assoc.* 7:484–502.

Greenson, R.R. (1972). Beyond transference interpretation *Int. J. Psychoanal* 53:213–217.

Heimann, P. (1950). On counter-transference *Int. J. Psychoanal.* 31:81–84.

Kanzer, M. (1953). Past and present in the transference *J. Am. Psychoanal Assoc.* 1:144–154.

Kernberg, O. (1965) Notes on countertransference *J. Am. Psychoanal. Assoc.* 13: 38–56.

Kris, E. (1956). The recovery of childhood memories in psychoanalysis *Psychoanal Study Child* 11:54–88.

Lampl-de Groot, J. (1976). Personal experience with psychoanalytic technique and theory during the last half-century *Psychoanal. Study Child* 31:*283–296.*

Leites, N. (1977). Transference interpretation only *Int. J. Psychoanal* 58:275–287.

Little, M. 1951 Counter-transference and the patient's response to it *Int. J. Psychoanal.* 32:32–40.

Loewenstein, R.M. 1957 Some thoughts on interpretation in the theory and practice of psychoanalysis *Psychoanal. Study Child* 12:127–150.

Rangell, L. (1979). Contemporary issues in the theory of therapy *J. Am. Psychoanal. Assoc.* 27 (Suppl.):81–112.

——— (1981). Psychoanalysis and dynamic psychotherapy: similarities and differences twenty-five years later *Psychoanal. Q.* 50:665–693.

Stone, L. (1961). The Psychoanalytic Situation New York: Int. Univ. Press.

——— (1967). The psychoanalytic situation and transference: postscript to an earlier communication *J. Am. Psychoanal. Assoc.* 15:3–58.

——— (1981). Some thoughts on the here-and-now in psychoanalytic technique and process *Psychoanal. Q.* 50:709–733.

Strachey, J. (1934). The nature of the therapeutic action of psychoanalysis *Int. J. Psychoanal.* 50:275–292.

Ticho, E. (1972). Termination of psychoanalysis: treatment goals, life goals *Psychoanal. Q.* 41:315–333.

CHAPTER 27

The Concept of Termination and the Evolution of Psychoanalytic Thought

(1989). J. Amer. Psychoanal. Assn., (37):275–295; Plenary Address, Annual Meeting of the American Psychoanalytic Association, Montreal, Canada, May 8, 1987.

ABSTRACT: Termination is a post-Freud contribution to the psychoanalytic process, which is never complete. The concept is illuminated in its analytic history and development. A formal well-defined terminal phase led to a tripartite psychoanalytic process which derived from and contributed to advances in psychoanalytic theory and knowledge. The terminal phase is a valuable addition and conclusion, but may be invested with irrational expectation and analytic myth. Various features and formulations of the terminal phase are explored, and the limitations of termination are noted.

Freud left a magnificent psychoanalytic edifice, but one to be completed by succeeding generations of psychoanalysts. It is not generally appreciated that one of the areas left incomplete was the conclusion of clinical psychoanalysis in the form that we take for granted today. During Freud's lifetime, there was an opening and a middle phase of clinical analysis. There was no description of a concluding or termination phase in an otherwise open-ended, timeless analytic process. Analysis was compared to a chess game which could be brought to a successful end (not a stalemate), but the criteria, characteristics, and management of the ending were never discussed (Freud, 1913). Toward the end of his life, Freud (1937) pondered termination from many different viewpoints without ever introducing the concept of a terminal phase. After

Freud, a historic change led to the current tripartite psychoanalysis, consisting of an opening phase initiating the process; a middle phase of the major analytic work; and a terminal phase with its own criteria and characteristics. This paper will deal with that clinical and conceptual change which is an overlooked area of the history and theory of the analytic process.

Why was a termination phase so long delayed in the development of the psychoanalytic process? How, when, and why did the concept emerge, and how did termination reciprocally influence theory and practice? Is termination itself sometimes traumatic, and is terminal mourning of special theoretical or therapeutic significance? And what are the contributions of the concluding phase to the final outcome and to the achievement of the goals of analysis? I shall offer an approach and orientation to these questions and to the general concept and characteristics of termination in relation to the evolution of psychoanalytic thought.

Some of the important issues are convergent with issues in the termination of training analysis. However, the termination of training analysis, so similar and yet so different from ordinary therapeutic analysis, will not be considered except where it is particularly pertinent to the concept. I have previously referred to some historic interrelations of training and termination (Blum, 1987). Certainly, the analyst's own analysis is a model, and supervisory and analytic experience will influence ideas about termination. Analytic education, and a rapidly growing relevant literature (e.g., Firestein, 1978) also contribute to the analyst's own formulations, values, and assumptions about the length of analysis and termination. The termination of training analysis is complicated by the training situation and the post-analytic relationship. The candidate may not feel free to terminate, and the same may be true for the training analyst. The candidate and his own patient may terminate simultaneously, and analyses will generally be burdened by multiple terminations. Termination is particularly painful for the analyst if he has very few analysands and is faced with not fulfilling his analytic goals and ideals. In addition, with insufficient analytic practice, the analyst will not be eligible to become a training analyst. Training may not be truly terminated until the analyst becomes a training analyst in his own right, equal with his own analyst (unconsciously, a parent-analyst with his own child-candidate).

Perhaps psychoanalysts did not deal with termination until they had to confront Freud's demise and their own termination from Freud. His reassuring presence and authority may well have left analysts with a feeling that the psychoanalytic process had been securely and finally formulated; change might be associated with anxiety and guilt. The formulation of the transference neurosis (Freud, 1914) had an enduring impact on all subsequent views of the psychoanalytic process. The end of analysis coincided with the resolution and genetic reduction of the transference neurosis, an ideal cure of the ideal illness created by the analytic process. The paradigm of the analytic process neither included nor required a terminal phase (Hurn, 1971). The criteria for termination were phenomenological, dynamic, and structural, manifest in symptomatic relief and a sense of well-being, an understanding of the unconscious conflicts and their derivatives, and improved personality organization and functions, respectively. Freud's topographic and structural aphorisms, "transforming what is unconscious into what is conscious" (1917b, p. 280) and "Where id was there shall ego be" (1933, p. 80) were both process and outcome goals related to termination. The topographic formulation also referred to the acquisition of insight as a condition for ego dominance and structural change. Freud's well known maxim, referring to the patient's healthy capacity to work and love as a measure of analytic improvement, appears to be based on his statement, "whether the subject is left with a sufficient amount of capacity for enjoyment and of efficiency" (Freud, 1917b, p. 457). Efficiency, rather than ability to work (*Leistungsfahigkeit*) or productivity, is probably an example of Strachey's tendency to recast Freud's lucid language and pragmatic observations in more scientific/mechanistic terms. Freud's early "experience-close" depiction of analytic goals complemented the metapsychological formulations. (His preanalytic comment is still applicable: "much will be gained if we succeed in transforming … hysterical misery into common unhappiness" (Breuer and Freud, 1895, p. 305). Process and outcome goals, means and ends, were gradually elucidated, but without a concluding phase. As late as 1938, Glover's questionnaire survey of British analysts indicated that the majority of respondents lacked criteria for termination and used intuition, a feeling that the end had arrived.

Freud had pondered issues of termination from the beginning of analysis to his final paper on the subject. In order to understand Freud's propositions about termination, it is necessary to consider his self-analysis. Freud's monumental self-analysis embodied the discovery of the psychoanalytic method and the psychoanalytic process as a treatment, and as a mode of investigation and research. By 1937, the psychoanalytic process was expected to create the conditions for its perpetuation in the form of self-analysis. Self-analysis was now the outcome rather than the inception of the analytic process: "… we reckon on the stimuli that he has received in his own analysis not ceasing when it ends and on the process of remodeling the ego continuing spontaneously in the analyzed subject and making use of all subsequent experiences in this newly-acquired sense" (Freud, 1937, p. 249). The continuing process was epitomized in self-analysis. Self-analysis was for Freud a lifelong process, an interminable undertaking. There was no limit to self-knowledge. A different translation of "Analysis Terminable and Interminable" as analysis finite or infinite might be related to the self-analytic theme and the self-analytic paradigm of the creator of psychoanalysis. But self-analysis also has its limitations, and it has its differences from clinical psychoanalysis, then and now. Freud was aware of the problems at the very time of his self-analysis. He wrote to Fliess on November 14, 1897, "I have realized why I can analyze myself only with the help of knowledge obtained objectively (like an outsider). True self-analysis is impossible; otherwise there would be no neurotic illness" (Freud, 1900, p. 281). It is immediately apparent that self-analysis does not deal with termination. Freud did not take leave of himself. As his own analyst and his own patient, Freud continued the analytic work. Issues of mourning and the meaning of separation would await a much later period of psychoanalytic exposition. Even after Freud (1917a) dealt with object loss in "Mourning and Melancholia," he did not refer to the loss of the analyst and the meaning of the loss of the analyst's direct participation in the analytic process.

The loss and dissolution of Freud's friendship with Fliess and the understanding of the transference relationship to Fliess were associated with progressive self-analysis. Freud's separation from and identification with his lost transference object was a problem for his further analysis; identifications with Fliess did not facilitate the acquisition and development of analytic functions. The pioneer analysts who followed after Freud had the experience of being analyzed by another analyst; nevertheless, the development of independent self-analytic functions and internalization of the analytic process were not studied until the advent of ego psychology.

Another feature of the early analyses which was doubtless linked to the lack of a termination phase was that so many of these analyses were didactic and time-limited. When Freud (1937) later wrote of the pressures and problems of psychoanalytic practice and the potential for countertransference difficulties, he suggested, "Every analyst should periodically—at intervals of five years or so —submit himself to analysis once more …" (p. 249). The periodic return was associated with very short periods of analysis by today's standards. These recommendations to analysts for pieces of analysis, or intermittent "reanalysis" would, in effect, deepen and compensate for the short introductory training analysis. The regular resumption of analysis would be facilitated by former analysis and a burgeoning self-analytic process. However, short analyses such as six to twelve months hardly allowed for more than an opening phase; the analysis closed just after it had opened.

As a result of the issues raised by Freud and the increasing experience of analysts, analyses tended to become longer. Referring to Ferenczi's later comforting assurance that with sufficient analytic skill and patience, analysis can be brought to a natural end, Freud (1937, p. 247) echoed similar sentiments and stated (p. 249), "I am not intending to assert that analysis is altogether an endless business. Whatever one's theoretical attitude to the question may be, the termination of an analysis is, I think a practical matter" (p. 249). Termination, then, was a matter of clinical judgment and the responsibility of the analyst in case there was not a convergence of views between analyst and patient. Freud (April 16, 1900) had drawn the same inferences in a remarkable letter to Fliess written in the pretermination of their relationship: "I am beginning to understand that the apparent endlessness of the treatment is something that occurs regularly and is connected with the transference. I hope that this remnant will not detract from the practical success. I could have continued the treatment, but I had the feeling that such prolongation is a compromise between illness and health that patients themselves desire, and the physician must therefore not accede to it" (p. 409).

Paradoxically, the paradigm of a fixed future date of termination was historically and specifically introduced in a stalemated rather than a successfully completed analysis. This was a terminal period, but the changed process was to become the precursor of a regular terminal phase. I refer to the case of the Wolf Man which left its stamp in so many ways on psychoanalytic theory. consistent with a coerced conclusion, Ferenczi and Rank (1924), in a forerunner of Rank's birth trauma and terminal rebirth, advised a final interval of treatment when the original neurosis has been replaced by the transference neurosis, regardless of the analysand's progress. Freud (1937) returned to the Wolf Man case to discuss the fixing of a time limit as well as considerations of reanalysis and interminability. In the case of the Wolf Man, the fixing of the time limit and the final phase of treatment was first described as a "heroic measure" (p. 217). The original case report actually became the model for termination as an impetus to the analytic process. "Under the inexorable pressure of this fixed limit his resistance … gave way, and … the analysis produced all the material which made it possible to clear up his inhibitions and remove his symptoms. All the information, too, which enabled me to understand his infantile neurosis is derived from this last period of work …" (Freud, 1918, p. 11). The bulk of the analytic work as it was then conceptualized was carried out during termination, and analytic understanding and progress coincided with the terminal six-month period of the patient's four-year treatment.

In retrospect, the Wolf Man appears to have reacted to the imposed termination (hardly the later aim of termination by mutual agreement) with characteristic pseudo-compliance. Relying on enemas to break the veil or caul in which he was enveloped, he presumably heard the message, in part, as "shit or get off the pot," "shape up or ship out." Twenty years later Freud noted fixing time limits in other cases as well; he referred to it as a blackmailing device: "But it cannot guarantee to accomplish the task completely. On the contrary, we may be sure that, while part of the material will become accessible under the pressure of the threat, another part will be kept back and thus become buried, as it were, and lost to our therapeutic efforts. For once the analyst has fixed the time-limit he cannot extend it; otherwise the patient would lose all faith in him … Nor can any general rule be laid down as to the right time for resorting to this forcible technical device; the decision must be left to the analyst's tact. A miscalculation cannot be rectified. The saying that a lion only springs once must apply here" (Freud, 1937, pp. 218–219).

Freud then questioned the meaning of a completed analysis and whether there was such a thing as a natural end to the analysis beyond the practical change that analyst and patient ceased to meet with each other. A completed analysis, Freud (1937, p. 219) decided, referred to the analyst judging that so much has been made conscious and so much internal resistance conquered that a repetition of a pathological process was unlikely; a more far-reaching and idealized meaning of the end of an analysis meant that no further change could be expected in the patient if the analysis were to be continued. The ideal situation of a complete analysis or finished analysis could never be met. No analysis was ever complete, and conflict was always actual or potential. Freud observed that analysis could not guarantee against recurrence or obliterate the pathogenic conflicts that had been previously analyzed, nor could it immunize the patient against new pathogenic conflicts. Not all conflicts could be expressed in the transference at any one time. And it was not possible to activate dormant conflicts. Actually, this limited conflict activation in analysis may have been partially a function of the short analyses of that period. And while conflicts might not be activated in the patient's transference. Freud remarked that dormant unconscious conflict could be activated in the analyst's countertransference. Soberly and somberly reflecting on the depth and permanence of analytic change, Freud (1937, p. 250) summarized, "Our aim will be not to rub off every peculiarity of human character for the sake of a schematic 'normality', nor yet to demand that the person who has been 'thoroughly analyzed' shall feel no passions and develop no internal conflicts. The business of the analysis is to secure the best possible psychological conditions for the functions of the ego; with that it has discharged its task."

The ideal of a complete analysis was championed by Ferenczi (1927, p. 84) for future analysts, "on whom the fate of so many others depends." Therapeutic zeal found reason, and in degree, rationalization. Termination after thorough analysis was fused with a latent myth of complete analysis. It is of interest that Ferenczi (1927, p. 85) had then proposed that, "neither the physician nor the patient puts an end to it, but it [analysis] just dies of exhaustion." The candidate's conflicts and analytic needs became determinants of the duration of training analysis. Longer training analysis then led reciprocally to the increasing length of therapeutic analysis (Balint, 1954). As analysis extended, the pitfalls and side effects of very prolonged analysis were at first only minimally considered along with the advantages. Current studies of transference-countertransference were also stimulated by termination of training analysis. No other patient might expose the analyst's frailties and vulnerabilities to the analytic community, greatly intensifying related transference-countertransference problems. It was probably not coincidence that an upsurge of interest in both countertransference and termination developed simultaneously.

The issues of termination resurfaced in 1950 with the publication of a symposium on termination in the *International Journal of Psycho-Analysis*. Reich (1950) wrote, "Astonishingly, the topic of termination has very rarely been the subject of psychoanalytic investigation," and cited the only two papers on the subject by Ferenczi and Freud. Nevertheless, the value and necessity of adding a well-defined terminal phase was almost immediately regarded as regular and crucial. Discussions quickly centered on the criteria for termination, the unique, typical, and yet individual characteristics of the terminal phase, the analyst's technique during termination, and possible technical variations. Perhaps no amendment of the psychoanalytic process was so readily and unquestioningly accepted by psychoanalysts.

Previously, termination had not been taught or supervised in analytic training. Prior to 1950 it had been assumed that anyone who could conduct analysis properly could terminate it correctly. A terminated case was not required for institute graduation, nor for membership (certification) in the American Psychoanalytic Association. Termination was only later correlated with analyzability and outcome (Weiss and Fleming, 1980). Glover (1955, p. 140) insisted, "Unless the terminal phase has been passed through, it is very doubtful whether any case has been psychoanalyzed." Glover's position reflected and was endorsed as the standard of analytic teaching and practice. Termination became the "touchstone" of completed analysis. After a long period in which analysis was practiced without a characteristic terminal phase and with more or less intuitive, pragmatic considerations for ending, the concept of termination was rapidly assimilated into the psychoanalytic process, practice, and education. It was almost as if there were a need for closure in a well-defined analytic process. Influenced by an ideal model of technique, analysis was then also compared to and differentiated from psychotherapy, which lacked analysis of a transference neurosis and a regular phase sequence. The termination phase was formalized when analytic training was rapidly expanding, and when psychoanalysis was idealized, at peak popularity.

Was the terminal phase really equal to the opening phase and the major middle phase in importance? Could the theory of technique account for a terminal phase and phenomena which followed after attainment of analytic goals? Since the transference neurosis was relatively resolved as a criterion for termination, termination could be merely an epilogue or final repetition and review. How was the analytic process crucially effected by the terminal phase? Given an analytic process without a terminal phase, as sometimes occurred, for example, because of an abrupt change in the patient's reality circumstances or because of the illness or death of the analyst, did that vitiate the previous analytic work? Was termination necessary to lock in gains? Did termination diminish later needs for reanalysis? Could a good ending correct prior problems in analytic work? Analytic evidence elicits many reservations and, as usual, no simple answers. In one sense, termination began the day the analysis commenced. The selection of an appropriate patient and the opening introduction would all influence the termination. Errors or chronic countertransferences that were introduced early in the analysis and that might persist throughout were likely to be of far more consequence than difficulties of the analytic process to which the analyst had contributed significantly only during termination. Though the ending has its own very valuable contributions, to my mind it is not really on a par with the preceding phases, or essential to progressive analytic work.

Termination will usually have been anticipated from the very beginning of analysis. Patients may have had their own timetable or brought up termination in terms of resistance, and interruption, but termination becomes an appropriate issue as patient and analyst assess the achievements and limits of analytic goals. Termination is set in motion during its discussion in a preterminal period. It is accelerated and given reality with the establishment of the termination date. The terminal phase duration has been highly variable, depending on the particular patient and analytic judgment. Reactions to terminating may be quite different from separations and cancellations which are followed by ongoing analysis. The reactions are colored by the particular patient's problems and progress, and by the decision itself, whether mutual or unilateral, or imposed by extra-analytic circumstances (Novick, 1982). Autonomy is both sought and feared. Historically, it seemed paradoxical that after many signs of symptomatic and characterological improvement, termination should promote as well as reverse regression. Such regression has been interpreted as both a warning signal and as a concomitant of closing efforts at mastery (Firestein, 1978). Currently, termination is not usually considered to be unalterable, a sealed fate, and the decision or date may be changed if necessary.

The analyst may be bribed, blackmailed, and begged to continue, as in the Biblical "entreat me not to leave you nor to refrain from following after you." Fantasies of becoming a therapist are common. The fantasy of giving a gift to express gratitude and leave a part of oneself in contact with the analyst is occasionally translated into reality. We know that patients still hope for transference gratifications, and that many patients find reasons to consult the analyst after termination. While the earlier literature emphasized the reorganization of the drives and alterations of the defenses, there is currently greater awareness of the importance of unconscious fantasy organization (Arlow, 1969); (Abend, 1987); (Boesky, 1987) and ego integration. The fantasies which appear during the terminal phase of analysis have often been worked through during the heart of the analysis itself and are now subjected to final scrutiny. However, some fantasies, such as death, birth, and rebirth; separation and reunion; pregnancy and abortion; punishment and redemption; castration, elimination, and weaning are ubiquitous in termination.

Fantasies and feelings about mortality and finality, along with loss and change, can be readily discerned as part of the background of termination. The timeless and seemingly goalless nature of analysis is changed, occasionally by the analyst's explicit direction. Setting a termination date might be theoretically regarded as a departure from analytic neutrality. Patients become aware of time. Anticipation is intensified and often disguised and displaced onto other issues. There are specific references to the past, present, and future, to future plans, to permanence and transience, to time lapses and limits. Associations frequently involve temporal organization and expression, as in racing against time, stopping the clock, countdowns, and overtime. Time may be freedom or tyranny—manipulated, saved, lost, killed—all referring to time as a transference object and to the analytic process and separation. The time limit itself has its own influence and unconscious meaning. Patients may be mobilized (or occasionally immobilized) by deadlines, reminiscent of Samuel Johnson's observation, "When a man knows he is to be hanged in a fortnight, it concentrates his mind wonderfully."[1]

It is apparent that the phenomena of termination could not have been observed until there was a formal setting of the date with sufficient time between the setting of the date and the end of the treatment for a termination phase—a phase that, on the other hand, was not so long that it was in itself interminable. The concept of a terminal phase grew out of the closest correlation of clinical observation and theoretical inference.

One chronically angry patient with reactivated infantile hostility engendered by the impending termination complained bitterly of being forced to work overtime. He spoke of laborers leisurely taking their time working on the floor while nevertheless producing a "hard finish." He disliked commuting and battling traffic. As he arrived at his own office, he had told his secretary

---

1 In "Epitaph on Goldsmith," September 17, 1777. [Appearing on a monument in Westminster Abbey, the epitaph, written by Samuel Johnson, reads: "Oliver Goldsmith: A Poet, Naturalist, and Historian, who left scarcely any style of writing untouched, and touched nothing that he did not adorn."]

"Today's trip was a fight to the finish." Another patient with unexpressed thoughts of forbidden, incestuous love, described a parapraxis which occurred during sexual relations. Her husband interrupted foreplay and said, "time out," while he put on a condom. The patient misheard her husband's comment as "time's up," and was momentarily bewildered until she realized and analyzed her misperception. This was a situation where several members of the family, including her husband, had been or were in analysis. Past and present terminations, time out and time up, had reverberating meanings for everyone in the family. The expectations and achievements, disappointments and frustrations, were directly and indirectly shared within the family.

The theme of disappointment during and after termination is of particular significance and may tend to be hidden during the termination phase proper only to surface in the important period which Rangell (1966) has designated as the post-termination phase. Disappointment and disillusionment are essentially universal, with rational and irrational sources. Analysts have repeatedly echoed Freud's caution about analytic outcome. There are the inherent real limitations of the patient, analyst, and the analytic process. Painful regrets and necessary renunciations come to the fore during and after termination. The patient cannot return to the past and long-lost objects and opportunities. Some hopes and dreams can never be fulfilled. The phase of life may prevent biological motherhood or conversely the opportunity to avoid detrimental influences on one's children. Timeless infantile wishes require renunciation or sublimated transformation. Termination leads to a new confrontation with magical expectations and infantile omnipotence. Infantile omnipotence is an important issue in all analytic termination (Schmideberg, 1938), but is especially significant in the termination of the so-called narcissistic neuroses and borderline conditions. Disappointments are all too often associated with unanalyzed negative transference and narcissistic mortifications. Patient and analyst may have convergent wishes for perfection and praise.

The Wolf Man's inability to terminate, his paranoid regression when his omnipotent object developed cancer, and his subsequent therapeutic needs confirmed Freud's (1918), (1937) final formulations of severe narcissistic trends and developmental disorder. Similar interminable cases lead to related considerations of borderline conditions, structural fragility or malformation, and developmental deficit (Freud, 1937); (Blum, 1974).

Some patients, and not necessarily borderline personalities, could not terminate at all; others terminated only to resume treatment with the same or another therapist sooner or later.[2] It became clear that there were some patients for whom the presence of the analyst and the continuation of treatment was the condition for their adaptation or stability. Analysis could even become a way of life. In addition to unmanageable transference and countertransference configurations, unusual forms of pathological object and reality relations were identified. Investigations of modified and interminable analysis would contribute to a deeper understanding of termination. Pertinent to analytic training, a rare candidate group decompensated only after termination and graduation, when required to function independently.

At termination, the stability of analytic achievements is tested and, sometimes, hitherto unsuspected vulnerabilities, structural faults, and primordial transference may emerge. Initial diagnosis and analyzability may be evaluated again in ending, along with the decision to terminate (Shane and Shane, 1984). Termination is a trial analysis of the patient's progress, and a trial of the analysis itself. An oedipal transference neurosis may give way to preoedipal regression, and object dependency. This may be a final defense against resolution of oedipal conflict or it may represent hitherto unrecognized oedipal distortions, developmental deviations, ego fragility, etc. Some patients are impelled to "wreck" a successful analysis, or require a final negative therapeutic reaction. Here a host of contributions relevant to ego development and object relations have reciprocally illuminated issues of analyzability, terminability, and the limitations of psychoanalysis (Stone, 1954); (Weil, 1956); (Arlow and Brenner, 1964); (Rangell, 1966); (Mahler, 1971); (Kohut, 1971); (Kernberg, 1975).

In ways not anticipated in the early literature, the analyst may represent an auxiliary ego (A. Freud, 1965), an organizing object and beacon of

---

2 Reanalysis is a misnomer if it implies a previously complete or separate analytic experience. Cumulative pieces of analytic work can be very valuable.

orientation (Mahler et al., 1975), and the analysis may represent a holding environment (Winnicott, 1965). In these situations, the underlying personality disturbance comes to the fore at termination. The inevitable supporting and suggestive elements in the analytic situation may have been particularly important. Sometimes a pseudo-analytic process has been unrecognized, and psychotherapy on the couch proceeds as analysis. While long analyses are not necessarily interminable, refractory cases are not necessarily resolved with more analysis. Many analyses are ended because of diminishing or vanishing returns, or the lack of new or enduring insights. Patients who hear only the music need the words, too, "For you it's best that we be parted" (Bach, cantata 108, paraphrase).

Developmental considerations became important in the termination of child analysis, and were proposed for adult analysis. Expanding analytic knowledge of separation, individuation, and of object loss at different levels of development stimulated new thinking about termination. Termination is experienced differently at different phases of development and of life. The anticipated loss of the analyst is frequently associated with mourning, and many analysts have regarded mourning as an essential feature of the terminal phase of analysis. For some patients, especially those with a history of object loss, mourning may be facilitated by the analytic process, and activated by termination. Patients with a history of separation trauma are especially likely to experience symptom reappearance at termination (S. Keiser in Panel, 1975). Some patients, traumatized by loss, e.g., through suicide or homicide, may not accept or tolerate termination. In termination, there is analysis of anticipated separation, but not of actual separation. The analysis is not over until it is over. Mourning cannot be completed prior to real separation. But is mourning really necessary for analytic result? Arlow (1971) questioned the significance of mourning in termination, and in Kramer's (1986) clinical exposition of termination, issues of separation and mourning were not particularly prominent. The analysis of unconscious conflict took precedence to the end. It follows that termination issues are not invariably the central theme of the terminal phase.

However, the severance of such an intimate relationship is bound to have deep-seated repercussions. After all, the analyst has represented all of the original objects, and the loss of any close relationship will be mourned. The analyst also faces loss, and unanalyzed countertransference can delay, hasten, or otherwise impinge on termination. Mourning contributes to the patient's independence, and to his relinquishing infantile objects and illusions. But mourning is not the essential instrument of analytic structural change. There can be mourning with persistent regression, mourning without understanding, and mourning without ego mastery.

What survives of the object relationship and of the identifications with the analyst after termination? Does the representation of the analyst remain particularly distinct, as seems likely, or does it tend, perhaps more so with candidates, to coalesce with other object representations associated with insight and mastery? The analyst may be experienced as a presence, his image summoned in times of stress, his voice heard, certain interpretations remembered. Under these circumstances, the analyst may be more of an introject. Yet, the analysis may be forgotten, the insights not consciously recalled, and structural change and synthesis may have silently occurred, independent of recall of the analysis (Kris, 1956). Follow-up studies of terminated analysis (Pfeffer, 1961), (1963); (Oremland et al., 1975) show that what is revived is not simply the transference neurosis, but analytic efforts at mastery of the unconscious conflicts. There is a miniature revival of symptoms and of the analytic process in the follow-up situation. I suggest that the follow-up consultations may particularly revive termination, resuming the end phase of the analysis.

From whom does the patient terminate—the analyst as transference object, interpreting object, or the real person-analyst? In this connection, Freud (1920, p. 36) noted: "This same compulsion to repeat frequently meets us as an obstacle to our treatment when at the end of an analysis we try to induce the patient to detach himself completely from his physician." The transference repetition is central, and the analyst is primarily mourned as transference object. Experience at termination, in reanalysis, and in follow-up confirms the importance of transference residues; the transference and neurosis are never fully resolved. At the same time, two people have worked together in the unique intimacy of the analytic situation. The analyst as participant-observer has shared a profound experience with the patient. A real relationship has developed, concomitant with the analysis of transference distortion, and realistic revision of self- and object representations. The patient is aware of the analyst's skills and dedication; the patient may feel the analyst understands him better than anyone else. Loss of the analyzing object (and analysis) is also mourned, but not in the depth and poignancy of the transference object loss. In training analysis, analyst and analysand remain real objects in life after termination. Freud (1937) regarded their continuing friendly relationship as a highly rewarding outcome.

Termination spans developmental experience from resonances of separation-individuation, through the persisting oedipal organization to adolescent transition (Silverman, 1971), to adulthood. During the terminal phase, the patient is increasingly able to take over the analytic work, and endeavors to find mature solutions to problems (Dewald, 1982). The patient has actively contributed to the acquisition of insight and to the working through leading to change inside and outside the analysis (Rangell, 1981). After the analysis, the representation of the analyst and identification with his analyzing functions may or may not persist unchanged. Improved ego function and a continued unconscious analytic process facilitate the attainment of life goals through the patient's analytic achievements (Ticho, 1972). My own impression is that self-analysis is highly variable. It is a requirement for termination only in training analysis.

The bittersweet last hour, so meaningful (Lipton, 1961), often patently concerns plans involving replacement of or reunion with the analyst. Though there is loss, termination is a maturational experience, with pride in achievement and new satisfactions and sublimations (M. Kanzer in Panel, 1975). The positive gains, however, may defend against terminal reactivation of trauma. The termination itself may be traumatic. A patient with a flare for evocative dramatization had a daydream of being rocketed (from Mother Earth) on a trip into outer space, returning to final splashdown. That was the penultimate session. In the final hour she reviewed many of the gains she had made in understanding her inner conflicts and their unconscious influence on her own life and on her children, including her children's enuresis (Blum, 1970). Shortly before the "end," she had a fantasy on the couch: "I took out a bottle of champagne and broke the bottle over her head." The poor, humiliated Jewish girl was christened and launched into a new life. The head injury had many important determinants which by no means all referred to the crowning achievements of the analysis, or for that matter, to clobbering interpretation. The patient had been stunned previously by learning of her husband's infidelity and had in earlier life felt betrayed and disappointed in love. There were many infantile and later traumata. Stunned by traumatic experience, she had compensatory fantasies of stunning beauty. What I wish to emphasize here is the insistent, and often disguised repetition of trauma at termination, and its analytic recognition. All trauma, not only separation trauma, will likely be reactivated, and even typical fantasies may incorporate real trauma.

The patient's analytic progress is best served by analysis to the end. Much depends on new synthesis and inner freedom for mature choice and decision. Coincident with Freud's loss of Fliess, his "only audience," he overcame his inhibition and went to Rome. Rome (like Jerusalem) was the eternal city of eternal laws where he and Fliess promised to have a congress. Reconstructing the traumatic primeval past, he replaced Fliess with Moses, and promptly "visited" Moses. Freud's termination with Fliess and his turn to Moses as his heroic, idealized object contributed to self-confident independence with a new guiding framework, continuing self-analysis, and incipient concepts of clinical termination. Analytic exploration, however, remained essentially unlimited and interminable; we never reach the promised land.

REFERENCES

Abend, S.M. (1987). The relationship of unconscious fantasies to issues of termination of analysis In *Unconscious Fantasy, Myth, and Reality* ed. H. Blum, Y. Kramer, A. Richards. Hillsdale, NJ: Analytic Press.

Arlow, J.A. (1969). Unconscious fantasy and disturbances of conscious experience *Psychoanal. Q.* 38:1–27.

——— (1971). Some problems in current psychoanalytic thought In *The World Biennial of Psychiatry and Psychotherapy* Vol. 1. ed. S. Arieti. New York: Basic Books, pp. 34–54.

——— & Brenner, C. (1964). Psychoanalytic Concepts and the Structural Theory New York: Int. Univ. Press.

Balint, M. (1954). Analytic training and training analysis *Int. J. Psychoanal.* 35: 157–162.

Blum, H.P. (1970). Maternal psychopathology and enuresis *Psychoanal. Q.* 39: 609–619.

——— (1974). The borderline childhood of the Wolf Man *J. Am. Psychoanal. Assoc.* 22:721–742.

——— (1987). Analysis terminable and interminable: a half-century retrospective *Int. J. Psychoanal.* 68:37–47.

Boesky, D. (1987). Termination as orgasm In *Unconscious Fantasy, Myth, and Reality.* ed. H.P. Blum, Y. Kramer, A. Richards. Hillsdale, NJ: Analytic Press.

Breuer, J. & Freud, S. (1895). Studies on hysteria *S.E.* 2.

Dewald, P. (1982). The clinical importance of the terminal phase *Psychoanal. Inq.* 2:441–462.

Ferenczi, S. (1927). *The problem of the termination of the analysis In Final Contributions to the Problems and Methods of Psycho-Analysis.* New York: Brunner/Mazel, 1980 pp. *77–86.*

——— & Rank, O. (1924). *The Development of Psychoanalysis* New York: Nervous Mental Disease Publishing Co.

Firestein, S. (1978). *Termination in Psychoanalysis* New York: Int. Univ. Press.

Freud, A. (1965). Normality and Pathology in Childhood. *Writings* 6 New York: Int. Univ. Press.

Freud, S. (1900). *The Complete Letters of Sigmund Freud to Wilhelm Fliess.*, ed J. Masson. Cambridge: Harvard Univ. Press, 1985.

——— (1913). On beginning the treatment *S.E.* 12.

——— (1914). Remembering, repeating, and working-through *S.E.* 12.

——— (1917a). Mourning and melancholia *S.E.* 14.

——— (1917b). Introductory lectures on psycho-analysis *S.E.* 16.

——— (1918). From the history of an infantile neurosis *S.E.* 17.

——— (1920). Beyond the pleasure principle *S.E.* 18.

——— (1933). New introductory lectures on psycho-analysis *S.E.* 22.

——— (1937). Analysis terminable and interminable *S.E. 23.*

Glover, E. (1955). *The Technique of Psychoanalysis.* New York: Int. Univ. Press.

Hurn, H. (1971). Toward a paradigm of the terminal phase *J. Am. Psychoanal. Assoc.* 19:332–348.

Kernberg, O.F. (1975). *Borderline Conditions and Pathological Narcissism.* New York: Aronson.

Kohut, H. (1971). *The Analysis of the Self* New York: Int. Univ. Press.

Kramer, Y. (1986). Aspects of Termination: Theory and Practice. In *Psychoanalysis: The Science of Mental Content.* eds. A. Richards, M. Willick. Hillsdale, NJ: Analytic Press.

Kris, E. (1956). On some vicissitudes of insight in psychoanalysis *Int. J. Psychoanal.* 37:445–455.

Lipton, S.D. (1961). The last hour *J. Am. Psychoanal. Assoc. 9*:325–330.

Mahler, M.S. 1971 A study of the separation-individuation process: and its possible application to borderline phenomena in the psychoanalytic situation. *Psychoanal. Study Child* 26:403–424.

——— Pine, F. & Bergman, A. (1975). *The Psychological Birth of the Human Infant* New York: Basic Books.

Novick, J. (1982). Termination: themes and issues *Psychoanal. Inq.* 2 329–365.

Oremland, J., Blacker, K.H. & Norman, H.F. (1975). Incompleteness in "successful" psychoanalysis: a follow-up study *J. Am. Psychoanal. Assoc.* 23: 819–844.

Panel (1975). Termination: problems and techniques W. Robbins, reporter. *J. Am. Psychoanal. Assoc.* 23:166–176.

Pfeffer, A.Z. 1961 Follow-up study of a satisfactory analysis *J. Am. Psychoanal. Assoc.* 9:698–718.

——— (1963). The meaning of the analyst after analysis *J. Am. Psychoanal. Assoc.* 11:229–244.

Rangell, L. (1966). *An Overview of The Ending of an Analysis in Psychoanalysis in the Americas* ed. R. Litman. New York: Int. Univ. Press.

——— (1981). From insight to change *J. Am. Psychoanal. Assoc.* 29: 119–14.

——— (1982). Some thoughts on termination *Psychoanal. Inq.* 2 367–392.

Reich, A. (1950). On the termination of analysis. *Int. J. Psychoanal.*30:179–183.

Schmideberg, M. (1938). After the analysis … *Psychoanal. Q.*7:122–142.

Shane, M. & Shane, F. (1984). The end phase of analysis: indications, functions, and tasks of termination *J. Am. Psychoanal. Assoc.* 32:739–777.

Silverman, J. (1971). Termination of analysis: graduation-initiation rite and mythopoetic aspects. In *The Unconscious Today*. ed. M. Kanzer. New York: Int. Univ. Press, pp. 288–305.

Stone, L. (1954). The widening scope of indications for psychoanalysis *J. Am. Psychoanal. Assoc.* 2:567–594.

Ticho, E. (1972). Termination of psychoanalysis: treatment goals, life goals *Psychoanal. Q.* 41:315–333.

Weil, A. (1956). Some evidence of deviational development in infancy and early childhood *Psychoanal. Study Child* 11:292–299.

Weiss, S. & Fleming, J. (1980). On the teaching and learning of termination in psychoanalysis *Annual of Psychoanalysis* 8:37–55.

Winnicott, D. (1965). *The Maturational Processes and the Facilitating Environment.* New York: Int. Univ. Press.

CHAPTER 28

Discussion on the Erotic Transference: Contemporary Perspectives

(1994). *Psychoanal. Inq.*, (14)(4):622–635.

It is a privilege to read and review a series of papers that explore a topic of special interest with new and enlarged perspectives of contemporary psychoanalysis. The subject of erotic transference elicits transference as well as reality-oriented reactions to both the topic and the review task. Given the wealth of ideas and observations and the often convergent yet very different papers under review, it is impossible to do justice to their contributions. And for those papers representative of other frames of reference and alternate analytic theories, I will generally limit comment to ways in which the paper has stimulated my own analytic thinking and reaction.

The terms "erotic transference," "erotized transference, and "instinctualized transference" continue to be used without sharp conceptual differentiation. The analytic situation and process facilitates the development of erotic transference with expressions of love and demands for reciprocal love from the analyst. Freud (1915) early distinguished transference love from positive, aim-inhibited, friendly transference, but he did not specifically refer to erotized transference. Since transference has been classically categorized according to its manifest positive or negative appearance, I still believe it is useful to delineate manifest "erotized transference" as I did in 1973. I focused as Hill notes in his paper in this issue, "The Special Place of the Erotic Transference in Psychoanalysis," on the spectrum of erotic transferences. Erotized transference is an extreme sector of the erotic transference spectrum. The positive part of the spectrum stretches from a useful and manageable transference of affection and friendliness to a form that is extremely erotized: "an intense, vivid, irrational, erotic preoccupation with the analyst characterized by overt seemingly ego-syntonic demands for love and sexual fulfillment from the analyst" (Blum, 1973, p. 63). Although there are always underlying aggressive and negative transferential elements in erotized transference, I see no gain in the use of the term "instinctualized transference" at this time. All transferences, such as angry transference, are instinctualized in degree, with ego and superego elements as well. Typically, transference love has an "as-if" quality, and its unrequited frustration also contributes to its potential analysis to its infantile, genetic roots.

The ego-syntonic erotized transference is not recognized by the patient to be unrealistic and inappropriate and is more likely to be associated with impediments and severe resistance to analytic work. Patients with this type of transference may insist on recognition and gratification of their demands and are not inclined to seek understanding of their transference fantasy. They often reject genetic interpretations that indicate that a regressive repetition of the past is being recapitulated in the analytic situation. The patient's attempt to evoke and provoke erotic enactments with the analyst are not recognized as a disguised repetition of fantasied or actual infantile object relations. Freud (1915) was aware of the special problems of female patients who declared themselves to be in love with the analyst and who were "children of nature," with an "elemental passionateness" (p. 166). Some of these patients understood only "the logic of soup, with dumplings for arguments" (p. 167). And although they were not necessarily totally refractory to psychoanalytic change, Freud (1915) suggested that a change to another analyst might be necessary. He noted that the erotized transference is overdetermined by many complicated factors. Hill perceptively notes that Freud recognized the study of transference love as capable of yielding special insights. The case of Anna O probably provided Freud with emerging insights into transference and countertransference, which were to evolve and consolidate in the course of his self-analysis and enlarging clinical experience.

Freud (1915) questioned the difference between transference love and "real love," since falling in love is based on infantile prototypes in both analysis and real life. The resistance, as Freud further noted, does not create transference love, but finds it ready at hand and makes use of it in aggravated forms. Hill infers a defensive change of function and unveils transference love as a case of infantile love "masquerading as love." Infantile wishes are disguised within an adultomorphic masquerade. Conceptual as well as technical problems may be formidable, and Hill differentiates between manifest and latent content, as well as between the form and content of erotized transference. Though erotic transferences are regressive, they may be a pathway toward maturity, implying the mastery of fixation and trauma. Hill highlights papers that changed previously established views, for example, that patients with erotized transference were necessarily unanalyzable. Falling in love with the analyst was not a requirement for analytic success, nor always a harbinger of analytic failure. Transference love may be inhibited, displaced, or acted out with other objects. I had pointed out (1971, 1973) that refractory patients with erotized transference often displayed defective object and reality ties. The intensity and tenacity of the manifest erotized transference was not necessarily in lock-step with oedipal conflict, but might also involve ego impairment and preoedipal developmental disturbance.

Coen (1981) also recognized that sexual fantasy and behavior may be blatantly expressed for defensive purposes and elaborated the concept of sexualization. Coen observed that "sexualization" is used imprecisely, and he especially emphasized sexualization as defense, not just in perverse behavior, but as a predominant constellation in narcissistic, borderline, and psychotic patients. Sexualization prominently appeared in the erotized transference of such patients. I had emphasized the multiple functions of the erotized transference: drive gratification of oedipal and preoedipal strivings; repetition of trauma, especially parental seduction; narcissistic demands and the regulation of self-esteem and regard; and defense and adaptation. A generalized seductive style may represent character pathology, and a formidable resistance to analysis.

The defense could be against oedipal strivings through preoedipal regression, but also against preoedipal issues in their own right; sexual dangers, particularly homosexuality; aggression and hostility; object loss; and narcissistic frustration and injury. Coen (1981) and Nydes (1950) emphasized the illusory actualization of fantasies, with a need for concrete manipulation of the representational world to maintain fantasied omnipotence.

Transference love is understood as simultaneously progressive and regressive, transitional between fantasy and reality, and facilitating the emergence of the new coordinated with the old. Old experiences are made accessible and new experiences made possible through the analytic understanding and work on the erotic transference (Schafer, 1977).

In highlighting the development of psychoanalytic thought about erotized transference, Hill then turns to the relationship of erotized transference manifestations and the actual gender of the analyst. Freud considered the problems of transference love only in the case of a woman falling in love with her male analyst. Hill cites Person's (1985) views that for men there is a conflict between dependency and phallic sexuality; tending to split the object of erotic desire and dependency, the male confuses power with sexuality. According to Person, men avoid dependency on an erotic object, where as women use dependency-laced eroticism to defend against aggression and preoedipal loss while maintaining the object relationships that sustain their gender identity; women use the erotic transference as a resistance, and men resist the erotic transference.

The issue of gender at this point will serve as an introduction to the realities of the analytic situation. These realities, are contrapuntal to our usual intrapsychic focus and emphasis on unconscious fantasy. The transference is indiscriminately repetitive—why should it have any relationship to the real gender of the analyst, or the age of the analyst, or the race of the analyst? In my earlier papers on transference, I focused attention on the unconscious fantasy as well as on the need to consider the influence of realities. I raised questions about the effect of gender on the intensity and sequence of the transference manifestations. These included the patient's preferences and prejudices for an analyst of a particular gender, the patient's oedipal and narcissistic conflicts, social and cultural factors, the readiness of an analyst to deal with his or her own bisexuality, and the capacity to understand cross-gender transference in same-sex analytic dyads. I noted the importance of the analyst's countertransference, which could stimulate, validate, and reinforce a patient's erotized transference. Countertransference might make a patient's erotized transference unmanageable and unanalyzable.

The patient's experience of the analyst's countertransference is, however, a reality within the analytic situation. The countertransference may not be just the fantasy of the analyst, but is often an actual set of responses on the part of the analyst, which the patient registers and to which he or she reacts. Today we would talk of a transference-countertransference field and a continuum of transference-countertransference responses. It would be hoped that the countertransference would be analyzed, muted, and modulated. Analytic self-scrutiny and self-analysis provide further sources of information about the patient and about the analytic process that may be used to facilitate analytic progress. The erotized countertransference in which the analyst may fall in love with the patient, initiate seductive overtures to the patient, and make subtle or not-so-subtle requests for reciprocal love from the patient, needed further elaboration. Sometimes both analytic partners have regressive reactions to frustrated transference love and oedipal/preoedipal disappointment. This problem has now come into central attention, with current reports of sexual seduction and abuse of patients. Although Freud was aware of the dangers of countertransference enactments, today we are particularly cognizant, not only of the serious psychological damage sustained by patients who have sexual relationships with their therapists, but also of familial, ethical, and legal issues and consequences.

Confirming the traumatic core of many erotized transferences, both patients with erotized transference and therapists with erotized countertransference often have histories of incestuous relationships and other forms of traumatic experience in childhood. These people are also at risk for repeating such overstimulated and deviant experiences with their own children. Therapists who have been traumatized in childhood are apparently at risk for possible forms of seduction trauma with their vulnerable patients. The attempt to repeat in the service of mastery all too often turns out to be a failed effort with fresh traumatic repetition and new complications. Some patients or therapists campaign to seduce and be seduced. The realization of an incestuous transference-countertransference relationship may also serve narcissistic conquest and self-aggrandizement or disguised rage and revenge. Narcissistic patients may be particularly demanding, entitled, coercive, and vindictive. A patient may unconsciously wish to seduce in order to castrate and destroy the analyst. Guilt, shame, and disgrace coalesce with self punishment and self defeat. Sexual relations between patient and therapist may prove to be more pathogenic than less complete forms of incestuous seduction in childhood. Much depends on the patient's ego state and developmental phase, personality resources and resilience, and the overall nature of the patient's psychopathology and the relationship with the therapist. Basic trust is inevitably eroded and superego standards corrupted, after which patients may be very difficult to treat and may resist becoming deeply involved in a new therapeutic process, though a poor prognosis is not always the rule. The rage of frustration of an erotized transference may also mask relief and respect for analytic work and ethics.

The issue of gender is present in the choice of the referring analyst or therapist and in the patient's own preferences in choosing a therapist. Gender may be a consideration in transfer to and choice of a second analyst. The issue of gender of the analyst tends to recede as analysis proceeds and as deeper layers of transference are exposed and analyzed. Furthermore, as indicated earlier, because of human bisexuality, both parties in the analytic relationship have masculine and feminine tendencies and identifications (Blum and Blum, 1986). The possibility that the human female may be prewired for earlier empathic relatedness than the male and may retain a greater interest in relationships should stimulate further psychoanalytic research. Aware of the mingling of oedipal and preoedipal themes, Gould believes that her patient's narcissistic needs for self-assertion and symbiotic-like union were central. Oedipal interpretations of his erotized transference were experienced by the patient as failures on the part of the analyst to understand him.

This patient had been in psychoanalytic psychotherapy twice-weekly for 6 years, and was now 68 years of age. He was in his third marriage, had been alcoholic, had lost his second wife through her suicidal behavior, and had suffered from impotence. There were clearly powerful dependency needs and conflicts over orality and autonomy. This patient, with many overt and covert entreaties for soothing, comforting, and both preoedipal and oedipal mothering, developed a full-fledged erotized transference. This included expressions of love, proposals of marriage, cards and letters, love songs to the answering machine, invitations to dinner and the opera, and so forth. The patient was childless, and be announced he was making his therapist the beneficiary of his will.

Gould asserts that the erotized transference functioned as the vehicle through which the patient could sustain a sense of himself as strong and masterful. Interpretations of the patient's incestuous longings for his mother, or his being an oedipal loser, were experienced as empathic failures of the analyst by the patient.

Such patients do, indeed, try the soul of the therapist, especially when the patient is so seductive and when his escalating demands are relentless. The magical nature of the transference for him and his longings for omnipotence were evident in the transference replacement of his previous reliance on alcohol and his praying in church before each session. The treatment might be considered as analogous to the patient's religious conversion when he gave up alcoholism. Gould is aware of the powerful preoedipal underpinnings of the transference, but I would also emphasize more the narcissistic onslaught of the patient's age and his desperate fear of loss of the object, the object's nurturance, and love. There was probably a major regressive defense against oedipal conflict, but also profound oral dependent needs that were expressed in disguised form in the erotized transference fantasies. The fact that his wife was ill and emotionally unavailable, and that aging threatened his ego and sexual functioning, were major influences in his erotized transference. This man may have been longing for a "last fling" and narcissistic supplies. This is the type of patient for whom the relationship is sustaining, while interpretation, especially in an analytic psychotherapy, may be more problematic for the analyst and more difficult for the patient to assimilate.

In a recent review and reconsideration of transference in male patients with a female analyst, Goldberger and Holmes (1993) note that the countertransference with a particular analyst rather than the biases of analysis and of culture tends to be the major issue. There is a potential for limitation of the full range of transference constellations and conflicts in all analytic gender pairs, depending on a variety of factors. Male patients have now been noted to display the full range of transference phenomena, including erotized transference to female analysts (Karme, 1979; Lester, 1985; Meyers, 1986) and erotized homosexual transference to male analysts. Homosexual transference may also be found in patients with analysts of the opposite sex, provided that defenses against its expression and recognition are adequately analyzed.

At this point, it is appropriate to consider Siegel's "Clinical Observations of Sexual and Sensual Aspects of the Transference in Women." Siegel distinguishes the sensual from the sexual transference. In the former, she sees a strong evocation of the unity of the mother-child dyad with wishes for bodily intimacy, oral gratification, and yearnings for merger. Siegel excludes narcissistic needs for mirroring and admiration and more developmentally advanced sexual desires. According to Siegel, these subspecies of transference are present in attenuated form in all female analysands but occur with special strength in homosexual women. While Siegel notes that the sensual and sexual transferences are often comingled, she regards erotism as part of object relationships throughout development, a view consistent with the psychoanalytic theory of libidinal phases and infantile sexuality.

A female analyst may prefer a role of maternal nurturance, whereas a male analyst may prefer to be cast as an oedipal father. Siegel clearly describes the problems of the patient who demands the all-giving mother, where aggression fuels the sexual transference demands. The analyst is expected to know every thought of the analysand, and the inability of such understanding is experienced as the analyst being mean and withholding from the patient. Though the homosexual patients Siegel describes had successful careers, they regressed in the face of overwhelming needs and then literally did not know how to soothe themselves or integrate their thoughts, feelings, and yearnings.

That female homosexual patients do not develop oedipal transferences seems doubtful, although the preoedipal transference problems, so well described by Siegel, are often so powerful and predominant. In considering the range of "homosexualities," there is a variation in each individual case of oedipal, preoedipal, narcissistic, and constitutional determinants. Although these patients had borderline features, oedipal conflicts and regression from such conflicts would likely be an important factor in their analysis.

Analysis necessarily involves the nonverbal sphere of the transference and the preverbal elements to the extent that they can be distinctively recognized, articulated, and genetically interpreted. What Siegel calls "pretransference" is controversial and would require separate elaboration and discussion. Her view of the defense against transference might be further conceptualized as resistance to a particular form of transference, and as the acting out of the erotized transference, but primarily as a defense against hostile, negative preoedipal and oedipal maternal transference.

In "The Challenge of Erotized Transference to Psychoanalytic Technique," Bergmann observes that the women who developed erotized transference early in the treatment departed from the expected transference patterns and were also without guilt. This is an essentially ego-syntonic type of erotized transference more commonly found today in the wider scope of analysis with more seriously ill patients. Bergmann astutely questioned Freud's (1915) technical approaches to these difficult female patients. That genuine love would make them more docile, as Freud argued, introduces cultural values and minimizes the imperious qualities of love. Freud's second argument, that transference love is not currently "genuine," but composed of repetitions of earlier reactions, is true only in degree. Bergmann remarks that the very fact that the analyst responds differently from all other persons gives transference love a new quality. Freud also acknowledged that the genuineness of love was not disproved by resistance and that all love consists of new additions to old traits, though based on infantile models. Erotized transference, however, is pervasively infantile in its insatiable, imperative demands, the lack of more realistic and mature modifications, the lack of developmental transformation, and its hidden aggressive and defensive dimensions.

In this connection, erotized transference may or may not represent strictly neurotic phenomena. There is a variable range, from neurotic repetition of oedipal seduction to the borderline case (which may be closer to an episode of transference psychosis). I suggest that aggressive erotization may also take the form of a highly sadistic or masochistic transference. The transference repetition of traumatic sexual abuse is not the same as the sexualization of other forms of trauma or the erotization of danger, pain, or anxiety. The reconstruction of the trauma that may be repeated within the erotized transference will be of technical importance in the analysis of the transference. If childhood traumatic sexual overstimulation can be reconstructed, this will help the patient to understand childhood erotic repetition rather than assuming adult passionate love.

Bergmann importantly notes, and is in accord with Person (1985) and McDougall (1986), that the transition from the girl's earlier homosexual to later heterosexual attachments is not simple. Women analysts sometimes found their own analysis with male analysts did not sufficiently prepare them to deal with homosexual transference in their female patients. Analysis involves a two-person process, and Bergmann cites the case of a woman who realized in her second analysis that she had divorced her husband because she thought the first analyst had been attracted to her and would eventually marry her. She had not verbalized her conscious fantasies about her analyst, and his behavior had indicated that his being attracted to her was not entirely her fantasy.

In the earlier one-person psychology of the analytic process, only the women developed erotized transferences, and Bergmann interpolated that it was never indicated what the analyst did or did not do. Countertransference issues were not considered, and technical management was usually not described. The patients who were seduced in childhood showed impairment of reality testing, superego regulation, and capacities to delay and to sublimate. An erotomania may be an urgent attempt to forestall a psychotic break, or may represent a borderline psychotic regression. These formulations advance new perspectives. Contemporary experience with erotomania indicates that it is often associated with splitting of the representations, protecting an idealized love object from murderous aggression. A patient may be paranoid toward one narcissistic object while maintaining erotic attachment to another narcissistic object.

Technically, Bergmann very appropriately emphasizes the need to maintain an analytic attitude, whether in the face of an erotized transference or in confronting an extremely negative, hostile transference. He feels that the symbiotic longing behind oedipal incestuous love is often a basic issue, though the level of developmental disturbance and analyzability is variable.

Wolf considers erotized transference within the theoretical framework of self psychology. Self psychology treats infantile sexuality and drive motivation quite differently from classical Freudian theory and regards the intensification of sexual fantasy and the performance of sexual activities and exploits as forestalling the danger of self-fragmentation (Kohut, 1971). Wolf presents a fascinating account of a homosexual patient who would cruise the streets in search of visual contact with a man's penis. This would occur when he felt terribly anxious and, during the analysis, after disappointment with the analyst and disruption of the therapeutic relationship. The clinical material suggests castration and object loss anxieties, but what is of special interest for the purpose of this discussion of erotized transference is the importance of defensive sexualization and of narcissistic needs and narcissistic rage. The narcissistic dimension of erotized transference is often of major importance. It may present in terms of a patient feeling entitled to all the analyst's love and affection, time, attention, comforting, and nurturance. The patient may wish to be an exception, a privileged character for whom the ordinary analytic rules do not apply. The wish to be the favorite of the analyst and earlier of the parents, with persisting infantile omnipotence and self-aggrandizement, may be thinly disguised in erotized transference fantasy. The rage of the disappointed, frustrated narcissist may reach violent or paranoid proportions, and Wolf calls our attention to the dangerous coexistence of narcissistic lust and narcissistic rage in the same individual. This is a potentially explosive mixture of violence and sexuality from which antisocial threats of rape and mayhem may ensue.

Bollas introduces "Aspects of the Erotic Transference" with a vivid description of a female patient using the couch as "erotic territory." In an erotic script, she tells the analyst of her fantasies of making love, and their going together to concerts, plays, and parties. Bollas remarks that reporting erotic fantasies may be erotic in its own right, as well as that the analyst, "the figure with whom she has just been making passionate love," is actually there. Bollas cogently regards the verbal seduction as a derivative form of sexual enactment.

591

This patient's intense passions contributed to her difficulty in differentiating fantasy from reality. Bollas proposes that the patient's erotic interests in him helped her emerge from a narcissistic shell. He was an "internal object" derived from the patient's instinctual urges, from her inner world—not fundamentally from the analyst's inner world or suggestive behavior. In terms of Winnicott's (1965) clinical metaphors, the patient needed the analyst's actual presence and holding environment to release the inner object. Stated in a different frame of reference, transference fantasy is allowed full analytic expression. A negative transference may also both express and defend against erotic transference. Erotic wishes intensify in relation to the analyst's maintenance of abstinence and neutrality. Bollas describes hate breaking through the analytic barrier and the internal fantasy linked to the analyst's body. Bollas depicts the analysand's trying to touch the body-self of the analyst by hating him and thereby arousing his affects. Of course, love, envy, jealousy, panic, and anger may also arouse the analyst's own affects and sensory experience. The presence of the analyst as a real object and the intersubjective aspects of the analytic situation are noted. The analyst may feel intensely guilty if he has revealed his true feelings from behind the screen of analytic neutrality. Bollas also distinguishes between typical erotic transference and the sexualized transference. In the sexualized transference, the analysand's urgent demand for intercourse with the analyst is fundamentally not an erotic or love relationship. His contribution here is reminiscent of Ferenczi (1933) and pertinent to the transference repetition of childhood sexual trauma. Although erotized transference may be couched in the language of love and tenderness, it is rooted in infantile psychopathology and should not be confused with a mature love relationship.

I should again draw attention here to the background of preoedipal maternal transference that often gives special coloring and intensity to the erotized transference. The patient may be pining for a nurturant, protective, and comforting mother, disguised as adult sexual cravings. While the manifest erotization may even lead to orgiastic like experiences, the latent transference may be more oral, associated with desperate narcissistic, object, and affect hunger. In such cases, sexual excitement may culminate in an anxiety or anger orgasm or defensive avoidance of explosive rage and terror. The patient's history may indicate addiction or addictive clinging, compulsive masturbation, or episodic promiscuity.

Very much in sympathy with Bollas is Benjamin, who also found the formulations of Winnicott useful for her elaboration of erotized transference. In "What Angel Would Hear Me? The Erotics of Transference," Benjamin invokes poetry, lines from Rilke, and the metaphor of the angel, a creature who completed the transformation from inarticulate, unrealized being to perfect consciousness. This poetic, mystical metaphor is introduced to somehow demystify the mysterious force of the transference. For Benjamin, the core of erotized transference is no longer to be understood in an oedipal triangular configuration, but in terms of preoedipal maternal transference. Invoking Winnicott's (1965) true and false self, Benjamin's discussion does not make clear what the relationship of erotized transference has been to actual incestuous experience or other traumata, the role of oedipal conflict and regression, or how we recognize "the primary intersubjectivity of direct presymbolic recognition." Benjamin describes the two phases of the angel as maternal and paternal, with both analytic discourses perhaps simultaneously representing both oedipal and preoedipal considerations.

Benjamin proposes that subsequent to Freud there was a major change in the theory of technique. The analyst's empathy, attunement, and identification with the patient is described as decisive for change, as are interpretation, insight, and self-knowledge. This shift to "intersubjective space," the desire of the patient to be known, and the experience of being known, places emphasis on the analytic relationship and the analytic experience.

However, what is unique about an analytic relationship and what differentiates it from all other relationships, is that the relationship itself is analyzed, and the patient's childhood is reconstructed. The unconscious infantile transference fantasies and the disguised traumatic experiences that the patient attempts to repeat in the transference are uncovered and interpreted. If erotized transference is "a blue or fallen angel," I believe it is interpretation and insight, particularly into the oedipal and preoedipal roots of erotized transference and their relation to regression and resistance, that demystify the patient's experience. The scrutiny of the intersubjective and interactive aspects of the analytic relationship and a careful analysis of the reciprocal influence of transference and countertransference have enriched the theory of technique. The real verbal and nonverbal interactions of analyst and patient have provided further insight into the nuances of unconscious communication in analytic work. It is important to recognize that patients benefit from the prolonged analytic relationship and experience, without slighting the primacy of analytic understanding and interpretation.

REFERENCES

Blum, H. (1971), On the conception and development of the transference neurosis. *J. Amer. Psychoanal. Assn.* 19:41–53.

——— (1973). The concept of erotized transference. *J. Amer. Psychoanal. Assn.* 21:61–76.

——— & Blum, E. (1986). Reflections on transference and countertransference in the treatment of women. In: *Between Analyst and Patient*, ed. H. Meyers. Hillsdale, NJ: The Analytic Press. pp. 177–192.

Coen, S. (1981). Sexualization as a predominant mode of defense. *J. Amer. Psychoanal. Assn.*, 29:893–920.

Ferenczi, S. (1933). Confusion of tongues between adults and the child. In: *Final Contributions to the Problems and Methods of Psycho-Analysis*, ed. M. Balint (tr. E. Mosbacher). London: Karnac Books pp. 156–167, 1980.

Freud, S. (1915). Observations on transference love. *Standard Edition* 12:157–168, 1958.

Goldberger, M. & Holmes, D. (1993). Transferences in male patients with female analysts: An update. *Psychoanal. Inq.* 13:173–191.

Karme, L. (1979). The analysis of a male patient by a female analyst: The problem of the negative oedipal transference. *Int. J. Psycho-Anal.* 60:253–261.

Lester, E. (1985). The female analyst and the eroticized transference. *Int. J. Psycho-Anal.*, 66:283–293.

McDougall, J. (1986). Eve's reflection. On the homosexual components of female sexuality. In: *Between Analyst and Patient*. ed. H. Meyers. Hillsdale, NJ: The Analytic Press, pp. 213–228.

Meyers, H. (1986). Analytic work by and with women: The complexity and the challenge. In: *Between Analyst and Patient*, ed. H. Meyers. Hillsdale, NJ: The Analytic Press, pp. 159–176.

Nydes, J. (1950). The magical experience of the masturbation fantasy. *Amer. J. Psychother.*, 4:303–310.

Person, E. (1985). The erotic transference in women and in men: Differences and consequences. *J. Amer. Acad. Psychoanal.* 13:159–180.

Schafer, R. (1977). The interpretation of transference and the condition of loving. *J. Amer. Psychoanal. Assn.*, 25:335–362.

Winnicott, D. (1965). *The Maturational Processes and the Facilitating Environment*. New York: IUP.

CHAPTER 29

Repression, Transference, and Reconstruction

(2003). *Int. J. Psychoanalysis* 84(3):497–503.

Whereas Peter Fonagy almost dismisses the importance of repression and the recovery of repressed and suppressed memory, the author believes that the analysis of repression retains importance in clinical psychoanalysis.

Transference is a return of the repressed, with repressed memories embedded within a fundamental unconscious fantasy constellation. Moreover, transference is an essential, but not the only, route to the understanding and analysis of the patient. Nor should transference be confused with the real or new analytic relationship. The author does not regard the dynamic unconscious as definitely registered and retrieved in procedural memory, awaiting further research. A focus on the present 'self with other' model of therapeutic action neglects pathogenesis and the importance of childhood and its psychoanalytic reconstruction.

In 1999 Peter Fonagy published a guest editorial in the pages of this *Journal* that addressed current psychoanalytic controversies regarding the link between memory and therapeutic action. A renowned colleague, he has made important contributions to psychoanalytic theory and research. Fonagy proposed major shifts in psychoanalytic thought, requiring careful exploration and evaluation. Challenging the role of repression, the recovery of repressed memories and the value of reconstruction in the therapeutic action of psychoanalysis, he regards the archeological metaphor of bringing the buried past to light as misleading and theoretically incorrect. While relying exclusively on the current transference, he proposes a new theory of therapeutic change through the experience of 'self with other', rather than the primary analysis of unconscious intrapsychic conflict, trauma and their genetic determinants. The Editors have invited me to present my concerns about Fonagy's thesis and present my own opposing views in this new *IJP* format.

Fonagy's proposed shift away from the personal past is illustrated by his statement: "therapies that focus on the recovery of memory pursue a false god. Psychoanalysts should carefully and consistently avoid the archeological metaphor (1999, pp. 217, 220). It is the false god Freud who declared, "The theory of repression is the corner-stone on which the whole structure of psychoanalysis rests" (1914b, p. 16). Fonagy disregards the crucial connection of transference and resistance with repression. Perhaps we are dealing with different concepts of transference, complicating and impeding contemporary psychoanalytic discourse. Do traditional concepts and formulations such as transference need to be modified or supplanted and, if so, in what way? Fonagy's concept of therapeutic action would be welcome if it represented an advance in the theory of technique.

In respectfully dissenting from Fonagy's editorial views I regard the following clinical vignette as illustrative of the mutative value of the lifting of repression and reconstruction. A patient, deeply troubled by her hostility toward her infant, dreamed that *her sibling had died on his birthday*. She gradually recognized in analysis that her infant represented her sibling. In the transference I represented her ambivalently loved mother with whom she was identified. Fragmented memories of her greeting her sibling's arrival with enmity and rage, intensified by severe illness at that time, were recovered from screen memories, dreams and transference. What was not gradually remembered was laboriously reconstructed in the analysis. This reconstruction, which was very helpful to the patient in the resolution of her hostility to her own infant and in her marriage, was confirmed by family members. She affectively re-experienced her childhood trauma and reworked her adaptation to it in the immediacy and safety of the analytic process and in the context provided by reconstruction (Blum, 1994).

Memory, accurate or unreliable, tormenting or pleasurable, is essential to and stimulated by psychoanalytic work. Beginning with conscious memories, free association releases preconscious memories into awareness. These memories, including screen memories, distorted memories, memory gaps, fragments and lapses, become grist for the mill, advancing the analytic process. The revision of memory including associated affects is an intermediate analytic goal. In addition to the analytic goal of progressive intrapsychic structural change, there are external goals of improved capacities for work, love and play. For Fonagy intrapsychic structural change seems to be equivalent to modified object relations.

Everyday parapraxes of memory are ordinarily related to unconscious conflicts that are active in the transference, and other important life experience, linking past to present relationships. What is Fonagy's basis for concluding that the recovery of repressed memory is therapeutically inert, an epiphenomenon? 'Hysterics suffer from reminiscences' (Breuer and Freud, 1895, p. 7). The gain in popularity of psychoanalysis after the two World Wars was in no small measure due to the therapeutic value of the psychodynamic treatment of 'shell shock' and 'war neuroses'. In abundant documented cases of war neuroses repressed traumatic memories were recovered during treatment, with marked symptomatic relief and functional improvement (Karon and Widener, 1998). Similarly, findings of the therapeutic efficacy of the interpretation and reconstruction of repressed past unconscious conflicts and trauma have been reported by many psychoanalysts (Greenacre, 1956; Schimek, 1977; Wetzler, 1985; Reed, 1993).

According to Fonagy the only way we could know 'what goes on in our patients' minds, what might have happened to them, is how they are with us in the transference' (1999, p. 217). What is the evidence for this viewpoint? Without the patient's life history, including education, family and culture, as well as character, the transference cannot be fully understood and vice versa. The repetitive reactions of childhood are important patterns, often vital to full comprehension of the adult analytic transference. Moreover, what is acted out, outside the analytic situation, may not directly appear in transference. The analysis of character is only loosely related to transference. The same character traits and attitudes are present everywhere, inside and outside the analytic process. We do not know our patients' character through transference alone, and the analyst is not the only transference object. The analyst may represent the father; the patient's wife may represent his mother. In this sense extra transference interpretations involve extra-analytic transferences. How does a patient feel when only transference is interpreted and other issues are ignored? All associations, interventions and reactions are forced into the Procrustean bed of transference. A strictly analytic transference focus is consistent with a narcissistic position of the analyst; he/she is not only a very important person, but is considered the most important person in the patient's life. The patient identifies with the idealized analyst and the narcissism of the analytic dyad is then gratified and promoted. This is especially problematic in a long analysis if real-life relationships have been devalued, and cannot compare to the exceptional status and satisfactions of the analytic situation. An enduring dependency on the analyst and analysis may be unwittingly fostered and encouraged. In such instances the analysis could easily be isolated from the fabric of the patient's life, in an analytic *folie-á-deux*(Blum, 1983).

Arlow (2003), also critical of a one-dimensional stress on transference, noted that limiting attention to the manifest transference misses the underlying conflicts and the defensive compromise aspect of transference. His patient experienced mounting feelings of murderous rage toward her parents and then protected her parents by shifting her rage to fantasies of tearing the analyst apart. Severing the transference from its defensive context may deprive the patient of an opportunity to comprehend the persistent genetic roots of the transference. The transference is a transfer from unconscious childhood fantasy into the analytic present, and cannot be understood without its infantile character and origins.

Fonagy introduced his transference concept as:

a kind of model—a network of unconscious expectations or mental models of self-other relationships. The models exist non-consciously as procedures…. The models are not replicas of actual experience but are undoubtedly defensively distorted by wishes and fantasies current at the time of the experience. Thus in no sense can they be thought of as bearing testament to historical truth (1999, p. 217).

His formulation explicitly refers to non-conscious models, existing non-consciously as procedures, becoming accessible if the individual directs attention to them. Yet, in the same paragraph he has confusingly stated that these expectations are unconscious. He referred to experiences which are preverbal, but paradoxically also to fantasies current at the time of the experience. Autobiographical memory is said to be secondarily activated. Departing from the dynamic unconscious to the non-conscious, non-repressed, Fonagy has given priority to hypothetical procedural memories over autobiographical memory. Moreover, infantile self and object representations alone do not take into account the complexity of development. While self- and object-representations and their linked affects (Kernberg, 1988) are basic to psychic structure, these micro-structures interact with ego development and maturation, and with facilitating as well as traumatic life experience.

Transference is not a literal recapitulation of the patient's early object relations. Transference is a compromise formation, an unconscious fantasy, including components of real experience, self- and object-representations, defense, superego factors, and associated affects. The unconscious conflicts are embedded in the fantasy. Fonagy's self-other models and ways of being with the other do not address the developmental path from narcissism to object constancy. Though Fonagy later remarks about the significance of childhood fantasy, the analysis of self-other models appears to have precedence over the analysis of unconscious fantasy. I concur with his own suggestion that his model of therapeutic action could be criticized as implicitly non-dynamic. The manifest transference of the patient is no more reliable for understanding the patient than the manifest content of dreams, behavior or symptoms. As Freud (1914a) long ago inferred, transference has a resistance dimension, a resistance to recognizing, remembering and understanding the past as persisting in the present.

The defensive nature of manifest transference is well known. An erotic transference may defend against hostile transference and vice versa. How can 'self and other relationships' be modified without analysis of unconscious fantasy? Further, Fonagy has not elaborated the complexity of different unconscious internal self-other models which may conflict or compete, for example, phallic and castrated self- or object-representations. The meaning and unconscious structure of the self-other relationships are ill defined.

Fonagy stated that 'deeply pathological ways of experiencing the other may antedate the memory systems …' (1999). Why and how does he infer the imprint of such archaic experience in procedural memory? Is he implying that such unaltered infant experience is reflected and repeated in the later analytic transference through procedural memory? What does Fonagy think about the significance of autobiographical memory in 'Remembering, repeating and working-through' (Freud, 1914a)? While we no longer expect to recover repressed memories in the manner Freud then described, the lifting of repression facilitates the analysis of distortions of memory and unconscious fantasy. Reconstruction is synergistic with and may substitute for memory retrieval, and provides a developmental context for genetic interpretation. Fonagy cited the supportive literature, but then minimized the importance of repressed memory and reconstruction. Fonagy is aware that proposed procedural memory is unknowable until it enters the realm of autobiographical experience. He did not indicate how his analytic use of procedural memory articulates with traditional transference analysis. What significance does Fonagy attach to endowment or instinctual drives? How does his model of 'self with other' relationships, with their affects, articulate with the transformations and reorganization of later developmental phases? If his model has been influenced by attachment theory, with its working models of the infant's relationship expectations, clarity would be enhanced by making this explicit. Fonagy has presented an object-relations paradigm isolated from other theoretical perspectives, rather than encompassed within a cohesive psychoanalytic theory (Rangell, 2000).

The importance of transference and of object relations is not in question, but the psychoanalytic process can be derailed when any one component, such as transference, dominates. The transference, however, is a major guide toward the reconstruction of the patient's childhood, and reconstruction is also essential to understanding the transference (Blum, 1980; Brenman, 1980) and the influence of childhood on later life. A major task of psychoanalysis is to reconstruct relevant dimensions of the patient's childhood from the traces left behind (Freud, 1937). In contrast, Fonagy stated, 'It is hard to envision the formulation of an accurate reconstruction on the basis of a patient's distorted memories and symptoms' (1999, p. 216). Fonagy then relies upon an affective self-other procedural model, which seems to be in itself his own hypothetical reconstruction. As far as I am concerned, genetic interpretation and reconstruction of the unconscious conflicts and trauma of childhood significantly contribute to therapeutic action. For example, I do not think it possible to really understand an adult's master–slave fantasies in life and in the analytic transference without the recollection and reconstruction of his/her experience as the child of servants.

The countertransference of the analytic 'self with the patient other' also has unconscious determinants. The adult neurosis includes later development, but is built on childhood psychopathology and vulnerabilities. A patient's conscious anamnesis is not simply discarded as though it were entirely inaccurate and irrelevant. The patient's conscious account of his/her life history with its inevitable gaps, inconsistencies, distortions and personal myths provides the context in which the analyst begins to understand the patient. Reconstruction proceeds in an analytic and historical context from surface to depth, from present to past and back again. Reconstruction integrates reality and fantasy, past and present, cause and effect. Paradoxically, the past is recreated in an integrated form that never existed as such (Blum, 2000).

The present or past may defend against each other, but a traumatized patient must reconstruct the past as past and not continually present. An adult patient, who had a series of injuries and fractures beginning in childhood that he regarded as accidental, had to be shown that these were not the result of accidents but self-injuries. I do not believe this accident-prone patient could have been successfully treated without transference interpretation and reconstruction. Whether or not labeled as such, I regard reconstruction as intrinsic to clinical psychoanalysis.

For Fonagy, the chief agent of change appears to be the resolution of difficulties in the experience of oneself with another. How is treatment accomplished based on this model (Goldberg, 1999)? Is Fonagy advocating intersubjective, interpersonal interventions based on a parent–infant paradigm? He does not indicate whether analytic anonymity and neutrality are to be maintained. Fonagy's focus on the experience of the analytic relationship is distantly reminiscent of Ferenczi and Rank (1924). His formulations of therapeutic action may evoke the *Controversial discussions* (King and Steiner, 1991). Principal controversies then involved polarized questions regarding exclusive focus on transference, and whether analytic results were primarily from the therapeutic modification of internal objects rather than from the undoing of repression.

Is Fonagy indicating a beneficial real relationship in the here and now, or the analyst as a new object? A curative experiencing of self and other might have been previously conceptualized as a corrective emotional experience (Alexander, 1956; Migone, 2000). In a modified analysis of a developmentally deviant or arrested patient, or in child analysis, the analyst might necessarily also function as an educator. In Fonagy's construct of therapeutic action, it is not clear if the therapeutic action of self with the analyst-other is largely achieved through experience, education or insight into the infantile unconscious. How is new understanding of the discrepancy between internal self and object representations and the real external persons, between transference and reality, to be attained? Changes are effected in many ways, but it is affective insight into the dynamic unconscious that is specifically psychoanalytic. Analytic insight is broadened and deepened through reconstruction.

Fonagy's propositions about procedural memory and neuroscience are very thoughtful considerations and would be a major contribution if confirmed. Fonagy differentiated between declarative memory, which is conscious, or preconscious, and which can achieve symbolic representation in images and words, from procedural or implicit memory, which is outside conscious awareness and verbalization. He assumed that initial paradigms of selfobject relationships are registered within and can be retrieved from procedural memory (Clyman, 1991). Stern et al. (1998) proposed the concept of 'implicit relational knowing', a type of procedural memory based upon an infant's learning what approach will elicit a desired parental response. These expectations of self with other then become the model procedures rather than the anlage of the adult patient's transference. However, procedural memories for skills are usually regarded as non-conscious, rather than dynamically unconscious. Skills such as automatically riding a bicycle are consciously learned with awareness of the skill. The repressed unconscious is not accounted for in non-conscious procedural memory. Even if the conjectured infantile patterns of procedural memory could be inferred and interpreted in nonverbal transference phenomena, this would not necessarily support Fonagy's virtual dismissal of the therapeutic value of uncovering of repressed memory and its fantasy elaboration. To the contrary, I would maintain the critical importance of the repressed in pathogenesis, and the lifting of repression in the therapeutic action of psychoanalysis.

Fonagy asserted that our explanations are very likely to presume what we really do not know, simultaneously questioning whether psychoanalysis has any effect. Although I do not question the therapeutic effect of analysis where appropriately indicated, much remains to be learned about how and why psychoanalysis is effective and with which patient and disorder. We both hope to enrich our understanding of process, outcome and their relationship while avoiding premature conclusions and closure.

REFERENCES

Alexander, F. (1956). *Psychoanalysis and Psychotherapy: Developments in Theory, Technique, and Training.* New York: Norton.

Arlow, J. (2003). Transference as a defense compromise formation. *J. Amer. Psychoanal. Assn.* 50(4):1139–50. doi: 10.1177/00030651020500040101.

Blum, H. (1980). The value of reconstruction in adult psychoanalysis. *Int. J. Psycho-Anal.* 61:39–54.

——— (1983). The position and value of extra transference interpretation. *J. Amer. Psychoanal. Assn.* 31:587–618.

——— (1994). Reconstruction in psychoanalysis: Childhood revisited and recreated. New York: Int. Univ. Press.

——— (2000). The reconstruction of reminiscence. *J. Amer. Psychoanal. Assn.* 47:1125–44.

Brenman, E. (1980). The value of reconstruction in adult psychoanalysis. *Int. J. Psycho-Anal*.61: 53–66.

Breuer, J. & Freud, S. (1895). Studies on hysteria. *S.E.* 2.

Clyman R (1991). The procedural organization of emotions: A contribution from cognitive science to the psychoanalytic theory of therapeutic action. *J. Amer. Psychoanal. Assn.* 39(S):349–82.

Ferenczi, S. & Rank, O. (1924). The development of psychoanalysis. *New York: Nervous and Mental Disease,* Monograph Series, 1925.

Fonagy, P (1998). Moments of change in psychoanalytic theory: Discussion of a new theory of psychic change. *Infant Ment Health J.* 19:163–171.

——— (1999). Memory and therapeutic action. *Int. J. Psycho-Anal.* 80:215–223.

Freud, S, (1914a). Remembering, repeating and working-through. *S.E.* 12.

——— (1914b). On the history of the psycho-analytic movement. *S.E.* 14.

——— (1937). Constructions in analysis. *S.E.* 23.

Goldberg, A. (1999). A memory and therapeutic action. Letter to the Editor. *Int. J. Psycho-Anal.* 80:1011.

Greenacre, P. (1956). Re-evaluation of the process of working through. In *Emotional Growth,* New York: Int. Univ. Press.

Holmes, J. (2000). Memory and therapeutic action. Letter to the Editor. *Int. J. Psycho-Anal*.81:353–354.

Karson B. & Widener A (2001). Repressed memories: Avoiding the obvious. *J. Psychoanal Psychol.* 18:161–4.

Kernberg, O. (1988). Psychic structure and structural change: An ego psychology-object relations theory viewpoint. *J. Amer. Psychoanal. Assn* .36(S):315–37.

King P. & Steiner, R. (Eds) (1991). Controversial discussions. New York: W.W. Norton.

Migone, P. (2000). Memory and therapeutic action. Letter to the Editor. *Int. J. Psycho-Anal.* 81:356.

Rangell, L. (2000). Psychoanalysis at the millennium: A unitary theory. *Psychoanal. Psychol.*17:451–66.

Reed, G. (1993). On the value of explicit reconstruction. *Psychoanal. Q.* 62:52–73.

Schimek, J. (1977). The interpretations of the past: Childhood trauma, psychical reality, and historical truth. *J. Amer. Psychoanal. Assn.* 25:845–65.

Stern, D. et al. (1998). Non-interpretive mechanisms in psychoanalytic therapy: The something more than interpretation. *Int. J. Psycho-Anal.* 79: 903–921.

Wetzler, S. (1985). The historical truth of psychoanalytic reconstruction. *Int. Rev. Psycho-Anal.* 12: 187–97.

CHAPTER 30

Psychoanalytic Understanding and Psychotherapy of Borderline Regression

(1972). International Journal of Psychoanalytic Psychotherapy 1(1):47-60.

The borderline personality is on a continuum between neurosis and psychosis, with varied deficits and alterations of psychic structure. Given this often fragile and vulnerable personality organization, borderline regression can be understood as decompensation and defense, as regressive flight from more advanced tasks, and as enfeebled, deviant infantile adaptation. There are often disguised elements of early traumatic experience.

Selective assessment of the regressed, distorted, and intact ego functions is of fundamental importance in both diagnosis and treatment. Precipitating and predisposing factors, frequently confused and condensed, can be separately evaluated in a dynamic and developmental framework. Developmental deviation or arrest apparently occurs in the later separation-individuation phase, with further disturbance as a consequence, or is superimposed in succeeding periods of life.

These patients display ego passivity rather than the fragmentation of psychosis. Depending upon their personality, strengths, and resources, some borderline patients are analyzable. With careful attention to their underlying distrust and impaired object and reality relationships, borderline cases can be beneficially involved in psychotherapy. An example is offered of a reintegrative style of psychoanalytic psychotherapy appropriate to a particularly severe borderline regression.

Psychoanalytic thinking has contributed to the conceptualization, differentiation, and treatment of the borderline patient. The borderline personality may present a facade of blandly normal functioning or may manifest a variety of serious symptoms. The diagnostic category is a poorly defined transitional zone between neurosis and psychosis, with special proximity to psychosis. Freud (1937), considering the difficulty of therapeutic cooperation with psychotics, envisioned a continuum between normality and psychosis.

Every normal person, in fact, is only normal on the average. His ego approximates to that of the psychotic in some part or other and to a greater or lesser extent; and the degree of its remoteness from one end of the series and of its proximity to the other will furnish us .with a provisional measure of what we have so indefinitely termed an alteration of the ego.

Because of this continuum, overlapping types of disturbance, and our present lack of diagnostic precision, I shall not distinguish borderline personality from borderline state, character, or condition. This continuum does not exclude the possibility of discrete borderline or psychotic. conditions, with possible organic predispositions, such as cyclothymia.

The borderline state is also relatively undifferentiated from the psychotic category of "schizoid personality," "latent psychosis," or "psychotic character" (Frosch, 1970); the term borderline cuts across the usual classification of addiction, depression, or paranoia. The common denominator is the ego defect, the fragility or impairment of important ego functions (Knight, 1953). This is a psychoanalytic concept and it would be even more difficult to define and demarcate borderline personality without the psychoanalytic study of ego function and psychic structure. Freud's formulation of a continuum of ego deficit becomes a forerunner to the diagnosis and classification of borderline states.

Borderline patients have disturbed object relations, narcissistic features, intolerance of frustration, and a lack of affect modulation. They have rigid and often brittle archaic defensive constellations which contribute to confusion and loneliness. There are omnipotent expectations and an underlying reliance on magical controls. Along with signs of developmental deviation and arrest, a stable rigidity or fluid instability may be evident. Psychic equilibrium may be covertly dependent on a key object relationship or supportive situation.

The pathology of object relations may not always be apparent until some internal or external change in the patient's life disrupts his flimsy adaptation. The patient has established tenuous boundaries between self and object, but neither the self or object representation is firmly integrated. Early difficulties in the separation-individuation phase lead to a lack of confidence in reality and identity. Aggressive devaluations lead to defenses over idealization with untamed narcissistic glorification. Moreover, as Kernberg (1967) has emphasized, there may be a defensive splitting of the devalued and idealized self and object representations. Grandiose wishful attitudes of the self and/or object are retained. This lack of synthesis of the loved and hated, omnipotent and impotent object leads to impairment of object constancy. The object tie is not maintained in frustration or disappointment and in the absence of actual support from the object. The borderline's inner aggression constantly threatens the survival of the relationship and the danger of estrangement. Object contact is both sought and feared and there is a pervasive ambivalence.

Some borderlines seem self-sufficient in their narcissism and display a lifelong aloofness; others struggle with intense symbiotic conflicts. They are afraid of both loss of the object and a fusion with the object with loss of identity. These patients may show a diffuse disturbance in many areas of personality functioning. Impaired reality testing may be complicated by extensive denial and wishful (primary process) thinking. Contact and avoidance of objects may be in the service of separation and/or symbiosis. In contrast to the psychotic, the borderline usually preserves object ties and his own identity. A borderline young man would grotesquely arrange to phone his girlfriend while he was defecating, discarding her even as he attempted contact, introjecting and projecting in unending ambivalence. One borderline female disregarded her social relationships while addicted to mood-elevating drugs, which represented an idealized, omnipotent, comforting mother. She magically restored self-regard while denying feelings of depression. and dissolution.

Various types of pathological object relationships (Grinker, Werble, and Drye, 1968) are correlated with distorted internal self and object representations. These defective internal representations predispose to a bewildering variety of pathological manifestations. There may be continuing adult attachment to transitional objects; oscillating object contacts; isolated relationships with a "good object" and a "bad object" simultaneously; promiscuous search for an object following inevitable disappointment and provoked rejection; or fixation to a specific supportive object which is the ego counterpart to what Freud (1937) called "libidinal adhesion." The use and abuse of objects may be primarily for oral narcissistic gratification. Narcissistic object choices may protect against devaluation and loss of omnipotence. The object representations in the borderline, unlike the psychotic, are neither fragmented nor fused, but are distorted and lacking in full depth and differentiation. It is as if separation-individuation has progressed, but is incomplete and deviant (Mahler, 1967). Borderline characters in search of an author may go from therapist to therapist in a distorted separation-individuation process. These borderlines, despite other therapeutic progress, are often unable to terminate.

Other disturbed ego functions, such as defense, identification, and synthesis, participate in the final, unique, complex borderline condition. The lifestyle may range from bizarre alienation to "as if" conventionality. The level of personality function. will also depend upon the selective use of regression and the degree to which such regression is reversible. Borderline personalities are often capable of advanced integrated functioning in selected areas, and at times may show either more mature or more primitive aspects of representation and relationship. Infantilisms can coexist with advanced sublimations, such as creative writing and acting. The syndrome of social isolation and seclusion is usually overdetermined. Important contributions from preoedipal levels of childhood conflict combine with avoidance of unconscious temptations toward incest or homosexuality.

Many borderline patients demonstrate a severe regressive tendency, which may be regarded as an aspect of their ego defect. In addition, the borderline patient not only regresses to earlier levels of fixation, but from more advanced, though tenuous, development. This is a flight from unbearable conflict which can serve defense. Although tendency to regression is a frequent aspect of the fragility of the borderline personality, there may be a line of advantage as well as of least resistance. The escape from danger is precariously balanced against the danger of poorly controlled regression.

In analytic psychotherapy, study of the onset of regression can be used in an attempt at "reconstruction upward" (Loewenstein, 1957) to the more recent sources of stress. The therapeutic focus is shifted outward from transference to the patient's contemporary life. Rediscovery of the precipitating and related "danger situations" aids the tenuous treatment interest and the adaptive efforts of the ego. This presupposes the maintenance of some positive transference and rapport. Irrational reactions to the therapist, reflections of the past, may be utilized as paradigms of tendencies toward conflict and distorted object relations, with parallels in present life. The predisposition, the current external reality, and elements of intrapsychic danger can be clarified and differentiated. I believe that partial understanding of the superficial derivatives of unconscious conflict may have psychotherapeutic value, apart from providing defensive rationalization. A little understanding goes a long way! With help the patient can glimpse the current danger which precipitated the regression. Reason and synthesis are supported even though the unconscious derivation is neither truly interpreted nor reconstructed. These analytically derived modes of ego support help to sort out fantasy and reality, subjective past and objective present.

I would like to offer a clinical vignette of psychotherapy (twice-weekly sessions for two years) with a borderline patient. A fifty-five-year-old male chemist was frantically referred after prior unsuccessful psychotherapy and pharmacotherapy for fanatic compulsive handwashing. He dismissed the exploration of his childhood in previous psychotherapy; he felt nothing had been pertinent to his present problems. Recent electroshock and carbon dioxide treatments were valueless. The shock treatments reminded him of short circuits, and the carbon dioxide stirred thoughts of the Jews in gas chambers. He too felt hopeless and despaired of any relief from his relentless washing, which had begun seven months before. He was obsessed with ideas of contacting and transmitting cancer with his hands, by touching "contaminated" articles. He demanded that these articles and contacted clothes be washed repeatedly. He held in abeyance the belief that he could spread deadly disease. This was a borderline delusion because he basically knew this was impossible and unreal, and was aware he had chosen a noncontagious disease. There was no thought disorder (in Bléuler's sense) or definite loss of the sense of reality or identity. Yet magic permeated many areas of his thinking and action. Gesture and touch 'could be tragedy or salvation, and his washing also represented both prevention and penance. There was a progressive constriction of both human and inanimate contact. His hands were tied and he literally could not handle ordinary problems or objects. Primitive conflicts, involving guilt and undoing, magical controls, and both grandiose and devalued self and object representations were apparent. Good and bad, clean and contaminated, affection and sex were never adequately integrated (Greenson, 1954; Kernberg, 1967). With borderline regression, further desynthesis and instability of object representations threaten object constancy and cohesive object relations.

In treatment I initially functioned as an auxiliary ego and' organizing object for this patient. I tolerated and tried to clarify his extraordinary feelings of ambivalence and danger. I represented reality, consistency, and reason, offering assistance and response but not direct reassurance. Despite his deep distrust, doubt, and dread of contact, he began to develop a "psychotherapeutic alliance" (Zetzel, 1965). Such distrust and apprehension are primary issues with borderline patients. His hostile distrust and fear of retaliatory desertion were in constant focus. He wanted to ritually control our meetings, free of the destructive contamination he feared from within. His belief in the passive power of magical word and gesture was repeatedly confronted. He recognized his disappointment in my not providing immediate omnipotent restoration and cure. His communication became. more animated, direct, and personal. He relinquished his fear of contamination or contagious engulfment in my office chair. With the establishment of. a therapeutic dialogue, his washing became less intense. It became possible to recognize more current conflicts, which were colored by and condensed within the deeply regressive trends. The picture of his contemporary life situation slowly emerged, with spontaneous glimpses of his past.

As a young man he was inhibited and lonely, with few friends or dates. His only romance was with the girl he later married. She was receptive, submissive, and singularly supportive and interested in him. He regarded himself as relatively content. and. secure within the narrow and familiar limits of his marriage and family. He was not aware of his unconscious anxieties about both intimacy and separation, since he had established a conventional marriage and now had two married children.

Actually, a new daughter-in-law had recently moved temporarily into his home with her infant. I learned that his first frightening obsessions had previously appeared with ideas of German measles threatening his other pregnant daughter-in-law. His wife, with her sons married and free of maternal responsibility, went to work for the first time. During my observation of this patient and in his history there were. severe relapses of compulsive handwashing following separation. For example, his wife's return to work after vacations. He had a fantasy of replacing his aging, "deserting'* wife with his pretty daughter-in-law. Here was a man feeling. the decline of age, with jealousy of his sons' sexuality and young wives. His malignant obsessions were primarily concerned with cancer of the female sex organs; that is, with invasion and impregnation. His oedipal strivings (positive and negative) had been pathogenically. influenced by preoedipal sadomasochism and devouring. Also, in relation to separation, his own parents were in advanced old age and he felt he was losing his wife, his grown children, and his senile parents. His "delicate balance" was threatened by the evolution and erosion of the life cycle. The obsessive facade both concealed and bolstered the borderline personality structure. His crippling symptoms had determinants in disturbed ego functions, which regressively evaluated and reacted to intrapsychic danger. His oedipal strivings and avoidance bore the stamp of unresolved earlier oscillation between omnipotent possession and separation from the object. His conflicts over touch and contact not only reflected punitive prohibitions but also related to the protection and preservation of object relations and ego boundaries. The disruptive symptoms had important defensive and adaptive roles (for example, undoing, grasping, and a "holding operation") and were approached with caution. Even when his hands were abraded, 1 never suggested he stop washing.

In the psychotherapy some aspects of his sexual and aggressive conflicts and the symbolism of cancerous growth and decay became apparent. We talked about his omnipotent fantasies (that is, his confusion of thought and deed), his rage at his working wife, and his fear and guilt in relation to current incestuous objects, such as his daughters-in-law. He slowly recognized his veiled fear of loss of manhood, family, and status; his anxiety about age and change; and his yearnings to hold and sever past relationships. His struggles to both retain and relinquish his objects were core conflicts. Never confident or independent, he lived a rigidly controlled life of ambivalent activities and relationships.

For this man separation from wife or therapist aroused disorganizing anxiety and anger. The lack of stability of self and object representations left him with the danger of loss of object ties and ego identity. He needed the presence of the object, as a toddler does before full consolidation of object constancy, in order to secure integrated ego functions and support autonomy. His fear of inner dissolution and of regression and disorganization were associated with extraordinary ego passivity.

I believe the infantile omnipotence, fear of change, rigidity, and instability of the borderline condition are closely tied to ego passivity. I am speaking of ego passivity in relation to the imperatives of reality as well as to internal demands and pressures (Gray, 1967). While ego passivity is related to the problem of passive behavior and masochism, I am referring here to relative ego helplessness, to difficulty in maintaining ego controls, achievements, and goal direction. Speaking metaphorically, this is a borderline ego that anticipates defeat and accedes to regressive retreat. The borderline patient does not suffer the fragmentation of the psychotic process, but displays the regression and immobilization of passivity toward intrapsychic conflict. The passivity of such vital functions as ego synthesis may be the result of the primary disturbance of separation-individuation or may be a cause or concomitant of developmental failure. Resilience of borderline ego function is indicated in the capacity to control and reverse regression and in the adaptive use of regression.

Many borderline patients have a severely traumatic history. Their fantasies of overwhelming danger have the historical truth of childhood threats to their psychic survival (Frosch, 1967). Such traumas in early life sometimes provide a clear-cut etiology for subsequent developmental deviation and arrest. Borderline regressions in later life, from this viewpoint, represent modified reactivations of such earlier traumatic experience along with enfeebled efforts at mastery. Attempts at active mastery may be as basic an ego function as delay of discharge or anticipation. It is in being active, where formerly passive, in relation to traumatic anxiety that the borderline ego is particularly vulnerable. While ego efforts toward active mastery are far more persistent and efficient than in psychosis, they are passive and weak compared to the neurotic normal. This has pathogenic consequences for all later development with its unavoidable conflict and normative crises.

I have not said anything of the childhood of my patient with respect to developmental disturbance. There are important implicit issues of predisposition and pathogenesis. Was this adult patient a borderline case in childhood, or in adolescence? Should there not be early signs of developmental disorder? Was there a discrete traumatic experience or early traumas, or pathological patterns of development due to crippling constitutional or environmental factors? How did this patient really appear during the childhood phases of separation-individuation and later oedipal development? These and many related questions cannot be answered without further longitudinal studies of deviant children, reconstructions from adult psychoanalyses, and inferences from the psychoanalytic psychotherapy of borderline patients. Data from my patient pointed to a childhood of empathic deprivation with an alcoholic father and a seductive, but insensitive, narcissistic mother. I picture him as a tense and rigid toddler with premature apparent "pseudo" independence, which rested upon narcissistic detachment and fantasies of omnipotence. There was unresolved conflict over loss of control of impulse and object. Some differentiation of self and object had occurred, but with persistent splitting into idealized and devaluated representation along the anal lines of precious or worthless, pure or poisonous. An inflexible, punitive sphincter morality, which did not distinguish any nuances between clean and dirty, was associated with a poorly internalized and insufficiently abstracted superego.

My patient had a life-threatening attack of diphtheria, probably at four to five years of age. This occurred during the infancy of a younger sister, whose birth had already precipitated a depression with increasing distance from and jealous desire for his The patient was isolated and quarantined in what must have been a setting of profound anxiety for him and the whole family. This was more than half a century ago before the great therapeutic advances of medical science, particularly in relation to such infectious diseases as diphtheria. No doubt he was a potential menace to society, if we consider his immediate family and infant sister as this little patient's social world. Can we construct the family washing rituals, the dread of contamination and spread of disease? Were his clothes and possessions removed and destroyed? What power did this invalid child have, and what influence on the magical fantasies stirred by his contagious illness? We can see how the frantic handwashing of his adult illness appeased a cruel conscience, which demanded the cleansing and flushing of his contaminated thinking. During his diphtheritic illness anyone who had contact with him probably had to ritually wash, and undoubtedly there were attempts to wash and sterilize his clothes and room articles. In what way did this trauma contribute to oedipal disruption, regression, and later repetition?

From a taut, temperamental preschooler he developed into a pseudo-compliant, reticent, and retiring schoolboy. Detached and daydreaming, he was early left back in school despite excellent intelligence. His passive behavior became even more overt in adolescence. He was aloof and relatively friendless with narrow interests and activities, acquiescent without any enthusiasm. He did not consciously masturbate at all, often a borderline symptom in male adolescence. He then rationalized wearing gloves at night because of a contact dermatitis of his hands, and he was afraid of both irritation and contamination.

His hands were washed and salved frequently and meticulously. Here was the adolescent forerunner of the unresolved masturbatory conflicts, which were expressed in the regressive. handwashing syndrome some forty years later. Moreover, it is possible to sense the continuity of this patient's disruptive conflicts, despite their different manifestations at different periods. of, life. In his teens he had never been able to reach out assertively for friendship or, fulfillment He displayed a resigned indifference instead of the challenging and testing of adolescent exploration. His hands were. tied, and he could not readily maintain social ties or actively develop and consolidate his stunted masculine ego identity. I believe this patient is not atypical, and that the borderline adult personality emerges from a seriously disturbed childhood development and what is usually a borderline adolescence.

The treatment of the borderline regression evolves from grasp of the diagnosis and dynamics, within a developmental framework. There are arrests and deviations, in psychic structure which are pathogenic and predisposed to later conflict and regression. These early and often severe impairments in object relations and ego synthesis imply a guarded therapeutic prognosis. These patients vary in their ego resources and in their fixity and proximity to psychosis. In their severe regressions they are usually closer to psychosis. Some borderline patients are analyzable, or become analyzable in protracted analysis, or can be prepared for analysis. The others may be treated by an individually appropriate and psychoanalytically derived psychotherapy. Frequent appointments and careful attention to ego states may be very helpful in the initial approach to borderline regression. Though these patients may be fearful of emotional closeness and intimacy, I do not agree with Zetzel's (1971) view that these patients should not be seen more than once a week. A few may need an indefinite period of treatment.

The clinical vignette I presented was of an application of ego psychology in a reintegrative style of treatment with a particular borderline patient (who was not suitable for psychoanalysis). The psychotherapy shifted the patient's orientation to his more advanced and integrated development. The therapist is an organizing object for the patient's intensely ambivalent and tenuous attachments, promoting higher levels of ego integration and superego tolerance. The therapist may be both an auxiliary ego and superego, but must always recognize and support the patient's own efforts at individuation and adaptation. This patient's struggle against masturbation and separation was also a plea "to have and to hold." In my patient's handwashing, he wanted to free his hands and protect his objects, not only to wash his hands of them and his problems. Also, before the regression, the patient had functioned with modest achievement and advance, with some subtly limited autonomy. It is therefore important not to undermine higher level defenses and organization as well as consistently to interpret' primitive disruptive defenses. I am in general agreement: with Kernberg's (1968) and Knight's (1953) views on the treatment of the borderline patient, and would emphasize the need to interpret negative transference and the current gross distortions in the therapeutic relationship without regard to specific genetic interpretation. I would be very cautious, however, about efforts to actively structure or direct the patient's outside life, despite possible apparent benefits to the treatment effort. These patients are extremely fearful of being engulfed and controlled, of surrendering a fragile identity and independence. Their ego functions are not fragmented, as in schizophrenia, and their own exercise of their executive ego: functions must be encouraged. The therapist need not be remote, but should certainly not be excessively active or directive. Intact ego functions can be mobilized when ego passivity has been a cause and consequence of borderline regression. Within the limits of his ego impairment, the patient can participate in the therapeutic work and can be supported in his own progress toward reintegration. The multiple meanings of the therapist to the patient, including the overdetermined and often shifting transferences, should be understood by the therapist. The gross transference distortions of the therapist should be not only clarified but used to elucidate analogous distortions of the patient's current object relations and external reality. The primary emphasis is on the patient's immediate problems, and conflict and danger are clarified in terms of the current situation in which the patient regressed. The precipitating stress is related to the predisposition and underlying borderline psychopathology. With my patient the regression was considered first as a decompensation, and then as a defense. Surface danger (for example, the fantasied desertion by his wife and hidden desire to replace her with his daughter-in-law) was brought into widened awareness with support of active ego assimilation.

The therapist's own appreciation of the unconscious infantile danger situation and related early ego disturbance is often not interpreted in psychotherapy. Many subtle aspects of the patient's transference ties, so vital to his psychotherapeutic progress, will be humbly and deliberately left uninterpreted. There must be careful dosage of speech and silence, of appointments and separations. The borderline personality, so often traumatized and vulnerable, is especially sensitive to the therapist's empathy and real attitudes. This may supersede other therapeutic considerations.

The doctor's patience and perseverance are required and tested. To remain objective and understanding, calm and accepting, and to be neither manipulated nor provoked may provide new models for identification and object relationship. The therapist who is not seduced or intimidated into acting out with the patient may prevent an induced repetition of previous traumatic experience. The regressed patient can then use the stable and understanding therapist as an auxiliary ego and organizing object, permitting more mature and possibly new types of psychic problem-solving activity.

My own patient made a functional recovery and returned from the regressive borderline of involutional psychosis. He resumed his ordinary activities and interests, with restoration of his life facade of ordered rigidity and narcissistic constriction. He is undoubtedly prone to severe regression under stress, with a functional but fragile recovery.

The application of modern psychoanalytic concepts can lead to the understanding and scientific therapy of borderline regression. These patients, so often puzzling, challenging, and relatively refractory, can respond to insightful treatment and have much to teach us.

REFERENCES

Freud, S. (1937). Analysis terminable and interminable. In *Standard Edition*: 23:209–253, 1964.

Frosch, J. (1967). Severe regressive states during analysis. *J. Amer. Psychoanal. Assoc.* 15:491–507.

——— (1970). Psychoanalytic considerations of the psychotic character. *J. Amer. Psychoanal. Assoc.* 18:24–50.

Gray, P. (1967), Panel report: activity-passivity. *J. Amer. Psychoanal. Assoc.* 15:709–728.

Greenson, R. (1954). The struggle against identification. *J. Amer. Psychoanal. Assoc.* 2:200–217.

Grinker, R., Werble, B., & Drye, R. (1968). *The Borderline Syndrome*. New York: Basic Books.

Kernberg, O. (1967). Borderline personality organization. *J. Amer. Psychoanal. Assoc.* 15:641–685.

——— (1968). The treatment of patients with borderline personality organization. Int. J. Psycho-anal. 49 :600–619.

Knight, R. (1953). Borderline states. Management and psychotherapy of the borderline schizophrenic patient. In *Psychoanalytic Psychiatry and Psychology,* eds. R. Knight & C. Friedman, 97–109, 1 10–112. New York: International Universities Press, 1954.

Loewenstein, R. (1957). Some thoughts on interpretation in the theory and practice of psychoanalysis. *Psychoanalytic Study of the Child* 12:127–150.

Mahler, M. (1967). On human symbiosis and the vicissitudes of individuation. *J. Amer. Psychoanal. Assoc.* 1 5:740–763.

Zetzel, E. (1965). Theory of therapy in relation to a developmental model of the psychic apparatus. *Int. J. Psychoanal.* 46: 39–52.

(1971). A developmental approach to the borderline patient. Amer. J. Psych., 127:867–871.

Acknowledgments

This article is an expanded version of a brief paper, "Contribution of Psychoanalytic Thinking to the Psychotherapy of Borderline Patients," given at a joint panel of the American Psychiatric Association and the American Psychoanalytic Association in May, 1970.

CHAPTER 31

Seduction Trauma: Representation, Deferred Action, and Pathogenic Development

(1996). *J. Amer. Psychoanal. Assn.*, (44):1147–1164.

Historical Introduction

Seduction trauma refers to a range of phenomena currently described under the rubric of child abuse. Freud elucidated the fantasy distortion and elaboration of traumatic experience and retained the importance of actual trauma. Psychic trauma is associated with the alteration of self and object representations and ensuing new identifications, e.g., with victim and aggressor. The "deferred action" of psychic trauma is an antiquated concept and psychic trauma has immediate effects as well as far reaching developmental consequences. Prior trauma predisposes to later traumatic vulnerability and to trauma linked to phase specific unconscious conflict. The pathogenesis of child sex abuse and the enactment of oedipal incest extends before and after the oedipal phase, is often associated with other forms of abuse, and has a history of pathogenic parent-child relationship.

This is the 100th anniversary of the publication of *Studies on Hysteria* (Breuer and Freud, 1893-1895) with its exploration of seduction trauma and treatment through abreaction or "catharsis." The seduction theory proposed that the psychopathology of adults stems from repressed childhood sexual trauma.

Childhood seduction trauma is now designated as the sexual abuse of children, a problem of enormous psychological and social importance. Currently the term *seduction* may be regarded as an umbrella concept which includes seductive behavior, sexual harassment, coercive molestation, sexual abuse, and child rape. No child can give informed consent to a sexual relationship.

The discarded seduction theory was a theory of etiology with a unitary pathogenic agent. Traumatic seduction, however, was never actually abandoned as pathogenic. Repressed traumatic memories were regarded as similar to encapsulated harmful foreign bodies that could cause later disorder. Freud gradually recognized that the reports by his patients of childhood incest were often fantasies, or as he came to understand, admixtures of fantasy and reality. Freud certainly appreciated the importance of incest and other forms of abusive behavior involving children. No doubt child molestation, child prostitution, and child pornography flourished in turn-of-the-century Vienna, as it did throughout the world.

This paper will address the importance of both psychic and external reality, that is, the importance of both reality and fantasy in the overdetermination of incestuous traumatic abuse and subsequent developmental disturbance. There is a continuous overlap and interplay between psychic reality and external reality, and unconscious fantasy codetermines actual experience (Arlow, 1969). I shall stress the anchoring of unconscious fantasy in external reality; the role of identifications, especially identification with the aggressor, and with the defenses of the aggressor; and pathogenic development. The concept of deferred action will be questioned, highlighting issues of traumatic memory and the immediate and persisting effects of trauma. Incest trauma in protean form will be considered in conjunction with changing psychic representations of self and object, and the subsequent transformation of the personality.

Traumatic experience tends to produce a fixation to trauma, a fear or phobia of the traumatic situation; or, in contrast, a traumatophilia, an attraction to and often unconscious seduction of trauma; that is, a seeking after traumatic experience, repetition of the trauma in thought, feeling, and action, as well as a vulnerability to regression and retraumatization. A traumatized person may try to avoid or to arrange potential traumatic revivals.

Breuer and Freud (1893-1895) observed, "hysterics suffer mainly from reminiscences" (p. 7), referring particularly to traumatic memories of "seduction." There was generally not "the single traumatic cause but a group of similar ones" and therapy required "taking all the provoking causes into account" (p. 173). "The particular nature of the symptoms is explained by their relation to the traumatic scenes which were their cause" (p. 14). Freud (1896) also wrote of partial traumas, "which have only been able to exercise a traumatic effect by summation" (p. 6). One may recognize here the forerunner of the later concepts of strain trauma (Kris, 1956), cumulative trauma (Khan, 1963), and deferred action. When siblings were involved in actual incest, Freud (1896) concluded that these siblings had already been seduced by an adult. This was an early example of the repetition of trauma and the child's identification with the abuser or aggressor in repeating the traumatic experience. Those who were seduced became seducers, and seduction trauma led to the seduction of trauma. Abuser and abused were then alternated or amalgamated. Children who have been abused are at risk for abusing themselves or others.

Modern concepts of trauma derive from Freud's discoveries and formulations. Myths and folklore testify to the cross-cultural importance of childhood "seduction traumas." Freud had encouraged Otto Rank to present his studies of incest drama to the first three meetings of the Wednesday night group in Freud's apartment (October 1906). This work became Rank's 600-page volume, *The Incest Theme in Literature and Legend*(1912). Rank provided extensive literary confirmation of Freud's clinical formulations. Freud's studies led him to elaborate the preconditions and predisposition to "seduction trauma," the cause, content, and consequences of trauma, assimilation, and later recovery from trauma. Fixation to trauma implied "unfinished business" and a tendency for trauma to have an organizing effect (Greenacre, 1952), for trauma to be cumulative, repeated, with the interweaving of shock and strain trauma (Kris, 1956; Blum, 1986). Constitutional factors and innate predisposition were important considerations in both parent and child. Defining trauma in psychobiological terms, Freud (1917) referred to "an increase of stimulus too powerful to be dealt with or worked off in the normal way, and this must result in permanent disturbances of the manner in which the energy operates" (p. 275). Freud's (1926) definition of trauma emphasized the experience of traumatic anxiety and ego helplessness and was linked to unconscious conflict: "we have a perfect right to describe repression, which lies at the basis of every neurosis, as a reaction to trauma—as an elementary traumatic neurosis..." (1919b, p. 210). The introduction of structural theory further emphasized universal unconscious conflict, with determinants from all three psychic agencies and reality. The two theories of psychic trauma and psychic conflict were interrelated, though sometimes isolated and sometimes integrated in subsequent theory and practice.

Psychic trauma had damaging consequences. The concept of permanent disturbance remains important, but different from the attenuation, sublimation, and mastery of trauma. Freud (1937) later paradoxically proposed that neuroses in which trauma was a prominent factor had a far more positive prognosis. Freud's multiple perspectives, shifting emphases, and sometimes paradoxical positions contributed to later analytic controversy over his own and subsequent views of endowment versus experience, and oedipal fantasy versus actual traumatic seduction. Furthermore, discrete incidents of traumatic seduction were not equivalent to pathological incestuous relationships and sexual abuse extending over time and different phases of development (Neubauer, 1967). The concept of cumulative trauma coalesced with later concepts of developmental disorder and deviation.

Freud's formulations concerning the fantasy or reality of childhood seduction were inconsistent, and on occasion he proposed that differentiation might not only be impossible but perhaps did not matter (1917, p. 370). Isolated statements were often cited; for example, "neurotic symptoms were not related directly to actual events but to wishful phantasies, and that as far as the neurosis was concerned psychical reality was of more importance than material reality" (Freud, 1925, p. 34) and "hysterical symptoms had derived from phantasies and not from real occurrences" (Freud, 1933, p. 120). He had also learned (1905, p. 274) that seduction fantasies might fend off "memories of the subjects' own sexual activity (infantile masturbation)," but he also questioned his possible personal influence in some patients' reports of childhood seduction.

The notion that Freud abandoned the significance of real experience and attended only to isolated fantasy is contradicted in the corpus of his scientific writing (Schimek, 1987). His case histories and papers are replete with references to actual incestuous seduction. Freud continued to seek historical truth in his final papers on "Constructions in Analysis" (1937) and "Moses and Monotheism" (1939). Freud (1917) had stated:

> If the infantile experiences brought to light by analysis were invariably real, we should feel that we were standing on firm ground; if they were regularly falsified and revealed as inventions, as phantasies of the patient, we should be obliged to abandon this shaky ground and look for salvation elsewhere. But neither of these things is the case: the position can be shown to be that the childhood experiences constructed or remembered in analysis are sometimes indisputably false and sometimes equally certainly correct, and in most cases compounded of truth and falsehood [p. 367].

In this connection he stated (Freud, 1900), "Hysterical symptoms are not attached to actual memories, but to phantasies erected on the basis of memories" (p. 491). Freud (1917) repeatedly stressed the reality of trauma: "Fantasies of being seduced are of particular interest, because so often they are not fantasies but real memories" (p. 370). Freud (1931) later stated, "Actual seduction is common enough ... it invariably disturbs the natural course of the developmental processes, and it often leaves behind extensive and lasting consequences" (p. 232). Half a century later, Anna Freud (1981) reasserted her father's findings: "Far from existing only as a fantasy, incest is thus also a fact. ... It would be a fatal mistake to underrate either the importance or the frequency of its actual occurrence" (p. 34). The traumatic, pathogenic effects of incest are compounded because the child cannot turn to the parent for help when the parent has sexually abused the child.

Although it is sometimes very difficult or impossible to differentiate the fantasy from the reality of child abuse, there has been an attempt to use this issue to inflict abuse on Freud and psychoanalysis. Freud was accused in his lifetime of often suggesting fantasies and false memories of seduction to his patients.

Freud has now been misinterpreted and misrepresented as the parent who abuses the child and conceals the abuse, or as the colluding parent who inflicts parallel or further abuse on the child by denial and disavowal of the reality of sexual abuse. Freud is depicted by detractors as living in a fantasy world where no actual incestuous or abusive behavior has occurred. This form of Freud denigration is also related to treating his insights as unconfirmed conjecture and to attempts at character assassination as if thereby to kill his ideas.

Freud's preanalytic seduction theory was replaced by the formulation of the Oedipus complex in which incest is a universal fantasy. While both parent and child have incestuous fantasies, the parents are responsible for maintaining intrafamilial boundaries and for not responding inappropriately to a child's immature seductiveness or provocation. Analytic recognition of both preexisting sexual fantasy and actual incest experience provided an intrapsychic focus and unconscious meaning of the trauma without disregarding real trauma. Beyond the simple concept of passive victimization, psychic trauma was related to intrapsychic representation and fantasy as well as real life experience.

Deferred Action

There were actually several seduction theories of pathogenesis (Blass and Simon, 1994). Freud's formal seduction hypothesis of 1895 and 1896 centered upon memories of infantile seduction which, at the time of registration, were not necessarily experienced as traumatic. The earlier event registered in memory becomes traumatic as a result of deferred action in which a provocative, later experience modified the memory. Freud (1895) wrote: "We invariably find that a memory is repressed that has only become a trauma by deferred action" (p. 356). Deferred action then occurred when an unconscious memory of seduction was revived and altered after puberty. This deferred action (*Nachträglichkeit, aprés coup*) of childhood trauma is a form of retroactive or retrospective effect. The concept has been generalized to refer to retrospective resignification or changed meaning, or a later reinterpretation or construction which results in a fresh trauma. Freud had referred to the "retranscription of memory" in accordance with fresh circumstances in a letter to Fliess (Masson, 1985, p. 208), a more general concept of the mutative effects of later experiences upon memory not tied to trauma. This conceptual modification was retained by Laplanche and Pontalis (1973, p. 111) who defined Nachträglichkeit as: "experiences, impressions and memory-traces may be revised at a later date to fit in with fresh experiences or with the attainment of a new state of development." This reformulation was elaborated by Modell (1990) who proposed that the ego can constantly remodel memory, emphasizing the progressive therapeutic impact of the analytic experience and relationship. Deferred action has also been viewed as an attempt to reconcile intrapsychic fantasy and actual trauma and to reconcile past and present theory (Thoma and Cheshire, 1991; Kunstlicher, 1994). The modification of memory with life experience and analytic experience, and its retrieval, report, and reintegration at different phases of analysis, is not equivalent to the deferred action which transforms memory-fantasy into new trauma. Traumatic regression and therapeutic progression are paired, but opposite views of deferred action.

Expansion of developmental theory raised questions about the relationship of trauma to the process of development as well as to unconscious fantasy and conflict. Transformation of an earlier, benign experience into a malignant trauma was largely an intrapsychic process, dependent upon maturation and development, and not requiring new external traumatization. Freud also noted reparative efforts at mastery in the nightmares, transference, and sublimations of traumatized patients. Initial developmental interference, deviation, and arrest due to trauma was in contrast to the general idea of deferred action which indicated that the trauma would first become pathogenic at a later phase. The concepts of deferred action and seduction trauma, fantasy and/or reality, were historically linked together and to early theories of pathogenesis.

Deferred action was then revived and extended in the Wolf Man case history. Freud (1918) inferred that the single, actual parental primal scene experience and associated sexual seduction by his sister and nursemaid shattered the Wolf Man's psychosexual development via deferred action. Freud proposed that this primal scene at 18 months was not traumatic then, not traumatic until a developmental reorganization at age 4. An earlier memory ostensibly became a "retrospective trauma" under present conditions (Sandler, 1967; Mahony, 1984; Schimek, 1987). What is more remarkable is that this altered representation and understanding which resulted in traumatic experience, occurred during a dream on the Wolf Man's fourth birthday—a dream which activated and altered the Wolf Man's presumed primal scene experience at the age of 18 months.

This famous dream is important because of its significance in psychoanalytic history and theory and its role as the centerpiece of the Wolf Man case report. The dream (a nightmare) became a "fresh trauma" which, on analysis, led to the classic exposition of primal scene oedipal trauma. It is doubtless the cardinal example of deferred action, and is also relevant to important, contemporary issues concerning, for example, psychic reality and external reality; memory and myth; and developmental arrest and progression.

The complexity and daring of Freud's conjectures and formulations, the presentation of his own assertions, doubts, conflicts, and changes in psychoanalytic theory, suggest that *"nachträglichkeit"* requires the most careful and critical evaluation. The deferred effects were described as a "deferred revision" (Freud, 1918, p. 38). The deferred traumatic consequences, both depending upon development and promoting regression, are perhaps without parallel in the elucidation of the psychic trauma of "seduction." Freud (1918, p. 38) wondered whether it was possible at the age of 4 for deferred revision of the impressions at 18 months to later penetrate the child's understanding. He then assigned an extraordinary developmental significance and function to the Wolf Man's dream and asserted, "During the dream he had reached a new phase in his sexual organization. … The activation of the primal scene in the dream now brought him back to the genital organization. He discovered the vagina and the biological significance of masculine and feminine" (pp. 46-47). Freud (1918) then stated that the psychosexual development was "diverted by the scene of observation of the coitus, which in its deferred action, operated like a second seduction" (p. 47). To be sure, Freud did not eliminate immediate effects of the primal scene, and he noted the infantile appetite disturbance as well as an acceleration of sexual maturation. He regarded these effects, however, as "insignificant in appearance" (p. 107), that is, compared to the effects of traumatization by the "second seduction." The traumatic effect of the

Wolf Man's infantile malaria, inappropriate, multiple mothering, and paternal psychosis was overlooked at that time (Blum, 1974).

The Wolf Man's dream fantasy, however, was presumed to transform an earlier nontraumatic preoedipal memory into a new trauma. Development here largely occurs in a fantasy world, isolated from the child's life. The enduring psychic reality of the dream became more important than the actual past experience or its memory, ongoing developmental change, or current pathogenic experience. Deferred action may paradoxically deny past trauma and yet assert its unconscious fantasy evocation and elaboration. Real preoedipal trauma may be denied, devalued, reduced to a dream. As in the expression, "It's only a dream," the "real" traumatic overstimulation is shorn of reality and importance and could invite an exclusive fantasy focus.

"Deferred action" is an ambiguous concept, a dubious, antiquated, theoretical legacy. Deferred action overlooks the immediate and potentially powerful effects of preoedipal trauma and is dissociated from considerations of cumulative trauma and developmental disturbance. Deferred action tended to force pathogenesis into an entirely oedipal configuration. The Wolf Man's preoedipal "seduction trauma" and intervening development were propelled into a phase-specific oedipal trauma. Later trauma actually reactivates early traumatic memories (e.g., infantile seduction), rather than merely indifferent or "provocative" memories. Because of its relation to temporal and causal issues, I propose "nachträglichkeit" or deferred action as an unrecognized precursor of the contemporary concept of developmental transformation. In the prototypical Wolf Man case an out of phase preoedipal primal scene "trauma" at 18 months of age was later transformed into a phase specific oedipal trauma, concurrent with developmental progression. For example, the Wolf Man's preoedipal fears of separation and object loss were revived and were reexperienced as threats of castration and death at the time of his fourth birthday nightmare. Much important development occurred between 1 1/2 years and the Wolf Man's nightmare at his fourth birthday. Preoedipal developmental disturbance was then minimized, but the case presaged the preoedipal influence on oedipal and subsequent conflict and development. Trauma not only influenced subsequent development but was influenced by development. Developmental accretions and transformations altered the preconditions for the representation and meaning of traumatic experience. "Deferred action" emphasized traumatic events and memory rather than cumulative developmental effects of shock and strain trauma, and pathogenic object relationships. The concept of deferred action deterred consideration of real infantile experience and the complex overdetermination of pathogenesis through development. In my view, deferred action should refer to developmental alterations which may not only have traumatic effects but may be detrimental or beneficial, regressive or progressive. Transformations occur through the different phases of development, and recapitulations are new editions rather than replications (Novick and Novick, 1994).

Freud (1911) repeatedly considered "the difficulty of distinguishing unconscious phantasies from memories which have become unconscious" (p. 225). This was a general theoretical problem, and Freud (1911) had noted, "every neurosis has as its result, and probably therefore as its purpose, a forcing of the patient out of real life, an alienating of him from reality" (p. 218). He later added, "We are in doubt to begin with whether we are dealing with reality or phantasies. Later, we are enabled by certain indications to come to a decision and we are faced by the task of conveying it to the patient" (1917, p. 368). Technical as well as theoretical issues in the analytic differentiation of fantasy and reality have continued to be of great importance. The problems of the parents' contribution to the child's distortion of reality and memory, and the analyst's possible similar distortions, surfaced in and far beyond the Freud-Ferenczi controversy (Kirshner, 1993; Blum, 1994a).

Controversy continues in contemporary questions of narrative versus historical truth (Spence, 1982), and "false memory syndrome" (Brenneis, 1994). "False memories" are reminiscent of the seductive stories of incestuous seduction which contributed to the seduction theory or which were attributed to the therapist's suggestion or seduction. Either parent or analyst could be a "false witness." Both patient and therapist might unwittingly collude in their illusory belief, cocreating new pseudomemories and new "innocent victims." Parents and caregivers have claimed to be victimized by false accusations of child abuse. Trauma can be invoked as a defense to mask conflict, to blame others for abuse, disappointments, mistakes, and misfortunes, and to avoid personal guilt and responsibility. Traumatic memory can serve as a screen memory for earlier or later traumas. Traumatic memory may also be registered and retrieved differently from other memories and subject to greater screening and defensive alteration. Defense and memory may be impaired by structural damage with threats to psychic survival (Laub and Auerhahn, 1993). Preverbal memories may not be encoded in symbolic or linguistic forms, but in visual, affective, or sensorimotor forms. This may be related to the difficulty in retrieving verbal recall of infantile trauma, and the intrusion of frightening, visual flashbacks which are experienced without the psychological distance experienced with other memories (Greenberg and Van der Kolk, 1987). Horrifying "daymares" may take the place of pleasant, wishful dreams. In their vivid intensity and sense of reality, they represent derivative reproductions of traumatic experience. Trauma has overwhelmed repression.

In some instances incest has never been forgotten, though such conscious memory has not been correlated with the type of severity of damage. There may also be isolated areas of amnesia, with gaps and discontinuities in memory and in the sense of self. Periods of amnesia may alternate with disguised flashbacks, fragments, or isolated memories of the sexual abuse. A number of memories may be screened and telescoped into a singular recollection. Implicit aspects of memory in which the person has no conscious awareness of remembering (Shevrin, 1994) are an indication of the compromise between the unrememberable and the unforgettable (Frank, 1969). Any traumatic experience may be secondarily erotized, complicating the specific differentiation of actual incest. Furthermore, incestuous abuse is commonly associated with other forms of trauma and developmental disorder, complicating the evaluation of pathogenic consequences of incest. Though the incidence of incest is far greater than previously known, the problems of conscious and unconscious falsification of memory require separate discussion.

It may be noted that analytic assessment of incest no longer depends upon recovered memories, direct recall, or external confirmation. Conscious memory is only more or less a reliable record versus an incomplete, distorted revision of the past. Establishing childhood incest and sexual abuse requires reconstruction. The reconstruction of trauma depends upon the totality, cohesion, and logical fit of the analytic and anamnestic data (Greenacre, 1975; Blum, 1994b; Person and Klar, 1994). It is, nevertheless, not always possible to determine the reality of sexual abuse or to unravel cause, consequence, developmental transformations, and retrospective alterations of experience.

Intrapsychic Representation and Real Experience

Incest is multidimensional in cause and effect and does not have the same meaning or influence in different phases of life (e.g., latency versus adolescence). The fantasy system of the child or adolescent is altered by the traumatic experience and ego efforts toward adaptation and recovery. There is a continuous reciprocal influence between fantasy and reality. The child's reaction to sexual abuse is related to developmental phase, vulnerability to trauma, and to his or her unconscious fantasies. The reaction also depends upon the nature, onset, and duration of abuse; on caregiver response, such as threats, and/or concealment; the child's ego development, personality organization, resilience, and ego resources; the relationship of the child to the abuser (e.g., whether the sexual abuse was inflicted by a parent, relative, or a sibling; and the availability of protective, comforting, and rescuing objects).

Fantasy construction in which memories are altered and distorted may continue through life, thus rewriting and rationalizing history and shaping personal myth. The sexual abuse of children has protean effects without any uniform etiology or pathognomonic syndrome. Similar disturbances are found in nonabused individuals. There are always both psychological and psychosomatic residues of incest (Levine, 1990; Kramer and Akhtar, 1991). There may also be neurophysiological sequellae, affecting the regulation of pleasure and pain, anxiety and sexual arousal. Pyrrhic oedipal victory, guilt, shame, and narcissistic injury are often of massive magnitude. With all severe trauma such as incest, the traumatized individual is never the same person. Given traumatic and regressive vulnerability, are some parents retraumatized by repeating their own childhood incest trauma with their children?

The fantasy distortions of the seduced and abused child have more than a grain of truth. The fantasies have present and past reality coordinates and determinants. Shared fantasies may be enacted in an incestuous partnership with its own rewards and punishments. Fantasy and reality interpenetrate with mutual influence, and intrapsychic alterations occur without "deferred action." Identification with aggressor, victim, and protectors/rescuers contribute to changing self and object representations and to alterations in identity and character. Inevitable identification with the aggressor includes the motives, defenses, affects, and aggression of the aggressor. Identification with the aggressor may be included in the role of identification in recovery from trauma, but it is a significant factor in the proclivity to repeat and provoke trauma. The seduced child may then seduce or induce further trauma to the self or others, but only a minority of such abused children appear to become abusive parents. The repetition may also be in the service of turning passive into active and of attempting reparative mastery of traumatic experience. Incestuous abuse may be followed by a protective attachment and allegiance to the abuser, masochistic subjugation, or demands for justice, punishment, and revenge, etc. There may be a global identification with the aggressor or a more selective identification with his or her defenses, traits, attitudes, and particular behaviors such as denial or evasion, fellatio or anal penetration.

The self and object representations of the sexually abused child are often dissociated or "split" in various ways, with a pathogenic internalization of the incestuous self and object relationship. Sexually abused children use dissociation to preserve a representation of a good parent and self-worth.

Contradictory images and attitudes may exist in consciousness, and an abusive mother may be described both as "mommy dearest" and as a despised witch. The contradictory representations of a parent and child incest dyad represent the confusion and reversal of the generations. However, the parent may actually display inconsistent attitudes and contradictory behavior. The "parentified child" is expected to comfort and gratify the parent and is a metaphor which also represents realistic aspects of the parent as an overgrown child. Parents may alternate between affectionate interest and incestuous abuse of their child. Some seduced patients remain fixated to their incest partner in all subsequent erotic fantasy.

Pathogenic Developmen

The pathogenesis of incest is vastly overdetermined and often encompasses more than core oedipal conflict. I shall focus here on preoedipal influence and the continuing pathogenic parent-child relationship throughout development rather than "deferred action." Incest gradually emerges in disordered families, exacerbates the disorder, and may repeat previous incest in the parent's childhood. The predisposition to act out oedipal fantasy, however, may depend upon preoedipal (and oedipal) disturbances and traumatic life experience, including adult trauma. Such acting out may be precipitated by psychosis or drug addiction, but is not limited to a specific diagnostic category. The sexual abuse of children is, at times, predictable on the basis of prior parental traumatization and parental fantasies even before the child is born (Steele, 1994). It should be noted that a colluding nonprotective parent actually protects the parents! The abusive parent is protected and the colluding parent is also self-protective. "Unknowing" collusion avoids conscious guilt and is self-exonerating while condoning vicarious incest and child abuse.

Incest behaviors range along a continuum from unconscious to conscious, from inhibited arousal to orgasm, from remote derivatives to incest enactments of intercourse. Immature, irresponsible parents may exploit the child for their own gratification and their own defensive needs. Empathy and appreciation of the child's developmental needs are deficient or impaired. Some parents are sexually excited by babies, others by adolescents. Some are only fixated on an incestuous relationship, others are generally pedophilic and also molest children outside the family. Some parents only gradually initiate incest through years of excessive hugging, kissing, and caressing. Others sporadically rape their sons and daughters and may or may not seek to continue an incest relationship. Daughters who are impregnated through incest constitute a separate subgroup. A father and daughter may be incestuous allies against the mother just as mother and son may be incestuous allies against the father. A parent may seek infantile love and simultaneously seek to avenge or punish the child's other parent and his own parent through repeated incestuous abuse. An entire family may directly as well as vicariously participate in incest. Those children who are neglected, callously mistreated, rejected, and affection starved are more vulnerable to sexual exploitation. Incest also serves the parent's infantile narcissism and the narcissistic love or rage of the parent. Some cases highlight the lack of maternal bonding, holding, attunement, and the lack of appropriate physical stimulation. Parents who cannot permit separation- individuation and who retain omnipotent ownership of the child's body and the child's personality, are at much greater risk for erotization of the parent-child relationship. Neither parent nor child can separate and individuate, and the child may be a fetish object for such a pedophile parent (Mahler, Pine, and Bergman, 1975). Parents may bed, bathe, and toilet with the infant, and continue to possessively engulf the child; their incestuous behavior is suffused with pregenital aims.

The mother who masturbates her infant, or has oral genital contact with her infant, or the father who invites the toddler to play with his genitals or rubs his penis against his baby, is sexually abusive prior to the child's oedipal phase. Incestuous parents may stimulate and invite the child's seduction and cannot set limits for the child or themselves, so that unconscious collusion ensues. Through projection and identification they may regressively confuse their child's needs and wishes with their own narcissistic and sexual gratification. Though outwardly presenting a strong, supportive facade, an incestuous parent may be starved for affection and nurturance and symbiotically dependent. Oedipal jealousy and incestuous demands may simultaneously represent preoedipal infantile envy, rage, and omnipotent control of a narcissistic object.

I differ with those who have proposed that incest may be benign or adaptive or a "love affair." To my mind, incest may promote certain ego functions such as anticipation and vigilance, but there is usually far greater ego injury. Family secrets and the "conspiracy of silence" about incest add severe insult to injury. Since incest tends to be associated with multiple traumas (physical abuse, spouse abuse, etc.) it may superficially appear to be the "lesser evil." Resilient individuals may surmount, in degree, such pathogenic life experiences. Perhaps spurred by the need to master trauma and to overcome shame and guilt, they may develop highly refined artistic and scientific sublimations.

The psychoanalytic literature on cases of actual incest with sexual intercourse (e.g., Shengold, 1989; Margolis, 1984; Richards, 1988; Gabbard and Twemlow, 1994) is continuing to enlarge with important new observations and formulations. The vast psychoanalytic literature on incest and related sexual abuse of children initially derives from Freud's initial investigation of seduction trauma. These fertile studies promise new, expanded analytic understanding and treatment of sexually abused patients.

REFERENCES

Arlow, J. (1969). Fantasy, memory and reality testing. *Psychoanal. Q.*, 38:1–17.

Blass, R. & Simon, B. (1994). The value of the historical perspective to contemporary psychoanalysis: Freud's "Seduction Hypothesis." Int. J Psychoanal. 75:677–694.

Blum, H. (1974). The borderline childhood of the Wolf Man, *J Amer. Psychoanal. Assn.*, 22:721–742.

——— (1983). Splitting of the ego and its relation to parent loss. *J Amer. Psychoanal. Assn.*, (Suppl.) 31:301–324.

——— (1986). The concept of the reconstruction of trauma. In *The Reconstruction of Trauma*, ed. A. Rothstein. Madison, CT: Int. Univ. Press, pp. 7–27.

——— (1987). The role of identification in the resolution of trauma: The Anna Freud Memorial Lecture. *Psychoanal. Q.*, 56:609–627.

——— (1989). Punitive parenthood and childhood trauma: the psychoanalytic core. In *Festschrift in Honor of Leo Rangell*. Madison, CT: Int. Univ. Press.

——— (1994a). The confusion of tongues and psychic trauma. *Int. J Psychoanal.*, 71:871–882.

——— (1994b). Reconstruction in Psychoanalysis: Childhood Revisited and Recreated. Madison, CT: Int. Univ. Press.

Brenneis, C. (1994). Memories of childhood sexual abuse. *J Amer. Psychoanal. Assn.,* 42:1027–1054.

Breuer, J., & Freud, S. (1893–1895). Studies on hysteria. *S.E.,* 2.

Ferenczi, S. (1933). Confusion of tongues between the adult and the child. In *Final Contributions to the Problems and Methods of Psychoanalysis.* London: Ho- garth, 1955, pp. 156–167.

Frank, A. (1969). The unrememberable and the unforgettable: passive primal repression. *Psychoanal. Study Child,* 24:48–77.

Freud, A. (1981). A psychoanalyst's view of sexual abuse by parents. In *Sexually Abused Children and Their Families,* ed. P. Mrazek & C. Kempe. Oxford, U.K.: Pergamon, p. 34.

Freud, S. (1895). Project for a scientific psychology. *S.E.,* 1:283–397.

——— (1896). The aetiology of hysteria. *S.E.,* 3:187–221.

——— (1900). The interpretation of dreams. *S.E.,* 4 & 5.

——— (1905). Three essays on the theory of sexuality. *S.E.,* 7:125–245.

——— (1911). Formulations on the two principles of mental functioning. *S.E.,* 12:213–226.

——— (1917). Introductory lectures on psycho-analysis. *S.E.,* 15 & 16.

——— (1918). From the history of an infantile neurosis. *S.E.,* 17:1–122.

——— (1919a). A child is being beaten: a contribution to the study of the origin of sexual perversions. *S.E.,* 17:175–204.

——— (1919b). Introduction to *Psycho-analysis and the War Neuroses. S.E.,* 205–210.

——— (1925). An autobiographical study. *S.E.,* 20:1–71.

——— (1926). Inhibitions, symptoms, and anxiety. *S.E.,* 20:75–172.

——— (1931). Female sexuality. *S.E.,* 21:221–243.

——— (1933). New introductory lectures on psychoanalysis. *S.E.,* 7:7–182.

——— (1937). Analysis terminable and interminable. *S.E.,* 23:209–253.

——— (1939). Moses and monotheism. *S.E.,* 23:1–137.

Gabbard, G. & Twemlow, W.W. (1994). Mother-son incest in the pathogenesis of narcissistic personality disorder. *J Amer. Psychoanal. Assn.,* 42:171–190.

Greenacre, p. (1952). *Trauma, Growth, and Personality.* New York: Norton.

——— (1975). On reconstruction.] *Amer. Psychoanal. Assn.,* 23:693–712.

Greenberg, M. & van Der Kolk, B. (1987). Retrieval and integration of traumatic memories with the "Pointing Cure." In *Psychological Trauma,* ed. B. Van der Kolk. Washington, DC: Amer. Psychiatric Press.

Khan, M. (1963). The concept of cumulative trauma. Psychoanal. Study Child, 18:286–306.

Kirshner, L. (1993). Concepts of reality and psychic reality in psychoanalysis as illustrated by the disagreement between Freud and Ferenczi. *Int. J Psychoanal.,* 74:219–230.

Kramer, S. & Akhtar, S. (1991). *The Trauma of Transgression.* New York: Aronson.

KRIS, E. (1956). The recovery of childhood memories in psychoanalysis. *Psychoanal. Study Child,* 11:54–88.

Kunstlicher, R. (1994). *Nachtraglichkeit*: the intermediary of an unassimilated impression and experience. *Scand. Psychoanal. Rev.,* 17:101–118.

l.aplanche, J. & Pontalis, j. (1973). *The Language of Psychoanalysis.* New York: Norton.

l. Aus, D. & Auerhahn, N. (1993). Knowing and not knowing massive psychic trauma: forms of traumatic memory. *Int. J Psychoanal.,* 74:287–302.

Levine, h., Ed. (1990). *Adult Analysis and Childhood Sexual Abuse.* Hillsdale, NJ: Analytic Press.

Mahler, M., Pine, F. & Bergman, a. (1975). *The Psychological Birth of the Human Infant.* New York: Basic Books.

Mahony, p. (1984). *The Cries of the Wolf-Man.* New York: Int. Univ. Press.

Margolis, M. (1984). A case of mother-adolescent son incest: a follow up study. *Psychoanal. Q.,* 53:355–385.

Masson, j., Ed. (1985). *The Complete Letters of Sigmund Freud to Wilhelm Fliess.* Cam- bridge, MA: Harvard Univ. Press.

Modell, A. (1990). *Other Times, Other Realities.* Cambridge, MA: Harvard Univ. Press.

Neubauer, P. (1967). Trauma and psychopathology. In *Psychic Trauma,* ed. S. Furst. New York: Basic Books, pp. 85–107.

NovicK, K. & NovicK, J. (1994). Postoedipal transformations. *J Amer. Psychoanal. Assn.*, 42:143–170.

——— & Federn, E., Eds. (1962). *Minutes of the Vienna Psychoanalytic Society,* Vol. I (1906–1908). New York: Int. Univ. Press.

Person, E. & Klar, H. (1994). Establishing trauma. *J Amer. Psychoanal. Assn.*,42:1055–1082.

Rank, O. (1912). *The Incest Theme in Literature and Legend: Fundamentals of a Psychology of Literary Creation.* Baltimore, MD: John Hopkins Univ. Press, 1992.

Richards, A. (1988). Self-mutilation and father-daughter incest. In *Fantasy, Myth and Reality: Essays in Honor of Jacob A. Arlow,* ed. H. Blum, Y. Kramer, A. Richards, & A. Richards. Madison, CT: Int. Univ. Press, pp. 465–480.

Sandler, J. (1967). Trauma, strain and development. In *Psychic Trauma,* ed. S. Furst. New York: Basic Books, pp. 154–174.

Schimek, J. (1987). Fact and fantasy in the seduction theory: a historical review. *J Amer. Psychoanal. Assn.,* 35:937–965.

Shengold, L. (1989). *Soul Murder.* New Haven: Yale Univ. Press.

Shevrin, H. (1994). The use and abuses of memory. *J Amer. Psychoanal. Assn.,* 42:991–996.

Spence, D. (1982). *Narrative Truth and Historical Truth.* New York: Norton.

Steele, B. (1994). Psychoanalysis and the maltreatment of children. *J Amer. Psychoanal. Assn.,* 42:1001–1026.

Thoma, H. & Cheshire, N. (1991). *Nachtraglichkeit* and deferred action. *Int. Rev. Psychoanal.,* 18:407–427.

CHAPTER 32

Object Relations in Contemporary Psychoanalysis: Contrasting Views

(2010). *Contemp. Psychoanal.*, (46)(1):32–47.

Object relations perspectives have contributed greatly to the contemporary concept of a two-person analytic process, even among traditional psychoanalysts. With the recognition of intersubjectivity, the caricatured ideal of the affectless, neutral analyst has been replaced by a model of an empathic analyst with therapeutic interest and sufficient neutrality and objectivity. Object relations theories have also been important in the changed understanding of countertransference from a focal blind spot to a ubiquitous influence that can advance analytic progress. "Minding the gap" between the different schools, I describe and briefly comment on the contrasting views of relatively traditional or mainstream theory and practice, and object relations theory and practice. I discuss the shift from a one-person focus on the intrapsychic conflicts of the patient to both a one and a two-person analytic process. I consider countertransference as well as transference; the emphasis on "here-and-now" analytic relationships; analytic change effected through interpretation and insight versus change through the dyadic object relationship and experience; and the analyst as new and real object alongside the analyst as a transference object. From a theoretical perspective I address object relationships as the necessary precursor and foundation for psychic structure formation within the tripartite structural theory and as contrasted with and contributed to by object relations theory. Object relations versus instinctual drive theory and the notions of external object relationships versus unconscious self- and object representation and internalized object relations are also discussed.

Psychoanalysis has always encompassed a theory of object relationships, for example in the understanding of development and psychopathology. Parallel to the development of analytic theory, the role and meaning of the analytic relationship in the analytic process has also always been considered. A major divide in psychoanalysis between traditional theory and object relations theories has become even more pronounced in the 21st century. Object relations has taken center stage in psychoanalytic papers and discussions, challenging prior theoretical concepts and the technical role of abstinence, neutrality, and objectivity in the analytic process. Suggestions to abandon technical neutrality could all too easily derail a patient's own associations, gratify infantile transference demands, and promote joint acting out.

Freud (1915) noted that a drive has an object of attraction as well as an aim, which is the act through which the drive tends to achieve gratification with the object. For him, the first object was essentially a human maternal caregiver, even if the object could be most variable in the search or urge for drive satisfaction. Freud (1940) in his final, incisive comments, anticipated a generally accepted contemporary formulation concerning the development of object relationships: "[T]he mother is established unalterably for a whole lifetime as the first and strongest love-object and as the prototype of all later love-relations —for both sexes" (p. 188). It should be noted that the definition of an object and its conceptual variations depends on the analytic framework and context. The terms part objects and whole objects, need satisfying objects; narcissistic objects, selfobjects, split objects, and object constancy have not been used with consistency or consensual meaning. For example, a selfobject is defined within the framework of self psychology but has been loosely extended to more general use. For the sake of clarity, I use the term object relationship to connote relationships with others and the term object relations to connote the theory and practice of the different object relations frameworks.

Regarding the analytic process I discuss the shift from a one-person focus on the intrapsychic conflicts of the patient to both a one- and a two-person analytic process. I consider countertransference as well as transference; emphasis on "here-and-now" analytic relationships with little attention to the genetic past and childhood; analytic change effected through interpretation and insight versus change through the dyadic object relationship and experience; and the analyst as new and real object alongside the analyst as a transference object. In contemporary psychoanalysis the shared experience of analyst and patient is complementary to interpretation and insight. For very disturbed infantile patients, patients with ego deficits, and severely regressed patients, the experience of the analyst's intimacy, empathy, attention, and being listened to may be more important over time than assimilating insight. Nor do borderline and narcissistic personalities necessarily change into analyzable neurotics consequent to prolonged analytic psychotherapy.

From a theoretical perspective, I address the issues of object relationships as the necessary precursor and foundation for psychic structure formation within the tripartite structural theory and as contrasted with and contributed to by object relations theory. Object relations versus instinctual drive theory and notions of external object relationships versus unconscious self- and object representation and internalized object relations are also discussed.

Regrettably, over the years, there have been few forums and conferences to compare and contrast theories of object relationships within traditional psychoanalytic theory; object relations theories have evolved from other schools of psychoanalysis. The dearth of meetings and the absence of any meeting of the minds have been compounded over the years by the fact that there are two literatures. Traditional psychoanalytic literature and the literatures from the other schools of analysis grew apart from and in relative isolation from each other.

Some of the positive, important influences of object relations theory on traditional psychoanalysis have often been overlooked. The natural science model of the objective analyst observing the free-associating patient that was in vogue during the first decade or two after World War II came under siege thereafter and has now been discarded. The old idealizing metaphors of the analyst as a blank screen for the patient or as a mirror accurately reflecting only the patient's psyche, uninfluenced by the analyst or the analytic situation, like a surgeon operating in a sterile field without any affective response of his or her own, have been abandoned. The analyst is no longer a cold, impersonal, detached scientist or a stony-faced, silent automaton, occasionally issuing lofty insights through finely formulated interpretations. Analyst and patient are emotionally involved and perceptive of each other's character and reactions. The analyst is, indeed, a participant observer (Sullivan, 1953). a presence that is felt in a variety of ways. Object relations theorists have particularly emphasized the interpersonal and intersubjective nature of the analytic process and the analytic situation.

Object relations theories have contributed significantly to a change in the ambiance and atmosphere of the psychoanalytic situation. Critical of any intimations of rigid orthodoxy, object relations theorists foster a non-dogmatic, benevolent attitude, stressing a flexible technique that recognizes the analyst's inevitable transmission of hopes and expectations regarding the patient, the process, and treatment outcome. The presumed authoritarian attitude of the traditional psychoanalyst would have applied to certain analysts but was not the usual stance. Many "traditional analysts" actually have long been inclined toward a flexible technique, which at times encompasses advice, education, and humor, as well as urgent admonitions. The analyst is an authority, but is not an authoritarian personality; not overly zealous therapeutically, he or she nevertheless has a definite interest in the patient's welfare and therapeutic benefit.

Object relations analysts advocating an equality and symmetry in analytic work tend to exaggerate the putative previous analytic position of aggrandized superiority. The analytic situation is bound to be asymmetrical: the analyst learns the patient's private thoughts and feelings, but the patient is not privy to the analyst's free associations and private reflections. The analyst has technical expertise and analytic knowledge and is competent to clarify and interpret the patient's free associations. The superficially appealing concept of a democratic, friendly psychoanalytic process disregards the analyst's greater knowledge about the conduct of the analytic process gained from his or her analytic education, personal analysis, and capacity for self-analysis. Why should a patient pay for treatment with an analyst who does not have analytic expertise and an understanding of the patient's conflicts and problems? This critique of a clinical democracy does not imply an appeal to an idealized authority, nor is it intended to suggest a lack of regard and respect for each patient's unique personality, values, and, aspirations. Technical approaches, varying with each analytic dyad, become more specific with greater understanding of diagnosis, personality strengths, vulnerabilities, and deficits.

Among the various analytic schools there is acknowledgment of bilateral unconscious communication, projective identification, and interpersonal influence between analyst and analysand. Analytic technique has become more flexible and more oriented toward friendly, conjoint analytic exploration, with less emphasis on overcoming the resistances of patient and analyst. To be sure, these trends were underway in mainstream psychoanalysis 50 years ago, evident in the formulations of Spitz's (1956) diatrophic attitude, Stone's (1961) benevolent neutrality, Gitelson's (1962) anaclitic support, and Winnicott's (1965) holding environment. Later formulations of the working alliance (Greenson, 1965) were built on Freud's (1913) early formulations of the positive affectionate transference, proper rapport, and "everything an analyst should do in a positive sense" (p. 252).

Freud's (1940) analytic pact could be sustained even in the presence of a negative transference and bound the patient in the search for the affective meaning of the analytic data. Freud (1905). in the process of discovering and uncovering transference in the Dora case, pondered whether he had done or said anything to evoke Dora's transference reactions. Thus, the two-person analytic process rather than a focus on the patient's intrapsychic conflicts and fantasies had many early sources inside and outside traditional psychoanalysis. A two-person process taking into account bilateral, interpersonal influence had been variously considered in the literature by a number of authors, including Balint and Balint (1939). Winnicott (1965). Klein (1957). and, more recently, Renik (1998) and Gill (1994). Kohut (1977) stressed the importance of analytic empathy, and currently there is appreciation of attunement in both developmental and clinical psychoanalysis.

It is impossible to do justice to all the many contributions of present-day object relations theories, and particularly to the important role of the countertransference in psychoanalysis. As psychoanalysis evolved, countertransference came to the fore alongside the critical role of transference analysis. Far from the original notion of countertransference as representing a focal blind spot of the analyst, it is now recognized as ubiquitous, universal, and potentially advantageous to the analytic process (Hermann, 1950; Racker, 1968).

Similarly, consideration of the analyst as a real object and as a new object (Loewald, 1960) emerged concurrently with object relations theories of the interpersonal, intersubjective aspects of the psychoanalytic process. If a patient alleges that his or her analyst is critical or insensitive, the patient may have correctly perceived the analyst's real attitude. Transference has to be distinguished from reality, and transference to the analyst from transference displaced to other objects. The extreme of considering only transference devalues external object relationships and fosters an analytic narcissistic dyad (e.g., mutual admiration) especially in a prolonged analysis (Blum, 1983). Extratransference influence and interpretation can be very significant. A narcissistic dyad is representative of unconscious collusion in analytic work; collusion may take many other, subtle forms. In psychoanalytic psychotherapy, the real dyadic object relationship attains greater importance because the analysis of unconscious conflict has greater limitations.

In listening to object relations presentations and discussions of clinical material by proponents of object relations theory, major differences in theory and practice with traditional psychoanalysis become apparent. The lack of a developmental scheme in nontraditional analytic object relations theories leaves the notion of the object relationship very close to an unmodified model of the early dyadic relationship. This formulation takes little account of the development of the object from the first libidinal, or love object, attachment to the primary object all the way to the development of self- and object constancy at the conclusion of the process of separation-individuation (Mahler, 1971). Separation-individuation is superseded by the triadic oedipal objects of the oedipal phase of development, but object constancy is necessary for the full development and consolidation of the Oedipus complex. Developmental progression, with consideration of both continuities and transformations, is crucial to the mainstream concepts of self- and object representation.

Discussions among colleagues from the object relations schools tend to disregard unconscious primary-process thought, unconscious conflict, and both unconscious and preconscious fantasy. Attention is paid to the conscious and interpersonal, intersubjective shaping influence of the patient and analyst on each other. What is listened to, selected, and formulated in the analytic process, and clarified and interpreted about the analytic relationship and understanding of the patient's conflicts, tends to be oriented toward present problems. The patient is helped to verbally identify, communicate, clarify, reflect, and resolve these problems and current conflicts. Interpretation and insight into the patient's unconscious conflicts, unconscious fantasy, and unconscious transference reactions are largely ignored. Instead rupture and repair of the relationship, the matrix of the relationship, the communication network, and articulation of unformulated thoughts and feelings in the analytic process are emphasized. Analytic change is effected through the experience of the relationship rather than through insight and working through of unconscious conflict and trauma. Nor is there any systematic attempt to analyze the genetic determinants of the patient's conflicts in the infantile unconscious. The childhood of the patient receives minimal attention, and the importance of childhood experience, fixations, and fantasy on the adult personality is hardly addressed.

Given the diversity that exists both in traditional psychoanalysis and among the various schools of object relations, I am nevertheless impressed by the disregard or minimization of unconscious conflict and fantasy. A narrow focus on object relations in the here-and-now pays little heed to the repetition of past trauma and subsequent developmental disturbance, nor are shifts in the analytic work between regression and progression noted. The adherents of object relations schools tend to focus analytic work on the conscious over the unconscious, the present over the past, reality over fantasy. What Freud (1912) referred to as the use of the "Doctor's unconscious" to reconstruct "that unconscious which determines the patient's free associations" (p. 116) is neglected. Instead of such reconstruction, present-day conscious and preconscious conflicts are elaborated in the reciprocal, relatively realistic shaping influence that the partners of the analytic dyad have on each other.

649

Reconstruction, also devalued in the current analytic emphasis on the here-and-now, becomes co-construction. In object relations frameworks, the transference, counter-transference, and analytic field are commonly regarded as the co-construction of the analytic process is conceptually interwoven with an overemphasis on the here and now, and devaluation of the infantile dynamic unconscious. The patient's life history tends to be shorn of reality and either too largely reduced to personal myth or lightly treated as almost irrelevant. The classical historical and genetic dimensions of psychoanalysis are replaced by a new emphasis on a co-constructed analytic narrative. Parallel to inattention to unconscious fantasy, the role of the sexual and aggressive drives are devalued or dismissed (Rangell, 2004). Object relations in development and in clinical work have largely supplanted consideration of the instinctual drives and desfenses. Contrary to some object relations schools, contemporary mainstream psychoanalysis recognizes the importance and interrelation of sexual and aggressive drives, affects, and object relationships.

From the outset, Freud employed relational concepts in the theory and practice of psychoanalysis (Breuer and Freud, 1895). A division between object relationships and drive theory is artificial as both are interwoven in psychoanalytic developmental theory (Mills, 2005). Drives and affects are biologically based, innate, essential elements of human development and object relatedness. It seems to me that it is an oversimplification to ignore biologically endowed drives and affects in favor of object relatedness. The primary object relationship and the processes of attachment and separation/individuation cannot normally evolve without oral and hunger gratification as well as caregiver-infant communication and affect regulation. Mainstream psychoanalytic theory conceptualizes the interaction of drive, affect, and object relations in the development of psychic structure.

Affect theory now takes into account differentiation, modulation, regulation, and reciprocal communication rather than discharge phenomena. In current mainstream theory, motivation and impetus for action involve drive and affect within the context of object relationships. Intrapsychic object and self-representations are no longer regarded as static, but as evolving in conjunction with drive, affect, memory, and cognitive processes. Self- and object representation concepts are interdependent, so that those representations may be conceptualized as internalized affectively invested object relations (Kernberg, 2004). Most traditional contemporary psychoanalysts affirm both unconscious 'psychic reality' as well as the significance of external reality in development and disorder. Clinically, and to an extent theoretically, two extreme perspectives of the analytic process have now appeared. At one extreme, only unconscious fantasy and unconscious meaning are significant; at the other pole, only interpersonal, realistic influences are importantly acknowledged. The first neglects reality, and the other neglects the unconscious. Neither aspect of this dichotomy does justice to the complexity of the intrapsychic representations of the object in later development and in clinical psychoanalysis. A related issue concerns the fantasy character of primary object representations, for example, splitting them into all good and all bad, idealized and persecutory objects or part-objects. In traditional psychoanalysis, self-and object representations have components derived from fantasy and reality. The intrapsychic representational world is thus quite different from the real, external object world, though it is partly derived from external objects. Hence the need for the term object" rather than "person." In development, intrapsychic self- and object relations are only gradually differentiated and only gradually become more consolidated, integrated, realistic, and mature. The initial formulations of the psychoanalytic drive object, however, did not sufficiently take into account the real attributes of the object and identification with the real object. In addition, the term libidinal object can no longer be equated with love object; love embraces much more than libidinal investment.

Currently psychoanalysts consider the internalizations of the relationships of self and object rather than self- and object representations per se (Sandler and Sandler, 1998). These desired and feared self- and object relationships, "internalized object relations," codetermined by unconscious conflicts, appear in the transference and countertransference fantasies of patient and analyst. The intrapsychic representations of self and object, the relationship between them, and associated affects are important components and building blocks of the ego. The world of internalized object relations coexists and contributes to other ego functions, such as differentiation, integration, affect regulation, and adaptation to reality. Technically, repressed unconscious fantasy, with the important component of internalized object relations, has been the focus of analytic work with dreams, transference and acting out. With the decline of American ego psychology, there is greater interest in primitive defenses. Work with borderline patients and with severely traumatized patients has led to a new emphasis on dissociation, splitting, and fragmentation. For example, memories and fantasies associated with traumatic child abuse may be repressed or dissociated. The divided self may also be kept from awareness of other relationships. This division is similar to ego denial and simultaneous acknowledgment of trauma. Doubt about the reality of the abuse is often associated with identification with the aggressor and with the aggressor's denial and lies. In another form of dissociation, idealized and denigrated self- and object representations can be kept in consciousness without full awareness, or without a sense of contradiction and incompatibility. These incompatible self- and object relationships may rapidly alternate in borderline transference reactions. The analyst may alternately represent the patient's self and object or narcissistic object (Kernberg, 2004).

The wish for actualization of the unconscious fantasy in the here-and-now of the analytic transference (as well as in the countertransference) and the recognition of unconscious enactments on both sides of the analytic dyad have contributed to the contemporary formulation of co-construction of the analytic process. The analysand's life history is similarly viewed as co-constructed. I believe that elements of co-construction are ubiquitous, but there are definite limits to co-construction. Co-construction tends to overlook the evocation of the patient's preexisting character and unconscious transference fantasy. The unconscious transference fantasy, however, contains elements of current reality, analogous to the day residue of a dream.

Clinical Illustrations

Consider the case of an obese woman whose obesity long preceded her becoming an analytic patient. Were her eating disorder and other symptoms co-constructed? Not only was her obesity already present long before her analysis, but she had a personality of her own; character disorder, depressive and masochistic trends in her personality also preceded her psychoanalysis.

Critical dimensions of her life history, such as familial obesity or predisposition to diabetes, were important factors, which genetically and experientially significantly influenced her own obesity and diabetic vulnerability. One of her first dreams was that she was being fed dog food. Are we surprised that an obese woman dreams that she is being improperly fed? Did the analyst cocreate the dream, or was "not being properly fed" a red thread throughout her life? This dream was co-constructed to the extent that the transference was influenced by the self-disclosure of the analyst's lack of experience in treating eating disorders, and the patient's being offered a low fee to make the analysis possible. The patient was suspicious of the analyst's motives and concerned that she might receive poor treatment.

For her, a major undercurrent of the treatment was being either well fed or badly fed, nurturance or starvation, feast or famine. At one point, to appease the analyst, whom she felt she had degraded and who she fantasized might starve or abandon her, she brought her homemade cupcakes as a gift to the analyst. Reversing roles, she was now the feeding mother, nurturing the depleted analyst-self. Her need for narcissistic supplies and emotional feeding extended to her husband and children. She was inevitably disappointed and disgruntled because neither her present family nor her family of origin provided the narcissistic and oral supplies of which she had always felt deprived. That deprivation left her particularly vulnerable to traumatic seductive overstimulation. These patterns of interaction of being needy and demanding, on one hand, and being overly indulgent and emotionally overfeeding, on the other, preceded and continued during the analysis. Her hunger for incestuous love was condensed within her oral greed. She was unable to effect impulse regulation and was prone to episodic impulsive behavior. To be sure, there was continual pressure on the analyst to be nurturant and talkative and to be used as a superego figure who would provide the controls the patient lacked. When feeling particularly depleted, the patient sought an emotionally nurturing relationship, a desperately needed snack, which also served oedipal fantasy gratification. She wished for reassurance of no reprisal for her oral and oedipal hunger for love and her rage at disappointment and frustration. The analyst's neutrality and objectivity were being tested, and the patient feared and wanted the analyst's indulgence and punishment.

Such a situation does not, in my opinion, call for abandonment of analytic neutrality and objectivity, but, rather, for maintaining as much of an enacted, but analyzed and modulated. Health issues, such as dietary restrictions because of the obesity and diabetic tendency, complicate the picture, as does envy of the analyst's apparent good health and normal weight. The social stigma associated with obesity is not a matter primarily of analytic co-construction; it is an issue that may subtly enter the transference and countertransference. Context is always significant, as may be complications of medical treatment. In the dyadic relationship of patient and analyst, over time minor and often unnoticed subtle enactments are bound to occur. Yet the major facets of the patient's psychopathology are genetically determined by the patient's early experience and all her preadult life. Her conflicts will be present whoever the analyst might be, although they will be colored by intersubjectivity. Much in the traditional theory of technique has stood the test of time. I concur with traditional technique that the analyst's subjective influence should be minimized. The analyst's minimal intrusion, noninterference in patients' life situation, and technical neutrality allow patients to understand their own symptoms, character, behavior, and fantasy life and to take responsibility for their character, symptoms, and behavior.

In another case, an emotionally detached depressed mother, in effect, pushed her daughter (now an adult patient) toward an incestuously seductive father. In childhood the patient not only was subjected to sexual abuse and witnessed physical abuse but also suffered verbal abuse in the form of crude obscenities and vivid, aggressively erotic communication. The child was also exposed to her parents' extramarital affairs.

With such a patient, in addition to transference and countertransference interpretation, the analytic understanding of psychogenesis and psychoanalytic reconstruction are essential. The seduced child and adolescent may be afraid of seduction yet may act seductively, both disappointed and relieved that the analyst is not seduced. The childhood experience is repeated in transference fantasy elaboration with more or less disguise. The analyst's silence, failure to interpret, failures of interpretation, or unconscious excitement or disapproval of the patient's enactments may contribute to co-construction of the analytic process. But the basic issues are largely determined by this patient's infantile unconscious fantasy, childish fixations, and developmental disturbance in the context of her social and familial relationships and abusive experience.

Current life experience and analytic experiences may evoke or provoke transference reactions, including reactivated past traumatic experience. Consider the case of a battle-scarred veteran who overreacts to a fire alarm or police siren. The following associations were elicited in the here-and-now of a young man's associations. The patient verbalized thoughts and feelings about public education and the problem of matching teachers who are dedicated to teaching with students who really want to learn. He then went on to discuss a willingness to pay for fine education, but noted that good teachers are hard to find and often lacked sufficient training and expertise. With respect to public education, he commented that teachers often had the very difficult task of dealing with an overflow of students in overcrowded classrooms. This led the patient to thoughts of overcrowded classrooms, birth control, and population control. The world's population was increasing at an alarming rate and might outgrow the available food and water supplies. Too many children in a family would virtually guarantee indigence and ignorance.

The patient's rather obvious transference reactions were triggered by his unconscious perception of his female analyst's pregnancy. She had chosen not to announce her pregnancy, but to allow the patient's responses to her pregnancy to emerge spontaneously as she became more obviously pregnant. The analyst had her own conscious and unconscious reactions to her pregnancy, but the spontaneous transference reactions could hardly have been simply co-constructed. His transference reactions were based on his childhood

655

sibling rivalry and jealousy, and his anger at his mother for her pregnancy and bringing his sibling into the family. Despite being a psychologically mature adult in some areas of his personality, his reaction to his analyst's pregnancy was hardly pleasant. He did not offer congratulations or pleasant associations. The patient's associations were largely endogenously determined and similar to many other patients' reactions to their analysts' pregnancies.

This patient's associations are reminiscent of Freud's discovery of his own reactions to the birth of a sibling in his self-analysis. Freud wrote to Fliess, how he sobbed, as a little boy, when he observed his mother's pregnancy and then the arrival of a new sibling (Masson, 1985, letter of October 15, 1897). His mother tried to console him, but, of course, she did not understand Freud's fears of abandonment or his rage at his sibling's birth. Probably his incomplete self-analysis condensed his mother's successive pregnancies and the births of later siblings. Freud's dreams indicated his repudiated unconscious wish to eliminate all sibling rivals. Freud thought he had recovered his jealousy of his older brother, Philip, whom he held responsible for his mother's pregnancy, jealousy that was displaced from his father. Freud, like Little Hans and many first-born children, reacted to his mother's pregnancy and childbirth with intrafamilial jealousy, rivalry, and anxiety over loss of the object and loss of the object's love.

To return to the prior analytic case (with the pregnant analyst): there were indications of as yet unanalyzed transference and countertransference fantasies of the patient's having impregnated the analyst. To conceptualize the patient's associations and transference reactions as primarily co-constructed with the analyst, however, is to avoid the patient's individual transference reaction and turn the analysis into an a-historic encounter. The analyst's pregnancy would be meaningful only in the here-and-now, bypassing the crucial analysis of the unconscious fantasy, with its component memories, thoughts, affects, wishes, and so on. The transference, then, would not be essentially transferred from the past into the present analytic situation, but it would be an altered concept based on the present analyst-patient relationship. The genetic roots of the transference would be missed, and the unconscious parent and sibling conflicts would be left in large measure unanalyzed. The patient would hardly understand how much his childhood experience and fantasies continued to influence his present life, inside and outside the analysis. This patient was particularly competitive with and jealous of colleagues, a pattern that was not simply co-constructed in analysis but preexisted his coming into treatment. Being prone to being very anxious and angry was one of his reasons for seeking treatment. Another reason for anticipating abandonment was that he recognized that his analyst was very likely to take maternity leave without his being sure of when she would return. Meanwhile, her love and attention would be centered on her baby and not on him. The patient felt as though he should have been her only, if not at least her preferred, child. In my view, transference can be anchored, interwoven, or seemingly validated in reality. However, it is fundamentally a compromise formation derived from unconscious childhood fantasy and trauma, with the coalescence of day residues and intersubjective experience.

It would be appropriate for the analyst eventually to disclose her plans about maternity leave in advance, so that the patient has a chance to prepare for the analytic interruption and at least partially work through some of his conflicts about her pregnancy and motherhood. In this situation the analyst did later confirm her pregnancy and her concern about the patient's feelings of hurt and anger. The question remains, though, is self-disclosure for the benefit of the patient or for the benefit of the analyst?

Here the self-disclosure was indicated for the benefit of both analysis and patient. Self-disclosures of illness, errors, and enactments that may impinge on the analysis are important events and may be necessary to facilitate the analytic process and preserve the values of psychoanalysis. There are no simple rules or forms of self-disclosure, as is evident in the varied literature on the analyst's illness. If the analyst's self-disclosure is used for narcissistic, exhibitionistic, or sadomasochistic purposes, the disclosure will impede or subvert the analytic process, and often represents a form of countertransference enactment (Abend, 2003). If the analyst reveals that he has recovered from alcoholism, or was a juvenile delinquent, it may inspire the patient to try to master such a problem. It may however, also gratify the analyst's narcissistic omnipotence, while defending against fear of his or her own vulnerability. Disclosure of the analyst's acting out may convey possible quasi-unconscious approval of or stimulation of acting out by the patient. Highly erotic self-disclosure by the analyst is a countertransference enactment and may seductively invite boundary violations.

To assert that self-disclosure is a reliably useful analytic intervention is to drastically oversimplify and minimize the possible detrimental consequences. Transference reactions to the analyst's inappropriate or radical self-disclosure may be very difficult to analyze and difficult to differentiate from realistic responses. The free associations of the patient may be coopted in the service of the analyst's issues, and the listening of both parties' may become selectively organized around the highly charged countertransference and the real radical intrusion of the analyst's own conflicts and problems into the analytic situation.

The importance of transference as transferred from the past into the present relationship tends to be lost when the psychoanalytic relationship is primarily understood in terms of its interpersonal and intersubjective dimensions. Transference love and hate may be accentuated in the interactive analytic relationship if the relationship is misunderstood as constructed in the present. As Freud (1905) early noted, "[T]he finding of an object is the re-finding of it" (p. 222). In this sense, the object is never just a new object but a new edition of childhood self- and object representations and relationships. Transference has an essential core of repetition, and both the erotic and the aggressive transference relationships encompass internalized infantile object relationships in addition to day residues and current analytic intersubjective experience.

To fall in love is to reencounter one's original loved ones coalescing with the real attributes of the current love object. Our original objects live on within us in memory and in our conscious and unconscious fantasies. This means that no person is ever free of transferences to external persons and institutions; the realities of life are always colored by transference fantasy and by attempts to actualize the fantasy if only in derivative form. We are unable to perceive our object relationships totally accurately and realistically, just as we are limited in our ability to see ourselves objectively and as others may see us. Nevertheless, we should try to be as objective as possible both in analytic work with patients and in self-analysis. Technical neutrality facilitates recognition and appreciation of transference, but also appreciation of the real qualities and attitudes of each dyadic participant observer. By maintaining an analytic attitude, with good enough analytic neutrality, objectivity, and attunement, it is possible to do competent and appropriate analytic work even with the imperfections, uncertainties, and limitations of the analytic process. The analytic relationship is continually buffeted by unconscious conflicts that may be actualized in the analytic situation and test the maintenance of therapeutic boundaries. Ideally, the history and variety of our internalized object relationships is revived in psychoanalysis as we work toward rewarding object relationships on higher levels of development and maturity.

REFERENCES

Abend, S. (2003). Relational influences on modern conflict theory. *Contemp. Psychoanal.*, 39:*367–377.*

Balint, A. & Balint, M. (1939). On transference and countertransference. *Int. J. Psycho-Anal.*, 20:*223–230.*

Blum, H. (1983). The position and value of extra-transference interpretation. *J. Amer. Psychoanal. Assn.*, 31:*587–618.*

Blum, H. (1998). An analytic inquiry into inter-subjectivity. *Journal of Clinical Psychoanalysis*, 7:*189–208.*

Breuer, J. & Freud, S. (1895). Studies on Hysteria. *Standard Edition* 2, 1955.

Freud, S. (1905). Fragment of an analysis of a case of hysteria. *Standard Edition* 7:*7–122,* 1953.

Freud, S. (1912). Recommendations to physicians practicing psychoanalysis. *Standard Edition* 12:*111–120.*

——— (1913). The dynamics of transference. *Standard Edition* 12:*97–108,* 1968.

——— (1915). Instincts and their vicissitudes. *Standard Edition* 4:*109–140,* 1957.

——— (1940). An outline of psycho-analysis. *Standard Edition* 23:*144–207,* 1964.

Gill, M. (1994). Psychoanalysis in Transition. Hillsdale, NJ: Analytic Press.

Gitelson, M. (1962). The curative factors in psychoanalysis. *Int. J. Psycho-Anal.*, 43:*194–205.*

Greenson, R. (1965). The working alliance and the transference neurosis. *Psychoanal. Q.*, 34:*155–181*.

Heimann, P. (1950). On countertransference. *Int. J. Psycho-Anal.*, 31:*81–84*.

Kernberg, O. (2004). Contemporary Controversies in Psychoanalytic Theory, Technique, and Their Applications. New Haven, CT: Yale University Press.

Klein, M. (1957). Envy and Gratitude. New York: Basic Books.

Kohut, H. (1977). The Restoration of 'the Self'. New York: International Universities Press.

Loewald, H. (1960). On the therapeutic action of psychoanalysis. *Int. J. PsychoAnal.*, 41:*16–33*.

Mahler, M. (1971). A study of the separation-individuation process and its possible application to borderline phenomena in the psychoanalytic situation. *Psychoanal. St. Child*, 26: *403–424*. New Haven, CT: Yale University Press.

Masson, J., trans. & ed. (1985). *The Complete letters of Sigmund Freud to Wilhelm Fliess, 1887–1904*. Cambridge, MA: Harvard University Press.

Mills, J. (2005). A critique of relational psychoanalysis. *Psychoanal. Psychol.*, 22:*155–188*.

Racker, H. (1968). Transference and Countertransference. New York: International Universities Press.

Rangell, L. (2004). My life in Theory. New York: Other Press.

Renik, O. (1998). The analyst's subjectivity and the analyst's objectivity. *Int. J. Psycho-Anal.*, 79:*487–497*.

Sandler, J. & Sandler, M. (1998). Internal Objects Revisited. London: Karnac Books.

Spitz, R.A. (1956). Transference: The analytic setting and its prototype. *Int. J. Psycho-Anal.*, 37:*380–385*.

Stone, L. (1961). The Psychoanalytic Situation. New York: International Universities Press.

Sullivan, H. (1953). The Interpersonal Theory of Psychiatry. New York: Norton.

Winnicott, D.W. (1960). Countertransference. *Brit. J. Med. Psychol.*, 33:*17–21*.

Winnicott, D.W. (1965). The Maturational Process and the Facilitating Environment. New York: International Universities Press.

Appendix

Van Gogh Correspondence

DOCTEUR SERGE LEBOVICI
ANCIEN INTERNE DES HOPITAUX DE PARIS
MÉDECIN ASSISTANT DES HOPITAUX DE PARIS

3. AV. DU PRÉSIDENT WILSON. XVIᵉ

KLEBER 17·16

Paris, le 19 juin 1957

Mon cher Confrère,

Madame Marie Bonaparte m'a transmis l'article
que vous avez écrit sur les chaises de Van Gogh; j'ai le
plaisir de vous annoncer qu'il sera publié dans la Revue
Française de Psychanalyse.

Vous serez aimable de me dire si vous désirez
des tirés à part et combien, le cas échéant.

Il va sans dire que cette publication restera
probablement encore assez éloignée, vu l'abondance des
matières dans la Revue.

Je vous prie de croire, mon cher Confrère, à
mes meilleurs sentiments.

S. Lebovici
Rédacteur en Chef de la
Revue Française de Psychanalyse

P. BLUM, M.D.
11 Circle
nn.) U.S.A.

APPENDIX

Doctor Serge Lebovici*
Former Intern of Hopitaux de Paris [Paris Hospitals]
Assistant Physician of Hopitaux de Paris [Paris Hospitals]

Paris, 19 June 1957

My Dear Colleague,

Madame Marie Bonaparte has submitted to me your article about Van Gogh's chairs; it is my pleasure to inform you that it will be published in the Revue Française de Psychanalyse [French Review of Psychoanalysis.]

Please let me know if you would like reprints, and if so, how many.

It goes without saying that the publication date may be somewhat delayed, given the abundance of material scheduled to appear in the Revue.

Please accept, my dear colleague, my best regards.

S. Lebovici
Editor in Chief of the
Revue Française de Psychanalyse

—

Annotation:

*Serge Lebovici, MD (1915 - 2000) became a prominent French child psychiatrist and psychoanalyst. Dr. Lebovici published extensively and was renowned among French psychoanalysts for his work on the relationship between mothers and children. The World Association for Infant Mental Health established an award in his name which continues to be given for significant contributions to the field of child psychiatry. From 1973 to 1977, Dr. Lebovici was president of the International Psychoanalytic Association, a society originally founded by Sigmund Frued.

** The masthead of the Revue Française de Psychanalyse (see banner on the left of the original letter) is a veritable "who's who" of famous psychoanalysts and intellectuals of the twentieth century

Monsieur,

En réponse à votre lettre du 3 septembre, concernant le suicide de mon ami Vincent van Gogh, je peux Vous dire qu'en l'absence d'autopsie, le trajet de la balle de révolver ne peut être précisé exactement.

Entré dans la poitrine au-dessous du mamelon gauche, le projectile a dû dévier sur une côte et se diriger vers le bas, dans l'hypocondre gauche, peut-être jusqu'à l'aine, cependant sans lésions internes entrainant la mort immédiate.

Il n'a rien dit à ce sujet et seules l'extraction de la balle ou l'autopsie auraient pu déceler avec certitude le chemin parcouru par le projectile.

Veuillez agréer, Monsieur, mes Salutations distinguées.

Auvers-sur-Oise (S et O.)
12. IX. 55.

Paul Gachet

Letter of Dr. Paul Gachet*

Sir,

In response to your letter of 3 September, concerning the suicide of my friend Vincent Van Gogh, I can tell you that in the absence of an autopsy, the trajectory of the bullet from the revolver cannot be traced with precision.

Entering the chest below the left nipple, the projectile must have hit a rib and deviated lower into the left hypochondrium, possibly as far down as the groin, all without producing internal wounds that would have proved immediately fatal.

He said nothing about this. and only extraction of the bullet or an autopsy could have revealed with certainty the path of the projectile.

Please accept, dear sir, my esteemed regards.

Paul Gachet

Auvers-sur-Oise (S et O) [Seine et Oise]
12.IX.55 [12 September 1955]

—

Annotation:
*The author of the letter, Dr. Paul Gachet (fils, 1873–1962) was the son of the physician, Dr. Paul Gachet (père, 1828-1909) who treated Vincent Van Gogh upon his release from the Saint-Paul-de-Mausole asylum in Saint-Rémy-de-Provence in 1890. Dr. Gachet (père) followed Van Gogh until his death later that year. In fact, Dr. Gachet became Van Gogh's friend as well as his subject. A well-known portrait of the doctor is one of many paintings produced by Van Gogh in his last months. Dr. Gachet was an amateur painter and art collector who entertained many well-known artists at his house in Auvers-sur Oise, the address noted in his son's letter. In 1955, at the suggestion of the French art historian, Charles Terrasse, Harold wrote to Dr. Gachet's son for details about the suicide attempt that ultimately killed Van Gogh. (An infection in the wound proved deadly, not the actual shooting.) Dr Gachet's son would have been about 17 years old when Van Gogh died, while the latter was 37. Notably, in this response to Harold, the son refers to the painter as "my friend Vincent Van Gogh."

Harold P. Blum, M.D., F.A.P.A.
23 The Hemlocks
Roslyn Estates, NY 11576
516 621-6850
hpblum1@gmail.com

January 31, 20013

Dr. Alex Ruger, Director
Van Gogh Museum

Dear Dr. Ruger:

I am in possession of a very significant letter, sent to my by V.W. Van Gogh, nephew of the artist and founder of the Van Gogh Museum. The letter sent to me in 1957, was a response to an inquiry I made as a young physician interested in Van Gogh's art and life. The letter was lost for decades as a result of moves to different locations and demanding professional activities.
I was delighted to at last find the letter which had been misfiled by secretarial error.

I am a psychiatrist and psychoanalyst and have have published papers on Vincent van Gogh. I regard this letter as most interesting and valuable from historical, biographical and psychological perspectives. I feel the original document should be preserved in the Van Gogh Museum. Could you kindly indicate whether your are interested in possessing the original letter and what you would consider as a payment. I am enclosing a photocopy of the letter with the signature of Theo's son, Vincent.

IR. V. W. VAN GOGH
ROZENLAANTJE
LAREN N.H. Feb. 5th '57.

Dear Dr. Blum,

Many thanks for the reprint of your article on van Gogh's Chairs! It took me some time before I came to writing you and even now I don't have the leisure to mention all the points to which one comes when reading it. Good psycho-analytical essais on art matters or on artists are rare! Therefor I appreciate you writing the more.

The question of the chairs has been treated before by Bataille, in Documents 2nd volume (2ième Année) nr 8, page 11 (1930). Westerman Holsteyn once mentioned this article in a lecture, and Kraus knew about it for he mentions it in his literature-list in 1941. Kraus died last year; he was professor in Groningen and wrote on van Gogh's sickness in a Dutch monthly: Psychiatrische en Neurologische Bladen, nr 5, 1941 with an up to date list of literature.

Nor Meier-Graefe, nor Nordenfalk (who is [2] a good friend of mine,) nor Terrasse, nor Shapiro know anything original about the question. They only copy or use their phantasy in a non-scientific way — Specially the first one mentioned! Gauguin's Avant et après probably is not untrue but it seems not to be the whole truth and therefor it needs interpretation.

As to the facts and specially the time when they happened there is some more. The quarel with Gauguin came about when Vincent heard of Theo's intention to get married. Further crises were caused by the actual marriage, by the anouncement a baby would come, when the baby was born — at least that seems a very important cause. That Vincent painted his own chair after he „ran out on the fields for six hours after pleading with Gauguin to „be a good chap" (your page 2, no 18) should be provided with a question-mark — it seems doubtful — where does Meyer Graefe take this from? He never investigated as far as I know.

The symbolic significance of the chairs, the pipe, tobacco-pouch, etc. is not to be doubted. On page 315 you mention that van Gogh wrote that his chair was of white wood — I may mention that that does not refer to the colour but the

IR. V. W. VAN GOGH
ROZENLAANTJE
LAREN N.H.

French use „bois blanc" for what we call „fir" or/and „pine". Probably the chair in reality had been covered either with wax or with „brou" – I cannot find the English expression just now, but it is liquid fo impregnate the wood giving it a brownish or yellowish colour.

I don't know if (pale) yellow represents for van Gogh the inadequate father identification, impotence and castration. It might also be the only warmth (and love) that he had within him, that means the feeling for his brother Theo.

Your quotation on p. 316 (39) is a little different! „ Fortunately Gauguin, I (this ought to be „myself") and other painters are not yet armed with machine guns, ..." This relates to accusing Gauguin as being the representative of the enemy impressionism (or something to that effect).

All this I mention just to show my interest to you. With the last paragraph of your article I am in agreement! In your

last words you mention the big 4.
question: what (, who and under
what circumstances) makes great
Art come into being? Or, wider
field: what is the cause of
development of the creative
abilities of the (every) individual?
So far I have only a negative
reply: mankind is gifted — everybody
is — in the beginning but society,
family, school, convention, &
associations of every kind, etc. do
their best to bring the creative
ability to as little as possible and
one has only to wonder that so
much is left. Can a more general
acceptance of psycho-analyses
bring a better situation about?
Study of art can put us more
wise in many respects. I wonder
if you know the writings of Charles
Mauron, the blind major of St. Rémy,
who wrote a psycho-analytical book
on Mallarmé, and also some
articles on Vincent van Gogh?
I am much obliged for your
reprint and remain
     sincerely
     V. W. van Gogh.

APPENDIX

Ministry   Fontainebleau Palace
Of The National Education   etc.
—

Arts and Letters
—

Museum of France
—

Fontainebleau Museum

      Sir:

        I apologize for the delay in responding to your letter. I have been away for quite some time.

        I believe that you may be able to contact Dr. Gachet, the son of the physician who treated Van Gogh, for details concerning the end of Van Gogh's life. As far as I am aware, he would know more than anyone about the painter's final moments.

        Please be assured, dear sir, of my most distinguished regard.

        Charles Terrasse*

Address of Doctor Gachet: at Auvers-sur-Oise, (Seine et Oise)

—

Annotation:
*Charles Terrasse (1893-1982), attaché to the Minister of Education, secretary general of the Paris Conservatory and assistant curator of the Fontainebleau Museum, was a noted French art historian and historiographer who wrote extensively about art history and artists, including Van Gogh.